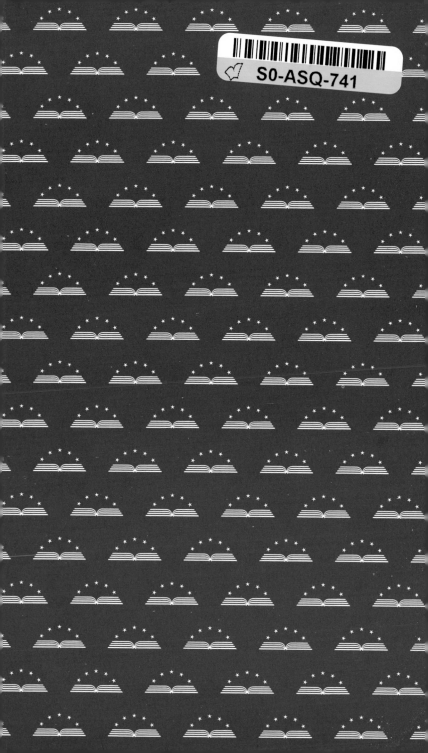

JOHN MARSHALL

JOHN MARSHALL

WRITINGS

THE LIBRARY OF AMERICA

Excerpts from THE PAPERS OF JOHN MARSHALL, VOLUMES
I THROUGH 12 edited by Charles F. Hobson, et al. Published for the
Omohundro Institute of Early American History and Culture.
Copyright © by the University of North Carolina Press. Used
in this Library of America edition by arrangement
with the publisher. www.uncpress.edu

The paper used in this publication meets the
minimum requirements of the American National Standard for
Information Sciences—Permanence of Paper for Printed
Library Materials, ANSI z39.48—1984.

Distributed to the trade in the United States
by Penguin Group (USA) Inc.
and in Canada by Penguin Books Canada Ltd.

Library of Congress Control Number: 2009933071
ISBN 978–1–59853–064–3

———

First Printing
The Library of America—198

Manufactured in the United States of America

CHARLES F. HOBSON
SELECTED THE CONTENTS AND
WROTE THE NOTES FOR THIS VOLUME

Contents

DIPLOMAT, CONGRESSMAN, AND SECRETARY OF STATE, 1798–1801

CHIEF JUSTICE OF THE SUPREME COURT, 1801–1819

SOLDIER, STATE LEGISLATOR, LAWYER, AND FEDERALIST
1779–1797

To Thomas Posey

Dear Major   Smith's Clove, N.Y., September 1, 1779
    Yours, inclosing Genl. Wayne's second letter to Congress rel-
ative to the reduction of Stony Point, I received just as I was
setting out from Ramapough. I read the Genl.'s letter with
attention & will give my sincere sentiments upon it. You recollect that in your letter to Genl. Washington you only complaind because you was not mentioned. You did not claim
particular attention. Your sole wish was not to be totally neglected. You are now mentioned. The cause of your complaint
is removed, & you cannot, in my opinion, without acting in-
consistantly demand anything farther. Though I say you can
demand nothing farther yet I must confess that I think Genl.
Wayne ought to have done more. When the Man who possesses a great, a generous Soul has inadvertently injured another
he will not stop at barely giving him such satisfaction as will
prevent his discovering resentment. He will repair the injury in
the most ample manner immaginable. Was Genl. Wayne regardless of you he ought I think to have said more for his own
sake. He committed an error in omitting you. This he did not
attempt to correct till your complaints obliged him to it, &
even then he has said nothing which he could possibly avoid.
Your being mentioned appears to proceed from constraint as
much as choice. The Man who has seen with what a liberal
hand the Genl. has, in his first letter, dealt out praises to Men
who could not have deserved much more than yourself will
confess that he has been rather sparing in his encomiums on
Major Posey.
    I have shewn the letter to several of your Friends. They per-
fectly agree with me in thinking that you can ask nothing farther but that Genl. Wayne might & ought to have done more.
What news have you Major? What does our movement to this
place indicate? Is an attack on West Point apprehended? I
assure I am somewhat fearful we may yet have bloody noses.
Never was I a witness to such a scene of lewdness as about
Ramapough particularly at the very venerable Mrs. Sydmon's.

I should certainly have thought had I staid there much longer that all the virtue of the fair sex was centered in our Camp Ladies & should very possibly have begun to think of choosing one of them as a Partner for life.

You have heard that Congress have at length done something cleaver for us by way of subsistence. One hundred Dollars per Month for each ration will do pretty well. It will serve to purchase *milk & sopaun* for some time. Farewell I am dear Major with much esteem, Yours

RAISING MEN AND MONEY

To William Pierce

Richmond, February 12, 1783

Never more dear Pierce shall pique at your not answering my letters deprive me of the pleasure of writing to the soldier I esteem. I will not again think myself neglected or beleive that our friendship had on your part lost its former warmth. You shall have my thoughts as freely as they rise in my own bosom.

What, says my friend, is Virginia about? Upon my word I can scarcely tell you. The grand object of the people is still, as it has ever been, to oppose successfully our British enemies & to establish on the firm base of certainty the independence of America. But in the attainment of this object an attention to a variety of little interests & passions produces such a distracted contrariety of measures that tis sometimes difficult to determine whether some other end is not nearer the hearts of those who guide our Counsels. We have not perhaps so much virtue as we ought to have but we are possessed of much more than our neighbors will give us credit for. But you wish to know what measures we have taken to bring men into the field & Money into the Treasury. You are acquainted with our recruiting bill. It has producd a considerable sum & the money has been religiously applied to the purpose for which it was raised. We have not however been so successful as I could have wished. We have not yet recruited in the course of the winter 300 men. Those officers who have been most successful are continued in the business & the money is taken out of the hands of those who have raised no men. The financier tis said has discontinued the post at Winchester in consequence of which our continental recruits have no provisions or are a burthen on the state. We have paid into the continental Treasury 37000 Dollars. The Continent will receive from us in the Spring £50000. Other States have paid more money than Virginia & other States exult in having done so. It is not remembered that the property of our citizens to an immense amount, has been wrested from them for Continental purposes, that could accounts ever be fairly settled (a thing I know to be impossible) the Continent could now have no demands on Virginia. We are exerting ourselves to put our arms in repair & to place ourselves in a defensible situation. So much for politics.

How my dear Pierce in that relaxation from business which is the consequence of the evacuation of Charles Town is your time employed? But I need not ask. You are in a Country where your *gallantry* may be as serviceable in peace as in war. I know your skill maneuvering under the banners of Venus & I doubt not but several hearts can testify your success. But have you among the rice birds & polloos of Carolina a particular object? Have you totally forgot the Virginia *genius* to whom you was so long an humble Servant? Write me everything which interests you. I expect it because you know 'twill interest me: Am I not uncommonly dull? I'll give you a reason for it. I have been setting up all night at an Assembly. We have them in Richmond regularly once a fortnight. The last was a brilliant one; 'twas on the Generals birth night. Never did I see such a collection of handsome Ladies. I do not beleive that Versailles or saint James's ever displayed so much beauty. I wish you had been present. The Virginians would have retained their high place in your opinion.

Adieu my dear Sir. Mrs. Marshall presents her compliments to you. I am your

We have vague accounts of peace but they will reach you as soon as this letter. [   ]

FAILINGS OF THE VIRGINIA ASSEMBLY

To Charles Simms

Dear Colo.   Richmond June 22d. 1783

Yours by Major Powel came too late to enable me to draw any thing for you. There is now no flour in the Treasury—if there was any the price is rais'd to 16/8—per Ct. You will never receive commutables when you limit me to a certain price. By the time you will agree to give what is demanded the commutables are either rais'd or sold—perhaps both; for the quantity in the Treasury is so unequal to the demand that neither money or commutables can remain there for a week. I flatter'd myself some little time past that I shou'd be able to draw cash for you. A motion had pass'd the house of Delegates directing the Treasurer to sell some Hemp in his possession for what cash he cou'd get & pay it to the Officers. I shou'd have exerted myself for you & being on the spot might have succeeded, tho' the supply was small, but the resolution was drop'd in the Senate. Tis now impossible to determine when I shall get any thing for you as it depends on the payments to be made by the Sheriffs. If tis possible to procure money or commutables on good terms by August Loudoun Court I will bring whatever I draw with me to that place where I hope to have the pleasure of seeing you, but I rather incline to think you will get nothing till September or October next. The House of Delegates have pass'd a bill which tis suppos'd will meet no opposition in the Senate appropriating £70000 per Annum for the payment of the interest & principal of Military certificates till the whole shall be discharg'd. This will make them immediately equal to specie in real value tho' markets in General will not yet estimate them at their true worth. The Circuit Court bill will not pass. A bill is introduc'd for paying a few Magistrates to do the business of County Courts. I am uncertain what will be its fate. Shou'd it pass the value of the general Court practise will be greatly lessen'd. A bill for regulating the practise of Attornies is refer'd to the next session of Assembly. You have hear'd that the collection of the taxes is suspended till November. The Gentlemen of this Country have invincible objections to every tax on property. They are desirous of burthening trade & of laying duties on the necessaries of life. The Legislature concentres in itself at pleasure the Legislative, Judiciary, & Executive Authorities. They hesitate not an instant to pass laws with a retrospective tendency, if the whim of the moment impels them to do so. If Men of Virtue & abilities do not come into the Assembly those liberties for the attainment of which we have made such noble exertions will be destroyd in their birth. Adieu. Will you present my best compliments to your Lady, to my Unkle Keith & to his family. I shou'd be glad to correspond with him. I am Your

PATRICK HENRY'S INFLUENCE

To James Monroe

Dear Sir   December 12, 1783
    The letters to Genl. Clarke & Mr. Banks enclosed in yours of the 5th. inst. I yesterday delivered. Should a letter to Majr. Crittenden arrive by the next post I can give it a certain & immediate conveyance. I gave you in my last some account of the proceedings of the Assembly. The Commutable bill has at length passed & with it a suspension of the collection of taxes till the first of January next. I told you the principle speakers for & against the measure. Colo. R. H. Lee has not attended this Session. This is not all. His services in the Assembly are lost for ever. 'Tis conjectured that Colo. Harry Lee of the Legionary corps, will take his place. You know the character of that Gentleman better than I do & can best determine whether the public will be injured by the change. The idea of rendering Members of Congress eligible to the Genl. Assembly has not been taken up. Indeed the attention of the house since the passage of the Commutable bill has been so fixed on the citizen bill that they have scarcely thought on any other subject. Since the rejection of the bill introduced by Taylor, Colo. Nicholas (a politician not famed for hitting a medium) introduced one admitting into this Country every species of Men except natives who had borne arms against the state. When the house

went into Committee on this bill Mr. Jones introduced by way of amendment, one totally new & totally opposite to that which was the subject of deliberation. He spoke with his usual sound sense & solid reason. Mr. Henry opposed him. The Speaker replied with some degree of acrimony & Henry retorted with a good deal of tartness but with much temper; 'tis his peculiar excellence when he altercates to appear to be drawn unwillingly into the contest & to throw in the eyes of others the whole blame on his adversary. His influence is immense. The house rose for the day without coming to any determination & the bill is yet in suspense. The principle point on which they split is the exclusion of the Statute Staple men. I really am uncertain what will be the determination on this subject.

The Officers will soon begin to survey their lands on the Cumberland. Has Crittenden your Military warrant? The report from Congress with respect to the 'cession has not yet reached us; of course the Assembly can have determined nothing about it. My Father set out for the western Country about the 5th. of Novr. I have not heard a syllable from Crittenden since his departure. Adieu, I am, with the greatest esteem, Your

"THE GREATEST MAN ON EARTH"

To James Monroe

Dear Sir Richmond, January 3, 1784

At length then the military career of the greatest Man on earth is closed. May happiness attend him whereever he goes. May he long enjoy those blessings he has secured to his Country. When I speak or think of that superior Man my full heart overflows with gratitude. May he ever experience from his Countrymen those attentions which such sentiments of themselves produce.

Let me assure you that I will punctually comply with every requisition you may make on pecuniary subjects or any other within my reach. Your letter to Majr. Crittenden shall be put today into the hands of Genl. Clarke who will be in the western

country in February next, or in march at furthest. I will request his particular attention to your military warrant. I am
sure his friendship for you will induce him to pay it chearfully.
The Speaker has for some time left Richmond & may not perhaps be here till the next session. Should I see him I will mention to him your certificate. I lament as sincerely as you can do
the exclusion of our Delegates in Congress from a seat in our
Legislature. There is no one quality perhaps which we more
need than wisdom. Severely very severely indeed have we experienced the want of it. And surely no one measure can have
a greater tendency to continue & even increase the misfortune
than those exclusions, those unnecessary exclusions of men
whose virtue & abilities have secured the esteem & good opinion of their Country. Fears of the power of Congress I have
ever considerd as chimerical. I never could bring myself to think
that Gentlemen who urged really felt them but conceived they
were usd as a political engine to effect particular purposes. And
I have ever observed that our Countrymen in the general may
be persuaded from an apprehension of a distant evil, to adopt
measures which may must produce a certain one. This arises
from refining too much, & this they will do in all cases except
those where money is to be drawn from their purses.

While the sending the resolution of Congress with respect
to our cession of Western territory shews your attention to the
information & interests of your Country, I cannot but lament
that my letter should have produced to you unnecessary trouble & to us expense. For the thursday after I had written to
you the Resolutions of Congress made their appearance under
a cover from our friend Colo. Mercer dated in Septr. last.
Adeiu I am with the most affectionate esteem, Your

MATRIMONIAL NEWS

To James Monroe

Dear Sir　　　　　　　　　　Richmond, February 24, 1784
I wish it was possible to releive your wants by your Boy, but
it is impossible. The exertions of the Treasurer & of your other

friends here have been ineffectual. There is not one shilling in the Treasury & the keeper of it coud not borrow one on the faith of government. The extreme inclemency of the season has rendered it impossible for the Sheriffs to make collections and I have my fears that you will not receive an adequate supply till some time in April. I transmitted to you by post three weeks past a bill for a small sum drawn since the £100. I hope you have received it.

I am pressed warmly by Ege for money & your old Land-Lady Mrs. Shera begins now to be a little clamarous. I shall be obligd I apprehend to negotiate your warrants at last at a discount. I have kept them up thus long in hopes of drawing Money for them from the Treasury & shall keep them up till about April next by which time I may receive some instructions from you on the subject.

This excessive cold weather has operated like magic on our youth. They feel the necessity of artificial heat, & quite wearied with lying alone, are all treading the broad road to Matrimony. Little Stewart, (coud you beleive it?) will be married on thursday to Kitty Hair & Mr. Dunn will bear of your old acquaintance Miss Shera. Tabby Eppes has grown quite fat & buxom, her charms are renovated & to see her & to love her are now synonimous terms. She has within these six weeks seen in her train at least a score of Military & civil characters. Carrington, Young, Selden, Wright (a merchant) & Foster Webb have alternately bowed before her & been discarded. Carrington tis said has drawn off his forces in order to refresh them & has marched up to Cumberland where he will in all human probability be reinforced with the dignified character of Legislator. Webb has returnd to the charge & the many think from their similitude of manners & appetites that they were certainly designd for each other.

The other Tabby is in high spirits [   ] success of her antique sister & firmly beleives her time will come next, she looks quite spruce & speaks of matrimony as of a good which she yet means to experience. Lomax is in his County. Smith is said to be electioneering. Nelson has not yet come to the board. Randolph is here & well. Short has a certain complaint which you will probably be a judge of before you return from Annapolis. Farewell, I am your

"A CANDIDATE AT THE NEXT ELECTION"

To James Monroe

Dear Sir   Richmond, April 17, 1784

Yours of the 12th. of March I did not till yesterday receive.

I had made a small excursion into Fauquier to enquire into the probability of my being chosen by the people should I offer as a Candidate at the next election.

I am no longer a member of the Executive, the opinion of the Judges with respect to a Counsellors standing at the bar determined me to retire from the Council board. Every person is now busied about the ensuing election. Your friend Wilson Nicholas is the first Representative of Albemarle. Grayson is chosen with Bullitt for Prince William. Carrington will certainly come for Cumberland & either Wallace or Brent for Stafford. Mann Page is I am told a candidate for the chair. Dick Lee I expect will come from Loudoun. In almost every County except this changes have taken place. Here Wilkinson supports himself against every attack Mayo & the town can make on him. I had forgot to tell you that Hawes with Taylor are chosen for Caroline. I have been maneuvering amazingly to turn your warrants into cash. If I succeed I shall think myself a first rate speculator. I can tell you that you will not lose more [   ]

The ten shillings added to the £100 is the discount on the negotiation of the bill which I have insisted on your being allowd for.

REFORMING THE COUNTY COURTS

To Charles Simms

Dear Sir   Richmond, June 16, 1784

I received your two favors the one on the subject of the petition & the other enclosing a bond. Mr. Henderson promisd to write you immediately to let you know that by a standing order of the house no petition concerning private property could be received till it had been publishd in the County & in the Gazette. If this is done by the next session I flatter myself we may be able to carry it through the house. I see no prospect of amending the mode of distributing justice in this Commonwealth. The circuit Court system meets with too much opposition from selfish individuals to be adopted. Those Magistrates who are tenacious of authority will not assent to any thing which may diminish their ideal dignity & put into the hands of others a power which they will not exercise themselves. Such of the County Court lawyers too as are suspicious that they do not possess abilities or knowledge sufficient to enable them to stand before judges of law are opposd from motives of interest to any plan which may put the distribution of justice into the hands of judges. Every attempt to alter & amend the County Court establishment has been alike ineffectual. Indeed there are many members who really appear to be determind against every Measure which may expedite & facilitate the business of recovering debts & compelling a strict compliance with contracts. These are sufficient to throw impediments in the way of any improvements on our judiciary system tho they are not so powerful as to shut up our courts altogether.

A bill is now under the consideration of the house which has employd its ablest members & will I beleive end in being printed for the consideration of the people. Tis to restrict vessels from foreign nations to certain ports. Norfolk & Alexandria are the two which are now in contemplation. Tis calculated to agrandize very much those two commercial Towns & shoud it be adopted will I trust produce many happy effects.

We seem at length to have determined to hold but one session in the year. A bill for that purpose has gone through a committee of the whole house, it has not yet passd into a law but the greatest obstacles are I hope surmounted.

As soon as the Assembly rises I shall go up to Fauquier. My present plan is to pass my summers there & my winters here. I am uncertain whether or not 'twill hold in practise.

Present my compliments to your Lady. I am dear Sir with the greatest esteem, Your

BRITISH DEBTS AND THE CONFEDERATION

To James Monroe

Dear Sir   Richmond, December 2, 1784
   Yours of the 14th. of Novr. I have just received. I congratulate you sincerely on your safe return to the Atlantic part of
our world.
   I wish with you that our Assembly had never passed those
resolutions respecting the British debts which have been so
much the subject of reprehension throughout the States. I wish
it because it affords a pretext to the British to retain possession
of the forts on the lakes but much more because I ever considered it as a measure tending to weaken the federal bands
which in my conception are too weak already. We are about,
though reluctantly to correct the error. Some resolutions have
passed a Committee of the whole house & been received by
the house on which a bill is to be brought in removing all impediments in the way of the treaty & directing the payment of
debts by instalments. The resolutions were introduced by your
Unkle. As the bill at present stands there are to be seven annual payments, the first to commence in April 1786.
   We have as yet done nothing finally. Not a bill of public importance, in which an individual was not particularly interested
has passd. The exclusive privilege given to Rumsey & his assigns to build & navigate his new invented boats, is of as much
perhaps more consequence than any other bill we have passed.
We have rejected some which in my conception woud have
been advantageous to this country. Among these I rank the bill
for encouraging intermarriages with the Indians. Our prejudices
however oppose themselves to our interests & operate too
powerfully for them. The two subjects which now most engross
the attention of the Legislature are the General Assessment &
circuit court bills. I am apprehensive they will both be thrown
out. When supported by all the Oratory & influence of Mr.
Henry the former coud scarcely gain admission into the house
& now, when he is about moving in sphere of less real importance & power his favorite measure must miscarry. I am sorry
the members of Council were appointed before your letter

recommending Colo. Mercer had reachd me. Had I known that that Gentleman wished an appointment in the Executive I should certainly not have been unmindful of the debt I contracted with him on a former similar occasion. Mr. Jones supplies the vacancy made by the resignation of Mr. Short & Mr. Roane & Mr. Selden take the places of our old friend Smith & of Colo. Christian. I exerted myself though ineffectually for Carrington. He was excessively mortified at his disappointment & the more as he was within one vote of Selden & as that vote was lost by the carelessness of Colo. Jack Nicholas who walked out just as we were about to ballot the last time & did not return till it was too late to admit his ticket. I endeavored too to promote the interests of your friend Wilson Nicholas who is just about to form a matrimonial connexion with Miss Smith of Baltimore, but he was *distanced*.

I shewd my Father that part of your letter, which respects the western Country. He says he will render you every service of the kind you mention which is within his power with a great deal of pleasure. He says tho that Mr. Humphry Marshall a Cousin & Brother of mine is better acquainted with the lands & would be better enabled to work for your advantage than he woud. If however you wish rather to depend on my Father I presume he may avail himself of the knowledge of his son in law.

I do not know what to say to your scheme of selling out. If you can execute it you will have made a very capital sum, if you can retain your lands you will be poor during life unless you remove to the western country but you will have securd for posterity an immense fortune. I shoud prefer the selling business & if you adopt it I think you have fixd on a very proper price.

Adieu. May you be very happy is the wish of your

AFFAIRS IN KENTUCKY

To George Muter

Dear Sir: Richmond, January 7, 1785

Let me thank you for the full account you have given me of the situation of affairs in the western country. I begin to think that the time for a separation is fast approaching, and has perhaps actually arrived. All I am solicitous about is, that the business be done with wisdom and temperance. If honor and public faith should be distinguished features in the character of the new State, she will soon attract very many of the wise and virtuous from her sister States, and Kentucky may be the seat of happiness as well as wealth. It is impossible that we can, at this distance, legislate wisely for you, and it is proper that you should legislate for yourselves. I presume you heard that Mr. Innes was chosen attorney general for your district court. We had you nominated as judge in his place, and I am persuaded you would have been appointed in preference to any other person who was in nomination, had not Cyrus Griffin been put on the list. Your friends withdrew you. There is some doubt whether that gentleman will serve or not. If he should decline it, you may depend on my applying for you to the executive, and using my best endeavors to procure the appointment for you. The salary is £300 per annum.

We have passed two bills this session of the utmost consequence both to you and us. They are, to open the communication between the James and Potomac rivers with the western waters. Should this succeed, and should Mr. Rumsey's scheme for making boats to work against the stream answer the expectation of our sanguine gentlemen, the communication between us will be easy, and we shall have but little occasion to contest the navigation of the Mississippi. My father sets out early in the spring. Will you present my compliments to my acquaintances in your country, and believe me to be, dear colonel, with esteem and affection, yours,

To James Wilkinson

Dear Sir,   Richmond, January 5, 1787

It is with a great deal of mortification I tell you that I have failed in obtaining the passport I applied for. On my mentioning the subject to the Governor he said he was acquainted with you and would with great pleasure do any thing which was proper to serve you. He took time to consider the subject and after several applications, told me to-day that to grant the passport as an official act was entirely improper because it could only extend to the limits of Virginia to which you had a right to go without his permit and that he could not write a private letter of recommendation to the Governor without having some acquaintance with him. On these reasons sir, my application in your favor was rejected. I am much chagrined at my disappointment.

I am much indebted to you for the clear and succinct account you have given me of the two expeditions against the Indians. I fear with you that so long as you remain connected with Virginia it will be absolutely impossible to act on any great occasion with reputation or success. Just information from such a distance will never be obtained by government without a solicitude about intelligence which seldom exists in a proper degree on the eve of a separation. You are considered as being certainly about to part with us and therefore less attention will be given to any regulations respecting your country than if the disunion was not expected.

All is gloom in the eastern states. Massachusetts is rent into two equal factions and an appeal I fear has by this time been made to the God of battles. Three of the leaders of the opponents to Government have been taken and imprisoned in Boston. The whole force of the party is collected for their releif. The last intelligence gives us reason to fear that before this time the attempt to relieve them has been made with the whole power of one party and opposed by the whole power of the other. But of this I suppose you receive better information than I can give you. We have contradictory accounts of the motives and views of the insurgents. We are sometimes informed that they are a British faction supported secretly from Canada whose immediate object is to overthrow the present and restore the former government, at other times we are told that it is a mere contest for power between Bowdoin and Hancock and that the Hancock faction are aiming at the destruction of all public securities and the subversion of all public faith. Whatever may be the cause of these dissentions or however they may terminate, in their present operation they deeply affect the happiness and reputation of the United States. They will, however, I presume tend to people the western world if you can govern yourselves so wisely as to present a safe retreat to the weaker party. These violent, I fear bloody, dissentions in a state I had thought inferior in wisdom and virtue to no one in the union, added to the strong tendency which the politics of many eminent characters among ourselves have to promote private and public dishonesty cast a deep shade over that bright prospect which the revolution in America and the establishment of our free governments had opened to the votaries of liberty throughout the globe. I fear, and there is no opinion more degrading to the dignity of man, that those have truth on their side who say that man is incapable of governing himself. I fear we may live to see another revolution. I am dear sir, with high esteem and respect, Your obed't serv't.

KENTUCKY AND THE MISSISSIPPI

To George Muter

My dear Sir   Richmond, February 11, 1787
    How do you approve of the measures of the last assembly so far as they affect your district? But before you can answer this I expect to hear your sentiments & those of your country. A separation I expect either has or will be decided on. I had the other day some conversation with Colo. Carrington one of our Delegates in Congress on the subject and he seems to entertain some doubt whether Congress will consent to your admission into the union. Do not imagine that any difficulties will be

generated by virginia or her Delegates—I beleive I can assure you that you will experience from them every good office. What prospect have you of obtaining the navigation of the Mississipi & what are your sentiments of the treaty about the cession of it for a term of years? People in general here are decidedly against it & yet some who are deeply interested in the prosperity of the western country appear to wish for it as being beneficial to you. I cannot conjecture how this opinion is to be supported but I assure it is the opinion of some very rational men who are I beleive sincere friends to the prosperity of the western country. I suppose you have before this collected all the comfortable things of this world except one to share them with you. How do you feel on that subject? Are you not beginning to think tis time to take up the consideration of that subject? Farewell I am my dear Sir with the warmest wishes for your happiness, your

RELATIONS WITH SPAIN

To Arthur Lee

Dear Sir   Richmond, March 5, 1787
   Your favor of the 10th of Jany. is now before me. I have not sent the letter you enclosed me in search of Mr. Imlay because I am told by my brother who is much better acquainted with him than I am that he either now is or will very soon be in New York.
   I have in my possession the notes you enquire for. I very much fear that the conduct of some unthinking men in the western country will embroil us with Spain unless there be some more vigorous interposition of government than we seem disposed to make. A memorial signed by some of the most respectable persons of Kentucky has lately been presented to the Governor on this subject in which the conduct of General Clarke I am told is a good deal criminated. Whether the cession for a time of the navigation of the Mississipi would conduce to the interests of the western country or not must depend on facts of which I have but little information & therefore have never

formed a decided opinion on the subject; but the people of this as well as of the Kentucky country who seem to form no adequate ideas of the magnitude of danger while at a distance have pronounced upon it without hesitation.

Mr. Henry whose opinions have their usual influence has been heard to say that he would rather part with the confederation than relinquish the navigation of the Mississipi—but as we have been fortiter in modo, I dare say we shall be suaviter in re.

I congratulate you on the prospect of reestablishing order & good government in Massachusetts. I think their government will now stand more firmly than before the insurrection provided some examples are made in order to impress on the minds of the people a conviction that punishment will surely follow an attempt to subvert the laws & government of the Commonwealth.

Our attention is now entirely turned towards the next elections—the debtors as usual are endeavoring to come into the Assembly & as usual I fear they will succeed. I am dear Sir with the highest esteem, your obedt Servt.

Speech in the Virginia Ratifying Convention on the Necessity of Adopting the Constitution

MR. *John Marshall.*—Mr. Chairman,—I conceive that the object of the discussion now before us, is, whether Democracy, or Despotism, be most eligible. I am sure that those who framed the system submitted to our investigation, and those who now support it, intend the establishment and security of the former. The supporters of the Constitution claim the title of being firm friends of liberty, and the rights of mankind. They say, that they consider it as the best means of protecting liberty. We, Sir, idolize Democracy. Those who oppose it have bestowed eulogiums on Monarchy. We prefer this system to any Monarchy, because we are convinced that it has a greater tendency to secure our liberty and promote our happiness. We admire it, because we think it a well regulated Democracy. It is recommended to the good people of this country—They are, through us, to declare whether it be such a plan of Government, as will establish and secure their freedom. Permit me to attend to what the Honorable Gentlemen (Mr. *Henry*) has said. He has expatiated on the necessity of a due attention to certain maxims—to certain fundamental principles, from which a free people ought never to depart. I concur with him in the propriety of the observance of such maxims. They are necessary in any Government, but more essential to a Democracy than to any other. What are the favourite maxims of Democracy? A strict observance of justice and public faith, and a steady adherence to virtue. These, Sir, are the principles of a good Government. No mischief—no misfortune ought to deter us from a strict observance of justice and public faith. Would to Heaven that these principles had been observed under the present Government! Had this been the case, the friends of liberty would not be so willing now to part with it. Can we boast that our Government is founded on these maxims? Can we pretend to the enjoyment of political freedom, or security, when we are told, that a man has been, by an act of Assembly, struck out of existence, without a trial by jury—without examination—

without being confronted with his accusers and witnesses—
without the benefits of the law of the land? Where is our safety,
when we are told, that this act was justifiable, because the
person was not a Socrates? What has become of the worthy
member's maxims? Is this one of them? Shall it be a maxim,
that a man shall be deprived of his life without the benefit of
law? Shall such a deprivation of life be justified by answering,
that the man's life was not taken *secundum artem*, because he
was a bad man? Shall it be a maxim, that Government ought
not to be empowered to protect virtue?

The Honorable member, after attempting to vindicate that
tyrannical Legislative act to which I have been alluding, proceeded to take a view of the dangers to which this country is
exposed. He told us, that the principal danger arose, from a Government, which if adopted, would give away the Mississippi. I
intended to proceed regularly, by attending to the clause under
debate, but I must reply to some observations which were dwelt
upon, to make impressions on our minds, unfavourable to the
plan upon the table. Have we no navigation in, or do we derive
no benefit from, the Mississippi? How shall we attain it? By retaining that weak Government which has hitherto kept it from
us? Is it thus that we shall secure that navigation? Give the
Government the power of retaining it, and then we may hope
to derive actual advantages from it. Till we do this, we cannot
expect that a Government which hitherto has not been able to
protect it, will have power to do it hereafter. Have we not attended too long to consider whether this Government would
be able to protect us? Shall we wait for further proofs of its inefficacy? If on mature consideration, the Constitution will be
found to be perfectly right on the subject of treaties, and containing no danger of losing that navigation, will he still object?
Will he object because eight States are unwilling to part with
it? This is no good ground of objection. He then stated the
necessity and probability of obtaining amendments. This we
ought to postpone till we come to that clause, and make up our
minds, whether there be any thing unsafe in the system. He
conceived it impossible to obtain amendments after adopting
it. If he was right, does not his own argument prove, that in
his own conception, previous amendments cannot be had; for,
Sir, if subsequent amendments cannot be obtained, shall we get

amendments before we ratify? The reasons against the latter do not apply against the former. There are in this State, and in every State of the Union, many who are decided enemies of the Union. Reflect on the probable conduct of such men. What will they do? They will bring amendments which are local in their nature, and which they know will not be accepted. What security have we, that other States will not do the same? We are told, that many in the States are violently opposed to it. They are more mindful of local interests. They will never propose such amendments, as they think would be obtained. Disunion will be their object. This will be attained by the proposal of unreasonable amendments. This, Sir, though a strong cause, is not the only one that will militate against previous amendments. Look at the comparative temper of this country now, and when the late Federal Convention met. We had no idea then of any particular system. The formation of the most perfect plan was our object and wish. It was imagined that the States would accede to, and be pleased with the proposition that would be made them. Consider the violence of opinions, the prejudices and animosities which have been since imbibed. Will not these greatly operate against mutual concessions, or a friendly concurrence? This will, however, be taken up more properly at another time. He says, we wish to have a strong, energetic, powerful Government. We contend for a well regulated Democracy. He insinuates, that the power of the Government has been enlarged by the Convention, and that we may apprehend it will be enlarged by others. The Convention did not in fact assume any power. They have proposed to our consideration a scheme of Government which they thought advisable. We are not bound to adopt it, if we disapprove of it. Had not every individual in this community a right to tender that scheme which he thought most conducive to the welfare of his country? Have not several Gentlemen already demonstrated, that the Convention did not exceed their powers? But the Congress have the power of making bad laws it seems. The Senate, with the President, he informs us, may make a treaty which shall be disadvantageous to us—and that if they be not good men, it will not be a good Constitution. I shall ask the worthy member only, if the people at large, and they only, ought to make laws and treaties? Has any man this in contemplation? You

cannot exercise the powers of Government personally yourselves. You must trust agents. If so, will you dispute giving them
the power of acting for you, from an existing possibility that
they may abuse it? As long as it is impossible for you to transact your business in person, if you repose no confidence in delegates, because there is a possibility of their abusing it, you can
have *no* Government; for the power of doing good, is inseparable from that of doing some evil.

We may derive from Holland, lessons very beneficial to ourselves. Happy that country which can avail itself of the misfortunes of others—which can gain knowledge from that source
without fatal experience! What has produced the late disturbances in that country? The want of such a Government as
is on your table, and having in some measure such a one as
you are about to part with. The want of proper powers in the
Government—The consequent deranged and relaxed administration—The violence of contending parties, and inviting foreign powers to interpose in their disputes, have subjected them
to all the mischiefs which have interrupted their harmony. I
cannot express my astonishment at his high-coloured eulogium on such a Government. Can any thing be more dissimi-
lar than the relation between the British Government, and the
Colonies, and the relation between Congress and the States.
We *were not* represented in Parliament. Here we are represented.
Arguments which prove the impropriety of being taxed by
Britain, do not hold against the exercise of taxation by Congress. Let me pay attention to the observation of the Gentleman who was last up, that the power of taxation ought not to
be given to Congress. This subject requires the undivided attention of this House. This power I think essentially necessary,
for without it, there will be no efficiency in the Government.
We have had a sufficient demonstration of the vanity of depending on requisitions. How then can the General Government exist without this power? The possibility of its being
abused, is urged as an argument against its expediency. To very
little purpose did Virginia discover the defects in the old system
—To little purpose indeed did she propose improvements—
and to no purpose is this plan constructed for the promotion
of our happiness, if we refuse it now, because it is possible that
it may be abused. The Confederation has nominal powers, but

no means to carry them into effect. If a system of Government were devised by more than human intelligence, it would not be effectual if the means were not adequate to the power. All delegated powers are liable to be abused. Arguments drawn from this source go in direct opposition to every Government, and in recommendation of anarchy. The friends of the Constitution are as tenacious of liberty as its enemies. They wish to give no power that will endanger it. They wish to give the Government powers to secure and protect it. Our enquiry here must be, whether the power of taxation be necessary, to perform the objects of the Constitution, and whether it be safe and as well guarded as human wisdom can do it. What are the objects of the national Government? To protect the United States, and to promote the general welfare. Protection in time of war is one of its principal objects. Until mankind shall cease to have ambition and avarice, wars will arise. The prosperity and happiness of the people depend on the performance of these great and important duties of the General Government. Can these duties be performed by one State? Can one State protect us, and promote our happiness? The Honorable Gentleman who has gone before me (Governor *Randolph*) has shewn that Virginia cannot do these things. How then can they be done? By the national Government only. Shall we refuse to give it power to do them? We are answered, that the powers may be abused. That though the Congress may promote our happiness, yet they may prostitute their powers to destroy our liberties. This goes to the destruction of all confidence in agents. Would you believe that men who had merited your highest confidence would deceive you? Would you trust them again after one deception? Why then hesitate to trust the General Government? The object of our inquiry is,—*Is the power necessary— and is it guarded*? There must be men and money to protect us. How are armies to be raised? Must we not have money for that purpose? But the Honorable Gentleman says, that we need not be afraid of war. Look at history, which has been so often quoted. Look at the great volume of human nature. They will foretell you, that a defenceless country cannot be secure. The nature of man forbids us to conclude, that we are in no danger from war. The passions of men stimulate them to avail themselves of the weakness of others. The powers of Europe are jealous of us. It is our interest to watch their conduct, and guard against them. They must be pleased with our disunion. If we invite them by our weakness to attack us, will they not do it? If we add debility to our present situation, a partition of America may take place. It is then necessary to give the Government that power in time of peace, which the necessities of war will render indispensable, or else we shall be attacked unprepared. The experience of the world, a knowledge of human nature, and our own particular experience, will confirm this truth. When danger will come upon us, may we not do what we were on the point of doing once already, that is, appoint a Dictator? Were those who are now friends of this Constitution, less active in the defence of liberty on that trying occasion, than those who oppose it? When foreign dangers come, may not the fear of immediate destruction by foreign enemies impel us to take a most dangerous step? Where then will be our safety? We may now regulate and frame a plan that will enable us to repel attacks, and render a recurrence to dangerous expedients unnecessary. If we be prepared to defend ourselves, there will be little inducement to attack us. But if we defer giving the necessary power to the General Government, till the moment of danger arrives, we shall give it then, and with an *unsparing hand*. America, like other nations, may be exposed to war. The propriety of giving this power will be proved by the history of the world, and particularly of modern Republics. I defy you to produce a single instance where requisitions on the several individual States composing a confederacy, have been honestly complied with. Did Gentlemen expect to see such punctually complied with in America? If they did, our own experience shews the contrary. We are told, that the Confederation carried us through the war. Had not the enthusiasm of liberty inspired us with unanimity, that system would never have carried us through it. It would have been much sooner terminated had that Government been possessed of due energy. The inability of Congress, and the failure of the States to comply with the Constitutional requisitions, rendered our resistance less efficient than it might have been. The weakness of that Government caused troops to be against us which ought to be on our side, and prevented all the resources of the community from being called at once into action. The extreme readiness of the people to make their utmost exertions to ward off the pressing danger, supplied the place of requisitions. When they came solely to be depended on, their inutility was fully discovered. A bare sense of duty, or a regard to propriety is too feeble to induce men to comply with obligations. We deceive ourselves if we expect any efficacy from these. If requisitions will not avail, the Government must have the sinews of war some other way. Requisitions cannot be effectual. They will be productive of delay, and will ultimately be inefficient. By direct taxation, the necessities of the Government will be supplied in a peaceable manner without irritating the minds of the people. But requisitions cannot be rendered efficient without a civil war—without great expence of money, and the blood of our citizens. Are there any other means? Yes, that Congress shall apportion the respective quotas previously, and if not complied with by the States, that then this dreaded power shall be exercised. The operation of this has been described by the Gentleman who opened the debate. He cannot be answered. This great objection to that system remains unanswered. Is there no other argument which ought to have weight with us on this subject? Delay is a strong and pointed objection to it. We are told by the Gentleman who spoke last, that direct taxation is unnecessary, because we are not involved in war. This admits the propriety of recurring to direct taxation if we were engaged in war. It has not been proved, that we have no dangers to apprehend on this point. What will be the consequence of the system proposed by the worthy Gentleman? Suppose the States should refuse. The worthy Gentleman who is so pointedly opposed to the Constitution, proposes remonstrances. Is it a time for Congress to remonstrate, or compel a compliance with requisitions, when the whole wisdom of the Union, and the power of Congress are opposed to a foreign enemy? Another alternative is, that if the States shall appropriate certain funds for the use of Congress, that Congress shall not lay direct taxes. Suppose the funds appropriated by the State for the use of Congress, should be inadequate; it will not be determined whether they be insufficient till after the time at which the quota ought to have been paid, and then after so long a delay, the means of procuring money which ought to have been employed in the first instance, must be recurred to. May they not be amused by such ineffectual and temporising alternatives, from year to year, till America shall be enslaved? The failure of one State will authorise a failure in another. The calculation in some States that others will fail, will produce general failures. This will also be attended with all the expences which we are anxious to avoid. What are the advantages to induce us to embrace this system? If they mean that requisitions should be complied with, it will be the same as if Congress had the power of direct taxation. The same amount will be paid by the people.

It is objected, that Congress will not know how to lay taxes so as to be easy and convenient for the people at large. Let us pay strict attention to this objection. If it appears to be totally without foundation, the necessity of levying direct taxes will obviate what Gentlemen say, nor will there be any colour for refusing to grant the power. The objects of direct taxes are well understood—They are but few—What are they? Lands, slaves, stock of all kinds, and a few other articles of domestic property. Can you believe that ten men selected from all parts of the State, chosen because they know the situation of the people, will be unable to determine so as to make the tax equal on, and convenient for, the people at large? Does any man believe, that they would lay the tax without the aid of other information, besides their own knowledge, when they know that the very object for which they are elected, is to lay the taxes in a judicious and convenient manner? If they wish to retain the affection of the people at large, will they not inform themselves of every circumstance that can throw light on the subject? Have they but one source of information? Besides their own experience— their knowledge of what will suit their constituents, they will have the benefit of the knowledge and experience of the State Legislatures. They will see in what manner the Legislature of Virginia collects its taxes. Will they be unable to follow their example? The Gentlemen who shall be delegated to Congress will have every source of information that the Legislatures of the States can have, and can lay the tax as equally on the people and with as little oppression as they can. If then it be admitted, that they can understand how to lay them equally and conveniently, are we to admit that they will not do it; but that in violation of every principle that ought to govern men, they will lay them so as to oppress us? What benefit will they have by it? Will it be promotive of their re-election? Will it be by wantonly imposing hardships and difficulties on the people at large, that they will promote their own interest, and secure their re-election? To me it appears incontrovertible, that they will settle them in such a manner, as to be easy for the people. Is the system so organized as to make taxation dangerous? I shall not go to the various checks of the Government, but examine whether the immediate representation of the people be well constructed. I conceive its organization to be sufficiently satisfactory to the warmest friend of freedom. No tax can be laid without the consent of the House of Representatives. If there be no impropriety in the mode of electing the Representatives, can any danger be apprehended? They are elected by those, who can elect Representatives in the State Legislature. How can the votes of the electors be influenced? By nothing but the character and conduct of the man they vote for. What object can influence them when about choosing him? They have nothing to direct them in the choice, but their own good. Have you not as pointed and strong a security as you can possibly have? It is a mode that secures an impossibility of being corrupted. If they are to be chosen for their wisdom, virtue and integrity, what inducement have they to infringe on our freedom? We are told that they may abuse their power. Are there strong motives to prompt them to abuse it? Will not such abuse militate against their own interest? Will not they and their friends feel the effects of iniquitous measures? Does the Representative remain in office for life? Does he transmit his title of Representative to his son? Is he secured from the burthen imposed on the community? To procure their re-election, it will be necessary for them to confer with the people at large, and convince them that the taxes laid are for their good. If I am able to judge on the subject, the power of taxation now before us, is wisely conceded, and the Representatives are wisely elected.

The Honorable Gentleman said, that a Government should ever depend on the affections of the people. It must so. It is the best support it can have. This Government merits the confidence of the people, and I make no doubt will have it. Then he informed us again, of the disposition of Spain with respect to the Mississippi, and the conduct of the Government with regard to it. To the debility of the Confederation alone, may justly be imputed every cause of complaint on this subject. Whenever Gentlemen will bring forward their objections, I trust we can prove, that no danger to the navigation of that river can arise from the adoption of this Constitution. I beg those Gentlemen who may be affected by it, to suspend their judgment till they hear it discussed. Will, says he, the adoption of this Constitution pay our debts? It will compel the States to pay their quotas. Without this, Virginia will be unable to pay.— Unless all the States pay, she cannot. Though the States will not coin money, (as we are told) yet this Government will bring forth and proportion all the strength of the Union. That oeconomy and industry are essential to our happiness will be denied by no man. But the present Government will not add to our industry. It takes away the incitements to industry, by rendering property insecure and unprotected. It is the paper on your table that will promote and encourage industry. New-Hampshire and Rhode-Island have rejected it, he tells us. New-Hampshire, if my information be right, will certainly adopt it. The report spread in this country, of which I have heard, is, that the Representatives of that State having, on meeting, found they were instructed to vote against it, returned to their Constituents without determining the question, to convince them of their being mistaken, and of the propriety of adopting it. The extent of the country is urged as another objection, as being too great for a Republican Government. This objection has been handed from author to author, and has been certainly misunderstood and misapplied. To what does it owe its source? To observations and criticisms on Governments, where representation did not exist. As to the Legislative power, was it ever supposed inadequate to any extent? Extent of country may render it difficult to execute the laws, but not to Legislate. Extent of country does not extend the power. What will be sufficiently energetic and operative in a small territory, will be feeble when extended over a wide extended country. The Gentleman tells us, there are no checks in this plan. What has become of his enthusiastic eulogium on the American spirit? We should find a check and controul when oppressed, from that source. In this country, there is no exclusive personal stock of interest. The interest of the community is blended and inseparably connected with that of the individual.—When he promotes his own, he promotes that of the community. When we consult the common good, we consult our own. When he desires such checks as these, he will find them abundantly here. They are the best checks. What has become of his eulogium on the Virginia Constitution? Do the checks in this plan appear less excellent than those of the Constitution of Virginia? If the checks in the Constitution be compared to the checks in the Virginian Constitution, he will find the best security in the former.

The temple of liberty was complete, said he, when the people of England said to their King, that he was their servant. What are we to learn from this? Shall we embrace such a system as that? Is not liberty secure with us, where the people hold all powers in their own hands, and delegate them cautiously, for short periods, to their servants, who are accountable for the smallest mal-administration? Where is the nation that can boast greater security than we do? We want only a system like the paper before you, to strengthen and perpetuate this security.

The Honorable Gentleman has asked, if there be any safety or freedom, when we give away the sword and the purse? Shall the people at large hold the sword and the purse without the interposition of their Representatives? Can the whole aggregate community act personally? I apprehend that every Gentleman will see the impossibility of this. Must they then not trust them to others? To whom are they to trust them but to their Representatives who are accountable for their conduct? He represents secrecy as unnecessary, and produces the British Government as a proof of its inutility. Is there no secrecy there? When deliberating on the propriety of declaring war, or on military arrangements, do they deliberate in the open fields? No, Sir. The British Government affords secrecy when necessary, and so ought every Government. In this plan, secrecy is only used when it would be fatal and pernicious to publish the schemes of Government. We are threatened with the loss of our liberties by the possible abuse of power, notwithstanding the maxim, that those who give may take away. It is the people that give power, and can take it back. What shall restrain them? They are the masters who give it, and of whom their servants hold it.

He then argues against this system, because it does not resemble the British Government in this, that the same power that declares war has not the means of carrying it on. Are the people of England more secure, if the Commons have no voice in declaring war, or are we less secure by having the Senate joined with the President? It is an absurdity, says the worthy member, that the same man should obey two masters—that the same collector should gather taxes for the General Government and the State Legislature. Are they not both the servants of the people? Are not Congress and the State Legislatures the agents of the people, and are they not to consult the good of the people? May not this be effected by giving the same officer the collection of both taxes? He tells you, that it is an absurdity to adopt before you amend. Is the object of your adoption to amend solely? The objects of your adoption are Union, and safety against foreign enemies—Protection against faction— against what has been the destruction of all Republics. These impel you to its adoption. If you adopt it, what shall restrain you from amending it, if in trying it, amendments shall be found necessary? The Government is not supported by force, but depending on our free will. When experience shall shew us any inconveniences, we can then correct it. But until we have experience on the subject, amendments, as well as the Constitution itself, are to try. Let us try it, and keep our hands free to change it when necessary. If it be necessary to change Government, let us change that Government which has been found to be defective. The difficulty we find in amending the Confederation, will not be found in amending this Constitution. Any amendments in the system before you, will not go to a radical change—a plain way is pointed out for the purpose. All will be interested to change it, and therefore all will exert themselves in getting the change. There is such a diversity of sentiments in human minds, that it is impossible we shall ever concur in one system, till we try it. The power given to the General Government over the time, place, and manner of election, is also strongly objected to. When we come to that clause, we can prove that it is highly necessary, and not dangerous.

The worthy member has concluded his observations by many eulogiums on the British Constitution. It matters not to us whether it be a wise one or not. I think, that for America at least, the Government on your table is very much superior to it. I ask you, if your House of Representatives would be better than it is, if a hundredth part of the people were to elect a majority of them? If your Senators were for life, would they be more agreeable to you? If your President were not accountable to you for his conduct; if it were a constitutional maxim, that he could do no wrong, would you be safer than you are now? If you can answer *yes* to these questions, then adopt the British Constitution. If not, then good as that Government may be, this is better. The worthy Gentleman who was last up, told us, that the Confederacies of ancient and modern times were not similar to ours, and that consequently reasons which applied against them, could not be urged against it. Do they not hold out one lesson very useful to us? However unlike in other respects, they resemble it in its total inefficacy. They warn us to shun their calamities, and place in our General Government, those necessary powers, the want of which destroyed them. I hope we shall avail ourselves of their misfortunes, without experiencing them. There was something peculiar in one observation he made. He said, that those who governed the cantons of Switzerland were purchased by foreign powers, which was the cause of their uneasiness and trouble. How does this apply to us? If we adopt such a Government as theirs, will it not be subject to the same inconvenience? Will not the same cause produce the same effect? What shall protect us from it? What is our security? He then proceeded to say, that the causes of war are removed from us—that we are separated by the sea from the powers of Europe, and need not be alarmed. Sir, the sea makes them neighbours to us. Though an immense ocean divides us, we may speedily see them with us. What dangers may we not apprehend to our commerce? Does not our naval weakness invite an attack on our commerce? May not the Algerines sieze our vessels? Cannot they, and every other predatory or maritime nation, pillage our ships and destroy our commerce, without subjecting themselves to any inconvenience? He would, he said, give the General Government all necessary powers. If any thing be necessary, it must be so, to call forth the strength of the Union, when we may be attacked, or when the general purposes of America require it. The worthy Gentleman then proceeded to shew, that our present exigencies are greater than they will ever be again. Who can penetrate into futurity? How can any man pretend to say, that our future exigencies will be less than our present? The exigencies of nations have been generally commensurate to their resources. It would be the utmost impolicy to trust to a mere possibility of not being attacked, or obliged to exert the strength of the community. He then spoke of a selection of particular objects by Congress, which he says must necessarily be oppressive. That Congress for instance, might select lands for direct taxes, and that all but landholders would escape. Cannot Congress regulate the taxes so as to be equal on all parts of the community? Where is the absurdity of having thirteen revenues? Will they clash with, or injure, each other? If not, why cannot Congress make thirteen distinct laws, and impose the taxes on the general objects of taxation in each State, so as that all persons of the society shall pay equally as they ought?

He then told you, that your Continental Government will call forth the virtue and talents of America. This being the case, will they encroach on the powers of the State Governments? Will our most virtuous and able citizens wantonly attempt to destroy the liberty of the people? Will the most virtuous act the most wickedly? I differ in opinion from the worthy Gentleman. I think the virtue and talents of the members of the General Government will tend to the security, instead of the destruction of our liberty. I think that the power of direct taxation is essential to the existence of the General Government, and that it is safe to grant it. If this power be not necessary, and as safe from abuse as any delegated power can possibly be, then I say, that the plan before you is unnecessary; for it imports not what system we have, unless it have the power of protecting us in time of peace and war.

June 10, 1788

Speech in the Virginia Ratifying Convention on the Militia

Mr. *John Marshall*, asked if Gentlemen were serious, when they asserted that if the State Governments had power to interfere with the militia, it was by implication? If they were, he asked the Committee, whether the least attention would not shew that they were mistaken? The State Governments did not derive their powers from the General Government. But each Government derived its powers from the people; and each was to act according to the powers given it. Would any Gentleman deny this? He demanded if powers not given, were retained by implication? Could any man say so? Could any man say, that this power was not retained by the States, as they had not given it away? For, says he, does not a power remain till it is given away? The State Legislatures had power to command and govern their militia before, and have it still, undeniably, unless there be something in this Constitution that takes it away. For Continental purposes Congress may call forth the militia; as to suppress insurrections and repel invasions. But the power given to the States by the people is not taken away: For the Constitution does not say so. In the Confederation Congress had this power. But the State Legislatures had it also. The power of Legislation given them within the ten miles square is exclusive of the States, because it is expressed to be exclusive. The truth is, that when power is given to the General Legislature, if it was in the State Legislatures before, both shall exercise it; unless there be an incompatibility in the exercise by one, to that by the other; or negative words precluding the State Governments from it. But there are no negative words here. It rests therefore with the States. To me it appears then unquestionable, that the State Governments can call forth the militia, in case the Constitution should be adopted, in the same manner as they could have done, before its adoption. Gentlemen have said, that the States cannot defend itself without an application to Congress, because Congress can interpose! Does not every man feel a refutation of the argument in his own breast? I will shew, that there could not be a combination between those who formed the Constitution, to take away this power. All the restraints intended to be laid on the State Governments (besides where an exclusive power is expressly given to Congress) are contained in the tenth section, of the first article. This power is not included in the restrictions in that section.—But what excludes every possibility of doubt, is the last part of it.—That "no State shall engage in war, *unless actually invaded, or in such imminent danger as will not admit of delay.*" When invaded, they can engage in war; as also when in imminent danger. This clearly proves, that the States can use the militia when they find it necessary. The worthy Member last up, objects to the Continental Government possessing the power of disciplining the militia, because, though all its branches be derived from the people, he says, they will form an Aristocratic Government, unsafe and unfit to be trusted.

Mr. *Grayson* answered, that he only said it was so constructed as to form a great Aristocratic body.

Mr. *Marshall* replied, that he was not certain whether he understood him. But he thought he had said so. He conceived that as the Government was drawn from the people, the feelings and interests of the people would be attended to, and that we would be safe in granting them power to regulate the militia. When the Government is drawn from the people, continued Mr. *Marshall*, and depending on the people for its continuance, oppressive measures will not be attempted, as they will certainly draw on their authors the resentment of those on whom they depend. On this Government, thus depending on ourselves for its existence, I will rest my safety, notwithstanding the danger depicted by the Honorable Gentleman. I cannot help being surprised that the worthy Member thought this power so dangerous. What Government is able to protect you in time of war? Will any State depend on its own exertions?—The consequence of such dependance and withholding this power from Congress will be, that State will fall after State, and be a sacrifice to the want of power in the General Government. *United we are strong, divided we fall.* Will you prevent the General Government from drawing the militia of one State to another, when the consequence would be, that every State must depend on itself? The enemy possessing the water, can quickly go from one State to another. No State will spare to another its militia, which it conceives necessary for itself. It requires a superintending power, in order to call forth the resources of all to protect all. If this be not done, each State will fall a sacrifice. This system merits the highest applause in this respect. The Honorable Gentleman said, that a general regulation may be made to inflict punishments. Does he imagine that a militia law is to be engrafted on the scheme of Government, so as to render it incapable of being changed? The idea of the worthy Member supposes, that men will renounce their own interests. This would produce general inconveniences throughout the Union, and would be equally opposed by all the States. But the worthy Member fears, that in one part of the Union they will be regulated and disciplined, and in another neglected. This danger is enhanced by leaving this power to each State; for some States may attend to their militia, and others may neglect them. If Congress neglect our militia, we can arm them ourselves. Cannot Virginia import arms? Cannot she put them into the hands of her militia men? He then concluded by observing, that the power of governing the militia was not vested in the States by implication; because being possessed of it antecedent to the adoption of the Government, and not being divested of it, by any grant or restriction in the Constitution, they must necessarily be as fully possessed of it as ever they had been: And it could not be said, that the States derived any powers from that system, but retained them, though not acknowledged in any part of it.

June 16, 1788

Speech in the Virginia Ratifying Convention on the Judiciary

Mr. *John Marshall*,—Mr. Chairman.—This part of the plan before us, is a great improvement on that system from which we are now departing. Here are tribunals appointed for the decision of controversies, which were before, either not at all, or improperly provided for.—That many benefits will result from this to the members of the collective society, every one confesses. Unless its organization be defective, and so constructed as to injure, instead of accommodating the convenience of the people, it merits our approbation. After such a candid and fair discussion by those Gentlemen who support it—after the very able manner in which they have investigated and examined it, I conceived it would be no longer considered as so very defective, and that those who opposed it, would be convinced of the impropriety of some of their objections.—But I perceive they still continue the same opposition. Gentlemen have gone on an idea, that the Federal Courts will not determine the causes which may come before them, with the same fairness and impartiality, with which other Courts decide. What are the reasons of this supposition?—Do they draw them from the manner in which the Judges are chosen, or the tenure of their office?—What is it that makes us trust our Judges?—Their independence in office, and manner of appointment. Are not the Judges of the Federal Court chosen with as much wisdom, as the Judges of the State Governments?—Are they not equally, if not more independent?—If so, shall we not conclude, that they will decide with equal impartiality and candour?—If there be as much wisdom and knowledge in the United States, as in a particular State, shall we conclude that that wisdom and knowledge will not be equally exercised in the selection of the Judges?

The principle on which they object to the Federal jurisdiction, seems to me to be founded on a belief, that there will not be a fair trial had in those Courts. If this Committee will consider it fully, they will find it has no foundation, and that we are as secure there as any where else. What mischief results from some causes being tried there?—Is there not the utmost reason to conclude, that Judges wisely appointed, and independent in their office, will never countenance any unfair trial? —What are the subjects of its jurisdiction? Let us examine them with an expectation that causes will be as candidly tried there, as elsewhere, and then determine. The objection, which was made by the Honorable Member who was first up yesterday (Mr. *Mason*) has been so fully refuted, that it is not worth while to notice it. He objected to Congress having power to create a number of Inferior Courts according to the necessity of public circumstances. I had an apprehension that those Gentlemen who placed no confidence in Congress, would object that there might be no Inferior Courts. I own that I thought, that those Gentlemen would think there would be no Inferior Courts, as it depended on the will of Congress, but that we should be dragged to the centre of the Union. But I did not conceive, that the power of increasing the number of Courts could be objected to by any Gentleman, as it would remove the inconvenience of being dragged to the centre of the United States. I own that the power of creating a number of Courts, is, in my estimation, so far from being a defect, that it seems necessary to the perfection of this system. After having objected to the number and mode, he objected to the subject matter of their cognizance.—(Here Mr. *Marshall* read the 2d section.)—These, Sir, are the points of Federal jurisdiction to which he objects, with a few exceptions. Let us examine each of them with a supposition, that the same impartiality will be observed there, as in other Courts, and then see if any mischief will result from them.—With respect to its cognizance in all cases arising under the Constitution and the laws of the United States, he says, that the laws of the United States being paramount to the laws of particular States, there is no case but what this will extend to. Has the Government of the United States power to make laws on every subject?—Does he understand it so?—Can they make laws affecting the mode of transferring property, or contracts, or claims between citizens of the same State? Can they go beyond the delegated powers? If they were to make a law not warranted by any of the powers enumerated, it would be considered by the Judges as an infringement of the Constitution which they are to guard:—They would not consider such a law as coming under their jurisdiction.—

They would declare it void. It will annihilate the State Courts, says the Honorable Gentleman. Does not every Gentleman here know, that the causes in our Courts are more numerous than they can decide, according to their present construction? Look at the dockets.—You will find them crouded with suits, which the life of man will not see determined. If some of these suits be carried to other Courts, will it be wrong? They will still have business enough. Then there is no danger, that particular subjects, small in proportion, being taken out of the jurisdiction of the State Judiciaries, will render them useless and of no effect. Does the Gentleman think that the State Courts will have no cognizance of cases not mentioned here? Are there any words in this Constitution which excludes the Courts of the States from those cases which they now possess? Does the Gentleman imagine this to be the case? Will any Gentleman believe it? Are not controversies respecting lands claimed under the grants of different States, the only controversies between citizens of the same State, which the Federal Judiciary can take cognizance of? The case is so clear, that to prove it would be an useless waste of time. The State Courts will not lose the jurisdiction of the causes they now decide. They have a concurrence of jurisdiction with the Federal Courts in those cases, in which the latter have cognizance.

How disgraceful is it that the State Courts cannot be trusted, says the Honorable Gentleman! What is the language of the Constitution? Does it take away their jurisdiction? Is it not necessary that the Federal Courts should have cognizance of cases arising under the Constitution, and the laws of the United States? What is the service or purpose of a Judiciary, but to execute the laws in a peaceable orderly manner, without shedding blood, or creating a contest, or availing yourselves of force? If this be the case, where can its jurisdiction be more necessary than here? To what quarter will you look for protection from an infringement on the Constitution, if you will not give the power to the Judiciary? There is no other body that can afford such a protection. But the Honorable Member objects to it, because, he says, that the officers of the Government will be screened from merited punishment by the Federal Judiciary. The Federal Sheriff, says he, will go into a poor man's house, and beat him, or abuse his family, and the

Federal Court will protect him. Does any Gentleman believe this? Is it necessary that the officers will commit a trespass on the property or persons of those with whom they are to transact business? Will such great insults on the people of this country be allowable? Were a law made to authorise them, it would be void. The injured man would trust to a tribunal in his neighbourhood. To such a tribunal he would apply for redress, and get it. There is no reason to fear that he would not meet that justice there, which his country will be ever willing to maintain. But on appeal, says the Honorable Gentleman, what chance is there to obtain justice? This is founded on an idea, that they will not be impartial. There is no clause in the Constitution which bars the individual member injured, from applying to the State Courts to give him redress. He says that there is no instance of appeals as to fact in common law cases. The contrary is well known to you, Mr. Chairman, to be the case in this Commonwealth. With respect to mills, roads, and other cases, appeals lye from the Inferior to the Superior Court, as to fact as well as law. Is it a clear case, that there can be no case in common law, in which an appeal as to fact might be proper and necessary? Can you not conceive a case where it would be productive of advantages to the people at large, to submit to that tribunal the final determination, involving facts as well as law? Suppose it should be deemed for the convenience of the citizens, that those things which concerned foreign Ministers, should be tried in the Inferior Courts—If justice would be done, the decision would satisfy all. But if an appeal in matters of fact could not be carried to the Superior Court, then it would result, that such cases could not be tried before the Inferior Courts, for fear of injurious and partial decisions.

But, Sir, where is the necessity of discriminating between the three cases of chancery, admiralty, and common law? Why not leave it to Congress? Will it enlarge their powers? Is it necessary for them wantonly to infringe your rights? Have you any thing to apprehend, when they can in no case abuse their power without rendering themselves hateful to the people at large? When this is the case, something may be left to the Legislature freely chosen by ourselves, from among ourselves, who are to share the burdens imposed upon the community, and who can be changed at our pleasure. Where power may be trusted, and there is no motive to abuse it, it seems to me to be as well to leave it undetermined, as to fix it in the Constitution.

With respect to disputes between a State, and the citizens of another State, its jurisdiction has been decried with unusual vehemence. I hope no Gentleman will think that a State will be called at the bar of the Federal Court. Is there no such case at present? Are there not many cases in which the Legislature of Virginia is a party, and yet the State is not sued? It is not rational to suppose, that the sovereign power shall be dragged before a Court. The intent is, to enable States to recover claims of individuals residing in other States. I contend this construction is warranted by the words. But, say they, there will be partiality in it if a State cannot be defendant—if an individual cannot proceed to obtain judgment against a State, though he may be sued by a State. It is necessary to be so, and cannot be avoided. I see a difficulty in making a State defendant, which does not prevent its being plaintiff. If this be only what cannot be avoided, why object to the system on that account? If an individual has a just claim against any particular State, is it to be presumed, that on application to its Legislature, he will not obtain satisfaction? But how could a State recover any claim from a citizen of another State, without the establishment of these tribunals?

The Honorable Member objects to suits being instituted in the Federal Courts by the citizens of one State, against the citizens of another State. Were I to contend, that this was necessary in all cases, and that the Government without it would be defective, I should not use my own judgment. But are not the objections to it carried too far? Though it may not in general be absolutely necessary, a case may happen, as has been observed, in which a citizen of one State ought to be able to recur to this tribunal, to recover a claim from the citizen of another State. What is the evil which this can produce?—Will he get more than justice there?—The independence of the Judges forbids it. What has he to get?—Justice. Shall we object to this, because a citizen of another State can obtain justice without applying to our State Courts? It may be necessary with respect to the laws and regulations of commerce, which Congress may make. It may be necessary in cases of debt, and some other controversies. In claims for land it is not necessary, but it is not dangerous. In the Court of which State will it be instituted, said the Honorable Gentleman? It will be instituted in the Court of the State where the defendant resides,—where the law can come at him, and no where else. By the laws of which State will it be determined, said he? By the laws of the State where the contract was made. According to those laws, and those only, can it be decided. Is this a novelty?—No—it is a principle in the jurisprudence of this Commonwealth. If a man contracted a debt in the East-Indies, and it was sued for here, the decision must be consonant to the laws of that country.—Suppose a contract made in Maryland, where the annual interest is at six per centum; and a suit instituted for it in Virginia—What interest would be given now, without any Federal aid?—The interest of Maryland most certainly; and if the contract had been made in Virginia, and suit brought in Maryland, the interest of Virginia must be given without doubt.—It is now to be governed by the laws of that State where the contract was made. The laws which governed the contract at its formation, govern it in its decision. To preserve the peace of the Union only, its jurisdiction in this case ought to be recurred to.—Let us consider that when citizens of one State carry on trade in another State, much must be due to the one from the other, as is the case between North-Carolina and Virginia. Would not the refusal of justice to our citizens, from the Courts of North-Carolina, produce disputes between the States? Would the Federal Judiciary swerve from their duty in order to give partial and unjust decisions?

The objection respecting the assignment of a bond to a citizen of another State, has been fully answered. But suppose it were to be tried as he says, what could be given more than was actually due in the case he mentioned? It is *possible*, in our Courts as they now stand, to obtain a judgment for more than justice. But the Court of Chancery grants relief. Would it not be so in the Federal Court? Would not depositions be taken, to prove the payments, and if proved, would not the decision of the Court be accordingly?

He objects in the next place to its jurisdiction in controversies between a State, and a foreign State. Suppose, says he, in such a suit, a foreign State is cast, will she be bound by the decision? If a foreign State brought a suit against the Commonwealth of Virginia, would she not be barred from the claim if the Federal Judiciary thought it unjust? The previous consent of the parties is necessary. And, as the Federal Judiciary will decide, each party will acquiesce. It will be the means of preventing disputes with foreign nations. On an attentive consideration of these Courts, I trust every part will appear satisfactory to the Committee.

The exclusion of trial by jury in this case, he urged to prostrate our rights. Does the word Court only mean the Judges? Does not the determination of a jury, necessarily lead to the judgment of the Court? Is there any thing here which gives the Judges exclusive jurisdiction of matters of fact? What is the object of a jury trial? To inform the Court of the facts. When a Court has cognizance of facts, does it not follow, that they can make enquiry by a jury? It is impossible to be otherwise. I hope that in this country, where impartiality is so much admired, the laws will direct facts to be ascertained by a jury. But, says the Honorable Gentleman, the juries in the ten miles square will be mere tools of parties, with which he would not trust his person or property; which, he says, he would rather leave to the Court. Because the Government may have a district ten miles square, will no man stay there but the tools and officers of the Government?—Will no body else be found there? —Is it so in any other part of the world, where a Government has Legislative power?—Are there none but officers and tools of the Government of Virginia in Richmond?—Will there not be independent merchants, and respectable Gentlemen of fortune, within the ten miles square?—Will there not be worthy farmers and mechanics?—Will not a good jury be found there as well as any where else?—Will the officers of the Government become improper to be on a jury?—What is it to the Government, whether this man or that man succeeds?—It is all one thing. Does the Constitution say, that juries shall consist of officers, or that the Supreme Court shall be held in the ten miles square? It was acknowledged by the Honorable Member, that it was secure in England. What makes it secure there?—Is it their Constitution? What part of their Constitution is there, that the Parliament cannot change?—As the preservation of this right is in the hands of Parliament, and it has ever been held sacred by them, will the Government of America be less honest

than that of Great Britain? Here a restriction is to be found.
The jury is not to be brought out of the State. There is no
such restriction in that Government; for the laws of Parliament
decide every thing respecting it. Yet Gentlemen tell us, that
there is safety there, and nothing here but danger. It seems to
me, that the laws of the United States will generally secure trials
by a jury of the vicinage, or in such manner as will be most safe
and convenient for the people.

But it seems that the right of challenging the jurors, is not
secured in this Constitution. Is this done by our own Constitution, or by any provision of the English Government? Is it
done by their Magna Charta, or Bill of Rights? This privilege is
founded on their laws. If so, why should it be objected to the
American Constitution, that it is not inserted in it? If we are
secure in Virginia, without mentioning it in our Constitution,
why should not this security be found in the Federal Court?

The Honorable Gentleman said much about the quitrents
in the Northern Neck. I will refer it to the Honorable Gentleman himself. Has he not acknowledged, that there was no
complete title? Was he not satisfied, that the right of the legal
representative of the proprietor did not exist at the time he
mentioned? If so, it cannot exist now. I will leave it to those
Gentlemen who come from that quarter. I trust they will not
be intimidated on this account, in voting on this question. A
law passed in 1782, which secures this. He says that many poor
men may be harrassed and injured by the representative of
Lord Fairfax. If he has no right, this cannot be done. If he has
this right and comes to Virginia, what laws will his claims be
determined by? By those of this State. By what tribunals will
they be determined? By our State Courts. Would not the poor
man, who was oppressed by an unjust prosecution, be abundantly protected and satisfied by the temper of his neighbours,
and would he not find ample justice? What reason has the
Honorable Member to apprehend partiality or injustice? He
supposes, that if the Judges be Judges of both the Federal and
State Courts, they will incline in favour of one Government. If
such contests should arise, who could more properly decide
them, than those who are to swear to do justice? If we can expect a fair decision any where, may we not expect justice to be
done by the Judges of both the Federal and State Govern-

ments? But, says the Honorable Member, laws may be executed tyrannically. Where is the independency of your Judges?
If a law be executed tyrannically in Virginia, to what can you
trust? To your Judiciary. What security have you for justice?
Their independence. Will it not be so in the Federal Court?

Gentlemen ask what is meant by law cases, and if they be not
distinct from facts. Is there no law arising on cases in equity
and admiralty? Look at the acts of Assembly.—Have you not
many cases, where law and fact are blended? Does not the jurisdiction in point of law as well as fact, find itself completely
satisfied in law and fact? The Honorable Gentleman says, that
no law of Congress can make any exception to the Federal
appellate jurisdiction of fact as well as law. He has frequently
spoken of technical terms, and the meaning of them. What is the
meaning of the term *exception*? Does it not mean an alteration
and diminution? Congress is empowered to make exceptions
to the appellate jurisdiction, as to law and fact, of the Supreme
Court.—These exceptions certainly go as far as the Legislature
may think proper, for the interest and liberty of the people.—
Who can understand this word, *exception*, to extend to one
case as well as the other? I am persuaded, that a reconsideration of this case will convince the Gentleman, that he was mistaken. This may go to the cure of the mischief apprehended.
Gentlemen must be satisfied, that this power will not be so
much abused as they have said.

The Honorable Member says, that he derives no consolation
from the wisdom and integrity of the Legislature, because we
call them to rectify defects which it is our duty to remove. We
ought well to weigh the good and evil before we determine—
We ought to be well convinced, that the evil will be really produced before we decide against it. If we be convinced that the
good greatly preponderates, though there be small defects in
it, shall we give up that which is really good, when we can
remove the little mischief it may contain, in the plain easy
method pointed out in the system itself?

I was astonished when I heard the Honorable Gentleman
say, that he wished the trial by jury to be struck out entirely. Is
there no justice to be expected by a jury of our fellow citizens?
Will any man prefer to be tried by a Court, when the jury is to
be of his countrymen, and probably of his vicinage? We have

reason to believe the regulations with respect to juries will be such as shall be satisfactory. Because it does not contain all, does it contain nothing? But I conceive that this Committee will see there is safety in the case, and that there is no mischief to be apprehended.

He states a case, that a man may be carried from a federal to an antifederal corner, (and *vice versa*) where men are ready to destroy him. Is this probable? Is it presumeable that they will make a law to punish men who are of different opinions in politics from themselves? Is it presumeable, that they will do it in one single case, unless it be such a case as must satisfy the people at large? The good opinion of the people at large must be consulted by their Representatives; otherwise mischiefs would be produced, which would shake the Government to its foundation. As it is late, I shall not mention all the Gentleman's argument: But some parts of it are so glaring, that I cannot pass them over in silence. He says that the establishment of these tribunals, and more particularly in their jurisdiction of controversies between citizens of these States, and foreign citizens and subjects, is like a retrospective law. Is there no difference between a tribunal which shall give justice and effect to an existing right, and creating a right that did not exist before? The debt or claim is created by the individual. He has bound himself to comply with it. Does the creation of a new Court amount to a retrospective law?

We are satisfied with the provision made in this country on the subject of trial by jury. Does our Constitution direct trials to be by jury? It is required in our Bill of Rights, which is not a part of the Constitution. Does any security arise from hence? Have you a jury when a judgment is obtained on a replevy bond, or by default? Have you a jury when a motion is made for the Commonwealth, against an individual; or when a motion is made by one joint obligor against another, to recover sums paid as security? Our Courts decide in all these cases, without the intervention of a jury; yet they are all civil cases. The Bill of Rights is merely recommendatory. Were it otherwise, the consequence would be, that many laws which are found convenient, would be unconstitutional. What does the Government before you say? Does it exclude the Legislature from giving a trial by jury in civil cases? If it does not forbid its exclusion, it is on the same footing on which your State Government stands now. The Legislature of Virginia does not give a trial by jury where it is not necessary. But gives it wherever it is thought expedient. The Federal Legislature will do so too, as it is formed on the same principles.

The Honorable Gentleman says, that unjust claims will be made, and the defendant had better pay them than go to the Supreme Court. Can you suppose such a disposition in one of your citizens, as that to oppress another man, he will incur great expences? What will he gain by an unjust demand? Does a claim establish a right? He must bring his witnesses to prove his claim. If he does not bring his witnesses, the expences must fall upon him. Will he go on a calculation that the defendant will not defend it; or cannot produce a witness? Will he incur a great deal of expence, from a dependance on such a chance? Those who know human nature, black as it is, must know, that mankind are too well attached to their interest to run such a risk. I conceive, that this power is absolutely necessary, and not dangerous; that should it be attended by little inconveniences, they will be altered, and that they can have no interest in not altering them. Is there any real danger?—When I compare it to the exercise of the same power in the Government of Virginia, I am persuaded there is not. The Federal Government has no other motive, and has every reason of doing right, which the Members of our State Legislature have. Will a man on the Eastern Shore, be sent to be tried in Kentuckey; or a man from Kentuckey be brought to the Eastern Shore to have his trial? A Government by doing this, would destroy itself. I am convinced, the trial by jury will be regulated in the manner most advantageous to the community.

June 20, 1788

DECLINING A FEDERAL APPOINTMENT

To George Washington

Sir   Richmond, October 14, 1789

Not having been in Richmond when your Excellencys letter arrived, enclosing me a commission as Attorney for the United States in the Virginia district, I coud not, sooner, acknowlege the receit of it.

I thank you sir very sincerely for the honor which I feel is done me by an appointment flowing from your choice, & I beg leave to declare that it is with real regret I decline accepting an office which has to me been rendered highly valuable by the hand which bestowed it. Coud a due attention to the duties of the office have consisted with my practice in the superior courts of this state I shoud with great satisfaction have endeavord to discharge them, but the session of the foederal & state courts being at the same time in different places an attendance on the one becomes incompatible with the duties of an Attorney in the other.

With every sentiment of respect & real attachment, I remain Sir, Your most obedt. Servt.

"THE ILLIBERAL USE OF CONTRACTED PREJUDICE"

To Archibald Stuart

My dear Sir

I have just receivd yours by Mr. Patteson & shall with great pleasure attend to the injunction as you have directed. I forgot I beleive in my former letter to tell you that the suit Syme v Johnston as determind in favor of the latter on which there is an appeal which will I trust yield a few guineas more. I do not think Maeze will prosecute his appeal so that Hambleton may commence his liberality as soon as he pleases. Nothing coud come amiss with me now.

I am not surprizd at the news you tell me about Zach. & yet
I do not beleive he has one iota of real esteem for the man he
so lavishly praises. The instant that character departs from a
slavish observance of every dictum of a particular party he will
lose their good opinion & they will think themselves licensd to
brand him with what appellations they may chuse to bestow
on him. I wish you coud be with us next session but if your interest pronounces a loud & firm negative to your coming you
will be right to stay. Notwithstanding the illiberal abuse of
contracted prejudice I can tell you that the lawyers of the last
assembly preservd the little reputation which is still left to the
old dominion.

How comes on McClures business. Certificates are now at
8/ in the pound. I wish he woud pay the certificate itself. I am
sure my father woud prefer it to 10/ in the pound. A client is
just come in—pray heaven he may have money. I wish much to
see you & am with sincere esteem & affection Your

c. December 1789

THE VIRGINIA JUDICIAL SYSTEM

To Albert Gallatin

Dear Sir   Richmond, January 3, 1790
I have receivd yours of the 23d of Decr. & wish it was in my
power to answer satisfactorily your questions concerning our
judiciary system but I was myself in the army during that period concerning the transactions of which you enquire & have
not since informd myself of the reasons which governd in
making those changes which took place before the establishment of that system which I found on my coming to the bar.
Under the colonial establishment the judges of common law
were also judges of chancery, at the revolution these powers
were placd in different persons. I have not understood that
there was any considerable opposition to this division of jurisdiction. Some of the reasons leading to it I presume were that
the same person coud not appropriate a sufficiency of time
to each court to perform the public business with requisite

dispatch—that the principles of adjudication being different in the two courts, it was scarcely to be expected that eminince in each coud be attaind by the same man.

That there was an apparent absurdity in seeing the same men revise in the characters of Chancellors the judgements they had themselves renderd as common law judges. There are however many who think that the chancery & common law jurisdiction ought to be united in the same persons. They are actually united in our inferior courts & I have never heard it suggested that this union is otherwise in convenient than as it produces delay to the chancery dockett. I never heard it proposd to give the judges of the genl. court chancery jurisdiction. When the district system was introduced in 82 it was designd to give the district judges the powers of chancellors but the act did not then pass, tho the part concerning the court of chancery formed no objection to the bill. When again introducd it assumd a different form, nor has the idea ever been revived.

The first act constituting a high court of chancery annexd a jury for the trial of all important facts in the cause. To this I presume we were led by that strong partiality which the citizens of America have for that mode of trial. It was soon parted with & the facts submitted to the judge with a power to direct an issue where-ever the fact was doubtful. In most chancery cases the law & fact are so blended together that if a jury was impaneld of course the whole must be submitted to them or every case must assume the form of a special verdict which woud produce inconvenience & delay.

The delays of the court of chancery have been immense & those delays are inseparable from the court if the practise of England be observd. But that practise is not necessary. Tis greatly abridgd in virginia by an act passd in 1787 & great advantages result from the reform. There have been instances of suits depending for twenty years but under our present regulations a decision woud be had in that court as soon as any other in which there were an equal number of weighty causes. The parties may almost immediately set about collecting their proofs & so soon as they have collected them they may set the cause on the court dockett for a hearing.

It has never been proposd to blend the principles of common law & chancery so as for each to operate at the same trial in the same cause & I own it woud seem to me to be very difficult to effect such a scheme but at the same time it must be admitted that coud it be effected it woud save considerable sums of money to the litigant parties. I enclose you a copy of the act you request. I most sincerely condole with you on your heavy loss. Time only aided by the efforts of philosophy can restore you to yourself. I am dear Sir with much esteem, Your obedt. Servt.

Resolutions in Support of the Neutrality Proclamation

At a numerous meeting of the Citizens of Richmond, and its vicinity, held at the capitol on Saturday the 17th of August, 1793, agreeable to notification; and in order to take under consideration the late Proclamation of the President of the United States.

The Proclamation of the President being read, the following resolutions were offered, discussed, and unanimously agreed to:

1st. That it is the interest and duty of these United states to conform to their several subsisting treaties, and to maintain a strict neutrality towards the belligerent powers of Europe, on the due and faithful observance of which the happiness and prosperity of our common country very greatly depend.

2dly. That our illustrious fellow citizen, GEORGE WASHINGTON, to whose eminent services, great talents, and exalted virtues, all America pays so just a tribute, has given an additional proof of his watchful attention to his own duty, and the welfare of his country, by his Proclamation notifying to all that these United States are in perfect neutrality with respect to the belligerent powers of Europe, and enjoining our citizens to an observance thereof.

3dly. That it is our duty as well as our interest to conduct ourselves conformably to the principles expressed in the said Proclamation, and to use our best endeavours to prevent any infringement of them by others; and we hereby declare that it is our firm intention to do so.

And a committee was appointed to draw up an address conformable to said resolutions, consisting of the following gentlemen: J. Marshall, C: Braxton, A. Ronald, J. M'Clurg, A. Campbell, and J. Steele. The Committee returned, and Mr. Marshall reported an address, which being read, was unanimously agreed to.

The meeting continuing to sit, the following Resolutions were offered, discussed, and unanimously agreed to:

1st. That the constitution of our country has provided a proper and adequate mode of communication between these United States and foreign nations, or their ministers, whereby the sense of these United States or of foreign nations on any subject concerning either may be conveyed or received.

2dly. That if at any time this constitutional authority should be abused, & the Supreme Executive of the United States should misconstrue treaties, violate the laws, or oppose the sense of the union, there exists among the people of America, without the intervention of foreign ministers, discernment to detect the abuse, and ability to correct the mischief.

3dly. That any communication of foreign ministers on national subjects, with the citizens of these United States, or any of them, otherwise than through the constituted authority; any interference of a foreign minister with our internal government or administration; any intriguing of a foreign minister with the political parties of this country; would violate the laws and usages of nations, would be a high indignity to the government and people of America, and would be great and just cause of alarm, as it would be at once a dangerous introduction of foreign influence, and might, too probably lead to the introduction of foreign gold and foreign armies, with their fatal consequences, dismemberment and partition.

GEORGE WYTHE, *President*.
A. DUNSCOMB, *Secretary*.

August 17, 1793

Address in Support of
the Neutrality Proclamation

SIR,   Richmond, August 17, 1793

IMPRESSED with a full conviction of the wisdom of your administration in general, and especially approving that system of conduct which you have adopted, and steadily observed towards the belligerent powers of Europe, we, the Inhabitants of Richmond and its Vicinity, in the Commonwealth of Virginia, are happy in an opportunity of conveying to you these our genuine sentiments.

When propitious Heaven had crowned with victory the efforts of your country and yourself, while rejoicing America enumerated the blessings to be derived from so important a revolution, it was not reckoned among the least of them that, in future, the people of this favored land might in peace pursue their own happiness though war and violence should desolate the European world, or drench it in human blood—so too, when the good genius of America had devised that change in our government, which her wisdom has since adopted, it was held an argument of some weight against the necessity of this change, and all in opposition to it with one voice declared, that, situated as this country is, no madness or folly could ever be so supreme as to involve us again in European contests. Nor was this opinion, so uniform and universal, in favor of peace, derived from any other source than a knowledge of the real situation and a conviction of the real interests of America. It is impossible for the eye of cool and temperate reason to survey these United States without perceiving, that, however dreadful the calamities of war may be to other nations, they are still more dreadful to us, and however important the benefits of peace to others, to us it must be still more beneficial.

From those whose province it is to make war, we expect every effort to avoid it consistent with the honor, interest and good faith of America; from you, Sir, to whom is assigned the important task of, "taking care that the laws be faithfully executed," we have already experienced the most active and watchful attention to our dearest interests.

Ever since the period when a just respect for the voice of

your country induced you to abandon the retirement you loved, for that high station to which your fellow-citizens unanimously called you, your conduct has been uniformly calculated to promote their happiness and welfare: And in no instance has this been more remarkable, or your vigilant attention to the duties of your office more clearly discovered, than in your Proclamation respecting the neutrality of the United States.

As genuine Americans, with no other interest at heart but that of our country, unbiassed by foreign influence, which history informs us has been the bane of more than one republic, our minds are open to a due sense of the propriety, justice, and wisdom of this measure; and we cannot refrain from expressing our pleasure at its adoption.

We recollect too well the calamities of war, not to use our best endeavours to restrain any wicked citizen, if such indeed can he found among us, who, disregarding his own duty, and the happiness of the United States, in violation of the law of the land and the wish of the people, shall dare to gratify his paltry passions at the risk of his country's welfare, perhaps of his existence.

We pray Heaven to manifest its providential care of these states, by prolonging to them the blessings of your administration—and may the pure spirit of it continue to animate the government of America through a succession of ages.

Signed by desire and on behalf of the meeting,

(Teste) GEORGE WYTHE, *President*.
ANDREW DUNSCOMB, *Secretary*.

Aristides No. I

MR. DAVIS,   Richmond, September 8, 1793

When a gentleman, whose style of composition is respectable, and who seems not to be impelled by the mere vanity of becoming an author, presses forward with a bold venture on the conduct of his fellow-citizens, his charge demands our consideration, under a title not to be overlooked.

Persuaded that the present real disposition of our country differed essentially from the representations which had industriously been made of it; and, that much mischief had resulted, and more was to be feared from these misrepresentations, the citizens of Richmond and its vicinity deemed it proper that the people should declare their own sentiments. Thus thinking they, as a part of the people, convened together to express their opinions on subjects all important to us,—the neutrality and complete sovereignty of these United States. This proceeding has brought forth a criminating address signed AGRICOLA. The writer will not venture to say, that the people had a right peaceably to meet together and to declare their opinions on any political subject whatever, or that this right can only be properly exercised by calumniating public measures. His disapprobation, therefore, of those resolutions, goes not to the right of framing them, but to the matter they contain. To the public they are submitted, and the public will judge of them. They consist of two parts—the one approving the conduct of the President of the United States, towards the belligerent powers of Europe—the other declaring a detestation and abhorrence of any interference whatever of a foreign nation or minister with our political contests or internal government. Can the American exist who, like Agricola, professes himself the friend of neutrality, and yet does not most cordially unite with the citizens of Richmond and its vicinity in these sentiments? Is there a man among us who has so buried the love of country under a zeal for party or affection for a foreign nation, that he could stoop to be dictated to by the minister of that nation or could witness his dangerous efforts to create divisions among us, and opposition to our government, without feeling himself as the citizen of an independent republic, degraded and insulted? For what then is the conduct of the people of Richmond and its vicinity to be reprehended? This we are to learn from Agricola. Let us attend to him—He tells us that a game is playing by the enemies of the French revolution and of liberty, who under specious and wholesome appearances, cover from the view of those for whom the dose is intended, the poison it contains. That the French minister, in pressing the cause of his country, and of *liberty* upon the President, has in his zeal intimated a belief that the sentiments of the people were more favorable to his country and to her *cause* than our executive councils were; and that he would appeal to this sentiment. That the operations of the executive must be in some measure secret, and that a disagreement with a foreign minister, while there was a prospect of compromise, should be peculiarly so. That as the best interests of both countries required a secret discussion of these subjects, some object unfriendly to both dictated the publication. This object is to effect the destruction of our present government, by dissolving all connection with France, and uniting with England. This was the true and genuine object of the publication of Mr. Jay and Mr. King. That a train has been laid for disseminating the variance, and extending it to the community at large, is with certainty to be inferred. "How, (says Agricola) account for the prompt and correspondent publications at Richmond and Burlington, if they were not dictated, or at least suggested from the same source." The citizens of these places are not more zealous than their countrymen for the national honor, nor have they exhibited stronger proofs of patriotism, that they should thus step forward to foment this unhappy division—they ought rather to have held aloof, and as impartial but afflicted spectators, deplored the occasion which gave birth to it. Agricola then prescribes to us the resolutions we ought to adopt.

These are the substantial parts of his publication. He will pardon me that I have not repeated his own words, and that I have totally omitted many insinuations which appeared to be entirely unfounded and unjust. To you, my countrymen, who have no object but the common good, whose happiness, whose existence perhaps, is staked upon your present conduct, who have only to be rightly informed to judge rightly, to you I submit this defence of the conduct of your fellow citizens, and this comment on the censure of Agricola.

If there be among us men who are enemies to the French revolution, or who are friends to monarchy, I know them not. If I might judge from the extent of my own information, I should disbelieve the assertion. If Mr. Jay, and Mr. King, entertain these opinions, Agricola would not censure them more severely than myself. I can only say, that however he may feel himself warranted to adduce so heavy a charge by the possession of other proofs, that which he vouchsafes to exhibit to the public will by no means authorise it. When a foreign minister shall dare to pursue measures calculated to raise a party to oppose our government under his banners, the men who give notice of such measures, are not for that only reason to be considered as the enemies of America. Much more is he to be suspected who looks on as an impartial spectator, and thinks himself unaffected by the efforts of a foreign minister to sow dissention in his country.

These gentlemen are charged too with having improperly and for vicious purposes divulged the secrets of the Executive. If the declaration alluded to was made in secret, if it was a private threat, the secret must have been divulged to them before they could have communicated it to others. But let it be, if this will gratify Agricola, that Mr. Jay and Mr. King, are foes to our happy government, that they have acted improperly in publishing the improper conduct of a foreign Minister—yet America is possessed of the fact. We have it supported by the Minister himself. How ought we to act upon it? Should we manifest our disapprobation of such conduct, or should we hold aloof, as impartial spectators unconnected with our own government, and silently deplore the attempt to engage us against it, without censuring that attempt? The first has been the conduct of the people wherever they have spoken or acted, the last is recommended by Agricola.

When the people of Richmond and its vicinity, without naming the Minister of France, or applying their resolutions to him, otherwise than as the fact they censured might be adopted by him, proceed to declare that the interference of a Foreign Minister with our internal government would be dangerous, alarming and degrading to us—Agricola is warm in his condemnation of them. He attributes their resolutions, to the same source, if I understand him rightly, to which he had before attributed the publication of Mr. Jay and Mr. King; that is to an enmity to the French revolution and the cause of liberty, and to the desire of establishing a Monarchy on the ruins of our present happy constitution. If this be the idea of Agricola, the calumny grows not out of the fact, and merits no other reply, than that Agricola himself, though he may be less a friend to America, is not more attached to the cause of France or the rights of mankind in general, than a great majority of the meeting he ventures to defame. If, by saying the resolutions at Richmond and Burlington were dictated or suggested from the same source, he means that one common prompter moved the puppets at each place, and that the people think and speak not for themselves, but as they are directed by a hand behind the curtain, the slander is equally contemptible, and could never have been fabricated, had no person in America been better versed in the business of dancing puppets, than the people Agricola condemns. But passing over these indecent insinuations, as unworthy of further notice, I mean to shew that the conduct Agricola censures was highly proper, and that the strongest human motives urge you, my countrymen, to the adoption of similar measures.

Happily separated from the people of Europe, by an immence ocean, America is at peace with all of them. Almost every nation of that quarter of the globe is at war with France. We universally consider that gallant people as contending for the rights of human nature, and our best wishes attend their efforts. But we have treaties with her enemies not less obligatory on us, than those with France, and until it shall be the will of Congress to dissolve them by a declaration of war, it is not less the duty of the Supreme Executive of the United States, faithfully to observe them. No one of these treaties is offensive and defensive;—they place us in a state of perfect neutrality. With this situation Agricola professes himself to be content. A breach of this neutrality by individuals, if not disavowed and punished by the nation, would be a just cause of war, as being a breach of that faith which America has pledged to every power with whom she has a treaty. To attend to the observance of these treaties is the province of the President of the United States, and to notify their obligation and the penalties annexed to the violation of them, was surely his duty. A regard to this duty, produced his Proclamation. For this was he most industriously insulted and defamed. The public ear was every day offended by the most malignant charges against their beloved Chief Magistrate. He was treated in a scandalous paper (could you hear it Americans and be silent?) as if he had sacrificed the interests of his own country, to those of Britain, as if neutrality was pusillanimity, as if, while exerting his utmost powers to comply faithfully with all our engagements, he was dictated to by a nation, unfriendly to us, and feared to discharge our obligations to our best and most esteemed ally. An active, but I trust not a numerous party, incessant in their efforts to disgust America with the government of her choice, had the boldness to erect themselves into the proclaimers of the public opinion, and to declare that the people universally condemned the conduct of their President, and universally wished for those measures, which every reflecting man must know lead directly to war. Silence was misconstrued into approbation, and these hardy men already plumed themselves upon it. The minister of our beloved ally seems to have been credulous enough to believe them. They have seduced him into a conduct which his country must condemn, because his country is friendly to ours. They have tempted him to measures, which if persisted in, must destroy that friendship, because they lead directly to the ruin of one of the parties. Weigh, I beseech you, the consequences of a foreign minister in a republic, appealing to the people from the constitutional decisions of their government. How is this appeal to be supported? Must it not be by raising a party to oppose the government? If one foreign minister may make the appeal, what shall restrain every other from making it? If one foreign minister may raise parties against the government, what shall restrain others? If foreign ministers be permitted to proceed thus, what must be the situation of our country? Attend to the effects of such proceedings in the antient world; attend to them in Sweden, in Holland, and above all, in Poland. Our safety, my fellow-citizens, as well as our honour, urges us to be prompt in discountenancing such dangerous measures. They are produced by an opinion, that the people will support them. This opinion can only be eradicated by the declarations of the people themselves. If the minister of France has been deceived, it is our duty to undeceive him, that he may pursue a conduct more worthy of the nation he represents, and more worthy of that to which he is deputed. He knows that the people of America love France, we all know it, we all feel and avow it; but it has become necessary for us to intermingle with such an avowal declarations of our respect for ourselves, and for our own government. It has now become necessary for us to say, that however devoted we may be to France, we cannot permit her to interfere in our internal government, nor can we allow her minister to set an example to others, so dangerous to our independence, and so destructive of our happiness. These motives impelled the people of Richmond and its vicinity to assemble together, and to pass the resolutions, which you my countrymen have seen, and which Agricola ascribes to such disreputable views. In expressing them they have condemned the act without ascribing it to any individual.

The people of Richmond and its vicinity, claim no pre-eminence of patriotism over their fellow-citizens—they only demand an equality with them. They pretend not to have rendered more signal services to their country than others, but they fear no comparison of character. They have acted like their countrymen, they think like their countrymen, and they claim an equal right to speak their sentiments. Every subject which begins at all, must begin with some one, and it is unjust to charge those who do begin, with assuming to themselves any superiority over others. The people of Richmond and its vicinity have spoken only for themselves. Agricola undertakes to prescribe to others. With much more propriety might his countrymen enquire, what Agricola have been your great achievements? What pre-eminent display of talents and patriotism have you ever made which shall authorize you thus to censure some, and dictate to others? What unbounded services have you rendered to the community, that may justify you in assuming that exalted seat in which you have placed yourself? Forbear, Agricola, forbear to indulge yourself in sarcasm and invective against your fellow-citizens! If your object be a worthy one, you should rather seek to convince, than to irritate.

ARISTIDES.

Virginia Gazette, and General Advertiser,
September 11, 1793

Aristides No. II

MR. DAVIS,

Feeling as I do feel the most perfect conviction of the purity of motive which dictated the resolutions of the citizens of Richmond and its vicinity, and thinking the wisdom and propriety of those resolutions too well established to be now assailed, but for the mere purpose of imitation, I had hoped that they were not again to be arraigned at the bar of the public. But to have been forward in approving the pacific system of the government of the United States, and to have manifested a determination to support that system, tho' a bold and daring faction should enlist itself under the banners of a foreign minister to force us out of it, was an offence too great to be forgiven. That respite which was considered as an abandonment of an unprovoked and unjustifiable attack upon the honest opinions of the people, was, it seems only a pause, for the collection of that virulent matter which has now burst forth with a violence proportioned to the time of its confinement. While Agricola was labouring by every species of misrepresentation, and by sophistry not to be dignified with the title of argument, to excite in the public mind a baneful irritation against the government of his country, I had not supposed that he was thus warring with his most sacred duties, solely to possess himself of advantageous ground from which he might renew his assault on a respectable body of his fellow-citizens, and display his malice against Aristides. In the notice I feel it now incumbent on me to take of him, I shall not pursue him through that circuitous route by which he has chosen to travel because the poison he has so industriously administered was quickly succeeded by its antidote, & he has been quickly followed by a writer who has sufficiently exposed the fallacy and weakness of those statements on which he professes to rely. It has been shewn that the charges exhibited against the government of the United States were as unfounded, as the wanton attack on the people of Richmond and its vicinity, was unprovoked and indecent. In his progress he has been as liberal of abuse as he has been parsimonious of reason and from the President of the United States to the supposed proposer of the resolutions in Richmond, no character has been touched but to be slandered. Where facts could not be directly alledged, the most foul and unwarrantable insinuations have been resorted to, and a degree of malice has been displayed in hinting calumnies, which could only be equalled by the infamy of fabricating them. If the opinions Agricola thought proper to combat had been really such as ought not to have been avowed, and he had thought it his duty to step forward, a volunteer for their suppression, arguments to prove their impropriety could not have been wanting, nor would those arguments have needed for their support the insinuation of an untruth concerning the source from which the resolutions were dictated or suggested. It is much to be regretted that a public question cannot be discussed without the introduction of private slander, nor is it an extenuation of the mischief that this forces a tartness of reply irksome to the injured person compelled to use it; but there will ever be a marked distinction between the instrument of faction and the person who writes for the honorable purpose of being useful to his fellow-citizens, and perhaps there is not a more certain criterion by which it is to be determined than the substitution of particular calumny for general reasoning.

Altho' so much of Agricola as seems to have been designed by himself for argument has been sufficiently refuted, it may not be improper to notice a principle which being unable to prove, he seems to have assumed. It is that those only (with the exception of a few who are deceived) wish well to the French nation who support the conduct of Mr. Genet in America, and that those who express their approbation of the government of the United States, and declare their determination to oppose the introduction of foreign influence, are bowing obsequiously to Britain and endeavoring to assimilate our government to her's. This it is true has not been in express terms asserted, but it seems to be the vital principle which animates every paper, and I know not how otherwise to account for his *crusade* against the people of Richmond in particular, and against that great body of people throughout the United States in general, whose only sin is, that they have avowed these sentiments. For the injustice of this principle I need only appeal to the judgment and feelings of my fellow-citizens throughout the community. To notice the conduct of Mr. Genet from his arrival in the United States to the present moment, would give me no pleasure, and would be unnecessary, because I believe the public mind is sufficiently impressed with its extreme impropriety. Even the *desperadoes* of his party but faintly support him, and after a very feeble defence, either declare that they do not mean to advocate his appeal to the people, or endeavour to turn our resentment on those who have first noticed his efforts to govern our politics, while they seek his apology in our love for his country and her cause. I ask each individual who is so much of an American as to resent the indignity offered to us by the minister of France, and to ward off the mischiefs which must result from it if submitted to, whether he connects in his mind the French people or the French cause with Mr. Genet? Whether his disapprobation of the conduct of that gentleman arises from, or has produced an enmity towards France? I am persuaded there is scarcely an individual who would not answer each question in the negative. If the publications on this subject be resorted to, It will, I believe, appear that those who have defended the measures of the government of the United States, and who have reprobated the intermeddling of foreigners with our political concerns, have in no instance, charged France with the conduct of her minister, or sought to weaken our attachment to that country. Our own safety made it necessary to manifest a firm determination to be guided only by ourselves, but in manifesting that determination, America has shewn and felt her affection for France to be undiminished. Notwithstanding the demonstration this procedure affords, we find it contended in the face of truth, and in opposition to the knowledge of those who read, that the public declarations on this subject proceed from a desire to separate these states from France, and unite them with Britain, in the hope of thereby wounding the cause of liberty and equality every where, and of paving the way for the establishment of the English form of government here, on the ruin of our own. If it could be justifiable to follow the example of Agricola in any thing, I would ask what can be the motive of such conduct? It cannot be to strengthen our attachment to France, because Agricola himself is not so miserable an advocate as not to discern, that, if any thing could impair the affection of America for that nation, it would be a belief that she countenanced the conduct of her minister, and sought, by leaguing herself with a faction, to distract or govern the politics of these United States. What then can be the motive? Is there a party determined to strengthen itself by foreign aid, for the establishment of its own views? Are they (still to follow Agricola) tho' not holders of, hunters after, public office? I do not myself believe there is such a party, because I do not believe that many can be found who will go through with Agricola; I am persuaded he will stand alone, the desperate advocate of such desperate measures. I believe the good sense and upright intention of my countrymen will every where prevail, and that with one voice we shall say, *we will govern ourselves, we will preserve our faith with all nations, and we will be at peace with the world.*

Enraged that these sentiments should be advocated, Agricola can spare none who have advanced them, and therefore condescends to think some parts of Aristides worthy of notice. He introduces his observations by saying "the contradictions and absurdities which appear in this essay obviously betray the embarrassment of the writer."

In the habit of saying rash things and of failing to support them, Agricola would not have been uniform, had he, with respect to Aristides, departed from this system. It would not be surprising, if, in this assertion, he should even think himself correct, for, as to a jaundiced eye every object seems tinged with yellow, it may be that to a confused mind every proposition appears embarrassed. But we will attend to his proofs. "It will be observed (says he) that instead of disproving the views of this faction he (Aristides) denies its existence." If I should admit this, it would be difficult to shew that it was either contradictory, absurd or embarrassed. To disprove the views of a party, whose existence is denied is a task I shall not undertake however Agricola may censure my declining it. But he is to support himself by quotation. In answer to his charge that a powerful faction in our government and country were seeking to embroil us with France, in order to establish a monarchy here, Aristides had said, "If there be among us men who are enemies to the French revolution, or who are friends to the monarchy, I know them not." By any but Agricola this would have been understood, rather as a declaration that Aristides knew of no such faction, than as an averment that none such existed. This was the more certain because he proceeds immediately to say, "If Mr. Jay and Mr. King be of this description, Agricola would not censure them more severely than myself." But he rushes on to comment on this quotation too precipitately to give himself time to understand it. He supposes that bitterness will be received in the place of justice, and that if an observation be sufficiently harsh it need not apply correctly. Agricola effects to understand this expression from Aristides as avering that he did not know a man in the United States, of any nation, who was either a friend to monarchy or an enemy to the French revolution, and having assumed this exposition, he triumphs in his supposed victory, as if he had proved thereby, that the Richmond resolutions were improper, or that the pacific system they approve, was a sacrifice of the honor and interests of the people of America. But as his triumph will be unenvied, neither, I believe, will it ever be imitated. It is impossible to understand this observation otherwise than as applying to Americans. In a neutral country there will ever reside persons born in and belonging to other nations who may be at war with each other. It is not to be supposed that such men do not retain some partiality for their native country and its government. When speaking of our own government and of those concerned in the administration of it, no general expression is understood as extending to them. Nor is it any proof when reasoning against the existence of a powerful and extensive faction, that a denial of it, or of a knowledge of men of such principles, is not seriously made, because there exists an individual, a foreigner, who pretends not to influence in the government or among the people, to whom Agricola or common fame may chuse to ascribe antirepublican opinions. Whether the person supposed to be alluded to, would wish to establish a monarchy, or to assimilate our government in any degree to the British, I do not to this moment, know, nor do I suppose Agricola could inform me. The observation as applied to the people of America is strictly true, nor do I know or believe that there exists in the government such a faction as Agricola has stated, or, that there are Americans within the circle of my acquaintance, who would support it if it existed. Is it possible that Aristides can be otherwise construed? Is Agricola the only reader who could mistake him? Or did he understand rightly the sentence quoted, but wished to impose a misconstruction on others? "Candor startles at the charge! Was his party zeal so violent as to hide so flagrant a truth from his eyes? This perhaps the best apology, but a bad one for a man who assumes the task he has chosen, and who imputes to others the same weakness." He forfeits however his apology by betraying his consciousness that he had in his own mind construed the assertion differently from his statement of it, when he says himself that he quotes this passage in order to prove that Aristides denied the existence of the faction he had spoken of. Nor is he more fortunate in searching for an idea contradictory to that which has been mentioned, or more correct in his statement of it. It has been said by Aristides that "Agricola, tho' he may be less a friend to America, is not more attached to the cause of France or the rights of mankind in general, than a great majority of the meeting he had ventured to defame"—having cited this, he asks what characters then composed the minority? That is if they were not as much attached to France, and the rights of mankind as Agricola, what must have been their characters? If I had said that they were not, I should have beg'd pardon of my fellow-citizens, I should probably have injured them. But I have not said so. I have vouched for a great majority, because I know them, but have not condemned those I did not know. For there were some among the American citizens with whom I am not acquainted. This perfectly consists with the former assertion, for there it is stated, that if the faction spoken of by Agricola, existed, I knew them not, and here it is averred, that I did know a great majority of the meeting defamed, and that in patriotism they yielded not to their accuser. I forbear to comment on these plain mistatements, or assign a motive for them. I will proceed to his further criticisms.

The state of the public mind when those resolutions were entered into, cannot be forgotten. No means were unessayed to induce an opinion that the constitution had been violated, and the honor and interests of the community sacrificed by the Executive of the United States. Measures which could not fail to produce a war, in which America would have been considered as, in some degree, the aggressor, were zealously supported in private and through the medium of the press. The public mind was supposed to have been prepared sufficiently for the condemnation of every act of the government, and for the support of the new system to be urged upon us. The appeal of Mr. Genet to the people was then announced. The fact was not then supported by that complete and ample testimony which he has since afforded, but there was too much cause to give it credence. Whether Mr. Genet had himself created the faction, or was imposed on by it—whether he had instigated the various libels which have appeared against the pacific system of the government, or had been really induced by them to suppose that the people at large were opposed to that system—it was alike necessary for the people to speak. If Mr. Genet had mistaken the sense of America, it was proper to undeceive him, and if he was about to form a party in opposition to the government, we could not be too early in telling him the American temper would not brook it. There was still a possibility that this gentleman might not have been criminal to the extent of the charge. The people of Richmond and its vicinity did not choose to aver that he was. It had however become necessary to assert the principle, and, if it applied to Mr. Genet, the principle was not the less true or the less proper on that account. This in the usual stile of Agricola is termed an uncandid and unbecoming evasion. But Agricola cannot do such violence to his propensities as to be just for a moment. By any but him it would be admitted, that an attempt to use the people as the instruments of their own calamity, could not be more properly repelled, than by a declaration that they would not be so used, and that this declaration could not be made with more delicacy, or less offensively, than by forbearing to mingle with it any assertion, that the attempt had actually been made, and that it had been made by the minister of France. The one perhaps can only be justified by actual conviction of guilt; the other is proper when there is just cause of fear; for I can never admit with Agricola, that it is time enough to guard against a mischief, when it has actually befallen us. What could have tempted Agricola to ask whether the resolutions are not vindicated on the ground of the certificate is only to be discovered by himself, since he could not have read Aristides and have considered him as supporting the resolutions by that testimony. In avering that this piece of evidence was relied on, it is difficult to believe that Agricola could either have imposed on himself, or could have hoped to escape detection in his attempt to impose on others. It might therefore have been treated as an idle enquiry, had he not in the succeeding paragraph assumed it as a fact.

It is painful to myself and tedious to others, in a discussion which ought only to contain matters useful and interesting to the public, to be compelled to waste so much of their time in correcting the mistatements of Agricola—mistatements, unimportant to the public because they do not in any degree affect the argument, but only concern the personal reputation of Aristides. Without reflecting that if the measures supported by Aristides, had even been defended with as much weakness and passion as they have been assailed, they would not be the less proper on that account; he has deserted the argument, and exerted all his talents at misrepresentation to shew contradictions and untruths in the writer he attacks, which would only affect the person, and not the subject. This compels me to ask the indulgence of noticing one other criticism of the same complexion. He charges Aristides with "advocating the resolutions on a supposition that they contain what in reality they do not contain, and for which they are censured." The quotation in support of this assertion is "he (the French minister) knows that the people of America love France, we all know it, we all feel and avow it, but it has become necessary for us to intermingle with such an avowal, declarations of our respect for ourselves and for our own government." Not choosing to hazard a denial of the truth of this proposition, Agricola contents himself with saying that a reader would suppose "that an avowal of our attachments to France, was the ground-work of these resolutions, and that the censure on her minister was only reluctantly intermingled with it." It is for Agricola alone not to discern that Aristides speaks of the continuing language of the people of America. It is for Agricola alone not to perceive that when the people of America are universally avowing their attachment to France, any declaration in support of our own government, must be intermingled with the avowals which are continually made of that attachment, altho' not expressed in the same resolutions.—But it is time to take leave, I trust forever, of such unessential criticisms, and to notice an argument which more deserves the public attention.

Agricola affects to consider the appeal of a foreign minister from the government to the people of America, as an event unimportant in itself, and not threatening, in its consequences, those dangers to our future welfare, which throughout the history of man, have invariably attended the introduction of foreign influence. This is not a mere invective against Aristides, but is the avowal of a political opinion seriously interesting to every citizen of the United States. It is impossible to divest this appeal of the means by which it is to be prosecuted. The mind cannot trace without shuddering at them. Upon this subject the good sense of America will not be misguided by the examples cited by Agricola, and, to our astonishment, said by him to be analogous to this. The two great revolutions of 1776 and 1788 are spoken of as cases where an appeal was made to the people, and the subjects proposed to them deliberately discussed, and I think wisely decided on. By whom were those appeals made? By whom were they prosecuted? By whom and by what were they or could they be supported? What interests or what motives did or could lead us to either important crisis and conduct us through it? The first was the united voice and united strength of America, appealing to the supreme director of all human affairs against foreign oppression. The second was the deliberate consultation of the people of America among themselves, unimpelled by foreigners, unsupported by foreign influence, foreign interests, or foreign force, on a subject uninteresting to them, but all important to us. It was the deliberate exercise of American wisdom, for the purpose of correcting those defects which experience had marked in our ancient system. In this there was and can be no danger while we exclude foreign influence. In such a case, whatever difference of opinion might prevail, there can be but one party, and that is the people of America; there can be but one object, and that is the happiness of our common country; there can be but one power exerted to produce or conduct us through the crisis, and that is the power of reason exerted in and on the American mind. How different the case this is cited to support. The person appealing to the people is a foreigner. The first proposition would be an attempt to seduce us into a violation of the constitution of our country. The interests to be discussed are foreign interests. The parties concerned are foreign nations at war with each other. The object is a foreign good. The power exerted in support of and opposition to the claims of the appellant, is a foreign power, aided by such factions as either might, by any means, be able to excite in the bosom of our country. To dilate on the obvious vice and folly of countenancing or admitting such an appeal would be an indignity to the common sense of my countrymen. What dangerous paths must he already have trodden, who cannot perceive them! But we are told that no mischief is to be feared from this measure of Mr.

Genet, because his nation is republican. That is, that foreign influence may be admitted when conjoined with Agricola, and when they are to afford reciprocal aid to each other. Let it be remembered that Agricola has affirmed the existance of a powerful British faction in America. If this be true would not that faction call in the aid of British influence to oppose French influence so improperly applied? Admitting it not to be true (and I believe it is not) if the powers at war with France should perceive, that claims in which they were deeply interested, were to be decided, not by a reference to the constituted authority, but by parties among the people, they would certainly endeavor to strengthen themselves by the same means. Our country, instead of pointing its united efforts to the promotion of its own happiness, might be found divided into parties struggling under the direction, and for the views of foreigners. How incumbent then is it on those, who are unconnected with party and unstained by faction, who can have no object but the public good, no interest distinct from that of the community, to step forward and resist in its first advance, so baneful and so dangerous a measure. Foreign influence to be exerted on the people, in a republican government, can only be repelled by the conduct of the people themselves. Admit it once and it may be found too mighty for our best endeavors to exclude it.

ARISTIDES.

Virginia Gazette, and General Advertiser,
November 20, 1793

"FOLLY, ENVY, MALICE & DAMND RASCALITY"

To Archibald Stuart

My dear Sir   Richmond, March 27, 1794
    I enclose you a letter to Bell which I wish you to seal & send to him as soon as possible. I have examind the record & suppose it to be a full one. The errors suggested in the petition are

1st. That the value of the land ought to have been estimated by a jury, &

2dly. That so much of the original purchase money as remaind unpaid ought to have been deducted. If there is anything among the papers to cure these defects let me know it that I may apply for a certiorari. I am inclind to think the decree will be opend tho I am not certain of it & I suppose be it so or not the ultimate determination will be for Mills.

I am not employd for Matthews. He has chosen Counsellor Duval. No person has appeard for Mrs. Burns. Unless the answer makes its appearance before the commencement of the next term a motion cannot be then made to dissolve the injunction. I cannot appear for Donaghoe. I do not decline his business from any objection to his *bank*: to that I shoud like very well to have free access & woud certainly discount *from* it as largely as he woud permit, but I am already fixd by Rankin & as those who are once in the bank do not I am told readily get out again I despair of being ever able to touch the guineas of Donaghoe.

Shall we never see you again in Richmond? I was very much rejoiced when I heard that you were happily married but if that amounts to a ne exeat which is to confine you entirely to your side of the mountain I shall be selfish enough to regret your good fortune & almost to wish you had found some little crooked rib among the fish & oysters which woud once a year drag you into this part of our terraqueous globe. You have forgotten I beleive the solemn compact we made to take a journey to Philadelphia together this winter & superintend for a while the proceedings of Congress. I wish very much to see you. I want to observe [   ] how much honester men you & I are than half our acquaintance. Seriously there appears to me every day to be more folly, envy, malice & damnd rascality in the world than there was the day before & I do verily begin to think that plain downright honesty & unintriguing integrity will be kickd out of doors.

We fear & not without reason a war. The man does not live who wishes for peace more than I do, but the outrages committed upon us are beyond human bearing. Farewell—pray Heaven we may weather the storm. Your

"KISS OUR CHILDREN"

To Mary W. Marshall

My dearest Polly   Philadelphia, February 3, 1796

After a journey which woud have been beyond measure tedious but for the agreeable company with which I came I am at length safe at this place. My business woud be spedily determind if Mr. Campbell woud come on. We wait only for him to enter on the cause concerning British debts. My own cause I greatly fear will not be taken up & I shall be under the very disagreeable necessity of returning without any decision. It is a cruel thing on me to be kept here extremely against my inclination because Mr. Campbell will not come on.

I have not yet heard from my beloved wife & children. You ought not to keep me in any suspense about you. I was at the play last night & very much admird Mrs. Marshall who is the favorite of the town but with all her good qualities she does not equal our Mrs. Bignal.

No information has yet been receivd of the arrival of the vessel which carried my brother & his wife. We expect every day to receive inteligence from them.

Kiss our children & especially our sweet little Poll for me & tell Tom I expect him to attend to his brother & to write to me. I count on Jaquelines great improvement before my return. I am my dearest Polly your affectionate

Argument in the U.S. Supreme Court in Ware v. Hylton

Marshall, (of *Virginia*) for the Defendant in error. The case resolves itself into two general propositions: 1st, That the act of assembly of *Virginia,* is a bar to the recovery of the debt, independent of the treaty. 2d, That the treaty does not remove the bar.

1. That the act of Assembly of *Virginia* is a bar to the recovery of the debt, introduces two subjects for consideration:

1st. Whether the Legislature had power to extinguish the debt? 2d. Whether the Legislature had exercised that power?

1st. It has been conceded, that independent nations have, in general, the right of confiscation; and that *Virginia*, at the time of passing her law, was an independent nation. But, it is contended, that from the peculiar circumstances of the war, the citizens of each of the contending nations, having been members of the same government, the general right of confiscation did not apply, and ought not to be exercised. It is not, however, necessary for the Defendant in error to show a parallel case in history; since, it is incumbent on those, who wish to impair the sovereignty of *Virginia*, to establish on principle, or precedent, the justice of their exception. That State being engaged in a war, necessarily possessed the powers of war; and confiscation is one of those powers, weakening the party against whom it is employed, and strengthening the party that employs it. War, indeed, is a state of force; and no tribunal can decide between the belligerent powers. But did not *Virginia* hazard as much by the war, as if she had never been a member of the *British* empire? Did she not hazard more, from the very circumstance of its being a civil war? It will be allowed, that nations have equal powers; and that *America*, in her own tribunals at least, must from the 4th of *July* 1776, be considered as independent a nation as *Great Britain*: then, what would have been the situation of *American* property, had *Great Britain* been triumphant in the conflict? Sequestration, confiscation and proscription would have followed in the train of that event; and why should the confiscation of British property be deemed less just in the event of the *American* triumph? The rights of war clearly exist between members of the same Empire, engaged in a civil war. Vatt. B. 3, s. 292, 295. But, suppose a suit had been brought during the war by a *British* subject against an *American* citizen, it could not have been supported; and if there was a power to suspend the recovery, there must have been a power to extinguish the debt: they are, indeed, portions of the same power, emanating from the same source. The legislative authority of any country, can only be restrained by its own municipal constitution: This is a principle that springs from the very nature of society; and the judicial authority can have no right to question the validity of a law, unless such a jurisdiction is expressly given by the constitution. It is not necessary to enquire, how the judicial authority should act, if the Legislature were evidently to violate any of the laws of God; but property is the creature of civil society, and subject, in all respects, to the disposition and controul of civil institutions. There is no weight in the argument founded on what is supposed to be the understanding of the parties at the place and time of contracting debts; for, the right of confiscation does not arise from the understanding of individuals, in private transactions, but from the nature and operation of government. Nor does it follow, that because an individual has not the power of extinguishing his debts, the community, to which he belongs, may not, upon principles of public policy, prevent his creditors from recovering them. It must be repeated, that the law of property, in its origin and operation, is the offspring of the social state; not the incident of a state of nature. But the revolution did not reduce the inhabitants of *America* to a state of nature; and, if it did, the Plaintiff's claim would be at an end. Other objections to the doctrine are started: It is said, that a debt, which arises from a contract, formed between the subjects of two belligerent powers, in a neutral country, cannot be confiscated; but the society has a right to apply to its own use, the property of its enemy, wherever the right of property accrued, and wherever the property itself can be found. Suppose a debt had been contracted between two *Americans*, and one of them had joined *England*, would not the right of confiscation extend to such a debt? As to the case of the ransom bill, if the right of confiscation does not extend to it, (which is, by no means, admitted) it must be on account of the peculiar nature of the contract, implying a waiver of the rights of war. And the validity of capitulations depends on the same principle. But, let it be supposed, that a government should infringe the provisions of a capitulation, by imprisoning soldiers, who had stipulated for a free return to their home, could an action of trespass be maintained against the gaoler? No: the act of the government, though disgraceful, would be obligatory on the judiciary department.

2d. But it is now to be considered, whether, if the Legislature of *Virginia* had the power of confiscation, they have exercised it? The third section of the act of Assembly discharges the debtor; and, on the plain import of the term, it may be asked, if he is discharged, how can he remain charged? The expression is, he shall be discharged from the debt; and yet, it is contended, he shall remain liable to the debt. Suppose the law had said, that the debtor should be discharged from the commonwealth, but not from his creditor, would not the Legislature have betrayed the extremest folly in such a proposition? and what man in his senses would have paid a farthing into the treasury, under such a law? Yet, in violation of the expressions of the act, this is the construction which is now attempted. It is, likewise, contended, that the act of Assembly does not amount to a confiscation of the debts paid into the treasury; and that the Legislature had no power, as between creditors and debtors, to make a substitution, or commutation, in the mode of payment. But what is a confiscation? The substance, and not the form, is to be regarded. The state had a right either to make the confiscation absolute, or to modify it as she pleased. If she had ordered the debtor to pay the money into the treasury, to be applied to public uses; would it not have been, in the eye of reason, a perfect confiscation? She has thought proper, however, only to authorize the payment, to exonerate the debtor from his creditor, and to retain the money in the treasury, subject to her own discretion, as to its future appropriation. As far as the arrangement has been made, it is confiscatory in its nature, and must be binding on the parties; though in the exercise of her discretion, the state might chuse to restore the whole, or any part, of the money to the original creditor. Nor is it sufficient to say, that the payment was voluntary, in order to defeat the confiscation. A law is an expression of the public will; which, when expressed, is not the less obligatory, because it imposes no penalty. Banks, Canal Companies, and numerous associations of a similar description, are formed on the principle of voluntary subscription. The nation is desirous that such institutions should exist; individuals are invited to subscribe on the terms of the law; and, when they have subscribed, they are entitled to all the benefits, and are subject to all the inconveniences of the association, although no penalties are imposed. So, when the government of *Virginia* wished to possess itself of the debts previously owing to *British* subjects, the debtors were invited to make the payment into the treasury; and, having done so, there is no reason, or justice, in contending that the law is not obligatory on all the world, in relation to the benefit, which it promised as an inducement to the payment. If, subsequent to the act of 1777, a law had been passed confiscating *British* debts, for the use of the state, with orders that the Attorney General should sue all *British* debtors, could he have sued the defendants in error, as *British* debtors, after this payment of the debt into the treasury? Common sense and common honesty revolt at the idea; and, yet, if the *British* creditor retained any right or interest in the debt, the state would be entitled, on principles of law, to recover the amount.

II. Having thus, then, established, that at the time of entering into the Treaty of 1783, the Defendant owed nothing to the Plaintiff, it is next to be enquired, whether that treaty revived the debt in favour of the Plaintiff, and removed the bar to a recovery, which the law of *Virginia* had interposed? The words of the fourth article of the Treaty are, "that creditors on either side, shall meet with no lawful impediment to the recovery of the full value, in sterling money, of all *bona fide* debts heretofore contracted." Now, it may be asked, who are creditors? There cannot be a creditor where there is not a debt; and *British* debts were extinguished by the act of confiscation. The articles, therefore, must be construed with reference to those creditors, who had *bona fide* debts, subsisting, in legal force, at the time of making the Treaty; and the word *recovery* can have no effect to create a debt, where none previously existed. Without discussing the power of Congress to take away a vested right by treaty, the fair and rational construction of the instrument itself, is sufficient for the Defendant's cause. The words ought, surely, to be very plain, that shall work so evident a hardship, as to compel a man to pay a debt, which he had before extinguished. The treaty, itself, does not point out any particular description of persons, who were to be deemed debtors; and it must be expounded in relation to the existing state of things. It is not true, that the fourth article can have no meaning, unless it applies to cases like the present. For instance;— there was a law of *Virginia*, which prohibited the recovery of *British* debts, that had not been paid into the treasury: these were *bona fide* subsisting debts; and the prohibition was a legal impediment to the recovery, which the treaty was intended to remove. So, likewise, in several other states, laws had been passed authorizing a discharge of *British* debts in paper money, or by a tender of property at a valuation, and the treaty was calculated to guard against such impediments to the recovery of the sterling value of those debts. It appears, therefore, that at the time of making the treaty, the state of things was such, that *Virginia* had exercised her sovereign right of confiscation, and had actually received the money from the *British* debtors. If debts thus paid were within the scope of the fourth article, those who framed the article knew of the payment; and upon every principle of equity and law, it ought to be presumed, that the recovery, which they contemplated, was intended against the receiving state, not against the paying debtor. *Virginia* possessing the right of compelling a payment for her own use, the payment to her, upon her requisition, ought to be considered as a payment to the attorney, or agent, of the *British* creditor. Nor is such a substitution a novelty in legal proceedings: a foreign attachment is founded on the same principle. Suppose judgment had been obtained against the Defendants in error, as garnishee in a foreign attachment brought against the Plaintiff in error, and the money had been paid, accordingly, to the Plaintiff in the attachment; but it afterwards appeared that the Plaintiff in the attachment had, in fact, no cause of action, having been paid his debt before he commenced the suit. If the treaty had been made in such a state of things, which would be the debtor contemplated by the fourth article, the Defendants in error, who had complied with a legal judgment against them, or the Plaintiff in the attachment, who had received the money? This act of *Virginia* must have been known to the *American* and *British* commissioners; and, therefore, cannot be repealed without plain and explicit expressions directed to that object. Besides, the public faith ought to be preserved. The public faith was plighted by the act of *Virginia*; and, as a revival of the debt in question, would be a shameful violation of the faith of the state to her own citizens, the treaty should receive any possible interpretion to avoid so dishonorable and so pernicious a consequence. It is evident, that the power of the government, to take away a vested right, was questionable in the minds of the *American* commissioners, since they would not exercise that power in restoring confiscated real estate; and confiscated debts, or other personal estate must come within the same rule. If Congress had the power of divesting a vested right, it must have arisen from the necessity of the case; and if the necessity had existed, the *American* commissioners, explicitly avowing it, would have justified their acquiescence to the nation. But the commissioners could have no motive to form a treaty such as the opposite construction supposes; for, if the stipulation was indispensable to the attainment of peace, the object was national, and so should be the payment of the equivalent: the commissioners, in such case, would have agreed, at once, that the public should pay the *British* debts; since the public must, on every principle of equity, be answerable to the *Virginia* debtor, who is now said to be the victim. The case cited from *Jenkins*, does not apply; as there is no article of the treaty, that declares the law of Virginia void. See *Old Law of Evidence*, 196.

February 9, 1796

SUPPORTING THE JAY TREATY

To Alexander Hamilton

Dear Sir   Richmond, April 25, 1796

Yours of the 14th only reachd me by the mail of this evening. I had been informd of the temper of the house of representatives & we had promptly taken such measures as appeard to us fitted to the occasion. We coud not venture an expression of the public mind under the violent prejudices with which it had been impressd so long as a hope remaind that the house of representatives might ultimately consult the interest or honor of the nation. But now when all hope of this has vanishd, it was deemd adviseable to make the experiment however hazardous it might be. A meeting was calld which was more numerous than I have ever seen at this place & after a very ardent & zealous discussion which consumd the day a decided majority declard in favor of a resolution that the welfare & honor of the nation requird us to give full effect to the treaty negotiated with Britain.

This resolution with a petition drawn by an original opponent of the treaty will be forwarded by the next post to Congress. The subject will probably be taken up in every county in
the state or at any rate in very many of them. It is probable
that a majority of the counties will avow sentiments opposd to
ours, but the division of the state will appear to be much more
considerable than has been stated. In some of the districts there
will certainly be a majority who will concur with us & that perhaps may have some effect. As Man is a gregarious animal we
shall certainly derive much aid from declarations in support of
the constitution & of appropriations if such can be obtaind
from our sister States. The ground we take here is very much
that of Mr. Hillhouse. We admit the discretionary constitutional power of the representatives on the subject of appropriations but contend that the treaty is as completely a valid &
obligatory contract when negotiated by the President & ratified
by him with the assent & advice of the Senate as if sanctiond
by the house of representatives also under a constitution requiring such sanction. I think it woud be very difficult perhaps
impossible to engage Mr. H. on the right side of this question.

If you have any communications which might promote a
concurrence of action we shall be proud to receive them. With
much respect & esteem I am dear Sir your obedt.

PRESIDENTIAL ELECTION RESULTS

To James Iredell

Dear Sir   Richmond, December 15, 1796

I had not the pleasure of receiving til yesterday your favor of
the 3d. inst. Since then I have seen the votes of North Carolina
& you I presume have seen those of Virginia. Mr. Adams woud
have receivd one other vote had Mr. Eyre really been elected,
but he was left out by accident. There was supposd to be no
opposition to him & in consequence of that opinion the people
in one county on the eastern shore did not vote at all & in the
other a very few assembled. On the day of election the people
of Princess Ann whose court day it happend to be assembled in

numbers & elected Mr. Nimmo who voted for Mr. Jefferson. For that gentleman you will have heard there were twenty votes, for Mr. Saml. Adams 15, for Mr. Clinton 3, for Burr 1, Genl. Washington 1, Mr. Pinkney 1, & Mr. John Adams 1. I receivd a letter from Philadelphia stating that five votes south of Potowmack woud be necessary to secure the election of Mr. Adams. It is then certain that he cannot be elected.

Our assembly which you know is in session displays its former hostility to foederalism. They have once more denied *wisdom* to the administration of the President & have gone so far as to say in argument that we ought not by any declarations to commit ourselves so as to be bound to support his measures as they respect France. To what has America fallen! Is it to be hopd that North Carolina will in this particular rather adopt such measures as have been pursued by other states than tread the crooked path of Virginia?

I have receid a letter from Mr. Dallas & will furnish him with my argument in the case of the British debts.

I expect to be under the necessity of [   ] the opinions of the judges except yours from Mr. Dallas whose report of the case will be publishd before mine. With very much respect & esteem I am dear Sir your obedt

"THE TWO HAPPIEST PERSONS ON EARTH"

To Mary W. Marshall

My dearest Polly   Alexandria, June 24, 1797
I am thus far on my way to Philadelphia & have come without any inconvenience from a starting horse. All your other fears will be as foundationless as this & I shall soon see you again to be the two happiest persons on earth. I came this morning from Mount Vernon where I was pressd to pass the day & which is certainly one of the most delightful places in our country. Had you been with me I shoud have been there as happy as I coud be any where. I shoud have been quite happy as it was coud I have been certain—quite certain that your mind was perfectly at ease. Nothing distresses me but that. Let

me hear from you by the time I have been two days at Philadelphia & do tell me & tell me truly that the bitterness of parting is over & your mind at rest—that you think of me only to contemplate the pleasure of our meeting & that you will permit nothing to distress you while I am gone. I cannot help feeling a pang when I reflect that every step I take carrys me further & further from what is to me most valuable in this world but I will suppress such sensations & will be at quiet if I can only be certain that you are so. Even sending away Dick wounds me because it looks like parting with the last of the family—but I will not yield to these sensations—only let me know that you have conquerd them & all is well. I am now at my unkle Keiths where every body treats me with the utmost affection & friendship. They always have done so. I dine here to day with kind friends who make the time as agreeable as possible—but this is not Richmond.

I shall write to you as soon as I get to Philadelphia & am thinking of you always. Farewell. I never was peremptory but I must now give you one positive order. It is be happy. Once more, Farewell. I am ever your affectionate truely affectionate

I brought away by mistake two letters. The one to Genl. Young send to Mr. Hopkins. That which is unseald send to my brother. Again I am your

                                        J M

DINNER WITH PRESIDENT ADAMS

To Mary W. Marshall

My dearest Polly   Philadelphia, July 3, 1797
    I am here after a passage up the bay from Baltimore which woud have been very unpleasant but for the company of a very agreeable family which greatly alleviated the vexatious calamity of a dead calm under an excessive hot sun. I dind on saturday in private with the President whom I found a sensible plain candid good temperd man & was consequently much pleasd with him. I am not certain when I shall sail nor have I yet taken a vessel but I conjecture it will be early in the next week. Do

you however my dearest life continue to write to me as your letters will follow me shoud I be gone before their arrival & as my heart clings with real pleasure & delight only to what comes from you.

I dind yesterday with Mr. Morris. That family receives me with precisely the same friendship & affection as formerly & seems to preserve in a great degree its vivacity but it must be discernible that a heavy gloom hangs around them which only their good sense restrains them from showing. They live what we shoud style most elegantly nor is there in the house any apparent change except in the croud of company which formerly frequented it. I wish most earnestly for their sake they may be able to rtrieve their affairs nor am I without some hope of its being possible.

I was on friday evening at the Vauxhall of Philadelphia. It is indeed a most elegant place. I woud attempt to describe it to you but shoud fail. The amusements were walking, sitting punch ice creams etc. Music & conversation. I rode out yesterday to see Mrs. Heyward but she was not at home. She lives in the neighborhood of Philadelphia on the bank of the schuylkil at one of the most enchanting spots you ever saw.

Thus my dearest Polly do I when not engagd in the very serious business which employs a large portion of my time endeavor by amusements to preserve a mind at ease & [   ] it from brooding too much over my much lovd & absent wife. By all that is dear on earth, I entreat you to do the same. Our separation will not I trust be long & letters do everything to draw its sting. I am my dearest life your affectionate

PREPARING TO SAIL OVERSEAS

To Mary W. Marshall

My dearest Polly   Philadelphia, July 5, 1797
    I have been extremely chagrind at not having yet receivd a letter from you. I hope you are well as I hear nothing indicating the contrary but you know not how sollicitous how anxiously sollicitous I am to hear it from yourself. Write me

that you are well & in good spirits & I shall set out on my voyage with a lightend heart. I beleive I shall sail in the course of the next week for Amsterdam where it is expected that I shall join Genl. Pinckney. I have not taken my passage but I think I shall go in the brig Grace Capt. Wills. However you will hear from me more than once before my departure. I dind yesterday in a very large company of Senators & members of the house of representatives who met to celebrate the 4th. of July. The company was really a most respectable one & I experiencd from them the most flattering attention. I have much reason to be satisfied & pleasd with the manner in which I am receivd here but something is wanting to make me happy. Had I my dearest wife with me I shoud be delighted indeed. Not having that pleasure why do you not give me what is nearest to it. I am just calld off. Farewell. Your affectionate

"THIS DELAY IS SO CRUEL"

To Mary W. Marshall

My dearest Polly   July 10, 1797
    I have had the pleasure of receiving by the last post your letter of the 30th. of June. I thank Heaven that your health is better. To know that it is so, will take off one half from the unpleasantness of a voyage over the Atlantic. In your next I promise myself the delight of receiving assurances that your mind has become tranquil & as sprightly as usual. Good health will produce good spirits & I woud not on any consideration relinquish the hope that you will possess both. Remember that, if your situation shoud be as suspected, melancholy may inflict punishment on an innocent for whose sake you ought to preserve a serene & composed mind.
    Colo. Gamble a day or two before I parted with you expressd the wish of Mrs. Gamble to see you frequently & by her good & cheerful spirits to aid yours but that she felt some difficulty on account of your not encouraging an acquaintance. I mention the fact & leave it to yourself to decide what you will do.

I have been delayd extremely & very much to my mortification. Every day which passes before I set out threatens to make it a day longer before I return & is therefore most irksome to me. If my journey was to be postpond for any considerable time I woud certainly visit Richmond & all that is dearest in the world & which Richmond contains once more before my departure, but I expect to sail in the course of the present week or at any rate in the commencement of the next. This delay is so cruel as to retard my business without the consolation of seeing you. It is as yet out of my power to speak positively concerning my return. Indeed it will not be in my power until I reach Paris. The time depends so much on the course of business there as to make it impossible to know here what its length will be. I still hope however to return as early as we contemplated. Of this I know I will be certain; All my efforts will be usd to shorten as much as possible an absence the full misery of which I did not calculate til I felt it. Remember me affectionately to your mother & to all our good friends & relations. Tell the boys I please myself with the hopes of their improvement during my absence & kiss little Mary for your ever affectionate

Congress rises to day.

"BEYOND EXPRESSION IMPATIENT"

To Mary W. Marshall

My dearest Polly   July 11, 1797
Altho Mr. Marshall does not go directly to Richmond so that a letter by tomorrows post may perhaps reach you before this yet I cannot avoid writing to you because while doing so I seem to myself to be in some distant degree enjoying your company. I was last night at the play & saw the celebrated Mrs. Merry in the character of Juliet. She performs that part to admiration indeed but I really do not think Mrs. West jr. is far her inferior in it. I saw Mrs. Heyward there. I have paid that Lady one visit to one of the most delightful & romantic spots

on the river Schuylkil. She expressd much pleasure to see me & has pressed me very much to repeat my visit. I hope I shall not have time to do so. Tis said she is about to be married to a very wealthy young Englishman named Baring. This I think improbable as he is not more than four & twenty & being rich himself has no temptation to marry meerly for money.

I know nothing more concerning myself than I did yesterday. I am beyond expression impatient to set out on the embassy. The life I lead here does not suit me. I am weary of it. I dine out every day & am now engagd longer I hope than I shall stay. This dissipated life does not long suit my temper. I like it very well for a day or two but I begin to require a frugal repast with good cool water. This is my present situation. I woud give a great deal to dine with you to day on a piece of cold meat with our boys beside us & to see little Mary running backwards & forwards over the floor playing the sweet little tricks she is full of. But I can have no such pleasure. I wish to Heaven the time which must intervene before I can repass these delightful scenes was now terminated & that we were looking back on our separation instead of seeing it before us. Farewell my dearest Polly. Make yourself happy & you will bless, your ever affectionate

PHILADELPHIA THEATER AND FASHION

To Mary W. Marshall

My dearest Polly   Philadelphia, July 14, 1797
    Tomorrow the Grace in which I am to embark for Amsterdam will sail from this port. I shall go down to New Castle & go on board there on sunday. All concur that the vessel is a very fine & very safe one & that the season is most favorable for a good voyage. I hope therefore to reach Amsterdam by the latter end of August & from thence I will write to you as soon as possible. My letters however cannot be calculated on till some time in October. You must not therefore after I sail count on hearing from me till october. Unless there shoud be extraordinary & unlookd for delay you will I think receive

letters from me in that month. I shall then have it in my power to give you some more certain inteligence concerning my return. At present I can add nothing to what I have always said. My utmost endeavors will be usd to get back by christmass. If that shoud be practicable you will see me; if it shoud be impracticable you must not permit your fears in any situation to subdue you. If you will only give me this assurance I shall be happy. Mr. Brown came in the last stage & says he was too much hurried to give you information of his journey but I am satisfied all was well or he woud have heard it was not so. My son Tom wrote to me on the 6th. of the month & I was pleasd with his letter. I am happy to perceive from it that you retain your better health. I flatter myself you do because he does not mention your health. Thus will I continue to please myself concerning you & to beleive that you are well & happy. This beleif smooths the way before me & beguiles the melancholy of many an hour.

I dind yesterday with Mr. Bingham at his celebrated country seat on the Schuylkill. The entertainment was elegant but not by any means so expensive as I had been led to expect. It is the practice here to place in the center of the table a large oval vase almost like the waiter of a tea table but of silver or gold & ornamented with Cupids on which are glasses with flours. The table is then coverd all round with small dishes, none being placed in the center. In consequence of this large dinners here are not so expensive as with us. Mrs. Bingham is a very elegant woman who dresses at the height of the fashion. I do not however like that fashion. The sleeve does not reach the elbow or the glove come quite to it. There is a vacancy of three or four inches & just above the naked elbow is a gold clasp. Independent of relationship I like no body so well as the family of Mr. Morris. There is among them throughout a warmth & cordiality which is extremely pleasing. But Virginia & my own dear connections are not only more belovd but appear to me more to deserve love than any body else.

Farewell my much loved wife. Once more before I go on board will you hear from your

To Mary W. Marshall

My dearest Polly   Bay of Delaware, July 20, 1797
    The land is just escaping from my view the pilot is about to leave us & I hasten from the deck into the cabin once more to give myself the sweet indulgence of writing to you. On the 17th. as I mentiond in my last we left Philadelphia in order to join our vessel at New Castle & on the 18th. we came on board & weighd anchor at about 10 OClock. There has been so little wind that we are not yet entirely out of the bay. It is so wide however that the land has the appearance of a light blue cloud on the surface of the water & we shall very soon lose it entirely. The wind is now fair & tolerably fresh. I have been so long on board that I can form a very tolerable estimate of the accomodations to be expected on the voyage. The cabin is neat & clean, my birth a commodious one in which I have my own bed & sheets of which I have a plenty so that I lodge as conveniently as I coud do in any place whatever & I find that I sleep very soundly altho on water. We have for the voyage the greatest plenty of salt provisions, live stock & poultry & as we lay in our own liquors I have taken care to provide myself with a plenty of excellent porter wine & brandy. The Captain is one of the most obliging men in the world & the vessel is said by every body to be a very fine one. In addition to Mr. Brown Mr. Gamble & myself two dutch Gentlemen are passengers who appear to be intelligent men well disposd to make the voyage agreeable. I have then my dearest Polly every prospect before me of a passage such as I coud wish in every respect but one. At this season of the year there are such frequent calms as to create fear of a lengthy passage. We have met in the bay several vessels. One from Liverpool had been at sea nine weeks, & the others from other places had been out proportionably long. I hope we shall do better but in spite of me fears mingle with my hopes. I shall be extremely impatient to hear from you & our dear children. I have written a letter to Tom which I sent to Winchester in expectation that he might be there. If he is at Fauquier court house let him know it that he may endeavor to

have it sent to him. Colo. Carrington or Mr. Hopkins will give your letters a conveyance to me. I think it better for the present that they shoud some go by the way of London to the care of Rufus King esquire our minister there, some by the way of Amsterdam or the Hague to the care of William Vanns Murry esquire our minister at the Hague & perhaps some directed to me as Envoy extraordinary of the United States to the French Republic at Paris. Do not I intreat you omit to write. Some of your letters may miscarry but some will reach me & my heart can feel till my return no pleasure comparable to what will be given it by a line from you telling me that all remains well. Farewell my dearest life. Your happiness will ever be the first prayer of your unceasingly affectionate

DIPLOMAT, CONGRESSMAN,
AND SECRETARY OF STATE
1797–1801

To Mary W. Marshall

My dearest Polly   At sea, August 3, 1797
    A vessel is just in sight which appears to be sailing for Amer-
ica & with the hope that I may get it on board her I hasten to
scribble a few lines to you. We are now 12 or 1300 miles from
the capes of Delaware in the direct course for the channel &
have had yet a while a favorable voyage except that we have in
the general too little wind. We have not made quite a third of
our way to Amsterdam. We had for three days a strong breeze
but all is calm again & we scarcely creep along. I shoud disregard this if I did not so greatly fear that a long passage may too
much delay my return. I have had scarcely any sea sickness &
am now perfectly well. My only sollicitudes are for the success
of my mission & for the much loved persons I leave behind me
in my own country. Sometimes I am melancholy & sink into
fears concerning you but I shake them off as fast as possible &
please myself with the delightful picture of our meeting on my
return. I fancy myself by your side with our children round us
& seem to myself to have such a hold on happiness that it cannot slip from me. I have with me more books than I can read
during the passage & that circumstance tends very much to diminish the tediousness of such a voyage. The Captain is remarkably obliging & we have abundant stores of everything which
can tend to make our situation comfortable. Indeed if I coud
know that you were perfectly well & happy I shoud feel as
much content & satisfaction as can be felt with the prospect
before me of so long a separation from you. I will indulge the
sweet hope of hearing from you very soon after my arrival in
Europe & I will beleive that your letters will all assure me that
you are well & happy. Tis that beleif alone which can keep up
my spirits.

                                                    August 29th. 97
    The vessel by which I expected to have sent the above did
not give me an opportunity of putting it on board. I have this
instant arrived in Holland & seen a vessel whose Captain will

sail for america as soon as the wind permits. I sieze the opportunity to let you know that I am safe & perfectly well. I can
add nothing further as I have not yet reachd a place where I
can collect any inteligence & as I detain the captain while I add
with what affection I am your

THE HAGUE

To Mary W. Marshall

My dearest Polly   The Hague, September 9, 1797
    I have just heard that a vessel sails so soon as the wind will
permit from Rotterdam for the United States & I sieze the opportunity of writing to you.
    I reachd this place on the 3d. instant & immediately saw Genl.
Pinckney with whom I am very much pleasd. We had agreed
to set out immediately for Paris for which place the minister of
France is authorizd to give us passports. Genl. Pinckney however two days after my arrival receivd a letter from Mr. Gerry
written at Boston informing of his intention to embark immediately & of his expectation to join us here the latter end of
August. He has not yet come but we anxiously wait for him.
We shall wait a week or ten days longer & shall then proceed
on our journey. You cannot conceive (yes you can conceive)
how these delays perplex & mortify me. I fear I cannot return
until the spring & that fear excites very much uneasiness &
even regret at my having ever consented to cross the Atlantic.
I wish extremely to hear from you & to know your situation.
My mind clings so much to Richmond that scarcely a night
passes in which during the hour of sleep I have not some interesting conversation with you or concerning you.
    This place was formerly the residence of the Prince & Princess
of orange & being the court was also the residence of all the
foreign ministers. It is still the latter. The former palace is bestowd on the Minister from France. There are at the Hague a
great many elegant walks which are very unusual in the midst
of a city but the pride & boast of the place is a very extensive

wood adjoining the city which extends to the sea. This is I beleive the only natural wood in Holland. It is intersected with a variety of walks & is indeed in the summer one of the most delightful situations in the world. The society at the Hague is probably very difficult, to an American it certainly is & I have no inclination to attempt to enter into it. While the differences with France subsist the political characters of this place are probably unwilling to be found frequently in company with our countrymen. It might give umbrage to France. Genl. Pinckney has with him a daughter who appears to be about 12 or 13 years of age. Mrs. Pinckney informs me that only one girl of her age has visited her since the residence of the family at the Hague. In fact we seem to have no communication but with Americans or those who are employd by America or who have property in our country. Near my lodgings is a theatre in which a french company performs three times a week. I have been frequently to the play & tho I do not understand the language I am very much amusd at it. The whole company is considerd as having a great deal of merit but there is a Madame deGazon who is considerd as one of the first performers in Paris who bears the palm in the estimation of every person.

The Directory with the aid of the soldiery have just put in arrest the most able & leading members of the legislature who were considerd as moderate men & friends of peace. Some conjecture that this event will so abridge our negotiations as probably to occasion my return to America this fall. A speedy return is my most ardent wish but to have my return expedited by the means I have spoken of is a circumstance so calamitous that I deprecate it as the Greatest of evils. Remember me affectionately to our friends & kiss for me our dear little Mary. Tell the boys how much I expect from them & how anxious I am to see them as well as their beloved mother. I am my dearest Polly unalterably, Your,

NEWS OF HOLLAND AND FRANCE

To George Washington

Dear Sir   The Hague, September 15, 1797
  The flattering evidences I have receivd of your favorable
opinion, which have made on my mind an impression only to
wear out with my being, added to a conviction that you must
yet feel a deep interest in all that concerns a country to whose
service you have devoted so large a portion of your life, induce
me to offer you such occasional communications as, while in
europe I may be enabled to make, & induce a hope too that
the offer will not be deemd an unacceptable or unwelcome
intrusion.
  Until our arrival in Holland we saw only British & neutral
vessels. This added to the blockade of the dutch fleet in the
Texel, of the french fleet in Brest & of the spanish fleet in
Cadiz manifests the entire dominion which one nation at present possesses over the seas. By the ships of war which met us
we were three times visited & the conduct of those who came
on board was such as woud proceed from general orders to
pursue a system calculated to conciliate America. Whether this
be occasiond by a sense of justice & the obligations of good
faith, or solely by the hope that the perfect contrast which it
exhibits to the conduct of France may excite keener sensations at that conduct, its effects on our commerce are the
same.
  The situation of Holland is truely interesting. Tho the face
of the country still exhibits a degree of wealth & population
perhaps unequald in any other part of Europe its decline is visible. The great city of Amsterdam is in a state of blockade. More
than two thirds of its shipping ly unemployd in port. Other
seaports suffer tho not in so great a degree. In the meantime
the requisitions made upon them are enormous. They have just
completed the payment of the 100,000,000 of florins (equal
to 40,000,000 of dollars) stipulated by treaty; they have sunk,
on the first entrance of the French, a very considerable sum in
assignats; they made large contributions in specifics; & they
pay feed & cloath an army estimated, as I am informd, at near

three times its real number. It is supposd that France has by various means drawn from Holland about 60,000,000 of dollars. This has been paid, in addition to the national expenditures, by a population of less than 2000,000. Nor, shoud the war continue, can the contributions of Holland stop here. The increasing exigencies of France must inevitably increase her demands on those within her reach. Not even peace can place Holland in her former situation. Antwerp will draw from Amsterdam a large portion of that commerce which is the great source of its wealth, for Antwerp possesses in the existing state of things, advantages which not even weight of capital can entirely surmount. The political divisions of this country & its uncertainty concerning its future destiny must also have their operation. Independent of the grand division between those for & against the stadtholder; between those who favor an indivisible & those who favor a foederal republic, there is much contrariety of opinion concerning the essential principles of that indivisible consolidated republic which the influence of France imposes on the nation. A constitution which I have not read, but which is stated to me to have contain all the great fundamentals of a representative government, & which has been prepard with infinite labor, & has experienced an uncommon length of discussion was rejected in the primary assemblies by a majority of nearly five to one of those who voted. The objections do not accompany the decision, but they are said to be to the duration of the constitution which was to remain five years unalterd, to the division of the legislature into two chambers, & to its power of definitive legislation. The substitute wished for by its opponents is a legislature with a single branch having power only to initiate laws which are to derive their force from the sanction of the primary assemblies. I do not know how they woud organize their executive, nor is it material how they woud organize it. A constitution with such a legislature woud live too short a time to make it worth the while to examine the structure of its other parts. It is remarkable that the very men who have rejected the form of government proposed to them have reelected a great majority of the persons who prepard it & who will probably make from it no essential departure. Those elected are now assembled in convention at this place, but we know not in what manner they are proceeding. It is also worthy of notice that more than two thirds of those intitled to suffrage including perhaps more than four fifths of the property of the nation & who wishd, as I am told, the adoption of the constitution, withheld their votes on this very interesting question. Many were restraind by an unwillingness to take the oath requird before a vote coud be received; many, disgusted with the present state of things, have come to the unwise determination of revenging themselves on those whom they charge with having occasiond it by taking no part whatever in the politics of their country, & many seem to be indifferent to every consideration not immediately connected with their particular employments.

The political opinions which have producd the rejection of the constitution, & which, as it woud seem, can only be entertaind by intemperate & ill informd minds unaccustomd to a union of the theory & practice of liberty, must be associated with a general system which if brought into action will produce the same excesses here which have been so justly deplored in France. The same materials exist tho not in so great a degree. They have their clubs, they have a numerous poor & they have enormous wealth in the hands of a minority of the nation. On my remarking this to a very rich & inteligent merchant of Amsterdam, & observing that if one class of men withdrew itself from public duties & offices it woud immediately be succeeded by another which woud acquire a degree of power & influence that might be exercisd to the destruction of those who had retired from society, he replied that the remark was just, but that they relied on France for a protection from those evils which she had herself experiencd. That france woud continue to require great supplies from Holland & knew its situation too well to permit it to become the prey of anarchy. That Holland was an artificial country acquird by persevering industry & which coud only be preservd by wealth & order. That confusion & anarchy woud banish a large portion of that wealth, woud dry up its sources & woud entirely disable them from giving France that pecuniary aid she so much needed. That under this impression very many who, tho friends to the revolution, saw with infinite mortification french troops garrison the towns of Holland, woud now see their departure with equal regret. Thus they willingly relinquish national independence for individual safety. What a lesson to those who woud admit foreign influence into the United States!

You have observd the storm which has been long gathering in Paris. The thunder bolt has at length been launched at the heads of the leading members of the legislature & has, it is greatly to be feard, involved in one common ruin with them the constitution & liberties of their country.

The inclosd papers will furnish some idea of a transaction which may be very interesting to America as well as to France. Complete & *impartial* details concerning it will not easily be obtaind as the press is no longer free. The journalists who had venturd to censure the proceedings of a majority of the directory are seizd & against about forty of them a sentence of transportation is pronouncd. The press is placd under the superintendence of a police appointed by & dependent on the executive. It is supposd that all private letters have been seized for inspection.

From some Paris papers it appears that on the first alarm several members of the legislature attempted to assemble in their proper halls, which they found closd & guarded by an armd force. Sixty or seventy assembled at another place & began to remonstrate against the violence offerd to their body but fear soon dispersd them. To destroy the possibility of a rallying point the municipal administrations of Paris & the central administration of the seine were immediately suspended & forbidden by an arrêté of the directoire, to assemble themselves together. Many of the administrators of the departments through France elected by the people, had been previously removd & their places filld by persons chosen by the directory. Moreau who commanded the army of the Sambre & the Meuse by which he was deservedly beloved & who was considered as attached to the fallen party was, as is reported, invited from his army to Paris under the pretext of a personal consultation. We have not heard of his arrival or of his fate. The command of his army during his absence did not, we learn, devolve on the oldest officer but was given to Genl. Hoche who also commands the army of the interior. Carnot is at one time said to have been killd in defending himself from some soldiers who pursued & attempted to take him, at another time he is said to have effected his escape. The fragment of the legislature convokd by

the directory at L'odeon & L'ecole de santé, hastend to repeal
the law for organizing the national guards, & authorized the
directory to introduce into Paris as many troops as shoud be
judged necessary. The same day the liberty of the press was
abolished by a line, property taken away by another & personal
security destroyd by a sentence of transportation against men
unheard & untried. All this is stild the triumph of liberty & of
the constitution.

To give a satisfactory statement of the origin & progress of
the contest between the executive & legislative departments
woud require more time than coud be devoted to the subject,
did I even possess the requisite information, & to you, sir, it
woud be unnecessary because I have no doubt of your having
received it through other channels. I shall briefly observe that
the controversy has embraced a variety of interesting subjects.
Since the election of the new third, there were found in both
branches of the legislature a majority in favor of moderate measures, &, apparently, wishing sincerely for peace. They have
manifested a disposition which threatend a condemnation of
the conduct of the directory towards America, a scrutiny into
the transactions of Italy, particularly those respecting Venice &
Genoa, an enquiry into the disposition of public money & a
regular arrangement of the finances as woud prevent in future
those dilapidations which are suspected to have grown out
of their disorder. They have sought too by their laws to amelio-
rate the situation of those whom terror had driven out of France,
& of those priests who had committed no offence. Carnot &
Barthelemy two of the directory were with the legislature.

The cry of a conspiracy to reestablish royalism was immediately raised against them. An envoy was dispatchd to the army
of Italy to sound its disposition. It was represented that the
legislature was hostile to the armies, that it withheld their pay
& subsistence, that by its opposition to the directory it encouraged Austria & Britain to reject the terms of peace which
were offered by France & which but for that opposition woud
have been accepted, & finally that it had engagd in a conspiracy for the destruction of the constitution & the republic &
for the restoration of royalty. At a feast given to the armies of
Italy to commemorate their fellow soldiers who had fallen in
that country the Generals addressed to them their complaints,

plainly spoke of marching to Paris to support the directory against the Councils & receivd from them addresses manifesting the willingness of the soldiers to follow them. The armies also addressd the directory & each other, & addresses were dispatchd to different departments. The directory answerd them by the strongest criminations of the legislature. Similar proceedings were had in the army of the interior commanded by Genl. Hoche. Detachments were moved within the limits prohibited by the constitution, some of which declard they were marching to Paris "to bring the legislature to reason." Alarmd at these movements the council of five hundred called on the directory for an account of them. The movement of the troops within the constitutional circle was attributed to accident & the discontents of the army to the falts committed by the legislature who were plainly criminated as conspirators against the army & the republic. This message was taken up by Tronçon in the council of antients & by Thibideau in the council of five hundred. I hope you have seen their speeches. They are able, & seem to me to have entirely exculpated the legislature. In the mean time the directory employd itself in the removal of the administrators of many of the departments & cantons & replacing those whom the people had elected by others in whom it coud confide, & in the removal generally of such officers both civil & military as coud not be trusted to make room for others in whom it coud rely. The legislature on its part, passed several laws to enforce the constitutional restrictions on the armies & endeavord to organize the national guards. On this latter subject especially Pichegru great & virtuous I beleive in the cabinet as in the field, was indefatigable. We understand that the day before the law for their organization woud have been carried into execution the decisive blow was struck.

To support the general charge of a conspiracy in favor of royalty I know of no particular facts alledgd against the arrested members except Pichegru & two or three others. An abridgement of the paper constituting the whole charge against Pichegru will be found in the inclosd supplement. I have seen the paper at full length. The story at large is still more improbable than its abridgement because Pichegru is made in the first moment of conversation to unbosom himself entirely to a perfect stranger who had only told him that he came from the

Prince of Condé & coud not exhibit a single line or testimonial of any sort to prove that he had ever seen that Prince or that he was not a spy employed by some of the enemies of the General.

This story is repeld by Pichegru's character which has never before been defild. Great as were the means he possessed of personal aggrandizement he retird clean handed from the army, without adding a shilling to his private fortune. It is repeled by his resigning the supreme command, by his numerous victories subsequent to the alledgd treason, by its own extreme absurdity & by the fear which his accusers show of bringing him to trial according to the constitution even before a tribunal they can influence & overawe, or of even permitting him to be heard before that prostrate body which is still termed the legislature, & which in defiance of the constitution has pronounced judgement on him.

Yet this improbable & unsupported tale seems to be receivd as an establishd truth by those who, the day before his fall bowed to him as an idol. I am mortified as a man to learn that even his old army which conquerd under him, which adord him, which partook of his fame & had heretofore not joind their brethren in accusing the legislature, now unite in bestowing on him the heaviest execrations & do not hesitate to pronounce him a traitor of the deepest die.

Whether this conspiracy be real or not, the wounds inflicted on the constitution by the three directors seem to me to be mortal. In opposition to the express regulations of the constitution the armies have deliberated, the result of their deliberations addressd to the directory has been favorably received, & the legislature since the revolution has superadded its thanks.

Troops have been marchd within those limits which by the constitution they are forbidden to enter but on the request of the legislature.

The directory is forbidden to arrest a member of the legislature unless in the very commission of a criminal act & then he can only be tried by the high court, on which occasion forms calculated to protect his person from violence or the prejudice of the moment are carefully prescribed. Yet it has seizd by a military force about fifty leading members not taken in a criminal act & has not pursued a single step marked out by the constitution.

The councils can inflict no penalty on their own members other than reprimand, arrest for eight & imprisonment for three days. Yet they have banishd to such place as the directory shall chuse a large portion of their body without the poor formality of hearing a defence.

The legislature shall not exercise any judiciary power or pass any retrospective law. Yet it has pronounced this heavy judgement on others as well as its own members & has taken from individuals property which the law had vested in them.

The members of the directory are personally securd by the same rules with those of the legislature. Yet three directors have deprivd two of their places, the legislature has then banishd them without a hearing & has proceeded to fill up the alledged vacancies. Merlin late minister of justice & François de Neufchatel have been elected.

The constitution forbids the house of any man to be enterd in the night. The orders of the constituted authorities can only be executed in the day. Yet many of the members were seized in their beds.

Indeed sir the constitution has been violated in so many instances that it woud require a pamphlet to detail them. The detail woud be unnecessary for the great principle seems to be introduced that the government is to be administerd according to the will of the armies & not according to the will of the nation.

Necessity the never to be worn out apology for violence, is alledgd—but coud that necessity go further than to secure the persons of the conspirators? Did it extend to the banishment of the printers & to the slavery of the press? If such a necessity did exist it was created by the disposition of the people at large, & it is a truth which requires no demonstration that if a republican form of government cannot be administerd by the general will, it cannot be administerd against that will by an army.

After all the result may not be what is apprehended. France possesses such enormous power, such internal energy, such a vast population that she may possibly spare another million &

preserve or reacquire her liberty. Or, the form of the Government being preservd, the independence of the legislature may be gradually recoverd.

With their form of Government or revolutions we have certainly no right to intermeddle, but my regrets at the present state of things are increasd by an apprehension that the rights of our country will not be deemd so sacred under the existing system as they woud have been had the legislature preservd its legitimate authority.

Genl. Pinckney (with whom I cannot but be very much pleasd) have waited impatiently for Mr. Gerry & shall wait until monday the 18th inst. On that day we set out for Paris.

The negotiations with Austria & Britain are still pending & are of very uncertain issue.

This letter has extended itself to an unexpected length. I have fatigued you sir & will only add that I remain, with sincere & respectful attachment, Your obedt. Servt.

I just now learn that fifteen hundred persons have been arrested at Lyons. That resistance is made at Avignon & that Massena is marching to quel it.

THE FIRST "XYZ" DISPATCH

To Timothy Pickering

No. 1
Dear Sir   Paris, October 22, 1797
    All of us having arrived at Paris on the evening of the fourth instant, on the next day we verbally and unofficially informed the Minister of Foreign Affairs therewith, & desired to know when he would be at leisure to receive one of our Secretaries with the official notification; he appointed the next day at two o'Clock, when Major Rutledge waited on him with the following Letter.

Citizen Minister,
    The United States of America being desirous of terminating all differences between them and the French Republic, and of restoring that harmony and good understanding, and that commercial and friendly

intercourse which from the commencement of their political connection until lately have so happily subsisted, the President has nominated and by and with the advice and consent of the Senate has appointed us, the undersigned, jointly and severally Envoys extraordinary and Ministers Plenipotentiary to the French Republic, for the purpose of accomplishing these great objects. In persuance of such nomination and appointment and with such view having come to Paris, we wish, Citizen Minister, to wait on you at any hour you will be pleased to appoint, to present the Copy of our Letters of Credence; and whilst we evince our sincere and ardent desire for the speedy restoration of friendship and harmony between the two Republics, we flatter ourselves with your concurrence in the accomplishment of this desirable event. We request you will accept the assurances of our perfect esteem and consideration.

Paris October 6th in   Signed, CHARLES COTESWORTH PINCKNEY
the 22d year of   JOHN MARSHALL
American Independence   ELBRIDGE GERRY

To this letter the Minister gave a verbal answer that he would see us the day after the morrow (the 8th.) at one o'Clock. Accordingly at that hour and day we waited on the Minister at his home where his office is held, when being informed he was not at home, the Secretary General of the Department told Major Rutledge that the Minister was obliged to wait on the Directory & requested we would suspend our visit till three o'Clock. At which hour we called; the Minister we found was then engaged with the Portuguese Minister, who retired in about ten minutes, when we were introduced and produced the copy of our Letters of credence, which the Minister perused and kept. He informed us "that the Directory had required him to make a report relative to the situation of the United States with regard to France which he was then about, and which would be finished in a few days, when he would let us know what steps were to follow." We asked if cards of hospitality were in the mean time necessary, he said they were and that they should be delivered to us: and he immediately rung for his Secretary and directed him to make them out. The Conversation was carried on by him in French, and by us in our own language.

The next day Cards of Hospitality were sent to us and our Secretaries, in a Style suitable to our official Character.

On Saturday the 14th Major Mountflorence informed

General Pinckney that he had a conversation with mr. Osmond, the private and confidential Secretary of the Minister of Foreign Affairs, who told him that the Directory were greatly exasperated at some parts of the President's Speech at the opening of the last Session of Congress, and would require an explanation of them from us. The particular parts were not mentioned. In another Conversation on the same day the Secretary informed the Major that the Minister had told him it was probable we should not have a public Audience of the Directory till such time as our negociation was finished; that probably persons might be appointed to treat with us, but they would report to him, and he would have the direction of the negociation. The Major did not conceal from mr. Osmond his intention to communicate these conversations to us.

In the morning of October the eighteenth M. Hubbard of the House of Van Stophorsts and Hubbard of Amsterdam called on General Pinckney and informed him that a Mr. Horttinguer who was in Paris and whom the General had seen at Amsterdam was a gentleman of considerable credit and reputation; that he had formerly been a banker at Paris and had settled his affairs with honor; that he had then formed connections in America; had married a native of that country; intended to settle there; was supported by some capital houses in Holland; and that we might place great reliance on him. In the evening of the same day M. Horttinguer called on General Pinckney and after having sat some time in a room full of company whispered to him that he had a message from M. Talleyrand to communicate when he was at leisure. General Pinckney immediately withdrew with him into another room; and when they were alone, M. Horttinguer said, that he was charged with a business in which he was a novice; that he had been acquainted with M. Talleyrand in America; and that he was sure he had a great regard for that country and its citizens; and was very desirous that a reconciliation should be brought about with France: that to effectuate that end, he was ready, if it was thought proper, to suggest a plan, confidentially, that M. Talleyrand expected would answer the purpose. General Pinckney said he should be glad to hear it. M. Horttinguer replied, that the Directory, and particularly two of the members of it, were exceedingly irritated at some passages of the President's speech, and desired that they should be softened; and that this step would be necessary previous to our reception; that besides this, a sum of money was required for the pocket of the Directory and ministers, which would be at the disposal of M. Talleyrand; and that a loan would also be insisted on. M. Horttinguer said if we acceded to these measures, M. Talleyrand had no doubt that all our differences with France might be accommodated. On enquiry, M. Horttinguer could not point out the particular passages of the speech that had given offence, nor the quantum of the loan; but mentioned that the douceur for the pocket was twelve hundred thousand livres, about fifty thousand pounds sterling. General Pinckney told him his colleagues and himself from the time of their arrival here had been treated with great slight and disrespect; that they earnestly wished for peace and reconciliation with France; and had been entrusted by their country with very great powers to obtain these ends on honourable terms; that with regard to the propositions made, he could not even consider of them before he had communicated them to his colleagues; that after he had done so, he should hear from him. After a communication and consultation had, it was agreed that General Pinckney should call on M. Horttinguer and request him to make his propositions to us all; and for fear of mistakes or misapprehension, that he should be requested to reduce the heads into writing. Accordingly, on the morning of October the nineteenth, General Pinckney called on M. Horttinguer, who consented to see his colleagues in the evening, and to reduce his propositions to writing. He said his communication was not immediately with M. Talleyrand, but through another gentleman, in whom M. Talleyrand had great confidence: this proved afterwards to be M. Bellamy, a native of Geneva, of the house of Bellamy Riccia and Company of Hamburg.

At six in the evening, M. Horttinguer came and left with us the first set of propositions which, translated from the French, are as follows. "A person who possesses the confidence of the Directory, on what relates to the affairs of America, convinced of the mutual advantages which would result from the reestablishment of the good understanding between two nations, proposes to employ all of his influence to obtain this object. He will assist the commissioners of the United States in all the demands which they may have to make from the government of France, in as much as they may not be contradictory to those which he proposes himself to make, and of which the principal will be communicated confidentially. It is desired, that in the official communications there should be given a softening turn to a part of the President's speech to Congress, which has caused much irritation. It is feared that in not satisfying certain individuals in this respect, they may give way to all their resentment. The nomination of commissioners will be consented to on the same footing as they have been named in the treaty with England, to decide on the reclamations which individuals of America may make on the government of France, or on French individuals. The payment which agreably to the decisions of the commissioners, shall fall to the share of the French Government, are to be advanced by the American government itself. It is desired that the funds which by this means shall enter again into the American trade, should be employed in new supplies for the French colonies. Engagements of this nature on the part of individuals reclaming will always hasten in all probability the decisions of the French commissioners; and perhaps it may be desired that this clause should make a part of the instructions which the government of the United States should give to the commissioners they may chuse. The French government desires besides to obtain a loan from the United States; but so that that should not give any jealousy to the English government, nor hurt the neutrality of the United States this loan shall be masked, by stipulating That the government of the United States consents to make The advances for the payment of the debts contracted by the agents of the French government with the citizens of the United States; and which are already acknowledged, and the payment ordered by the Directory, but without having been yet effectuated. There should be delivered a note to the amount of these debts. Probably this note may be accompanied by ostensible peices which will guarantee to the agents the responsability of the United States in case any umbrage should cause an enquiry. There shall also be first taken from this loan certain sums for the purpose of making the customary distributions in diplomatic affairs." The person of note mentioned in the minutes who had the confidence of the Directory, he said before us all, was M. Talleyrand. The amount of the loan he could not ascertain precisely but understood it would be according to our ability to pay. The sum which would be considered as proper according to diplomatic usage was about twelve hundred thousand livres. He could not state to us what parts of the President's speech were excepted to, but said he would enquire and inform us. He agreed to breakfast with M. Gerry the morning of the twenty first in order to make such explanations as we had then requested or should think proper to request: but on the morning of the twentieth M. Horttinguer called and said that M. Bellami, the confidential friend of M. Talleyrand, instead of communicating with us through M. Horttinguer, would see us himself and make the necessary explanations. We appointed to meet him the evening of the twentieth, at seven o'clock, in General Marshalls room. At seven M. Bellami and M. Horttinguer entered: and the first mentioned gentleman being introduced to us as the confidential friend of M. Talleyrand, immediately stated to us the favorable impressions of that gentleman toward our country, impressions which were made by the kindness and civilities he had personally received in America. That impressed by his solicitude to repay these kindness, he was willing to aid us in the present negociation by his good offices with the Directory, who were, he said, extremely irritated against the government of the United States, on account of some parts of the Presidents speech, & who had neither acknowledged nor received us, and consequently have not authorised M. Talleyrand to have any communications with us. The Minister therefore could not see us himself but had authorized his friend M. Bellami to communicate to us certain propositions and to receive our answers to them, and to promise on his part that if we would engage to consider them as the basis of the proposed negociation, he would intercede with the Directory to acknowledge us and to give us a public audience. M. Bellami stated to us explicitly and repeatedly that he was cloathed with no authority; that he was not a diplomatic character; that he was not even a Frenchman; he was only the friend of M. Talleyrand, and trusted by him. That with regard to himself, he had landed property in America on which he hoped his children would reside: and that he earnestly wished well to the United States. He then took out of his pocket a French translation of the President's speech, the parts of which objected to by the Directory were marked agreeably to our request to M. Horttinguer and are contained in the exhibit A. Then he made us the second set of propositions, which were dictated by him & written by M. Horttinguer in our presence, and delivered to us, and which, translated from the French, are as follows: "There is demanded a formal disavowal in writing, declaring that the speech of the citizen President Barras did not contain any thing offensive to the government of the United States, nor any thing which deserved the epithets contained in the whole paragraph. Secondly, reparation is demanded for the article by which it shall be declared that the decree of the Directory there mentioned did not contain any thing contrary to the treaty of 1778, and had none of those fatal consequences that the paragraph reproaches to it. Thirdly, it is demanded that there should be an acknowledgement in writing of the depredations exercised on our trade by the English and French privateers. Fourthly, the government of France, faithful to the profession of public faith which it has made not to intermeddle in the internal affairs of foreign governments with which it is at peace, would look upon this paragraph as an attack upon its loyalty, if this was intended by the President. It demands, in consequence, a formal declaration that it is not the government of France, nor its agents that this paragraph meant to designate. In consideration of these reparations, the French Republic disposed to renew with the United States of America, a treaty which shall place them reciprocally in the same state that they were in 1778. By this new treaty, France shall be placed, with respect to the United States, exactly on the same footing as they stand with England, in virtue of the last treaty which has been concluded between them. A secret article, of this new treaty would be a loan, to be made by the United States to the French Republic: and once agreed upon the amount of the loan, it would be endeavoured to consult the convenience of the United States with respect to the best method of preventing its publicity." On reading the speech, M. Bellami dilated very much upon the keenness of the resentment it had produced, and expatiated largely on the satisfaction he said was indispensably necessary as a preliminary to negociation. But said he, gentlemen, I will not disguise from you, that this satisfaction, being made, the essential part of the treaty remains to be adjusted: "il faut de l'argent—il faut beaucoup d'argent." You must pay money—you must pay a great deal of money. He spoke much of the force, the honor and the jealous republican pride of France; and represented to us strongly the advantages which we should derive from the neutrality thus to be purchased. He said that the receipt of the money might be so disguised as to prevent its being considered as a breach of neutrality by England; and thus save us from being embroiled with that power. Concerning the twelve hundred thousand livres, little was said; that being completely understood, on all sides, to be required for the officers of government; and therefore needing no further explanation. These propositions, he said, being considered as the admitted basis of the proposed treaty, M. Talleyrand trusted that, by his influence with the Directory, he could prevail on the government to receive us. We asked whether we were to consider it as certain that without previous stipulation to the effect required we were not to be received. He answered, that M. Talleyrand himself was not authorised to speak to us the will of the Directory and consequently could not authorise him. The conversation continued until after nine, when they left us; having engaged to breakfast with M. Gerry the next morning. October the twenty first, M. Horttinguer came before nine o'clock. M. Bellami did not come until ten: he had passed the morning with M. Talleyrand. After breakfast the subject was immediately resumed. He represented to us, that we were not yet acknowledged or received; that the Directory were so exasperated against the United States, as to have come to a determination to demand from us, previous to our reception, those disavowals, reparations and explanations, which were stated at large last evening. He said that M. Talleyrand and himself were extremely sensible of the pain we must feel in complying with this demand: but that the Directory would not dispense with it: that therefore we must consider it as the indispensable preliminary, to obtain our reception: unless we could find the means to change their determination in this particular. That if we satisfied the Directory in these particulars, a letter would be written to us to demand the extent of our powers, and to know whether we were authorized to place them precisely on

the same footing with England: whether, he said, our full
powers were really and substantially full powers; or, like those
of Lord Malmesbury, only illusory powers. That if, to this demand, our answer should be affirmative, then France would
consent that commissioners should be appointed to ascertain
the claims of the United States, in like manner as under our
treaty with England: but from their jurisdiction must be withdrawn those which were condemned for want of a rôle
d'equipage; that being a point on which Merlin, while minister
of justice, had written a treatise and on which the Directory were
decided. There would however be no objection to our complaining of these captures in the course of the negociation; and
if we could convince Merlin by our reasoning, the Minister
would himself be satisfied with our so doing. We required an
explanation of that part of the conversation in which M. Bellami had hinted at our finding means to avert the demand concerning the President's speech. He answered that he was not
authorised to state those means; but that we must search for
them and propose them ourselves. If however we asked his
opinion as a private individual, and would receive it as coming
from him, he would suggest to us the means which in his opinion would succeed. On being asked to suggest the means, he
answered—money. That the Directory were jealous of its own
honor and of the honor of the nation; that it insisted on receiving from us the same respect with which we had treated
the king; that this honor must be maintained in the manner
before required; unless we substituted in the place of those
reparations something perhaps more valuable that was money.
He said further, that if we desired him to point out the sum
which he believed would be satisfactory, he would do so. We
requested him to proceed: and he said that there were thirty
two millions of florins of Dutch inscriptions, worth ten
shillings in the pound, which might be assigned to us at twenty
shillings in the pound: and he proceeded to state to us the certainty, that after a peace the Dutch government would repay
us the money; so that we should ultimately lose nothing: and
the only operation of the measure would be, an advance from
us to France of thirty two millions, on the credit of the government of Holland. We asked him whether the fifty thousand
pounds sterling, as a douceur to the Directory, must be in ad-

dition to this sum. He answered in the affirmative. We told him, that on the subject of the treaty, we had no hesitation in saying that our powers were ample: that on the other points proposed to us, we would retire into another room, and return in a few minutes with our answer.

We committed immediately to writing the answer we proposed, in the following words: "Our powers respecting a treaty are ample: but the proposition of a loan, in the form of Dutch inscriptions, or in any other form, is not within the limits of our instructions: upon this point therefore the government must be consulted: one of the American Ministers will for the purpose forthwith embark for America: provided the Directoire will suspend all further captures on American vessels, and will suspend proceedings on those already captured, as well where they have been already condemned, as where the decisions have not yet been rendered: and that where sales have been made, but the money not yet received by the captors, it shall not be paid until the preliminary questions proposed to the ministers of the United States be discussed and decided:" which was read as a verbal answer; and we told them they might copy it if they pleased. M. Bellamy refused to do so; disappointment was apparent: he said we treated the money part of the proposition as if it had proceeded from the Directory; whereas in fact it did not proceed even from the Minister but was only a suggestion from himself, as a substitute to be proposed by us, in order to avoid the painful acknowledgement that the Directory had determined to demand of us. It was told him, that we understood that matter perfectly; that we knew the proposition was in form to be ours; but that it came substantially from the minister. We asked what had led to our present conversation? And General Pinckney then repeated the first communication from M. Horttinguer (to the whole of which that gentleman assented) and we observed that those gentlemen had brought no testimonials of their speaking any thing from authority; but that relying on the fair characters they bore, we had believed them when they said they were from the minister; and had conversed with them in like manner as if we were conversing with M. Talleyrand himself; and that we could not consider any suggestion M. Bellamy had made, as not having been previously approved of: but yet, if he did not choose to take a memorandum in writing of our answer, we had no wish that he should do so: and further, if he chose to give the answer to his proposition the form of a proposition from ourselves, we could only tell him that we had no other proposition to make, relative to any advance of money on our part. That America had sustained deep and heavy losses by French depredations on our commerce, and that France had alledged some complaints against the United States, that on those subjects we came fully prepared; and were not a little surprized to find France unwilling to hear us; and making demands upon us which could never have been suspected by our government; and which had the appearance of our being the aggressing party. M. Bellami expressed himself vehemently on the resentment of France; and complained that instead of our proposing some substitute for the reparations demanded of us, we were stipulating certain conditions to be performed by the Directory itself. That he could not take charge of such propositions and that the Directory would persist in its demand of those reparations which he at first stated. We answered, that we could not help it; it was for the Directory to determine what course its own honor and the interests of France required it to pursue: it was for us to guard the interests and honor of our country. M. Bellamy observed, that we had taken no notice of the first proposition, which was, to know whether we were ready to make the disavowal reparations and explanations concerning the President's Speech. We told him that we supposed it to be impossible that either he or the minister could imagine that such a proposition could require an answer: that we did not understand it as being seriously expected; but merely as introductory to the subjects of real consideration.

He spoke of the respect which the Directory required, and repeated, that it would exact as much as was paid to the antient kings. We answered, that America had demonstrated to the world, and especially to France, a much greater respect for her present government than for her former monarchy; and that there was no evidence of this disposition which ought to be required, that we were not ready to give. He said that we should certainly not be received; and seemed to shudder at the consequences. We told him that America had made evey possible effort to remain on friendly terms with France; that she was still making them: that if France would not hear us; but would make war on the United Slates; nothing remained for us, but to regret the unavoidable necessity of defending ourselves.

The subject of our powers was again mentioned; and we told him, that America was solicitous to have no more misunderstandings with any republic, but especially with France; that she wished a permanent treaty; and was sensible that no treaty could be permanent which did not comport with the interests of the parties; and therefore that he might be assured, that our powers were such as authorized us to place France on an equal ground with England, in any respects in which an inequality might be supposed to exist at present between them, to the disadvantage of France. The subject of the rôle d'equipage was also mentioned; and we asked what assurance we could have, if France insisted on the right of adding to the stipulations of our our treaty, or of altering them by municipal regulations, that any future treaty we could make should be observed. M. Bellamy said, that he did not assert the principle of changing treaties by municipal regulations; but that the Directory considered its regulation concerning the rôle d'equipage as comporting with the treaty. We observed to him, that none of our vessels had what the French termed a rôle d'equipage; & that if we were to surrender all the property which had been taken from our citizens in cases where their vessels were not furnished with such a rôle, the government would be responsible to its citizens for the property so surrendered; since it would be impossible to undertake to assert that there was any plausibility in the allegation, that our treaty required a rôle d'equipage.

The subject of disavowals etc. concerning the Presidents speech was again mentioned; and it was observed, that the constitution of the United States authorised and required our President to communicate his ideas on the affairs of the nation; that in obedience to the constitution he had done so; that we had not power to confirm or invalidate any part of the President's speech; that such an attempt could produce no other effect than to make us ridiculous to the government and to the citizens at large of the United States; and to produce, on the part of the President, an immediate disavowal and recall of us as his agents: that independent of this, all America was acquainted with the facts stated by the President; and our disavowing them would not change the public sentiment concerning them.

We parted with mutual professions of personal respect, and with full indications, on the part of M. Bellamy, of his expectation that we should immediately receive the threatened letter.

The nature of the above communication will evince the necessity of secrecy; and we have promised Messrs. Horttinguer and Bellami that their names shall in no event be made public.

We have the honor to be, with great respect & esteem, your most obedient humble Servants

CHARLES COTESWORTH PINCKNEY

J MARSHALL

E GERRY

P. S. October 27th. 1797. The Definitive Articles of Peace are signed between the French Republic and the Emperor, the particulars you will find in the public prints. The Portuguese Minister is ordered to quit France as the Treaty with Portugal has not been yet ratified by the Queen. The Treaty itself is declared by the Directory to be void. Since our arrival at Paris the Tribunal of Cassation has rejected Capt: Scott's petition complaining of the condemnation of his vessel by the Civil tribunal for the want of a Role d'Equipage. Mr. Duclos, the Advocate employed in behalf of the owners of the American Vessels who have appealed in the last report to the Tribunal of Cassation, informs that notwithstanding all the arguments he made use of to the Reporter and Commissary of the Executive Directory to put off the hearing of the Rosanna as a diplomatic case, till the issue of our negociations is known, that case is set down for hearing and will come on the 29th. or 30th. instant. The same Advocate also says that it is obvious that the Tribunal have received instructions from the Officers of the Government to hasten their decisions, and that it was hardly worth while to plead, for all our petitions in Cassation would be rejected. Our Advocates however decline giving their Sentiments on this subject in writing under an apprehension of committing themselves.

Exhibit A

No. 1. With this conduct of the French Government, it will be proper to take into view, the public audience given to the late minister of the United States, on his taking leave of the Executive Directory. The speech of the President discloses sentiments more alarming than the refusal of a Minister, because more dangerous to our independence and union, and at the same time studiously marked with indignities towards the Government of the United States. It evinces a disposition to separate the people of the United States from the Government; to persuade them that they have different affections, principles and interests from those of their fellow citizens, whom they themselves have chosen to manage their common concerns; and thus to produce divisions fatal to our peace. Such attempts ought to be repelled, with a decision which shall convince France & the world, that we are not a degraded people, humiliated under a colonial spirit of fear and sense of inferiority, fitted to be the miserable instruments of foreign influence and regardless of national honor, character & interest.

No. 2. The diplomatic intercourse between the United States & France being at present suspended, the Government has no means of obtaining official information from that Country: nevertheless there is reason to believe that the Executive Directory passed a decree on the second of March last, contravening in part the treaty of Amity and Commerce of 1778, injurious to our lawful commerce and endangering the lives of our Citizens. A Copy of this Decree will be laid before you.

No. 3. While we are endeavoring to adjust all our differences with France; by amicable negociation, the progress of the war in Europe, the Depredations on our Commerce, the personal injuries to our Citizens and the general complexion of affairs, render it my indispensable duty to recommend to your consideration effectual measures of defence.

No. 4. It is impossible to conceal from ourselves or the world, what has been before observed, that endeavors have been employed to foster & establish a division between the Government and the people of the United States. To investigate the causes which have encouraged this attempt is not necessary. But to repel by decided and united Councils, in situations so derogatory to the honor, and agressions so dangerous to the Constitution, Union, and even Independence of the nation, is an indispensable duty.

ECONOMIC CONDITIONS IN FRANCE

To George Washington

Dear Sir   Paris, October 24, 1797

I did myself the honor of addressing to you from the Hague
by Capt Izzard, a very long letter which I hope you have received. The offer therein made of occasionally communicating
to you my observations on the great & interesting events of
europe was not even intitled to the small value which in my
own mind I had bestowd upon it. Causes, which I am persuaded you have anticipated, forbid me to allow myself that
free range of thought & expression which coud alone apologize for the intrusive character my letters bear. Having however
offerd what I cannot furnish, I go on to substitute something
else perhaps not worth receiving.

You have heard it said in the United States that the agriculture of France has in the course of the present war been considerably improved. On this subject I am persuaded there has
been no exaggeration. In that part of the country through
which I have passd the evidences of plenty abound. The whole
earth appears to be in cultivation & the harvests of the present
year appear to be as productive as the fields which yield them
are extensive. I am informd that every part of the country exhibits the same aspect. If this be the fact, there will probably
remain, notwithstanding the demands of the armies, a surplus
of provisions. Manufactures have declind in the same ratio that
the cultivation of the soil has increased. War has been made
upon the great manufacturing towns & they are in a considerable degree destroyed. With manufactures France does not supply herself fully from her internal resources. Those of Britain
flow in upon her notwithstanding the most severe prohibitory
laws. The port of Rotterdam is purposely left open by the English & their goods are imported by the Dutch under Prussian
& other neutral colors. They are smuggled in great quantities
into France. Peace then will find this nation entirely competent to the full supply of her colonies with provisions & needing
manufactures to be imported for her own consumption. This
state of things will probably change; but it is unquestionably

the state of things which will exist at, & for some time after the termination of the present war. France can take from America tobacco & raw cotton, she can supply us with wines, brandies & silks.

The papers which I transmitted to you contained the evidence on which were founded the transactions of the 18th. fructidor or 4th of September. Since then a letter has been publishd bearing the signature of Genl. Moreau & produced as an unequivocal testimonial of the treason alledged to have existed. You will have seen the letter & have made upon it your own comments, but you will be astonishd to hear that perhaps a majority of the people do not beleive that Moreau ever wrote it.

The existing political state of France is connected with certain internal & powerfully operating causes by which it has been & will continue to be greatly influenced. Not the least of these is the tenure by which property is held.

In the course of the revolution it is beleivd that more than half the land of France has become national. Of this a very considerable proportion has been sold at a low rate. It is true that much of this property formerly belonged to the church but it is also true that much of it belongd to those who have fallen under the guillotine or have been termd emigrants. Among the emigrants are many whose attachments to their country has never been shaken; & what is remarkable, among them are many who were never out of France. The law upon this subject is worthy of attention. Any two persons, no matter what their reputation, may, to some authority, I beleive the municipality of the district, write & subscribe against any person whatever a charge, that such person is an emigrant, on receipt of which the person so chargd is without further investigation inscribd on the list of emigrants. If the person so inscribed be afterwards apprehended while his name remains on the list, the trial, as I understand, is not of the fact of emigration, but of the identity of the person, & if this identity be establishd, he is instantly fusillerd. This law is either rigidly executed or permited to be relaxed, as the occasion or the temper of the times may direct.

During intervals of humanity some disposition has been manifested to permit the return of those who have never offended, who have been banishd by a turn which the government itself has reprobated, & to permit in cases of arrestation, an investigation of the fact of emigration as well as of the identity of the person accused.

There is too a great deal of property which has been sold as national but which in truth was never so, & which may be reclaimd by the original proprietors.

In this state of things the acquirers of national property are of course extremely suspicious. They form a vast proportion of the population of France. They are not only important in consequence of their numbers, but in consequence of their vigor, their activity & that unity of interest which produces a unity of effort among them. The armies too have been promisd a milliard. This promise rests upon the national property for its performance. The effect of these circumstances cannot escape your observation. Classes of citizens are to be disfranchisd against the next elections.

Our ministers have not yet, nor do they seem to think it certain that they will be, receivd. Indeed they make arrangements which denote an expectation of returning to America immediately. The captures of our vessels seem to be only limited by the ability to capture. That ability is increasing, as the government has let out to hardy adventurers the national frigates. Among those who plunder us, who are most active in this infamous business, & most loud in vociferating criminations equally absurd & untrue, are some unprincipled apostates who were born in America. These sea rovers by a variety of means seem to have acquird great influence in the government. This influence will be exerted to prevent an accommodation between the United States & France & to prevent any regulations which may intercept the passage of the spoils they have made on our commerce, to their pockets. The government I beleive is but too well disposd to promote their views. At present it seems to me to be radically hostile to our country. I coud wish to form a contrary opinion, but to do so I must shut my eyes on every object which presents itself to them, & fabricate in my own mind nonexisting things, to be substituted for realities, & to form the basis of my creed. Might I be permited to hazard an opinion it woud be that the Atlantic only can save us, & that no consideration will be sufficiently powerful to check the extremities to which the temper of this government will carry it, but an apprehension that we may be thrown into the arms of Britain.

The negotiations with the Emperor are said not to have been absolutely broken off. Yesterday it was said that peace with him was certain. Several couriers have arrivd lately from Buonaparte & the national debt rose yesterday from seven to ten livres in the hundred. Whether this is founded on a real expectation of peace with Austria or is the meer work of stock jobbers is not for me to decide. We are told that Mantua is no longer the obstacle to peace, that it is surrenderd by the Emperor & that the contest now is for Istria & Dalmatia.

October 27th.

The definitive peace is made with the Emperor. You will have seen the conditions. Venice has experiencd the fate of Poland. England is threatend with an invasion.

THE SECOND "XYZ" DISPATCH

To Timothy Pickering

No. 2

Dear Sir   Paris, November 8, 1797

We now enclose you in thirty six quarto pages of Cypher, and in eight pages of cyphered exhibits the sequel to the details commenced in No 1 dated the 22d of last month, and have the honor to be Your most obedt hble Servts

CHARLES COTESWORTH PINCKNEY
J MARSHALL
E GERRY

Account of Negotiation Proceedings

October 27, 1797 About twelve we received another visit from M. Horttinguer. He immediately mentioned the great event announced in the papers and then said that some proposals from us had been expected on the subject on which we had before conversed; that the Directory were becoming impatient and would take a decided course with regard to America, if we could not soften them. We answered, that on that subject we had already spoken explicitly, and had nothing further to add. He mentioned the change in the state of things which had been produced by the peace with the Emperor, as warranting an expectation of a change in our system: to which we only replied, that this event had been expected by us, and would not in any degree affect our conduct. M. Horttinguer urged that the Directory, had since this peace, taken a higher and more decided tone with respect to us and all other neutral nations, than had been before taken; that it had been determined that all nations should aid them, or be considered and treated as their enemies. We answered, that such an effect had already been contemplated by us as probable; and had not been overlooked when we gave to this proposition our decided answer: and further that we had no powers to negociate for a loan of money; that our government had not contemplated such a circumstance in any degree whatever; that if we should stipulate a loan, it would be a perfectly void thing, and would only deceive France and expose ourselves. M. Horttinguer again expatiated on the power and violence of France; he urged the danger of our situation; and pressed the policy of softening them, and of thereby obtaining time. The present men he said would very probably not continue long in power and it would be very unfortunate if those who might succeed, with better dispositions towards us, should find the two nations in actual war. We answered, that if war should be made on us by France, it would be so obviously forced on us, that on a change of men, peace might be made with as much facility as the present differences could be accomodated: we added, that all America deprecated a war with France; but that our present situation was more ruinous to us than a declared war could be; that at present our commerce was plundered unprotected; but that if war was declared, we should seek the means of protection. M. Horttinguer said he hoped we should not form a connection with Britain; and we answered that we hoped so too; that we had all been engaged in our revolution war, and felt its injuries; that it had made the deepest impression on us; but that if France should attack us we must seek the best means of self-defence. M. Horttinguer again returned to the subject of money: said he, gentlemen you do not speak to the point; it is money; it is expected that you will offer money: we said we had spoken to that point very explicitly: we had given an answer. No, said he, you have not: what is your answer? We replied, it is no, no, not a six pence. He again called our attention to the dangers which threatened our country; and asked if it would not be prudent, though we might not make a loan to the nation, to interest an influential friend in our favor. He said we ought to consider what men we had to treat with; that they disregarded the justice of our claims and the reasoning with which we might support them; that they disregarded their own colonies; and considered themselves as perfectly invulnerable with respect to us; that we could only acquire an interest among them by a judicious application of money; and it was for us to consider whether the situation of our country did not require that these means should be resorted to. We observed, that the conduct of the French government was such as to leave us much reason to fear, that should we give the money, it would effect no good purpose; and would not produce a just mode of thinking with respect to us. Proof of this must first be given us. He said, that when we employed a lawyer, we gave him a fee, without knowing, whether the cause could be gained or not; but it was necessary to have one; and we paid for his services, whether those services were successful or not: so in the present state of things, the money must be advanced for the good offices the individuals were to render, whatever might be the effect of those good offices. We told him there was no parallel in the cases; that a lawyer not being to render the judgement, could not command success: he could only endeavor to obtain it; and consequently, we could only pay him for his endeavours: but the Directory could decide on the issue of our negociation. It had only to order that no more American vessels should be seized, and to direct those now in custody to be restored; and there could be no opposition to the order. He said that all the members of the Directory were not disposed to receive our money; that Merlin, for instance, was paid from another quarter, and would touch no part of the douceur which was to come from us. We replied that we had understood, that Merlin was paid by the owners, of the privateers; and he nodded an assent to the fact. He proceeded to press this subject with vast perseverance. He told its that we paid money to obtain peace with the Algerines and with the Indians; and that it was doing no more to pay France for peace. To this it was answered, that when our government commenced a treaty with either Algiers or the Indian tribes, it was understood that money was to form the basis of the treaty and was it's essential article; that the whole nation knew it, and was prepared to expect it, as a thing of course; but that in treating with France, our government had supposed that a proposition, such as he spoke, of, would, if made by us, give mortal offence. He asked if our government did not know that nothing was to be obtained here without money? We replied, that our government had not even suspected such a state of things. He appeared surprized at it, and said, there was not an American in Paris who could not have given that information. We told him that the letters of our Minister had indicated a very contrary temper in the government of France; and had represented it as acting entirely upon principle, and as feeling a very pure and disinterested affection for America. He looked somewhat surprized; and said briskly, to General Pinckney—Well; Sir; you have been a long time in France and in Holland, what do you think of it? General Pinckney answered, that he considered M. Horttinguer and M. Bellamy as men of truth, and of consequence he could have but one opinion on the subject. He stated, that Hamburg and other States of Europe were obliged to buy a peace; and that it would be equally for our interest to do so. Once more he spoke of the danger of a breach with France, and of her power which nothing could resist. We told him, that it would be in vain for us to deny her power, or the solicitude we felt to avoid a contest with it; that no nation estimated her power more highly than America, or wished more to be on amicable terms with her; but that one object was still dearer to us than the friendship of France, which was our national independence: that America had taken a neutral station: she had a right to take it: no nation had a right to force us out of it: that to lend a sum of money to a belligerent power abounding in everything requisite for war but money, was to relinquish our neutrality, and take part in the war: to lend this money under the lash and coercion of France, was to relinquish the government of ourselves, and to submit to a foreign government imposed upon us by force: that we would make at least one manly struggle before we thus surrendered our national independence: that our case was different from that of one of the minor nations of Europe; they were unable to maintain their independence, and did not expect to do so: America was a great, and so far as concerned her self defence, a powerful nation: She was able to maintain her independence; and must deserve to lose it, if she permitted it to be wrested from her; that France and Britain had been at war for near fifty years of the last hundred; and might probably be at war for fifty years of the century to come: that America had no motives which could induce her to involve herself in those wars; and that if she now preserved her neutrality and her independence, it was most probable that she would not in future be afraid, as she had been for four years past: but if she now surrendered her rights of self government to France, or permitted them to be torn from her, she could not expect to recover them, or to remain neutral in any future war. He said that France had lent us money during our revolution war, and only required that we should now exhibit the same friendship for her. We answered that the cases were very different; that America solicited a loan from France, and left her at liberty to grant or refuse it; but that France demanded it from America, and left us no choice on the subject. We also told him there was another difference in the cases; that the money was lent by France for great national and French objects. It was lent to maim a rival, and an enemy whom she hated; that the money, if lent by America, would not be for any American objects, but to enable France to extend still further her conquests. The conversation continued for nearly two hours and the public & private advance of money was pressed and repressed in a variety of forms. At length M. Horttinguer said that he did not blame us; that our determination was certainly proper, if we could keep it: but he showed decidedly his opinion to be, that we could not keep it. He said that he would communicate, as nearly as he could, our conversation to the Minister; or to M. Bellamy, to be given by him to the Minister; we are not certain which. We then separated. On the 22nd of October, M. Hautval a French Gentleman of respectable character, informed Mr. Gerry, that M. Talleyrand, Minister of foreign relations, who professed to be well disposed towards the United States had expected to have seen the American Ministers frequently, in their private capacities, and to have confered with them individually on the objects of their mission; and had authorized M. Hautval to make this communication to M. Gerry. The latter sent for his colleagues; and a conference was held with M. Hautval on the subject; in which General Pinckney and General Marshall expressed their opinions, that not being acquainted with M. Talleyrand, they could not with propriety call on him; but that according to the custom of France, he might expect this of M. Gerry, from a previous acquaintance in America. This M. Gerry reluctantly complied with on the 23rd; and with M. Hautval called on M. Talleyrand; who not being then at his office, appointed the 28th for the interview. After the first introduction, M. Talleyrand began the conference. He said, that the Directory had passed an arrête, which he offered for perusal, in which they had demanded of the envoys an explanation of some parts, and a reparation for others, of the President's speech to Congress, of the 16th. of May last: he was sensible, he said, that difficulties would exist on the part of the envoys relative to this demand; but that by their offering money, he thought he could prevent the effect of the arrête. M. Hautval, at the request of M. Gerry, having stated that the envoys have no such powers; M. Talleyrand replied; they can in such case take a power on themselves: and proposed that they should make a loan. M. Gerry then addressed M. Talleyrand distinctly in English, which he said he understood and stated, that the uneasiness of the Directory resulting from the Presidents speech, was a subject unconnected with the objects of the mission; that M. Barras in his speech to M. Munroe, on his recall, had expressed himself in a manner displeasing to the government and citizens of the United States; that the President, as the envoys conceived, had made such observations on M. Barras's speech as were necessary to vindicate the honor of the United States; that this was not considered by our government as a subject of dispute between the two nations; that having no instructions respecting it, we could not make any explanations or reparations relating to it; and that M. Talleyrand himself was sufficiently acquainted with the constitution of the United States to be convinced of the truth of these observations. M. Gerry further stated, that the powers of the

Envoys, as they conceived, were adequate to the discussion and adjustment of all points of real difference between the two nations; that they could alter and amend the treaty; or if necessary, form a new one: that the United States were anxiously desirous of removing all causes of complaint between themselves and France, and of renewing their former friendship and intercourse, on terms which should be mutually honorable and beneficial to the two nations; but not on any other terms: that as to a loan, we had no powers whatever to make one; that if we were to attempt it, we should deceive himself and the Directory likewise, which as men of honor we could not do; but that we could send one of our number for instructions on this proposition, if deemed expedient; provided that the other objects of the negociation could be discussed and adjusted: that as he had expressed a desire to confer with the envoys individually, it was the wish of M. Gerry that such a conference should take place, and their opinions thus be ascertained, which he conceived corresponded with his own in the particulars mentioned. M. Talleyrand, in answer, said he should be glad to confer with the other envoys individually, but that this matter about the money must be settled directly, without sending to America; that he would not communicate the arrête for a week; and that if we could adjust the difficulty respecting the speech, an application would nevertheless go to the U. States for a loan. A courier arriving at this moment from Italy and M. Talleyrand appearing impatient to read the letters, M. Gerry took leave of him immediately. He followed to the door, and desired M. Hautval to repeat to M. Gerry what he, M. Talleyrand, had said to him. M. Gerry then returned to his quarters, with M. Hautval, took down the particulars of this interview, as before stated, sent for Generals Pinckney and Marshall, and read it to them in the presence of M. Hautval, who confirmed it. Generals Pinckney and Marshall then desired M. Hautval to inform M. Talleyrand, that they had nothing to add to this conference; and did not wish that the arrête might be delayed on their account.

October the twenty ninth, M. Horttinguer again called on us. He said M. Talleyrand was extremely anxious to be of service to us, and had requested that one more effort should be made to induce us to enable him to be so. A great deal of the same conversation which had passed at our former interviews was repeated. The power and the haughtiness of France was again displayed to us. We were told that the destruction of England was inevitable; and that the wealth and arts of that nation would naturally pass over to America, if that event should find us in peace. To this observation we replied; that France would probably forbid America to receive them, in like manner as she had forbid Switzerland to permit the residence in its country of a British Minister. We told him also, that we were sensible of the value of peace, and therefore sought it unremittingly, but that it was real peace we sought for; and real peace only which could be desirable.

The sum of his proposition was, that if we would pay, by way of fees, that was his expression, the sum of money demanded for private use, the Directory would not receive us; but would permit us to remain in Paris as we now were; and we should be received by M. Talleyrand, until one of us could go to America and consult our government on the subject of the loan. These were the circumstances he said under which the minister of Portugal had treated. We asked him if in the mean time the Directory would order the American property not yet passed into the hands of the privateers-men, to be restored? He said explicitly, that they would not. We asked him whether they would suspend further depredations on our commerce? He said they would not: but M. Talleyrand observed, that on this subject we could not sustain much additional injury, because the winter season was approaching, when few additional captures could be made. We told him that France had taken violently from America more than fifteen millions of dollars, and treated us in every respect as enemies, in return for the friendship we had manifested for her; that we had come to endeavour to restore harmony to the two nations, and to obtain compensation for the injuries our countymen had sustained; and that in lieu of this compensation, we were told that if we would pay twelve hundred thousand livres, we might be permitted to remain in Paris (which would only give us the benefit of seeing the plays and operas of Paris, for the winter), that we might have time to ask from our country to exhaust her resources for France, whose depredations would be continued. He again stated, that by this procedure we should suspend a war; and that perhaps in five or six months, power might change hands.

We told him, that what we wished to see in France, was a temper sincerely friendly to the United States, and really disposed to do us justice. That if we could perceive this, we might not so much regard a little money, such as he stated to be usual; although we should hazard ourselves by giving it. But that we saw only evidences of the most extreme hostility toward us. War was made upon us so far as France could make it in the present state of things; and it was not even proposed that on receiving our money this war should cease. We had no reason to beleive that a possible benefit could result from it; and we desired him to say that we would not give a shilling, unless American property unjustly captured was previously restored, and further hostilities suspended; and that unless this was done, we did not conceive that we could even consult our government concerning a loan. That if the Directory would receive us and commence negociations, and any thing occurred which rendered a consultation of the government necessary, one of us would return to America for that purpose. He said, that without this money we should be obliged to quit Paris; and that we ought to consider the consequences.

The property of the Americans would be confiscated, and their vessels in port embargoed. We told him that unless there was a hope of real reconciliation, these evils could not be prevented by us; and the little delay we might obtain would only increase them. That our mission had induced many of our countrymen to trust their vessels into the ports of France; and that we remained in Paris, that very circumstance would increase the number; and consequently the injury which our countrymen would sustain, if France could permit herself so to violate her own engagements and the laws of nations. He expressed a wish that M. Bellamy should see us once more. We told him that a visit from M. Bellamy, as a private gentleman would always be agreeable to us; but if he came only with the expectation that we should stipulate advances of money, without previously establishing a solid and permanent reconciliation, he might save himself the trouble of the application; because it was a subject we had considered maturely, and on which we were immovable. He parted with us, saying if that was the case, it would not be worthwhile for M. Bellamy to come. In the evening, while Genl. Pinckney and Genl. Marshall were absent, M. Bellamy and M. Horttinguer called, and were invited by M. Gerry to breakfast with us the next morning.

October the thirtieth. Immediately after breakfast, the subject was resumed. M. Bellamy spoke without interuption for near an hour. He said that he was desirous of making a last effort to serve us, by proposing something which might accomodate the differences between the two nations. That what he was now about to mention had not by any means the approbation of the Directory; nor could M. Talleyrand undertake further than to make from us the proposition to the Directory, and use his influence for its success. That last week, M. Talleyrand could not have ventured to have offered such propositions; but that his situation had been very materially changed by the peace with the emperor. By that peace he had acquired, in an high degree, the confidence of the Directory, and now possessed great influence with that body; that he was also closely connected with Bonaparte and the generals of the army in Italy; and was to be considered as firmly fixed in his post, at least for five or six months. That under these circumstances, he could undertake to offer in our behalf, propositions which before this increase of influence he could not have hazarded. M. Bellamy then called our attention to our own situation, and to the force France was capable of bringing to bear upon us. He said that we were the best judges of our capacity to resist, so far as depended on our own resources; and ought not to deceive ourselves on so interesting a subject.

The fate of Venice was one which might befall the United States. But, he proceeded to observe, it was probable we might rely on forming a league with England: If we had such a reliance, it would fail us. The situation of England was such as to compel Pitt to make peace on the terms of France. A variety of causes were in operation which made such an effect absolutely certain. To say nothing of the opposition in England to the minister and to the war, an opposition which the fears of the nation would encrease; to say nothing of a war against England which was preparing in the north; an army of one hundred and fifty thousand men, under the command of Bonaparte, spread upon the coast of France; and aided by all the vast resources of his genius, would most probably be enabled to invade England; in which event their government would be overturned: but should this invasion not be absolutely effected, yet the alarm it would spread, through the nation, the enormous expence it must produce, would infallibly ruin them, if it was to be continued, and would drive them to save themselves by a peace: that independant of this, France possessed means which would infallibly destroy their bank and their whole paper system. He said he knew very well it was generally conjectured that Bonaparte would not leave Italy, and the army which had conquered under him, and which adored him; he assured us that nothing could be more unfounded than the conjecture; that Bonaparte had for more than ten days left Italy for Rastadt, to preside over the Congress which was formed for adjusting the affairs of the empire. He said that Pitt himself was so confident of the absolute necessity of peace, that after the naval victory over the Dutch, he had signified his readiness to treat on the same terms which he had offered before that action: we could not then rely on the assistance of England. What, he asked, would be our situation if peace should be made with England before our differences with France would be accommodated? But he continued: if even England should be able to continue the war, and America should unite with her, it would not be in our power to injure France. We might indeed wound her ally; but if we did, it would be so much the worse for us. After having stated the dangers attending us, if we should engage in the war, he proceeded to the advantages we might derive from a neutral situation: and insisted at large on the wealth which would naturally flow into our country from the destruction of England. He next proceeded to detail the propositions which are in substance in the paper annexed marked (A;) except that he insisted that we should engage to use our influence with our government for the loan. He stated expressly that the propositions were to be considered as made by us; that Mr Talleyrand would not be responsible for the success of any one of them: He would only undertake to use his influence with the Directory in support of them. The proposition, he said, concerning a suspension of hostilities on the part of France, was one which proceeded entirely from himself: Mr Talleyrand had not been consulted upon it; and he could not undertake to say that that Gentleman would consent even to lay it before the Directory. The proposition for an advance to the government of France of as much money as was due from it to our citizens on contract, and as might be determined to be due for Vessels improperly captured and condemned, was, he said indispensible: unless we made that, it was unnecessary to make any other; for the others would not be received. He expatiated on the vast advantages we should derive from delay: it was, he said, absolutely to gain our cause. He returned to the danger of our situation, and the policy of making with France any accommodation which France would assent to. Perhaps, said he, you believe that in returning and exposing to your countrymen the unreasonableness of the demands of this government, you will unite them in their resistance to those demands: you are mistaken: you ought to know that the Diplomatic skill of France, and the means she possesses in your country, are sufficient to enable her, with the French party in America, to throw the blame which will attend the rupture of the negociations on the Federalists, as you term yourselves, but on the British party, as France terms you: and you may assure yourselves this will be done. He concluded with Declarations of being perfectly disinterested; and declared that his only motives for speaking thus freely were his friendship for Mr Talleyrand and his wish to promote the Interests and Peace of the United States. We told him that the freedom with which he had spoken, and which was agreeable to us, would induce us to speak freely also; and for once to accompany our view of the present state of things with a retrospect of the past: that America was the only nation upon earth which felt and had exhibited a real friendship for the Republic of France: That among the empires round her which were compelled to bend beneath her power and to obey her commands, there was not one which had voluntarily acknowledged her government; or manifested for it, spontaneously, any mark of regard: America alone had stepped forward and given the most unequivocal proofs of a pure and sincere friendship, at a time when almost the whole European world, when Austria, Germany, Prussia, Russia, Spain, Sardinia, Holland and Britain were leagued against France; when her situation was in truth hazardous, and it was dangerous to hold even friendly intercourse with her, America alone stood forward and openly and boldly avowed her enthusiasm in favour of the Republic, and her deep and sincere interest in its fate. From that time to the present, the government and people of the United States have uniformly manifested a sincere and ardent friendship for France, and have, as they conceive, in no single instance given to this Republic just cause of umbrage: if they have done so, they wish it to be pointed out to them. After the Determination of France to break off all regular intercourse with them, they have sent three Envoys Extraordinary to endeavour to make such explanations as might produce reconciliation: these Envoys are prepared to investigate, and wish to investigate any measures which may have given offence; and are persuaded that they can entirely justify the conduct of their government. To this distant, unoffending, friendly Republic what is the conduct and the Language of France? Wherever our property can be found she seizes and takes it from us; unprovoked, she determines to treat us as enemies; and our making no resistance produces no Diminution of hostility against us; she abuses and insults our government, Endeavours to weaken it in the estimation of the people, recalls her own minister, refuses to receive ours, and when Extraordinary means are taken to make such explanations as may do away misunderstandings, and such alterations in the existing relations of the two countries as may be mutually satisfactory, & may tend to produce harmony, the Envoys who bear these powers are not received; they are not permitted to utter the amicable wishes of their country, but in the haughty style of a master, they are told that unless they will pay a sum to which their resources scarcely extend, that they may expect the vengeance of France, and like Venice be erazed from the list of nations; that France will annihilate the only free Republic upon earth, and the only nation in the universe which has voluntarily manifested for her a cordial and real friendship! What impression must this make on the mind of America, if without provocation France was determined to make war upon us, unless we purchased peace? We could not easily believe that even our money would save us: our independence would never cease to give offence; and would always furnish a pretext for fresh demands. On the advantages of neutrality it was unnecessary to say anything: all the efforts of our government were Exerted to maintain it; and we would never willingly part with it. With respect to a political connection with Britain, we told him that America had never Contemplated it. Whether the danger he represented that government to be in was or was not real we should not undertake to decide: Britain we believed had much reason to wish for peace; and France had much reason to wish for peace also: if peace already existed it would not change the course America would pursue. Mr Bellamy manifested the most excessive impatience: he interrupted us and said, This eloquent dissertation might be true: America might have manifested, and he believed had manifested great friendship for France, and had just complaints against her; but he did not come to listen to those complaints. The Minister would on our request make for us certain propositions to the Directory: he had stated them to us; and all the answer he wished was yes or no: did we or did we not sollicit the Minister to make the propositions for us? We told him that without going farther into the discussion we chose to remark one or two things: they were, that the existing treaties gave to France certain advantages which were very essential; that especially the American coast afforded a protection near two thousand miles in extent to the prizes made by France on her Enemies, and refused that protection to the prizes taken from her; that she might be assured that in case of war these advantages would be lost for ever. We also told him we were convinced that France miscalculated on the parties in America: that the extreme injustice offered to our country would unite every man against her. Mr. Hortinguer informed us, that Mr Talleyrand would not consent even to lay this proposition before the Directory without previously receiving the fifteen thousand pounds, or the greater part of it. Mr Bellamy left in writing his propositions; and we returned the answer annexed and marked (B).

Nov. 1st. It was at length agreed that we would hold no more indirect intercourse with the government.

Nov. 3d. Mr. Hortinguer called on us and told General Pinckney and General Marshall (Mr Gerry not being within) that Mr Bellamy wished once more to see us. We answered, that we should at any time be glad to see Mr Bellamy as a private Gentleman: but that if his object was only to repeat his propositions for money, it was perfectly unnecessary to do so; because on that subject it was impossible for us to change the answer we had already given. We told him further, that we considered it as degrading our country to carry on farther such an indirect intercourse as we had for sometime submitted to, and had determined to receive no propositions, unless the persons who bore them had acknowledged authority to treat with us. He said that perhaps Mr Bellamy might have written powers from the Minister; and we replied, that if he had, we should receive his communications with pleasure. He spoke of a probable peace with England; and having requested us to be at home in the afternoon, left us.

About three o Clock he came; and after some conversation, in which we repeated in substance what is stated above, He shewed us a paper which he said was a copy of a letter prepared for us by Mr. Talleyrand, requesting an explanation of part of the President's speech, and which he said would be sent, unless we came into the propositions which had been made us. We wished to take a copy of it; which he declined permitting, saying he was forbidden to allow it. We spoke of the letter coming to us as a measure we had no expectation of preventing: and he said he could not understand, that we wished it delayed. To which we answered, that the delay of a few days could not be desired; unless a hope existed that the Directory might become more friendly to our country. He said that intelligence had been received from the United States that if Colonel Burr and Mr Madison had constituted the mission, the differences between the two nations would have been accommodated before this time. He added, as a fact he was not instructed to communicate, that Mr Talleyrand was preparing a memorial to be sent out to the United States complaining of us as being unfriendly to an accommodation with France. We replied to his intelligence from the United States that the Ministers correspondents in America took a good deal on themselves when they undertook to say how the Directory would have received Colonel Burr and Mr Madison and that with respect to the memorial of Mr Talleyrand, it would not be easy for him to convince our countrymen, that the statements we should make were untrue: if however we were confident that our conduct would be condemned, Mr Talleyrand might be assured that the fear of Censure would not induce us to deserve it: but that we should act in a manner which our own Judgments and consciences would approve of; and we trusted we should be supported by the great body of candid and honest men. In this conversation we again stated that America had taken a neutral position; that she had faithfully sought to preserve it; that a loan of money to one of the belligerent powers was directly to take part in the war; and that to take part in the war against her own Judgment and will, under the coercion of France, was to surrender our independence.

Exhibit A

1. The American envoys shall remain here for six months in the same manner and upon the same footing with regard to etiquette as did M. D'Aranjo the envoy of Portugal.

2. There shall be named a commission of five members, agreably to a form to be established, for the purpose of deciding upon the reclamations of the Americans relative to the prizes made on them by the French privateers.

3. The American envoys will engage that their government shall pay the indemnifications, or the amount of the sums already decreed to the American creditors of the French republic, and those which shall be adjudged to the claimants by the commissioners. This payment shall be made under the name of an advance to the French Republic, who will repay it in a time and manner to be agreed upon.

4. One of the American envoys shall return to America to demand of his government the necessary powers to purchase for cash the thirty two millions of dutch rescriptions belonging to the French Republic, in case the envoys should conclude a treaty which shall be approved by the two nations.

5. In the interval, the definitive treaty shall proceed for the termination of all differences existing between the French republic and the United States; so as that the treaty may be concluded immediately on the return of the deputy.

6. The question of the rôle d'equipage shall remain suspended, untill the return of the deputy and the commission shall not pronounce upon any reclamation where this point shall be in question.

7th. During the six months granted for the going and returning of the deputy, hostilities against the Americans shall be suspended, as well as the process for condemnation before the tribunals; and the money of the prizes already condemned, in the hands of the civil officers of the nation, shall remain there without being deliverd to the privateers-men until the return of the deputy.

Exhibit B

The envoys extraordinary and ministers Plenipotentiary of the United States cannot avoid observing the very unusual situation in which they are placed by the manner in which they are alone permitted to make communications on the objects of their mission. They are called upon to pledge their country to a very great amount, to answer demands which appear to them as extraordinary as they were unexpected, without being permitted to discuss the reason, the justice, or the policy on which those demands are founded, and not only without assurances that the rights of the United States will in future be respected, but without a document to prove that those to whom they required to open themselves without reserve, and at whose instance they are called on to sacrifice so much, are empowered even by the Minister to hold any communication with them: yet such is the anxious and real solicitude of the envoys to seize any occasion which may afford a hope, however distant, of coming to those explanations which they so much wish to make with this Republic, that they pass over the uncommon and informal modes which have been adopted, and will only consider the propositions themselves.

1. The Ministers of the United States will permit no personal considerations to influence their negociations with the French Republic. Although they expected that the extraordinary means adopted by their government to reconcile itself to that of France would have been received with some degree of attention, yet they are too solicitous to enter upon the important and interesting duty of their mission to permit themselves to be restrained by forms or etiquette.

2. On this article it is believed there can be no disagreement.

3. This Article, as explained, would oblige the United States to advance, not to their own citizens, but to the government of France, sums equivalent to the depredations made by the

corsaires of the Republic on the American commerce and to the contracts made with their citizens by France, and this advance, instead of benefiting the citizens of the United States would leave them precisely what they now are, the creditors of the French Republic: the more extensive the depredations and the more considerable the contracts uncomplied with, the more would the government of France receive from the United States. Independant of these objections, the Ministers of the United States cannot engage to assume in any form the debts due from France to their fellow citizens: they have no such power.

4th. If the negociations be opened, and the propositions for a loan, or any other propositions exceeding the powers of the Ministers be made, the government of the United States will be consulted thereon with expedition.

5th. This or any proposition having for its object the claims of the two nations on each other, or an accommodation of differences, will be embraced with ardor by the Ministers of the United States.

6th. It cannot escape notice that the question of the role d'equipage may involve in it every vessel taken from the United States: the Ministers however consider it, & wish to take it up as a subject of negociation.

7th. On this Article it is only to be observed, that the season of the year is such as probably to render a return, within six months, of the envoy who might sail to the United States impracticable; provision should be made for such an event.

If the difficulties attending the propositions for a loan and a compensation for past Injuries be such as to require time for their removal, the Ministers of the United States propose that the discussions on the relative situation of the two countries may commence in the usual forms; that the relation to each other may be so regulated as to obviate future misunderstandings; and that the adjustment of the claims of the citizens of the United States whose vessels have been captured, may be made, after a decision on the point first mentioned.

No diplomatic gratification can precede the ratification of the treaty.

"AMUSEMENT & DISSIPATION" IN PARIS

To Mary W. Marshall

My dearest Polly   Paris, November 27, 1797
   I have not since my departure from the United States receivd a single letter from you or from any one of my friends in
America. Judge what anxiety I must feel concerning you. I do
not permit myself for a moment to suspect that you are in any
degree to blame for this. I am sure you have written often to
me but unhappily for me your letters have not found me. I fear
they will not. They have been thrown over board or intercepted. Such is the fate of the greater number of the letters addressed by Americans to their friends in France, such I fear will
be the fate of all that may be addressed to me.
   In my last letter I informd you that I counted on being at
home in march. I then expected to have been able to leave this
country by christmass at furthest & such is my impatience to
see you & my dear children that I had determined to risk a
winters passage: I now apprehend that it will not be in my
power to reach America til April or May—but on this subject
all is yet uncertain. I wish you woud present my compliments
to Mr. Wickham & express to him my wish that the case of
Randolphs exrs. & Colo. Meade may ly til my return. I think
nothing will prevent my being at the chancery term in May.
Oh God how much time & how much happiness have I thrown
away!
   Paris presents one incessant round of amusement & dissipation but very little I beleive even for its inhabitants of that
society which interests the heart. Every day you may see something new magnificent & beautiful, every night you may see a
spectacle which astonishes & inchants the imagination. The
most lively fancy aided by the strongest description cannot
equal the reality of the opera. All that you can conceive & a
great deal more than you can conceive in the line of amusement is to be found in this gay metropolis but I suspect it
woud not be easy to find a friend. I would not live in Paris to
be among the wealthiest of its citizens.
   I have changed my lodgings much for the better. I lived till

within a few days in a house where I kept my own apartments perfectly in the style of a miserable old batchelor without any mixture of female society. I now have rooms in the house of a very accomplishd a very sensible & I beleive a very amiable lady whose temper, very contrary to the general character of her country women, is domestic & who generally sets with us two or three hours in the afternoon. This renders my sitation less unpleasant than it has been but nothing can make it eligible. Let me see you once more & then I can venture to assert that no consideration will induce me ever again to consent to place the Atlantic between us. Adieu my dearest Polly. Preserve your health & be as happy as possible till the return of him who is ever yours.

I inclose this letter under cover to Colo. Carrington. Whenever that happens you will advert to paying the postage.

EUROPEAN DEVELOPMENTS

To George Washington

Dear Sir   Paris, March 8, 1798
Before this reaches you it will be known universally in America that scarcely a hope remains of accomodating on principles consistent with justice, or even with the indepence of our country, the differences subsisting between France & the United States. Our ministers are not yet, & it is known to all that they will not be, recognizd, without a previous stipulation on their part, that they will accede to the demands of France. It is as well known that those demands are for money—to be usd in the prosecution of the present war. It was some little time past expected that, convinced of the unpracticability of effecting the objects of their mission, our ministers were about to demand their passports & to return to the United States. But this determination if ever made is, I am persuaded, suspended if not entirely relinquishd. The report has been that so soon as it shall be known that they will not add a loan to the mass of american property already in the hands of the government,

they will be ordered out of France & a nominal as well as actual war will be commenced against the United States. My opinion has always been that this depends on the state of the war with England. To that object the public attention is very much turnd, & it is perhaps justly beleivd that on its issue is stakd the independence of Europe & America. The preparations for an invasion are immense. A numerous & veteran army lines the coast & it is said confidently that if the landing of 50,000 men can be effected, no force in England will be able to resist them. The often repeated tale that the war is made not against the people but the government, maintains, in spite of experience some portion of its credit, & it is beleivd here that a formidable & organizd party exists in Britain ready, so soon as a landing shall be effected, to rise & demand a reform. It is supposed that England revolutionizd under the protection of a french army, will be precisely in the situation of the batavian & cisalpine republics & that its wealth, its commerce, & its fleets will be at the disposition of this government. In the meantime this expedition is not without its hazards. An army which arriving safe woud sink England may itself be encounterd & sunk in the channel. The effect of such a disaster on a nation already tired of the war & groaning under the pressure of an enormous taxation, which might discern in it the seeds of another coalition, & which perhaps may not be universally attachd to existing arrangements, might be extremely serious to those who hold the reins of government.

It is therefore beleivd by many who do not want inteligence that these formidable military preparations cover & favor secret negotiations for peace. It is rumord (but this is meer rumor) that propositions have been made to England to cede to her the possessions of Portugal in America, in consideration of her restoring the conquests she has made in France Spain & Holland & of her consent that Portugal in Europe shall be annexd to the spanish monarchy. This report is derivd from no source in any degree to be relied on & is supported by no circumstance rendering it in any degree probable other than the existing disposition for partitioning & disposing of empires. I am however persuaded that some secret negotiation with England is now on the tapis. I know almost certainly that a person high in the confidence of this government, who is frequently employd in unofficial negotiation, has passed over into that island. We can only conjecture his objects.

You probably know that the affairs of Rastadt are substantially decided. The Emperor & the King of Prussia have declard themselves in favor of ceding to France the whole territory on the left of the rhine on the principle of compensation in the interior of Germany. This woud seem to me to take from England the hope of once more arming Austria & Prussia in her favor, for certainly had those powers contemplated such an event they woud not have effected the pacification of the empire. This circumstance will probably influence the secret negotiations with England. It will probably too very much influence the affairs of Swisserland. The determination of France to revolutionize the helvetic body has been long known. In the pais de vaud belonging to the Canton of Berne the revolution has commenced & is completely effected under the protection & guidance of a french army for which that little country has already paid about 800,000 livres Swiss. France has insisted on extending the revolution throughout Swisserland. The existing governments in some of the cantons & especially in Bern declare their willingness to reorganize their constitution on the base of an equality of rights & a free representation, but they protest against foreign interposition & against a revolutionary intermediate government. In support of this resolution they have collected all their force & most of the cantons which have already changed their form of government have furnishd their contingents. The mass of the people in Bern are firmly united & seem to join the government in saying that they will to the last man bury themselves under the ruins of their country rather than submit to the intermeddling of foreigners in the formation of their constitutions. Such is the present truely interesting state of Swisserland. A powerful military force is advancing upon them & at the same time it is said that the negotiations are to be opend. The terms offerd however are supposd to be such as if accepted will place that country in the same situation as if conquerd. A revolutionary government is insisted on.

The Swiss have observd an exact neutrality throughout the late war on the continent & have even since the peace sought to preserve the forbearance of France by concessions not perfectly compatible with the rights of an independent nation.

On the side of Italy it is beleivd that materials are preparing to revolutionize Sardinia & Naples. Some jealousies exist with respect to Spain. Augereau has been orderd sometime since to Perpignan a position from which he may with advantage overawe that monarchy, invade Portugal or preserve order in the south during the insuing elections. It is the common opinion that shoud the elections in any respect disappoint the wishes of the Directory it will be on the side of Jacobinism. The existing government appears to me to need only money to enable it to effect all its objects. A numerous brave & well disciplind army seems to be devoted to it. The most military & the most powerful nation on earth is entirely at its disposal. Spain Italy & Holland with the Hanseatic towns obey its mandates. Yet there is a difficulty in procuring funds to work this vast machine. Credit being annihilated, the actual empositions of the year must equal the disbursements. The consequence is that notwithstanding the enormous contributions made by foreign nations France is overwhelmed with taxes. The proprietor complains that his estate yields him nothing. Real property pays in taxes nearly a third of its produce & is greatly reduced in its price. The patriotic gifts for the invasion of England to which men have been stimulated by all possible means have not exceeded by the highest calculation 100 000 livres. This is the amount stated by a person who charges the officers of the treasury with peculation. The treasury admits 65,000 livres. It is supposd that recourse will be had to a forced loan & that the neighbors of the republic will be requird to contribute still further to its wants. A very heavy beginning has been made with Rome.

March 10th.
The papers announce that the troops of France & Swisserland have had some severe encounters in which those of the latter have been worsted & the french have enterd Fribourg & Soleure. Report (which as yet wants confirmation & indeed is disbeleivd) also says that Berne has submitted.

To Citizens of Richmond

Richmond, August 11, 1798

I will not, Gentlemen, attempt to describe the emotions of joy which my return to my native country, and particularly to this city, has excited in my mind; nor can I paint the sentiments of affection and gratitude towards you, which my heart has ever felt, and which the kind and partial reception now given me by my fellow citizens, cannot fail to increase. He only who has been long absent from a much loved country and from friends greatly and deservedly esteemed—whose return is welcomed with expressions which, dictated by friendship, surpass his merits or his hopes, will judge of feelings to which I cannot do justice.

The situation in which the late envoys from the United States to the French republic found themselves in Paris, was indeed attended with the unpleasant circumstances which you have traced. Removed far from the councils of their country, and receiving no intelligence concerning it, the scene before them could not fail to produce the most anxious and disquieting sensations. Neither the ambition, the power, nor the hostile temper of France, was concealed from them:—nor could they be unacquainted with the earnest and unceasing solicitude felt by the government and people of the United States for peace. But amidst these difficulties, they possessed as guides, clear and explicit instructions, a conviction of the firmness and magnanimity, as well as of the justice and pacific temper of their government, and a strong reliance on that patriotism and love of liberty, which can never cease to glow in the American bosom. With these guides, however thorny the path of duty might be, they could not mistake it. It was their duty, unmindful of personal considerations, to pursue peace with unabating zeal, through all the difficulties with which the pursuit was embarrassed by a haughty and victorious government, holding in perfect contempt the rights of others, but to repel with unhesitating decision, any propositions, an acceptance of which would subvert the independence of the United States. This they have endeavored to do. I delight to believe that their endeavors have not dissatisfied their government or country, and it is most grateful to my mind to be assured that they receive the approbation of my fellow citizens in Richmond, and its vicinity.

I rejoice that I was not mistaken in the opinion I had formed of my countrymen. I rejoice to find, though they know how to estimate, and therefore seek to avoid the horrors and the dangers of war, yet they know also how to value the blessings of liberty and national independence: They know that peace would be purchased at too high a price by bending beneath a foreign yoke, and that peace so purchased could be but of short duration. The nation thus submitting, would be soon involved in the quarrels of its master, and would be compelled to exhaust its blood and its treasure, not for its own liberty, its own independence, or its own rights, but for the aggrandizement of its oppressor. The modern world unhappily exhibits but too plain a demonstration of this proposition. I pray Heaven that America may never contribute to its still further elucidation.

Terrible to her neighbors on the continent of Europe, as all must admit France to be, I believe that the United States, if indeed united, if awake to the impending danger, if capable of employing their whole, their undivided force—are so situated as to be able to preserve their independence. An immense ocean placed by a gracious providence, which seems to watch over this rising empire, between us and the European world, opposes of itself such an obstacle to invading ambition, must so diminish the force which can be brought to bear upon us, that our resources, if duly exerted, must be adequate to our protection, and we shall remain free, if we do not deserve to be slaves.

You do me justice, gentlemen, when you suppose that consolation must be derived from a comparison of the administration of the American government, with that which I have lately witnessed. To a citizen of the United States, so familiarly habituated to the actual possession of liberty, that he almost considers it as the inseparable companion of man, a view of the despotism, which, borrowing the garb and usurping the name of freedom, tyrannizes over so large and so fair a portion of the earth, must teach the value which he ought to place on the solid safety and real security he enjoys at home. In support of these, all temporary difficulties, however great, ought to be encountered and I agree with you, that the loss of them would poison and embitter every other joy; and that deprived of them, men who aspire to the exalted character of free men, would turn with loathing and disgust from every other comfort in life.

To me, gentlemen, the attachment you manifest to the government of your choice, affords the most sincere satisfaction. Having no interests separate from, or opposed to, those of the people, being themselves subject in common with others, to the laws they make, being soon to return to that mass from which they are selected for a time in order to conduct the affairs of the nation, it is by no means probable that those who administer the government of the United States can be actuated by other motives than the sincere desire of promoting the real prosperity of those whose destiny involves their own, and in whose ruin they must participate. Desirable as is at all times a due confidence in our government, it is peculiarly so in a moment of peril like the present, in a moment when the want of that confidence must impair the means of self defence, must increase a danger already but too great, and furnish, or at least give the appearance of furnishing, to a foreign real enemy, those weapons which have so often been so successfully used.

Accept, gentlemen, my grateful acknowledgements for your kind expressions concerning myself, and do me the justice to believe, that your prosperity, and that of the city of Richmond and its vicinity, will ever be among the first wishes of my heart.

Virginia Gazette, and General Advertiser,
August 14, 1798

PUBLIC OPINION REGARDING FRANCE

To Timothy Pickering

Dear Sir   Richmond, August 11, 1798
On my return to Richmond a very few days past I had the pleasure of receiving your letter of the 15th. of July inclosing the copy of one addressed to Mr. Gerry & also that of the 24th. of the same month transmiting several copies of the dispatches

from the late envoys to the french republic, for both of which I thank you.

I shoud scarcely suppose it possible that the letter to Mr. Gerry coud find him in France, but as I know he is so extremely cautious as often to be dilatory I am apprehensive that complete information of the present temper of the United States will be acquird by the french government before he sails & that possessd of such information insiduous propositions will be hinted, not with real pacific views, but for the purpose of dividing the people of this country & separating them from their government. I shall therefore continue to feel considerable anxieties on this subject until I hear of his arrival & that he has brought with him either real peace which I am sure is impossible, or no seductive intimations. The people of this country generally, so far as I can judge in the very short time I have been here, are pretty right as it respects France. Few are desperate enough to defend her conduct or to censure that of our government with respect to her. Some leading characters have reprobated slightly the conduct of the envoys for not having in a more explicit manner offerd to abandon the claim for spoliations on our commerce on condition of an abandonment on the part of France of the demand of a loan, & others have endeavord to spread the opinion that the fairest prospect existed of an accomodation through the means of Mr. Gerry with whom there was every reason to beleive that a negotiation was opend so soon as Genl. Pinckney & myself left Paris. These representations however make so little impression that I beleive France will be given up & the attack upon the government will be supported by the alien & sedition laws. I am extremely sorry to observe that here they are more successful & that these two laws, especially the sedition bill, are viewd by a great many well meaning men, as unwarranted by the constitution. I am entirely persuaded that with many the hate of the Government of our country is implacable & that if these bills did not exist the same clamor woud be made by them on some other account, but there are also many who are guided by very different motives & who tho less noisy in their complaints are seriously uneasy on this subject.

I am extremely anxious to hear from Genl. Pinckney & cannot

restrain a fear that his distance from Paris may prevent his sailing til his embarkation may be opposed by serious difficulties.

The derangements produced by my absence & the dispersion of my family oblige me to make either sales which I do not wish, or to delay payments of money which, I ought not to delay, unless I can receive from the treasury. This state of things obliges me to apply to you & to ask whether you can furnish me either with an order from the Secretary of the treasury on Colo. Carrington with your request to him to advance money to me. The one or the other will be sufficient. With very much respect & esteem, I am dear Sir your obedt. Servt.

When you can with convenience do so you will much oblige by forwarding to me the hastyly sketchd journal which I kept in France.

"SWEET LITTLE MARY"

To Mary W. Marshall

My dearest Polly   Richmond, August 18, 1798
I reached this place about a week past & have scarcely had time to look into any business yet there are so many persons calling every hour to see me. I have been a little indisposd by the hot & disagreeable ride but am now perfectly well & if I coud only learn that you were entirely restord I shoud be happy. Your mama & friends are in good health & your mama is as chearful as usual except when some particular conversation discomposes her. Your sweet little Mary is one of the most fascinating little creatures I ever beheld. She has improved very much since I saw her & I cannot help agreeing that she is a substitute for her lovely sister. She talks in a way not easily to be understood tho she comprehends very well every thing that is said to her & is the most coquetish little prude & the most prudish little coquet I ever saw. I wish she was with you as I think she woud entertain you more than all the rest of your children put together. Poor little John is cuting teeth & of course is

sick. He appeard to know me as soon as he saw me. He woud not come to me but he kept his eyes fixed on me as on a person he had some imperfect recollection of. I expect he has been taught to look at the picture & had some confusd idea of a likeness. He is small & weakly but by no means an ugly child. If as I hope we have the happiness to raise him I trust he will do as well as the rest. Poor little fellow, the present hot weather is hard on him cutting teeth, but great care is taken of him & I hope he will do well.

I hear nothing from you my dearest Polly but I will cherish the hope that you are getting better & will indulge myself with expecting the happiness of seeing you in october quite yourself. Remember my love to give me this pleasure you have only to take the cold bath, to use a great deal of exercise to sleep tranquilly & to stay in chearful company. I am sure you will do every thing which can contribute to give you back to yourself & me. This hot weather must be very distressing to you—it is so to every body—but it will soon be cooler. Let me know in time every thing relative to your coming down. Farewell my dearest Polly, I am your ever affectionate

To a Freeholder

Dear Sir,   Richmond, September 20, 1798

I have received your letter of yesterday, and shall, with equal candor, and satisfaction, answer all your queries. Every citizen has a right to know the political sentiments of the man who is proposed as his representative; and mine have never been of a nature to shun examination. To those who think another gentleman more capable of serving the district than myself, it would be useless to explain my opinions, because whatever my opinions may be, they will, and ought, to vote for that other; but I cannot help wishing, that those who think differently, would know my real principles, and not attribute to me those I never possessed, and with which active calumny has been pleased to asperse me.

Answ. 1. In heart and sentiment, as well as by birth and interest, I am an American, attached to the genuine principles of the constitution, as sanctioned by the will of the people, for their general liberty, prosperity and happiness. I consider that constitution as the rock of our political salvation, which has preserved us from misery, division and civil wars;—and which will yet preserve us if we value it rightly and support it firmly.

2d. I do not think the interest and prosperity of America, at all dependent on an alliance with any foreign nation; nor does the man exist who would regret more than myself the formation of such an alliance. In truth, America has, in my opinion, no motive for forming such connections, and very powerful motives for avoiding them.—Europe is eternally engaged in wars in which we have no interest; and with which the soundest policy forbids us to intermeddle. We ought to avoid any compact which may endanger our being involved in them. My sentiments on this subject, are detailed at large, in the beginning of the memorial addressed by the late envoys from the U. States to the minister of foreign affairs of the French republic, where the neutrality of the United States is justified, and the reasons for that neutrality stated.

3d. I am not in favor of an alliance offensive and defensive with G. Britain, nor for any closer connection with that nation, than already exists. No man in existence is more decidedly opposed to such an alliance, or more fully convinced of the evils that would result from it. I never have, in thought, word or deed, given the smallest reason to suspect I wished it; nor do I believe any man acquainted with me does suspect it. Those who originate and countenance such an idea, may (if they know me) design to impose on others, but they do not impose on themselves. The whole of my politics respecting foreign nations are reducible to this single position. We ought to have commercial intercourse with all, but political ties with none. Let us buy as cheap and sell as dear as possible. Let commerce go wherever individual, and consequently national interest, will carry it: but let us never connect ourselves politically, with any people whatever. I have not a right to say, nor can I say positively, what are the opinions of those who administer the government of the U. States; but I believe firmly, that neither the President, nor any one of those with whom he advises, would consent to form a close and permanent political connection with any nation upon earth. Should France continue to wage an unprovoked war against us, while she is also at war with Britain, it would be madness and folly not to endeavour to make such temporary arrangements as would give us the aid of the British fleets to prevent our being invaded; but I would not, even to obtain so obvious a good, make such a sacrifice as I think we should make, by forming a permanent political connection with that, or any other nation on earth.

4th. The measures of the administration and government of the U. States with respect to France, have in my opinion, been uniformly directed by a sincere and unequivocal desire to observe, faithfully, the treaties existing between the two nations, and to preserve the neutrality and independence of our country. Had it been possible to maintain peace with France without sacrificing those great objects, I am convinced that our government would have maintained it. Unfortunately it has been impossible. I do not believe that any different line of conduct, on our part, unless we would have relinquished the rights of self-government, and have become the colonies of France, could have preserved peace with that nation. Be assured that the primary object of France is, and for a long time past has been, dominion over others. This is a truth only to be disbelieved by those who shut their eyes on the history and conduct of that nation. The grand instruments by which they effect this end, to which all their measures tend, are immense armies on their part, and divisions, which a variety of circumstances have enabled them to create, among those whom they wish to subdue. Whenever France has exhibited a disposition to be just towards the United States, an accurate attention to facts now in possession of the public, will prove, that this disposition was manifested in the hope of involving us in her wars as a dependent and subordinate nation.

5th. I am not an advocate for the alien and sedition bills: had I been in congress when they passed, I should, unless my judgment could have been changed, certainly have opposed them. Yet, I do not think them fraught with all those mischiefs which many gentlemen ascribe to them. I should have opposed them, because I think them useless; and because they are calculated to create, unnecessarily, discontents and jealousies at a time when our very existence, as a nation, may depend on our union

—I believe that these laws, had they been opposed on these principles by a man, not suspected of intending to destroy the government, or of being hostile to it, would never have been enacted. With respect to their repeal, the effort will be made before I can become a member of congress. If it succeeds, there will be an end of the business—if it fails, I shall, on the question of renewing the effort, should I be chosen to represent the district, obey the voice of my constituents. My own private opinion is, that it will be unwise to renew it for this reason: The laws will expire of themselves, if I recollect rightly the time for which they are enacted, during the term of the ensuing congress. I shall, indisputably, oppose their revival; and I believe that opposition will be more successful, if men's minds are not too much irritated by the struggle about a repeal of laws which will, at the time, be expiring of themselves.

Virginia Herald, October 2, 1798

"SERIOUS & ALARMING" SENTIMENTS

To George Washington

Dear Sir   Richmond, January 8, 1799

I had the pleasure of receiving your letter of the 30th. of Decr. while Genl. Pinckney was at this place & of delivering to him the packet it inclos'd. He left us with the ladies of his family on the 4th. in health & spirits.

I thank you for the charge of Judge Addison; 'tis certainly well written & I wish that as well as some other publications on the same subject coud be more generally read. I beleive that no argument can moderate the leaders of the opposition —but it may be possible to make some impression on the mass of the people. For this purpose the charge of Judge Addison seems well calculated. I shall forward it to Mr. Washington.

However I may regret the passage of one of the acts complaind of, I am firmly persuaded that the tempest has not been raised by them. Its cause lies much deeper & is not easily to be removed. Had they never pass'd, other measures woud have been selected which woud have been attackd with equal virulence. The misfortune is that an act operating on the press in any manner, affords to its opposers arguments which so captivate the public ear, which so mislead the public mind that the efforts of reason to correct false impressions will often fail of success.

Two very interesting subjects have during the present session peculiarly engag'd the attention of the legislature. The first was a paper produc'd by Colo. Taylor of Caroline, & which you must have seen, containing resolutions which take advantage of the irritation excited by the alien & sedition laws, to criminate the whole conduct of our administration & charge it with the design of introducing monarchy; the other was a proposition from Mr. George K. Taylor of Prince George expressive of sentiments similar to those which have been declard by other legislatures of the union on our controversy with France, in the place of which was substituted by a majority of twenty nine a counter proposition termd an amendment which was offerd by Colo. Nicholas of Albemarle & which seems calculated to evince to France & to the world that Virginia is very far from harmonizing with the American government or her sister States.

The debates on these subjects were long & animated. In the course of them sentiments were declard & (in my judgement) views were developed of a very serious & alarming extent. To me it seems that there are men who will hold power by any means rather than not hold it; & who woud prefer a dissolution of the union to the continuance of an administration not of their own party. They will risk all the ills which may result from the most dangerous experiments rather than permit that happiness to be enjoy'd which is dispensd by other hands than their own. It is more than ever essential to make great exertions at the next election, & I am persuaded that by making them we obtain a legislature if not foederal, so divided as to be moderate.

I am by no means certain who will be elected for this district. Whatever the issue of the election may be I shall neither reproach my self nor those at whose instance I have become a candidate, for the step I have taken. I feel with increasd force the obligations of duty to make sacrafices & exertions for the preservation of American union & independence, as I am more convinc'd of the reality of the danger which threatens them. The exertions made against me by particular characters throughout this state & even from other States have an activity & a malignancy which no personal considerations woud excite. If I fail I shall regret the failure more on account of the evidence it will afford of the prevalence of a temper hostile to our government & indiscriminately so to all who will not join in that hostility, than of the personal mortification which woud be sustaind. With the most respectful attachment, I remain Sir your obedt.

DEBASEMENT BY FACTION

To James M. Marshall

My dear brother   April 3, 1799

I have receivd your letters by Mr. Smith & by the post. I approve entirely of the ejectment in the winchester case & shoud never have suggested the distress but on your informing me that the lott holders woud not abide by the decision of one case. There has been no express decision of a court stating Lord Fairfax to have been siezed in fee of the northern neck, the Judges have expressd that opinion but not formally. There can therefore be no objection to finding the title of Lord Fairfax. In the district court of Winchester you will perceive the case agreed between Hunter & Fairfax in which his title is found & which you may translate into your present case with the necessary alterations fitted to your being plaintiff instead of defendent. I will endeavor to send you by Mr. Smith so much of the case agreed in the Fedl. court in which Fairfax was plaintiff as relates to his title. If however I shoud not do so you may form one very readily from that which you will find in Peytons office. The alteration in the finding relative to the old town is not I think essential tho perhaps it may be proper & necessary to alter it so as to show that the particular lot in question was sold.

I shall bring in chancery the suit against Pendleton &

others. I have no doubt myself of the jurisdiction of the court but I think our court of appeals very ill instructed on that subject & I fear its decisions.

I had wish'd to encourage Davies after his loss of the place of public printer & took two papers. As one answerd all my purposes I subscrib'd for the other in your name. I will examine the sum I receivd for you at the treasury & inform you of its amount. I wish you not to mention to Mr. Marshall the money lent to him as I am confident he is not in a situation to repay it.

I never suspected Doctor Conrod of having stated any thing as coming from me which was not strictly true nor shoud I have written to him on the subject had it not been absolutely necessary to do so in order to show that the authority I was told Mr Hite woud resort to woud not support him. I have no right to object to any thing the Doctor might have stated as his conjecture of my opinion since it was unconnected with any evidence proceeding from myself & only founded on his own opinions of the conduct of Mr. Gerry himself. I have always thought highly of Doctor Conrod nor is my good opinion of him in any degree diminish'd.

The fate of my election is extremely uncertain. The means used to defeat it are despicable in the extreme & yet they succeed. Nothing I believe more debases or pollutes the human mind than faction.

I shall not prevent the ejectment you deem necessary to secure the payment of rent arrear on any of the property.

I regret very sincerely the situation of Genl. Morgan & wish you shoud you see him to present me respectfully & affectionately to him.

I understand that my sister Jane while here was addressd by Major Taylor & that his addresses were encouraged by her. I am not by any means certain of the fact nor did I suspect it until we had separated the night preceeding her departure & consequently I coud have no conversation with her concerning it. I beleive that tho Major Taylor was attachd to her it woud probably have had no serious result if Jane had not manifested some partiality for him. This affair embarasses me a good deal. Major Taylor is a young gentleman of talents & integrity for whom I profess & feel a real friendship. There is no person with whom I shoud be better pleasd if there were not other considerations which ought not to be overlookd. Major Taylor possesses but little if any fortune & is encumberd with a family & does not like his profession. Of course he will be so eminent in it as from his talents he ought to be. These are facts now unknown to my sister but which ought to be known to her. Had I conjecturd that Mr. Taylor was contemplated in the character of a lover I shoud certainly have made to her all the proper communications. I regret that it was conceald from me. I have a sincere & real affection & esteem for Major Taylor but I think it right in affairs of this sort that the real situation of the parties shoud be mutually understood. Present affectionately to my sister, Your

Since writing the above I have receivd your letter with the certificates. I regret much that they do not state the truth more fairly.

Speech in Congress on
the Case of Thomas Nash

MR. MARSHALL said, believing, as he did most seriously—
that in a government constituted like that of the United States,
much of the public happiness depended, not only on its being
rightly administered, but on the measures of administration
being rightly understood:—On rescuing public opinion from
those numerous prejudices with which so many causes might
combine to surround it:—he could not but have been highly
gratified with the very eloquent,—and what was still more valuable, the very able, and very correct argument, which had been
delivered by the gentleman from Delaware (Mr. Bayard) against
the resolutions now under consideration. He had not expected
that the effect of this argument would have been universal, but
he had cherished the hope, and in this he had not been disappointed, that it would be very extensive. He did not flatter
himself with being able to shed much new light on the subject,
but, as the argument in opposition to the resolutions had been
assailed, with considerable ability, by gentlemen of great talents, he trusted the house would not think the time misapplied, which would be devoted to the re-establishment of the
principles contained in that argument, and to the refutation of
those advanced in opposition to it. In endeavouring to do this,
he should notice the observations in support of the resolutions, not in the precise order in which they were made, but as
they applied to the different points he deemed it necessary to
maintain, in order to demonstrate, that the conduct of the executive of the United States, could not justly be charged with
the errors imputed to it by the resolutions.

His first proposition, he said, was that the case of Thomas
Nash, as stated to the President, was completely within the
27th article of the treaty of amity, commerce, and navigation,
entered into between the United States of America and Great
Britain.

He read the article and then observed—The casus foederis
of this article occurs, when a person, having committed murder or forgery within the jurisdiction of one of the contracting

parties, and having sought an asylum in the country of the other, is charged with the crime, and his delivery demanded, on such proof of his guilt as according to the laws of the place where he shall be found, would justify his apprehension and commitment for trial, if the offence had there been committed.

The case stated is, that Thomas Nash, having committed a murder on board a British Frigate, navigating the high seas under a commission from his Britannic Majesty, had sought an asylum within the United States, and on this case his delivery was demanded by the minister of the King of Great Britain.

It is manifest that the case stated, if supported by proof, is within the letter of the article, provided a murder committed in a British frigate, on the high seas, be committed within the jurisdiction of that nation.

That such a murder is within their jurisdiction, has been fully shown by the gentleman from Delaware. The principle is, that the jurisdiction of a nation extends to the whole of its territory, and to its own citizens in every part of the world. The laws of a nation are rightfully obligatory on its own citizens in every situation, where those laws are really extended to them. This principle is founded on the nature of civil union. It is supported every where by public opinion, and is recognized by writers on the law of nations. Rutherforth in his second volume page 180 says, "The jurisdiction which a civil society has over the persons of its members, affects them immediately, whether they are within its territories or not."

This general principle is especially true, and is particularly recognized, with respect to the fleets of a nation on the high seas. To punish offences committed in its fleet, is the practice of every nation in the universe; and consequently the opinion of the world is, that a fleet at sea, is within the jurisdiction of the nation to which it belongs. Rutherforth 2 vol. page 491, says, "There can be no doubt about the jurisdiction of a nation over the persons, which compose its fleets, when they are out at sea, whether they are sailing upon it, or are stationed in any particular part of it."

The gentleman from Pennsylvania, (Mr. Gallatin) tho' he has not directly controverted this doctrine, has sought to weaken it, by observing, that the jurisdiction of a nation at sea could not be compleat even in its own vessels;—and in support of this position he urged the admitted practice, of submitting to search for contraband—a practice not tolerated on land, within the territory of a neutral power. The rule is as stated; but is founded on a principle which does not affect the jurisdiction of a nation over its citizens or subjects in its ships. The principle is, that in the sea, itself, no nation has any jurisdiction. All may equally exercise their rights, and consequently the right of a belligerent power to prevent aid being given to his enemy, is not restrained by any superior right of a neutral in the place. But if this argument possessed any force, it would not apply to national ships of war, since the usage of nations does not permit them to be searched.

According to the practice of the world then, and the opinions of writers on the law of nations, the murder committed on board a British frigate navigating the high seas, was a murder committed within the jurisdiction of the British nation.

Altho such a murder is plainly within the letter of the article, it has been contended not to be within its just construction, because at sea, all nations have a common jurisdiction, and the article correctly construed, will not embrace a case of concurrent jurisdiction.

It is deemed unnecessary to controvert this construction, because the proposition—*that the United States had no jurisdiction over the murder committed by Thomas Nash*, is believed to be completely demonstrable.

It is not true that all nations have jurisdiction over all offences committed at sea. On the contrary no nation has any jurisdiction at sea, but over its own citizens or vessels, or offences against itself. This principle is laid down in 2d. Ruth. 488, and 491.

The American government has on a very solemn occasion, avowed the same principle. The first minister of the French republic asserted and exercised powers of so extraordinary a nature, as unavoidably to produce a controversy with the United States. The situation in which the government then found itself was such, as necessarily to occasion a very serious and mature consideration of the opinions it should adopt. Of consequence, the opinions then declared, deserve great respect. In the case alluded to, Mr. Genet had asserted the right of fitting out privateers in the American ports, and of manning them with American citizens, in order to cruize against nations with whom America was at peace. In reasoning against this extravagant claim, the then secretary of state, in his letter of the 17th of June, 1793, says "For our citizens then to commit murders and depredations on the members of nations at peace with us, or to combine to do it, appeared to the executive and to those whom they consulted, as much against the laws of the land, as to murder or rob, or combine to murder or rob, its own citizens; and as much to require punishment, if done, within their limits, where they have a territorial jurisdiction, or on the high seas, where they have a *personal jurisdiction*, that is to say, one which reaches *their own citizens only*; this being an *appropriate part* of each nation, on an element where all have a common jurisdiction."

The well considered opinion then of the American government on this subject is, that the jurisdiction of a nation at sea is "*personal*," reaching its "*own citizens only*," and that this is "*the appropriate part* of each nation" on that element.

This is precisely the opinion maintained by the opposers of the resolutions. If the jurisdiction of America at sea be personal —reaching its own citizens only, if this be its appropriate part, then the jurisdiction of the nation cannot extend to a murder committed by a British sailor, on board a British frigate navigating the high seas under a commission from his Britannic majesty.

As a further illustration of the principle contended for, suppose a contract made at sea, and a suit instituted for the recovery of money which might be due thereon. By the laws of what nation would the contract be governed? The principle is general, that a personal contract follows the person, but is governed by the law of the place where it is formed. By what law then would such a contract be governed! If all nations had jurisdiction over the place, then the laws of all nations would equally influence the contract but certainly no man will hesitate to admit, that such a contract ought to be decided according to the laws of that nation, to which the vessel or contracting parties might belong.

Suppose a duel attended with death, in the fleet of a foreign nation, or in any vessel which returned safe to port, could it be pretended that any government on earth, other than that to which the fleet or vessel belonged, had jurisdiction in the case; or that the offender could be tried by the laws, or tribunals, of any other nation whatever.

Suppose a private theft by one mariner from another and the vessel to perform its voyage and return in safety, would it be contended that all nations have equal cognizance of the crime; and are equally authorized to punish it?

If there be this common jurisdiction at sea, why not punish desertion from one belligerent power to another, or correspondence with the enemy, or any other crime which may be perpetrated? A common jurisdiction over all offences at sea, in whatever vessel committed, would involve the power of punishing the offences which have been stated. Yet all gentlemen will disclaim this power. It follows then that no such common jurisdiction exists.

In truth the right of every nation to punish, is limited, in its nature, to offences against the nation inflicting the punishment. This principle is believed to be universally true.

It comprehends every possible violation of its laws on its own territory, and it extends to violations committed elsewhere by persons it has a right to bind. It extends also to general piracy.

A pirate under the law of nations, is an enemy of the human race. Being the enemy of all he is liable to be punished by all. Any act which denotes this universal hostility, is an act of piracy. Not only an actual robbery therefore, but cruizing on the high seas without commission, and with intent to rob, is piracy. This is an offence against all and every nation and is therefore alike punishable by all. But an offence which in its nature affects only a particular nation, is only punishable by that nation.

It is by confounding general piracy with piracy by statute, that indistinct ideas have been produced, respecting the power to punish offences committed on the high seas.

A statute may make any offence piracy, committed within the jurisdiction of the nation passing the statute, and such offence will be punishable by that nation. But piracy under the law of nations, which alone is punishable by all nations, can only consist in an act which is an offence against all. No particular nation can increase or diminish the list of offences thus punishable.

It had been observed by his colleague (Mr. Nicholas) for the purpose of showing that the distinction taken on this subject by the gentleman from Delaware, (Mr. Bayard) was inaccurate, that any vessel robbed on the high seas, could be the property only of a single nation, and being only an offence against that nation could be, on the principle taken by the opposers of the resolutions no offence against the law of nations: But in this his colleague had not accurately considered the principle. As a man, who turns out to rob on the high way, and forces from a stranger his purse with a pistol at his bosom, is not the particular enemy of that stranger, but alike the enemy of every man who carries a purse, so those, who, without a commission, rob on the high seas, manifest a temper hostile to all nations, and therefore become the enemies of all. The same inducements which occasion the robbery of one vessel, exist to occasion the robbery of others, and therefore the single offence is an offence against the whole community of nations, manifests a temper hostile to all, is the commencement of an attack on all, and is consequently, of right, punishable by all.

His colleague had also contended that all the offences at sea, punishable by the British Statutes from which the act of Congress was in a great degree copied, were piracies at common law, or by the law of nations, and as murder is among these, consequently murder was an act of piracy by the law of nations, and therefore punishable by every nation. In support of this position he had cited 1. Hawk. P. C. 267 and 271. 3d Inst. 112 and 1st Woodison 140.

The amount of these cases is, that no new offence is made piracy by the statutes; but that a different tribunal is created for their trial, which is guided by a different rule, from that which governed, previous to those Statutes. Therefore, on an indictment for piracy, it is still necessary to prove an offence which was piracy before the Statutes. He drew from these authorities a very different conclusion from that which had been drawn by his colleague. To show the correctness of his conclusion, it was necessary to observe, that Statute did not indeed change the nature of piracy since it only transferred the trial of

the crime to a different tribunal, where different rules of decision prevailed, but having done this, other crimes committed
on the high seas, which were not piracy, were made punishable
by the same tribunal, but certainly this municipal regulation
could not be considered as proving, that those offences were
before, piracy by the law of nations. Mr. Nicholas insisted that
the law was not correctly stated, whereupon Mr. Marshall
called for 3d inst. and read the statute. "All treasons, felonies
robberies, murders, and confederacies committed in or upon
the seas, &c. shall be enquired, tried, heard, determined and
judged in such shires, &c. in like form and condition as if any
such offence had been committed on the land, &c."

"And such as shall be convicted &c. shall have and suffer
such pains of death, &c. as if they had been attainted of any
treason, felony, robbery, or other the said offences done upon
the land."

This statute it is certain, does not change the nature of
piracy, but all treasons, felonies, robberies, murders and confederacies committed in or upon the sea, are not declared to
have been, nor are they, piracies. If a man be indicted as a pirate, the offence must be shown to have been piracy before the
statute, but if he be indicted for treason, felony, robbery, murder, or confederacy committed at sea, whether such offence
was or was not a piracy, he shall be punished in like manner as
if he had committed the same offence at land. The passage
cited from 1. Woodison 140, is a full authority to this point.
Having stated that offences committed at sea were formerly
triable before the Lord high Admiral, according to the course
of the Roman civil law, Woodison says "but by the Statutes 27.
H. 8th. C 4. and 28. H. 8. C. 15. all treasons, felonies, piracies
and other crimes committed on the sea or where the Admiral
has jurisdiction, shall be tried in the realm as if done on land.
But the Statutes referred to affect only the manner of the trial
so far as respects piracy. The nature of the offence is not changed.
Whether a charge amounts to piracy or not, must still depend
on the law of nations, except where, *in the case of British subjects*, express acts of Parliament have declared that the crimes
therein specified shall be adjudged piracy, or shall be liable to
the same mode of trial and degree of punishment."

This passage proves not only that all offences at sea are not piracies by the law of nations, but also that all indictments for piracy must depend on the law of nations, "except where, *in the case of British subjects, express acts of Parliament*" have changed the law. Why do not these "express acts of Parliament" change the law as to others than "British subjects"? The words are general—"All treasons, felonies &c." Why are they confined in construction to British subjects? The answer is a plain one. The jurisdiction of the nation is confined to its territory and to its subjects.

The gentleman from Pennsylvania (Mr. Gallatin) abandons, and very properly abandons, this untenable ground. He admits that no nation has a right to punish offences against another nation, and that the United States can only punish offences against their own laws, and the laws of nations. He admits too, that if there had only been a mutiny (and consequently if there had only been a murder) on board the Hermoine, that the American courts could have taken no cognizance of the crime. Yet mutiny is punishable as piracy by the law of both nations. That gentleman contends that the act commited by Nash was piracy according to the law of nations. He supports his position by insisting, that the offence may be constituted by the commission of a single act, that unauthorized robbery on the high seas is this act, and that the crew having seized the vessel and being out of the protection of any nation, were pirates.

It is true that the offence may be complete by a single act—but it depends on the nature of that act. If it be such as manifests general hostility against the world, an intention to rob generally, then it is piracy; but if it be merely a mutiny and murder in a vessel, for the purpose of delivering it up to the enemy, it seems to be an offence against a single nation, and not to be piracy. The sole object of the crew might be to go over to the enemy, or to free themselves from the tyranny experienced on board a ship of war, and not to rob generally.

But should it even be true, that running away with the vessel to deliver her up to an enemy, was an act of general piracy, punishable by all nations, yet the mutiny and murder was a distinct offence.—Had the attempt to seize the vessel failed, after the commission of the murder, then, according to the argument of the gentleman from Pennsylvania, the American courts could have taken no cognizance of the crime. Whatever then might have been the law respecting the piracy, of the murder there was no jurisdiction. For the murder, not the piracy, Nash was delivered up. Murder, and not piracy, is comprehended in the 27th article of the treaty between the two nations. Had he been tried then, and acquitted on an indictment for the piracy, he must still have been delivered up for the murder, of which the court could have no jurisdiction. It is certain that an acquittal of the piracy, would not have discharged the murder; and therefore in the so much relied on trials at Trenton, a separate indictment for murder was filed, after an indictment for piracy. Since then, if acquitted for piracy, he must have been delivered to the British government on the charge of murder, the President of the United States might, very properly, without prosecuting for the piracy, direct him to be delivered up on the murder.

All the gentlemen who have spoken in support of the resolutions, have contended that the case of Thomas Nash is within the purview of the act of Congress, which relates to this subject, and is, by that act, made punishable in the American courts. That is, that the act of Congress designed to punish crimes committed on board a British frigate.

Nothing can be more completely demonstrable than the untruth of this proposition.

It has already been shewn, that the legislative jurisdiction of a nation, extends only to its own territory, and to its own citizens, wherever they may be. Any general expression in a legislative act, must, necessarily be restrained to objects within the jurisdiction of the legislature passing the act. Of consequence, an act of Congress can only be construed to apply to the territory of the United States, comprehending every person within it, and to the citizens of the United States.

But independent of this undeniable truth, the act itself affords complete testimony of its intention and extent. (See Laws of the U. S. vol. I. P. 100.)

The title is, "An act for the punishment of certain crimes against the United States." Not against Britain—France—or the World;—but singly "against the United States."

The first section relates to treason, and its objects are "any person or persons owing allegiance to the United States." This description comprehends only the citizens of the United States, and such others as may be on its territory, or in its service.

The second section relates to mis-prison of treason, and declares, without limitation, that any person or persons, having knowledge of any treason, and not communicating the same, shall be guilty of that crime. Here then is an instance of that limited description of persons in one section, and of that general description in another, which has been relied on to support the construction contended for by the friends of the resolutions. But will it be pretended that a person can commit mis-prison of treason, who cannot commit treason itself? That he would be punishable for concealing a treason, who could not be punished for plotting it? Or can it be supposed that the act designed to punish an Englishman or a Frenchman, who, residing in his own country, should have knowledge of treasons against the United States, and should not cross the Atlantic to reveal them?

The same observations apply to the 6th section which makes "any person or persons" guilty of mis-prison of felony, who having knowledge of murder or other offences enumerated in that section, should conceal them. It is impossible to apply this to a foreigner, in a foreign land, or to any person not owing allegiance to the United States.

The 8th section, which is supposed to comprehend the case, after declaring that if any person or persons shall commit murder on the high seas, he shall be punishable with death, proceeds to say, that if any captain or mariner shall piratically run away with a ship or vessel, or yield her up voluntarily to a pirate, or if any seaman shall lay violent hands on his commander, to prevent his fighting, or shall make a revolt in the ship, every such offender shall be adjudged a pirate, and a felon.

The persons who are the objects of this section of the act, are all described in general terms, which might embrace the subjects of all nations. But is it to be supposed, that if, in an engagement between an English and a French ship of war, the crew of the one or the other, should lay violent hands on the captain, and force him to strike, that this would be an offence against the act of Congress punishable in the courts of the United States? On this extended construction of the general terms of the section, not only the crew of one foreign vessel forcing their captain to surrender to another, would incur the penalties of the act, but if in the late action between the gallant Truxton and a French frigate, the crew of that frigate had compelled the captain to surrender, while he was unwilling to do so, they would have been indictable as felons in the courts of the United States. But surely the act of Congress admits of no such extravagant construction.

His colleague, Mr. Marshal said, had cited, and particularly relied on the 9th section of the act. That section declares, that if a citizen shall commit any of the enumerated piracies, or any act of hostility on the high seas, against the United States, under color of a commission from any foreign Prince or State, he shall be adjudged a pirate, felon and robber, and shall suffer death.

This section is only a positive extension of the act to a case, which might otherwise have escaped punishment. It takes away the protection of a foreign commission, from an American citizen who, on the high seas robs his countrymen. This is no exception from any preceding part of the law, because there is no part which relates to the conduct of vessels commissioned by a foreign power; it only proves that, in the opinion of the legislature, the penalties of the act could not, without this express provision, have been incurred by a citizen holding a foreign commission.

It is then most certain, that the act of Congress does not comprehend the case of a murder committed on board a foreign ship of war.

The gentleman from New-York has cited 2d Woodison 428, to show that the courts of England extend their jurisdiction to piracies committed by the subjects of foreign nations.

This has not been doubted. The case from Woodison is a case of robberies committed on the high seas by a vessel without authority. There are ordinary acts of piracy, which, as has been already stated, being offences against all nations, are punishable by all. The case from 2d Woodison, and the note cited from the same book by the gentleman from Delaware, are strong authorities against the doctrines contended for by the friends of the resolutions.

It has also been contended that the question of jurisdiction was decided at Trenton, by receiving indictments against persons there arraigned for the same offence, and by retaining them for trial after the return of the habeas corpus.

Every person in the slightest degree acquainted with judicial proceedings, knows, that an indictment is no evidence of jurisdiction; and that in criminal cases, the question of jurisdiction will seldom be made, but by arrest of judgement after conviction.

The proceedings after the return of the habeas corpus, only prove, that the case was not such a case as to induce the Judge immediately to decide against his jurisdiction. The question was not free from doubt, and therefore might very properly be postponed until its decision should become necessary.

It has been argued by the gentleman from New-York, that the form of the indictment is, itself evidence of a power in the court to try the case. Every word of that indictment said the gentleman, gives the lie, to a denial of the jurisdiction of the court.

It would be assuming a very extraordinary principle indeed to say, that words inserted in an indictment for the express purpose of assuming the jurisdiction of a court, should be admitted to prove that jurisdiction. The question certainly depended on the nature of the fact, and not on the description of the fact. But as an indictment must necessarily contain formal words in order to be supported, and as forms often denote what a case must substantially be, to authorize a court to take cognizance of it, some words in the indictments at Trenton, ought to be noticed. The indictments charge the persons to have been within the peace, and the murder to have been committed against the peace of the United States. These are necessary averments, and, to give the court jurisdiction, the fact ought to have accorded with them. But who will say that the crew of a British frigate on the high seas, are within the peace of the United States, or a murder committed on board such a frigate, against the peace of any other than the British government.

It is then demonstrated that the murder with which Thomas Nash was charged, was not committed within the jurisdiction of the United States, and, consequently, that the case stated was completely within the letter, and the spirit, of the 27th article of the treaty between the two nations. If the necessary evidence was produced, he ought to have been delivered up to justice. It was an act to which the American Nation was bound by a most solemn compact. To have tried him for the murder would have been mere mockery. To have condemned and executed him, the court having no jurisdiction, would have been murder:—to have acquitted and discharged him, would have been a breach of faith and a violation of national duty.

But it has been contended that altho' Thomas Nash ought to have been delivered up to the British Minister, on the requisition made by him in the name of his government, yet the interference of the President was improper.

This Mr. Marshall said led to his second proposition, which was—That the case was a case for executive and not judicial decision. He admitted implicitly the division of powers stated by the gentleman from New York, and that it was the duty of each department to resist the encroachments of the others.

This being established, the enquiry was, to what department was the power in question allotted?

The gentleman from New-York had relied on the 2d section of the 3d article of the constitution, which enumerates the cases to which the judicial power of the United States extends,—as expressly including that now under consideration. Before he examined that section, it would not be improper to notice a very material mis-statement of it, made in the resolutions offered by the gentleman from New York. By the constitution, the judicial power of the United States is extended to all *cases in law and equity* arising under the constitution, laws and treaties of the United States; but the resolutions declare the judicial power to extend to *all questions* arising under the constitution, treaties and laws of the United States. The difference between the constitution and the resolutions was material and apparent. A case in law or equity was a term well understood, and of limited signification. It was a controversy between parties which had taken a shape for judicial decision. If the judicial power extended to every *question* under the constitution it would involve almost every subject proper for legislative discussion and decision; if to every *question* under the laws and treaties of the United States it would involve almost every subject on which the executive could act. The division of power which the gentleman had stated, could exist no longer, and the other departments would be swallowed up by the judiciary. But it was apparent that the resolutions had essentially misrepresented the constitution. He did not charge the gentleman from New-York, with intentional misrepresentation; he would not attribute to him such an artifice in any case, much less in a case where detection was so easy and so certain. Yet this substantial departure from the constitution, in resolutions affecting substantially to unite it, was not the less worthy of remark for being unintentional. It manifested the course of reasoning by which the gentleman had himself been misled, and his judgement betrayed into the opinions those resolutions expressed.

By extending the judicial power to all *cases in law and equity*, the constitution had never been understood, to confer on that department, any political power whatever. To come within this description, a question must assume a legal form, for forensic litigation, and judicial decision. There must be parties to come into court, who can be reached by its process, and bound by its power; whose rights admit of ultimate decision by a tribunal to which they are bound to submit.

A case in law or equity proper for judicial decision, may arise under a treaty, where the rights of individuals acquired or secured by a treaty, are to be asserted or defended in court. As under the 4th or 6th article of the treaty of peace with Great Britain, or under those articles of our late treaties with France, Prussia and other nations, which secure to the subjects of those nations, their property within the United States: or as would be an article which, instead of stipulating to deliver up an offender, should stipulate his punishment, provided the case was punishable by the laws, and in the courts of the United States. But the judicial power cannot extend to political compacts—as the establishment of the boundary line between the American and British dominions; the case of the late guarantee in our treaty with France; or the case of the delivery of a murderer under the 27th article of our present treaty with Britain.

The gentleman from New-York has asked, triumphantly asked, what power exists in our courts to deliver up an individual to a foreign government? Permit me, said Mr. Marshall, but not triumphantly, to retort the question.—By what authority can any court render such a judgement? What power does a court possess to seize any individual, and determine that he shall be adjudged by a foreign tribunal? Surely our courts possess no such power, yet they must possess it, if this article of the treaty is to be executed by the courts.

Gentlemen have cited and relied on that clause in the constitution, which enables Congress to define and punish piracies, and felonies; committed on the high seas, and offences against the law of nations; together with the act of Congress declaring the punishment of those offences; as transferring the whole subject to the courts. But that clause can never be construed to make to the government a grant of power, which the people making it, did not themselves possess. It has already been shown that the people of the United States have no jurisdiction over offences, commited on board a foreign ship, against a foreign nation. Of consequence, in framing a government for themselves, they cannot have passed this jurisdiction to that government. The law therefore cannot act upon the case. But this clause of the constitution cannot be considered and need not be considered, as affecting acts which are piracy under the law of nations. As the judicial power of the United States extends to all cases of admiralty and maritime jurisdiction, and piracy under the law of nations is of admiralty and maritime jurisdiction, punishable by every nation, the judicial power of the United States of course extends to it. On this principle the courts of admiralty under the Confederation, took cognizance of piracy, altho' there was no express power in Congress to define and punish the offence.

But the extension of the judicial power of the United States to all cases of admiralty and maritime jurisdiction, must necessarily be understood with some limitation. All cases of admiralty and maritime jurisdiction which, from their nature, are triable in the United States, are submitted to the jurisdiction of the courts of the United States. There are, cases of piracy by the law of nations, and cases within the legislative jurisdiction of the nation. The people of America possessed no other power over the subject, and could consequently transfer no other to their courts, and it has already been proved that a murder committed on board a foreign ship of war, is not comprehended within this description.

The consular convention with France has also been relied

on, as proving, the act of delivering up an individual to a foreign power, to be in its nature judicial and not executive.

The 9th article of that convention authorizes the consuls and vice consuls of either nation, to cause to be arrested all deserters from their vessels, "for which purpose the said consuls and vice consuls shall address themselves to the courts, judges and officers competent."

This article of the convention does not, like the 27th article of the treaty with Britain, stipulate a national act, to be performed on the demand of a nation; it only authorizes a foreign minister to cause an act to be done, and prescribes the course he is to pursue. The contract itself is, that the act shall be performed by the agency of the foreign consul, through the medium of the courts; but this affords no evidence that a contract of a very different nature, is to be performed in the same manner.

It is said that the then President of the United States declared the incompetency of the courts, judges and officers to execute this contract without an act of the legislature. But the then President made no such declaration. He has said that some legislative provision is requisite, to carry the stipulations of the convention into *full* effect. This however is by no means declaring the incompetency of a department to perform an act stipulated by treaty, until the legislative authority shall direct its performance.

It has been contended that the conduct of the executive on former occasions, similar to this in principle, has been such, as to evince an opinion even in that department, that the case in question is proper for the decision of the courts.

The fact adduced to support this argument is, the determination of the late President, on the case of prizes made within the jurisdiction of the United States, or by privateers fitted out in their ports.

The nation was bound to deliver up those prizes in like manner as the nation is now bound to deliver up an individual demanded under the 27th article of the treaty with Britain. The duty was the same, and devolved on the same department.

In quoting the decision of the executive on that case, the gentleman from New-York has taken occasion to bestow high encomium on the late President, and to consider his conduct as furnishing an example worthy the imitation of his successor.

It must be cause of much delight to the real friends of that great man,—to those who supported his administration while in office, from a conviction of its wisdom and its virtue, to hear the unqualified praise which is now bestowed on it, by those who had been supposed to possess different opinions. If the measure now under consideration, shall be found, on examination, to be the same in principle, with that which has been cited, by its opponents, as a fit precedent for it, then may the friends of the gentleman now in office indulge the hope, that when he, like his predecessor, shall be no more, his conduct too may be quoted as an example for the government of his successors.

The evidence relied on to prove the opinion of the then executive on the case, consists of two letters from the Secretary of State, the one of the 29th of June 1793 to Mr. Genet, and the other of the 16th of August 1793 to Mr. Morris.

In the letter to Mr. Genet, the Secretary says, that the claimant having filed his libel against the ship William, in the court of Admiralty, there was no power which could take the vessel out of court, until it had decided against its own jurisdiction, that having so decided, the complaint is lodged with the executive, and he asks for evidence to enable that department to consider and decide finally on the subject.

It will be difficult to find in this letter an executive opinion, that the case was not a case for executive decision. The contrary is clearly avowed. It is true that when an individual claiming the property as his, had asserted that claim in a court, the executive acknowledges in itself a want of power, to dismiss or decide upon the claim thus pending in court. But this argues no opinion of a want of power in itself to decide upon the case, if instead of being carried before a court as an individual claim, it is brought before the executive as a national demand. A private suit instituted by an individual, asserting his claim to property, can only be controled by that individual. The executive can give no direction concerning it. But a public prosecution carried on in the name of the United States, can without impropriety be dismissed at the will of the government. The opinion therefore given in this letter is unquestionably correct, but it is certainly misunderstood when it is considered as being an opinion that the question was not, in its nature, a question for executive decision.

In the letter to Mr. Morris the secretary asserts the principle, that vessels taken within our jurisdiction ought to be restored; but says it is yet unsettled whether the act of restoration is to be performed by the executive or judicial department.

The principle then according to this letter is not submitted to the courts, whether a vessel captured within a given distance of the American coast was or was not captured within the jurisdiction of the United States, was a question not to be determined by the courts, but by the executive. The doubt expressed is, not what tribunal shall settle the principle, but what tribunal shall settle the fact. In this respect a doubt might exist in the case of prizes, which could not exist in the case of a man. Individuals on each side claimed the property, and therefore their rights could be brought into court, and there contested as a case in law or equity. The demand of a man made by a nation stands on different principles.

Having noticed the particular letters cited by the gentleman from New-York, permit me now said Mr. Marshall to ask the attention of the house to the whole course of executive conduct on this interesting subject.

It is first mentioned in a letter from the secretary of state to Mr. Genet of the 25th of June 1793. In that letter, the secretary states a consultation between himself and the secretaries of the treasury and war, (the President being absent) in which (so well were they assured of the President's way of thinking in those cases) it was determined, that the vessels should be detained in the custody of the consuls in the ports, "until the government of the United States shall be able to *enquire into and decide on the fact.*"

In his letter of 12th of July 1793 the secretary writes that the President has determined to *refer* the questions concerning prizes "to *persons learned in the laws.*" And he requests that certain vessels enumerated in the letter should not depart "until *his* ultimate determination shall be made known."

In his letter of the 7th of August 1793, the Secretary informs Mr. Genet that the President considers the U. States as bound to "*to effectuate the restoration of*, or to make compensation for, prizes which shall have been made of any of the parties at war with France, subsequent to the 5th day of June last, by privateers fitted out of our ports." That it is consequently expected that Mr. Genet will cause restitution of such prizes, to be made. And that the United States "will cause restitution" to be made "of all such prizes as shall be hereafter brought within their ports by any of the said privateers."

In his letter of the 10th of November 1793 the Secretary informs Mr. Genet, that, for the purpose of obtaining testimony to ascertain the fact of capture within the jurisdiction of the United States, the Governors of the several states were requested on receiving any such claim, immediately to notify thereof the Attornies of their several districts; whose duty it would be to give notice "to the principal agent of both parties and also to the consuls of the nations interested, and to recommend to them, to appoint by mutual consent, arbiters to decide whether the capture was made within the jurisdiction of the United States as stated in my letter of the 8th. inst. according to whose award the Governor may proceed to deliver the vessel to the one or the other party." If either party refuses to name arbiters then the attorney is to take depositions on notice, which "he is to transmit for the *information and decision of the President*." "This prompt procedure is the more to be insisted on, as it will enable the President, *by an immediate delivery* of the vessel and cargo to the party having title, to prevent the injuries consequent on long delay."

In his letter of the twenty-second of Nov. 1793 the Secretary repeats, in substance, his letter of the 12th of July and 7th of August, and says that the determination to deliver up certain vessels, involved the brig Jane of Dublin, the brig Lovley Lass, and the brig Prince William Henry. He concludes with saying, "I have it in charge to enquire of you, sir, whether these three brigs have been given up, according to the *determination of the President*, and if they have not to repeat the requisition that they be given up to their former owners."

Ultimately it was settled that the fact should be investigated in the courts, but the decision was regulated by the principles established by the executive department.

The decision then on the case of vessels captured within the

American jurisdiction, by privateers fitted out of the American ports, which the gentleman from New-York has cited with such merited approbation; and which he has declared to stand on the same principles, with those which ought to have governed, in the case of Thomas Nash; which deserves the more respect, because the government of the United States was then so circumstanced as to assure us, that no opinion was lightly taken up, and no resolution formed but on mature consideration. This decision quoted as a precedent and pronounced to be right, is found, on fair and full examination, to be precisely and unequivocally the same, with that which was made in the case under consideration. It is a full authority to show, that, in the opinion always held by the American government, a case like that of Thomas Nash, is a case for Executive and not judicial decision.

The clause in the constitution which declares that "the trial of all crimes, except in cases of impeachment, shall be by jury," has also been relied on as operating on the case, and transferring the decision on a demand for the delivery of an individual, from the executive to the judicial department.

But certainly this clause in the constitution of the United States cannot be thought obligatory on, and for the benefit of, the whole world. It is not designed to secure the rights of the people of Europe and Asia, or to direct and controul proceedings against criminals throughout the universe. It, can then, be designed only, to guide the proceedings of our own courts, and to prescribe the mode of punishing offences committed against the government of the United States, and to which the jurisdiction of the nation may rightfully extend.

It has already been shown that the courts of the United States were incapable of trying the crime for which Thomas Nash was delivered up to justice, the question to be determined was not how his crime should be tried and punished but whether he should be delivered up to a foreign tribunal which was alone capable of trying and punishing him. A provision for the trial of crimes in the courts of the United States is clearly not a provision for the performance of a national compact, for the surrender to a foreign government of an offender against that government.

The clause of the constitution declaring that the trial of all

crimes shall be by jury, has never even been construed to extend to the trial of crimes committed in the land and naval
forces of the United. States. Had such a construction prevailed,
it would most probably have prostrated the constitution itself,
with the liberties and the independence of the nation, before
the first disciplined invader who should approach our shores.
Necessity would have imperiously demanded the review and
amendment of so unwise a provision. If then this clause does
not extend to offences committed in the fleets and armies of
the United States, how can it be construed to extend to offences
committed in the fleets and armies of Britain or of France, of
the Ottoman or Russian empires?

The same argument applies to the observations on the 7th
article of the amendments to the constitution. That article relates only to trials in the courts of the United States, and not
to the performance of a contract for the delivery of a murderer
not triable in those courts.

In this part of the argument, the gentleman from New-York
has presented a dilemma of a very wonderful structure indeed.
He says that the offence of Thomas Nash was either a crime or
not a crime. If it was a crime, the constitutional mode of punishment ought to have been observed—if it was not a crime,
he ought not to have been delivered up to a foreign government, where his punishment was inevitable.

It had escaped the observation of that gentleman, that if the
murder committed by Thomas Nash was a crime, yet it was
not a crime provided for by the constitution, or triable in the
courts of the United States: And that if it was not a crime, yet
it is the precise case in which his surrender was stipulated by
treaty. Of this extraordinary dilemma then, the gentleman
from New-York is, himself, perfectly at liberty, to retain either
form.

He has chosen to consider it as a crime, and says it has been
made a crime by treaty, and is punished by sending the offender out of the country.

The gentleman is incorrect in every part of his statement.
Murder on board a British frigate, is not a crime created by
treaty. It would have been a crime of precisely the same magnitude, had the treaty never been formed. It is not punished by
sending the offender out of the United States. The experience

of this unfortunate criminal, who was hung and gibbeted, evinced to him, that the punishment of his crime was of a much more serious nature, than mere banishment from the United States.

The gentleman from Pennsylvania and the gentleman from Virginia have both contended, that this was a case proper for the decision of the courts, because points of law occurred, and points of law must have been decided, in its determination.

The points of law which must have been decided, are stated by the Gentleman from Pennsylvania to be, first, a question whether the offence was committed within the British jurisdiction; and, secondly, whether the crime charged was comprehended within the treaty.

It is true, sir, these points of law must have occurred, and must have been decided: but it by no means follows that they could only have been decided in court. A variety of legal questions must present themselves in the performance of every part of executive duty, but these questions are not therefore to be decided in court. Whether a patent for land shall issue or not, is always a question of law, but not a question which must necessarily be carried into court. The gentleman from Pennsylvania seems to have permitted himself to have been misled, by the misrepresentation of the constitution, made in the resolutions of the gentleman from New York: and, in consequence of being so misled, his observations have the appearance of endeavouring to fit the constitution to his arguments, instead of adapting his argument to the constitution.

When the gentleman has proved that these are questions of law, and that they must have been decided by the President, he has not advanced a single step towards proving, that they were improper for executive decision. The question whether vessels captured within three miles of the American coast, or by privateers fitted out in the American ports, were legally captured or not, and whether the American government was bound to restore them if in its power, were questions of law, but they were questions of political law, proper to be decided and they were decided by the executive and not by the courts.

The casus foederis of the guaranty was a question of law but no man would have hazarded the opinion; that such a question must be carried into court, and can only be there decided.

So the casus foederis under the 27th article of the treaty with Britain is a question of law, but of political law. The question to be decided is whether the particular case proposed be one, in which the nation has bound itself to act, and this is a question depending on principles never submitted to courts.

If a murder should be committed within the United States, and the murderer should seek an asylum in Britain, the question whether the casus foederis of the 27th article had occurred, so that his delivery ought to be demanded, would be a question of law, but no man would say it was a question which ought to be decided in the courts.

When therefore the gentleman from Pennsylvania has established, that in delivering up Thomas Nash, points of law were decided by the President, he has established a position, which in no degree whatever, aids his argument.

The case was in its nature a national demand made upon the nation. The parties were the two nations. They cannot come into court to litigate their claims, nor can a court decide on them. Of consequence the demand is not a case for judicial cognizance.

The President is the sole organ of the nation in its external relations, and its sole representative with foreign nations. Of consequence the demand of a foreign nation can only be made on him.

He possesses the whole executive power. He holds and directs the force of the nation. Of consequence any act to be performed by the force of a nation, is to be performed through him.

He is charged to execute the laws. A treaty is declared to be a law. He must then execute a treaty, where he and he alone possesses the means of executing it.

The treaty which is a law enjoins the performance of a particular object. The person who is to perform this object is marked out by the constitution, since the person is named who conducts the foreign intercourse, and is to take care that the laws be faithfully executed. The means by which it is to be performed —the force of the nation, are in the hands of this person. Ought not the person to perform the object, altho' the particular mode of using the means, has not been prescribed? Congress unquestionably may prescribe the mode; and Congress may devolve on others the whole execution of the contract: but till this be done, it seems the duty of the executive department to execute the contract, by any means it possesses.

The gentleman from Pennsylvania contends that, altho' this should be properly an executive duty, yet it cannot be performed until Congress shall direct the mode of performance. He says that altho' the jurisdiction of the courts is extended by the Constitution, to all cases of admiralty and maritime jurisdiction, yet if the courts had been created without any express assignment of jurisdiction, they could not have taken cognizance of causes expressly allotted to them by the constitution. The executive he says can no more than courts,—supply a legislative omission.

It is not admitted that in the case stated courts could not have taken jurisdiction. The contrary is believed to be the correct opinion. And, altho' the executive cannot supply a total legislative omission, yet it is not admitted or believed that there is such a total omission in this case.

The treaty stipulating that a murderer shall be delivered up to justice, is as obligatory as an act of Congress making the same declaration. If then there was an act of Congress in the words of the treaty, declaring that a person who had committed murder within the jurisdiction of Britain, and sought an assylum within the territory of the United States, should be delivered up by the United States, on the demand of his Britannic Majesty, and such evidence of his criminalty, as would have justified his commitment for trial, had the offence been here committed; could the President who is bound to execute the laws have justified a refusal to deliver up the criminal, by saying that the legislature had totally omitted to provide for the case?

The executive is not only the constitutional department, but seems to be the proper department, to which the power in question may most wisely and most safely be confided.

The department which is entrusted with the whole foreign intercourse of the nation, with the negotiation of all its treaties, with the power of demanding a reciprocal performance of the article, which is accountable to the nation for the violation of its engagements, with foreign nations, and for the consequences resulting from such violation, seems the proper department, to be entrusted with the execution of a national contract, like that under consideration.

If at any time policy may temper the strict execution of the contract, where may that political discretion be placed so safely, as in the department, whose duty it is to understand precisely, the state of the political intercourse and connection between the United States and foreign nations; to understand the manner in which the particular stipulation is explained and performed by foreign nations; and to understand completely the state of the union?

This department too, independent of judicial aid which may, perhaps, in some instances be called in, is furnished with a great law officer, whose duty it is to understand and to advise, when the casus foederis occurs. And if the President should cause to be arrested under the treaty, an individual who was so circumstanced, as not to be properly the object of such an arrest, he may perhaps bring the question of the legality of his arrest, before a Judge by a writ of habeas corpus.

It is then demonstrated, that according to the practice, and according to the principles of the American government, the question whether the nation has or has not bound itself to deliver up any individual, charged with having committed murder or forgery within the jurisdiction of Britain, is a question the power to decide which, rests alone with the executive department.

It remains to enquire, whether in exercising this power, and in performing the duty it enjoins, the President has committed an unauthorized and dangerous interference with judicial decisions.

That Thomas Nash was committed originally, at the instance of the British consul at Charleston, not for trial in the American courts, but for the purpose of being delivered up to justice in conformity with the treaty, between the two nations, has been already so ably argued by the gentleman from Delaware, that nothing further can be added to that point. He would therefore, Mr. Marshall said, consider the case as if Nash, instead of having been committed for the purposes of the treaty, had been committed for trial. Admitting even this to have been the fact, the conclusions which have been drawn from it were by no means warranted.

Gentlemen had considered it as an offence against judicial authority, and a violation of judicial rights, to withdraw from their sentence a criminal against whom a prosecution had been commenced. They had treated the subject, as if it was the privilege of courts, to condemn to death, the guilty wretch arraigned at their bar, and that to intercept the judgement was to violate the privilege. Nothing can be more incorrect than this view of the case. It is not the privilege, it is the sad duty of courts to administer criminal justice. It is a duty to be performed at the demand of the nation, and with which the nation has a right to dispense. If judgment of death is to be pronounced, it must be at the prosecution of the nation, and the nation may at will stop that prosecution. In this respect the President expresses constitutionally the will of the nation, and may rightfully as was done in the case at Trenton, enter a nolle prosequi, or direct that the criminal be prosecuted no further. This is no interference with judicial decisions, nor any invasion of the province of a court. It is the exercise of an indubitable and a constitutional power. Had the President directed the judge at Charleston to decide for or against his own jurisdiction—to condemn or acquit the prisoner—this would have been a dangerous interference with judicial decisions and ought to have been resisted.

But no such direction has been given, nor any such decision been required. If the President determined that Thomas Nash ought to have been delivered up to the British government, for a murder committed on board a British frigate, provided evidence of the fact was adduced; it was a question which duty obliged him to determine, and which he determined rightly. If in consequence of this determination he arrested the proceedings of a court on a national prosecution, he had a right to arrest and to stop them, and the exercise of this right was a necessary consequence of the determination of the principal question. In conforming to this decision, the court has left open the question of its jurisdiction. Should another prosecution of the same sort be commenced, which should not be suspended but continued by the executive, the case of Thomas Nash would not bind as a precedent against the jurisdiction of the court. If it should even prove that, in the opinion of the executive, a murder committed on board a foreign fleet was not within the jurisdiction of the court, it would prove nothing more: and though this opinion might rightfully induce the executive to exercise its power over the prosecution, yet if the prosecution was continued, it could have no influence with the court in deciding on its jurisdiction.

Taking the fact then even to be, as the gentlemen in support of the resolutions would state it, the fact cannot avail them.

It is to be remembered too, that in the case stated to the President, the judge himself appears to have considered it as proper for executive decision, and to have wished that decision. The President and judge seem to have entertained, on this subject, the same opinion: and in consequence of the opinion of the judge, the application was made to the President.

It has then been demonstrated.

1st.   That the case of Thomas Nash, as stated to the President, was compleatly within the 27th article of the treaty between the United States of America and Great Britain.

2ly   That this question was proper for executive and not for judicial decision, and

3dly   That, in deciding it, the President is not chargeable with an interference with judicial decisions.

After trespassing so long Mr. Marshall said on the patience of the house, in arguing what had appeared to him to be the material points growing out of the resolutions, he regretted the necessity of detaining them still longer, for the purpose of noticing an observation, which appeared not to be considered, by the gentleman who made it, as belonging to the argument.

The subject introduced by this observation however was so calculated to interest the public feelings, that he must be excused for stating his opinion on it.

The gentleman from Pennsylvania had said, that an impressed American seaman, who should commit homicide for the purpose of liberating himself from the vessel in which he was confined, ought not to be given up as a murderer. In this, Mr. Marshall said, he concurred entirely with that gentleman. He believed the opinion to be unquestionably correct,—as were the reasons that gentleman had given in support of it. He had never heard any American avow a contrary sentiment, nor did he believe a contrary sentiment could find a place in the bosom of any American. He could not pretend, and did not pretend, to know the opinions of the executive on the subject, because he had never heard the opinions of that department, but he felt the most perfect conviction, founded on the general conduct of the government, that it could never surrender an impressed American to the nation, which, in making the impressment, had committed a national injury.

This belief was in no degree shaken, by the conduct of the executive in this particular case.

In his own mind it was a sufficient defence of the President, from an imputation of this kind, that the fact of Thomas Nash being an impressed American, was obviously not contemplated by him in the decision he made on the principles of the case. Consequently if a new circumstance occured, which would essentially change the case decided by the President, the judge ought not to have acted under that decision, but the new circumstance ought to have been stated. Satisfactory as this defence might appear, he should not resort to it, because to some it might seem a subterfuge. He defended the conduct of the President on other, and still stronger ground.

The President had decided that a *murder* committed on board a British frigate on the high seas, was within the jurisdiction of that nation, and consequently within the 27th. article of its treaty with the United States. He therefore directed Thomas Nash to be delivered to the British minister, if satisfactory evidence of the *murder* should be adduced. The sufficiency of the evidence was submitted entirely to the judge. If Thomas Nash had committed a murder, the decision was that he should be surrendered to the British minister, if he had not committed a murder, he was not to be surrendered.

Had Thomas Nash been an impressed American, the homicide on board the Hermoine, would, most certainly, not have been murder.

The act of impressing an American is an act of lawless violence. The confinement on board a vessel is a continuation of that violence, and an additional outrage. Death committed within the United States, in resisting such violence, would not have been murder, and the person giving the wound could not have been treated as a murderer. Thomas Nash was only to have been delivered up to justice on such evidence as, had the fact been committed within the United States, would have been sufficient to have induced his commitment and trial for murder. Of consequence the decision of the President was so expressed, as to exclude the case of an impressed American liberating himself by homicide.

He concluded with observing that he had already too long availed himself of the indulgence of the House, to venture further on that indulgence, by recapitulating, or reinforcing the arguments which had already been urged.

March 7, 1800

NEGOTIATIONS WITH GREAT BRITAIN

To Rufus King

No. 2
Dear Sir,   Washington, August 23, 1800

Your letter stating your negotiations with Lord Grenville respecting the differences which have arisen in executing the 6 Article of our treaty of Amity, Commerce and Navigation with Great Britain, have been laid before and considered by the President.

He still retains the opinion that an amicable explanation of that Article is greatly to be desired, and therefore receives with much regret the information, that the British cabinet is indisposed to enter on the discussion of this interesting subject.

He perceives with a concern not entirely unmixed with other sensations, that the secession of two commissioners from the Board lately sitting in Philadelphia has been attributed, not to its real cause, but to motives which in no instance have ever influenced the American Government.

That Government is, as it has ever been, sincerely desirous of executing, with perfect and scrupulous good faith, all its engagements with foreign Nations. This desire has contributed, not inconsiderably, to the solicitude it now manifests, for the explanatory articles you have been instructed to propose.

The efforts of the American commissioners to proceed and decide on particular cases, instead of laying down abstract principles believed to be untrue in themselves, ought to have rescued their government from suspicions so very unworthy, and so little merited by the general tenor of its conduct.

The resolutions maintained by a majority of the late Board of commissioners, are such as the government of the United States can never submit to. They are considered, not as constructive of an existing treaty, but as imposing new and injurious burthens, unwarranted by compact, and to which, if in the first instance plainly and intelligibly stated, this government never could and never would have assented.

This opinion is not lightly taken up. It is a deep and solemn conviction produced by the most mature and temperate consideration we are capable of bestowing on the subject.

This being the fixed judgment of the United States, it is impossible not seriously to apprehend, unless we could forget the past, that no attempt by arbitration to adjust the claims of individuals under the 6 Article of the treaty, previous to an explanation of it by the two governments, can be successful. A second effort at this adjustment by the proposed modification of the Board, while the principles heretofore contended for, receive the countenance of the British Government, would most probably, unless indeed the Board should again be dissolved, subject us to the painful alternative, of paying money which, in our best judgment, the commissioners had no power to award, or of submitting the public faith to imputations from which it could only be freed by a correct and laborious investigation of the subject. In a situation presenting to us only such an alternative, we are extremely unwilling to be placed.

It is then very seriously desired, that the explanations required by this Government, should be made. They are believed to be so reasonable in themselves, and to be so unquestionably in the spirit, and to the full extent to the existing treaty, that it is hoped the difficulties on the part of the British cabinet may yet be removed.

The President therefore requests that you will take any proper occasion, should one in your judgment present itself, to renew your application to Lord Grenville on this subject. Perhaps a change of temper may be produced by a change of circumstances, and there may be a state of things in which you may perceive a disposition favourable to the accomplishment of an object which ought to be desired by both nations, because it is just in itself, and because it will remove a subject of controversy which may, in the course of events, have a very unhappy influence on that good understanding and friendly intercourse, which it is the interest of both to preserve.

The note of the 18 of April addressed to you by Lord Grenville, stating the determination of the British cabinet, not to modify, but to reject without discussion, the explanatory Articles proposed by you, on the part of the United States, assumes as the base of its decision, a principle not only so different from those admitted by this government, but so different from those recognized by both Nations in the Treaty of Amity negotiated between them, and which ought therefore to be adhered to in all explanations of that treaty, as to warrant a hope, that the determination announced in that note, may not be unalterable.

His Lordship assumes as a fact that "the 4th Article of the treaty of Peace not having been duly executed on the part of the United States, the British Government withheld the delivery of the forts on the frontier of Canada, in order that these might serve as a pledge for the interests and rights secured to the British creditors under that Article."

But this is a fact which the American Government has ever controverted, and which has never yet been established.

Without entering into the always unavailing and now improper discussion of the question—which Nation committed the first fault?—it ought never to be forgotten that the treaty in which the claim of the British creditors on the United States originated, was avowedly entered into for the purpose of terminating the differences between the two Nations, "in such manner as, without reference to the merits of their respective complaints and pretensions, may be the best calculated to produce mutual satisfaction and good understanding."

In questions growing out of such a treaty neither nation can be permitted to refer to and decide the merits of those respective complaints and pretensions, by asserting that the other, and not itself has committed the first fault.

Lord Grenville then proceeds on the idea that the commissioners appointed by the American Government have withdrawn from the Board, merely because awards were rendered against their opinion, and on claims which they believed to be unjust.

But this idea is neither warranted by the conduct or declarations of the American Commissioners or of the government which appointed them. It has been and still is expressly disavowed. The commissioners and their government acquiesced under opinions which they conscientiously believed to be formed on erroneous principles, but on principles submitted by the treaty to their decision. Awards conforming to such opinions, unless by mutual consent the subject shall assume some other form, will be paid by the United States. It was not until a majority of the Board had proceeded to establish a system of rules for the government of their future decisions, which, in the opinion of this government, clearly comprehended a vast mass of cases never submitted to their consideration; that it was deemed necessary to terminate proceedings believed to be totally unauthorized, and which were conducted in terms and in a spirit, only calculated to destroy all harmony between the two Nations.

We understand the treaty differently from what Lord Grenville would seem to understand it, when he says that the decision of the Board constituted according to the provisions of that instrument "was expressly declared to be, in all cases, final and conclusive."

These terms have never been understood by us as authorizing the Arbiters to go out of the special cases described in the instrument creating and limiting their powers. The words "all cases" can only mean those cases which the two nations have submitted to reference. These are described in the preceding part of the Article, and this description is relied on by the United States, as constituting a boundary, within which alone the powers of the commissioners can be exercised. This boundary has, in our judgment, been so totally prostrated, that scarcely a trace of it remains. The reasoning on which we have formed this judgment, it would be unnecessary to detail to you, because you are in perfect possession of it.

Believing the British cabinet disposed to act justly and Honorably in a case, in which we conceive their reputation as well as ours to be concerned, we have been confident in the opinion, that to obtain their serious attention to the subjects of differences between the two Nations, was to secure the establishment of that reasonable and *liberal* construction of the Article, for which America has contended. We shall abandon this opinion with reluctance and regret.

Altho' the President decidedly prefers the amicable explanations which have been suggested, to any other mode of adjusting the differences which have arisen in executing the 6th. Article of our treaty with Great Britain, yet it is by no means the only mode to which he is willing to resort. He does not even require that you shall press this proposition in a manner which in your judgment may lessen the probability of settling existing differences, or further than may comport with the interests of the United States. Your situation—your full and near view of all the circumstances which can influence the negotiation, enable you to decide, more certainly than can be done on this side the Atlantic, on the precise course which it may be most advantageous to pursue. To your discretion therefore the President entirely submits this part of the subject.

If the explanatory Article so much desired by the United States be attainable, the substitution of a gross sum, in full compensation of all claims made or to be made on this goverment, under the 6th Article of our treaty of Amity, Commerce and Navigation with his Britannic Majesty, is deemed the most eligible remaining mode of accommodating those differences which have impeded the execution of that Article.

It is apparent that much difficulty will arise in agreeing on the sum which shall be received as compensation. The ideas of the two governments on this subject appear so different, that, without reciprocal sacrifices of opinion, it is probable they will be as far from agreeing on the sum which ought to be received, as on the merits of the claims for which it will be paid. This difficulty is perhaps increased by the extravagant claims which the British Creditors have been induced to file. Among them are cases believed to be so notoriously unfounded, that no commissioners retaining the slightest degree of self respect, can establish them. There are many others where the debtors are as competent to pay as any inhabitants of the United States. And there are others where the debt has been fairly and voluntarily compromised by agreement between creditor and debtor.

There are even cases where the money has been paid in specie and receipts in full given. I do not mention their distinct classes, as comprehending all the cases of claims filed, which can never be allowed, but as examples of the materials which compose that enormous mass of imagined debt, which may by its unexamined bulk obstruct a just and equitable settlement of the well founded claims which really exist.

The creditors are now proceeding, and, had they not been seduced into the opinion that the trouble and expense inseparable from the pursuit of old debts might be avoided by one general resort to the United States, it is believed they would have been still more rapidly proceeding in the collection of the very claims, so far as they are just, which have been filed with the commissioners. They meet with no obstructions either of law or fact which are not common to every description of creditors, in every country, unless the difficulty with respect to interest during the War, may be so denominated. Our judges are even liberal in their construction of the 4th Article of the treaty of Peace, and are believed in questions growing out of that treaty, to have manifested no sort of partiality for the debtors. Indeed it is believed that, with the exception of the contested Article of war interest, and possibly of claims barred by the Act of limitations during the War, the United States are justly chargeable with the debts of only such of their citizens, as have become insolvent subsequent to the peace, and previous to the establishment of the Federal Courts. This opinion is founded on a conviction that our Judges give to the 4th Article of the Treaty of Peace, a construction as extensive as ought to be given to it by commissioners appointed under the 6 Article of the Treaty of Amity, commerce & Navigation.

Those who have attended most to this subject are of opinion, that the sum which might properly be awarded against the United States, would fall far short of any estimate which has probably been made of it in England, or by the British creditors or agents in this Country. We are however sensible that commissioners acting within their powers may extend the sum further than justice or a fair construction of the Article would extend it, and we have been taught to apprehend a construction of which, at the ratification of the Treaty, no fear was entertained. From this persuasion and from a solicitude to perform what even rigid and unfavourable Judges may suppose to be injoined by good faith, the interests of the United States may require, and the President is therefore willing that the agreement should not be strictly limited by the sum for which in our own opinion we ought to be liable. He will be satisfied with *four million of Dollars*. He will not consent to exceed *One Million* sterling.

If a gross sum in satisfaction of all other claims be accepted, you will of course stipulate for the lowest possible sum, and for the most favourable instalments which may be attainable.

Should it be found impossible to negotiate reasonable explanatory articles, or to agree on a sum to be received as compensation for the claims of the creditors, much doubt is entertained concerning the proposition for new modeling the Board as proposed by the British Minister. While the government itself professes to approve the conduct of its late commissioners, much fear is entertained that their successors may bring with them, those extravagant and totally inadmissible opinions which have dissolved the past, and will most probably dissolve any future Board. Before the United States proceed to take a new step in a case where experience has done so much to teach them caution, some assurances of the temper in which the commissioners to be appointed will meet, ought to be received. And yet we are not satisfied that good faith does not require that, notwithstanding the past, we should consent to make a second effort for the execution of the 6th. Article of the treaty in the forms it has prescribed.

On this part of the subject however the President has come to no determination. So soon as his decision shall have been made, it shall be communicated to you. With very much respect & Esteem, I am Dear Sir, your Obt. Servt.

ANTI-BRITISH SENTIMENT

To Rufus King

Private
Dear Sir   Washington, August 23, 1800
   I have just addressd to you a letter on the subject of the differences existing between the United States & Great Britain
respecting the execution of the 6th. article of our treaty with
that nation. There are some statements omited in that letter
which I deem it proper to make.
   The gentlemen concernd in the administration of our government who are best informd respecting the claims of British
creditors under the article in question, are of opinion that, on
a fair & honorable construction of that article, they woud not
exceed two milion, or at most two & a half milion of dollars.
My own estimate accords with theirs. On that however I do
not much rely, because I have not examind the particular cases
of demand for compensation which have been on the United
States. You will readily perceive what *a sacrafice we make for
the preservation of peace* & of *the* public *faith* shoud we *appease*
the existing differences *by the payment of* such a *sum as is
contemplated.*
   There are other considerations (but these are my own sug-
gestions & have not even been communicated to those with
whom I act) which lead to a decisive *preference* of the *explanatory articles* shoud they *be attainable.*
   A variety of causes among wh I am sorry to place the *continued impressments of our seamen & the unpunished depredations
on our commerce have combined* to increase considerably the *irritation of the public mind in Amer at the British Govt an
agreement to pay even a reasonable sum in gross* will be considerd & represented as a *disgraceful sacrafice with wh the Govt
have purchased the* continuance of a *humiliating* [   ] *peace.*
   Any attainable *Sum will exceed* the calculations made in
America & being a *new Step voluntarily taken* shoud be enterd
into with caution.
   These considerations will not & ought not to induce the
government of the United States to decline a measure of pub-

lic utility. But they increase & justly increase our preference for the explanatory articles shoud it be found practicable to obtain them.

We are just informd tho not officially or certainly, that our negotiations with France have terminated, not in a treaty. The difficulties which are stated to have prevented the success of this mission were considerable, yet I am strongly inclind to the opinion that the successes of Buonaparte in Italy, & *the Election of N Y* have contributed to its failure. This event in the existing state of things renders the situation of the United States delicate & critical. Their conduct I trust will not vacillate—but will continue to be firm & moderate.

Your number 77 is just receivd. I am dear Sir with very much respect & esteem, Your obedt. Servt

AMERICAN COMPLAINTS AGAINST BRITAIN

To Rufus King

No. 5

Dear Sir   Washington, September 20, 1800

It is the hope & expectation of the President that your negotiation with Lord Grenville, concerning contraband of war & the impressment of our seamen, which had progressd considerably, & been broken off in consequence, as is here understood, of the differences between the two nations respecting the construction of the 6th. article of their treaty of amity, commerce & navigation, has been, or will now be, renewd.

Shoud it have been intended to proceed pari passu with these subjects, yet your instructions respecting the claims of British creditors on the United States, having, as we hope, enabled you to place that business in a train for adjustment, we are sanguine in our expectations concerning the other objects of the negotiation.

Shoud you be unable to obtain—what is most desird because most just—explanatory articles placing the original treaty on its true ground, or even to settle this difference on the terms stated in my No. 2, terms of the liberality of which I am more

& more convinc'd, yet we perceive no reason growing out of this misunderstanding, which shoud obstruct the progress of an agreement on subjects, the present practice on which so seriously threatens the peace of the two nations.

The 7th. article of the treaty of amity, commerce, & navigation, corresponds with the 6th., & proceedings under both have been suspended. It is not my purpose to show that these two measures, viewd together, are injurious to the United States, because we do not complain, for the present, of the suspension, which has taken place, of the proceedings of the board lately siting in London. But certainly, as the one measure completely balances the other, this misunderstanding can furnish to the British government no plausible pretext, for taking other steps unfriendly in themselves, or for refusing to take such as justice & friendship indispensably require.

We trust then that, whatever may be the fate of the propositions respectively made, concerning the differences under the 6th. & 7th. articles of our late treaty, the negotiations relative to contraband & impressments will now progress, without further interuption, to a happy conclusion.

Shoud this hope be disappointed the practices of depredating on our commerce & impressing our seamen, demand & must receive the most serious attention of the United States.

The unfeignd solicitude of this government to preserve peace with all, & to obtain justice by friendly representations to the party commiting injuries, rather than by a resort to other means, induces it now to wish, that any misjudgement respecting its views & intentions, which may have been formd in the british cabinet, & which may have promoted dispositions unfavorable to that perfect harmony which it is the interest of both nations to cherish, may be completely corrected. For this the President has great & just reliance on you. If impressions of any sort have been made, impairing that conciliatory temper which enables one nation to view with candor the proceedings of another, the President hopes that your perfect knowledge of the principles which influence the government you represent, will enable you to meet & to remove them.

That such impressions have been made by connecting two measures entirely independent of each other is greatly suspected.

The secession of the American commissioners from the

board lately siting at Philadelphia, & the recommencement of negotiations with France, may have been united together as parts of one system, & been considerd as evidencing a temper less friendly to Great-Britain than had heretofore guided our councils.

You have been assurd that the suspension of further proceedings on the claims of british creditors against the United States, is attributable, exclusively, to the wild, extensive, & unreasonable construction put, by the commissioners of that nation, on the article they were appointed to execute; a construction which, as we think, at once prostrated the words & spirit of the article, & overleapd all those bounds, within which, by common consent, their powers were limited. You know too well the integrity of this government to doubt the sincerity with which this opinion is avowd, & you possess too perfectly the reasoning on which it has been formd, to feel any difficulty in supporting it. In fact we beleive that the points of difference need only be considerd, to produce in every inteligent mind the conviction, that the American government is, at least, sincere in the opinion it has maintaind.

Being entirely persuaded of the vast injury & injustice which woud result from executing the 6th. article according to the strange system devisd by a majority of the commissioners, a sense of duty & of national honor, as well as a wish to preserve a solid & lasting peace between the two countries, renderd indispensable the step which has been taken. Had the United States been at open & declard war with France, without a prospect of speedy pacification, the same causes must have inducd the same measure.

The suspension then of the commission at Philadelphia was not influencd by the probability of negotiating with France, nor have these two measures any tendency to explain each other.

It is equally true that neither of them proceeds from a temper in the United States hostile to, or even indifferent about a good understanding with, the british government.

The one has been shown to be a necessary measure of defence against, what was beleivd to be, an unauthorizd attack on the interests of the United States, which, it was conceivd, the british government woud not have sanctiond. The other is a necessary consequence of the well digested political system which this government adopted early in the present war, & has uniformly sought to maintain.

The United States do not hold themselves, in any degree, responsible to France or to Britain, for their negotiations with the one or the other of those powers. But they are ready to make amicable & reasonable explanations with either.

In this spirit their political system may be reviewd.

It has been the object of the American government from the commencement of the present war, to preserve between the belligerent powers, an exact neutrality. Separated far from Europe, we mean not to mingle in their quarrels. This determination was early declard, & has never been changd. In pursuance of it we have avoided, & we shall continue to avoid, any political connections which might engage us further than is compatible with the neutrality we profess; and we have sought, by a conduct just & friendly to all, to be permited to maintain a position which, without offence to any, we had a right to take.

The aggressions, sometimes of one, & sometimes of another belligerent power, have forcd us to contemplate, & to prepare for, war, as a probable event. We have repeld, & we will continue to repel, injuries not doubtful in their nature, & hostility not to be misunderstood. But this is a situation of necessity, not of choice. It is one in which we are placd—not by our own acts—but by the acts of others; & which we change, so soon as the conduct of others will permit us to change it.

The regularly accumulating injuries sustaind from France had, in 1798, progressd to such a point, as to leave to the United States no reasonable ground of doubt, that war was to be expected, & that force & force only coud be relied on, for the maintenance of our rights as a sovereign & independent nation. Force therefore was resorted to: but in the very act of resorting to it our preference for peace was manifest, & it was apparent that we shoud return to our natural situation, so soon as the wrongs which forcd us from it shoud cease & security against their repetition be offerd. A reasonable hope that this state of things may be attaind, has been furnishd by the recent conduct & overtures of the french government. America meets these overtures, & in doing so, only adheres to her pacific system.

To impress more forcibly on the british cabinet the principles on which this government acts, it may not perhaps be improper, to point their attention to our conduct, during the
most critical periods of the present war.

In 1793, when the combination against France was most formidable, when, if ever, it was dangerous to acknowledge her
new government, & to preserve with it the relations of amity,
which, in a different state of things, had been formd with the
nation, the American government openly declard its determination to adhere to that state of impartial neutrality, which it
has ever since sought to maintain; nor did the clouds which,
for a time, lourd over the fortunes of the republic in any degree, shake this resolution.

When victory had changd sides, & France in turn threatend
those who did not arrange themselves under her banners,
America, pursuing, with undeviating step, the same steady
course, negotiated with his Britannic majesty, a treaty of amity,
commerce & navigation, nor coud either threats or artifices
prevent its ratification.

At no period of the war has France occupied such elevated
ground, as at the very point of time when America armd to resist her. Triumphant & victorious every where, she had dictated a peace to her enemies on the continent & had refusd
one to Britain.

In the reverse of her fortunes, when defeated both in Italy &
on the Rhine, in danger of losing Holland, before the victory
of Massena had changd the face of the last campaign, & before
Russia had receded from the coalition against her, the present
negotiation was resolvd on. During its pendency the state of
the war has changd, but the conduct of the United States sustains no alteration. Our terms remain the same. We still pursue
peace. We will embrace it if it can be obtaind without violating
our national honor or our national faith, but we will reject,
without hesitation, all propositions which may compromit the
one or the other.

I have thought it not entirely useless to notice thus briefly,
the relative situation of the belligerent powers, at the several eras
when important measures have been adopted by the American
government, because the review will mark, unequivocally, the

character of that government, & show how steadily it pursues its system, without regarding the dangers from the one side or the other, to which the pursuit may be exposd.

The present negotiation with France is a part of this system, & ought therefore to excite in Britain, no feeling unfriendly to the United States.

Perhaps the apprehension that an erroneous estimate may have been made in the british cabinet, of the views & intentions of this government, may be unfounded. If so, it will of course be unnecessary to attack prejudices which do not exist. If, however, such prejudices do exist, you will, by a plain & candid representation of the truth, endeavor to remove them.

The way being thus smoothd for the reception of our complaints, the peace & interests of the nation require, that they shoud be, temperately but very seriously, enforcd.

These complaints are occasiond by the conduct of the british government through its agents, towards our commerce & our seamen.

The depredations on our commerce have of late been so considerable, as even to give some countenance to the opinion, that orders have been receivd to capture every american vessel bound to an enemy port. It cannot be difficult for you to conjecture the effect of such a system.

In your correspondence with my predecessor I perceive that these subjects have been repeatedly taken up, & that, in your several representations to the ministers of his britannic majesty, you have done ample justice to your country.

I am directed by the President to express to you his wish that, unless this business be in a train for satisfactory adjustment, you once more call the very serious attention of the british government to the irritating & injurious vexations we sustain, & make one more solemn appeal to the justice, the honor, & the real interests of the nation.

Our complaints respecting the depredations on our commerce may be classd under the following heads.

1st.   The construction given to the article of our treaty relative to contraband of war.

2dly.   The extent given to the rule concerning blockaded ports.

3dly.   The unjust decisions of their courts of Vice Admiralty,

& the impunity which attends captures totally vexatious & without probable cause of siezure.

We will consider

1st. The interpretation given to the 18th. article of our treaty. Under the expression "and generally whatever may serve directly for the equipment of vessels" which closes the enumeration of prohibited articles, our merchant vessels have been siezd & condemnd, because a part of their cargoes consisted of such articles as may, by possibility, serve for the equipment of vessels, altho they are not generally so applied, but are most commonly usd for purposes of husbandry. Such are ticklenberg, oznaburgs, & small nails, which, in the courts of vice admiralty, have been adjudgd contraband of war.

This vexatious construction is beleivd to be as unjustifiable as it is unfriendly.

As the law of nations on this subject can only establish general principles, particular treaties supply this defect by defining, precisely, between the parties, the relative rights of each as a belligerent or neutral power.

Thus the law of nations is clearly understood to declare that articles exclusively usd in war, are contraband; & that all articles not usd in war are the objects of lawful commerce. But articles of promiscuous use, proper either for peace or war, may be, it has been contended, contraband or not, according to the circumstances.

Admiting this opinion to be correct, it woud seem to be a reasonable construction of the law, that the character of articles thus doubtful in themselves, shoud be determind by those circumstances which may ascertain the use to which they are to be applied. If the circumstances of the cargo & its destination show, unequivocally, that its application must be to military purposes, materials fit for both peace & war, may assume the character of contraband; but if those circumstances afford solid ground for the opinion that the suspected materials are designd only for the ordinary purposes of the nation, then there can be no just motive for interrupting a commerce which ought to be pronouncd lawful.

This principle woud seem to mark the boundaries of the conflicting rights of neutral & belligerent powers. For neutrals have a right to carry on their usual commerce & belligerents have a right to prevent them from supplying the enemy with instruments of war.

But in the application of the principle considerable difficulty exists. The two nations judge differently on the circumstances attending each case, & to prevent the quarrels which may grow out of this difference of judgement, a precise list of contraband is usually agreed on between them.

If however in the enumeration there can be an ambiguous expression, it ought to be expounded with a reference to those general principles, intended to have been renderd definite by the particular agreement, & the enquiry ought always to be made, whether the article was really designd for a prohibited object, or was transported for the ordinary purposes of commerce.

In the catalogue of contraband agreed on between the United States & Great Britain, there is one description which leaves to construction what specific articles it may comprehend. It is in the following words—"and generally whatever may serve *directly* to the equipment of vessels."

In construing this expression, the british courts of Vice Admiralty appear to consider it as including whatever might, by any possibility be applied to the equipment of vessels. Altho the article be in itself unfit & improper for that case, & therefore be not in common so applied, yet if it might by possibility, from a want of other proper materials, admit of such an application, the courts adjudge, altho such other materials be not wanting at the port of destination, that it is contraband of war.

This construction we deem alike unfriendly & unjust. We conceive that the expression which has been cited, comprehends only such articles, as in themselves are proper for, & in their ordinary use are applied to, "the equipment of vessels."

Under the british construction all operation is referrd to the word "directly." Expunge it from the sentence, and according to them, the sense will remain the same. But plain reason, & the soundest, & most universally admited rules of construction, forbid us to interpret by garbeling a compact. The word "directly" is an important word, which forms a necessary & essential part of the description, & must have been inserted for the purpose of having its due weight in ascertaining the sense of the article. We can discover no effect which is allowd to it, unless it be admited to limit the description to materials which in their ordinary use & common application are, in considerable quantities, proper for, or "serve directly to, the equipment of vessels." To exclude it, or to construe the article as if it was excluded, is to substitute another agreement for that of the parties.

We do not admit the expression we are considering to be in itself doubtful. But if it was so, rules of construction prescribd by reason, & adopted by common consent, seem to us, to reject the interpretation of the british courts.

As this contract is formd between a belligerent and neutral nation, it must have been designd to secure the rights of each, &, consequently, to protect that commerce which neutrals may lawfully carry on, as well as to authorize the seizure of articles which they may not lawfully carry to the enemy. But under the interpretation complaind of, not only articles of doubtful use with respect to the equipment of vessels, but such as are not proper for that purpose, or if proper only in very small quantities, & which therefore are not in common so applied, are, because they may by meer possibility admit of that application, classd with articles prohibited on the principle that they are for the purposes of war.

This construction ought to be rejected, because it woud swell the list of contraband to an extent which the laws & usages of nations do not authorize: it woud prohibit, as being for the equipment of vessels, articles plainly not destind for that purpose, but fited & necessary for, the ordinary occupations of men in peace: and it woud consequently presuppose a surrender on the part of the United States, of rights in themselves unquestionable, & the exercise of which is essential to themselves, & not injurious to Britain in the prosecution of the war in which she is engagd.

A construction so absurd & so odious ought to be rejected. The cases on which this reasoning is founded, have, many of them, been, already, stated to you, & they are, in some instances I beleive, now depending in the court of Admiralty in Great Britain.

In addition to the injury of condemning as contraband, goods which cannot properly, be so denominated, seizures & confiscations have been made in cases, where the condemnation even of contraband, coud not have been justified.

Articles of that description are, only, by the treaty declard to be "just objects of confiscation, whenever they are attempted to be carried to an enemy."

We conceive it certain that vessels bound to New Orleans & laden with cargoes proper for the ordinary use of the citizens of the United States who inhabit the Mississipi & its waters, cannot, meerly on account of the port to which they are bound, be justly said to carry those cargoes to an enemy.

By the treaty with Spain, New Orleans is made, for the present, a place of deposit for the merchandizes & effects of our citizens. Merchandizes designd for the consumption of those citizens who reside on the Mississipi or its waters, & which is to be transported up that river, will, in the present state of its commerce, be, almost universally, shipd for New Orleans. This port being by stipulation, & of necessity, common to the subjects of Spain, & to the citizens of the United States, the destination of the cargo can be no evidence of its being designd for an enemy, &, therefore, liable to confiscation when composd of articles that might be usd in war. In justice other testimony to this point out always to be receivd.

But the destination to New Orleans ought rather to exempt from confiscation articles of ordinary use but which may also serve to the equipment of vessels. It is well known not to be a port usually resorted to for that object. The Spaniards do not there build or equip vessels, nor has it ever been a depot for naval stores. When then a vessel bound for New Orleans, containing a cargo proper for the ordinary use of those citizens of the United States who are supplied through that port, & evidence that it is designd for them, shall be capturd, such cargo is not "a just object of confiscation" altho a part of it shoud also be deemd proper for "the equipment of vessels," because it is not "attempted to be carried to an enemy."

2dly.   The right to confiscate vessels bound to a blockaded port has been unreasonably extended to cases not coming within the rule as heretofore adopted.

On principle it might well be questiond, whether this rule can be applied to a place, not completely invested by land as well as by sea. If we examine the reasoning on which is founded the right to intercept & confiscate supplies designd for a blockaded town, it will be difficult to resist the conviction that its extension to towns invested by sea only, is an unjustifiable encroachment on the rights of neutrals. But it is not of this departure from principle—a departure which has receivd some sanction from practice—that we mean to complain. It is that ports not effectually blockaded by a force capable of completely investing them, have yet been declard in a state of blockade, & vessels attempting to enter them have been seizd, &, on that account, confiscated.

This is a vexation proceeding directly from the government, & which may be carried, if not resisted, to a very injurious extent. Our merchants have greatly complaind of it with respect to Cadiz & the ports of Holland.

If the effectiveness of the blockade be dispensd with, then every port of all the belligerent powers, may, at all times, be declard in that state, & the commerce of neutrals be, thereby, subjected to universal capture. But if this principle be strictly adherd to, the capacity to blockade will be limited by the naval force of the belligerent, &, of consequence, the mischief to neutral commerce cannot be very extensive. It is therefore of the last importance to neutrals that this principle be maintaind unimpaird.

I observe that you have pressd this reasoning on the british minister, who replies that an occasional absence of a fleet from a blockaded port, ought not to change the state of the place.

Whatever force this observation may be intitled to where that occasional absence has been producd by accident, as a storm which for a moment blows off the fleet & forces it from its station, which station it, immediately, resumes, I am persuaded that where a part of the fleet is applied, tho only for a time, to other objects, or comes into port, the very principle requiring an effective blockade, which is that the mischief can then only be coextensive with the naval force of the belligerent, requires that during such temporary absence, the commerce of neutrals to the place shoud be free.

The next subject of complaint is

3dly. The unjust decisions of their courts of admiralty, & the impunity which attends captures totally vexatious & without any probable cause.

No source has been more productive than this of injury to American commerce. From none are we to apprehend more serious mischief or more uncontrolable irritation.

It is not to be expected that all the commanders of national ships, much less that the commanders of privatiers, shoud be men of correct conduct & habits. The temptation which a rich neutral commerce offers to unprincipled avarice—at all times powerful—becomes irresistable, unless strong & efficient restraints be imposed by the government which employs it. It is the duty of the government to impose such restraints. Foreign friendly nations who do not exercise against such cruizers their means of self protection, have a right to expect & to demand it. The failure to impose them exposes the belligerent government to the just reproach, of causing the injuries it tolerates.

The most effectual restraint is an upright judiciary which will decide impartially between the parties, & uniformly condemn the captor in costs & damages, where the seizure has been made without probable cause. If this practice be not honestly & rigidly observd, there will exist no restraint on the captors. Their greediness for gain will be checkd by no fear of loss, & indiscriminate captures will, consequently, be made. If the vessel shoud be adjudgd good prize, of which before an unjust tribunal there is, in all cases, considerable probability, the profit is theirs; if the vessel even be acquited, the loss falls entirely on the capturd. The numerous depredations consequent on such a state of things are inevitable. The loss to the neutral merchant is immence. His voyage becomes not only unprofitable but injurious to him.

This is the state of things in the british possessions in America. Their courts of vice Admiralty, whatever may be the case, seldom acquit, & when they do, costs & damages for detention are never awarded.

We know well that Judges are appointed whose duty it is to award costs & damages for detention, instead of confiscation, in cases of vexatious seizure; but we know too the tenure by which they hold their offices, the source from which they derive their profits, & we know their practice. We can only attribute this practice to their government, for it has been notorious, has been of long continuance, & has never been checkd. It is not to be supposd that Judges circumstancd as are those of the courts of vice Admiralty, woud dare to pursue openly & invariably this vicious system, if it was known to be offensive to their government.

The existence of an appellate court does not remove the evil. The distance of that court, the expences & delays attendant on an appeal, the loss inseparable from a first condemnation tho it be afterwards reversd, render it a very inadequate remedy even in cases of unjust condemnation, & absolutely forbid any resort to it on a meer question of costs.

It is only by infusing a spirit of justice & respect for law into the courts of vice admiralty, that these excessive & irritating vexations can be restraind, & the imputations to which they subject the british government wipd away. This spirit can only be infusd by, uniformly discountenancing & punishing those who tarnish, alike, the seat of justice & the honor of their country, by converting themselves from Judges, into the meer instruments of plunder.

Until some such reform be made, the practices complaind of will continue, & must be considerd by foreign nations, as authorizd by, & proceeding from, the government which permits them.

The impressment of our seamen is an injury of very serious magnitude, which deeply affects the feelings & the honor of the nation.

This valuable class of men is composd of natives & foreigners who engage voluntarily in our service.

No right has been asserted to impress the natives of America. Yet they are impressd, they are dragd on board british ships of war with the evidence of citizenship in their hands, & forcd by violence there to serve, until conclusive testimonials of their birth can be obtaind. These must, most generally, be sought for on this side the Atlantic. In the mean time acknowledgd violence is practisd on a free citizen of the United States, by compeling him to engage, & to continue in, foreign service. Altho the Lords of the admiralty uniformly direct their discharge on the production of this testimony, yet many must perish unreleivd, & all are detaind a considerable time in lawless & injurious confinement.

It is the duty as well as the right of a friendly nation to require that measures be taken by the british government to prevent the continued repetition of such violence by its agents. This can only be done by punishing & frowning on those who perpetrate it. The meer release of the injurd, after a long course of service & of suffering, is no compensation for the past, & no security for the future. It is impossible not to beleive, that the decisive interference of the government in this respect, woud prevent a practice, the continuance of which must inevitably produce discord between two nations which ought to be the friends of each other.

Those seamen who, born in a foreign country have been adopted by this, were either the subjects of Britain or some other power.

The right to impress those who were british subjects has been asserted, & the right to impress those of every other nation has not been disclaimd.

Neither the one practice nor the other can be justified.

With the naturalization of foreigners, no other nation can interfere further, than the rights of that other are affected. The rights of Britain are certainly not affected by the naturalization of other than british subjects. Consequently those persons who, according to our laws, are citizens, must be so considerd by Britain, & by every other power not having a conflicting claim to the person.

The United States therefore require positively, that their seamen who are not british subjects, whether born in America or elsewhere, shall be exempt from impressments.

The case of british subjects, whether naturalizd or not, is more questionable; but the right even to impress them is denied. The practice of the british government itself, may, certainly in a controversy with that government, be relied on. The privileges it claims & exercises ought to be ceded to others. To deny this woud be to deny the equality of nations, & to make it a question of power & not of right.

If the practice of the british government may be quoted, that practice is to maintain & defend in their sea service, all those of any nation who have voluntarily engagd in it, or who, according to their laws, have become british subjects.

Alien seamen not british subjects, engagd in our merchant service, ought to be equally exempt with citizens, from impressment. We have a right to engage them, & have a right to,

& an interest in their persons, to the extent of the service contracted to be performd. Britain has no pretext of right to their persons or to their service. To tear them, then, from our possession is at the same time an insult & an injury. It is an act of violence for which there exists no palliative.

We know well that the difficulty of distinguishing between native Americans & British subjects, has been usd, with respect to natives, as an apology for the injuries complaind of. It is not pretended that this apology can be extended to the case of foreigners, & even with respect to natives we doubt the existence of the difficulty alledgd. We know well that among that class of people who are seamen, we can readily distinguish between a native American & a person raisd to manhood in Great Britain or Ireland; and we do not perceive any reason, why the capacity of making this distinction, shoud not be possessd in the same degree, by one nation as by the other.

If therefore no regulation can be formd which shall effectually secure all seamen on board american merchantmen, we have a right to expect from the justice of the british government, from its regard for the friendship of the United States & its own honor, that it will manifest the sincerity of its wishes to repress this offence, by punishing those who commit it.

We hope, however, that an agreement may be enterd into, satisfactory & beneficial to both parties. The article which appears to have been transmited by my predecessor, while it satisfies this country, will probably restore to the naval service of Britain, a greater number of seamen than will be lost by it. Shoud we ever be mistaken in this calculation, yet the difference cannot be put in competition with the mischief which may result from the irritation justly excited, by this practice, throughout the United States. The extent & the justice of the resentments it produces, may be estimated, in Britain, by enquiring what impressions woud be made on them by similar conduct on the part of this government.

Shoud we impress from the merchant service of Britain, not only Americans but foreigners, & even british subjects, how long woud such a course of injury unredressd, be permited to pass unrevengd? How long woud the government be content with unsuccessful remonstrance & unavailing memorials? I beleive, sir, that only the most prompt correction of, &

compensation for, the abuse, woud be admited as satisfaction in such a case.

If the principles of this government forbid it to retaliate by impressments, there is yet another mode which might be resorted to. We might authorize our ships of war, tho not to impress, yet to recruit, sailors on board british merchantmen. Such are the inducements to enter into our naval service, that we beleive even this practice woud, very seriously affect the navigation of Britain.

How, sir, woud it be receivd by the british nation?

Is it not more adviseable to desist from, & to take effectual measures to prevent, an acknowledgd wrong, than, by perseverance in that wrong, to excite against themselves the well founded resentments of America, & force our government into measures which may very possibly terminate in an open rupture?

As we are unacquainted with the present actual state of things in Europe, & the President has the most entire confidence in you, it is not his wish to injoin on you a representation to the ministers of his britannic Majesty, in the terms of this letter. It is only intended to convey to you the feelings & sentiments of the government & people of America, & to instruct you from the President himself, to call the very serious attention of the british government, in such terms of respect & earnestness as to yourself shall seem advisable, to the weighty subjects of complaint which have here been stated. With great & sincere respect & esteem, I am dear Sir your obedt. Servt.

"THE STRENGTH OF JACOBINISM"

To Richard Peters

Dear Sir   Washington, October 30, 1800
I thank you for the book which accompanied your letter of the 24th. inst.

I beleive with you that much of the strength of jacobinism is attributable to the direct tax—a snare which has been long set for the federalists & in which they have at length permited themselves to be taken. Yet that can not be considerd as the sole cause of the prevalence of opposition. Many others concur in effecting the work.

I do not however entirely despond. If the Legislature of Pennsylvania will elect by a concurrent vote our case is not absolutely desperate.

However the election may terminate good men ought still to continue their endeavors for the public happiness. I pray devoutly (which is no very common practice with me) that the future administration may do as little harm as the present & the past. Yours truely

PROSECUTIONS UNDER THE SEDITION ACT

To St. George Tucker

Dear Sir   Washington Novr. 18th. 1800

I receivd with much pleasure yours of the 6th. inst. I wish with all my soul that those with whom I have been formerly in habits of friendship, woud like you, permit me to retain for them that esteem which was once reciprocal. No man regrets more than I do, that intolerant & persecuting spirit which allows of no worth out of its own pale, & breaks off all social intercourse as a penalty on an honest avowal of honest opinions.

Fennos attack on Mr. Adams I never saw & that of Genl. Hamilton I wish for his sake had never been seen by any person. I have no doubt that it wounds & irritates the person at whom it is directed infinitely more than the Prospect before us, because its author is worthy of attention & his shaft may stick. Whether it is as properly the subject of judicial enquiry is a question on which I have no opinion because I have only given it one hasty reading & that not with a view to such an object. Be this as it may the proceeding, or omiting to proceed against him, can make no impression respecting the character of the executive because that is a subject over which the President exercises no control. The laws are made, & those who violate them are prosecuted by the proper officer without the knowledge or direction of the President. With respect to

Mr. Callendar I am mistaken if you & all the world, so far as the circumstances of the case are known, do not concur in the opinion, that nothing can render him an improper object for the punishment of the law but his being below its resentment. On that principle & on that only coud he I think, with any sort of propriety, be recommended for mercy. On that account my own private judgement woud have been against his being prosecuted, but I am not quite sure that it is a sufficient reason for interposing & arresting the course of the law. However this may be I do not think Mr. Adams woud take any step in the case while the election is uncertain. These acts are so often attributed to other than the real motives, that unless there were stronger reasons for them than exist at present, it woud not be adviseable to do any thing til the choice of future President shall be over.

The unconstitutionality of the law, cannot be urgd to the President because he does not think it so. His firm beleif is that it is warranted by the constitution. This opinion is confirmd by the judgement of the courts & is supported by as wise & virtuous men as any in the Union. Of consequence whatever doubts some of us may entertain, he who entertains none, woud not be & ought not to be influencd by that argument.

There will be a house of representatives to day. I beleive confidently that an accomodation has taken place with France tho we have as yet no official account of it. I think it is time for peace to be universal. I am dear Sir with much esteem & regard, yours &c.

THE CONSTITUTION AND THE COMMON LAW

To St. George Tucker

Dear Sir   Washington Novr. 27th. 1800
I had the pleasure a few days past of receiving a pamphlet written by you on the question how far the common law is the law of the United States for which I thank you. I have read it with attention, & you will perhaps be surprizd at my saying that I do not suppose we shoud essentially disagree.

In political controversy it often happens that the precise opinion of the adversary is not understood, & that we are at much labor to disprove propositions which have never been maintaind. A stronger evidence of this cannot I think be given than the manner in which the references to the common law have been treated. The opinion which has been controverted is, that the common law of England has not been adopted as the common law of America by the constitution of the United States. I do not beleive one man can be found who maintains the affirmative of this proposition. Neither in public nor in private have I ever heard it advocated, & I am as entirely confident as I can be of any thing of the sort, that it never has been advocated. This strange & absurd doctrine was first attributed to the judiciary of the United States by some frothy news paper publications which appeard in Richmond something more than twelve months past, but I never suspected that an attempt woud be made to represent this as a serious opinion entertaind by respectable men, until I saw the argument containd in the report of a committee of the house of Delegates in Virginia. You will pardon me for saying that notwithstanding the respectability of the author of this report I coud not read the part of it respecting the common law without being reminded of a ludicrous story told by Mr. Mason in the house of delegates in Williamsburg of a ram who amusd himself by taking such a position as to cast his shadow on a wall & then but at it as at a real enemy. So this report has gratuitously attributed to certain gentlemen an opinion never entertaind & has then very gravely demonstrated that the opinion is founded in error.

What the precise opinion entertaind on this subject may be I do not profess to know but I beleive that in the general definition of the principle sensible men of the two parties woud not disagree very materially. In the application of principles there woud perhaps be more difference than in their definition.

With respect to the case of Isaac Williams which you have mentiond in a note, I cannot beleive that you & Judge Ellesworth (if I understand that case rightly) woud disagree. Isaac Williams was prosecuted on two separate indictments—the one for privatiering under a french commission against the British & the other for privatiering under the same commission against

his own Country men. He was found guilty on both indictments. In the one case he was guilty of an offence against a
public treaty of the United States & in the other of an offence
against the United States on the high seas. I beleive it is not
controverted that both these crimes are clearly punishable in
the federal courts. The defence set up, so far as I understand it,
was that by taking a commission in the service of France which
was itself a crime, Isaac Williams withdrew himself from the
cognizance of our courts by ceasing to be an American citizen.
I mistake your opinions very much if you woud have counte-
nancd this defence.

In the case of Williams the common law was not relied on as
giving the court jurisdiction, but came in incidentally as part of
the law of a case of which the court had complete & exclusive
possession. I do not understand you as questioning the propriety of thus applying the common law, not of England, but, of
our own country.

My own opinion is that our ancestors brought with them
the laws of England both statute & common law as existing at
the settlement of each colony, so far as they were applicable to
our situation. That on our revolution the preexisting law of
each state remaind so far as it was not changd either expressly
or necessarily by the nature of the governments which we
adopted.

That on adopting the existing constitution of the United
States the common & statute law of each state remaind as
before & that the principles of the common law of the state
woud apply themselves to magistrates of the general as well as
to magistrates of the particular government. I do not recollect
ever to have heard the opinions of a leading gentleman of the
opposition which conflict with these. Mr. Gallatin in a very
acute speech on the sedition law was understood by me to
avow them. On the other side it was contended, not that the
common law gave the courts jurisdiction in cases of sedition
but that the constitution gave it. I am dear Sir yours truely

THE ELECTION OF 1800

To Charles Cotesworth Pinckney

My dear Sir   Washington Decr. 18th. 1800

According to our present inteligence Mr. Jefferson & Mr. Burr have an equal number of votes & of consequence the house of representatives must chuse between them. It is extremely uncertain on whom the choice will fall. Having myself no voice in the election, & in fact scarcely any wish concerning it, I do not intermeddle with it, but I hear what is said by others, & witness the anxiety of parties. Once more I suspect the contest (shoud one be made) will be decided by South Carolina. So far as I am enabled now to conjecture I think the person for whom your state votes will be President. Indeed if it shoud be decidedly for Mr. Jefferson I doubt whether Mr. Burr will not surrender so far as he can surrender all his pretensions to the office.

In the chagrin which I experiencd under our late defeat I had drawn much consolation from the opinion that the federalists throughout the continent had been faithful to themselves & to each other. I am extremely mortified to learn that this has not been completely the case. I beleive a Mr. Manton of Rhode Island threw away a vote. This is attributed in the letters from that State to Genl. Hamiltons pamphlet—but certainly the cause did not justify the effect.

The treaty with France is before the Senate. Many of that body appear to be by no means satisfied with it. I greatly suspect that an unconditional ratification will not be advisd.

Mr. Ellsworth has resignd his seat as chief justice & Mr. Jay has been nominated in his place. Shoud he as is most probable decline the office I fear the President will nominate the senior Judge.

I shall return to Richmond on the 3d. of March to recommence practice as a lawyer. If my present wish can succeed so far as respects myself I shall never again fill any political station whatever.

Present me respectfully to Mrs. Pinckney. I am dear Sir with much esteem & affection, your obedt. Servt

"A CHOICE OF EVILS"

To Edward Carrington

Dear Sir   Washington Decr. 28th. 1800

I am extremely desirous of selling my Buckingham land for the purpose of enabling me to raise money to pay for the Fairfax purchase.

It is divisible into two parts each of which may again be subdivided into two parts. Eppersons plantation comprehending the land south of bear branch & of snoddys spring branch contains about 1600 acres. For this my price is 50/ per acre. For the whole tract I will take 40/ per acre.

I inclose you a proposition receivd from Mr. Craig. I have referd him to you. I hope you will excuse this trouble. Mr. Hopkins on whose friendship I am accustomd to rely for things of this sort is in a state of distress which disinclines me to apply to him. As I shall have to sell the property again, its selling price must be regarded in any exchange which may be made. Copland is in possession of a bond given by my brother & myself for £3800 payable with interest from the date in three years. If he woud purchase any of the property with that bond I woud consider it as cash. You will much oblige me by writing on this subject.

It is understood that the votes for Mr. Jefferson & Colo. Burr are equal—tho there is a report that New York has given Burr a majority of two votes.

In the event of equality it is extremely doubtful who will be the President. I take no part & feel no interest in the decision. I consider it as a choice of evils & I really am uncertain which woud be the greatest. So far as I can learn however from what passes around me I really think the probability in favor of Burr. It is not beleivd that he woud weaken the vital parts of the constitution, nor is it beleivd that he has any undue foreign attachments. These opinions incline many who greatly disapprove of him yet to prefer him to the other gentleman who is offerd to their choice.

I have only to wish that the best for our common country may be done but I really do not know what that best is.

I hope it will be practicable for me to be in Richmond in February but I am not certain that I shall not be compeld to remain til the 3d. of march at this place. I am dear Sir with much esteem & affection, your Obedt. Servt.

JEFFERSON AND BURR

To Alexander Hamilton

Dear Sir   Jany 1st. 1801
    I receivd this morning your letter of the 26th of Decr. It is I beleive certain that Jefferson & Burr will come to the house of representatives with equal votes. The returns have been all receivd & this is the general opinion.
    Being no longer in the house of representatives, & consequently compeld by no duty to decide between them, my own mind had scarcely determind to which of these gentlemen the preference was due. To Mr. Jefferson whose political character is better known than that of Mr. Burr, I have felt almost insuperable objections. His foreign prejudices seem to me totally to unfit him for the chief magistracy of a nation which cannot indulge those prejudices without sustaining deep & permanent injury. In addition to this solid & immoveable objection Mr. Jefferson appears to me to be a man who will embody himself with the house of representatives. By weakening the office of President he will increase his personal power. He will diminish his responsability, sap the fundamental principles of the government & become the leader of that party which is about to constitute the majority of the legislature. The Morals of the Author of the letter to Mazzei cannot be pure.
    With these impressions concerning Mr. Jefferson I was in some degree disposd to view with less apprehension any other character, & to consider the alternative now offerd us as a circumstance not to be entirely neglected.
    Your representation of Mr. Burr with whom I am totally unacquainted shows that from him still greater danger than even from Mr. Jefferson may be apprehended. Such a man as you describe is more to be feard & may do more immediate if not

greater mischief. Beleiving that you know him well & are impartial my preference woud certainly not be for him—but I can take no part in this business. I cannot bring my self to aid Mr. Jefferson. Perhaps respect for myself shoud in my present situation deter me from using any influence (if indeed I possessd any) in support of either gentleman. Altho no consideration coud induce me to be the secretary of State while there was a President whose political system I beleivd to be at variance with my own, yet this cannot be so well known to others & it might be suspected that a desire to be well with the successful candidate had in some degree governd my conduct.

With you I am in favor of ratifying our treaty with france tho' I am far very far from approving it. There is however one principle which I think it right to explain.

Our Envoys were undoubtedly of opinion that our prior treaty with Britain woud retain its stipulated advantages & I think that opinion correct. Was our convention with any other nation than France I shoud feel no sollicitude on this subject. But France, the most encroaching nation on earth, will claim a literal interpretation & our people will decide in her favor. Those who coud contend that a promise not to permit privatiers of the enemy of France to be fitted out in our ports amounted to a grant of that privilege to France woud not hesitate to contend that a stipulation giving to France on the subject of privatiers & prizes the privileges of the most favord nation placd her on equal ground with any other nation whatever. In consequence of this temper in our own country I think the ratification of the treaty ought to be accompanied with a declaration of the sense in which it is agreed to. This however is only my own opinion. With very much respect & esteem, I am dear sir your Obedt

CHIEF JUSTICE OF
THE SUPREME COURT
1801–1819

To William Paterson

Dear Sir   Washington Feby. 2d. 1801

I had this instant the pleasure of receiving your letter of the 26th. of January.

For your polite & friendly sentiments on the appointment with which I have been lately honord I pray you to accept my warm & sincere acknowledgements.

I regret much that you cannot attend this session of the supreme court & still more the cause which detains you from us. I hope it will be of short duration & that the other members will be present. As yet however I have only seen Judge Cushing.

The question on the judicial bill will probably be taken in the Senate tomorrow, & we hope it will pass. It is substantially the same with that of the last session. Its most essential feature is the separation of the Judges of the supreme from those of the circuit courts, & the establishment of the latter on a system capable of an extension commensurate with the necessities of the nation. With great respect & esteem I am dear Sir, your obedt. Servt

ANTICIPATING JEFFERSON'S ADMINISTRATION

To Rufus King

private

Dear Sir   Washington Feb. 26th. 1801

You will undoubtedly receive from your correspondents in this country full & detaild accounts of the present state of our political system.

The strange revolution which has taken place in public opinion has I doubt not been attributed to various causes & it woud afford you no satisfaction that I shoud add my conjectures also to those which have been made by others.

The course to be pursued in future is of more importance & is not easily to be determind by those who have no place in the confidence of the President elect. So far as relates to our domestic situation it is beleivd & feard that the tendency of the administration will be to strengthen the state governments at the expence of that of the Union & to transfer as much as possible the powers remaining with the general government to the floor of the house of representatives.

The cabinet is suppos'd not to be perfectly form'd. Mr. Madison of Virginia is undoubtedly the Secretary of State. Mr. Dearbourne of Massachussetts it is conjectur'd will be the secretary of war. The Treasury has been suppos'd to be destind for Mr. Galatin, but doubts are now entertaind concerning this office & some beleive that it will be filld by Mr. Baldwin. It is as suppos'd that Genl. Smith of Baltimore was fixd on as the Secretary of the Navy—but this too is now brought into doubt. Mr. Lincoln of Massachussetts has been spoken of at one time as the Attorney General & at another Mr. Livingstone of New York.

What the conduct of Mr. Jefferson will be with respect to foreign powers is uncertain. Among those who have supported him are men who on this subject differ widely from each other. The most inteligent among them are in my opinion desirous of preserving peace with Britain but there is a mass of violence & passion in the party which seems to me dispos'd to press on to war. My private conjecture is that the government will use all its means to excite the resentment & hate of the people against England without designing to proceed to actual hostilities. For this the ill conduct of the british cruizers & still more of their courts of Vice Admiralty furnishes very abundant materials. Our merchants are preparing remonstrances on this subject which will pour in on the new administration & will have a great effect on the public mind.

If you have not yet concluded an agreement with the british minister I submit it privately to your consideration whether it will not be most wise to delay the completion of that business til you hear from the new Administration. Perhaps the agreement propos'd wd. not be ratified & it woud certainly be more desirable that it shoud not be made. I am dear Sir with great & sincere respect & esteem, your obedt

"THE NEW ORDER OF THINGS BEGINS"
To Charles Cotesworth Pinckney

Dear Sir   Washington March 4th. 1801
I had the pleasure of receiving a few days past your letter of
the 11th. Feb. For your friendly expressions on my late appointment I am infinitely obligd to you. Of the importance of the
judiciary at all times, but more especially the present I am very
fully impressd & I shall endeavor in the new office to which I
am calld not to disappoint my friends.

Before I receivd your letter Judge Bay had left us with the
intention of visiting the Mississipi territory. It was not in my
power to be otherwise useful to him than by giving him letters
to the governor & secretary of that country who will I hope
facilitate his enquiries concerning his property.

To day the new political year commences—The new order
of things begins. Mr. Adams I believe left the city at 4 OClock
in the morning & Mr. Jefferson will be inaugurated at 12.
There are some appearances which surprize me. I wish however more than I hope that the public prosperity & happiness
may sustain no diminution under democratic guidance. The
democrats are divided into speculative theorists & absolute
terrorists: With the latter I am not disposd to class Mr. Jefferson. If he arranges himself with them it is not difficult to foresee that much calamity is in store for our country—if he does
not they will soon become his enemies & calumniators.

4 OClock
I have administerd the oath to the President. You will before
this reaches you see his inauguration speech. It is in the general well judgd & conciliatory. It is in direct terms giving the
lie to the violent party declamation which has elected him; but
it is strongly characteristic of the general cast of his political
theory. With great & sincere esteem, I am dear Sir your Obedt

A DELAY IN ISSUING COMMISSIONS

To James M. Marshall

My dear Brother   Richmond March 18th. 1801
I learn with infinite chagrin the "developement of principle" mentiond in yours of the 12th. & I cannot help regreting it the more as I fear some blame may be imputed to me.

I did not examine Mr. Cranch's commission & do not know how the error coud have been commited unless the clerk who filld it up has omited some words intended to have been inserted. If this has happend it is probable that it has been recorded in the office of state with the proper words & if so no inconvenience I presume can occur.

I did not send out the commissions because I apprehended such as were for a fixd time to be completed when signd & seald & such as depended on the will of the President might at any time be revokd. To withhold the commission of the Marshal is equal to displacing him which the President I presume has the power to do, but to withhold the commission of the Justices is an act of which I entertaind no suspicion. I shoud however have sent out the commissions which had been signd & seald but for the extreme hurry of the time & the absence of Mr. Wagner who had been calld on by the President to act as his private Secretary.

I have passd Pennocks two first notes to Brown & Burton for their bills at 25 per cent exchange & shall remit them to Murdock with instructions to receive the money & hold it to be applied as instructed by you.

It will be advisable to bring the deed up to winchester with you where it may be acknowledgd & transmited to Norfolk.

I am excessively mortified at the circumstances relative to the appointment of the Chief Judge of the district. There was a negligence in that business arising from a confidence that Mr. Johnston woud accept, which I lament excessively. When Mr Swan parted with us at your house I thought he went to send an express the next morning. I wish to hear how principles continue to develope & am your affectionate brother

*

Let me know the day of meeting at winchester. Write also to Mr. Colston. I set out the 1st. of Apl or so to Buckingham & thence to winchester.

Pay Stewart six dollars for me which I forgot to do for myself. Ask Major Taylor for the money.

THE JUDICIARY BILL OF 1802

To William Paterson

Dear Sir   Richmond April 6th. 1802

Your favor of the 29th. of March reachd me last night. The letter addressd to Judge Washington I shall immediately inclose to him. Unfortunately the mail to Westmoreland is forwarded only once a week & had set out yesterday morning, so that a week will yet elapse before he can receive the letter. I have never seen that, the publication of which is sollicited & am entirely unacquainted with its contents.

I shall feel great pleasure in promoting so far as may be in my power the interests of Princeton College. I regret extremely the misfortune which has befallen it & wish very sincerely that the proper remedy may be applied.

You have I doubt not seen the arrangement of our future duties as markd out in a bill lately reported to the Senate. They are less burthensome than heretofore, or than I expected. I confess I have some strong constitutional scruples. I cannot well perceive how the performance of circuit duty by the Judges of the supreme court can be supported. If the question was new I shoud be unwilling to act in this character without a consultation of the Judges; but I consider it as decided & that whatever my own scruples may be I am bound by the decision. I cannot however but regret the loss of the next June term. I coud have wishd the Judges had convend before they proceeded to execute the new system. With great respect & esteem, I am dear Sir your Obedt.

To William Cushing

Dear Sir   Alexandria April 19th. 1802

A bill is now before Congress which will I am persuaded pass into a law by which the June term of the supreme court will be done away & the Judges directed to ride the circuits before they will again assemble.

For myself I more than doubt the constitutionality of this measure & of performing circuit duty without a commission as a circuit Judge. But I shall hold myself bound by the opinions of my brothers. I am not of opinion that we can under our present appointments hold circuit courts, but I presume a contrary opinion is held by the court & if so I shall conform to it. I am endeavoring to collect the opinion of the Judges & will when I shall have done so communicate the result. I will thank you to give me your opinion & direct your letter to me in Richmond. With very much respect I am dear Sir, Your Obedt. Servt

To William Paterson

Dear Sir   Alexandria April 19th. 1802

It having now become apparent that there will be no session of the supreme court of the United States holden in June next & that we shall be directed to ride the circuits, before we can consult on the course proper to be taken by us, it appears to me proper that the Judges shoud communicate their sentiments on this subject to each that they may act understandingly & in the same manner.

I hope I need not say that no man in existence respects more than I do, those who passd the original law concerning the courts of the United States, & those who first acted under it. So highly do I respect their opinions that I had not examind them & shoud have proceeded without a doubt on the subject, to perform the duties assignd to me if the late discussions had not unavoidably producd an investigation of the subject which from me it woud not otherwise have receivd. The result of this investigation has been an opinion which I cannot conquer that the constitution requires distinct appointments & commissions for the Judges of the inferior courts from those of the supreme court. It is however my duty & my inclination in this as in all other cases to be bound by the opinion of the majority of the Judges & I shoud therefore have proceeded to execute the law so far as that task may be assignd to me; had I not supposd it possible that the Judges might be inclind to distinguish between the original case of being appointed to duties markd out before their appointments & of having the duties of administering justice in new courts imposd after their appointments. I do not myself state this because I am myself satisfied that the distinction ought to have weight, for I am not—but as there may be something in it I am inducd to write to the Judges requesting the favor of them to give me their opinions which opinions I will afterwards communicate to each Judge. My own conduct shall certainly be regulated by them.

This is a subject not to be lightly resolvd on. The consequences of refusing to carry the law into effect may be very serious. For myself personally I disregard them, & so I am persuaded does every other Gentleman on the bench when put in competition with what he thinks his duty, but the conviction of duty ought to be very strong before the measure is resolvd on. The law having been once executed will detract very much in the public estimation from the merit or opinion of the sincerity of a determination, not now to act under it.

Not knowing how to direct to Judge Cushing I inclose my letter to him in this & ask the favor of you to forward it.

I shall be happy to hear from you in Richmond where I shall be in a few days & am dear Sir, With very much respect & esteem, your obedt servt

Will you also write to Mr. Cushing?

OPINIONS REGARDING CIRCUIT DUTY

To William Paterson

Dear Sir   Richmond May 3d. 1802

I receivd a few days past from Mr. Washington a letter of which the following is an extract.

"I am embarassd by Judge Bensons application because, altho my wishes are to oblige such a respectable number of Gentlemen, my judgement opposes & must prevent me from doing it. I formd a resolution shortly after the papers came to my possession, not to use or permit them to be usd, for party purposes. If I opend them to my political friends, I coud not refuse like access to those from whom I differd in opinion. How coud I, without incurring imputations of unfairness, & subjecting my self to charges which nothing but a resort to the papers coud remove. Suppose for instance I shoud be accusd of publishing partial parts of a correspondence, how coud I defend myself, & why shoud I involve myself in difficulties, from which I shoud never be able to extricate myself without opening the papers to both parties? The unmerited abuse of the democratic party I shoud disregard, but were I to use these papers as weapons against them, I shoud feel myself wrong when they sought aid from them, to refuse their request. I shoud not in short act as I beleive Genl. Washington woud have wishd, coud he have foreseen that I shoud be calld upon to act at all upon the case. From these considerations I declind complying with a request of General Hamiltons to send him copies of some papers, & I must be consistent (tho in error) in the present instance.

"I must get the favor of you to inform Judge Patteson that a resolution formd at the time I receivd the papers, not to use them for party purposes, to which I have hitherto adherd & upon which I have had occasion to act, will prevent me in the present instance, from complying with the request which has been made. That I have felt much embarassd by the application & feel still greater distress at being compelld to refuse the request of respectable men whose political conduct I admire,

& whose wishes I shoud take so much pleasure in gratifying coud it be done with propriety."

Mr. Washington also states it as his opinion that the question respecting the constitutional right of the Judges of the supreme court to sit as circuit Judges ought to be considerd as settled & shoud not again be movd. I have no doubt myself but that policy dictates this decision to us all. Judges however are of all men those who have the least right to obey her dictates. I own I shall be privately gratified if such shoud be the opinion of the majority & I shall with much pleasure acquiesce in it; tho, if the subject has never been discussd, I shoud feel greatly embarassd about it myself.

I have also receivd a letter from Judge Chase whose opinion is directly opposite to that of Judge Washington but he expresses an earnest desire, which he has requested me to communicate to every member of the bench, that we shoud meet in Washington for the purpose of determining on the course of conduct to be pursued, in August next when he is directed to hold a sort of a demi session at that place. I shall communicate this wish to Judge Moore & will thank you to correspond with Judge Cushing on the subject & let me know the result.

If we determine certainly to proceed to do circuit duty it will I presume be entirely unnecessary to meet in August. If we incline to the contrary opinion, or are undecided we ought to meet & communicate verbally our difficulties to each other.

After hearing from Judge Moore I will again write to you. With very much respect & esteem, I am dear Sir your Obedt

THE WAR IN THE SOUTH

To Charles Cotesworth Pinckney

My dear Sir   November 21. 1802—Richmond

In march last Mr. Washington placd the papers of our late respected & belovd General in my hands, & requested me to enter, as soon as possible, on the very difficult task of composing the history of his life. This I do not wish to be known;

but I have no difficulty in communicating it to you, & I do so now because there is much information, especially in relation to the war in the southern States, which the papers do not communicate & which I have some hope of being able to receive, at least in part from you.

General Lincoln was persimonious of his communications & of consequence his letters to the Commander in Chief do not contain so much as might have been expected.

In his letter stating the attempt on Savannah in 1779 he refers General Washington to Colonel Laurens for information & gives no other himself than that the attempt faild. Is it asking too much to request from you a statement of the facts respecting that affair within your knowledge? Was the American Column distinct from the french & if so who led it? Who led the different columns of french troops? What was the loss? Was the attempt rash & impracticable, or if not so to what causes is the failure to be attributed? What were the numbers of D Estaings army—what of the continental troops—& of the militia? What the order of attack & the situation of the works? Did the failure produce any animosity between the french & Americans? Anything further which may appear to you interesting I will thank you for. In what situation did Pulaski receive his wound? Where was his corps & how did it behave?

You will also greatly oblige me by any particulars respecting the seige of Charlestown which you may deem important. I have not however yet examind the papers of that transaction & do not know how far they may be defective. There are some enquiries respecting the first attack which I coud wish to make.

Who was the Enginier that directed the artillery from fort Moultrie on Sullivans island? What is the depth of water between Long island & Sullivans island, & what the communication between Long island & the continent? Coud Clinton have crossd over to Sullivans island to have attackd the fort by land & what was the force guarding the passage.

Shall we ever see you again in Richmond? I assure you few things woud give me greater pleasure. I have now scarcely any gratification which can be compard with the occasional conversation I have with the few friends I love & who deserve to be esteemd. There is so much in the political world to wound honest men who have honorable feelings that I am disgusted with it & begin to see things & indeed human nature through a much more gloomy medium than I once thought possible. This new doctrine of the perfectability of man, added to the practice of its votaries begins to exhibit him I think as an animal much less respectable than he has heretofore been thought.

It is whisperd among those who affect to know a great deal that a certain eminent personage is already fatigued almost beyond bearing with a great democratic & religious writer whose *useful* labors were of sufficient magnitude to entitle him to an invitation to cross the Atlantic in a national frigate. I cannot help feeling some gratification at this. I wish such deeds woud always bring their own reward. It woud induce infidels to beleive there was a possibility of there being a superintending providence.

Are you growing worse in South Carolina? In Virginia we are I think stationary. If our Legislature shoud not follow the example of Pennsylvania or establish a general ticket the elections for Congress will be very warmly contested in five or six districts, & federalism will I am inclind to think, prevail in three of them.

Mrs. Marshall requests me to present her respects to Mrs. Pinckney. I am dear General with much esteem & affection, Your obedt

TRAVEL MISADVENTURES

To Mary W. Marshall

My dearest Polly   Rawleigh Jany. 2d. 1803
    As I know you will feel the same pleasure in hearing from me that I do in writing to you I set down to tell you that I find everything here as pleasant as I coud expect & that my journey has been not a disagreeable one. The weather was uncommonly mild & tho rain was continually threatend it did not begin to fall till I was safely hous'd. This was extremely fortunate, but with this my good fortune ended. You will laugh at my vexation when you hear the various calamities that have befallen

me. In the first place when I came to review my funds, I had the mortification to discover that I had lost 15 silver dollers out of my waist coat pocket. They had worn through the various mendings the pocket had sustaind & sought their liberty in the sands of Carolina. I determind not to vex myself with what coud not be remedied & orderd Peter to take out my cloaths that I might dress for court when to my astonishment & grief after fumbling several minutes in the portmanteau, staring at vacancy, & sweating most profusely he turnd to me with the doleful tidings that I had no pair of breeches. You may be sure this piece of inteligence was not very graciously receivd; however, after a little scolding I determind to make the best of my situation & immediately set out to get a pair made. I thought I shoud be a sans culotte only one day & that for the residue of the term I might be well enough dressd for the appearance on the first day to be forgotten. But, 'the greatest of evils, I found, was followd by still greater!' Not a taylor in town coud be prevaild on to work for me. They were all so busy that it was impossible to attend to my wants however pressing they might be & I have the extreme mortification to pass the whole term without that important article of dress I have mentiond. I have no alleviation for this misfortune but the hope that I shall be enabled in four or five days to commence my journey homewards & that I shall have the pleasure of seeing you & our dear children in eight or nine days after this reaches you. In the meantime I flatter myself that you are well & happy. Adieu my dearest Polly, I am your ever affectionate

Opinion in Marbury v. Madison

A<small>T</small> the last term on the affidavits then read and filed with the clerk, a rule was granted in this case, requiring the Secretary of State to shew cause why a Mandamus should not issue, directing him to deliver to William Marbury his commission as a justice of peace for the County of Washington, in the district of Columbia.

No cause has been shewn, and the present motion is for a Mandamus. The peculiar delicacy of this case, the novelty of some of its circumstances, and the real difficulty attending the points which occur in it, require a complete exposition of the principles, on which the opinion to be given by the court, is founded.

These principles have been, on the side of the applicant, very ably argued at the bar. In rendering the opinion of the court, there will be some departure in form, though not in substance, from the points stated in that argument.

In the order in which the court has viewed this subject, the following questions have been considered and decided.

1st. Has the applicant a right to the commission he demands?

2dly. If he has a right, and that right has been violated, do the laws of his country afford him a remedy?

3dly. If they do afford him a remedy, is it a *Mandamus* issuing from this court?

The first object of enquiry is,

1st. Has the applicant a right to the commission he demands?

His right originates in an act of Congress passed in February 1801, concerning the district of Columbia.

After dividing the district into two counties, the 11th section of this law, enacts, "that there shall be appointed in and for each of the said counties, such number of discreet persons to be justices of the peace, as the President of the U. States, shall, from time to time, think expedient, to continue in office for five years."

It appears, from the affidavits, that in compliance with this law, a commission for William Marbury as a justice of peace for the county of Washington, was signed by John Adams, then President of the United States; after which the seal of the United States was affixed to it; but the commission has never reached the person for whom it was made out.

In order to determine whether he is intitled to this commission, it becomes necessary to enquire whether he has been appointed to the office. For if he has been appointed, the law continues him in office for five years; and he is entitled to the possession of those evidences of office, which, being completed, became his property.

The 2d section, of the 2d article of the Constitution, declares, that "the President shall nominate, and, by and with the advice and consent of the Senate, shall appoint ambassadors, other public ministers and consuls, and all other officers of the United States, whose appointments are not otherwise provided for."

The 3d section, declares, that "he shall commission all the officers of the United States."

An Act of Congress, directs the Secretary of State, to keep the seal of the United States, "to make out and record, and affix the said seal to all civil commissions to officers of the United States to be appointed by the President, by and with the consent of the Senate, or by the President alone; provided that the said seal shall not be affixed to any commission before the same shall have been signed by the President of the United States."

These are the clauses of the constitution and laws of the United States, which affect this part of the case. They seem to contemplate three distinct operations—

1st. The nomination. This is the sole act of the President, and is completely voluntary.

2d. The appointment. This is also the act of the President, and is also a voluntary act, though it can only be performed, by and with the advice and consent of the Senate.

3d. The commission. To grant a commission to a person appointed, might perhaps be deemed a duty, enjoined by the constitution. "He shall," says that instrument, "commission all the officers of the United States."

The acts of appointing to office, and commissioning the person appointed, can scarcely be considered as one and the same; since the power to perform them is given in two separate and distinct sections of the constitution. The distinction between the appointment and the commission, will be rendered more apparent, by adverting to that provision in the 2d section, of the 2d article of the constitution, which authorises Congress, "to vest, by law, the appointment of such inferior officers, as they think proper, in the President alone, in the courts of law, or in the heads of departments;" thus contemplating cases where the law may direct the President to commission an officer appointed by the courts, or by the heads of departments. In such a case, to issue a commission would be apparently a duty distinct from the appointment, the performance of which, perhaps, could not legally be refused.

Although that clause of the constitution which requires the President to commission all the officers of the U. States, may never have been applied to officers appointed otherwise than by himself, yet it would be difficult to deny the legislative power to apply it to such cases. Of consequence the constitutional distinction between the appointment to an office and the commission of an officer, who has been appointed, remains the same as if in practice the President had commissioned officers appointed by an authority other than his own.

It follows too, from the existence of this distinction, that, if an appointment was to be evidenced by any public act, other than the commission, the performance of such public act would create the officer; and if he was not removeable at the will of the President, would either give him a right to his commission, or enable him to perform the duties without it.

These observations are premised solely for the purpose of rendering more intelligible those which apply more directly to the particular case under consideration.

This is an appointment made by the President by and with the advice and consent of the Senate, and is evidenced by no act but the commission itself. In such a case therefore the commission and the appointment seem inseparable; it being almost impossible to show an appointment otherwise than by proving the existence of a commission; still the commission is not necessarily the appointment; tho' conclusive evidence of it.

But at what stage does it amount to this conclusive evidence?

The answer to this question seems an obvious one. The appointment, being the sole act of the President, must be completely evidenced, when it is shewn that he has done every thing to be performed by him.

Should the commission, instead of being evidence of an appointment, even be considered as constituting the appointment itself; still it would be made when the last act to be done by the President was performed, or, at furthest, when the commission was complete.

The last act to be done by the President, is the signature of the commission. He has then acted on the advice and consent of the Senate to his own nomination. The time for deliberation was then passed. He has decided. His judgment, on the advice and consent of the Senate concurring with his nomination, has been made, and the officer is appointed. This appointment is evidenced by an open, unequivocal act; and being the last act required from the person making it, necessarily excludes the idea of its being, so far as respects the appointment, an inchoate and incomplete transaction.

Some point of time must be taken when the power of the executive over an officer, not removeable at his will, must cease. That point of time must be when the constitutional power of appointment has been exercised. And this power has been exercised when the last act, required from the person possessing the power, has been performed—This last act is the signature of the commission.

This idea seems to have prevailed with the legislature, when the act passed converting the department of foreign affairs into the department of State. By that act it is enacted, that the Secretary of State, shall keep the seal of the United States, "and shall make out and record, and shall affix the said seal to all civil commissions, to officers of the United States, to be appointed by the President:" "Provided that the said seal shall not be affixed to any commission, before the same shall have been signed by the President of the United States; nor to any other instrument or act, without the special warrant of the President therefor."

The signature is a warrant for affixing the great seal to the commission; and the great seal is only to be affixed to an instrument which is complete. It attests, by an act supposed to be of public notoriety, the verity of the President's signature.

It is never to be affixed till the commission is signed because the signature, which gives force and effect to the commission, is conclusive evidence that the appointment is made.

The commission being signed, the subsequent duty of the Secretary of State is prescribed by law, and not to be guided by the will of the President. He is to affix the seal of the United States to the commission, and is to record it.

This is not a proceeding which may be varied, if the judgment of the executive shall suggest one more eligible; but is a precise course accurately marked out by law, and is to be strictly pursued. It is the duty of the Secretary of State to conform to the law, and in this he is an officer of the United States, bound to obey the laws. He acts, in this respect, as has been very properly stated at the bar, under the authority of law, & not by the instructions of the President. It is a ministerial act which the law enjoins on a particular officer for a particular purpose.

If it should be supposed, that the solemnity of affixing the seal, is necessary not only to the validity of the commission, but even to the completion of an appointment, still when the seal is affixed the appointment is made, and the commission is valid. No other solemnity is required by law; no other act is to be performed on the part of Government. All that the executive can do to invest the person with his office, is done; and unless the appointment be then made, the executive cannot make one without the co-operation of others.

After searching anxiously for the principles on which a contrary opinion may be supported, none have been found which appear of sufficient force to maintain the opposite doctrine.

Such as the imagination of the Court could suggest, have been very deliberately examined, and after allowing them all the weight which it appears possible to give them, they do not shake the opinion which has been formed.

In considering this question, it has been conjectured that the commission may have been assimilated to a deed, to the validity of which, delivery is essential.

This idea is founded on the supposition that the commission

is not merely *evidence* of an appointment, but is itself the actual appointment—a supposition by no means unquestionable. But for the purpose of examining this objection fairly, let it be conceded, that the principle, claimed for its support, is established.

The appointment being, under the constitution, to be made by the President *personally*, the delivery of the deed of appointment, if necessary to its completion, must be made by the President also. It is not necessary that the livery should be made personally to the grantee of the office: It never is so made. The law would seem to contemplate that it should be made to the Secretary of State, since it directs the Secretary to affix the seal to the commission *after* it shall have been signed by the President. If then the act of livery be necessary to give validity to the commission, it has been delivered when executed and given to the Secretary for the purpose of being sealed, recorded and transmitted to the party.

But in all cases of letters patent, certain solemnities are required by law, which solemnities are the evidences of the validity of the instrument. A formal delivery to the person is not among them. In cases of commissions the sign manual of the President, and the seal of the U. States, are those solemnities. This objection therefore does not touch the case.

It has also occurred as possible, and barely possible, that the transmission of the commission, & the acceptance thereof, might be deemed necessary to complete the right of the plaintiff.

The transmission of the commission, is a practice directed by convenience, but not by law. It cannot therefore be necessary to constitute the appointment which must precede it, and which is the mere act of the President. If the executive required that every person appointed to an office, should himself take means to procure his commission, the appointment would not be the less valid on that account. The appointment is the sole act of the President; the transmission of the commission is the sole act of the officer to whom that duty is assigned, and may be accelerated or retarded by circumstances which can have no influence on the appointment. A commission is transmitted to a person already appointed; not to a person to be appointed or not, as the letter inclosing the commission should happen to get into the post office and reach him in safety, or to miscarry.

It may have some tendency to elucidate this point, to enquire, whether the possession of the *original* commission be indispensably necessary to authorise a person, appointed to any office, to perform the duties of that office. If it was necessary, then a loss of the commission would lose the office. Not only negligence, but accident or fraud, fire or theft, might deprive an individual of his office. In such a case, I presume it could not be doubted, but that a copy, from the record of the office of the Secretary of State, would be, to every intent and purpose, equal to the original. The act of Congress has expressly made it so. To give that copy validity, it would not be necessary to prove that the original had been transmitted and afterwards lost. The copy would be complete evidence that the original had existed & that the appointment had been made, but, not that the original had been transmitted. If indeed it should appear that the original had been mislaid in the office of State, that circumstance would not affect the operation of the copy. When all the requisites have been performed which authorize a recording officer to record any instrument whatever, and the order for that purpose has been given, the instrument is, in law, considered as recorded, altho' the manual labour of inserting it in a book kept for that purpose may not have been performed.

In the case of Commissions, the law orders the Secretary of State to record them. When therefore they are signed and sealed, the order for their being recorded is given; and whether inserted in the book or not, they are in law recorded.

A copy of this record is declared equal to the original, and the fees, to be paid by a person requiring a copy, are ascertained by law. Can a keeper of a public record, erase therefrom a commission which has been recorded? Or can he refuse a copy thereof to a person demanding it on the terms prescribed by law?

Such a copy would, equally with the original authorize the justice of peace to proceed in the performance of his duty, because it would, equally with the original, attest his appointment.

If the transmission of a commission be not considered as necessary to give validity to an appointment; still less is its acceptance. The appointment is the sole act of the President; the acceptance is the sole act of the officer, and is, in plain common sense, posterior to the appointment. As he may resign, so may he refuse to accept: but neither the one, nor the other, is capable of rendering the appointment a non-entity.

That this is the understanding of the Government, is apparent from the whole tenor of its conduct.

A commission bears date, and the salary of the officer commences from his appointment; not from the transmission, or acceptance of his commission. When a person, appointed to any office, refuses to accept that office, the successor is nominated in the place of the person who has declined to accept, and not in the place of the person who had been previously in office, and had created the original vacancy.

It is therefore decidedly the opinion of the court, that when a commission has been signed by the President, the appointment is made; and that the commission is complete when the seal of the United States has been affixed to it by the Secretary of State.

Where an officer is removeable at the will of the executive, the circumstance which completes his appointment is of no concern; because the act is at any time revocable; and the commission may be arrested, if still in the office. But when the officer is not removable at the will of the executive, the appointment is not revocable, and cannot be annulled. It has conferred legal rights which cannot be resumed.

The discretion of the executive is to be exercised until the appointment has been made. But having once made the appointment, his power over the office is terminated in all cases, where, by law, the officer is not removable by him. The right to the office is *then* in the person appointed, and he has the absolute, unconditional, power of accepting or rejecting it.

Mr. Marbury, then, since his commission was signed by the President, and sealed by the Secretary of State, was appointed; and as the law creating the office, gave the officer a right to hold for five years, independent of the executive, the appointment was not revocable; but vested in the officer legal rights, which are protected by the laws of his country.

To withhold his commission, therefore, is an act deemed by

the court not warranted by law, but violative of a vested legal right.

This brings us to the second enquiry; which is,

2dly. If he has a right and that right has been violated, do the laws of his country afford him a remedy?

The very essence of civil liberty certainly consists in the right of every individual to claim the protection of the laws whenever he receives an injury. One of the first duties of government is to afford that protection. In Great Britain the king himself is sued in the respectful form of a petition, and he never fails to comply with the judgment of his court.

In the 3d vol. of his commentaries, p. 23, Blackstone states two cases in which a remedy is afforded by mere operation of law—

"In all other cases," he says, "it is a general & indisputable rule, that where there is a legal right, there is also a legal remedy by suit or action at law, whenever that right is invaded."

And afterwards, p. 109 of the same volume, he says, "I am next to consider such injuries as are cognizable by the courts of the common law. And herein I shall for the present only remark, that all possible injuries whatsoever, that did not fall within the exclusive cognizance of either the ecclesiastical, military, or maritime tribunals, are for that very reason, within the cognizance of the common law courts of justice; for it is a settled and invariable principle in the laws of England, that every right, when withheld, must have a remedy, and every injury its proper redress."

The government of the United States has been emphatically termed a government of laws, & not of men. It will certainly cease to deserve this high appellation, if the laws furnish no remedy for the violation of a vested legal right.

If this obloquy is to be cast on the jurisprudence of our country, it must arise from the peculiar character of the case.

It behoves us then to enquire whether there be, in its composition any ingredient which shall exempt it from legal investigation, or exclude the injured party from legal redress. In pursuing this enquiry the first question which presents itself, is, whether this can be arranged with that class of cases which come under the description of *damnum absque injuria*—a loss without an injury.

This description of cases never has been considered, and it is believed, never can be considered, as comprehending offices of trust, of honor or of profit. The office of justice of peace in the district of Columbia is such an office; it is therefore worthy of the attention and guardianship of the laws. It has received that attention & guardianship. It has been created by special act of congress, and has been secured, so far as the laws can give security to the person appointed to fill it, for five years. It is not then on account of the worthlessness of the thing pursued, that the injured party can be alleged to be without remedy.

Is it in the nature of the transaction? Is the act of delivering or withholding a commission to be considered as a mere political act, belonging to the executive department alone, for the performance of which, entire confidence is placed by our constitution in the supreme executive; & for any misconduct respecting which, the injured individual has no remedy?

That there may be such cases is not to be questioned; but that *every* act of duty, to be performed in any of the great departments of government, constitutes such a case, is not to be admitted.

By the act concerning invalids, passed in June, 1794, vol. 3 p. 112, the Secretary at war is ordered to place, on the pension list, all persons whose names are contained in a report previously made by him to congress. If he should refuse to do so, would the wounded veteran be without remedy? Is it to be contended that where the law in precise terms, directs the performance of an act, in which an individual is interested, that the law is incapable of securing obedience to its mandate? Is it on account of the character of the person against whom the complaint is made? Is it to be contended that the heads of departments are not amenable to the laws of their country?

Whatever the practice on particular occasions may be, the theory of this principle will certainly never be maintained. No act of the legislature confers so extraordinary a privilege, nor can it derive countenance from the doctrines of the common law. After stating that personal injury from the king to a subject is presumed to be impossible, Blackstone, vol. 3. page 255 says, "but injuries to the rights of property can scarcely be committed by the crown without the intervention of his officers; for whom, the law, in matters of right, entertains no respect or delicacy; but furnishes various methods of detecting the errors and misconduct of those agents, by whom the king has been deceived and induced to do a temporary injustice."

By the act passed in 1796, authorising the sale of the lands above the mouth of Kentucky river (vol. 3d p. 299) the purchaser, on paying his purchase money, becomes completely entitled to the property purchased; and on producing to the secretary of state, the receipt of the treasurer upon a certificate required by the law, the president of the United States is authorised to grant him a patent. It is further enacted that all patents shall be countersigned by the Secretary of state, and recorded in his office. If the secretary of state should chuse to withhold this patent; or the patent being lost, should refuse a copy of it, can it be imagined that the law furnishes to the injured person no remedy?

It is not believed that any person whatever would attempt to maintain such a proposition.

It follows then that the question whether the legality of an act of the head of a department be examinable in a court of justice or not, must always depend on the nature of that act.

If some acts be examinable, & others not, there must be some rule of law to guide the court in the exercise of its jurisdiction.

In some instances there may be difficulty in applying the rule to particular cases; but there cannot, it is believed be much difficulty in laying down the rule.

By the constitution of the United States, the president is invested with certain important political powers, in the exercise of which he is to use his own discretion, and is accountable only to his country in his political character, and to his own conscience. To aid him in the performance of these duties, he is authorised to appoint certain officers who act by his authority and in conformity with his orders.

In such cases, their acts are his acts; & whatever opinion may be entertained of the manner in which executive discretion may be used; still there exists, and can exist no power to controul that discretion. The subjects are political. They respect the nation, not individual rights, & being entrusted to the executive, the decision of the executive is conclusive. The application of this remark will be perceived, by adverting to the act of congress for establishing the department of foreign affairs. This officer, as his duties were prescribed by that act, is to conform precisely to the will of the president. He is the mere organ by whom that will is communicated. The acts of such an officer, as an officer, can never be examinable by the courts.

But when the legislature proceeds to impose, on that officer, other duties; when he is directed peremptorily to perform certain acts; when the rights of individuals are dependent on the performance of those acts; he is so far the officer of the law; is amenable to the laws for his conduct; and cannot at his discretion, sport away the vested rights of others.

The conclusion from this reasoning is, that where the heads of departments are the political, or confidential, agents of the executive, merely to execute the will of the president, or rather to act in cases, in which the executive possesses a constitutional, or legal discretion, nothing can be more perfectly clear, than that their acts are only politically examinable. But where a specific duty is assigned by law, and individual rights depend upon the performance of that duty, it seems equally clear that the individual who considers himself injured, has a right to resort to the laws of his country for a remedy.

If this be the rule, let us enquire how it applies to the case under the consideration of the court.

The power of nominating to the Senate, and the power of appointing the person nominated, are political powers, to be exercised by the president according to his own discretion. When he has made an appointment, he has exercised his whole power, and his discretion has been completely applied to the case. If, by law, the officer be removeable at the will of the president, then a new appointment may be immediately made, & the rights of the officer are terminated. But, as a fact, which has existed, cannot be made never to have existed, the appointment cannot be annihilated; and consequently, if the officer, is by law, not removeable at the will of the president; the rights he has acquired are protected by the law, and are not resumable by the president. They cannot be extinguished by executive authority, and he has the privilege of asserting them in like manner as if they had been derived from any other source.

The question whether a right has vested or not, is, in its nature, judicial, and must be tried by the judicial authority. If, for example, Mr. Marbury had taken the oaths of a magistrate and proceeded to act as one: in consequence of which a suit had been instituted against him, in which his defence had depended on his being a magistrate; the validity of his appointment must have been determined by judicial authority.

So, if he conceives that, by virtue of his appointment, he has a legal right, either to the commission which has been made out for him, or to a copy of that commission; it is equally a question examinable in a court, and the decision of the court upon it must depend on the opinion entertained of his appointment.

That question has been discussed, and the opinion is, that the latest point of time which can be taken as that at which the appointment was complete, and evidenced, was when after the signature of the president, the seal of the United States was affixed to the commission.

It is then the opinion of the court,

1st. That by signing the commission of Mr. Marbury, the president of the United States appointed him a justice of peace, for the county of Washington in the District of Columbia, & that the seal of the United States, affixed thereto by the Secretary of state, is conclusive testimony of the verity of the signature, and of the completion of the appointment; and that the appointment conferred on him a legal right to the office for the space of five years.

2dly. That, having this legal title to the office he has a consequent right to the commission; a refusal to deliver which is a plain violation of that right, for which the laws of his country afford him a remedy.

It remains to be enquired whether,

3dly. He is entitled to the remedy for which he applies. This depends on

1st The nature of the writ applied for, and

2dly The powers of this court.

1st. The nature of the writ.

Blackstone in the 3d volume of his commentaries, page 110, defines a Mandamus to be, "a command issuing in the king's name, from the court of King's bench, and directed to any person, corporation, or inferior court of judicature within the king's dominions, requiring them to do some particular thing therein specified, which appertains to their office and duty, and which the court of king's bench has previously determined, or at least supposes to be consonant to right and justice."

Lord Mansfield, in 3d Burrows 1266: in the case of the King vs Baker et al: states with much precision and explicitness, the cases in which this writ may be used.

"Whenever," says that very able judge, "there is a right to execute an office, perform a service, or exercise a franchise (more especially if it be in a matter of public concern, or attended with profit) and a person is kept out of possession, or dispossessed of such right, and has no other specific legal remedy, this court ought to assist by Mandamus, upon reasons of justice, as the writ expresses, & upon reasons of public policy to preserve peace, order, and good government." In the same case he says, "this writ ought to be used upon all occasions where the law has established no specific remedy, and where in justice & good government there ought to be one."

In addition to the authorities now particularly cited, many others were relied on at the bar, which show how far the practice has conformed to the general doctrines that have been just quoted.

This writ, if awarded, would be directed to an officer of government, and its mandate to him would be, to use the words of Blackstone, "to do a particular thing therein specified, which appertains to his office and duty, and which the court has previously determined, or at least supposes, to be consonant to right and justice." Or, in the words of Lord Mansfield, the applicant, in this case, has a right to execute an office of public concern, and is kept out of possession of that right.

These circumstances certainly concur in this case.

Still, to render the Mandamus a proper remedy, the officer to whom it is to be directed, must be one to whom, on legal principles, such writ may be directed; and the person applying for it must be without any other specific and legal remedy.

1st. With respect to the officer to whom it would be directed. The intimate political relation, subsisting between the president of the United States and the heads of departments, necessarily renders any legal investigation of the acts of one of those high officers peculiarly irksome, as well as delicate; and excites some hesitation with respect to the propriety of entering into such investigation. Impressions are often received without much reflection or examination, and it is not wonderful that in such a case as this, the assertion, by an individual, of his legal claims, in a court of justice; to which claims it is the duty of that court to attend; should at first view be considered by some, as an attempt to intrude into the cabinet, and to intermeddle with the prerogatives of the executive.

It is scarcely necessary for the court to disclaim all pretentions to such a jurisdiction. An extravagance, so absurd and excessive, could not have been entertained for a moment. The province of the court, is, solely, to decide on the rights of individuals, not to enquire how the executive, or executive officers, perform duties in which they have a discretion. Questions, in their nature political, or which are, by the constitution and laws, submitted to the executive, can never be made in this court.

But, if this be not such a question; if, so far from being an intrusion into the secrets of the cabinet, it respects a paper, which, according to law is upon record, and to a copy of which, the law gives a right, on the payment of ten cents—if it be no intermeddling with a subject, over which the executive can be considered as having exercised any controul—what is there in the exalted station of the officer, which shall bar a citizen from asserting, in a court of justice, his legal rights, or shall forbid a court to listen to the claim; or to issue a mandamus, directing the performance of a duty, not depending on executive discretion, but on particular acts of congress & the general principles of law?

If one of the heads of departments commits any illegal act, under color of his office, by which an individual sustains an injury, it cannot be pretended that his office alone exempts him from being sued in the ordinary mode of proceeding, and being compelled to obey the judgment of the law. How then can his office exempt him from this particular mode of deciding on the legality of his conduct, if the case be such a case as would, were any other individual the party complained of, authorise the process?

It is not by the office of the person to whom the writ is

directed, but the nature of the thing to be done, that the propriety or impropriety of issuing a mandamus, is to be determined. Where the head of a department acts in a case, in which executive discretion is to be exercised; in which he is the mere organ of executive will; it is again repeated, that any application to a court to controul, in any respect, his conduct, would be rejected without hesitation.

But where he is directed by law to do a certain act affecting the absolute rights of individuals in the performance of which he is not placed under the particular direction of the president, and the performance of which the president cannot lawfully forbid, and therefore is never presumed to have forbidden; as for example, to record a commission, or a patent for land, which has received all the legal solemnities; or to give a copy of such record; in such cases, it is not perceived on what ground the courts of the country are further excused from the duty of giving judgment, that right be done to an injured individual, than if the same services were to be performed by a person not the head of a department.

This opinion seems not now, for the first time, to be taken up in this country.

It must be well recollected that in 1792, an act passed, directing the Secretary at war to place on the pension list such disabled officers and soldiers as should be reported to him, by the Circuit courts; which act, so far as the duty was imposed on the courts, was deemed unconstitutional; but some of the judges, thinking that the law might be executed by them in the character of commissioners, proceeded to act and to report in that character.

This law being deemed unconstitutional at the circuits, was repealed, and a different system was established; but the question whether those persons, who had been reported by the judges, as commissioners were entitled, in consequence of that report, to be placed on the pension list, was a legal question, properly determinable in the courts, although the act of placing such persons on the list was to be performed by the head of a department.

That this question might be properly settled, congress passed an act in February, 1793, making it the duty of the Secretary of war, in conjunction with the Attorney General, to take such measures, as might be necessary to obtain an adjudication of the Supreme Court of the United States on the validity of any such rights, claimed under the act aforesaid.

After the passage of this act, a mandamus was moved for, to be directed to the Secretary at war, commanding him to place on the pension list, a person stating himself to be on the report of the judges.

There is therefore, much reason to believe, that this mode of trying the legal right of the complainant, was deemed by the head of a department, & by the highest law officer of the United States, the most proper which could be selected for the purpose.

When the subject was brought before the court the decision was, not that a mandamus would not lie to the head of a department, directing him to perform an act enjoined by law, in the performance of which an individual had a vested interest; but that a mandamus ought not to issue *in that case*; the decision necessarily to be made if the report of the commissioners did not confer, on the applicant a legal right.

The judgment in that case, is understood to have decided the merits of all claims of that description; and the persons on the report of the commissioners found it necessary to pursue the mode prescribed by the law subsequent to that which had been deemed unconstitutional, in order to place themselves on the pension list.

The doctrine, therefore, now advanced is by no means a novel one.

It is true that the mandamus, now moved for, is not for the performance of an act expressly enjoined by statute.

It is to deliver a commission; on which subject the acts of congress are silent. This difference is not considered as affecting the case. It has already been stated that the applicant has to that commission a vested, legal right, of which the executive cannot deprive him. He has been appointed to an office, from which he is not removeable at the will of the executive; and being so appointed, he has a right to the commission which the Secretary has received from the president for his use. The act of congress does not indeed order the secretary of state to send it to him, but it is placed in his hands for the person intitled to it; and cannot be more lawfully withheld by him, than by any other person.

It was at first doubted whether the action of detinue was not a specific legal remedy for the commission which has been withheld from Mr. Marbury; in which case a mandamus would be improper. But this doubt has yielded to the consideration that the judgment in detinue is for the thing itself, or its value. The value of a public office not to be sold, is incapable of being ascertained; and the applicant has a right to the office itself, or to nothing. He will obtain the office by obtaining the commission, or a copy of it from the record.

This then, is a plain case for a mandamus, either to deliver the commission, or a copy of it from the record; and it only remains to be enquired,

Whether it can issue from this court.

The act to establish the judicial courts of the United States authorises the supreme court "to issue writs of mandamus, in cases warranted by the principles and usages of law, to any courts appointed, or persons holding office, under the authority of the U. States."

The secretary of state, being a person holding an office under the authority of the United States, is precisely within the letter of the description; and if this court is not authorised to issue a writ of mandamus to such an officer, it must be, because the law is unconstitutional, and therefore absolutely incapable of conferring the authority, and assigning the duties which its words purport to confer and assign.

The constitution vests the whole judicial power of the United States in one Supreme court, and in such inferior courts as congress shall, from time to time, ordain and establish. This power is expressly extended to all cases arising under the laws of the United States: and consequently in some form may be exercised over the present case: because the right claimed is given by a law of the United States.

In the distribution of this power it is declared, that "The supreme court shall have original jurisdiction in all cases affecting ambassadors, other public ministers & consuls, and those in which a state shall be a party. In all other cases, the supreme court shall have appellate jurisdiction."

It has been insisted, at the bar, that as the original grant of jurisdiction, to the Supreme and inferior courts, is general, and the clause, assigning original jurisdiction to the supreme court, contains no negative or restrictive words; the power remains to the legislature, to assign original jurisdiction to that court in other cases than those specified in the article which has been recited; provided those cases belong to the judicial power of the United States.

If it had been intended to leave it in the discretion of the legislature to apportion the judicial power between the Supreme and inferior courts, according to the will of that body, it would certainly have been useless to have proceeded further than to have defined the judicial power, and the tribunals in which it should be vested. The subsequent part of the section is mere surplussage, is entirely without meaning, if such is to be the construction. If Congress remains at liberty to give this court appellate jurisdiction where the constitution has declared their jurisdiction shall be original—and original jurisdiction where the constitution has declared it shall be appellate—the distribution of jurisdiction, made in the constitution, is form without substance.

Affirmative words are often, in their operation, negative of other objects than those affirmed; and in this case, a negative or exclusive sense must be given to them or they have no operation at all.

It cannot be presumed that any clause in the constitution is intended to be without effect; and therefore such a construction is inadmissible, unless the words require it.

If the solicitude of the convention, respecting our peace with foreign powers, induced a provision that the Supreme Court should take original jurisdiction in cases which might be supposed to affect them—yet the clause would have proceeded no further than to provide for such cases, if no further restriction on the powers of congress had been intended. That they should have appellate jurisdiction in all other cases, with such exceptions as Congress might make, is no restriction; unless the words be deemed exclusive of original jurisdiction.

When an instrument organizing fundamentally a judicial system, divides it into one Supreme, and so many inferior courts as the legislature may ordain and establish; then enumerates its powers, and proceeds so far to distribute them, as to define the jurisdiction of the Supreme Court by declaring the cases in which it shall take original jurisdiction, and that in others it shall take appellate jurisdiction—the plain import of the words seems to be, that in one class of cases its jurisdiction is original, and not appellate; in the other it is appellate, and not original. If any other construction would render the clause inoperative, that is an additional reason for rejecting such other construction, & for adhering to their obvious meaning.

To enable this court then to issue a mandamus, it must be shewn to be an exercise of appellate jurisdiction, or to be necessary to enable them to exercise appellate jurisdiction.

It has been stated at the bar that the appellate jurisdiction may be exercised in a variety of forms, and that if it be the will of the legislature that a mandamus should be used for that purpose, that will must be obeyed. This is true—yet the jurisdiction must be appellate—not original.

It is the essential criterion of appellate jurisdiction, that it revises and corrects the proceedings in a cause already instituted, and does not create that cause. Although, therefore, a mandamus may be directed to courts, yet to issue such a writ to an officer for the delivery of a paper, is in effect the same as to sustain an original action for that paper, and therefore seems not to belong to appellate, but to original jurisdiction. Neither is it necessary in such a case as this, to enable the court to exercise its appellate jurisdiction.

The authority, therefore, given to the Supreme Court, by the act establishing the judicial courts of the United States, to issue writs of mandamus to public officers appears not to be warranted by the constitution—and it becomes necessary to enquire whether a jurisdiction, so conferred, can be exercised.

The question whether an act, repugnant to the constitution, can become the law of the land, is a question deeply interesting to the United States; but happily not of an intricacy proportioned to its interest. It seems only necessary to recognize certain principles, supposed to have been long and well established, to decide it.

That the people have an original right to establish, for their future government, such principles as, in their opinion, shall most conduce to their own happiness, is the basis, on which the whole American fabric has been erected. The exercise of this original right is a very great exertion; nor can it, nor ought it to be frequently repeated. The principles, therefore, so established, are deemed fundamental. And as the authority, from which they proceed, is supreme, and can seldom act, they are designed to be permanent.

This original and supreme will organizes the government, and assigns, to different departments, their respective powers. It may either stop here; or establish certain limits not to be transcended by those departments.

The government of the United States is of the latter description. The powers of the legislature are defined, and limited; and that those limits may not be mistaken, or forgotten, the constitution is written.

To what purpose are powers limited & to what purpose is that limitation committed to writing, if these limits may, at any time, be passed by those intended to be restrained? The distinction between a government with limited and unlimited powers, is abolished, if those limits do not confine the persons on whom they are imposed, and if acts prohibited and acts allowed, are of equal obligation. It is a proposition too plain to be contested, that the constitution controls any legislative act repugnant to it; or, that the legislature may alter the constitution by an ordinary act.

Between these alternatives there is no middle ground. The constitution is either a superior, paramount law, unchangeable by ordinary means, or it is on a level with ordinary legislative acts, & like other acts, is alterable when the legislature shall please to alter it.

If the former part of the alternative be true, then a legislative act contrary to the constitution is not law—if the latter part be true, then written constitutions are absurd attempts, on the part of the people, to limit a power, in its own nature, illimitable.

Certainly all those who have framed written constitutions, contemplate them as forming the fundamental and paramount law of the nation, and consequently the theory of every such government must be, that an act of the legislature, repugnant to the constitution, is void.

This theory is essentially attached to a written constitution, and is consequently to be considered, by this court, as one of the fundamental principles of our society. It is not therefore to be lost sight of in the further consideration of the subject.

If an act of the legislature repugnant to the constitution, is void, does it not withstanding its invalidity, bind the courts, and oblige them to give it effect? Or, in other words, though it be not law, does it constitute a rule as operative as if it was a law? This would be to overthrow in fact, what was established in theory; and would seem, at first view, an absurdity too gross to be insisted on. It shall, however, receive a more attentive consideration.

It is emphatically the province and duty of the judicial department to say what the law is. Those who apply the rule to particular cases, must of necessity expound, and interpret that rule. If two laws conflict with each other, the courts must decide on the operation of each.

So if a law be in opposition to the constitution; if both the law and the constitution apply to a particular case, so that the court must either decide that case conformably to the law, disregarding the constitution; or conformably to the constitution, disregarding the law; the court must determine which of these conflicting rules, governs the case. This is of the essence of judicial duty.

If then the courts are to regard the constitution; and the constitution is superior to any ordinary act of the legislature— the constitution, and not such ordinary act, must govern the case to which they both apply.

Those then who controvert the principle that the constitution is to be considered in court as a paramount law, are reduced to the necessity of maintaining that courts must close their eyes on the constitution, and see only the law.

This doctrine would subvert the very foundation of all written constitutions. It would declare that an act, which, according to the principles and theory of our government, is entirely void; is yet, in practice, completely obligatory. It would declare that if the legislature shall do what is expressly forbidden, such act, notwithstanding the express prohibition, is in reality effectual. It would be giving to the legislature a practical and real omnipotence, with the same breath which professes to restrict their powers within narrow limits. It is prescribing limits, and declaring that those limits may be passed at pleasure.

That it thus reduces to nothing what we have deemed the greatest improvement on political institutions—a written constitution—would of itself be sufficient, in America, where written constitutions have been viewed with so much reverence, for rejecting the construction. But the peculiar expressions of the constitution of the United States furnish additional arguments in favour of its rejection.

The judicial power of the United States is extended to all cases arising under the constitution.

Could it be the intention of those who gave this power, to say that, in using it, the constitution should not be looked into? That a case arising under the constitution should be decided without examining the instrument under which it arises?

This is too extravagant to be maintained.

In some cases then, the constitution must be looked into by the judges. And if they can open it at all, what part of it are they forbidden to read, or to obey?

There are many other parts of the constitution which serve to illustrate this subject.

It is declared that "no tax or duty shall be laid on articles exported from any state." Suppose a duty on the export of Cotton, of Tobacco, or of Flour; and a suit instituted to recover it. Ought judgment to be rendered in such a case? Ought the judges to close their eyes on the constitution, and only see the law.

The constitution declares, that "no bill of attainder or ex post facto law shall be passed."

If however such a bill should be passed and a person should be prosecuted under it; must the court condemn to death those victims whom the constitution endeavours to preserve?

"No person," says the constitution, shall be convicted of treason, "unless on the testimony of two witnesses to the same overt act, or on confession in open court."

Here the language of the constitution is addressed specially to the courts. It prescribes, directly for them, a rule of evidence not to be departed from. If the legislature should change that rule, and declare *one* witness, or a confession *out* of court, sufficient for conviction, must the constitutional principle yield to the legislative act?

From these, and many other selections which might be made, it is apparent, that the framers of the constitution contemplated that instrument, as a rule for the government of *courts*, as well as of the legislature.

Why otherwise does it direct the judges to take an oath to support it? This oath certainly applies, in an especial manner, to their conduct in their official character. How immoral to impose it on them, if they were to be used as the instruments, and the knowing instruments, for violating what they swear to support!

The oath of office, too, imposed by the legislature is completely demonstrative of the legislative opinion on this subject.

It is in these words, "I do solemnly swear that I will administer justice, without respect to persons, and do equal right to the poor and to the rich; and that I will faithfully and impartially discharge all the duties incumbent on me as according to the best of my abilities and understanding agreeably to *the constitution*, and laws of the United States."

Why does a judge swear to discharge his duties agreeably to the constitution of the United States, if that constitution forms no rule for his government? if it is closed upon him and cannot be inspected by him?

If such be the real state of things, this is worse than solemn mockery. To prescribe, or to take, this oath, becomes equally a crime.

It is also not entirely unworthy of observation, that in declaring what shall be the *Supreme* law of the land, the *constitution* itself is first mentioned; and not the laws of the United States generally, but those only which shall be made in *pursuance* of the constitution, have that rank.

Thus the particular phraseology of the constitution of the United States confirms & strengthens the principle, supposed to be essential to all written constitutions, that a law repugnant to the constitution is void; and that *courts*, as well as other departments, are bound by that instrument.

The rule must be discharged.

February 24, 1803

EDITING "THE LIFE OF GEORGE WASHINGTON"

To Caleb P. Wayne

Sir   Richmond Jany. 10th: 1804
   Your letter of the 2d. inst. has just reachd me.

   I think the note respecting the controversy between the house
of representatives & Governor of Massachussetts on the subject of a fixd salary may well be omitted: & it is probable there
are other notes which escape my memory & which may also be
passed over without injury to the work. Shoud such occur I
wish you to mention them, & I make no doubt of my perfect
concurrence with you on such subjects. I have no objection to
your plan of placing the long notes at the end of the volume in
the form of an appendix: indeed I think it the more eligible
mode of printing the work.

   My repugnance to permitting my name to appear in the title
still continues, but it shall yield to your right to make the best
use you can of the copy. I do not myself imagine that the name
of the author being given or withheld can produce any difference in the number of subscribers or of purchasers; but if you
think differently, I shoud be very unwilling by a pertinacious
adherence to what may be deemd a meer prejudice, to leave
you in the opinion that a real injury has been sustaind. I have
written to Mr. Washington on this subject & shall submit my
scruples to you & him, only requesting that my name may not
be given but on mature consideration & conviction of its propriety. If this shall be ultimately resolvd on I wish not my title
in the judiciary of the United States to be annexd to it. Mr.
Washington will probably write to you but I have requested
that no decision be made, unless it shall be necessary, till I see
him which will be at Washington early in february.

   With respect to punctuation I shall thank you to make such
corrections as may be judgd proper. I have no doubt of there
being frequent inaccuracies of this sort in the manuscript
which I shall regret my inability to correct when I see them in
print. I conjecture too that the same observation will apply
with equal justice to the paragraphs, & I request that you will
amend any obvious impropriety in this or any other respect

which you may discover. I am also willing to conform to Johnsons mode of spelling except where a well settled modern practice has so departed from his authority as to give an observance of it the appearance of affectation. I consider as of this description many words terminating in "our"—as Governour, in which the present establishd usage drops the "u." It is not however a subject on which I am solicitous, & in any doubtful case I woud decidedly prefer to follow Johnson. With respect to Capitals I wish common usage to be observd with this only regulation—that where it is matter of doubt or absolute indifference I woud rather the word shoud commence with a common than with a capital letter.

The two chapters taken from the first volume will not commence the second. The second volume will commence with a chapter beginning with the birth & ending with the marriage of General Washington. After which there will be one, perhaps two pages introductory to the 14th. which will form the 2d. chapter of the 2d. volume & I am not sure that it may not be necessary to make some slight alterations in the concluding part of the 15th. or 3d. chapter. Shoud Mr. Washington have contracted with Mr. Morgan these observations must be communicated to that Gentleman & only the 13 first chapters ought now to be deliverd to him.

The preliminary part of the history will properly have the same title with the residue of the work as there will be a continuation of the volumes, but I think it will be more correct to place on the top of each page the word "Introduction." I am not however anxious about it.

If you will let me know by what time you will be ready to commence the 2d. volume I will endeavor to transmit to Mr. Washington, certainly the first chapter, & probably the residue in time to prevent your being delayd. This however cannot be done further than respects the first chapter previous to my return from the february term of the supreme court. I am Sir very respectfully, Your obedt. Servt

Preface to
The Life of George Washington

A desire to know intimately those illustrious personages, who have performed a conspicuous part on the great theatre of the world, is, perhaps, implanted in every human bosom. We delight to follow them through the various critical and perilous situations in which they have been placed, to view them in the extremes of adverse and prosperous fortune, to trace their progress through all the difficulties they have surmounted, and to contemplate their whole conduct at a time when, the power and the pomp of office having disappeared, it may be presented to us in the simple garb of truth.

If among those exalted characters which are produced in every age, none can have a fairer claim to the attention and recollection of mankind than those under whose auspices great empires have been founded, or political institutions deserving to be permanent, established; a faithful representation of the various important events connected with the life of the favourite Son of America, cannot be unworthy of the general regard. Among his own countrymen it will unquestionably excite the deepest interest.

As if the chosen instrument of Heaven, selected for the purpose of effecting the great designs of Providence respecting this our western hemisphere, it was the peculiar lot of this distinguished man, at every epoch when the destinies of his country seemed dependent on the measures adopted, to be called by the united voice of his fellow citizens to those high stations on which the success of those measures principally depended. It was his peculiar lot to be equally useful in obtaining the independence, and consolidating the civil institutions, of his country. We perceive him at the head of her armies, during a most arduous and perilous war on the events of which her national existence was staked, supporting with invincible fortitude the unequal conflict. That war being happily terminated, and the political revolutions of America requiring that he should once more relinquish his beloved retirement, we find him guiding her councils with the same firmness, wisdom, and virtue, which had, long and successfully, been displayed in the field. We behold him her chief magistrate at a time when her happiness, her liberty, perhaps her preservation depended on so administering the affairs of the Union, that a government standing entirely on the public favour, which had with infinite difficulty been adopted, and against which the most inveterate prejudices had been excited, should conciliate public opinion, and acquire a firmness and stability that would enable it to resist the rude shocks it was destined to sustain. It was too his peculiar fortune to afford the brightest examples of moderation and patriotism, by voluntarily divesting himself of the highest military and civil honours when the public interests no longer demanded that he should retain them. We find him retiring from the head of a victorious and discontented army which adored him, so soon as the object for which arms had been taken up was accomplished; and withdrawing from the highest office an American citizen can hold, as soon as his influence, his character, and his talents, ceased to be necessary to the maintenance of that government which had been established under his auspices.

He was indeed "first in war,* first in peace, and first in the hearts of his fellow citizens."

A faithful detail of the transactions of a person so preeminently distinguished will be looked for with avidity, and the author laments his inability to present to the public a work which may gratify the expectations that have been raised. In addition to that just diffidence of himself which he very sincerely feels, two causes beyond his control combine to excite this apprehension.

Accustomed to look in the page of history for incidents in themselves of great magnitude, to find immense exertions attended with inconsiderable effects, and vast means employed in producing unimportant ends, we are in the habit of bestowing on the recital of military actions, a degree of consideration proportioned to the numbers engaged in them. When the struggle has terminated, and the agitations felt during its suspense have subsided, it is difficult to attach to enterprises, in

---

*The expressions of a resolution prepared by general Lee and passed in the house of representatives of the United States, on their being informed of the death of general Washington.

which small numbers have been concerned, that admiration which is often merited by the talents displayed in their execution, or that interest which belongs to the consequences that have arisen from them.

The long and distressing contest between Great Britain and these States did not abound in those great battles which are so frequent in the wars of Europe. Those who expect a continued succession of victories and defeats; who can only feel engaged in the movements of vast armies, and who believe that a Hero must be perpetually in action, will be disappointed in almost every page of the following history. Seldom was the American chief in a condition to indulge his native courage in those brilliant achievements to which he was stimulated by his own feelings, and a detail of which interests, enraptures, and astonishes the reader. Had he not often checked his natural disposition, had he not tempered his ardour with caution, the war he conducted would probably have been of short duration, and the United States would still have been colonies. At the head of troops most of whom were perpetually raw because they were perpetually changing; who were neither well fed, paid, clothed, nor armed; and who were generally inferior, even in numbers, to the enemy; he derives no small title to glory from the consideration, that he never despaired of the public safety; that he was able at all times to preserve the appearance of an army, and that, in the most desperate situation of American affairs, he did not, for an instant, cease to be formidable. To estimate rightly his worth we must contemplate his difficulties. We must examine the means placed in his hands, and the use he made of those means. To preserve an army when conquest was impossible, to avoid defeat and ruin when victory was unattainable, to keep his forces embodied and suppress the discontents of his soldiers, exasperated by a long course of the most cruel privations, to seize with unerring discrimination the critical moment when vigorous offensive operations might be advantageously carried on, are actions not less valuable in themselves, nor do they require less capacity in the chief who performs them, than a continued succession of battles. But they spread less splendour over the page which recounts them, and excite weaker emotions in the bosom of the reader.

There is also another source from which some degree of

disappointment has been anticipated. It is the impossibility of giving to the public in the first part of this work many facts not already in their possession.

The American war was a subject of too much importance to have remained thus long unnoticed by the literary world. Almost every event worthy of attention, which occurred during its progress, has been gleaned up and detailed. Not only the public, but much of the private correspondence of the commander in chief has been inspected, and permission given to extract from it whatever might properly be communicated. In the military part of this history, therefore, the author can promise not much that is new. He can only engage for the correctness with which facts are stated, and for the diligence with which his researches have been made.

The letters to and from the commander in chief during the war, were very numerous and have been carefully preserved. The whole of this immensely voluminous correspondence has, with infinite labour, been examined; and the work now offered to the public is, principally, compiled from it. The facts which occurred on the continent are, generally, supported by these letters, and it has therefore been deemed unnecessary to multiply references to them. But there are many facts so connected with those events, in which the general performed a principal part, that they ought not to be omitted, and respecting which his correspondence cannot be expected to furnish satisfactory information. Such facts have been taken from the histories of the day, and the authority relied on for the establishment of their verity has been cited. Doddesly's Annual Register, Belsham, Gordon, Ramsay, and Stedman have, for this purpose, been occasionally resorted to, and are quoted for all those facts which are detailed in part on their authority. Their very language has sometimes been employed without distinguishing the passages, especially when intermingled with others, by marks of quotation, and the author persuades himself that this public declaration will rescue him from the imputation of receiving aids he is unwilling to acknowledge, or of wishing, by a concealed plagiarism, to usher to the world, as his own, the labours of others.

In selecting the materials for the succeeding volumes, it was deemed proper to present to the public as much as possible of general Washington himself. Prominent as he must be in any history of the American war, there appeared to be a peculiar fitness in rendering him still more so in one which professes to give a particular account of his own life. His private opinions therefore; his various plans, even those which were never carried into execution; his individual exertions to prevent and correct the multiplied errors committed by inexperience, are given in more minute detail; and more copious extracts from his letters are taken, than would comport with the plan of a more general work. Many events too are unnoticed, which in such a composition would be worthy of being introduced, and much useful information has not been sought for, which a professed history of America ought to comprise. Yet the history of general Washington, during his military command and civil administration, is so much that of his country, that the work appeared to the author to be most sensibly incomplete and unsatisfactory, while unaccompanied by such a narrative of the principal events preceding our revolutionary war, as would make the reader acquainted with the genius, character, and resources of the people about to engage in that memorable contest. This appeared the more necessary as that period of our history is but little known to ourselves. Several writers have detailed very minutely the affairs of a particular colony, but the *desideratum* is a composition which shall present in one connected view, the transactions of all those colonies which now form the United States.

The materials for the complete execution of such a work are perhaps not to be found in America; and, if they do exist, their collection would require a length of time, and a labour of research, which neither the impatience of the public, nor the situation of the author would enable him to bestow on the subject. Yet he thought it more eligible to digest into one volume the most material of those facts which are now scattered through several books, than to commence his history abruptly with the war between Great Britain and her colonies.

The difficulties attending even such an undertaking as this, were soon perceived to be greater than had been expected. In several of the English colonies, either no accounts whatever, or such vague accounts of their transactions have been given, that long intervals of time pass away without furnishing a single document relative to their affairs. In others very circumstantial details of their original settlements have been published, but the relation stops at an early period. In New England alone has the history of any colony been continued to the war of our independence; mr. Belknap, mr. Hutchinson and mr. Minot have faithfully transmitted to those who succeed them, the events which occurred in New Hampshire and Massachussetts. Mr. Trumbull is engaged in a similar undertaking for Connecticut, but has not yet progressed far in its execution. In New York, mr. Smith has made a valuable commencement; and in Virginia mr. Stith, and mr. Beverly, have detailed at great length the hardships of the original settlers; but in the other colonies, until we reach South Carolina and Georgia, scarcely an attempt has been made at a history of any sort. To the reign of William and Mary, mr. Chalmer has furnished almost all the facts which the historian of the United States would require. It is much to be regretted that he has not prosecuted his very valuable work according to his original design. So far as it has been executed, it contains internal evidence of the means he possesses for its completion: means unattainable by any inhabitant of the United States. The author has made free use of the materials he has furnished, as well as of those collected by mr. Belknap, mr. Hutchinson, mr. Minot, mr. Smith, and the historian of South Carolina and Georgia. He has also made large extracts from the two chapters written by mr. Robertson and published since his decease. Had that gentleman lived to finish the work he began, an elegant and valuable history of our country would have been in possession of the public, and the author of the following sheets would have deemed it unnecessary to have introduced the Life of General Washington with any narrative of events preceding the time when that great man appeared on the theatre of action. But we have received from mr. Robertson only an account of the settlements of the two eldest colonies, and therefore the necessity of prefixing to this work some essay, though a crude one, towards a general history of the English settlements on this continent, still remained.

If mr. Chalmer, or any other person, shall complete the publication of that collection of facts which he has so successfully commenced, and intelligent individuals of other states could be induced to follow the example set them by mr. Belknap, mr. Hutchinson, mr. Minot, and mr. Trumbull, a fund of information would then be collected from which a correct and valuable history of the now United States might readily be compiled. Until one or both of these events occur, such a history is not to be expected. The author is by no means insensible of the insufficiency of that which is now presented to the public, but the Life of General Washington required some previous general knowledge of American affairs, and he thought it more advisable to accompany that work with even the imperfect sketch of our history which he has been enabled to draw, than to give it publicity unconnected with any narrative whatever of preceding events.

In executing the determination produced by this opinion, he soon perceived that though human nature is always the same, and consequently man will in every situation furnish useful lessons to the discerning politician; yet few would be willing to employ much time in searching for them through the minute details of the sufferings of an infant people, spreading themselves through a wilderness preoccupied only by savages and wild beasts. These details can interest themselves alone, and only the desire of knowing the situation of our own country in every stage of its existence, can stamp a value on the page which contains them. He has, therefore, omitted entirely many transactions deemed of great moment while passing, and yet he is more apprehensive of having overcharged his narrative with facts not of sufficient importance to be preserved, than of having contracted it too much.

For any inattention to composition an apology ought never to be necessary. A work of any importance ought never to be submitted to the public until it has been sufficiently revised and corrected. Yet the first part of the Life of General Washington goes into the world under circumstances, which might bespeak from candour less severity of criticism, than it will probably experience. The papers from which it has been compiled have been already stated to be immensely voluminous, and the public was already looking for the work, before the writer was fixed on and the documents from which it was to be composed placed in his hands. The impatience since discovered by many of the subscribers has carried the following sheets to the press much more precipitately than the judgment of the author would have permitted him to part with them, and he cannot flatter himself that they are free from many defects which on a re-perusal will attract even his own observation.

1804

THE IMPEACHMENT OF JUSTICE CHASE

To Samuel Chase

My dear Sir   Richmond Jany. 23d. 1804

On receiving your letter of the 13th. I instantly applied to my brother & to Mr. Wickham requesting them to state their recollection of the circumstances under which Colo. Taylors testimony was rejected. They both declared that they rememberd them very imperfectly but that they woud endeavor to recollect what passd & commit it to writing. I shall bring it with me to Washington in february. At the same time I shall take with me a list of the grand & petit jury, & a copy of the order of writ directing Callenders arrest.

The foreman of the Jury was Colo. Gamble & the juror who spoke to you was Mr. John Bassett. They are both men of character & intelligence.

Admitting it to be true that on legal principles Colo. Taylors testimony was admissible, it certainly constitutes a very extraordinary ground for an impeachment. According to the antient doctrine a jury finding a verdict against the law of the case was liable to an attaint; & the amount of the present doctrine seems to be that a Judge giving a legal opinion contrary to the opinion of the legislature is liable to impeachment. As, for convenience & humanity the old doctrine of attaint has yielded to the silent, moderate but not less operative influence of new trials, I think the modern doctrine of impeachment shoud yield to an appellate jurisdiction in the legislature. A reversal of those legal opinions deemd unsound by the legislature woud certainly better comport with the mildness of our character than a removal of the Judge who has renderd them unknowing of his fault. The other charges except the 1st. & 4th. which I suppose to be altogether unfounded, seem still less to furnish cause for impeachment. But the little finger of —— is heavier than the loins of ——.

I have not written to Mr. Moore because I count on his setting out for Washington before my letter coud reach him. Farewell—With much respect & esteem, I am dear Sir your Obedt

Mr. Nelson is unfortunately dead.

CRITICISMS OF "THE LIFE"

To Caleb P. Wayne

Sir   Richmond July 20th. 1804
I have received your letter with part of the sheets of the 2d. vol. & your resolution to postpone the 2d. edition of the first. I am just setting out for the upper country where I shall give the 1st. vol one considerate reading & then forward it to you by the post. You will please to direct to me at Front Royal, Frederick county Virginia. I will thank you to transmit me immediately at that place a copy of the corrections before made to the first volume, unless you shoud already have addressed the paper to me in Richmond in which case it will follow me.

I have no doubt that the errors noticed are principally if not entirely in the manuscript. Some very few I beleive are not but they are very few. I am confident of the care you have bestowd on the subject & wish every other person coud have performd his part with as much attention & exactness as you have done. I thank you for the two papers you sent me. I take the gazette of the United States & shall of course see anything which may appear in that paper. The very handsome critique in the political & commercial register was new to me. I coud only regret that there was in it more of pannegyric than was merited. The editor of that paper, if the author of the critique, manifests himself to be master of a style of a very superior order & to be of course a very correct Judge of the compositions of others.

Having, Heaven knows how reluctantly, consented against my judgement, to be known as the author of the work in question I cannot be insensible to the opinions entertaind of it, but I am much more sollicitous to hear the strictures upon it than to know what parts may be thought exempt from censure. As I am about to give a reading to the first volume & as not much time can be employed upon it the strictures of those who are either friendly or hostile to the work may be useful if communicated to me because they may direct my attention to defects which might other wise escape a single reading however careful that reading may be. I will therefore thank you to convey to me at Front Royal every condemnatory criticism which may reach you. It woud be impossible & I shall not attempt to polish every sentence. That woud require repeated readings & a long course of time; but I wish to correct obvious imperfections & the animadversions of others woud aid me very much in doing so.

I shall probably return about the beginning of october, but you will hear from me long before that time & will know when I shall leave the upper country. I am Sir very respectfully your Obedt

PUBLISHING DIFFICULTIES

To Caleb P. Wayne

Sir   Front Royal Septr. 3d. 1804

On my return from the Allegheny I received your letter of the 20th. of August with the magazine & paper which accompanied it.

I wish very sincerely that some of those objections which are now made to the plan of the work had been heard when the proposals for subscription were first published. I shoud very readily have relinquished my opinion respecting it if I had percieved that the public taste required a different course. I ought indeed to have foreseen that the same impatience which precipitated the publication woud require that the life & transactions of Mr. Washington shoud be immediately entered upon, &, if my original ideas of the subject had been preserved in the main, yet I ought to have departed from them so far as to have composed the introductory volume at leisure after the principal work was finished.

I have also to sustain increased mortification on account of the careless manner in which the work has been executed. I had to learn that under the pressure of constant application the spring of the mind loses its elasticity & that the style will be insensibly influenced by that of the authors we have been perusing. That compositions thus formed require attentive revisals when the impression under which they were written has worn off. But regrets for the past are unavailing. It is of more service to do what is best under existing circumstances. There will be great difficulty in retrieving the reputation of the first volume because there is a minuteness & a want of interest in details of the transactions of infant settlements which will always affect the book containing them however it may be executed. I have therefore some doubts whether it may not be as well to drop the first volume for the present—that is not to speak of a republication of it, & to proceed with the others. I shall at all events conform to your request & be silent respecting the corrections I have prepared.

I wish the third coud be reduced to the compass you mention. If it is not already in the press that might perhaps be done. I coud effect it if the copy was again in my possession. But I had no idea that the pages of the manuscript woud exceed those of the printed volume. Perhaps you might stop short of the chapter where the volume is now finishd.

I am very sorry that I cannot send on the 4th. Vol. by the time you request. Those whom I applied to as copyers have deserted the business in my absence, & I cannot return to Richmond to engage others till early in october. It will of consequence be perhaps the month of february before you can receive it. Independent of this untoward circumstance, experience has sufficiently admonished me of the indiscretion of sending another almost unexamined volume to the press.

Whatever might have been the execution, the work woud

have experienced unmerited censure. We must endeavor to rescue what remains to be done from such as is deserved. I wish you to consult Mr. Washington. I am very respectfully, your obedt

I shall give a very attentive perusal to the printed copy & render it much more fit for the public eye in case of another edition. But this must be postponed.

REVISING "THE LIFE"

To Caleb P. Wayne

Sir   Richmond June 27th. 1806
    I have received your letters of the 27th. of May & of the 6th. & 11th. of this month enclosing me five hundred dollars, two hundred dollars, & fifty dollars: and also informing me that seven hundred & fifty dollars were deposited for me in the bank of the United States. I have given a check for four hundred & fifty & shall to day give two checks for the balance. I have also received from Mr. Washington one hundred & forty one dollars three cents which were paid to him by one of your collectors in Baltimore.
    The last chapter will be copied this week & I am now watching for an opportunity to transmit it to Mount Vernon where the preceding chapters are, & whence it will be forwarded to you. The delay which is greater than I expected has been occasioned in part by my personal indisposition & in part by the necessity of going over the work & expunging about one third of it.
    I have always felt anxiety respecting a second edition & on that account have wished the copies of the first not to be multiplied. This will be to your advantage because the size of the volume may be reduced or the price augmented. Whether a second edition may ever be required or not I propose after returning from the springs to go over the first at my leisure & make many of those corrections which in the hurry of compo-

sition & even of that reading which I afterwards gave to the three first volumes, have certainly escaped my observation. I had proposed a short preface to this volume, but its size notwithstanding the diminutions it has sustained is still too large & I do not wish to stop it one day after an opportunity shall offer to send it forward. I am Sir respectfully, Your Obedt

Circuit Court Opinion in
United States v. Burr
Regarding a Motion for a Subpoena

THE object of the motion now to be decided is to obtain copies of certain orders understood to have been issued to the land & naval officers of the U.S. for the apprehension of the accused; and an original letter from Gen. Wilkinson to the President in relation to the accused, with the answer of the President to that letter, which papers are supposed to be material to the defence. As the legal mode of effecting this object, a motion is made for a subpœna duces tecum to be directed to the President of the U. States.

In opposition to this motion a preliminary point has been made by the counsel for the prosecution. It has been insisted by them that until the Grand Jury shall have found a true bill, the party accused is not entitled to subpœnas or to the aid of the court to obtain his testimony.

It will not be said that this opinion is now for the first time, advanced in the United States; but certainly, it is now for the first time advanced in Virginia. So far back as any knowledge of our jurisprudence is possessed, the uniform practice of this country has been to permit any individual who was charged with any crime, to prepare for his defence, and to obtain the process of the court, for the purpose of enabling him so to do. This practice is as convenient, and is as consonant to justice as it is to humanity. It prevents in a great measure those delays which are never desirable, which frequently occasion the loss of testimony, and which are often oppressive, that would be the inevitable consequence of withholding from a prisoner the process of the court, until the indictment against him was found by a Grand Jury. The right of an accused person to the process of the court, to compel the attendance of witnesses seems to follow necessarily from the right to examine those witnesses, and wherever the right exists, it would be reasonable that it should be accompanied with the means of rendering it effectual. It is not doubted, that a person who appears before a court, under a recognizance, must expect that a bill will be preferred against him, or that a question concerning the continuance of the recognizance, will be brought before the court. In the first event, he has the right, and it is perhaps his duty to prepare for his defence at the trial. In the second event, it will not be denied that he possesses the right to examine witnesses on the question of continuing his recognizance. In either case, it would seem reasonable that he should be entitled to the process of the court, to procure the attendance of his witnesses.

The genius and character of our laws and usages, are friendly, not to condemnation at all events, but to a fair and impartial trial; and they consequently allow to the accused the right of preparing the means to secure such a trial. The objection that the attorney may refuse to proceed at this time, and that no day is fixed for the trial, if he should proceed, presents no real difficulty. It would be a very insufficient excuse to a prisoner who had failed to prepare for his trial, to say that he was not certain the attorney would proceed against him. Had the indictment been found at the last term it would have been in some measure uncertain whether there would have been a trial at this, and still more uncertain on what day that trial would take place; yet subpœnas would have issued returnable to the first day of the term, and if, after its commencement, other subpœnas had been required, they would have issued returnable as the court might direct. In fact all process to which the law has affixed no certain return day, is made returnable at the discretion of the court.

General principles then, and general practice, are in favor of the right of every accused person so soon as his case is in court, to prepare for his defence, and to receive the aid of the process of the court to compel the attendance of his witnesses.

The constitution and laws of the U. States will now be considered for the purpose of ascertaining how they bear upon the question.

The 8th amendment to the constitution gives to the accused in all criminal prosecutions, a right to a speedy and public trial, and to compulsory process for obtaining witnesses in his favour. The right given by this article must be deemed sacred by the courts, and the article should be so construed as to be something more than a dead letter. What can more effectually elude the right to a speedy trial than the declaration that the

accused shall be disabled from preparing for it, until an indictment shall be found against him? It is certainly much more in
the true spirit of the provision which secures to the accused a
speedy trial, that he should have the benefit of the provision
which entitles him to compulsory process as soon as he is
brought into court.

This observation derives additional force from a consideration of the manner in which this subject has been contemplated by Congress. It is obviously the intention of the
national legislature that in all capital cases, the accused shall be
entitled to process before indictment found. The words of the
law are, "and every *such* person or persons accused or indicted
of the crimes aforesaid (that is of treason or any other capital
offence) shall be allowed and admitted in his said defence to
make any proof that he or they can produce, by lawful witness
or witnesses, and shall have the like process of the court where
he or they shall be tried, to compel his or their witnesses to appear at his or their trial, as is usually granted to compel witnesses to appear on the prosecution against them."

This provision is made for persons accused or indicted. From
the imperfection of human language it frequently happens that
sentences which ought to be the most explicit are of doubtful
construction, and in this case the words "accused or indicted"
may be construed to be synonimous, to describe a person in
the same situation or to apply to different stages of the prosecution. The word *or* may be taken in a conjunctive or a disjunc-
tive sense. A reason for understanding them in the latter sense
is furnished by the Sect: itself. It commences with declaring
that any person who shall be accused *and* indicted of treason,
shall have a copy of the indictment, and at least three days
before his trial. This right is obviously to be enjoyed after an
indictment, and therefore the words are "accused *and* indicted." So with respect to the subsequent clause which authorizes a party to make his defence and directs the court on his
application to assign him counsel. The words relate to any person accused *and* indicted. But when the section proceeds to
authorize the compulsory process for witnesses, the phraseology is changed. The words are "and every such person or persons accused or indicted" &c. thereby adapting the expression
to the situation of an accused person both before and after in-

dictment. It is to be remarked too, that the person so accused *or* indicted is to have "the like process to compel his or their witnesses to appear at his or their trial as is usually granted to compel witnesses to appear on the prosecution against them." The fair construction of this clause would seem to be that with respect to the means of compelling the attendance of witnesses to be furnished by the court, the prosecution and defence are placed by the law on equal ground. The right of the prosecutor to take out subpœnas or to avail himself of the aid of the court in any stage of the proceedings previous to the indictment, is not controverted. This act of Congress, it is true, applies only to capital cases; but persons charged with offences not capital have a constitutional and a legal right to examine their testimony, and this act ought to be considered as declaratory of the common law in cases where this constitutional right exists.

Upon immemorial usage then, and upon what is deemed a sound construction of the constitution and law of the land, the court is of opinion that any person charged with a crime in the courts of the United States has a right, before as well as after indictment, to the process of the court to compel the attendance of his witnesses. Much delay and much inconvenience may be avoided by this construction, no mischief which is perceived can be produced by it. The process would only issue, when according to the ordinary course of proceeding, the indictment would be tried at the term to which the subpœna is made returnable, so that it becomes incumbent on the accused to be ready for his trial at that term.

This point being disposed of, it remains to enquire whether a *subpœna Duces Tecum* can be directed to the President of the United States, and whether it ought to be directed in this case.

This question originally consisted of two parts. It was at first doubted whether, a subpœna could issue in any case to the chief magistrate of the nation; and if it could, whether that subpœna could do more than direct his personal attendance: whether it could direct him to bring with him a paper which was to constitute the gist of his testimony.

While the argument was opening, the attorney for the United States avowed his opinion that a general subpœna might issue to the President but not a subpœna *Duces Tecum*. This terminated the argument on *that* part of the question. The court, however, has thought it necessary to state briefly the foundation of its opinion that such a subpœna may issue.

In the provisions of the constitution and of the statute which give to the accused a right to the compulsory process of the court there is no exception whatever. The obligation, therefore, of those provisions is general; and it would seem that no person could claim an exemption from them but one who would not be a witness. At any rate, if an exception to the general principle exist, it must be looked for in the law of evidence. The exceptions furnished by the law of evidence (with one only reservation) so far as they are personal, are of those only whose testimony could not be received. The single reservation alluded to, is the case of the king. Although he may perhaps give testimony, it is said to be incompatible with his dignity to appear under the process of the court. Of the many points of difference which exist between the first magistrate in England and the first magistrate of the United States, in respect of the personal dignity conferred on them by the constitution of their respective nations, the court will only select and mention two. It is a principle of the English constitution that the king can do no wrong, that no blame can be imputed to him, that he cannot be named in debate.

By the constitution of the United States, the President as well as every other officer of the government, may be impeached, and may be removed from office on conviction of high crimes and misdemeanors.

By the constitution of Great-Britain the crown is hereditary and the monarch can never become a subject.

By that of the United States, the President is elected from the mass of the people, and on the expiration of the time for which he is elected, returns to the mass of the people again.

How essentially this difference of circumstances must vary the policy of the laws of the two countries in reference to the personal dignity of the executive chief, will be perceived by every person. In this respect, the first magistrate of the Union may more properly be likened to the first magistrate of a state—at any rate under the former confederation; and it is not known ever to have been doubted, that the chief magistrate of a state might be served with a subpœna ad testificandum.

If in any court of the United States, it has ever been decided, that a subpœna cannot issue to the President, that decision is unknown to this court.

If upon any principle, the President could be construed to stand exempt from the general provisions of the constitution, it would be because his duties as chief magistrate demand his whole time for national objects. But it is apparent that this demand is not unremitting, and if it should exist at the time when his attendance on a court is required it would be shown on the return of the subpœna, and would rather constitute a reason for not obeying the process of the court, than a reason against its being issued. In point of fact it cannot be doubted, that the people of England have the same interest in the service of the executive government, that is, of the cabinet counsel, that the American people have in the service of the executive of the United States, and that their duties are as arduous and as unremitting. Yet it has never been alledged that a subpœna might not be directed to them.

It cannot be denied, that to issue a subpœna to a person filling the exalted station of the chief magistrate, is a duty which would be dispensed with much more cheerfully than it would be performed; but if it be a duty the court can have no choice in the case.

If then, as is admitted by the counsel for the United States, a subpœna may issue to the President, the accused is entitled to it of course; and whatever difference may exist with respect to the power to compel the same obedience to the process, as if it had been directed to a private citizen, there exists no difference with respect to the right to obtain it. The guard furnished to this high officer to protect him from being harrassed by vexatious and unnecessary subpœnas, is to be looked for in the conduct of a court after those subpœnas have issued, not in any circumstance which is to precede their being issued.

If in being summoned to give his personal attendance to testify, the law does not discriminate between the President and a private citizen, what foundation is there for the opinion, that this difference is created by the circumstance that his testimony depends on a paper in his possession, not on facts which have come to his knowledge otherwise than by writing? The court can perceive no foundation for such an opinion. The propriety of introducing any paper into a case as testimony, must depend on the character of the paper, not on the character of the person who holds it. A subpœna *Duces Tecum* then may issue to any person to whom an ordinary subpœna may issue directing him to bring any paper of which the party praying it has a right to avail himself, as testimony, if indeed that be the necessary process for obtaining the view of such paper.

When this subject was suddenly introduced, the court felt some doubt concerning the propriety of directing a subpœna to the chief magistrate, and some doubt also concerning the propriety of directing any paper in his possession, not public in its nature, to be exhibited in court. The impression, that the questions which might arise in consequence of such process, were more proper for discussion on the return of the process than on its issuing, was then strong on the mind of the judges, but the circumspection with which they would take any step, which would in any manner relate to that high personage, prevented their yielding readily to those impressions, and induced the request that those points, if not admitted, might be argued. The result of that argument is a confirmation of the impression originally entertained. The court can perceive no legal objection to issuing a subpœna duces tecum, to any person whatever, provided, the case be such as to justify the process.

This is said to be a motion to the discretion of the court. This is true. But a motion to its discretion, is a motion not to its inclination, but to its judgement, and its judgement is to be guided by sound legal principles.

A subpœna duces tecum, varies from an ordinary subpœna only in this, that a witness is summoned for the purpose of bringing with him a paper in his custody. In some of our sister states whose system of jurisprudence is erected on the same foundation with our own, this process, we learn, issues of course. In this state it issues not absolutely of course, but with leave of the court. No case, however, exists, as is believed, in which the motion has been founded, on an affidavit, in which it has been denied, or in which it has been opposed. It has been truely observed, that the opposite party can regularly take no more interest in the awarding a subpœna duces tecum, than in the awarding an ordinary subpœna. In either case he may object to any delay, the grant of which, may be implied in granting the subpœna, but he can no more object regularly to the legal means of obtaining testimony, which exists in the mind, than in the papers of the person who may be summoned. If no inconvenience can be sustained by the opposite party he can only oppose the motion in the character of an amicus curiæ, to prevent the court from making an improper order, or from burdening some officer by compelling an unnecessary attendance. This court would certainly be very unwilling to say that upon fair construction the constitutional and legal right to obtain its process to compel the attendance of witnesses, does not extend to their bringing with them such papers as may be material in the defence. The literal distinction which exists between the cases, is too much attenuated to be countenanced in the tribunals of a just and humane nation. If then, the subpœna be used without enquiry into the manner of its application, it would seem to trench on the privileges which the constitution extends to the accused; it would seem to reduce his means of defence, within narrower limits than is designed by the fundamental law of our country, if an overstrained rigor should be used with respect to his right, to apply for papers deemed by himself to be material. In the one case the accused is made the absolute Judge of the testimony to be summoned; if in the other, he is not to judge absolutely for himself, his judgement ought to be controled only so far as it is apparent that he means to exercise his privileges, not really in his own defence, but for purposes which the court ought to discountenance. The court would not lend its aid to motions obviously designed to manifest disrespect to the government, but the court has no right to refuse its aid to motions for papers to which the accused may be entitled and which may be material in his defence.

These observations are made to show the nature of the discretion which may be exercised. If it be apparent that the papers are irrelative to the case, or that for state reasons, they cannot be introduced into the defence; the subpœna *duces tecum* would be useless; but if this is not apparent; if they may be important in the defence; if they may be safely read at the trial; would it not be a blot in the page which records the judicial proceedings of this country, if in a case of such serious import as this, the accused should be denied the use of them?

The counsel for the United States, take a very different view of this subject, and insist that a motion for process to obtain testimony, should be supported by the same full and explicit proof of the nature and application of that testimony, which would be required on a motion which would delay public justice; which would arrest the ordinary course of proceeding, or which would in any other manner affect the rights of the opposite party. In favor of this position, has been urged the opinion of one, whose loss as a friend and as a judge, I sincerely deplore; whose worth I feel, and whose authority I shall at all times greatly respect. If his opinion was really opposed to mine, I should certainly revise, deliberately revise the judgment I had formed: But I perceive no such opposition.

In the trials of Smith and Ogden, the court in which Judge Patterson presided, required a special affidavit in support of a motion made by the counsel for the accused for a continuance and for an attachment against witnesses who had been summoned and had failed to attend.

Had this requisition of a special affidavit been made as well a foundation for an attachment, as for a continuance, the cases would not have been parallel; because the attachment was considered by the counsel for the prosecution merely as a mean of punishing the contempt, and a court might certainly require stronger testimony to induce them to punish a contempt than would be required to lend its aid to a party in order to procure evidence in a cause. But the proof furnished by the case is most conclusive, that the special statements of the affidavit were required solely on account of the continuance.

Although the counsel for the United States considered the motion for an attachment merely as a mode of punishing for contempt, the counsel for Smith and Ogden considered it as compulsory process to bring in a witness, and moved a continuance until they could have the benefit of this process. The continuance was to arrest the ordinary course of justice, & therefore the court required a special affidavit, shewing the materiality of the testimony before this continuance could be granted. Prima faciæ evidence could not apply to the case, and there was an additional reason for a special affidavit. The object of this special statement was expressly said to be for a continuance.

COLDEN proceeded. "The present application is to put off the cause on account of the absence of witnesses whose testimony the defendant alledges is material for his defence, and who have disobeyed the ordinary process of the court. In compliance with the intimation from the bench yesterday, the defendant has disclosed, by the affidavit which I have just read, the points to which he expects the witnesses who have been summoned will testify.

"If the court cannot, or will not issue compulsory process to bring in the witnesses who are the objects of this application, then the cause will not be postponed.

"Or if it appears to the court that the matter disclosed by the affidavit might not be given in evidence if the witnesses were now here, then we cannot expect that our motion will be successful. For it would be absurd to suppose that the court will postpone the trial on account of the absence of witnesses whom they cannot compel to appear; and of whose voluntary attendance there is too much reason to despair, or on account of the absence of witnesses who if they were before the court, could not be heard on the trial." (Page 12.)

This argument states unequivocally the purpose for which a special affidavit was required.

The counsel for the U.S. considered the subject in the same light. After exhibiting an affidavit for the purpose of showing that the witnesses could not probably possess any material information, Mr. Sandford said "It was decided by the court yesterday that it was incumbent on the defendant, in order to entitle himself to a postponement of the trial, on account of the absence of these witnesses, to shew in what respect they are material for his defence. It was the opinion of the court that the general affidavit in common form would not be sufficient for this purpose; but that the particular facts expected from the witnesses must be disclosed, in order that the court might, upon those facts, judge of the propriety of granting the postponement." (Page 27.)

The court frequently treated the subject so as to show the opinion that the special affidavit was required only on account of the continuance; but what is conclusive on this point is, that after deciding the testimony of the witnesses to be such as could not be offered to the jury, Judge Patterson was of opinion, that a rule to show cause why an attachment should not issue ought to be granted. He could not have required the materiality of the witness to be shown on a motion, the success of which did not in his opinion, in any degree depend on that materiality; and which he granted after deciding the testimony to be such as the jury ought not to hear. It is then most apparent that the opinion of Judge Patterson has been misunderstood, and that no inference can possibly be drawn from it, opposed to the principle which has been laid down by the court. That principle will therefore be applied to the present motion.

The first paper required, is the letter of Gen. Wilkinson, which was referred to in the message of the President to Congress. The application of that letter to the case, is shown by the terms in which the communication was made. It is a statement of the conduct of the accused, made by the person who is declared to be the essential witness against him. The order for producing this letter is opposed,

1st: Because it is not material to the defence.

It is a principle universally acknowledged, that a party has a right to oppose to the testimony of any witness against him, the declarations which that witness has made at other times on the same subject. If he possesses this right, he must bring forward proof of those declarations. This proof must be obtained before he knows positively what the witness will say, for if he waits until the witness has been heard at the trial, it is too late to meet him with his former declarations. Those former declarations, therefore, constitute a mass of testimony which a party has a right to obtain by way of precaution, and the positive necessity of which, can only be decided at the trial.

It is with some surprize an argument was heard from the bar, insinuating that the award of a subpœna on this ground, gave the countenance of the court to suspicions, affecting the veracity of a witness who is to appear on the part of the United States. This observation could not have been considered. In contests of this description the court takes no part; the court has no right to take a part. Every person may give in evidence, testimony such as is stated in this case. What would be the feelings of the prosecutor, if in this case the accused should produce a witness completely exculpating himself, and the attorney for the U. States should be arrested in his attempt to prove what the same witness had said upon a former occasion, by a declaration from the bench, that such an attempt could not be permitted, because it would imply a suspicion on the court that the witness had not spoken the truth? Respecting so unjustifiable an interposition but one opinion would be formed.

The 2d objection is, that the letter contains matter which ought not to be disclosed.

That there may be matter, the production of which the court would not require, is certain; but that in a capital case, the accused ought not, in some form, to have the benefit of it, if it was really essential to his defence, is a position which the court would very reluctantly deny. It ought not to be believed, that the department which superintends prosecutions in criminal cases, would be inclined to withhold it. What ought to be done under such circumstances presents a delicate question, the discussion of which, it is hoped, will never be rendered necessary in this country. At present it need only be said, that the question does not occur at this time. There is certainly nothing before the court which shows, that the letter in question contains any matter, the disclosure of which, would endanger the public safety. If it does contain such matter, the fact may appear before the disclosure is made. If it does contain any matter which it would be imprudent to disclose, which it is not the wish of the executive to disclose, such matter, if it be not immediately and essentially applicable to the point, will, of course, be suppressed. It is not easy to conceive, that so much of the letter as relates to the conduct of the accused, can be a subject of delicacy with the President. Everything of this kind, however, will have its due consideration on the return of the subpœna.

3dly. It has been alledged that a copy may be received instead of the original, and the act of Congress has been cited in support of this proposition.

This argument pre-supposes that the letter required is a document filed in the department of state, the reverse of which may be and most probably is the fact. Letters addressed to the President are most usually retained by himself. They do not belong to any of the departments. But were the fact otherwise, a copy might not answer the purpose. The copy would not be superior to the original, and the original itself would not be admitted, if denied, without proof that it was in the hand writing of the witness. Suppose the case put at the bar, of an indictment on this letter for a libel, and on its production it should appear not to be in the hand writing of the person indicted. Would its being deposited in the department of state make it his writing or subject him to the consequence of having written it? Certainly not. For the purpose then of showing the letter to have been written by a particular person, the original must be produced and a copy could not be admitted.

On the confidential nature of this letter, much has been said at the bar, and authorities have been produced, which appear to be conclusive. Had its contents been orally communicated, the person to whom the communications were made could not have excused himself from detailing them so far as they might be deemed essential in the defence. Their being in writing gives no additional sanctity, the only difference produced by that circumstance is, that the contents of the paper must be proved by the paper itself, not by the recollection of the witness.

Much has been said about the disrespect to the chief magistrate which is implied by this motion and by such a decision of it as the law is believed to require.

These observations will be very truly answered by the declaration that this court feels many, perhaps peculiar motives, for manifesting as guarded a respect for the chief magistrate of the union as is compatible with its official duties. To go beyond these would exhibit a conduct which would deserve some other appellation than the term respect.

It is not for the court to anticipate the event of the present prosecution. Should it terminate as is expected on the part of the United States, all those who are concerned in it should certainly regret that a paper which the accused believed to be essential to his defence, which may, for aught that now appears, be essential, had been withheld from him. I will not say that this circumstance would in any degree tarnish the reputation of the government, but I will say that it would justly tarnish the reputation of the court which had given its sanction to its being withheld. Might I be permitted to utter one sentiment with respect to myself, it would be to deplore most earnestly, the occasion which should compel me to look back on any part of my official conduct with so much self-reproach as I should feel, could I declare on the information now possessed, that the accused is not entitled to the letter in question, if it should be really important to him.

The propriety of requiring the answer to this letter is more questionable. It is alledged that it most probably communicates orders showing the situation of this country with Spain, which will be important on the misdemeanor. If it contains matter not essential to the defence and the disclosure is unpleasant to the executive, it certainly ought not to be disclosed. This is a point which will appear on the return.

The demand of the orders which have been issued, and which have been, as is alleged, published in the Natchez Gazette, is by no means unusual. Such documents have often been produced in the courts of the U. States and the courts of England. If they contain matter interesting to the nation, the concealment of which is required by the public safety, that matter will appear upon the return. If they do not and are material, they may be exhibited.

It is said they cannot be material because they cannot justify any unlawful resistance which may have been employed or meditated by the accused.

Were this admitted, and were it also admitted that such resistance would amount to treason, the orders might still be material because they might tend to weaken the endeavor to connect such overt act with any overt act of which this court may take cognizance.

The court, however, is rather inclined to the opinion that the subpœna in such case ought to be directed to the head of the department in whose custody the orders are, and the court must suppose that the letter of the secretary of the navy which has been stated by the attorney for the U.S. to refer the counsel for the prisoner to his legal remedy for the copies he desired, alluded to such a motion as is now made.

The affidavit on which the motion is grounded has not been noticed. It is believed that such a subpœna as is asked ought to issue if there exist any reason for supposing that the testimony may be material and ought to be admitted. It is only because the subpœna is addressed to those who administer the government of this country, that such an affidavit was required as would furnish probable cause to believe that the testimony was desired for the real purposes of defence, and not for such as this court will forever discountenance.

June 13, 1807

LEGAL QUESTIONS IN THE BURR CASE

To William Cushing

Dear Sir   Richmond June 29th. 1807

It has been my fate to be engaged in the trial of a person whose case presents many real intrinsic difficulties which are infinitely multiplied by extrinsic circumstances. It would have been my earnest wish to consult with all my brethren of the bench on the various intricate points that occur, on which a contrariety of opinion ought not to prevail in the different circuits, but which cannot easily be carried before the supreme court. Sincerely do I lament that this wish cannot be completely indulged.

Several interesting enquiries were suggested during the session of the Grand Jury which I was unwilling to settle, & which I thought ought to be settled on consultation that a common rule might be adopted. One of these which may in future cases be of some consequence is the question whether a Grand Jury ought to require two witnesses to the same overt act to justify their finding a true bill on an indictment for treason. But the Grand Jury is now discharged, having found bills not only against Colo. Burr, but also against many others whose names you have seen in the papers. The court will meet on the first monday in August for their trial.

Many points of difficulty will arise before the petty jury which cannot be foreseen & on which I must decide according to the best lights I possess. But there are some which will certainly occur, respecting which considerable doubts may be entertained, & on which I most anxiously desire the aid of all the Judges. One of these respects the doctrine of constructive treasons. How far is this doctrine to be carried in the United

States? If a body of men assemble for a treasonable purpose, does this implicate all those who are concerned in the conspiracy whether acquainted with the assemblage or not? Does it implicate those who advised directed or approved of it? Or does it implicate those only who were present or within the district?

An argument of Judge Tucker on this subject which you will find in his appendix to his 4th. Blackstone may be worth perusing.

The opinion of the supreme court in the case of Bollman & Swartwout certainly adopts the doctrine of constructive treasons. How far does that case carry this doctrine? Ought the expressions in that opinion to be revised?

A second question of much importance is, how far may the declarations or confessions of one person be given in evidence against another who is proved to be connected with him in the same conspiracy? Is there a distinction between written & verbal declarations?

The English books contain many cases in which, for the purpose of proving the general objects of a conspiracy, the acts & writings of one conspirator have been given in evidence against others. But in England, treason may be committed by imagining the death of the King, & a conspiracy is an overt act of this treason. The general objects of the conspiracy may be proved by the conduct of any of the conspirators, and these general objects attach in a certain degree to every member. Yet, even in England, after proving the general objects of the conspiracy, the jury must enquire how far the individual whose case is before them participated in those objects; & in this enquiry I am not certain that the conduct or declarations of any person, not assented to by the prisoner, can be brought to bear upon him. I am inclined to beleive that this kind of testimony is admissible only in those prosecutions where the crime is consummated by the intention, & a conspiracy is an overt act. I do not know how far it can be allowed where the crime must be the embodying of men or any other open deed. The doctrine on this subject is well summed up in 2d. McNally, & is perhaps only applicable to indictments for a conspiracy. Of this however I do not pretend to be confident.

A third question which I shall certainly be compelled to

decide & on which I feel some doubt is whether an overt act of treason committed out of the district & consequently not laid in the indictment, can be given in evidence?

In England the Statute of William III enacts that no overt act not laid in the indictment shall be given in evidence. This is perhaps the sound doctrine of the common law independent of Statute. Yet in that country it has been decided that a fact which tends directly to prove an overt act laid in the indictment, altho it might have been laid as an overt act may be given in evidence. A case of this description is quoted by Foster. But, in England, the jurisdiction of the court being universal, an acquittal of the particular treason laid in the indictment would I presume be pleadable in bar to a second indictment for the same treason altho the overt acts should be differently laid; certainly it might be pleaded in bar to an indictment founded on matter which might have been given in evidence on the former trial.

In the United States, an acquittal in Virginia could not perhaps be pleaded in bar to an indictment in Kentucky for levying war in Kentucky. If upon an indictment in Virginia, evidence should be received of war levied in Kentucky for the purpose of proving that war was also levied in Virginia, & the prisoner should be acquitted, he might be again indicted in Kentucky, & the overt act committed in Virginia might be given in evidence to prove the overt act laid in Kentucky. Thus, notwithstanding the constitution, a man's life would in fact be twice put in jeopardy for the same offence; & he would, to every effectual purpose be tried in a district other than that in which the offence was committed. This objection does not ly to transactions which do not in themselves amount to overt acts of treason; but where they do amount to overt acts the difficulty appears to me to be considerable.

I am aware of the unwillingness with which a Judge will commit himself by an opinion on a case not before him & on which he has heard no argument. Could this case be readily carried into the supreme court I would not ask an opinion in its present stage. But these questions must be decided by the Judges separately on their respective circuits, & I am sure there would be a strong & general repugnance to giving contradictory decisions on the same points. Such a circumstance would be disreputable to the Judges themselves as well as to our judicial system. This consideration suggests the propriety of a consultation on new & difficult subjects & will I trust apologize for this letter. With respectful & affectionate esteem, I am dear Sir your obedt. Servt.

My letter to Judge Washington may perhaps not find him. Should you see him, be so obliging as to show him this & ask him to consider it as addressed also to himself.

Since writing the above another question has occurred to my mind which I will also take the liberty to state.

Must all the circumstances which tend to prove the treason —as for example declarations made by the prisoner of his intentions, be proved by two witnesses, or is it only necessary that the military assemblage should be proved by two witnesses?

Circuit Court Opinion in
United States v. Burr
on the Law of Treason

THE question now to be decided has been argued in a manner worthy of its importance, and with an earnestness evincing the strong conviction felt by the counsel on each side that the law is with them.

A degree of eloquence seldom displayed on any occasion has embellished a solidity of argument and a depth of research by which the court has been greatly aided in forming the opinion it is about to deliver.

The testimony adduced on the part of the United States, to prove the overt act laid in the indictment, having shown, and the attorney for the United States having admitted, that the prisoner was not present when that act, whatever may be its character, was committed, and there being no reason to doubt but that he was at a great distance and in a different state, it is objected to the testimony offered on the part of the United States, to connect him with those who committed the overt act, that such testimony is totally irrelevant and must therefore be rejected.

The arguments in support of this motion respect in part the merits of the case as it may be supposed to stand independent of the pleadings, and in part as exhibited by the pleadings.

On the first division of the subject two points are made:

1st. That conformably to the constitution of the United States, no man can be convicted of treason who was not present when the war was levied.

2nd. That if this construction be erroneous, no testimony can be received to charge one man with the overt acts of others, until those overt acts as laid in the indictment be proved to the satisfaction of the court.

The question which arises on the construction of the constitution, in every point of view in which it can be contemplated, is of infinite moment to the people of this country and to their government, and requires the most temperate and the most deliberate consideration.

"Treason against the United States shall consist only in levying war against them."

What is the natural import of the words "levying of war?" and who may be said to levy it? Had their first application to treason been made by our constitution, they would certainly have admitted of some latitude of construction. Taken most literally, they are perhaps of the same import with the words raising or creating war, but as those who join after the commencement are equally the objects of punishment, there would probably be a general admission, that the term also comprehended making war, or carrying on war. In the construction which courts would be required to give these words, it is not improbable that those who should raise, create, make or carry on war might be comprehended. The various acts which would be considered as coming within the term, would be settled by a course of decisions, and it would be affirming boldly to say, that those only who actually constituted a portion of the military force appearing in arms could be considered as levying war. There is no difficulty in affirming that there must be a war or the crime of levying it cannot exist, but there would often be considerable difficulty in affirming that a particular act did or did not involve the person committing it in the guilt and in the fact of levying war. If for example, an army should be actually raised for the avowed purpose of carrying on open war against the United States and subverting their government the point must be weighed very deliberately, before a judge would venture to decide that an overt act of levying war had not been committed by a commissary of purchases, who never saw the army, but who, knowing its object and leagueing himself with the rebels, supplied that army with provisions, or by a recruiting officer holding a commission in the rebel service, who, though never in camp, executed the particular duty assigned to him.

But the term is not for the first time applied to treason by the constitution of the U. States. It is a technical term. It is used in a very old statute of that country, whose language is our language, and whose laws form the substratum of our laws. It is scarcely conceivable that the term was not employed by the framers of our constitution in the sense which had been affixed to it by those from whom we borrowed it. So far as the meaning of any terms, particularly terms of art, is completely ascertained, those by whom they are employed must be considered as employing them in that ascertained meaning, unless the contrary be proved by the context. It is therefore reasonable to suppose, unless it be incompatible with other expressions of the constitution, that the term "levying war" is used in that instrument in the same sense in which it was understood in England and in this country, to have been used in the statute of the 25th of Edward, 3rd, from which it was borrowed.

It is said that this meaning is to be collected only from adjudged cases. But this position cannot be conceded to the extent in which it is laid down. The superior authority of adjudged cases will never be controverted. But those celebrated elementary writers, who have stated the principles of the law, whose statements have received the common approbation of legal men, are not to be disregarded. Principles laid down by such writers as Coke, Hale, Foster, and Blackstone, are not lightly to be rejected. These books are in the hands of every student. Legal opinions are formed upon them, and those opinions are afterwards carried to the bar, the bench and the legislature. In the exposition of terms, therefore, used in instruments of the present day, the definitions and the dicta of those authors, if not contradicted by adjudications, and if compatible with the words of the statute, are entitled to respect. It is to be regretted that they do not shed as much light on this part of the subject as is to be wished.

Coke does not give a complete definition of the term, but puts cases which amount to levying war. "An actual rebellion, or insurrection, he says is a levying of war." In whom?—Coke does not say whether in those only who appear in arms, or in all those who take part in the rebellion or insurrection by real open deed.

Hale in treating on the same subject puts many cases which shall constitute a levying of war, without which no act can amount to treason, but he does not particularize the parts to be performed by the different persons concerned in that war, which shall be sufficient to fix on each the guilt of levying it.

Foster says "the joining with rebels in an act of rebellion, or with enemies in acts of hostility will make a man a traitor."

"Furnishing rebels or enemies with money, arms, ammunition or other necessaries will *prima facie* make a man a traitor."

Foster does not say that he would be a traitor under the words of the statute independent of the legal rule which attaches the guilt of the principal to an accessary, nor that his treason is occasioned by that rule. In England this discrimination need not be made except for the purpose of framing the indictment, and therefore in the English books we do not perceive any effort to make it. Thus surrendering a castle to rebels, being in confederacy with them is said by Hale & Foster to be treason under the clause of levying war, but whether it be levying war in fact, or aiding those who levy it is not said. Upon this point Blackstone is not more satisfactory. Although we may find among the commentators upon treason enough to satisfy the enquiry, what is a state of internal war? Yet no precise information can be acquired from them which would enable us to decide with clearness whether persons not in arms, but taking part in a rebellion, could be said to levy war independent of that doctrine which attaches to the accessary the guilt of his principal.

If in adjudged cases this question has been taken up and directly decided, the court has not seen those cases. The argument which may be drawn from the form of the indictment, though strong is not conclusive. In the precedent found in Tremaine, Mary Speake, who was indicted for furnishing provisions to the party of the Duke of Monmouth, is indicted for furnishing provisions to those who were levying war, not for levying war herself. It may correctly be argued that, had this act amounted to levying war, she would have been indicted for levying war, and the furnishing of provisions would have been laid as the overt act. The court felt this when the precedent was produced. But the argument, though strong, is not conclusive, because in England, the enquiry whether she had become a traitor by levying war, or by giving aid and comfort to those who were levying war, was unimportant, and because too it does not appear from the indictment that she was actually concerned in the rebellion, that she belonged to the rebel party, or was guilty of any thing further than a criminal speculation in selling them provisions.

It is not deemed necessary to trace the doctrine that in treason all are principals to its source. Its origin is most probably stated correctly by Judge Tucker, in a work, the merit of which is with pleasure acknowledged. But if a spurious doctrine has been introduced into the common law, and has for centuries been admitted as genuine, it would require great hardihood in a judge to reject it. Accordingly, we find those of the English jurists who seem to disapprove the principle, declaring that it is now too firmly settled to be shaken.

It is unnecessary to trace this doctrine to its source for another reason. The terms of the constitution comprize no question respecting principal and accessary, so far as either may be truly and in fact said to levy war: Whether in England a person would be indicted in express terms for levying war, or for assisting others in levying war, yet if in correct and legal language he can be said to have levied war, and if it has never been decided that the act would not amount to levying war, his case may without violent construction be brought within the letter and the plain meaning of the constitution.

In examining these words the argument which may be drawn from felonies, as for example, from murder, is not more conclusive. Murder is the single act of killing with malice aforethought. But war is a complex operation composed of many parts, co-operating with each other. No one man or body of men can perform them all if the war be of any continuance. Although then, in correct and in law language, he alone is said to have murdered another who has perpetrated the fact of killing, or has been present aiding that fact, it does not follow that he alone can have levied war who has borne arms. All those who perform the various and essential military parts of prosecuting the war which must be assigned to different persons, may with correctness and accuracy be said to levy war.

Taking this view of the subject, it appears to the court, that those who perform a part in the prosecution of the war may correctly be said to levy war and to commit treason under the constitution. It will be observed, that this opinion does not extend to the case of a person who performs no act in the prosecution of the war, who counsels and advises it, or who being engaged in the conspiracy fails to perform his part. Whether such persons may be implicated by the doctrine, that whatever would make a man an accessary in felony makes him a principal in treason, or are excluded, because that doctrine is inapplicable to the United States, the constitution having declared that treason shall consist only in levying war, and having made the proof of *overt acts* necessary to conviction, is a question of vast importance which it would be proper for the supreme court to take a fit occasion to decide, but which an inferior tribunal would not willingly determine unless the case before them should require it.

It may now be proper to notice the opinion of the supreme court in the case of the United States against Bollman and Swartwout. It is said that this opinion in declaring that those who do not bear arms may yet be guilty of treason, is contrary to law, and is not obligatory, because it is extrajudicial, and was delivered on a point not argued. This court is therefore required to depart from the principle there laid down.

It is true, that in that case after forming the opinion that no treason could be committed, because no treasonable assemblage had taken place, the court might have dispensed with proceeding further in the doctrines of treason. But it is to be remembered, that the judges might act separately, and perhaps at the same time, on the various prosecutions which might be instituted, and that no appeal lay from their decisions. Opposite judgements on the point would have presented a state of things infinitely to be deplored by all. It was not surprising then that they should have made some attempt to settle principles which would probably occur, and which were in some degree connected with the point before them.

The court had employed some reasoning to show that without the actual embodying of men war could not be levied. It might have been inferred from this, that those only who were so embodied could be guilty of treason. Not only to exclude this inference, but also to affirm the contrary, the court proceeded to observe, "It is not the intention of the court to say that no individual can be guilty of this crime who has not appeared in arms against his country. On the contrary, if war be actually levied, that is, if a body of men be actually assembled for the purpose of effecting by force a treasonable object, all those who perform any part, however minute, or however remote from the scene of action, and who are actually leagued in the general conspiracy, are to be considered as traitors."

This court is told that if this opinion be incorrect it ought not to be obeyed, because it was extrajudicial. For myself, I can say that I could not lightly be prevailed on to disobey it, were I even convinced that it was erroneous; but I would certainly use any means which the law placed in my power to carry the question again before the supreme court for reconsideration, in a case in which it would directly occur and be fully argued.

The court which gave this opinion was composed of four judges. At the time I thought them unanimous, but I have since had reason to suspect that one of them, whose opinion is entitled to great respect, and whose indisposition prevented his entering into the discussions, on some of those points which were not essential to the decision of the very case under consideration, did not concur in this particular point with his brethren. Had the opinion been unanimous, it would have been given by a majority of the judges. But should the three who were absent concur with that judge who was present and who perhaps dissents from what was then the opinion of the court, a majority of the judges may overrule this decision. I should therefore feel no objection, although I then thought, and still think the opinion perfectly correct, to carry the point if possible again before the supreme court, if the case should depend upon it.

In saying that I still think the opinion perfectly correct, I do not consider myself as going further than the preceding reasoning goes. Some gentlemen have argued as if the supreme court had adopted the whole doctrine of the English books on the subject of accessaries to treason. But certainly such is not the fact. Those only who perform a part, and who are leagued in the conspiracy are declared to be traitors. To complete the definition both circumstances must concur. They must "perform a part," which will furnish the overt act, and they must be "leagued in the conspiracy." The person who comes within this description, in the opinion of the court levies war. The present motion, however, does not rest upon this point; for, if under this indictment, the U. States might be let in to prove the part performed by the prisoner, if he did perform any part, the court could not stop the testimony in its present stage.

2nd. The second point involves the character of the overt act which has been given in evidence, and calls upon the court to declare whether that act can amount to levying war. Although the court ought now to avoid any analysis of the testimony which has been offered in this case, provided the decision of the motion should not rest upon it, yet many reasons concur in giving peculiar propriety to a delivery, in the course of these trials, of a detailed opinion on the question, what is levying war? As this question has been argued at great length, it may probably save much trouble to the counsel now to give that opinion.

In opening the case it was contended by the Attorney for the United States and has since been maintained on the part of the prosecution, that neither arms nor the application of force or violence are indispensably necessary to constitute the fact of levying war. To illustrate these positions several cases have been stated, many of which would clearly amount to treason. In all of them, except that which was probably intended to be this case, and on which no observation will be made, the object of the assemblage was clearly treasonable: its character was unequivocal, and was demonstrated by evidence furnished by the assemblage itself; there was no necessity to rely upon information drawn from extrinsic sources, or in order to understand the fact, to pursue a course of intricate reasoning and to conjecture motives. A force is supposed to be collected for an avowed treasonable object, in a condition to attempt that object, and to have commenced the attempt by moving towards it. I state these particulars because although the cases put may establish the doctrine they are intended to support, may prove that the absence of arms, or the failure to apply force to sensible objects by the actual commission of violence on those objects, may be supplied by other circumstances, yet, they also serve to show that the mind requires those circumstances to be satisfied that war is levied.

Their construction of the opinion of the supreme court is, I think, thus far correct. It is certainly the opinion which was at the time entertained by myself, and which is still entertained. If a rebel army avowing its hostility to the sovereign power, should front that of the government, should march and countermarch before it, should manœuvre in its face, and should then disperse from any cause whatever without firing a gun, I confess I could not without some surprise, hear gentlemen seriously contend that this could not amount to an act of levying war. A case equally strong may be put with respect to the absence of military weapons. If the party be in a condition to execute the purposed treason without the usual implements of war, I can perceive no reason for requiring those implements in order to constitute the crime.

It is argued that no adjudged case can be produced from the English books where actual violence has not been committed. Suppose this were true. No adjudged case has, or it is believed, can be produced from those books in which it has been laid down, that war cannot be levied without the actual application of violence to external objects. The silence of the reporters, on this point may be readily accounted for. In cases of actual rebellion against the government, the most active and influential leaders are generally most actively engaged in the war, and as the object can never be to extend punishment to extermination, a sufficient number are found among those who have committed actual hostilities, to satisfy the avenging arm of justice. In cases of constructive treason, such as pulling down meeting houses, where the direct and avowed object is not the destruction of the sovereign power, some act of violence might be generally required to give to the crime a sufficient degree of malignity to convert it into treason, to render the guilt of any individual unequivocal.

But Vaughan's case is a case where there was no real application of violence, and where the act was adjudged to be treason. Gentlemen argue that Vaughan was only guilty of adhering to the king's enemies, but they have not the authority of the court for so saying. The judges unquestionably treat the cruizing of Vaughan as an overt act of levying war.

The opinions of the best elementary writers concur in declaring, that where a body of men are assembled for the purpose of making war against the government, and are in a condition to make that war, the assemblage is an act of levying war. These opinions are contradicted by no adjudged case and are supported by Vaughan's case. This court is not inclined to controvert them.

But although in this respect, the opinion of the supreme court has not been misunderstood on the part of the prosecution, that opinion seems not to have been fully adverted to in a very essential point in which it is said to have been misconceived by others.

The opinion I am informed, has been construed to mean, that any assemblage whatever for a treasonable purpose, whether in force, or not in force, whether in a condition to use violence or not in that condition, is a levying of war. It is this construction, which has not indeed been expressly advanced at the bar, but which is said to have been adopted elsewhere, that the court deems it necessary to examine.

Independent of authority, trusting only to the dictates of reason, and expounding terms according to their ordinary signification, we should probably all concur in the declaration that war could not be levied without the employment and exhibition of force. War is an appeal from reason to the sword, and he who makes the appeal evidences the fact by the use of the means. His intention to go to war may be proved by words, but the actual going to war is a fact which is to be proved by open deed. The end is to be effected by force, and it would seem that in cases where no declaration is to be made, the state of actual war could only be created by the employment of force or being in a condition to employ it.

But the term having been adopted by our constitution, must be understood in that sense in which it was universally received in this country, when the constitution was framed. The sense in which it was received is to be collected from the most approved authorities of that nation from which we have borrowed the term.

Lord Coke says, that levying war against the king was treason at the common law. "A compassing or conspiracy to levy war, he adds, is no treason, for there must be a levying of war in fact." He proceeds to state cases of constructive levying war, where the direct design is not to overturn the government but to effect some general object by force. The terms he employs in stating these cases, are such as indicate an impression on his mind, that actual violence is a necessary ingredient in constituting the fact of levying war. He then proceeds to say, "an actual rebellion or insurrection is a levying of war within this act." "If any with strength and weapons invasive and defensive doth hold and defend a castle or fort against the king and his power, this is levying of war against the king." These cases are put to illustrate what he denominates "a war in fact." It is not easy to conceive "an actual invasion or insurrection" unconnected with force, nor can "a castle or fort be defended with strength and weapons invasive and defensive" without the employment of actual force. It would seem then to have been the opinion of Lord Coke, that to levy war there must be an assemblage of men in a condition and with an intention to employ force. He certainly puts no case of a different description.

Lord Hale says (149.6) "what shall be said a levying of war is partly a question of fact, for it is not every unlawful or riotous assembly of many persons to do an unlawful act, though *de facto* they commit the act they intend, that makes a levying of war; for then every riot would be treason, &c." "but it must be such an assembly as carries with it *speciem belli*, the appearance of war, as if they ride or march *vexillis explicatis*, with colours flying, or if they be formed into companies or furnished with military officers, or if they are armed with military weapons as swords, guns, bills, halberds, pikes, and are so circumstanced that it may be reasonably concluded they are in a posture of war, which circumstances are so various that it is hard to describe them all particularly."

"Only the general expressions in all the indictments of this nature that I have seen are *more guerrino arraiati*, arrayed in warlike manner."

He afterwards adds, "If there be a war levied as is above declared, viz. an assembly arrayed in warlike manner, and so in the posture of war for any treasonable attempt, it is *bellum levatum but not percussum*."

It is obvious that Lord Hale supposed an assemblage of men in force, in a military posture, to be necessary to constitute the fact of levying war. The idea he appears to suggest, that the apparatus of war is necessary, has been very justly combatted by an able judge who has written a valuable treatise on the subject of treason; but it is not recollected that his position, that the assembly should be in a posture of war for any treasonable attempt, has ever been denied. Hawk. ch. 17, sec. 23, says, "That not only those who rebel against the king and take up arms to dethrone him, but also in many other cases, those who in a violent and forcible manner withstand his lawful authority are said to levy war against him, and therefore those that hold a fort or castle against the king's forces, or keep together armed numbers of men against the king's express command, have been adjudged to levy war against him."

The cases put by Hawkins are all cases of actual force and violence. "Those who rebel against the king and take up arms to dethrone him," in many other cases those "who in a violent and forcible manner withstand his lawful authority." "Those that hold a fort or castle against his forces, or keep together armed numbers of men against his express command."

These cases are obviously cases of force and violence.

Hawkins next proceeds to describe cases in which war is understood to be levied under the statute, although it was not directly made against the government. This Lord Hale terms an interpretative or constructive levying of war; and it will be perceived that he puts no case in which actual force is dispensed with.

"Those also, he says, who make an insurrection in order to redress a public grievance, whether it be a real or pretended one, and of their own authority attempt *with force* to redress it, are said to levy war against the king, although they have no direct design against his person, inasmuch as they insolently invade his prerogative by attempting to do that by private authority which he by public justice ought to do, which manifestly tends to a downright rebellion. As where great numbers *by force* attempt to remove certain persons from the king, &c." The cases here put by Hawkins of a constructive levying of war, do in terms require force as a constituent part of the description of the offence.

Judge Foster, in his valuable treatise on treason, states the opinion which has been quoted from Lord Hale, and differs from that writer so far as the latter might seem to require swords, drums, colours, &c. what he terms the pomp and pageantry of war, as essential circumstances to constitute the fact of levying war. In the cases of Damaree and Purchase, he says, "the want of those circumstances weighed nothing with the court although the prisoner's counsel insisted much on that matter." But he adds, "the number of the insurgents supplied the want of military weapons: and they were provided with axes, crows and other tools of the like nature, proper for the mischief they intended to effect. *Furor arma ministrat.*"

It is apparent that Judge Foster here alludes to an assemblage in force, or as Lord Hale terms it, "in a warlike posture" —that is in a condition to attempt or proceed upon the treason which had been contemplated. The same author afterwards states at large the cases of Damaree and Purchase from 8th state trials, and they are cases where the insurgents not only assembled in force, in the posture of war, or in a condition to execute the treasonable design, but they did actually carry it into execution, and did resist the guards who were sent to disperse them.

Judge Foster states, sec. 4, all insurrections to effect certain innovations of a public and general concern, *by an armed force*, to be in construction of law, high treason within the clause of levying war.

The cases put by Foster of constructive levying of war, all contain as a material ingredient, the actual employment of force. After going through this branch of his subject, he proceeds to state the law in a case of actual levying war, that is, where the war is intended directly against the government.

He says, sec. 9, "An assembly armed and arrayed in a warlike manner for a treasonable purpose is *bellum levatum* though not *bellum percussum*. Listing and marching are sufficient overt acts without coming to a battle or action. So cruizing on the king's subjects under a French commission, France being then at war with us, was held to be adherring to the king's enemies though no other act of hostility be proved."

"An assembly armed and arrayed in a warlike manner for any treasonable purpose," is certainly in a state of force; in a condition to execute the treason for which they are assembled. The words "enlisting and marching," which are overt acts of levying war, do in the arrangement of the sentence, also imply a state of force, though that state is not expressed in terms for the succeeding words, which state a particular event as not having happened, prove that event to have been the next circumstance to those which had happened—they are "without coming to a battle or action." "If men be enlisted and march," (that is, if they march prepared for battle or in a condition for action, for marching is a technical term applied to the movement of a military corps) it is an overt act of levying war though they do not come to a battle or action. This exposition is rendered the stronger by what seems to be put in the same sentence as a parallel case with respect to adhering to an enemy. It is cruising under a commission from an enemy without committing any other act of hostility. Cruizing is the act of sailing in warlike form and in a condition to assail those of whom the cruizer is in quest.

This exposition which seems to be that intended by Judge Foster, is rendered the more certain by a reference to the case in the state trials from which the extracts are taken. The words used by the Chief Justice are "when men form themselves into a body and march rank and file with weapons offensive and defensive, this is levying of war with open force, if the design be public." Mr. Phipps, the counsel for the prisoner afterwards observed, "Intending to levy war is not treason unless a war be actually levied." To this the Chief Justice answered, "Is it not actually levying of war, if they actually provide arms, and levy men, and in a warlike manner set out and cruize, and come with a design to destroy our ships?" Mr. Phipps still insisted "it wou'd not be an actual levying of war unless they committed some act of hostility." "Yes, indeed, said the Chief Justice, the going on board and being in a posture to attack the king's ships." Mr. Baron Powis added, "but for you to say that because they did not actually fight it is not a levying of war, is it not plain what they did intend? that they came with that intention, that they came in that posture, that they came armed, and had guns and blunderbusses and surrounded the ship twice; they came with an armed force, that is a strong evidence of the design."

The point insisted on by counsel in the case of Vaughan, as in this case, was, that war cou'd not be levied without actual fighting. In this the counsel was very properly overruled; but it is apparent that the judges proceeded entirely on the idea that a warlike posture was indispensable to the fact of levying war.

Judge Foster proceeds to give other instances of levying war. "Attacking the king's forces in opposition to his authority upon a march or in quarters is levying war." "Holding a castle or fort against the king or his forces, if *actual force be used in order to keep possession*, is levying war. But a bare detainer as suppose by shutting the gates against the king or his forces, without any other force from within, Lord Hale conceiveth will not amount to treason."

The whole doctrine of Judge Foster on this subject seems to demonstrate a clear opinion that a state of force and violence, a posture of war must exist to constitute technically as well as really the fact of levying war.

Judge Blackstone seems to concur with his predecessors. Speaking of levying war, he says, "This may be done by taking arms not only to dethrone the king, but under pretence to re-form religion, or the laws, or to remove evil counsellors, or other grievances, whether real or pretended. For the law does not, neither can it permit any private man or set of men to in-terfere *forcibly* in matters of such high importance."

He proceeds to give examples of levying war, which show that he contemplated actual force as a necessary ingredient in the composition of this crime.

It would seem then from the English authorities, that the words "levying war," have not received a technical different from their natural meaning, so far as respects the character of the assemblage of men which may constitute the fact. It must be a warlike assemblage, carrying the appearance of force, and in a situation to practice hostility.

Several judges of the United States have given opinions at their circuits on this subject, all of which deserve and will re-ceive the particular attention of this court.

In his charge to the grand jury when John Fries was in-dicted, in consequence of a forcible opposition to the direct tax, Judge Iredell is understood to have said, "I think I am war-ranted in saying, that if in the case of the insurgents who may come under your consideration, the intention was to prevent by force of arms the execution of any act of the Congress of the United States altogether, any *forcible opposition* calculated to carry that intention into effect, was a levying of war against the United States, and of course an act of treason." To levy war then, according to this opinion of Judge Iredell, required the actual exertion of force.

Judge Patterson, in his opinions delivered in two different cases, seems not to differ from Judge Iredell. He does not, in-deed, precisely state the employment of force as necessary to constitute a levying war, but in giving his opinion in cases in which force was actually employed, he considers the crime in one case as dependent on the intention, and in the other case he says, "combining these facts and this design," (that is, combining actual force with a treasonable design) "the crime is high treason."

Judge Peters has also indicated the opinion that force was necessary to constitute the crime of levying war.

Judge Chase has been particularly clear and explicit. In an opinion which he appears to have prepared on great consideration, he says, "the court are of opinion, that if a body of people conspire and meditate an insurrection to resist or oppose the execution of a statute of the United States by force, that they are only guilty of a high misdemeanor; but if they proceed to carry such intention into execution by force, that they are guilty of the treason of levying war; and the quantum of the force employed neither increases nor diminishes the crime; whether by one hundred or one thousand persons, is wholly immaterial.

"The court are of opinion, that a combination or conspiracy to levy war against the United States, is not treason unless combined with an attempt to carry such combination or conspiracy into execution, some actual force or violence must be used in pursuance of such design to levy war; but that it is altogether immaterial whether the force used be sufficient to effectuate the object. Any force connected with the intention will constitute the crime of levying of war."

In various parts of the opinion delivered by Judge Chase, in the case of Fries, the same sentiments are to be found. It is to be observed, that these judges are not content that troops should be assembled in a condition to employ force. According to them some degree of force must have been actually employed.

The Judges of the United States, then, so far as their opinions have been quoted, seem to have required still more to constitute the fact of levying war, than has been required by the English books. Our Judges seem to have required the actual exercise of force, the actual employment of some degree of violence. This however may be, and probably is, because in the cases in which their opinions were given the design not having been to overturn the government, but to resist the execution of a law, such an assemblage would be sufficient for the purpose, as to require the actual employment of force to render the object unequivocal.

But it is said all these authorities have been overruled by the decision of the supreme court in the case of the United States against Swartwout and Bollman.

If the supreme court have indeed extended the doctrine of treason, further than it has heretofore been carried by the judges of England, or of this country, their decision would be submitted to. At least this court could go no further than to endeavour again to bring the point directly before them. It would however be expected that an opinion which is to over-rule all former precedents, and to establish a principle never before recognized, should be expressed in plain and explicit terms. A mere implication, ought not to prostrate a principle which seems to have been so well established. Had the intention been entertained to make so material a change in this respect, the court ought to have expressly declared, that any assemblage of men whatever, who had formed a treasonable design, whether in force, or not, whether in a condition to attempt the design or not, whether attended with warlike appearances or not, constitutes the fact of levying war. Yet no declaration to this amount is made. Not an expression of the kind is to be found in the opinion of the supreme court. The foundation on which this argument rests is the omission of the court to state, that the assemblage which constitutes the fact of levying war ought to be in force, and some passages, which show that the question respecting the nature of the assemblage, was not in the mind of the court when the opinion was drawn, which passages are mingled with others, which at least show that there was no intention to depart from the course of the precedents in cases of treason by levying war.

Every opinion, to be correctly understood, ought to be considered with a view to the case in which it was delivered. In the case of the United States against Bollman and Swartwout, there was no evidence that even two men had ever met for the purpose of executing the plan, in which those persons were charged with having participated. It was therefore sufficient for the court to say that unless men were assembled war could not be levied. That case was decided by this declaration. The court might indeed have defined the species of assemblage which would amount to levying of war, but, as this opinion was not a treatise on treason, but a decision of a particular case, expressions of doubtful import should be construed in reference to the case itself; and the mere omission to state that a particular circumstance was necessary to the consummation of the crime, ought not to be construed into a declaration that the circumstance was unimportant. General expressions ought not to be considered as overruling settled principles without a direct declaration to that effect. After these preliminary observations the court will proceed to examine the opinion which has occasioned them.

The first expression in it bearing on the present question is "To constitute that specific crime for which the prisoner now before the court has been committed, war must be actually levied against the United States. However flagitious may be the crime of conspiracy to subvert by force the government of our country, such conspiracy is not treason. To conspire to levy war and actually to levy war, are distinct offences. The first must be brought into operation by the assemblage of men for a purpose treasonable in itself, or the fact of levying war cannot have been committed."

Although it is not expressly stated that the assemblage of men for the purpose of carrying into operation the treasonable intent, which will amount to levying war, must be an assemblage in force, yet it is fairly to be inferred from the context, and nothing like dispensing with force appears in this paragraph. The expressions are "to constitute the crime war must be actually levied." A conspiracy to levy war is spoken of as "a conspiracy to subvert by force the government of our country," speaking in general terms of an assemblage of men for this, or for any other purpose, a person would naturally be understood as speaking of an assemblage in some degree adapted to the purpose. An assemblage to subvert by force the government of our country, and amounting to a levying of war, should be an assemblage in force.

In a subsequent paragraph the court says, "It is not the intention of the court to say, that no individual can be guilty of this crime who has not appeared in arms against his country. On the contrary if war be actually levied, that is, if a body of men be actually assembled in order to effect by force a treasonable purpose, all those who perform any part, however minute, &c. and who are actually leagued in the general conspiracy, are traitors. But, there must be an actual assembling of men for the treasonable purpose to constitute a levying of war."

The observations made on the preceding paragraph apply to this. "A body of men actually assembled, in order to effect by force a treasonable purpose," must be a body assembled with such appearance of force as would warrant the opinion that they were assembled for the particular purpose; an assemblage to constitute an actual levying of war should be an assemblage with such appearance of force as would justify the opinion that they met for the purpose.

This explanation, which is believed to be the natural, certainly not a strained explanation of the words, derives some additional aid from the terms in which the paragraph last quoted commences. "It is not the intention of the court to say that no individual can be guilty of treason who has not appeared in arms against his country." These words seem to obviate an inference which might otherwise have been drawn from the preceding paragraph. They indicate that in the mind of the court the assemblage stated in that paragraph was an assemblage in arms. That the individuals who composed it had appeared in arms against their country. That is in other words that the assemblage was a military, a warlike assemblage.

The succeeding paragraph in the opinion relates to a conspiracy and serves to shew that force and violence were in the mind of the court, and that there was no idea of extending the crime of treason by construction beyond the constitutional definition which had been given of it.

Returning to the case actually before the court, it is said "a design to overturn the government of the U. States in New Orleans *by force*, would have been unquestionably a design which if carried into execution would have been treason, and the assemblage of a body of men for the purpose of carrying it into execution would amount to levying of war against the U.S."

Now what could reasonably be said to be an assemblage of a body of men for the purpose of overturning the government of the U.S. in New Orleans by force? Certainly an assemblage in force; an assemblage prepared and intending to act with force; a military assemblage. The decisions theretofore made by the judges of the United States, are then declared to be in conformity with the principles laid down by the supreme court. Is this declaration compatible with the idea of departing from those opinions on a point within the contemplation of the court? The opinions of Judge Patterson and Judge Iredell are said "to imply an actual assembling of men though they rather designed to remark on the purpose to which the force was to be applied than on the nature of the force itself." This observation certainly indicates that the necessity of an assemblage of men was the particular point the court meant to establish, and that the idea of force was never separated from this assemblage.

The opinion of Judge Chase is next quoted with approbation. This opinion in terms requires the employment of force.

After stating the verbal communications said to have been made by Mr. Swartwout to gen. Wilkinson, the court says "if these words import that the government of New-Orleans was to be revolutionized by force, although merely as a step to or a mean of exciting some greater projects, the design was unquestionably treasonable, and any assemblage of men for that purpose would amount to a levying of war."

The words "any assemblage of men" if construed to affirm that any two or three of the conspirators who might be found together after this plan had been formed, would be the act of levying war, would certainly be misconstrued. The sense of the expression, "any assemblage of men" is restricted by the words "for this purpose." Now could it be in the contemplation of the court that a body of men would assemble for the purpose of revolutionizing New-Orleans by force, who should not themselves be in force?

After noticing some difference of opinion among the judges respecting the import of the words said to have been used by Mr. Swartwout the court proceeds to observe: "But whether this treasonable intention be really imputable to the plan or not, it is admitted that it must have been carried into execution by an open assemblage for that purpose, previous to the arrest of the prisoner, in order to consummate the crime as to him."

Could the court have conceived "an open assemblage" "for

the purpose of overturning the government of New-Orleans by force" to be only equivalent to a secret furtive assemblage without the appearance of force?

After quoting the words of Mr. Swartwout, from the affidavit, in which it was stated that Mr. Burr was levying an army of 7,000 men, and observing that the treason to be inferred from these words would depend on the intention with which it was levied, and on the progress which had been made in levying it, the court say "the question then is, whether this evidence proves col. Burr to have advanced so far in levying an army as actually to have assembled them."

Actually to assemble an army of 7,000 men is unquestionably to place those who are so assembled in a state of open force.

But as the mode of expression used in this passage might be misconstrued so far as to countenance the opinion that it would be necessary to assemble the whole army in order to constitute the fact of levying war, the court proceeds to say, "It is argued that since it cannot be necessary that the whole 7,000 men should be assembled, their commencing their march by detachments to the place of rendezvous must be sufficient to constitute the crime."

"This position is correct with some qualification. It cannot be necessary that the whole army should assemble and that the various parts which are to compose it should have combined. But it is necessary there should be an actual assemblage; and therefore this evidence should make the fact unequivocal."

"The travelling of individuals to the place of rendezvous would perhaps not be sufficient. This would be an equivocal act, and has no warlike appearance. The meeting of particular bodies of men, and their marching from places of partial to a place of general rendezvous would be such an assemblage."

The position here stated by the counsel for the prosecution is, that the army "commencing its march by detachments to the place of rendezvous (that is of the army,) must be sufficient to constitute the crime."

This position is not admitted by the court to be universally correct. It is said to be "correct with some qualification." What is that qualification?

"The travelling of individuals to the place of rendezvous,"

(and by this term is not to be understood one individual by himself, but several individuals either separately or together but not in military form) "would perhaps not be sufficient." Why not sufficient? Because says the court, "this would be an equivocal act and has no warlike appearance." The act then should be unequivocal and should have a warlike appearance. It must exhibit in the words of Sir Matthew Hale *speciem belli*, the appearance of war. This construction is rendered in some measure necessary when we observe that the court is qualifying the position, "That the army commencing their march by detachments to the place of rendezvous must be sufficient to constitute the crime." In qualifying this position they say, "the travelling of individuals would perhaps not be sufficient." Now, a solitary individual travelling to any point, with any intent, could not, without a total disregard of language, be termed a marching detachment. The court, therefore, must have contemplated several individuals travelling together; and the words being used in reference to the position they were intended to qualify, would seem to indicate the distinction between the appearances attending the usual movement of a company of men for civil purposes, and that military movement which might in correct language be denominated "marching by detachments."

The court then proceeded to say, "the meeting of particular bodies of men and their marching from places of partial to a place of general rendezvous would be such an assemblage."

It is obvious from the context, that the court must have intended to state a case which would in itself be unequivocal, because it would have a warlike appearance. The case stated, is that of distinct bodies of men assembling at different places and marching from these places of partial to a place of general rendezvous. When this has been done, an assemblage is produced which would in itself be unequivocal. But when is it done? what is the assemblage here described? The assemblage formed of the different bodies of partial at a place of general rendezvous. In describing the mode of coming to this assemblage the civil term "travelling" is dropped, and the military term "marching" is employed. If this was intended as a definition of an assemblage which would amount to levying war, the definition requires an assemblage at a place of general rendezvous, composed of bodies of men who had previously assembled at places of partial rendezvous. But this is not intended as a definition, for clearly if there should be no places of partial rendezvous, if troops should embody in the first instance, in great force for the purpose of subverting the government by violence, the act would be unequivocal, it would have a warlike appearance, and it would, according to the opinion of the supreme court properly construed, and according to the English authorities, amount to levying war. But this, though not a definition, is put as an example; and surely it may be safely taken as an example. If different bodies of men, in pursuance of a treasonable design plainly proved, should assemble in warlike appearance at places of partial rendezvous, and should *march* from those places to a place of general rendezvous, it is difficult to conceive how such a transaction could take place without exhibiting the appearance of war, without an obvious display of force. At any rate, a court in stating generally such a military assemblage as would amount to levying war, and having a case before them in which there was no assemblage whatever, cannot reasonably be understood in putting such an example, to dispense with those appearances of war which seem to be required by the general current of authorities. Certainly they ought not to be so understood when they say in express terms, that "it is more safe as well as more consonant to the principles of our constitution, that the crime of treason should not be extended by construction to doubtful cases; and that crimes not already within the constitutional definition, should receive such punishment as the legislature in its wisdom may provide."

After this analysis of the opinion of the supreme court, it will be observed, that the direct question whether an assemblage of men which might be construed to amount to a levying of war, must appear in force or in military form was not in argument or in fact before the court, and does not appear to have been in terms decided? The opinion seems to have been drawn without particularly adverting to this question, and therefore upon a transient view of particular expressions, might inspire the idea that a display of force, that appearances of war were not necessary ingredients to constitute the fact of levying war. But upon a more intent and more accurate investigation of this opinion, although the terms force and violence are not employed as descriptive of the assemblage, such requisites are declared to be indispensable as can scarcely exist without the appearance of war and the existence of real force. It is said that war must be levied in fact, that the object must be one which is to be effected by force; that the assemblage must be such as to prove that this is its object, that it must not be an equivocal act, without a warlike appearance, that it must be an open assemblage for the purpose of force. In the course of this opinion, decisions are quoted and approved, which require the employment of force to constitute the crime. It seems extremely difficult, if not impossible, to reconcile these various declarations with the idea that the supreme court considered a secret unarmed meeting, although that meeting be of conspirators, and although it met with a treasonable intent, as an actual levying of war. Without saying that the assemblage must be in force or in warlike form, they express themselves so as to show that this idea was never discarded, and they use terms which cannot be otherwise satisfied.

The opinion of a single judge certainly weighs as nothing if opposed to that of the supreme court; but if he was one of the judges who assisted in framing that opinion, if while the impression under which it was framed was yet fresh upon his mind, he delivered an opinion on the same testimony, not contradictory to that which had been given by all the judges together, but showing the sense in which he understood terms that might be differently expounded, it may fairly be said to be in some measure explanatory of the opinion itself.

To the judge before whom the charge against the prisoner at the bar was first brought, the same testimony was offered with that which had been exhibited before the supreme court, and he was required to give an opinion in almost the same case. Upon this occasion he said, "War can only be levied by the employment of actual force. Troops must be embodied; men must be assembled in order to levy war." Again he observed, "The fact to be proved in this case is an act of public notoriety. It must exist in the view of the world or it cannot exist at all. The assembling of forces to levy war is a visible transaction, and numbers must witness it."

It is not easy to doubt what kind of assemblage was in the mind of the judge who used these expressions, and it is to be recollected that he had just returned from the supreme court and was speaking on the very facts on which the opinion of that court was delivered.

The same judge in his charge to the Grand Jury who found this bill, observed, "to constitute the fact of levying war, it is not necessary that hostilities shall have actually commenced by engaging the military force of the U.S. or that measures of violence against the government shall have been carried into execution. But levying war is a fact in the constitution of which force is an indispensable ingredient. Any combination to subvert by force the government of the U.S. violently to dismember the union, to compel a change in the administration, to coerce the repeal or adoption of a general law, is a conspiracy to levy war, and if the conspiracy be carried into effect by the actual employment of force, by the embodying and assembling of men for the purpose of executing the treasonable design which was previously conceived, it amounts to levying of war. It has been held that arms are not essential to levying war provided the force assembled be sufficient to attain, or perhaps to justify attempting the object without them." This paragraph is immediately followed by a reference to the opinion of the supreme court.

It requires no commentary upon these words to show that, in the opinion of the judge who uttered them, an assemblage of men which should constitute the fact of levying war must be an assemblage in force, and that he so understood the opinion of the supreme court. If in that opinion, there may be found in some passages, a want of precision, an indefiniteness of expression, which has occasioned it to be differently understood by different persons, that may well be accounted for when it is recollected that in the particular case there was no assemblage whatever. In expounding that opinion the whole should be taken together, and in reference to the particular case in which it was delivered. It is however not improbable that the misunderstanding has arisen from this circumstance. The court unquestionably did not consider arms as an indispensable requisite to levying war; an assemblage adapted to the object might be in a condition to effect or to attempt it without them. Nor did the court consider the actual application of the force to the object as, at all times, an indispensable requisite; for an assemblage might be in a condition to apply force, might be in a state adapted to real war, without having made the actual application of that force. From these positions, which are to be found in the opinion, it may have been inferred, it is thought too hastily, that the nature of the assemblage was unimportant, and that war might be considered as actually levied by any meeting of men, if a criminal intention can be imputed to them by testimony of any kind whatever.

It has been thought proper to discuss this question at large and to review the opinion of the supreme court, although this court would be more disposed to leave the question of fact, whether an overt act of levying war was committed on Blannerhassett's island to the jury under this explanation of the law, and to instruct them, that unless the assemblage on Blannerhassett's island was an assemblage in force, was a military assemblage in a condition to make war, it was not a levying of war, and that they could not construe it into an act of war, than to arrest the further testimony which might be offered to connect the prisoner with that assemblage, or to prove the intention of those who assembled together at that place. This point, however, is not to be understood as decided. It will, perhaps, constitute an essential enquiry in another case.

Before leaving the opinion of the supreme court entirely on the question of the nature of the assemblage which will constitute an act of levying war, this court cannot forbear to ask, why is an assemblage absolutely required? Is it not to judge in some measure of the end by the proportion which the means bear to the end? Why is it that a single armed individual entering a boat and sailing down the Ohio, for the avowed purpose of attacking New-Orleans could not be said to levy war? Is it not that he is apparently not in a condition to levy war? If this be so, ought not the assemblage to furnish some evidence of its intention and capacity to levy war before it can amount to levying war? And ought not the supreme court, when speaking of an assemblage for the purpose of effecting a treasonable object by force, be understood to indicate an assemblage exhibiting the appearance of force.

The definition of the Attorney for the United States, deserves notice in this respect. It is "when there is an assemblage of men, convened for the purpose of effecting by force a treasonable object, which force is meant to be employed before the assemblage disperses, this is treason."

To read this definition without adverting to the argument, we should infer that the assemblage was itself to effect by force the treasonable object, not to join itself to some other bodies of men and then to effect the object by their combined force. Under this construction it would be expected the appearance of the assemblage would bear some proportion to the object and would indicate the intention. At any rate that it would be an assemblage in force. This construction is most certainly not that which was intended, but it serves to show that general phrases must always be understood in reference to the subject matter, and to the general principles of law.

On that division of the subject which respects the merits of the case connected with the pleadings, two points are also made.

1st. That this indictment having charged the prisoner with levying war on Blannerhassett's island and containing no other overt act, cannot be supported by proof that war was levied at that place by other persons, in the absence of the prisoner, even admitting those persons to be connected with him in one common treasonable conspiracy.

2dly. That admitting such an indictment could be supported by such evidence, the previous conviction of some person who committed the act which is said to amount to levying war, is indispensable to the conviction of a person who advised or procured that act.

As to the first point, the indictment contains two counts, one of which charges that the prisoner with a number of persons unknown levied war on Blannerhassett's island, in the county of Wood, in the district of Virginia, and the other adds the circumstance of their proceeding from that island down the river for the purpose of seizing New-Orleans by force.

In point of fact, the prisoner was not on Blannerhassett's island nor in the county of Wood nor in the district of Virginia.

In considering this point the court is led first to enquire whether an indictment for levying war must specify an overt act or would be sufficient if it merely charged the prisoner in general terms with having levied war, omitting the expression of place or circumstance.

The place in which a crime was committed is essential to an indictment, were it only to show the jurisdiction of the court. It is also essential for the purpose of enabling the prisoner to make his defence. That, at common law, an indictment would have been defective which did not mention the place in which the crime was committed, can scarcely be doubted. For this, it is sufficient to refer to Hawkins B 2, ch. 25, sect. 84. & ch. 23, sect. 91. This necessity is rendered the stronger by the constitutional provision that the offender "shall be tried in the state and district wherein the crime shall have been committed," and by the act of Congress which requires that twelve petty jurors at least shall be summoned from the county where the offence was committed. A description of the particular manner in which the war was levied, seems also essential to enable the accused to make his defence. The law does not expect a man to be prepared to defend every act of his life which may be suddenly and without notice alleged against him. In common justice the particular fact with which he is charged ought to be stated, and stated in such a manner as to afford a reasonable certainty of the nature of the accusation, and the circumstances which will be adduced against him. The general doctrine on the subject of indictments is full to this point. Foster p. 149, speaking of the treason of compassing the king's death, says "From what has been said it followeth that in every indictment for this species of treason, and indeed for levying war and adhering to the king's enemies an overt act must be alledged and proved. For the overt act is the charge to which the prisoner must apply his defence."

In page 220, Foster repeats this declaration. It is also laid down in Hawk. B 8, ch. 17, sect. 29. 1st Hale 121. 1st East 116, and by the other authorities cited, especially Vaughan's case. In corroboration of this opinion, it may be observed that treason can only be established by the proof of overt acts, and that by the common law as well as by the statute of 7th of William 3d, those overt acts only which are charged in the indictment can be given in evidence, unless perhaps as corroborative testimony after the overt acts are proved. That clause in the constitution too which says that in all criminal prosecutions the accused shall enjoy the right "to be informed of the nature and cause of the accusation" is considered as having a direct bearing on this point. It secures to him such information as will enable him to prepare for his defence.

It seems then to be perfectly clear that it would not be sufficient for an indictment to alledge generally that the accused had levied war against the United States. The charge must be more particularly specified by laying what is termed an overt act of levying war. The law relative to an appeal as cited from Stamford, is strongly corroborative of this opinion.

If it be necessary to specify the charge in the indictment, it would seem to follow irresistibly, that the charge must be proved as laid.

All the authorities which require an overt act, require also that this overt act should be proved. The decision in Vaughan's case is particularly in point. Might it be otherwise, the charge of an overt act would be a mischief instead of an advantage to the accused. It would lead him from the true cause and nature of the accusation instead of informing him respecting it.

But it is contended on the part of the prosecution that, although the accused had been never with the party which assembled at Blannerhassett's Island, and was, at the time, at a great distance, and in a different state, he was yet legally present, and therefore may properly be charged in the indictment as being present in fact.

It is therefore necessary to enquire whether in this case the doctrine of constructive presence can apply.

It is conceived by the court to be possible that a person may be concerned in a treasonable conspiracy and yet be legally, as well as actually absent while some one act of the treason is perpetrated. If a rebellion should be so extensive as to spread through every state in the union, it will scarcely be contended that every individual concerned in it is legally present at every overt act committed in the course of that rebellion. It would be a very violent presumption indeed, too violent to be made without clear authority, to presume that even the chief of the rebel army was legally present at every such overt act. If the main rebel army with the chief at its head should be prosecuting war at one extremity of our territory, say in N.H. if this chief should be there captured and sent to the other extremity for the purpose of trial, if his indictment instead of alledging an overt act which was true in point of fact, should alledge that he had assembled some small party which in truth he had not seen, and had levied war by engaging in a skirmish in Georgia at a time when in reality he was fighting a battle in New-Hampshire, if such evidence would support such an indictment by the fiction that he was legally present though really absent, all would ask to what purpose are those provisions in the constitution which direct the place of trial, and ordain that the accused shall be informed of the nature and cause of the accusation?

But that a man may be legally absent who has counselled or procured a treasonable act, is proved by all those books which treat upon the subject, and which concur in declaring that such a person is a principal traitor, not because he was legally present, but because in treason all are principals. Yet the indictment I say upon general principles, would charge him according to the truth of the case. Lord Coke says "if many conspire to levy war and some of them do levy the same according to the conspiracy, this is high treason in all." Why? because all were legally present when the war was levied? No. "For in treason, continues Lord Coke, all be principals, and war is levied." In this case the indictment, reasoning from analogy, would not charge that the absent conspirators were present but would state the truth of the case. If the conspirator had done nothing which amounted to levying of war, and if by our constitution the doctrine that an accessary becomes a principal be not adopted, in consequence of which the conspirator could not be condemned under an indictment stating the truth of the case, it would be going very far to say that this defect, if it be termed one, may be cured by an indictment stating the case untruely.

This doctrine of Lord Coke has been adopted by all subsequent writers; and it is generally laid down in the English books that whatever will make a man an accessary in felony, will make him a principal in treason; but it is no where suggested that he is by construction to be considered as present when in point of fact he was absent.

Foster 3d has been particularly quoted, and certainly he is precisely in point. "It is well known, says Foster, that in the language of the law there are no accessaries in high treason, all are principals. Every instance of incitement, aid, or protection, which in the case of felony will render a man an accessary before or after the fact, in the case of high treason, whether it be treason at common law or by statute, will make him a principal in treason." The cases of incitement and aid are cases put as examples of a man's becoming a principal in treason, not because he was legally present, but by force of that maxim in the common law that whatever will render a man an accessary at common law will render him a principal in treason. In other passages the words "command" or "procure" are used to indicate the same state of things, that is a treasonable assemblage produced by a man who is not himself in that assemblage.

In point of law then, the man who incites, aids, or procures a treasonable act, is not merely in consequence of that incitement, aid or procurement, legally present when that act is committed.

If it does not result from the nature of the crime that all who are concerned in it are legally present at every overt act; then each case depends upon its own circumstances, and to judge how far the circumstances of any case can make him legally present who is in fact absent, the doctrine of constructive presence must be examined.

Hale in his 1 vol. p. 615 says "regularly no man can be a principal in felony unless he be present." In the same page he says "an accessary *before* is he that being absent at the time of the felony committed, doth yet procure, counsel, or command another to commit a felony." The books are full of passages which state this to be the law. Foster in showing what acts of concurrence will make a man a principal, says "he must be present at the perpetration, otherwise he can be no more than an accessary before the fact."

These strong distinctions would be idle in treason, at any rate they would be inapplicable, if they were to be entirely lost in the doctrine of constructive presence.

Foster adds (p. 349) "when the law requireth the presence of the accomplice at the perpetration of the fact in order to render him a principal, it doth not require a strict actual immediate presence, such a presence as would make him an eye or ear witness of what passeth." The terms used by Foster are such as would be employed by a man intending to show the necessity that the absent person should be near at hand, although from the nature of the thing no precise distance could be marked out. An inspection of the cases from which Foster drew this general principle will serve to illustrate it. Hale 439. In all these cases, put by Hale, the whole party set out together to commit the very fact charged in the indictment, or to commit some other unlawful act, in which they are all to be personally concerned at the same time and place, and are at the very time when the criminal act is committed, near enough to give actual personal aid and assistance to the man who perpetrated it. Hale in p. 449 giving the reason for the decision in the case of the lord Dacre says "they all came with an intent to steal the deer and consequently the law supposes that they came all with the intent to oppose all that should hinder them in that design." The original case says this was their resolution. This opposition would be a personal opposition. This case even as stated by Hale would clearly not comprehend any man who entered into the combination, but who, instead of going to the park where the murder was committed, should not set out with the others, should go to a different park, or should even lose his way. Hale 534.

In both the cases here stated, the persons actually set out together and were near enough to assist in the commission of the fact. That in the case of Pudsy the felony was as stated by Hale, a different felony from that originally intended is unimportant in regard to the particular principle now under consideration, so far as respected distance, as respected capacity to assist in case of resistance, it is the same as if the robbery had been that which was originally designed. The case in the original report shows that the felony committed was in fact in pursuance of that originally designed. Foster 350 plainly supposes the same particular design, not a general design composed of many particular distinct facts. He supposes them to be co-operating with respect to that particular design. This may be illustrated by a case which is perhaps common. Suppose a band of robbers confederated for the general purpose of robbing. They set out together, or in parties, to rob a particular individual, and each performs the part assigned to him. Some ride up to the individual and demand his purse, others watch out of sight to intercept those who might be coming to assist the man

on whom the robbery is to be committed. If murder or robbery actually take place, all are principals and all in construction of law are present. But suppose they set out at the same
time or at different times, by different roads, to attack and rob
different individuals or different companies: to commit distinct acts of robbery. It has never been contended that those
who committed one act of robbery or who failed altogether,
were constructively present at the act of those who were associated with them in the common object of robbery, who were
to share the plunder but who did not assist at the particular fact.
They do indeed belong to the general party, but they are not
of the particular party which committed this fact. Foster concludes this subject by observing that "in order to render a person an accomplice and a principal in felony, he must be aiding
and abetting at the fact, or ready to afford assistance if necessary." That is, at the particular fact which is charged; he must
be ready to render assistance to those who are committing that
particular fact; he must as is stated by Hawkins be ready to give
immediate and direct assistance.

All the cases to be found in the books go to the same point.
Let them be applied to that under consideration.

The whole treason laid in this indictment is the levying of
war in Blannerhassett's island, and the whole question to which
the enquiry of the court is now directed is whether the prisoner was legally present at that fact.

I say this is the whole question because the prisoner can only
be convicted on the overt act laid in the indictment. With respect to this prosecution it is as if no other overt act existed.

If other overt acts can be enquired into, it is for the sole purpose of proving the particular fact charged; it is as evidence of
the crime consisting of this particular fact, not as establishing
the general crime by a distinct fact.

The counsel for the prosecution have charged those engaged in the defence with considering the overt act as the treason, whereas it ought to be considered solely as the evidence
of the treason; but the counsel for the prosecution seem themselves not to have sufficiently adverted to this clear principle,
that though the overt act may not be itself the treason, it is
the sole act of that treason which can produce conviction. It
is the sole point in issue between the parties. And the only

division of that point, if the expression be allowed, which the court is now examining, is the constructive presence of the prisoner at the fact charged.

To return then to the application of the cases.

Had the prisoner set out with the party from Beaver for Blannerhassett's island, or perhaps had he set out for that place, though not from Beaver, and had arrived in the island, he would have been present at the fact; had he not arrived in the island, but had taken a position near enough to co-operate with those on the island, to assist them in any act of hostility, or to aid them if attacked, the question whether he was constructively present would be a question compounded of law and fact, which would be decided by the jury, with the aid of the court, so far as respected the law. In this case the accused would have been of the particular party assembled on the island, and would have been associated with them in the particular act of levying war said to have been committed on the island.

But if he was not with the party at any time before they reached the island; if he did not join them there, or intend to join them there; if his personal co-operation in the general plan was to be afforded elsewhere, at a great distance, in a different state; if the overt acts of treason to be performed by him were to be distinct overt acts; then he was not of the particular party assembled at Blannerhassett's island, and was not constructively present, aiding and assisting in the particular act which was there committed.

The testimony on this point, so far as it has been delivered, is not equivocal. There is not only no evidence that the accused was of the particular party which assembled on Blannerhassett's island, but the whole evidence shows he was not of that party.

In felony then, admitting the crime to have been completed on the island, and to have been advised, procured, or commanded by the accused, he would have been incontestably an accessary and not a principal.

But in treason it is said, the law is otherwise, because the theatre of action is more extensive.

The reasoning applies in England as strongly as in the United States. While in '15 and '45 the family of Stuart sought to regain the crown they had forfeited, the struggle was for the whole kingdom; yet no man was ever considered as legally present at one place, when actually at another; or as aiding in one transaction, while actually employed in another.

With the perfect knowledge that the whole nation may be the theatre of action, the English books unite in declaring, that he who counsels, procures or aids treason, is guilty accessorially and solely in virtue of the common law principle, that what will make a man an accessary in felony makes him a principal in treason. So far from considering a man as constructively present at every overt act of the general treason in which he may have been concerned, the whole doctrine of the books limits the proof against him to those particular overt acts of levying war with which he is charged.

What would be the effect of a different doctrine? Clearly that which has been stated. If a person levying war in Kentucky, may be said to be constructively present and assembled with a party carrying on war in Virginia, at a great distance from him; then he is present at every overt act performed any where; he may be tried in any state on the continent, where any overt act has been committed; he may be proved to be guilty of an overt act laid in the indictment in which he had no personal participation, by proving that he advised it, or that he committed other acts.

This is, perhaps, too extravagant to be in terms maintained. Certainly it cannot be supported by the doctrines of the English law.

The opinion of Judge Patterson in Mitchell's case has been cited on this point. 2 Dal. 348.

The indictment is not specially stated; but from the case as reported, it must have been either general for levying war in the county of Alleghany, and the overt act laid must have been the assemblage of men and levying of war in that county; or it must have given a particular detail of the treasonable transactions in that county. The first supposition is the most probable; but let the indictment be in the one form or the other, and the result is the same. The facts of the case are that a large body of men, of whom Mitchell was one, assembled at Braddock's field, in the county of Alleghany, for the purpose of committing acts of violence at Pittsburg. That there was also an assemblage at a different time at Couches fort, at which the prisoner also attended. The general and avowed object of that meeting was to concert measures for resisting the execution of a public law. At Couches fort, the resolution was taken to attack the house of the inspector, and the body there assembled marched to that house and attacked it. It was proved by the competent number of witnesses, that he was at Couches fort armed, that he offered to reconnoitre the house to be attacked, that he marched with the insurgents towards the house, that he was with them after the action attending the body of one of his comrades who was killed in it; one witness swore positively that he was present at the burning of the house, and a second witness said that "it ran in his head that he had seen him there." That a doubt should exist in such a case as this, is strong evidence of the necessity that the overt act should be unequivocally proved by two witnesses.

But what was the opinion of the judge in this case? Couches fort and Neville's house being in the same county, the assemblage having been at Couches fort and the resolution to attack the house having been there taken, the body having for the avowed purposes moved in execution of that resolution towards the house to be attacked, he inclined to think that the act of marching was in itself levying war. If it was, then the overt act laid in the indictment was consummated by the assemblage at Couches and the marching from thence, and Mitchell was proved to be guilty by more than two positive witnesses. But without deciding this to be the law, he proceeded to consider the meeting at Couches, the immediate marching to Neville's house, and the attack and burning of the house, as one transaction. Mitchell was proved by more than two positive witnesses to have been in that transaction, to have taken an active part in it, and the judge declared it to be unnecessary that all should have seen him at the same time and place.

But suppose not a single witness had proved Mitchell to have been at Couches, or on the march, or at Neville's. Suppose he had been at the time notoriously absent in a different state. Can it be believed by any person who observes the caution with which Judge Patterson required the constitutional proof of two witnesses to the same overt act, that he would have said Mitchell was constructively present, and might on that straining of a legal fiction, be found, guilty of treason? Had he delivered such an opinion what would have been the language of this country respecting it? Had he given this opinion, it would have required all the correctness of his life to strike his name from that bloody list in which the name of Jeffries is enrolled.

But to estimate the opinion in Mitchell's case, let its circumstances be transferred to Burr's case. Suppose the body of men assembled in Blannerhassett's island had previously met at some other place in the same county, and that Burr had been proved to be with them by four witnesses: That the resolution to march to Blannerhassett's island for a treasonable purpose had been there taken; that he had been seen on the march with them; that one witness had seen him on the island, that another thought he had seen him there; that he had been seen with the party directly after leaving the island; that this indictment had charged the levying of war in Wood county generally; the cases would then have been precisely parallel, and the decisions would have been the same.

In conformity with principle and with authority then the prisoner at the bar was neither legally nor actually present at Blannerhassett's island; and the court is strongly inclined to the opinion that without proving an actual or legal presence by two witnesses, the overt act laid in this indictment cannot be proved.

But this opinion is controverted on two grounds.

The first is, that the indictment does not charge the prisoner to have been present.

The second, that although he was absent, yet, if he caused the assemblage, he may be indicted as being present, and convicted on evidence that he caused the treasonable act.

The first position is to be decided by the indictment itself. The court understands the allegation differently from the attorney for the U. States. The court understands it to be directly charged, that the prisoner did assemble with the multitude and did march with them. Nothing will more clearly test this construction than putting the case into a shape which it may possibly take. Suppose the law to be, that the indictment would be defective unless it alledged the presence of the person indicted at the act of treason. If upon a special verdict facts should be found which amounted to a levying of war by the accused, and his counsel should insist that he could not be condemned because the indictment was defective in not charging that he was himself one of the assemblage which constituted the treason, or because it alledged the procurement defectively, would the attorney admit this construction of his indictment to be correct? I am persuaded that he would not, and that he ought not to make such a concession. If, after a verdict, the indictment ought to be construed to alledge that the prisoner was one of the assemblage at Blannerhassett's island, it ought to be so construed now. But this is unimportant, for if the indictment alledges that the prisoner procured the assemblage that procurement becomes part of the overt act and must be proved as will be shown hereafter.

The 2d position is founded on 1 Hale 214, 288 and 1. East 127.

While I declare that this doctrine contradicts every idea I had ever entertained on the subject of indictments, since it admits that one case may be stated and a very different case may be proved, I will acknowledge that it is countenanced by the authorities adduced in its support. To counsel or advise a treasonable assemblage, and to be one of that assemblage, are certainly distinct acts, and therefore ought not to be charged as the same act. The great objection to this mode of proceeding is, that the proof essentially varies from the charge in the character and essence of the offence, and in the testimony by which the accused is to defend himself. These dicta of Lord Hale therefore, taken in the extent in which they are understood by the counsel for the U.S. seem to be repugnant to the declarations we find every where, that an overt act must be laid, and must be proved. No case is cited by Hale in support of them, and I am strongly inclined to the opinion that, had the public received his corrected, instead of his original manuscript, they would, if not expunged, have been restrained in their application to cases of a particular description. Laid down generally, and applied universally to all cases of treason, they are repugnant to the principles for which Hale contends, for which all the elementary writers contend, and from which courts have in no case either directly reported or referred to in the books, ever departed. These principles are, that the indictment must give notice of the offence, that the accused is only bound to answer the particular charge which the indictment contains, and that the overt act laid is that particular charge. Under such circumstances, it is only doing justice to Hale to examine his dicta, & if they will admit of being understood in a limited sense, not repugnant to his own doctrines, nor to the general principles of law, to understand them in that sense.

"If many conspire to counterfeit, or counsel or abet it, and one of them doth the fact upon that counselling or conspiracy, it is treason in all, and they may be all indicted for counterfeiting generally within this statute, for in such case, in treason, all are principals."

This is laid down as applicable singly to the treason of counterfeiting the coin, and is not applied by Hale to other treasons. Had he designed to apply the principle universally he would have stated it as a general proposition, he would have laid it down in treating on other branches of the statute, as well as in the chapter respecting the coin, he would have laid it down when treating on indictments generally. But he has done neither. Every sentiment bearing in any manner on this point, which is to be found in Lord Hale, while on the doctrine of levying war, or on the general doctrine of indictments, militates against the opinion that he considered the proposition as more extensive than he has declared it to be. No court could be justified in extending the dictum of a judge beyond its terms, to cases in which he has expressly treated, to which he has not himself applied it, and on which he as well as others has delivered opinions which that dictum would overrule. This would be the less justifiable if there should be a clear legal distinction indicated by the very terms in which the judge has expressed himself between the particular case to which alone he has applied the dictum, and other cases to which the court is required to extend it.

There is this clear legal distinction. "They may, says Judge Hale, be indicted for counterfeiting generally." But if many conspire to levy war, and some actually levy it, they may not be indicted for levying war generally. The books concur in declaring that they cannot be so indicted. A special overt act of levying war must be laid. This distinction between counterfeiting the coins, and that class of treasons among which levying war is placed, is taken in the statute of Edward III. That statute requires an overt act of levying war to be laid in the indictment, and does not require an overt act of counterfeiting the coin to be laid. If in a particular case where a general indictment is sufficient, it be stated that the crime may be charged generally according to the legal effect of the act, it does not follow, that in other cases where a general indictment would be insufficient, where an overt act must be laid, that this overt act need not be laid according to the real fact. Hale then is to be reconciled with himself, and with the general principles of law, only by permitting the limits which he has himself given to his own dictum, to remain where he has placed them.

In page 238, Hale is speaking generally of the receiver of a traitor, and is stating in what such receiver partakes of an accessary. 1st. "His indictment must be special of the receipt, and not generally that he did the thing, which may be otherwise in case of one that is procurer, counsellor or consenter."

The words "*may* be otherwise" do not clearly convey the idea that it is universally otherwise. In all cases of a receiver the indictment *must* be special on the receipt, and not general. The words it "*may* be otherwise in case of a procurer, &c" signify that it may be otherwise in all treasons, or that it may be otherwise in some treasons. If it may be otherwise in some treasons without contradicting the doctrines of Hale himself, as well as of other writers, but cannot be otherwise in all treasons without such contradiction, the fair construction is, that Hale used these words in their restricted sense; that he used them in reference to treasons, in which a general indictment would lie, not to treasons where a general indictment would not lie, but an overt act of the treason must be charged. The two passages of Hale thus construed, may perhaps be law, and may leave him consistent with himself. It appears to the court to be the fair way of construing them.

These observations relative to the passages quoted from Hale apply to that quoted from East, who obviously copies from Hale, and relies upon his authority.

Upon this point Keeling 26, and 1st Hale 626, have also been relied upon. It is stated in both, that if a man be indicted as a principal and acquitted he cannot afterwards be indicted as accessary before the fact. Whence it is inferred, not without reason, that evidence of accessorial guilt may be received on such an indictment. Yet no case is found in which the question has been made and decided. The objection has never been taken at a trial and overruled, nor do the books say it would be overruled. Were such a case produced its application would be questionable. Keeling says, an accessary before the fact is *quodam modo* in some manner guilty of the fact. The law may not require that the manner should be stated, for in felony it does not require that an overt act should be laid. The indictment therefore may be general. But an overt act of levying war must be laid. These cases then prove in their utmost extent no more than the cases previously cited from Hale and East. This distinction between indictments which may state the fact generally, and those which must lay specially, bear some analogy to a general and a special action on the case. In a general action, the declaration may lay the assumpsit according to the legal effect of the transaction, but in a special action on the case the declaration must state the material circumstances truely, and they must be proved as stated. This distinction also derives some aid from a passage in Hale, 625, immediately preceding that which has been cited at the bar. He says "if A. be indicted as principal and B. as accessary *before* or *after*, and both be acquitted, yet B. may be indicted as principal, & the former acquittal as accessary is no bar."

The crimes then are not the same, and may not indifferently be tried under the same indictment. But why is it, that an acquittal as principal may be pleaded in bar to an indictment as accessary, while an acquittal as accessary may not be pleaded in bar to an indictment as principal? If it be answered that the accessorial crime may be given in evidence on an indictment as principal, but that the principal crime may not be given in evidence on an indictment as accessary, the question recurs, on what legal ground does this distinction stand? I can imagine only this. An accessary being *quodam modo* a principal, in indictments where the law does not require the manner to be stated, which need not be special, evidence of accessorial guilt, if the punishment be the same, may possibly be received; but every indictment as an accessary must be special. The very allegation that he is an accessary must be a special allegation, and must show how he became an accessary. The charges of this special indictment therefore must be proved as laid, and no evidence which proves the crime in a form substantially different can be received. If this be the legal reason for the distinction it supports the exposition of these dicta which has been given. If it be not the legal reason, I can conceive no other.

But suppose the law to be as is contended by the counsel for the United States. Suppose an indictment charging an individual with personally assembling among others and thus levying war, may be satisfied with the proof that he caused the assemblage. What effect will this law have upon this case?

The guilt of the accused, if there be any guilt, does not consist in the assemblage, for he was not a member of it. The simple fact of assemblage no more affects one absent man than another. His guilt then consists in procuring the assemblage, and upon this fact depends his criminality. The proof relative to the character of an assemblage must be the same whether a man be present or absent. In the general, to charge any individual with the guilt of an assemblage, the fact of his presence must be proved. It constitutes an essential part of the overt act. If then the procurement be substituted in the place of presence, does it not also constitute an essential part of the overt act? Must it not also be proved? Must it not be proved in the same manner that presence must be proved? If in one case the presence of the individual makes the guilt of the assemblage his guilt, and in the other case the procurement by the individual makes the guilt of the assemblage his guilt, then presence and procurement are equally component parts of the overt act, and equally require two witnesses.

Collateral points may, say the books, be proved according to the course of the common law, but is this a collateral point? Is the fact without which the accused does not participate in the guilt of the assemblage, if it was guilty, a collateral point? This cannot be. The presence of the party, where presence is necessary, being a part of the overt act, must be positively proved by two witnesses. No presumptive evidence; no facts from which presence may be conjectured or inferred, will satisfy the constitution and the law. If procurement take the place of presence, and become part of the overt act, then no presumptive evidence, no facts from which the procurement may be conjectured or inferred, can satisfy the constitution and the law. The mind is not to be led to the conclusion that the individual was present by a train of conjectures, or inferences, or of reasoning; the fact must be proved by two witnesses. Neither where procurement supplies the want of presence, is the mind to be conducted to the conclusion that the accused procured the assembly, by a train of conjectures, of inferences, or of reasoning; the fact itself must be proved by two witnesses, and must have been committed within the district.

If it be said that the advising or procurement of treason is a secret transaction which can scarcely ever be proved in the manner required by this opinion; the answer which will readily suggest itself is, that the difficulty of proving a fact will not justify conviction without proof. Certainly it will not justify conviction without a direct and positive witness in a case where the constitution requires two. The more correct inference from this circumstance would seem to be, that the advising of the fact is not within the constitutional definition of the crime. To advise or procure a treason is in the nature of conspiring or plotting treason, which is not treason in itself.

If then the doctrines of Keeling, Hale, and East, are to be understood in the sense in which they are pressed by the counsel for the prosecution, and are applicable in the U. States; the fact that the accused procured the assemblage on Blannerhassett's island must be proved, not circumstantially, but positively by two witnesses to charge him with that assemblage. But there are still other most important considerations which must be well weighed before this doctrine can be applied to the United States.

The 8th amendment to the constitution has been pressed with great force, & it is impossible not to feel its application to this point. The accused cannot be truly said to be "informed of the nature and cause of the accusation," unless the indictment shall give him that notice which may reasonably suggest to him the point on which the accusation turns, so that he may know the course to be pursued in his defence.

It is also well worthy of consideration, that this doctrine so far as it respects treason, is entirely supported by the operation of the common law which is said to convert the accessary before the fact into the principal, and to make the act of the principal his act. The accessary before the fact is not said to have levied war. He is not said to be guilty under the statute.

But the common law attaches to him the guilt of that fact which he has advised or procured; and as contended, makes it his act. This is the operation of the common law, not the operation of the statute. It is an operation then which can only be performed where the common law exists to perform it. It is the creature of the common law, and the creature presupposes its creator. To decide then that this doctrine is applicable to the U. States, would seem to imply the decision that the U. States, as a nation, have a common law which creates and defines the punishment of crimes accessorial in their nature. It would imply the further decision that these accessorial crimes are not, in the case of treason, excluded by the definition of treason given in the constitution. I will not pretend that I have not individually an opinion on these points, but it is one which I should give only in a case absolutely requiring it, unless I could confer respecting it, with the judges of the supreme court.

I have said that this doctrine cannot apply to the U.S. without implying those decisions respecting the common law which I have stated, because, should it be true as is contended, that the constitutional definition of treason comprehends him who advises or procures an assemblage that levies war, it would not follow that such adviser or procurer might be charged as having been present at the assemblage. If the adviser or procurer is within the definition of levying war, and, independent of the agency of the common law, does actually levy war, then the advisement or procurement is an overt act of levying war. If it be the overt act on which he is to be convicted, then it must be charged in the indictment, for he can only be convicted on proof of the overt acts which are charged.

To render this distinction more intelligible, let it be recollected that although it should be conceded that since the statute of William and Mary, he who advises or procures a treason may in England be charged as having committed that treason by virtue of the common law operation which is said, so far as respects the indictment, to unite the accessorial to the principal offence and permit them to be charged as one, yet it can never be conceded that he who commits one overt act under the statute of Edward, can be charged and convicted on proof of another overt act. If then procurement be an overt act of treason under the constitution, no man can be convicted for the procurement under an indictment charging him with actually assembling; whatever may be the doctrine of the common law in the case of an accessorial offender.

It may not be improper in this place again to advert to the opinion of the supreme court and to show that it contains nothing contrary to the doctrine now laid down. That opinion is that an individual may be guilty of treason "who has not appeared in arms against his country: that if war be actually levied, that is, if a body of men be actually assembled for the purpose of effecting by force a treasonable object, all those who perform any part however minute or however remote from the scene of action, and who are actually leagued in the general conspiracy, are to be considered as traitors."

This opinion does not touch the case of a person who advises or procures an assemblage and does nothing further. The advising certainly, and perhaps the procuring, is more in the nature of a conspiracy to levy war than of the actual levying of war. According to the opinion, it is not enough to be leagued in the conspiracy, and that war be levied, but it is also necessary to perform a part; that part is the act of levying war. This part, it is true, may be minute, it may not be the actual appearance in arms; and it may be remote from the scene of action, that is from the place where the army is assembled, but it must be a part, and that part must be performed by a person who is leagued in the conspiracy. This part however minute or remote constitutes the overt act on which alone the person who performs it can be convicted.

The opinion does not declare that the person who has performed this remote and minute part may be indicted for a part which was in truth performed by others and convicted on their overt acts. It amounts to this and nothing more, that when war is actually levied, not only those who bear arms, but those also who are leagued in the conspiracy and who perform the various distinct parts which are necessary for the prosecution of war, do in the sense of the constitution levy war. It may possibly be the opinion of the supreme court that those who procure a treason and do nothing further are guilty under the constitution; I only say that opinion has not yet been given; still less has it been indicated that he who advises, shall be indicted as having performed the fact.

It is then the opinion of the court that this indictment can be supported only by testimony which proves the accused to have been actually or constructively present when the assemblage took place on Blannerhassett's island, or by the admission of the doctrine that he who procures an act may be indicted as having performed that act.

It is further the opinion of the court that there is no testimony whatever which tends to prove that the accused was actually or constructively present when that assemblage did take place. Indeed the contrary is most apparent. With respect to admitting proof of procurement to establish a charge of actual presence, the court is of opinion that if this be admissible in England on an indictment for levying war, which is far from being conceded, it is admissible only by virtue of the operation of the common law upon the statute, and therefore is not admissible in this country unless by virtue of a similar operation; a point far from being established, but on which, for the present, no opinion is given. If, however, this point be established, still the procurement must be proved in the same manner and by the same kind of testimony which would be required to prove actual presence.

The second point in this division of the subject is the necessity of adducing the record of the previous conviction of some one person who committed the fact alledged to be treasonable.

This point pre-supposes the treason of the accused, if any has been committed, to be accessorial in its nature. Its being of this description according to the British authorities, depends on the presence or absence of the accused at the time the fact was committed. The doctrine on this subject is well understood, has been most copiously explained, and need not be repeated. That there is no evidence of his actual or legal presence is a point already discussed and decided. It is then apparent that, but for the exception to the general principle which is made in cases of treason, those who assembled at Blannerhassett's island, if that assemblage were such as to constitute the crime, would be principals, and those who might really have caused that assemblage, although in truth the chief traitors, would in law be accessories.

It is a settled principle in the law that the accessory cannot be guilty of a greater offence than his principal. The maxim is, accessorius sequitur naturam sui principalis; the accessory follows the nature of his principal. Hence results the necessity of establishing the guilt of the principal before the accessory can be tried. For the degree of guilt which is incurred by counselling or commanding the commission of a crime, depends upon the actual commission of that crime. No man is an accessory to murder unless the fact has been committed.

The fact can only be established in a prosecution against the person by whom a crime has been perpetrated. The law supposes a man more capable of defending his own conduct than any other person, and will not tolerate that the guilt of A shall be established in a prosecution against B. Consequently, if the guilt of B depends on the guilt of A, A must be convicted before B can be tried. It would exhibit a monstrous deformity, indeed, in our system, if B might be executed for being accessory to a murder committed by A, and A should afterwards, upon a full trial, be acquitted of the fact. For this obvious reason, although the punishment of a principal and accessory was originally the same, and although in many instances it is still the same, the accessory could in no case be tried before the conviction of his principal, nor can he yet be tried previous to such conviction, unless he requires it, or unless a special provision to that effect be made by statute.

If then, this was a felony, the prisoner at the bar could not be tried until the crime was established by the conviction of the person by whom it was actually perpetrated.

Is the law otherwise in this case, because in treason all are principals?

Let this question be answered by reason and by authority.

Why is it that in felonies however atrocious, the trial of the accessory can never precede the conviction of the principal? Not because the one is denominated the principal and the other the accessory, for that would be ground on which a great law principle could never stand. Not because there was in fact a difference in the degree of moral guilt, for in the case of murder committed by a hardy villain for a bribe, the person plotting the murder and giving the bribe, is perhaps, of the two the blacker criminal; and, were it otherwise, this would furnish no argument for precedence in trial.

What then is the reason?

It has been already given. The legal guilt of the accessory depends on the guilt of the principal; & the guilt of the principal can only be established in a prosecution against himself.

Does not this reason apply in full force to a case of treason?

The legal guilt of the person who planned the assemblage on Blannerhassett's island depends, not simply on the criminality of the previous conspiracy, but on the criminality of that assemblage. If those who perpetrated the fact be not traitors, he who advised the fact cannot be a traitor. His guilt then, in contemplation of law, depends on theirs, and their guilt can only be established in a prosecution against themselves. Whether the adviser of this assemblage be punishable with death as a principal or as an accessory, his liability to punishment depends on the degree of guilt attached to an act which has been perpetrated by others, and which, if it be a criminal act, renders them guilty also. His guilt therefore depends on theirs, and their guilt cannot be legally established in a prosecution against him.

The whole reason of the law then relative to the principal and accessory, so far as respects the order of trial, seems to apply in full force to a case of treason committed by one body of men in conspiracy with others who are absent.

If from reason we pass to authority, we find it laid down by Hale, Foster, and East, in the most explicit terms, that the conviction of some one who has committed the treason must precede the trial of him who has advised or procured it. This position is also maintained by Leach in his notes on Hawkins, and is not, so far as the court has discovered, any where contradicted.

These authorities have been read and commented on at such length that it cannot be necessary for the court to bring them again into view. It is the less necessary because it is not understood that the law is controverted by the counsel for the United States.

It is, however, contended that the prisoner has waved his right to demand the conviction of some one person who was present at the fact, by pleading to his indictment.

Had this indictment even charged the prisoner according to the truth of the case, the court would feel some difficulty in deciding that he had by implication waved his right to demand a species of testimony essential to his conviction. The court is not prepared to say that the act which is to operate against his rights, did not require that it should be performed with a full knowledge of its operation. It would seem consonant to the usual course of proceeding in other respects in criminal cases, that the prisoner should be informed that he had a right to refuse to be tried until some person who committed the act should be convicted, and that he ought not to be considered as waving the right to demand the record of his conviction, unless with the full knowledge of that right he consented to be tried. The court, however, does not decide what the law would be in such a case. It is unnecessary to decide it because pleading to an indictment in which a man is charged as having committed an act, cannot be construed to wave a right which he would have possessed, had he been charged with having advised the act. No person indicted as a principal can be expected to say I am not a principal, I am an accessary; I did not commit, I only advised the act.

The authority of the English cases on this subject depends in a great measure on the adoption of the common law doctrine of accessorial treasons. If that doctrine be excluded, this branch of it may not be directly applicable to treasons committed within the United States. If the crime of advising or procuring a levying of war be within the constitutional definition of treason, then he who advises or procures it must be indicted on the very fact, and the question whether the treasonableness of the act may be decided in the first instance in the trial of him who procured it, or must be decided in the trial of one who committed it, will depend upon the reason, as it respects the law of evidence, which produced the British decisions with regard to the trial of principal and accessary, rather than on the positive authority of those decisions.

This question is not essential in the present case, because if the crime be within the constitutional definition, it is an overt act of levying war, and to produce a conviction ought to have been charged in the indictment.

The law of the case being thus far settled, what ought to be the decision of the court on the present motion? Ought the court to sit and hear testimony which cannot affect the prisoner, or ought the court to arrest that testimony? On this question much has been said—much that may perhaps be ascribed to a misconception of the point really under consideration. The motion has been treated as a motion confessedly made to stop relevant testimony, and in the course of the argument, it has been repeatedly stated by those who oppose the motion, that irrelevant testimony may and ought to be stopped. That this statement is perfectly correct, is one of those fundamental principles in judicial proceedings which is acknowledged by all and is founded in the absolute necessity of the thing. No person will contend that in a civil or criminal case, either party is at liberty to introduce what testimony he pleases, legal or illegal, and to consume the whole term in details of facts unconnected with the particular case. Some tribunal then must decide on the admissibility of testimony. The parties cannot constitute this tribunal, for they do not agree. The jury cannot constitute it, for the question is whether they shall hear the testimony or not. Who then but the court can constitute it? It is of necessity the peculiar province of the court to judge of the admissibility of testimony. If the court admit improper, or reject proper testimony, it is an error of judgment, but it is an error committed in the direct exercise of their judicial functions.

The present indictment charges the prisoner with levying war against the United States, and alledges an overt act of levying war. That overt act must be proved, according to the mandates of the constitution and of the act of Congress, by two witnesses. It is not proved by a single witness. The presence of the accused has been stated to be an essential component part of the overt act in this indictment, unless the common law principle respecting accessaries should render it unnecessary; and there is not only no witness who has proved his actual or legal presence; but the fact of his absence is not controverted. The counsel for the prosecution offer to give in evidence subsequent transactions, at a different place, and in a different state, in order to prove what? The overt act laid in the indictment? That the prisoner was one of those who assembled at Blannerhassett's island? No; that is not alledged. It is well known that such testimony is not competent to establish such a fact. The constitution and law require that the fact should be established by two witnesses, not by the establishment of other facts from which the jury might reason to this fact. The testimony then is not relevant. If it can be introduced, it is only in the character of corroborative or confirmatory testimony, after the overt act has been proved by two witnesses, in such manner that the question of fact ought to be left with the jury. The conclusion that in this state of things no testimony can be admissible, is so inevitable, that the counsel for the U. States could not resist it. I do not understand them to deny, that if the overt act be not proved by two witnesses so as to be submitted to the jury, that all other testimony must be irrelevant, because no other testimony can prove the act. Now an assemblage on Blannerhassett's island is proved by the requisite number of witnesses, and the court might submit it to the jury, whether that assemblage amounted to a levying of war, but the presence of the accused at that assemblage being no where alledged except in the indictment, the overt act is not proved by a single witness, and of consequence all other testimony must be irrelevant.

The only difference between this motion as made, and the motion in the form which the counsel for the U. States would admit to be regular, is this. It is now general for the rejection of all testimony. It might be particular with respect to each witness as adduced. But can this be wished, or can it be deemed necessary? If enough is proved to show that the indictment cannot be supported, and that no testimony unless it be of that description which the attorney for the U. States declares himself not to possess, can be relevant, why should a question be taken on each witness?

The opinion of this court on the order of testimony has frequently been adverted to as deciding this question against the motion.

If a contradiction between the two opinions does exist, the court cannot perceive it. It was said that levying war is an act compounded of law and fact, of which the jury aided by the court must judge. To that declaration the court still adheres.

It was said that if the overt act was not proved by two witnesses, no testimony in its nature corroborative or confirmatory was admissible or could be relevant.

From that declaration there is certainly no departure. It has been asked, in allusion to the present case, if a general commanding an army should detach troops for a distant service, would the men composing that detachment be traitors, and would the commander in chief escape punishment?

Let the opinion which has been given answer this question. Appearing at the head of an army would, according to this opinion, be an overt act of levying war; detaching a military corps from it for military purposes might also be an overt act of levying war. It is not pretended that he would not be punishable for these acts, it is only said that he may be tried and convicted on his own acts, in the state where those acts were committed, not on the acts of others in the state where the others acted.

Much has been said in the course of the argument on points, on which the court feels no inclination to comment particularly, but which may, perhaps not improperly, receive some notice.

That this court dares not usurp power is most true.

That this court dares not shrink from its duty is not less true.

No man is desirous of placing himself in a disagreeable situation. No man is desirous of becoming the peculiar subject of calumny. No man, might he let the bitter cup pass from him without self-reproach, would drain it to the bottom. But if he has no choice in the case; if there is no alternative presented to him but a dereliction of duty or the opprobrium of those who are denominated the world, he merits the contempt as well as the indignation of his country who can hesitate which to embrace.

That gentlemen, in a case the utmost interesting, in the zeal with which they advocate particular opinions, & under the conviction in some measure produced by that zeal, should on each side press their arguments too far, should be impatient at any deliberation in the court, and should suspect or fear the operation of motives to which alone they can ascribe that deliberation, is perhaps a frailty incident to human nature; but if any conduct on the part of the court could warrant a sentiment that they would deviate to the one side or the other from that line prescribed by duty and by law, that conduct would be viewed by the judges themselves with an eye of extreme severity, and would long be recollected with deep and serious regret.

The arguments on both sides have been intently and deliberately considered. Those which could not be noticed, since to notice every argument and authority would swell this opinion to a volume, have not been disregarded. The result of the whole is a conviction as complete as the mind of the court is capable of receiving on a complex subject, that the motion must prevail.

No testimony relative to the conduct or declarations of the prisoner elsewhere and subsequent to the transaction on Blannerhassett's island can be admitted, because such testimony, being in its nature merely corroborative, and incompetent to prove the overt act in itself, is irrelevant, until there be proof of the overt act by two witnesses.

This opinion does not comprehend the proof by two witnesses that the meeting on Blannerhassett's island was procured by the prisoner. On that point the court, for the present, withholds its opinion for reasons which have been already assigned; and as it is understood from the statements made on the part of the prosecution that no such testimony exists. If there be such let it be offered and the court will decide upon it.

The jury have now heard the opinion of the court on the law of the case. They will apply that law to the facts, and will find a verdict of guilty or not guilty as their own consciences may direct.

It is true, that although no further testimony be offered, yet, it is in the power of the Jury to find its verdict of *guilty* or *not guilty*. The Court have given its opinion: it has said, that yet, if the Jury can satisfy themselves of the guilt of the prisoner, by the evidence of two witnesses, they have the right to find a verdict of *guilty*. The Court have done its duty: and it is for the Jury to do theirs.

August 31, 1807

"THE MOST UNPLEASANT CASE"

To Richard Peters

Dear Sir   Richmond Novr. 23d. 1807

Among the very few agreeable occurrences of the last nine months was your letter of the 10th. of August accompanying the reports of your admiralty decisions. I think with you that a publication of the judgements of our courts in that as well as in other branches of law is extremely desirable, & I am glad that you have set an example which will I hope be followed in the other great commercial cities. Had I known that the publication was about to be made I should certainly have been a subscriber provided it was made by subscription—but I perceive you have annexed no list of names to the work.

I have as yet been able only to peep into the book, not to read many of the cases. I received it while fatigued & occupied with the most unpleasant case which has ever been brought before a Judge in this or perhaps in any other country which affected to be governed by laws, since the decision of which I have been entirely from home. The day after the commitment of Colo. Burr for a misdemeanor I galloped to the mountains whence I only returned in time to perform my North Carolina circuit which terminates just soon enough to enable me to be here to open the court for the antient dominion. Thus you perceive I have sufficient bodily employment to prevent my mind from perplexing itself about the attentions paid me in Baltimore & elsewhere.

I wish I could have had as fair an opportunity to let the business go off as a jest here as you seem to have had in Pennsylvania: but it was most deplorably serious & I could not give the subject a different aspect by treating it in any manner which was in my power. I might perhaps have made it less serious to myself by obeying the public will instead of the public law & throwing a little more of the sombre upon others.

I thank you very sincerely for your reports. The proof they furnish that I am recollected by you with regard gives them peculiar value. I am my dear Sir with affectionate esteem, Your Obedt.

THE ELECTION OF 1808

To Charles Cotesworth Pinckney

My dear Sir   Richmond October 19th. 1808

You will perceive from the papers that a meeting of the federalists in Richmond has determined to recommend it to their
brethren throughout this state to support the Monroe ticket
for electors at the ensuing election. I was not at this meeting &
only reached town the day it was called. But I have been informed of the particular motives which led to this measure &
mention the subject to you that they may not be misunderstood.

The federalists of Virginia constitute you know a small &
oppressed minority of our state. Between the rival democratic
candidates for the Presidency they were divided, & about them
few were anxious. We found ourselves abused, insulted, &
maltreated by all, & perceived no assurance on which we could
confidently rely that the political system which has been adopted
would be changed by any of them. The superior talents of Mr.
Madison would probably have placed us in his scale had not
recent events induced the opinion that his prejudices with
respect to our foreign relations were still more inveterate & in-
curable than those of either of his competitors. This circumstance & this circumstance singly produced a considerable
diversity of sentiment & neither candidate was adopted with
sufficient earnestness by any to induce a wish to make it a party
question.

The elections to the East having induced a convention of the
federalists north of the Potowmack to suppose that we might
with some prospect of success offer from our own bosom candidates for the Presidency & Vice Presidency of the United
States, an electoral ticket for this state was contemplated
although we could not indulge the hope that our endeavors
would be crowned with success. Some correspondence was held
on this subject with the committee of Staunton in Augusta & a
ticket digested. Before this could be published, while it was
framing, a letter was received from the federal committee in
George town or the city of Washington or both, urging the
federalists of Virginia to support the Monroe ticket as the only

mode in which they could aid the federal cause. Many arguments some of which were entitled to great weight were urged in favor of this recommendation & it was I am told, declared to be the wish of the federalists in that part of the United States. Under the influence of this letter the meeting was called & the resolution taken to comply with the request it contained.

The mail of the next morning brought from Pennsylvania the unpleasant inteligence that Mr. Snyders election was secure. This induced the opinion that the federal candidates would not be announced & removed the objections which were before felt by many to the step which has been taken.

The federalists of course, & many of the democrats, are ardent in the cause of Spain. Yet it is apparent that many of our leading men with professions of liberty in their mouths do in their hearts devoutly pray for the subjugation of that gallant & injured country. They view with extreme mortification any event which may tend to defeat that system of war on British commerce which Bonaparte has enjoined on all his vassals & which our rulers have unfortunately adopted. Rather than relinquish it they would see national independence & consequently human liberty banished from Europe although the loss of our self government would be the infallible consequence. With affectionate esteem, I am my dear Sir, Your

Opinion in Fletcher v. Peck

THE pleadings being now amended, this cause comes on again to be heard on sundry demurrers and on a special verdict.

The suit was instituted on several covenants contained in a deed made by John Peck, the defendant in error, conveying to Robert Fletcher, the plaintiff in error, certain lands which were part of a large purchase made by James Gunn and others, in the year 1795, from the state of Georgia, the contract for which was made in the form of a bill passed by the legislature of that state.

The first count in the declaration sets forth a breach in the second covenant contained in the deed. The covenant is "that the legislature of the state of Georgia, at the time of passing of the act of sale aforesaid, had good right to sell and dispose of the same in manner pointed out by the said act." The breach assigned is that the legislature had no power to sell.

The plea in bar sets forth the constitution of the state of Georgia, and avers that the lands sold by the defendant to the plaintiff were within that state. It then sets forth the granting act and avers the power of the legislature to sell and dispose of the premises as pointed out by the act.

To this plea the plaintiff below demurred, and the defendant joined in demurrer.

That the legislature of Georgia, unless restrained by its own constitution, possesses the power of disposing of the unappropriated lands within its own limits, in such manner as its own judgement shall dictate, is a proposition not to be controverted. The only question, then, presented by this demurrer, for the consideration of the court, is this—did the then constitution of the state of Georgia prohibit the legislature to dispose of the lands, which were the subject of this contract, in the manner stipulated by the contract?

The question, whether a law be void for its repugnancy to the constitution, is at all times a question of much delicacy, which ought seldom, if ever, to be decided in the affirmative, in a doubtful case. The court, when impelled by duty to render such a judgment, would be unworthy of its station, could it be unmindful of the solemn obligations which that station imposes.

But it is not on slight implication and vague conjecture that the legislature is to be pronounced to have transcended its powers, and its acts to be considered as void. The opposition between the constitution & the law should be such that the judge feels a clear and strong conviction of their incompatibility with each other.

In this case the court can perceive no such opposition. In the constitution of Georgia, adopted in the year 1789, the court can perceive no restriction on the legislative power, which inhibits the passage of the act of 1795. The court cannot say that, in passing that act, the legislature has transcended its powers and violated the constitution.

In overruling the demurrer, therefore, to the first plea, the circuit court committed no error.

The 3d covenant is, that all the title which the state of Georgia ever had in the premises had been legally conveyed to John Peck, the grantor.

The 2d count assigns, in substance, as a breach of this covenant, that the original grantees from the state of Georgia promised and assured divers members of the legislature, then sitting in General Assembly, that, if the said members would assent to and vote for the passing of the act, and if, the said bill should pass, such members should have a share of, and be interested in all the lands purchased from the said state by virtue of such law. And that divers of the said members to whom the said promises were made, were unduly influenced thereby, and, under such influence, did vote for the passing of the said bill; by reason whereof the said law was a nullity, &c. and so the title of the state of Georgia did not pass to the said Peck, &c.

The plea to this count, after protesting that the promises it alleges were not made, avers that, until after the purchase made from the original grantees by James Greenleaf, under whom the said Peck claims, neither the said James Greenleaf nor the said Peck, nor any of the mesne vendors between the said Greenleaf and Peck had any notice or knowledge that any such promises or assurances were made by the said original grantees, or either of them, to any of the members of the legislature of the state of Georgia.

To this plea the plaintiff demurred generally, and the defendant joined in demurrer.

That corruption should find its way into the governments of our infant republics and contaminate the very source of legislation, or that impure motives should contribute to the passage of a law or the formation of a legislative contract, are circumstances most deeply to be deplored. How far a court of justice would, in any case, be competent, on proceedings instituted by the state itself, to vacate a contract thus formed, and to annul rights acquired, under that contract by third persons having no notice of the improper means by which it was obtained, is a question which the court would approach with much circumspection. It may well be doubted how far the validity of a law depends upon the motives of its framers, and how far the particular inducements, operating on members of the supreme sovereign power of a state, to the formation of a contract by that power, are examinable in a court of justice. If the principle be conceded, that an act of the supreme sovereign power might be declared null by a court in consequence of the means which procured it, still, would there be much difficulty in saying to what extent those means must be applied to produce this effect. Must it be direct corruption, or would interest or undue influence of any kind be sufficient? Must the vitiating cause operate on a majority, or on what number of the members? Would the act be null, whatever might be the wish of the nation, or would its obligation or nullity depend upon the public sentiment?

If the majority of the legislature be corrupted, it may well be doubted whether it be within the province of the judiciary to control their conduct; and, if less than a majority act from impure motives, the principle by which judicial interference would be regulated, is not clearly discerned.

Whatever difficulties this subject might present, when viewed under aspects of which it may be susceptible, this court can perceive none in the particular pleading now under consideration.

This is not a bill brought by the state of Georgia to annul the contract, nor does it appear to the court, by this count, that the state of Georgia is dissatisfied with the sale that has been made. The case, as made out in the pleadings, is simply this— One individual who holds lands in the state of Georgia, under a deed covenanting that the title of Georgia was in the grantor, brings an action of covenant upon this deed, and assigns, as a breach, that some of the members of the legislature were induced to vote in favor of the law, which constituted the contract, by being promised an interest in it, and that therefore the act is a mere nullity.

This solemn question cannot be brought thus collaterally and incidentally before the court. It would be indecent, in the extreme, upon a private contract between two individuals, to enter into an inquiry respecting the corruption of the sovereign power of a state. If the title be plainly deduced from a legislative act which the legislature might constitutionally pass, if the act be clothed with all the requisite forms of a law, a court sitting as a court of law cannot sustain a suit brought by one individual against another founded on the allegation that the act is a nullity, in consequence of the impure motives which influenced certain members of the legislature which passed the law.

The circuit court, therefore, did right in overruling this demurrer.

The 4th covenant in the deed is, that the title to the premises has been, in no way, constitutionally or legally impaired by virtue of any subsequent act of any subsequent legislature of the state of Georgia.

The third count recites the undue means practised on certain members of the legislature, as stated in the second count, and then alleges that, in consequence of these practices, and of other causes, a subsequent legislature passed an act annulling and rescinding the law under which the conveyance to the original grantees was made, declaring that conveyance void, and asserting the title of the state to the lands it contained. The count proceeds to recite, at large, this rescinding act, and concludes with averring that, by reason of this act, the title of the said Peck in the premises was constitutionally and legally impaired and rendered null and void.

After protesting, as before, that no such promises were made as stated in this count the defendant again pleads that himself and the first purchaser under the original grantees and all intermediate holders of the property were purchasers without notice.

To this plea there is a demurrer and joinder.

The importance and the difficulty of the questions, presented by these pleadings, are deeply felt by the court.

The lands in controversy vested absolutely in James Gunn, and others, the original grantees, by the conveyance of the Governor, made in pursuance of an act of assembly to which the legislature was fully competent. Being thus in full possession of the legal estate, they, for a valuable consideration, conveyed portions of the land to those who were willing to purchase. If the original transaction was infected with fraud, these purchasers did not participate in it, and had no notice of it. They were innocent. Yet the legislature of Georgia has involved them in the fate of the first parties to the transaction, and, if the act be valid, has annihilated their rights also.

The legislature of Georgia was a party to this transaction; and for a party to pronounce its own deed invalid, whatever cause may be assigned for its invalidity, must be considered as a mere act of power which must find its vindication in a train of reasoning not often heard in courts of justice.

But the real party, it is said, are the people, and when their agents are unfaithful, the acts of those agents cease to be obligatory.

It is, however, to be recollected that the people can act only by these agents, and that, while within the powers conferred on them, their acts must be considered as the acts of the people. If the agents be corrupt, others may be chosen, and, if their contracts be examinable, the common sentiment, as well as common usage of mankind, points out a mode by which this examination may be made, and their validity determined.

If the legislature of Georgia was not bound to submit its pretensions to those tribunals which are established for the security of property, and to decide on human rights, if it might claim to itself the power of judging in its own case, yet there are certain great principles of justice, whose authority is universally acknowledged, that ought not to be entirely disregarded.

If the legislature be its own judge in its own case, it would seem equitable that its decision should be regulated by those rules which would have regulated the decision of a judicial tribunal. The question was, in its nature, a question of title, and the tribunal which decided it was either acting in the character of a court of justice, and performing a duty usually assigned to a court, or it was exerting a mere act of power in which it was controlled only by its own will.

If a suit be brought to set aside a conveyance obtained by fraud, and the fraud be clearly proved, the conveyance will be set aside, as between the parties; but the rights of third persons, who are purchasers without notice, for a valuable consideration, cannot be disregarded. Titles, which, according to every legal test, are perfect, are acquired with that confidence which is inspired by the opinion that the purchaser is safe. If there be any concealed defect, arising from the conduct of those who had held the property long before he acquired it, of which he had no notice, that concealed defect cannot be set up against him. He has paid his money for a title good at law, he is innocent, whatever may be the guilt of others, and equity will not subject him to the penalties attached to that guilt. All titles would be insecure, and the intercourse between man and man would be very seriously obstructed, if this principle be overturned.

A court of chancery, therefore, had a bill been brought to set aside the conveyance made to James Gunn and others, as being obtained by improper practices with the legislature, whatever might have been its decision as respected the original grantees, would have been bound, by its own rules, and by the clearest principles of equity, to leave unmolested those who were purchasers without notice, for a valuable consideration.

If the legislature felt itself absolved from those rules of property which are common to all the citizens of the United States, and from those principles of equity which are acknowledged in all our courts, its act is to be supported by its power alone, and the same power may divest any other individual of his lands, if it shall be the will of the legislature so to exert it.

It is not intended to speak with disrespect of the legislature of Georgia or of its acts. Far from it. The question is a general question, and is treated as one. For although such powerful objections to a legislative grant, as are alleged against this, may not again exist, yet the principle, on which alone this rescinding act is to be supported, may be applied to every case to which it shall be the will of any legislature to apply it. The principle is this; that a legislature may by its own act, divest the vested estate of any man whatever, for reasons which shall, by itself, be deemed sufficient.

In this case the legislature may have had ample proof that the original grant was obtained by practices which can never be too much reprobated, and which would have justified its abrogation so far as respected those to whom crime was imputable. But the grant, when issued, conveyed an estate in fee simple to the grantee, clothed with all the solemnities which law can bestow. This estate was transferrable; and those who purchased parts of it were not stained by that guilt which infected the original transaction. Their case is not distinguishable from the ordinary case of purchasers of a legal estate without knowledge of any secret fraud which might have led to the emanation of the original grant. According to the well known course of equity, their rights could not be affected by such fraud. Their situation was the same, their title was the same with that of every other member of the community who holds land by regular conveyances from the original patentee.

Is the power of the legislature competent to the annihilation of such title, and to a resumption of the property thus held?

The principle asserted is, that one legislature is competent to repeal any act which a former legislature was competent to pass; and that one legislature cannot abridge the powers of a succeeding legislature.

The correctness of this principle, so far as respects general legislation, can never be controverted. But, if an act be done under a law, a succeeding legislature cannot undo it. The past cannot be recalled by the most absolute power. Conveyances have been made, those conveyances have vested legal estates, and, if those estates may be seized by the sovereign authority, still, that they originally vested is a fact, and cannot cease to be a fact.

When, then, a law is, in its nature, a contract, when absolute rights have vested under that contract, a repeal of the law cannot divest those rights; and the act of annulling them, if legitimate, is rendered so by a power applicable to the case of every individual in the community.

It may well be doubted whether the nature of society and of

government does not prescribe some limits to the legislative power; and, if any be prescribed, where are they to be found, if the property of an individual, fairly and honestly acquired, may be seized without compensation?

To the legislature all legislative power is granted; but the question, whether the act of transferring the property of an individual to the public, be in the nature of legislative power, is well worthy of serious reflection.

It is the peculiar province of the legislature to prescribe general rules for the government of society; the application of those rules to individuals in society would seem to be the duty of other departments. How far the power of giving the law may involve every other power, in cases where the constitution is silent, never has been, and perhaps never can be, definitely stated.

The validity of this rescinding act, then, might well be doubted, were Georgia a single sovereign power. But Georgia cannot be viewed as a single unconnected sovereign power on whose legislature no other restrictions are imposed than may be found in its own constitution. She is a part of a large empire, she is a member of the American union; and that union has a constitution, the supremacy of which all acknowledge, and which imposes limits to the legislatures of the several states, which none claim a right to pass. The constitution of the United States declares that no state shall pass any bill of attainder, *ex post facto* law, or law impairing the obligation of contracts.

Does the case now under consideration come within this prohibitory section of the constitution?

In considering this very interesting question, we immediately ask ourselves what is a contract? Is a grant a contract?

A contract is a compact between two or more parties, and is either executory or executed. An executory contract is one in which a party binds himself, to do or not to do a particular thing; such was the law under which the conveyance was made by the Governor. A contract executed is one in which the object of contract is performed; and this, says Blackstone, differs in nothing from a grant. The contract between Georgia and the purchasers was executed by the grant. A contract executed, as well as one which is executory, contains obligations binding on the parties. A grant, in its own nature, amounts to an extinguishment of the right of the grantor, and implies a contract not to reassert that right. A party is therefore always estopped by his own grant.

Since, then, in fact, a grant is a contract executed, the obligation of which still continues, and since the constitution uses the general term contract, without distinguishing between those which are executory and those which are executed, it must be construed to comprehend the latter as well as the former. A law annulling conveyances between individuals, and declaring that the grantors should stand seized of their former estates, notwithstanding those grants, would be as repugnant to the constitution, as a law discharging the vendors of property from the obligation of executing their contracts by conveyances. It would be strange if a contract to convey was secured by the constitution, while an absolute conveyance remained unprotected.

If under a fair construction of the constitution grants are comprehended under the term contracts, is a grant from the state excluded from the operation of the provision? Is the clause to be considered as inhibiting the state from impairing the obligation of contracts between two individuals, but as excluding from that inhibition contracts made with itself?

The words themselves contain no such distinction. They are general, and are applicable to contracts of every description. If contracts made with the state are to be exempted from their operation, the exception must arise from the character of the contracting party, not from the words which are employed.

Whatever respect might have been felt for the state sovereignties, it is not to be disguised that the framers of the constitution viewed, with some apprehension, the violent acts which might grow out of the feelings of the moment, and that the people of the U. States, in adopting that instrument, have manifested a determination to shield themselves and their property from the effects of those sudden and strong passions to which men are exposed. The restrictions on the legislative power of the states are obviously founded in this sentiment; and the constitution of the U. States contains what may be deemed a bill of rights for the people of each state.

No state shall pass any bill of attainder, *ex post facto* law, or law impairing the obligation of contracts.

A bill of attainder may affect the life of an individual, or may confiscate his property, or may do both.

In this form the power of the legislature over the lives and fortunes of individuals is expressly restrained. What motive then for implying in words which import a general prohibition to impair the obligation of contracts, an exception in favor of the right to impair the obligation of those contracts into which the state may enter?

The state legislatures can pass no *ex post facto* law. An *ex post facto* law is one which renders an act punishable in a manner in which it was not punishable when it was committed. Such a law may inflict penalties on the person, or may inflict pecuniary penalties which swell the public treasury. The legislature is then prohibited from passing a law by which a man's estate or any part of it shall be seized for a crime which was not declared, by some previous law, to render him liable to that punishment. Why, then, should violence be done to the natural meaning of words for the purpose of leaving to the legislature the power of seizing, for public use, the estate of an individual in the form of a law annulling the title by which he holds that estate? The court can perceive no sufficient grounds for making this distinction. This rescinding act would have the effect of an *ex post facto* law. It forfeits the estate of Fletcher for a crime not committed by himself, but by those from whom he purchased. This cannot be effected in the form of an *ex post facto* law or bill of attainder; why, then, is it allowable in the form of a law annulling the original grant?

The argument in favor of presuming an intention to except a case not excepted by the words of the constitution, is susceptible of some illustration from a principle originally ingrafted in that instrument, tho' no longer a part of it. The constitution, as passed, gave the courts of the U.S. jurisdiction in suits brought against individual states. A state, then, which violated its own contract was suable in the courts of the U.S. for that violation. Would it have been a defence in such a suit to say that the state had passed a law absolving itself from the contract? It is scarcely to be conceived that such a defence could be set up. And yet, if a state is neither restrained by the general principles of our political institutions, nor by the words of the constitution from impairing the obligation of its own contracts, such a defence would be a valid one. This feature is no longer found in the constitution; but it aids in the construction of those clauses with which it was originally associated.

It is, then, the unanimous opinion of the court that, in this case, the estate having passed into the hands of a purchaser for a valuable consideration, without notice, the state of Georgia was restrained, either by general principles which are common to our free institutions, or by the particular provisions of the constitution of the U. States, from passing a law whereby the estate of the plaintiff in the premises so purchased could be constitutionally and legally impaired and rendered null and void.

In overruling the demurrer to the 3d plea, therefore, there is no error.

The first covenant in the deed is that the state of Georgia, at the time of the act of the legislature thereof, entitled as aforesaid, was legally seized in fee of the soil thereof subject only to the extinguishment of part of the Indian title thereon.

The 4th count assigns as a breach of this covenant that the right to the soil was in the United States and not in Georgia.

To this count the defendant pleads that the state of Georgia was seized, and tenders an issue on the fact in which the plaintiff joins. On this issue a special verdict is found.

The jury find the grant of Carolina by Charles 2d to the Earl of Clarendon and others comprehending the whole country from 36 deg. 30 min. N. Lat. to 29 deg. N Lat. and from the Atlantic to the South sea.

They find that the northern part of this territory was afterwards erected into a separate colony, and that the most northern part of the 35 deg of N. Lat. was the boundary line between North and South Carolina.

That seven of the eight proprietors of the Carolinas surrendered to George 2d in the year 1729, who appointed a Governor of South Carolina.

That, in 1732, George the 2d granted to the Lord Viscount Percival and others seven eighths of the territory between the Savannah & the Altamaha, and extending west to the South sea, & that the remaining eighth part, which was still the property of the heir of Lord Carteret, one of the original grantees of Carolina, was afterwards conveyed to them. This territory was constituted a colony and called Georgia.

That the Governor of South Carolina continued to exercise jurisdiction south of Georgia.

That, in 1752, the grantees surrendered to the crown.

That, in 1754, a Governor was appointed by the crown, with a commission describing the boundaries of the colony.

That a treaty of peace was concluded between G Britain and Spain, in 1763, in which the latter ceded, to the former, Florida with Fort St. Augustin and the bay of Pensacola.

That, in October 1763, the King of G. Britain issued a proclamation creating four new colonies, Quebec, East Florida, West Florida and Grenada, and prescribing the bounds of each, & further declaring that all the lands between the Altamaha and St. Mary's should be annexed to Georgia. The same proclamation contained a clause reserving, under the dominion and protection of the crown, for the use of the Indians, all the lands on the western waters, and forbidding a settlement on them, or a purchase of them from the Indians. The lands conveyed to the plaintiffs lie on the western waters.

That, in November 1763, a commission was issued to the Governor of Georgia, in which the boundaries of that province are described as extending westward to the Mississippi. A commission, describing boundaries of the same extent, was afterwards granted in 1764.

That a war broke out between Great Britain and her colonies, which terminated in a treaty of peace acknowledging them as sovereign and independent states.

That, in April 1787, a convention was entered into between the states of South Carolina and Georgia settling the boundary line between them.

The jury afterwards describe the situation of the lands mentioned in the plaintiff's declaration, in such manner that their lying within the limits of Georgia, as defined in the proclamation of 1763, in the treaty of peace and in the convention between that state and South Carolina, has not been questioned.

The counsel for the plaintiffs rest their argument on a single proposition. They contend that the reservation for the use of the Indians, contained in the proclamation of 1763, excepts the lands on the western waters from the colonies within whose bounds they would otherwise have been, and that they were acquired by the revolutionary war. All acquisitions during the war, it is contended, were made by the joint arms, for the joint benefit of the United States, and not for the benefit of any particular state.

The court does not understand the proclamation as it is understood by the counsel for the plaintiffs. The reservation for the use of the Indians appears to be a temporary arrangement suspending, for a time, the settlement of the country reserved, and the powers of the royal governor within the territory reserved, but is not conceived to amount to an alteration of the boundaries of the colony. If the language of the proclamation be, in itself, doubtful, the commissions subsequent thereto, which were given to the governors of Georgia, entirely remove the doubt.

The question, whether the vacant lands within the United States became a joint property, or belonged to the separate states, was a momentous question which, at one time, threatened to shake the American confederacy to its foundation. This important and dangerous contest has been compromised, and the compromise is not now to be disturbed.

It is the opinion of the court that the particular land stated in the declaration appears, from this special verdict, to lie within the state of Georgia, and that the state of Georgia had power to grant it.

Some difficulty was produced by the language of the covenant and of the pleadings. It was doubted whether a state can be seized in fee of lands subject to the Indian title, and whether a decision, that they were seized in fee, might not be construed to amount to a decision that their grantee might maintain an ejectment for them, notwithstanding that title.

The majority of the court is of opinion that the nature of the Indian title, which is certainly to be respected by all courts until it be legitimately extinguished, is not such as to be absolutely repugnant to seizing in fee on the part of the state. *Judgement affirmed with costs.*

March 16, 1810

To Robert Smith

Dear Sir   Richmond July 27th. 1812

I had this morning the pleasure of receiving your letter of the 24th. The paper you mention reached me a few days past & was read with attention and approbation. Your wish respecting its republication will not be forgotten.

The view you take of the edict purporting to bear date on the 28th. of April 1811 appears to me to be perfectly correct. I am astonished, if in these times any thing ought to astonish, that the same impression is not made on all.

Although I have for several years forborn to intermingle with those questions which agitate & excite the feelings of party, it is impossible that I could be inattentive to passing events, or an unconcerned observer of them. As they have increased in their importance, the interest, which as an American I must take in them, has also increased; and the declaration of war has appeared to me, as it has to you, to be one of those portentous acts which ought to concentrate on itself the efforts of all those who can take an active part in rescuing their country from the ruin it threatens. All minor considerations should be waived; the lines of subdivision between parties, if not absolutely effaced, should at least be covered for a time; and the great division between the friends of peace & the advocates of war ought alone to remain. It is an object of such magnitude as to give to almost every other, comparative insignificance; and all who wish peace ought to unite in the means which may facilitate its attainment, whatever may have been their differences of opinion on other points.

On reading the decree of the 28th. of April I could not avoid asking myself questions such as these.

This decree having been obviously fabricated since the official declaration of the Prince Regent that the orders in council would stand repealed as soon as the decrees of Berlin & Milan should be proved by an authentic document to be revoked, why was it not dated on the 1st. of November 1810 instead of the 28th. of April 1811? Since the one date might have been affixed to it as readily as the other, why was not that date affixed which would have saved the feelings of the American government by supporting the assertion it has uniformly made in its diplomatic intercourse with foreign governments, in its domestic official communications, & in its legislative acts?—assertions on the truth of which our whole system stands? Had France felt for the United States any portion of that respect to which our real importance entitles us, could she have failed to give this proof of it? But, regardless of the assertion made by the President in his Proclamation of the 2d. of Novr. 1810, regardless of the communications made by the Executive to the Legislature, regardless of the acts of Congress, and regardless of the propositions which we have invariably maintained in our diplomatic intercourse with Great Britain, the Emperor has given a date to his decree, & has assigned a motive for its enactment, which in express terms contradict every assertion made by the American nation throughout all the departments of its government, & remove the foundation on which its whole system has been erected. The motive for this offensive & contemptuous proceeding cannot be to rescue himself from the imputation of continuing to enforce his decrees after their formal repeal, because this imputation is precisely as applicable to a repeal dated the 28th. of April 1811 as to one dated the 1st. of November 1810, since the execution of those decrees has continued after the one date as well as after the other. Why then is this obvious fabrication such as we find it? Why has Mr. Barlow been unable to obtain a paper which might consult the honor & spare the feelings of his government? The answer is not to be disguised. Bonaparte does not sufficiently respect us to exhibit for our sake, to France, to America, to Britain, or to the world, any evidence of his having receded one step from the position he had taken. He could not be prevailed on, even after we had done all he required, to soften any one of his acts so far as to give it the appearance of his having advanced one step to meet us. That this step, or rather the appearance of having taken it, might save our reputation was regarded as dust in the balance. Even now, after our solemn & repeated assertions that our discrimination between the belligerents is founded altogether on a first advance of France—on a decisive & unequivocal repeal of all her obnoxious decrees; after we have engaged in a war of the most calamitous character, avowedly, because France had repealed those decrees, the Emperor scorns to countenance the assertion or to leave it uncontradicted. He avers to ourselves, to our selected enemy, & to the world, that, whatever pretexts we may assign for our conduct, he has in fact ceded nothing, he has made no advance, he stands on his original ground & we have marched up to it. We have submitted, completely submitted; & he will not leave us the poor consolation of concealing that submission from ourselves. But not even our submission has obtained releif. His cruizers still continue to capture, sink, burn, & destroy.

I cannot contemplate this subject without excessive mortification as well at the contempt with which we are treated as at the infatuation of my countrymen. It is not however for me to indulge these feelings though I cannot so entirely suppress them as not sometimes though rarely to allow them a place in a private letter. With respectful esteem, I am Sir your Obedt. Servt.

Report of the
Virginia River Commission

To the Honorable, the Speaker and Members of the General Assembly, the undersigned Commissioners, named with others in the act, entitled "an act, appointing Commissioners for the purpose of viewing certain rivers within this commonwealth:"
RESPECTFULLY REPORT,

That, supposing the autumn to be the season which afforded the fairest prospects for giving effect to the views of the Legislature, as expressed in their act, your Commissioners agreed that a meeting should be called on the first of September, at Lynchburg. The number required by law for the execution of the service they were directed to perform, having assembled, and the necessary preparations having been made, your Commissioners began at the bridge at Lynchburg to view James River, and to take its level by sections to the mouth of Dunlop's creek. Mr. Andrew Alexander, the surveyor of Rockbridge county, had been engaged to execute this duty under their direction. To his report, which your commissioners believe to be accurate, they beg leave to refer, as exhibiting, in minute detail, the information required by law.

As an actual measurement of the whole river would have employed so much time as to defer the completion of the work, until high waters might defeat the object of the Legislature, and was rendered the less necessary by previous surveys, distances were in general conjectured. The eye, aided by a time piece, and occasionally corrected by actual measurement, furnished information which, though not perfectly exact, was believed not to vary much from the truth, and to be substantially sufficient. Those places which presented serious obstacles were measured by the chain, and the elevation was taken throughout by a spirit level.

On that part of the river which is comprised within the charter already granted, your Commissioners presume, that little, if any, information is expected from them, other than will be found in the annexed report of Mr. Alexander.

From Beau's bridge, or Crow's ferry, to the mouth of the

Cow Pasture, no difficulty presents itself, which may not be with certainty surmounted. The falls are no where formidable; there are long stretches of smooth water, and the shallows may be so deepened as to afford water for boats, bringing down from six to eight tons, and carrying up from four to six tons, if not throughout the year, through all but a very inconsiderable portion of it. Your Commissioners give the opinion, unanimously, and with great confidence, that the navigation from Crow's ferry to the mouth of the Cow Pasture may, with improvements by no means expensive, be rendered as certain, as useful, and as permanent, as the navigation from the same place to Lynchburg; and that it may be used at all times when the navigation to Lynchburg can be used, with boats carrying an equal burthen—Indeed that it may be rendered more safe, and less laborious than that from the mouth of the North Fork to Lynchburg now is.

From the mouth of the Cow Pasture to the mouth of Dunlop's creek, the difficulties become more considerable, and their removal will require greater expenditures of money. The mass of water diminishes, and the elevation increases. The shoals become longer and shallower, and the intervals of smooth water shorter. Yet this rugged navigation, though totally unimproved, is now used during high water. Boats laden with the produce of the country, pass every year from the mouth of Dunlop's creek to Richmond. It is therefore proved to be, even at this time, practicable for some portion of the year. This portion varies with the seasons. Most commonly, it commences in November and terminates late in May, or early in June.

That by the removal of rocks now lying promiscuously and irregularly through the bed of the river, which it will be necessary in only a few instances to blow, and by the judicious application of labour to the collection of water in narrower spaces than it now covers, this navigation may be rendered much more secure and beneficial, and the time during which it can be used may be considerably extended, will not admit of doubt. Whether this portion of the river may be rendered at all times boatable, depends on the depth of water to be collected in particular channels by such means as are applicable to the object.

Some of your Commissioners have been personally engaged

in opening the navigation of the North Fork of James river through Rockbridge. They are decidedly of opinion that the river denominated "Jackson's," contains, as far as Dunlop's creek, more water and less formidable obstructions than were found in the North Fork. Yet the North Fork, though its improvement is far from being complete, is now actually used to great advantage, and is not much inferior to the river below. Some experienced and judicious boatmen who were employed on the expedition, who are well acquainted with the river and its navigation, unite in the declaration that, if the means be taken which ought to be employed, that part of James river which is between the Cow Pasture and Dunlop's creek may be used by any boats which will be capable of continuing their voyage to Lynchburg.

Your Commissioners concur in this opinion; and they take occasion now to remark that, should it be deemed advisable still to adhere to the system of improvement heretofore used in the upper part of the river, the difficulties of this navigation would, they think, be much diminished by several facilities which might be given to it. They would particularly suggest chains with buoys, fastened in rocks or otherwise, or walls on which men may walk, of which boatmen might avail themselves to lessen the labor of ascending places of peculiar difficulty; and thus either to increase the load which may be carried up the river, or to diminish the number of persons necessary for carrying up a given load. They will also mention a fact deemed favorable to the object contemplated by the Legislature. It is this: although the cold may be more intense in the bosom of the mountains than below, this part of the river seldom freezes over.

It will perhaps save the honorable the members of the Legislature some calculation to observe, that the distance from Lynchburg to the commencement of the Blue ridge is stated, in the report of Mr. Alexander, to be 25 miles 1-4 & 30 poles; the elevation to be 111 feet 8 inches; shewing an average elevation of four and an half feet to the mile. The distance through the mountain, that is from Raccon Island to the mouth of the North Fork is 8 1-4 miles and 49 poles; and the elevation 101 feet 6 inches, giving an average elevation of upwards of 12 feet to the mile. The distance from the mouth of the North Fork to Crow's ferry, or Beall's bridge, the highest point to which navigation is to be carried by the James River Company, is stated at 26 miles, 38 poles; and the elevation is 131 feet 4 inches; making the average elevation five feet to a mile,

The distance from Beall's bridge or Crow's ferry, to the mouth of the Cow Pasture, is stated at 36 miles 59 poles—and the elevation is 190 feet 3 inches; making the average elevation 5 1-2 feet nearly to a mile. The distance from the mouth of the Cow Pasture to the mouth of Dunlop's creek is stated at 23 3-4 miles 20 poles; and the elevation is 228 feet 3 inches; making the average elevation 9 1-2 feet to the mile.

Having reached Dunlop's creek your Commissioners proceeded to view and mark out what appeared to them to be the best and most direct way for a turnpike road from the mouth of that creek to the most convenient navigable point on Greenbrier river.

With some inconsiderable deviation which will appear in the report of Mr. Alexander already referred to, and some others which will be suggested, the road now leading from the mouth of Dunlop's creek by Bowyer's Sulphur Spring to Anderson's Ford, over Greenbrier, at the mouth of Howard's creek, is believed to be the most eligible which can be made. To that part of the road which passes from the mouth of Dunlop's creek to the old iron works, a distance of about five miles, there are considerable objections which your Commissioners are inclined to believe may be diminished. The road crosses the creek eight times and the ground during the winter & spring would, if not much used and not well covered with stone or gravel, be much cut and be very deep. The creek too is frequently so high as not to be fordable.

Should it be found practicable, which your Commissioners believe to be the fact, to render Dunlop's creek navigable up to its falls, some distance below the old iron works, these inconveniences would be in a great measure moved.

Should it be deemed unadvisable to carry navigation up Dunlop's creek, a direction, as is understood from some of the inhabitants of that neighborhood, may be given to the road, so as to avoid five crossings of the creek, and at the same time shorten the distance. No attempt to view this way was made, because guides could not readily be procured, and your commissioners feared that, by devoting too much time to a minor object, on which complete information is attainable with care and certainly through various channels, they might hazard the failure of others which were believed to be of much importance.

The road from the Sulphur Spring to Greenbrier crosses Howard's creek, which is often not fordable, six times, and is in a few places attended with some difficulty. A small improvement may be made in it, and the steepest part avoided, by returning it near the river, to the ground over which it formerly passed, and from which it has been lately taken.

The road over the mountain has been attentively viewed, and the deviations, recommended from that now in use, carefully and plainly marked. Your Commissioners feel much satisfaction in stating that the elevation of this part of the road may, in the most unfavorable places, be reduced to an angle of five degrees with the horizon. By occasionally removing the earth for small distances, this angle may be still further diminished. It is believed to be susceptable of improvement on as easy terms as any other road, since the materials for a turnpike are every where convenient, & not more levelling will be necessary than must be expected in passing through a mountainous country.

Your Commissioners proceeded down the Greenbrier river in the boat in which they had ascended the James. The season had been remarkably dry, and the water was declared by the inhabitants to be as low as at any period within their recollection. It frequently spreads over a wide bed covered with large stone, and is, in its present unimproved state, and at the season when it was viewed, so very shallow, for the greater part of its course, as not to swim an empty boat. The labour of removing stones, and of dragging the boat over those which could not be removed without implements provided for the purpose, was so great that your Commissioners at one time were enabled to advance only three miles in two days, even with the assistance of a horse and of many additional laborers. In part of the river the shoals are frequent and long, and the falls, as the report of Mr. Alexander will show, considerable. At the great falls, which is the most important of them, the descent is twelve feet in 48 poles. There is no perpendicular fall at this place, but one continued rapid, with large rocks irregularly interspersed through the bed of the river. Near the mouth of the river is a flat rock which continues for about 240 poles, with many irregular apertures or fissures thro' which the water passes. Although, in the usual state of the river, this rock is covered with water of sufficient depth for navigation, yet, such was the drought of the last autumn, it was necessary to drag the boat over it's whole extent.

These difficulties present obstacles to navigation during a season when the waters are remarkably low, which can be surmounted only at a considerable expence.

But, from the best information your Commissioners can obtain, and they believe it to be correct, the Greenbrier is seldom so low at any season as it was during the last autumn; and it seldom if ever fails, for eight or nine months in the year, to be at least two feet higher than when viewed by your Commissioners; a depth of water unquestionably sufficient for the purpose of navigation. The testimony given by the inhabitants to this fact was corroborated by appearances on the river. The indications of a recent considerable diminution of water were not to be mistaken.

On an attentive consideration of the obstacles which were found by your commissioners to be great, while the river remains in the state in which they viewed it, they are unanimously and decidedly of opinion, that its navigation may be rendered as safe, as certain and easy as that of the James, at all times except when the water is unusually low. The rocks are generally loose, and may be removed without extraordinary difficulty, so as to afford a tolerably smooth passage to boats; and, by collecting the water into narrower channels, a sufficient depth may be obtained with the exception of a short period in a very dry year, to swim any boat which can be brought at the same time down James river. But so scanty is the supply of water in a time of uncommon drought, that doubts are entertained whether there may not be a short season of the year during which, unless a considerable expence be incurred, the navigation must be suspended. Though aided by men and horses, ten days of unremitting labour were consumed in passing from the mouth of Howard's creek to the mouth of Greenbrier river, a distance not much exceeding forty-eight miles. In the month of June, the same voyage, if not retarded by measuring the river, might have been performed in a single day. Some of your Commissioners, however, are of opinion, that the Greenbrier may, without great additional expense, be rendered at all times passable for boats carrying half a load.

In addition to the shallowness of the water, (an inconvenience which is common to all rivers as you approach their sources, and which disappears for eight or nine months in the year,) and to the rocks which have been mentioned, the obstructions to the navigation of the Greenbrier consists in its falls, and the general rapidity of its current.

The great falls alone are of sufficient magnitude to merit particular attention. These unquestionably admit of being rendered navigable, either by opening a sluice judiciously through them, or by locks. The latter would be most expensive, but would leave the navigation less laborious.

The rapidity of the current may be estimated by observing that the descent in forty eight miles and eighty-four poles is three hundred and sixty-two feet ten inches, between seven and eight feet to the mile.

This current will present no difficulty to a boat descending the river. To one ascending it, the labor will be considerable, but not so considerable as in some parts of James river.

The night of the 28th September, was passed among the islands in the mouth of Greenbrier; and on the morning of the 29th, your Commissioners entered New river.

The difficulties encountered in descending this river were of a character essentially different from those which were experienced in the Greenbrier. Uncommon as had been the drought, the supply of water was abundant. The boat sometimes, though rarely, rubbed upon a shoal; but in every such case it was apparent that a sufficient passage might be opened without much labor or expense. The velocity of the current, and the enormous rocks which often interrupt it, the number and magnitude of the rapids and falls, the steepness, cragginess and abruptness of the banks, constitute the great impediments which at present exist to navigation between the mouth of the Greenbrier and the Great Falls of Kanawha.

The New river, or that part of the Great Kanawha which is

above the mouth of Gauley, having to search its intricate way, and force a passage through a long chain of lofty and ragged mountains, whose feet it washes, exhibits an almost continued succession of shoals and falls, from which the navigator is sometimes, though rarely, relieved by a fine sheet of deep placid water.

The distance from the mouth of Greenbrier to Bowyer's ferry, is 40 miles one quarter and 46 poles, and the descent is 460 feet 7 inches; that is, 11 feet 6 inches in each mile. In general, there is much sameness in the appearance of this part of the river. Long rapids, frequently terminated by a fall from five to ten feet, in a distance of ten, twenty, thirty and sometimes a greater number of poles; an intervening space, sometimes more, sometimes less considerable, of swift or smooth water; rocks, sometimes above the surface, sometimes near it, so as to require great caution to save a boat from dashing on them; a copious stream with a current commonly impetuous, constitute it's leading characteristics.

Falls too great to come within this general description will be particularly noticed.

Brook's falls are about 4 1-4 miles below the mouth of Greenbrier. The water descends 18 feet 7 inches in 50 poles. In its most rapid part the descent is 5 feet 10 inches in 14 poles. The boat was navigated through this place.

A much more formidable obstruction is the falls at Richmond's mill. These are designated in the neighborhood by the name of the "Great Falls of New river," but are generally called at a distance, "Lick Creek Falls."

At this place the water may with propriety be said to fall perpendicularly 23 feet. For this distance, the sheet which dashes over the summit is intercepted only by huge fragments of broken rock, which having been successively disjoined from the brink of the precipice, have fallen into the foaming basin below, where, piled on each other, they form one or two benches that break the cataract. A small distance lower down is another fall of 3 or 4 feet.

Here, for the first time, the boat was taken out of the water and let down by skids.

The ground along which a canal may be carried around these

falls, pursuing the course of Richmond's mill race, was measured and the elevation taken. The descent was found to be 22
feet 9 inches in 181 poles.

This estimate excludes a part of the falls, between 5 and 6
feet of which are just above the head of Richmond's mill race.

The bottom of the river for some distance above these falls,
is a hard rock, often appearing above the surface, and much
covered with moveable stones, some of which are very large.
The bottom of the mill-race appears to be of the same
description.

From Bowyer's ferry to the falls of the Great Kanawha was
estimated at 19 miles and 58 poles, in which distance the river
falls 331 feet, that is 17 feet to a mile. The honorable the Legislature will perceive that below the ferry the descent, in the
same distance, is greater than above. For a part of this space,
the scene is awful and discouraging. The vast volume of water
which rolls down New river, and which, far above the ferry,
often spreads, without becoming shallow, over a bed 3 or 400
yards wide, is seldom more than 100 or 150 yards wide. In
some places, for a mile or more in continuation, it is compressed by the mountains on each side, into a channel from 20
to 60 yards wide; and even these narrow limits are still more
narrowed by enormous rocks which lie promiscuously in the
bed of the river, through which it is often difficult to find a
passage wide enough for the admission of a boat. In some
places, the bank is formed of rugged & perpendicular cliffs of
entire rock, which appear to be 20, 30 and 40 feet high; in
others, enormous but unconnected rocks dip into the water.

There are unequivocal indications of the river's having risen,
in these narrows, from 30 to 40 feet perpendicularly.

Immediately above the mouth of Gauley, the river opens
and presents a beautiful sheet of deep smooth water, which is
succeeded by the rock over which it dashes & forms the Great
Falls of Kanawha. The heights of these falls is twenty feet four
inches. With its name, the river loses its wild and savage aspect.
It is no longer confined by rugged cliffs, by mountains barely
separated by each other, nor interrupted by enormous masses
of rock which are scarcely to be avoided.

Within a short distance above the falls, the current is not un-
manageably swift, nor the rock over which it passes uneven.

Below, quite to the rocks which have fallen from the brink over which the cataract rushes, is a deep smooth and beautiful basin. The river is so wide as to rise, in the greatest freshes, only 6 or 7 feet. The falls themselves constitute the impediment, and the only impediment at this place.

Your Commissioners have deemed it proper to state in their full strength the difficulties which are to be surmounted in opening the intercourse between this part of the state of Virginia, and the western country; and to put the Legislature, as far as is possible, in possession of the testimony on which their opinion is formed, as well as of their opinion. If, misguided by their conviction of the importance of the object, they are too sanguine in their hopes of its accomplishment, the facts now communicated will enable the General Assembly to correct the mistaken conclusions which have been drawn, and to determine on the course which will best promote the interests of the public.

The practicability of rendering the Greenbrier navigable has already been stated. The system which may be found best adapted for the improvement of James river will be equally applicable to the Greenbrier, and will be equally successful. The one river and the other will be rendered more or less valuable as more or less labour and skill may be employed on them; but there can be no mistake in saying that, without incurring an expense which any would pronounce extravagant, they are both capable of being brought into extensive use. Not only in descending, but in ascending also, these rivers may be navigated to great advantage.

With respect to New river, a judgment cannot be formed quite so decisively, nor pronounced quite so confidently. The difficulties are great, and deserve to be seriously considered.

The boat which conveyed your Commissioners, passed from the mouth of Greenbrier, to the place where their expedition terminated, without being taken out of the water, except at the Great Falls of New river, and at the Great Falls of the Kanawha. It was navigated in the usual way through all the other difficult places which abound in New river, except two— both below Bowyer's ferry. Through these it was conducted by ropes.

The boat was not laden, nor was it empty. In addition to the number of hands usually employed in navigation, it carried between two and three thousand weight. The greater part of this burthen was taken out in the most difficult places; but, in many of considerable magnitude, it remained in the boat. Where the vessel was guided by ropes, the necessity of resorting to this expedient was occasioned solely by the intervention of rocks which can be removed.

It is also worthy of notice, that this voyage was performed by boatmen, who, having never before seen the river, were reduced to the necessity of selecting their way at the moment, without the aid of previous information.

The only impediments to the descent of the boat, except at the two great falls already mentioned, were rocks lying so near the surface of the water, as to strike the bottom while shooting over them. At the usual height of the river, these rocks would be entirely covered, and all danger from them be removed; but others would be placed in a situation to expose a boat to equal hazard. It is therefore necessary, even for the descending navigation, to open a plain and broad sluice through all the rapids and falls, so as to relieve boats navigating the river from all danger of being dashed against rocks. This may be effected by removing some and blowing others. This sluice may be so conducted as to graduate the falls where they are most sudden, and thereby, in some degree, to diminish the impetuosity of the current.

Brook's falls, the Great Falls of New river, and the Great Falls of Kanawha, will probably require and admit of a different course.

The first of these, which is the least formidable of the three, will present three alternatives to the election of those who may be engaged in improving the navigation.

First; One or more locks, which may unquestionably be constructed at this place.

Second; A canal, which is already almost formed, on the north side of the river. Its completion would require, that it be opened for a short distance, both where it would receive the water at the head of the falls, and where it would empty itself below them.

To the eligibility of this canal, there can be but one objection. There may be impracticable rock now hidden by the earth, so near the surface as to render this plan unadvisable.

Third. To open a sluice in the river along it's northern bank and to graduate the fall as far as may be compatible with that system of operation.

The Great Falls of New river must be turned, by using a canal to be cut on the southern side, pursuing nearly the tract of Richmond's mill race. Should locks be employed, it will most probably be found advisable to place them in this canal. Should locks be dispensed with, there will be no difficulty in descending through this channel, but the toil of ascending, must, at this place, be considerable.

At the Great Falls of Kanawha, there is, near Morris's mill, a very eligible place for locks. If a canal be preferred, there is every reason to believe, that the ground will admit of one which may be so extended, & the fall thereby so graduated, as to afford a safe passage to loaded boats.

These observations are formed on the state of the river when viewed by your Commissioners. It will readily occur, that they cannot judge with certainty of the changes which may be brought about by a great rise of water.

It would seem most probable that, by such rise, the falls would be diminished, because the water at their feet, would pass off less rapidly than at their head. But the apprehension cannot be entirely discarded that, in the narrows which have been mentioned, the torrent would, in a flood, be too impetuous to be trusted. It is probable, that a moderate elevation of the water would rather facilitate the passage of the boats; at least of those descending the river; but that great floods would suspend the navigation.

Having stated their view of this subject your Commissioners will only add their opinion, that the New river may be relied on with certainty, for the transportation of articles from the east to the west.

On the practicability of using this channel of conveyance for the transportation of articles from the western country towards the rivers which empty into the Atlantic, at least so much of it as lies between Bowyer's ferry and the Great Falls of Kanawha, they must speak with less confidence. The great difficulty consists in the velocity of the current. For several miles between Bowyer's ferry and the falls, it is believed that a canal would be impracticable. The river is susceptible of no other improvement than may be made in its channel, or in its banks. The current is often too rapid to be stemmed by a boat impelled by oars; and the water too deep to admit the use of poles. If a channel sufficient for the safe passage of vessels be opened, still some other means than oars and poles, must be devised for impelling them up the stream.

Your Commissioners submit with diffidence the following propositions.

1st. That boats impelled by steam may be employed successfully on New river.

With the capacities of this powerful agent they are too little acquainted to speak with confidence of the use which may be made of it in the waters of Virginia. Elsewhere, it has certainly been applied with great advantage to the purposes of navigation. Neither have they that intimate knowledge of the velocity of the currents, against which vessels have been propelled by it, to compare them with that of New river, and to hazard any decided opinion on the comparison. But they beg leave to say, that the currents of the Hudson, of the Mohawk, and of the Mississippi, are very strong; and that a practice so entirely novel as the use of steam in navigation will probably receive great improvements, and the power itself be so diversified in its modifications as to be applied in new and different situations, as their exigencies may require. It is believed, that a sufficient depth of water is certainly attainable; but whether sufficient employment may be found, to justify the use of a vessel which must, in any state of things, be constructed at considerable expence, is a question your commissioners cannot attempt to solve.

2d. Should it be found impracticable to apply steam with advantage to the navigation of New river, it is respectfully suggested that, between the Great falls of Kanawha, and Bowyer's ferry, resort may be had to horse labour.

To give this facility to the navigation, it will be necessary to construct a horse way along the bank of the river at different heights, or at the most common height of the water. The objection, that such way cannot be used at all times, will lose much of its force when it shall be recollected that the navigation up the river will admit of being suspended for considerable intervals with less injury to those who use it, than that which conveys to the western country articles imported for general consumption. The construction of this way, however, will require the blowing of a great quantity of rock, and will, consequently, be expensive.

3d. Should neither of these expedients be deemed eligible, it is respectfully suggested, that boats may be forced up the current, where it is too rapid for oars and too deep for poles, by the aid of chains fastened in the rocks on the bank.

Whatever doubts may be entertained respecting the navigation for boats ascending the river between the Great falls of Kanawha and Bowyer's ferry, your commissioners are entirely persuaded of the practicability of using it advantageously between the ferry and the mouth of Greenbrier.

In obedience to the law under which they have acted, your commissioners will now proceed to state their ideas of the sums of money which will probably be necessary to open the rivers and make the road they have viewed.

No part of their duty has been performed with less confidence than this.

It will readily occur to the Legislature that no estimate of the expense of executing so great a work as that which is to afford to the western parts of Virginia the means of conveying the produce of their lands to market, and probably to connect Virginia commercially with her sister States in the west, can have just pretensions to exactness. Were the system of improvement, and the extent to which that system is to be carried, accurately defined; any calculations which could now be made, even by professional men, of the sum necessary for its execution, might be found to vary widely from that which would be actually expended. Still less precision can be looked for in the calculations of your commissioners.

But it must be apparent that the expence of improvement will essentially depend on the object for which the improvement shall be made.

If the views of the Legislature, shall be limited to the conveyance of articles, the growth of the upper country, down James river, the cheapness of that conveyance will certainly depend much on the degree of perfection to which the improvement may be carried; but the river, being the only channel of conveyance, will, if merely practicable, be used to some extent.

If the views of the Legislature shall extend to a free commercial intercourse with the western states or any of them, the channel selected for that intercourse will come into competition with others which now exist or may be opened, and must recommend itself to a preference by the advantages it offers. With a view to the latter object, no improvement ought to be undertaken but with a determination to make it complete and effectual.

The estimates of expense were more particularly made by Mr. Caruthers who has been personally engaged in opening the North fork through Rockbridge. This gentleman made his calculations on the plan which has been adopted by the James river company, with such improvements as would better adapt that plan to up stream navigation. According to his estimate, one hundred and ninety thousand dollars will be sufficient to accomplish the work from Beall's bridge or Crow's ferry to the falls of the Great Kanawha, including the road. This estimate is formed on a comparison of the impediments to be removed with those he had himself encountered in opening the North fork of James river. Some others of your commissioners who have too little knowledge of the labor necessary for the accomplishment of objects of this description to confide, themselves, in their own judgment, much less to recommend it to the confidence of others, are so impressed with the magnitude of the difficulties they have seen as to be unable to persuade themselves that the work can be completed for the sum at which it has been estimated. That estimate does not appear to them to be extravagant, if the descending navigation alone be contemplated. To make the ascending navigation such as will entitle it to extensive use, and give this a preference over other routes, they submit, though with much diffidence, the opinion that at least half a million, perhaps six hundred thousand dollars will be requisite.

From the mouth of Dunlop's creek to the mouth of Howard's creek is twenty eight miles and forty four poles. From the first mentioned place to the summit of the Allegany mountain is sixteen miles and thirty six poles; and the elevation is nine hundred and forty eight feet; which makes an angle with the horizon of less than three quarters of a degree. From the summit of the mountain to the mouth of Howard's creek, the distance is twelve miles and eight poles, and the descent is eight hundred and thirty eight feet seven inches, making with the horizon an angle of about three quarters of a degree. There are no peculiarities attending this route which will render any plan the Legislature may prefer for turnpiking it more costly in its application to this road, than to others which have been constructed in various parts of the United States. It is now at least equal to, perhaps better, than any other of equal distance in the same part of the country.

In presenting to the honorable the Legislature the advantage which, in the opinion of your commissioners, will probably accrue to this State from executing the work to which their report relates, it will be necessary to divide the subject and to consider, separately, first those which may reasonably be expected to result from executing it in part; next those which are to be looked for from executing it in the whole.

Should the navigation of James river be carried up to the mouth of Dunlop's creek, and a turnpike road be made over the Allegany mountain, although nothing further should be done, a considerable impulse will be given to the agriculture, and a valuable effect produced on the wealth and population, of a considerable tract of country. It cannot reasonably be doubted that Bath, a part of Botetourt, and a great part of Greenbrier, Monroe, and perhaps even of Giles, would find a real interest in searching for a market on James river for the produce of their soil, if such safe and cheap conveyance were afforded them as might be given by the improvements which have been stated. Agriculture would mingle more than heretofore with grazing; and industry would flourish when the reward of industry should be attainable. Those more western counties whose distance might forbid the attempt to transport grain manufactured into flour, or distilled into spirit, to the markets on James river, might still be encouraged to bring to those markets, salt, salted provisions, and various manufactures of hemp. An increase of population would result, not only from the check which this state of things would give to emigration, but also from it's operation on the inhabitants in other respects.

Other parts of the State would derive corresponding advantages from their intercourse with a section of the country which would have more to sell and more to purchase than at present. By the augmentation of the wealth and population of a part, not only would those belonging to that part be improved in their circumstances, but the whole would be more powerful, and the public burdens, being more divided, might press less heavily on each individual.

These advantages would probably be extended by improving the navigation of the Greenbrier also.

Should New river be rendered a safe and easy channel of communication between the Ohio and the commercial towns on James river, the subject will assume a more important aspect, and the advantages may be estimated on a larger scale. Not only will that part of our own State which lies on the Kanawha and on the Ohio, receive their supplies and send much of their produce to market through James river, but an immense tract of fertile country, a great part of the States of Kentucky and Ohio, will most probably give their commerce the same direction. All that part of the State of Kentucky which lies above Louisville, & all that part of the State of Ohio whose trade would pass through the river of that name, might reasonably be expected to maintain a large portion of their commercial intercourse with the Atlantic States, through the James or the Potowmac. Certainly, in a contest for this interesting prize, the States thro' which those rivers run have geographical advantages, the benefits of which they can lose only by supineness in themselves or by extraordinary exertions in others. It is far from being impossible that even the south western parts of Pennsylvania may look down one of these rivers for their supplies of goods manufactured in Europe.

Let the importance attached by men best acquainted with the subject to the commerce of the West attest its value. The exertions which other States appear to be making to secure it will probably awaken the attention of Virginia to that part of it which should naturally belong to her.

There is still another aspect in which this subject deserves to be viewed.

That intimate connection which generally attends free commercial intercourse, the strong ties which are formed by mutual interest, and the interchange of good offices, bind together individuals of different counties, and are well calculated to cherish those friendly sentiments, those amicable dispositions which at present unite Virginia to a considerable portion of the Western people. At all times, the cultivation of these dispositions must be desirable; but, in the vicissitude of human affairs, in that mysterious future, which is in reserve, and is yet hidden from us, events may occur to render their preservation too valuable to be estimated in dollars and cents.

The advantages which may result to Virginia from opening this communication with the western country will be shared in common with her by the states of Kentucky & Ohio.

Considering it as a medium for the introduction of foreign articles into those states, it has claims to their serious attention.

The proposition that a nation finds its true interest in multiplying its channels of importation, admitting them to be equally convenient, is believed to be uncontrovertible. In addition to those arguments in support of this proposition which belong to every case, the situation of the western states suggests some which are peculiar to themselves, and which well deserve their consideration.

The whole of that extensive and fertile country, a country increasing in wealth and population with a rapidity which baffles calculation, must make its importations up the Mississippi alone, or through the Atlantic states. When we take into view the certain growth of the country, we can scarcely suppose it possible that any commercial city on the banks of that river can keep pace with that growth, and furnish a supply equal to the demand. The unfriendliness of the climate to human life will render this disparity between commercial and agricultural capital still more sensible. It will tend still more to retard a population of that sound mercantile character, which would render some great city on that majestic river, a safe emporium for the western world.

In times of profound peace, then, the states on the Ohio

would make sacrifices of no inconsiderable magnitude, by restricting their importations to a single river. But, in time of war, their whole trade might be annihilated. When it is recollected that the Mississippi empties itself into the gulph of Florida which is surrounded by foreign territory; that the island of Cuba and the coast of East Florida completely guard the passage from its mouth to the ocean; that the immense commerce flowing down its stream holds forth irresistible allurements to cruizers, the opinion seems well founded that scarcely a vessel making for that place could reach its port of destination.

But the length of the voyage up the Mississippi and the Ohio must be attended with delay so inconvenient to persons engaged in commerce, as to render a shorter route, though not less expensive, more eligible. For the importation of many articles, there is much reason to believe that a decided preference would always be given to the transportation through the United States, were that transportation rendered as easy as it is capable of being made.

The export trade during peace, so far as the articles exported were designed for a foreign market, would most probably pass exclusively down the Mississippi. But those articles which are consumed in the United States, as manufactures of hemp, would find their way to market thro' interior and shorter channels.

If the direct route through the Atlantic States, would, for many purposes, be more eligible than that thro' the gulph of Florida, which must be often connected with a coasting voyage to or from an Atlantic port, then the multiplication of those routes, if in themselves equal, by presenting a greater choice, and by accommodating more territory, must be desirable.

But your commissioners are sanguine in the opinion, that the communication thro' the rivers they have viewed, if properly made, will possess advantages over every other, which cannot fail to recommend it to a large portion of the States of Kentucky and Ohio. All that part of the Western country which draws its supplies, and transports it's produce through the river Ohio, and which lies east of Louisville and west of the Pennsylvania line, perhaps a part of the State of Pennsylvania, itself, could probably use this route more advantageously than any other; unless, indeed, that through the Powtomac connected with Monongahela, Cheat, or Yohaghany, should come into competition with it for the eastern part of the country just mentioned.

That it would, for the importation of articles from Europe, and from the East, (with a few exceptions) and for the exportation of those which are consumed in the United States, be preferred to the voyage through the Mississippi, unless the introduction of steam boats should essentially vary the present state of things, may safely be assumed, from the fact that a land carriage between Pittsburg and Philadelphia or Baltimore, and a carriage up or down the Ohio, are now used for the purposes described in preference to the route by New-Orleans.

The present price for the transportation of goods from Philadelphia or Baltimore, to Pittsburg, is understood to be from seven to ten dollars *per* hundred weight.

The price of transportation from Richmond, up James river to the mouth of Dunlop's creek, thence across the Alleghany to Greenbrier, and down to the mouth of the Great Kanawha, will certainly depend on the goodness of the road and the degree of perfection to which the navigation may be carried. Your commissioners believe that a sound national economy would dictate such improvements as would reduce the price of freight; altho' the labor employed in making them might be procured by an augmentation of toll, and some expenditure of public money.

Should the navigation of James river be rendered as safe & as easy as may be reasonably expected, and the Greenbrier and New rivers be improved in such manner as the object will justify, your commissioners believe they hazard nothing in saying that the expense of transporting one hundred weight from Richmond to the mouth of the Great Kanawha will not exceed half the price of transporting the same weight from Baltimore or Philadelphia to the same place.

The immense works meditated in New-York will certainly, if executed, give to that State great advantages in a competition for the trade of the lakes. But if other convenient and more direct channels be opened, it is not probable that the commerce of the Ohio will take the circuitous route by the lakes.

The expense of transportation from New-York through the canal contemplated can only be conjectured. The character of the rivers which would be used is not well understood; but they must possess many advantages, to give them a preference over the direct way through Virginia to the Ohio.

Your commissioners, however, take the liberty to repeat, that the success of any attempt to obtain that share of the commerce of the west to which this State, from her geographical situation, and her rivers, would seem to be entitled, must depend entirely on the safety and cheapness of her navigation. A mode of transportation by water, in itself insecure or so laborious as to be little less expensive than carriage by land, will never change the channels in which this trade already flows.

The advantages to accrue to the United States, from opening this new channel of intercourse between the eastern and the western States, are those which necessarily result to the whole body from whatever benefits its members, and those which must result to the United States, particularly, from every measure which tends to cement more closely the union of the eastern with the western States.

In those operations, too, which the exigencies of government may often require, this central channel of communication by water may be of great value. For the want of it, in the course of the last autumn, government was reduced to the necessity of transporting arms in waggons from Richmond to the falls of the Great Kanawha. A similar necessity may often recur.

All which is respectfully submitted to the General Assembly, by

> JOHN MARSHALL.
> JAMES BRECKENRIDGE.
> WILLIAM LEWIS.
> JAMES McDOWELL.
> WILLIAM CARUTHERS.
> ANDREW ALEXANDER.
> December 26, 1812

BANKRUPTCY LAW AND THE CONSTITUTION

To Bushrod Washington

My dear Sir   Richmond April 19th. 1814

Your letter of the 13th. reached me this morning. The question you propose had never before attracted my attention. Without examining the subject, I had taken it for granted that the power of passing bankrupt laws resided in the states. It now appears to me more doubtful than I had supposed it to be. Congress has power "to establish an uniform rule of naturalization & uniform laws on the subject of bankruptcies throughout the United States." This would seem to empower Congress to regulate the whole bankrupt system, & to require in all the states a conformity to the laws of the national legislature. But unless Congress shall act on the subject, I should feel much difficulty in saying that the legislative power of the states respecting it is suspended by this part of the constitution.

That part of the constitution which inhibits the passage of any "law impairing the obligation of contracts" was probably intended to prevent a mischief very different from any which grows out of a bankrupt law. Those laws exist in commercial countries where credit is in its most flourishing state, & were I believe common in the commercial states of the Union at the adoption of the constitution. I do not recollect that they excited any complaints or were considered as impairing credit in the states in which they were in operation. The fears & apprehensions which produced that limitation on the legislative power of the states were of a different description. Paper money, the tender of useless property, & other laws acting directly on the engagements of individuals were then objects of general alarm & were probably in the mind of the convention. Yet the words may go further; if they do on a fair & necessary construction, they must have their full effect.

The words of the Constitution are prospective. "No state shall" &c. They do not then act on the existing bankrupt system of any state. I should not willingly admit a construction which tolerated bankrupt laws in some states in which they already existed, but forbade their enactment in other states.

It may also be doubted whether a bankrupt law applying to contracts made subsequent to its passage may fairly be termed a law impairing the obligation of contracts. Such contract is made with a knowlege that it may be acted on by the law. But this would not apply to contracts made out of the state. I should fell no hesitation in saying that a particular act of the state legislature discharging a particular individual who had surrendered his property was invalid. But a general prospective act presents a question of considerable difficulty. I have not thought of the question long enough, nor viewed it in a sufficient variety of lights to have a decided opinion on it, but the biass of my mind at the moment is rather in favor of the validity of the law though I acknowlege I feel very great doubts whether I shall retain that opinion. Your own judgement, you having heard the argument, is much more to be relied on than mine. I am my dear Sir very sincerely, Your affectionate

"MY CULPABLE SON"

To an Unknown Correspondent

Sir   Richmond April 9th. 1815

I received two days past your favor of the 27th. of March. For the communication you have made, and for the interest you take in the fate of my culpable son, I pray you to receive my sincere thanks.

I have been excessively pained at his misconduct, & cannot entirely excuse myself for the unlimited confidence I placed in him. I think myself in some measure accessory to his disgrace.

I am anxious to give him an opportunity to retrieve his reputation & to restore himself to the affection & good opinion of his friends & connexions. I fear he will not avail himself of any opportunity which may be afforded him. I grieve to percieve in him no mark of sincere penitence, no deep conviction of his faults, no resolute determination to correct them. It is not the unavailing expression of regret unaccompanied by an exemplary performance of duty & a vigorous application to study, that can atone for his errors, or furnish a hope that they will not be repeated. If his conduct in the retirement to which he is sentenced shall be such as perfectly to satisfy the government of the University, if in his studies he shall outstrip the class of which he was a member until he proved himself unworthy of remaining in it, if he shall persevere without relaxation in that course of self improvement which will be the evidence & the sole evidence of real reformation, the past will be forgotten as well as forgiven, & he will be received by his parents & other friends as if no offense had been committed. But every thing depends on himself, & he may rest assured that it will not be in his power to practice imposition on me.

In the wounded feelings of a Father anxious for the welfare of a son of whose unworthiness he is unwilling to be convinced, your goodness will I trust find an apology for the trouble given you by this letter. Allow me to repeat my thanks for the interest you have taken in his affairs & to assure you that I am with very much respect, Your Obedt Servt.

SHARING AGRICULTURAL KNOWLEDGE

To Richard Peters

Dear Sir   Richmond July 21st. 1815
   In democracies, which all the world confesses to be the most perfect work of political wisdom, equality is the pivot on which the grand machine turns, & equality demands that he who has a surplus of any thing in general demand should parcel it out among his needy fellow citizens. It is therefore not only reasonable & just, but essential to the vital principles of our excellent institutions that celebrity in any thing especially in that which interests the community, should be burthened with the tax of communicating to all who hunt after knowlege, its superabundant stores. Consequently you cannot as a good patriot, be dissatisfied if every person anxious for instruction in the great & useful science of agriculture should be desirous of availing himself of the opportunity given by an occasional visit to Philadelphia, to draw upon your vast stock, & thus enable himself to show away to advantage among the small folks he

will on his return find in his own neighborhood eager to receive the lessons he will retail to them.

I hope I have now proved as plainly as a lawyer or rather a politician generally proves a proposition that a visit from & a conversation with every inquisitive traveller is entirely a thing of course, which belongs to your agricultural character & for which your mind is undoubtedly prepared. After this I need make no apology for the liberty I take in introducing to you my friend & neighbor Doctor Adams who is a sensible honorable man & one of our most successful farmers—especially in the cultivation of the grasses. I do this too in the confidence that you will yourself feel some satisfaction in hearing from him something of the practice of this part of the antient dominion. With great & sincere esteem I am dear Sir, Your Obedt

SETTING VERDICTS ASIDE

To Richard Peters

My dear Sir   Richmond Oct. 12th. 1815

On my return from a tour into the country to visit a plantation productive only of expence & vexation I was gratified by receiving your letter of the 4th. inst. Doctor Adams regretted much his not seeing you for half an hour, on many accounts, but more especially on account of losing a conversation on fioren grass from which he had anticipated pleasure & instruction. His disappointment was occasioned by the failure of more than one who had promised to accompany him to your farm previous to the session of your court.

On the question you propound I shall very freely communicate what occurs to my mind although I have no claims or pretensions to that *redundance* of knowledge on the subject which overflows its banks to the improvement of every thing around.

The setting aside of verdicts is very much within the discretion of the Judge who tries the cause. It must be a very strong case indeed in which his opinion given the one way or the other could be erroneous. Yet a man would wish to exercise this discretion soundly & in conformity with general usage. For a slight irregularity in the party in whose favor a verdict was found I should be disposed to set it aside, because it is important to justice that every attempt of the kind should be prevented, & the invariable rule to set aside a verdict in all such cases, whether it be right or wrong, is perhaps the only means of prevention in the power of the Judge. But for irregularities in the conduct of a juror in which the party does not participate, the necessity of observing this rule is not so obvious. The repetition of the practice may be prevented by a fine which is the appropriate punishment for the offence, & which reaches the guilty without touching the innocent.

There are I think considerable objections to setting aside a verdict where it conforms to the right of the cause. To say nothing of *precious* time consumed in a second trial of the same case, (time which might be so pleasantly employed on the farm) the justice of the case is committed to some hazard by being carried before another jury; &, in any event, a party who has committed no fault, is subjected to costs & delay. It can be of no real utility, if on principle it can be avoided, to send a cause to a new jury where a different verdict would not be received, or if received, would not be as acceptable as that already in possession of the court. I shall terminate these *wise* reflections by observing that if I approved the verdict I would let it stand; if I did not, although my disapprobation might not be sufficient to set it aside had all been perfectly *enregle*, I would avail myself of the irregularity to award a new trial. With much esteem I am dear Sir, Your Obedt

PLANS FOR REVISING "THE LIFE"

To Bushrod Washington

My dear Sir   Richmond Septr. 10th. 1816
    I had the pleasure of receiving on my return from the upper country your letter dated in August. I had not seen Brown & had formed an opinion of the civil admiralty jurisdiction from

the character of a case of piracy not from precedent. A pirate being an enemy of the human race & at war with the civilized world I had considered a libel for the condemnation of his vessel as partaking rather of the character of a prize cause than of one belonging to the civil admiralty side of the court. But I bow to precedent.

I should have deferred any communication respecting a revision of "The life" till I see you in Washington if I did not wish you to have some particular conversation with Mr. Wayne on the subject for which there may be an opportunity while you are in Philadelphia. I do not think a new edition ought to be hurried. It cannot be pressed on the publick. We must wait till it is required. I wish you to present this idea to Mr. Wayne & know what evidence he possesses if any that the work is really demanded.

The idea which presents itself to me as eligible is that the introduction be so much abridged as to comprehend the two chapters now inserted in the 2d. vol. respecting the controversies which preceded hostilities & the military operations anterior to the organization of a continental Army & the appointment of a commander in chief. The war may readily be comprized in two volumes. I mentioned to you formerly & I mention it again that I think the introduction may in a new edition be subscribed for distinctly from the residue of the work. That any person at his option subscribe for the whole, or for the introduction solely, or for the life of Washington exclusive of the introduction. If it is contemplated to bring the war within less than two volumes I could wish to know it. The volume respecting the civil administration may be somewhat reduced, particularly by excluding so much of the transactions of the government during Mr. Adams's Presidency as is unconnected with General Washington personally. I give you my ideas & should like to possess yours & Mr. Waynes.

As the alterations I presume will be considerable it would very much aid Mr. Wayne for me to mark them in the work itself. If Mr. Wayne has a set not bound it will be desirable that you should bring it with you to be applied in this manner. You can let me have it at Washington this winter or at any other time. It is a work which must be performed at liesure & I repeat my conviction that the edition ought not to be offered till it is really demanded. I am my dear Sir with much esteem, Your Obedt. Servt

A NEPHEW'S EDUCATION

To Louis Marshall

My dear brother   Richmond Decr. 23d. 1816
    Our Nephew the son of our Sister Taylor leaves us to day for Kentucky for the purpose of being educated under your superintendence. His mother was very desirous of committing him to your care & I have entirely approved her determination. His Father when dying requested me to supply his place as far as should be in my power & I accepted the trust with an earnest wish to fulfil the engagement. Had the state of my family allowed of my taking him into my own house I should still have preferred his being brought up in the country under your eye. This town is a dangerous place for youth & our seminaries are far from being respectable. I imagine my sister will write to you respecting the funds for his support & I will myself attend to the necessary arrangements. I have not conversed with her on the subject but will do so as soon as I see her. There will probably be no difficulty in your drawing on me; but if it should be more convenient the necessary funds shall be placed in a bank at this place, or Baltimore or Philadelphia or elsewhere as may be prescribed by yourself.

    My wife continues in wretched health. Her nervous system is so affected that she cannot set in a room while a person walks across the floor. I am now preparing to convey her out of town in order to escape the noisy rejoicings of the season which is approaching.

    Our legislature is entirely occupied with banks & conventions. But I am so withdrawn from the busy active world that I seldom know much of what is passing.

    It would give me great pleasure to see you here, but it is a pleasure which I scarcely expect. My Kentucky friends when they visit Virginia seldom take Richmond in their tour. With the best wishes for Mrs. Marshall & your family, I am my dear brother, Your affectionate

REPORTING SUPREME COURT DECISIONS

To Dudley Chase

Sir   Washington Feby. 7th. 1817

Your letter inclosing a copy of the bill "To provide for re-ports of the decisions of the Supreme court," in which you do me the honour to request, for the Committee, my views rela-tive to "the object and utility of the proposed act" was yesterday received &communicated to the Judges.

We all concur in the opinion that the object of the bill is in a high degree desirable.

That the cases determined in the Supreme court should be reported with accuracy & promptness is essential to correct-ness & uniformity of decision in all the courts of the United States. It is also to be recollected that from the same tribunal the public receives that exposition of the constitution laws & treaties of the United States as applicable to the cases of indi-viduals, which must ultimately prevail. It is obviously impor-tant that a knowledge of this exposition should be attainable by all.

It is a minor consideration, but not perhaps to be entirely overlooked, that even in cases where the decisions of the Supreme court are not to be considered as authority except in the courts of the United States, some advantage may be de-rived from their being known. It is certainly to be wished that independent tribunals having concurrent jurisdiction over the same subject, should concur in the principles on which they determine the causes coming before them. This concurrence can be obtained only by communicating to each the judge-ments of the other, & by that mutual respect which will prob-ably be inspired by a knowledge of the grounds on which their judgements respectively stand. On great commercial questions especially it is desirable that the judicial opinions of all parts of the Union should be the same.

From experience, the Judges think there is much reason to apprehend that the publication of the decisions of the Supreme court will remain on a very precarious footing, if the Reporter is to depend solely on the sales of his work for a reimbursement of the expenses which must be incurred in preparing it, & for his own compensation. The patronage of the government is beleived to be necessary to the secure & certain attainment of the object.

Law Reports can have but a limited circulation. They rarely gain admission into the libraries of other than professional gentlemen. The circulation of the decisions of the Supreme court will probably be still more limited than those of the courts of the states, because they are useful to a smaller number of the profession. Only a few of those who practise in the courts of the United States, or in great commercial cities, will often require them. There is therefore much reason to beleive that no Reporter will continue to employ his time & talents in preparing those decisions for the press, after he shall be assured that the government will not countenance his undertaking. With very great respect, I am Sir your obedt. Servt

HOPING FOR NEWS FROM HOME

To Mary W. Marshall

My dearest Polly   Washington Feb. 14th. 1817
    Since my being in this place I have been more in company than I wish & more than is consistent with the mass of business we have to go through. I have been invited to dine with the President with our own secretaries & with the minister of France & tomorrow I dine with the British minister. I have been very much pleased with the French minister & with his Lady. She is among the most simple & domestic women I ever saw. Speaks of the comfortable habits of our country with great approbation & with regret of the increasing luxury of those who possess but moderate fortunes. In the midst of these gay circles my mind is carried to my own fire side & to my beloved wife. I conjecture where you are sitting & who is with

you to cheer your solitary moments. I am most anxious to know how you do but nobody is kind enough to gratify my wishes. Mr. Wirt I understand came yesterday & I looked eagerly for a letter to day—but no letter came. I still retain some hope of receiving one tomorrow when I shall certainly see him.

Our weather continues intensely cold & I am the more grieved at it because I am sure it must prevent your riding out. You must not fail when you go to chiccahominy on the 21st. to carry out blankets enough to keep you comfortable. I am very desirous of hearing what is doing there but as no body is good enough to let me know how you do & what is passing at home I could not expect to hear what is passing at the farm. I am my dearest Polly, Your ever affectionate

AN AUTOBIOGRAPHICAL SKETCH

To Joseph Delaplaine

Sir   Richmond March 22d. 1818

I received while at Washington your letters requesting me to sit for my portrait to be taken first by Mr. Wood & afterwards by Mr. Lawrence. The first gentleman I could not see & the last did not reach Washington during my stay in the city. At your request my portrait was formerly taken by Mr. Wood, & I did suppose it was in your possession. His price I presume as well as that of Mr. Lawrence is forty dollars. If it is, & you can receive from him that which he has already painted, & you direct me to remit the money to him or yourself, I will do so.

I have also received your letter requesting some account of my birth parentage &c. I believe I answered the same or nearly the same queries two years past—but suppose my letter is mislaid. I shall again comply with your request. It is not however my wish to appear in your next half volume, nor is it my opinion that persons who are still in the view of the public ought to be placed in it. But I do not pretend to interfere with any mode of conducting your great work which to yourself shall seem eligible.

*

I was born on the 24th. of September 1755, in the county of Fauquier in Virginia. My Father Thomas Marshall was the eldest son of John Marshall who intermarried with a Miss Markham, & whose parents migrated from Wales, & settled in the county of Westmoreland in Virginia, where my Father was born. My mother was named Mary Keith. She was the daughter of a clergyman of the name of Keith who migrated from Scotland & intermarried with a Miss Randolph on James River. I was educated at home, under the direction of my Father, who was a planter, but was often called from home as a surveyor. From my infancy I was destined for the bar; but the contest between the mother country & her colonies drew me from my studies & my Father from the superintendence of them; & in September 1775, I entered into the service as a subaltern. I continued in the army until the year 1781, when, being without a command, I resigned my commission, in the interval between the invasions of Virginia by Arnold & Phillips. In the year 1782 I was elected into the legislature of Virginia, & in the fall session of the same year, was chosen a member of the Executive counsel of that state. In Jany. 1783 I intermarried with Mary Willis Ambler, the second daughter of Mr. Jaquelin Ambler, then Treasurer of Virginia, who was the third son of Mr. Richard Ambler a gentleman who had migrated from England, & settled at York Town in Virginia. In April 1784 I resigned my seat in the Executive counsel, & came to the bar, at which I continued, declining any other public office than a seat in the legislature, until the year 1797, when I was associated with General Pinkney & Mr. Gerry in a mission to France. In 1798 I returned to the United States, & in the spring of 1799 was elected a member of Congress, a candidate for which much against my inclination, I was induced to become by the request of General Washington. At the close of the first session I was nominated first to the Department of war, & afterwards to that of state, which last office I accepted, & in which I continued until the beginning of the year 1801; when, Mr. Ellsworth having resigned, & Mr. Jay having declined his appointment, I was nominated to the office of Chief Justice, which I still hold.

I am the oldest of fifteen children all of whom lived to be married & of whom nine are now living. My Father died when about seventy four years of age & my mother who survived

him about seven years, died about the same age. I do not recollect all the societies to which I belong, though they are very
numerous. I have written no book except the Life of Washington which was executed with so much precipitation as to require much correction.

I received also a letter from you requesting some expression
of my sentiments respecting your repository, & indicating an
intention to publish in some conspicuous manner, the certificates which might be given by Mr. Wirt & myself.

I have been ever particularly unwilling to obtain this kind of
distinction, & must insist on not receiving it now. I have however no difficulty in saying that your work is one in which the
nation ought to feel an interest, & I sincerely wish it may be
encouraged, & that you may receive ample compensation for
your labor & expence. The execution is I think in many respects praiseworthy. The portraits, an object of considerable
interest, are, so far as my acquaintance extends, good likenesses;
& the printing is neatly executed with an excellent type. In the
characters there is of course some variety. Some of them are
drawn with great spirit & justice—some are perhaps rather exaggerated. There is much difficulty in giving living characters
—at any rate until they shall have withdrawn from the public
view. The plan might perhaps have been improved by introducing a greater number of persons who were distinguished
for their exertions in [   ] settling & discovering our country. Sir Walter Raleigh & Capt Smith for example might have
been added with advantage to Columbus & Americas. Many
of those distinguished individuals who took an early part in
our revolutionary contest & whose portraits might probably
be obtained in their families or in Peales Museum, would have
been most desirable precursors to the lives of those who are
still in being. But as it is, we behold in it a great national
undertaking, & I cordially wish it success. Very respectfully I
am Sir, your obedt. Servt

Opinion in
Dartmouth College v. Woodward

This is an action of trover, brought by the Trustees of Dartmouth College against William H. Woodward, in the state court of New-Hampshire, for the book of records, corporate seal, and other corporate property, to which the plaintiffs allege themselves to be entitled.

A special verdict, after setting out the rights of the parties, finds for the defendant, if certain acts of the legislature of New-Hampshire, passed on the 27th of June, and on the 18th of December, 1816, be valid, and binding on the trustees without their assent, and not repugnant to the constitution of the United States; otherwise, it finds for the plaintiffs.

The superiour court of judicature of New-Hampshire rendered a judgment upon this verdict for the defendant, which judgment has been brought before this court by writ of error. The single question now to be considered is, Do the acts, to which the verdict refers, violate the constitution of the United States?

This court can be insensible neither to the magnitude nor delicacy of this question. The validity of a legislative act is to be examined; and the opinion of the highest law tribunal of a state is to be revised; an opinion, which carries with it intrinsic evidence of the diligence, of the ability, and the integrity, with which it was formed. On more than one occasion, this court has expressed the cautious circumspection, with which it approaches the consideration of such questions; and has declared, that, in no doubtful case, would it pronounce a legislative act to be contrary to the constitution. But the American people have said in the constitution of the United States, that "No state shall pass any bill of attainder, *ex post facto* law, or law impairing the obligation of contracts." In the same instrument they have also said, "that the judicial power shall extend to all cases in law and equity arising under the constitution." On the judges of this court, then, is imposed the high and solemn duty of protecting from even legislative violation those contracts, which the constitution of our country has placed beyond legislative controul; and however irksome the task may be, this is a duty, from which we dare not shrink.

The title of the plaintiffs originates in a charter dated the 13th day of December, in the year 1769, incorporating twelve persons therein mentioned, by the name of "The Trustees of Dartmouth College," granting to them and their successors the usual corporate privileges and powers, and authorizing the trustees, who are to govern the college, to fill up all vacancies, which may be created in their own body.

The defendant claims under three acts of the legislature of New-Hampshire, the most material of which was passed on the 27th of June 1816, and is entitled, "an act to amend the charter, and enlarge, and improve the corporation of Dartmouth College." Among other alterations in the charter, this act increases the number of trustees to twenty-one, gives the appointment of the additional members to the executive of the state, and creates a board of overseers with power to inspect and controul the most important acts of the trustees. This board consists of twenty-five persons. The president of the senate, the speaker of the house of representatives of New-Hampshire, and the governour and lieutenant-governour of Vermont, for the time being, are to be members *ex officio*. The board is to be completed by the governour and council of New-Hampshire, who are also empowered to fill all vacancies, which may occur. The acts of the 18th and 26th of December are supplemental to that of the 27th of June, and are principally intended to carry that act into *effect*.

The majority of the trustees of the college have refused to accept this amended charter, and have brought this suit for the corporate property, which is in possession of a person holding by virtue of the acts, which have been stated.

It can require no argument to prove, that the circumstances of this case constitute a contract. An application is made to the crown for a charter to incorporate a religious and literary institution. In the application it is stated, that large contributions have been made for the object which will be conferred on the corporation, as soon as it shall be created. The charter is granted, and on its faith the property is conveyed. Surely in this transaction every ingredient of a complete and legitimate contract is to be found.

The points for consideration are,

1st. Is this contract protected by the constitution of the United States?

2d. Is it impaired by the acts, under which the defendant holds?

1st. On the first point it has been argued, that the word "contract" in its broadest sense would comprehend the political relations between the government and its citizens, would extend to offices held within a state for state purposes, and to many of those laws concerning civil institutions, which must change with circumstances, and be modified by ordinary legislation, which deeply concern the publick, and which, to preserve good government, the publick judgment must controul. That even marriage is a contract, and its obligations are affected by the laws respecting divorces. That the clause in the constitution, if construed in its greatest latitude, would prohibit these laws. Taken in its broad unlimited sense, the clause would be an unprofitable and vexatious interference with the internal concerns of a state, would unnecessarily and unwisely embarrass its legislation, and render immutable those civil institutions, which are established for purposes of internal government, and which, to subserve those purposes, ought to vary with varying circumstances. That as the framers of the constitution could never have intended to insert in that instrument a provision so unnecessary, so mischievous and so repugnant to its general spirit, the term "*contract*" must be understood in a more limited sense. That it must be understood as intended to guard against a power of at least doubtful utility, the abuse of which had been extensively felt; and to restrain the legislature in future from violating the right to property. That anterior to the formation of the constitution, a course of legislation had prevailed in many, if not in all of the states, which weakened the confidence of man in man, and embarrassed all transactions between individuals, by dispensing with a faithful performance of engagements. To correct this mischief by restraining the power, which produced it, the state legislatures were forbidden "to pass any law impairing the obligation of contracts," that is, of contracts respecting property, under which some individual could claim a right to something beneficial to himself; and that since the clause in the constitution must in construction receive some limitation, it may be confined, and ought to be confined, to cases of this description; to cases within the mischief, it was intended to remedy.

The general correctness of these observations cannot be controverted. That the framers of the constitution did not intend to restrain the states in the regulation of their civil institutions, adopted for internal government, and that the instrument they have given us, is not to be so construed, may be admitted. The provision of the constitution never has been understood to embrace other contracts, than those, which respect property, or some object of value, and confer rights, which may be asserted in a court of justice. It never has been understood to restrict the general right of the legislature to legislate on the subject of divorces. Those acts enable some tribunal, not to impair a marriage contract, but to liberate one of the parties because it has been broken by the other. When any state legislature shall pass an act annulling all marriage contracts, or allowing either party to annul it without the consent of the other, it will be time enough to enquire, whether such an act be constitutional.

The parties in this case differ less on general principles, less on the true construction of the constitution in the abstract, than on the application of those principles to this case, and on the true construction of the charter of 1769. This is the point, on which the cause essentially depends. If the act of incorporation be a grant of political power, if it create a civil institution to be employed in the administration of the government, or if the funds of the college be publick property, or if the state of New-Hampshire, as a government, be alone interested in its transactions, the subject is one, on which the legislature of the state may act according to its own judgment, unrestrained by any limitation of its power imposed by the constitution of the United States.

But if this be a private eleemosynary institution, endowed with a capacity to take property for objects unconnected with government, whose funds are bestowed by individuals on the faith of the charter; if the donors have stipulated for the future disposition and management of those funds in the manner prescribed by themselves; there may be more difficulty in the case, although neither the persons, who have made these stipulations, nor those, for whose benefit they were made, should be parties to the cause. Those, who are no longer interested in the property, may yet retain such an interest in the preservation of their own arrangements, as to have a right to insist, that those arrangements shall be held sacred. Or, if they have themselves disappeared, it becomes a subject of serious and anxious inquiry, whether those, whom they have legally empowered to represent them forever, may not assert all the rights, which they possessed, while in being; whether, if they be without personal representatives, who may feel injured by a violation of the compact, the trustees be not so completely their representatives in the eye of the law, as to stand in their place, not only as respects the government of the college, but also as respects the maintenance of the college charter.

It becomes then the duty of the Court most seriously to examine this charter, and to ascertain its true character.

From the instrument itself, it appears, that about the year 1754, the Rev. Eleazer Wheelock established at his own expense, and on his own estate a charity school for the instruction of Indians in the christian religion. The success of this institution inspired him with the design of soliciting contributions in England for carrying on, and extending, his undertaking. In this pious work he employed the Rev. Nathaniel Whitaker, who, by virtue of a power of attorney from Dr. Wheelock, appointed the Earl of Dartmouth and others, trustees of the money, which had been, and should be, contributed; which appointment Dr. Wheelock confirmed by a deed of trust authorizing the trustees to fix on a site for the college. They determined to establish the school on Connecticut river, in the western part of New-Hampshire; that situation being supposed favourable for carrying on the original design among the Indians, and also for promoting learning among the English, and the proprietors in the neighbourhood having made large offers of land on condition that the college should there be placed. Dr. Wheelock then applied to the crown for an act of incorporation; and represented the expediency of appointing those, whom he had by his last will named, as trustees in America, to be members of the proposed corporation. "In consideration of the premises," "for the education and instruction of the youth of the Indian tribes, &c." "and also of English youth, and any others," the charter was granted, and the trustees of Dartmouth College were by that name created a body corporate, with power, *for the use of the said college,* to acquire real and personal property, and to pay the president, tutors, and other officers of the college such salaries as they shall allow.

The charter proceeds to appoint Eleazer Wheelock, "the founder of said college," president thereof, with power by his last will to appoint a successor, who is to continue in office, until disapproved by the trustees. In case of vacancy, the trustees may appoint a president, and in case of the ceasing of a president, the senior professor or tutor, *being one of the trustees,* shall exercise the office, until an appointment shall be made. The trustees have power to appoint and displace professors, tutors and other officers, and to supply any vacancies, which may be created in their own body by death, resignation, removal or disability; and also to make orders, ordinances, and laws, for the government of the college, the same not being repugnant to the laws of Great Britain, or of New-Hampshire, and not excluding any person on account of his speculative sentiments in religion, or his being of a religious profession different from that of the trustees.

This charter was accepted, and the property both real and personal, which had been contributed for the benefit of the college, was conveyed to, and vested in the corporate body.

From this brief review of the most essential parts of the charter, it is apparent, that the funds of the college consisted entirely of private donations. It is perhaps not very important, who were the donors. The probability is, that the Earl of Dartmouth and the other trustees in England were, in fact, the largest contributors. Yet the legal conclusion from the facts recited in the charter, would probably be, that Dr. Wheelock was the founder of the college.

The origin of the institution was, undoubtedly, the Indian charity school, established by Dr. Wheelock at his own expense. It was at his instance, and to enlarge this school, that contributions were solicited in England. The person soliciting these contributions was his agent; and the trustees, who received the money, were appointed by, and acted under his, authority. It is not too much to say, that the funds were obtained by him, in trust to be applied by him to the purposes of his enlarged school. The charter of incorporation was granted at his instance. The persons named by him in his last will, as the trustees of his charity school, compose a part of the corporation, and he is declared to be the founder of the college, and its president for life. Were the enquiry material, we should feel some hesitation in saying, that Dr. Wheelock was not, in law, to be considered as the founder (1) of this institution, and as possessing all the rights appertaining to that character. But be this as it may, Dartmouth college is really endowed by private individuals, who have bestowed their funds for the propagation of the christian religion among the Indians, and for the promotion of piety and learning generally. From these funds the salaries of the tutors are drawn; and these salaries lessen the expense of education to the students. It is then an eleemosynary, (2) and, as far as respects its funds, a private corporation.

Do its objects stamp on it a different character? Are the trustees and professors publick officers, invested with any portion of political power, partaking in any degree in the administration of civil government, and performing duties, which flow from the sovereign authority?

That education is an object of national concern, and a proper subject of legislation, all admit. That there may be an institution founded by government, and placed entirely under its immediate controul, the officers of which would be publick officers, amenable exclusively to government, none will deny. But is Dartmouth College such an institution? Is education altogether in the hands of government? Does every teacher of youth become a publick officer, and do donations for the purposes of education necessarily become publick property, so far that the will of the legislature, not the will of the donor, becomes the law of the donation? These questions are of serious moment to society, and deserve to be well considered.

Doctor Wheelock, as the keeper of his charity school, instructing the Indians in the art of reading, and in our holy religion; sustaining them at his own expense, and on the voluntary contributions of the charitable, could scarcely be considered, as a publick officer, exercising any portion of those

(1) 1 Black. Comm. 481.
(2) 1 Black. Comm. 471.

duties, which belong to government; nor could the legislature have supposed that his private funds, or those given by others, were subject to legislative management, because they were applied to the purposes of education. When, afterwards, his school was enlarged, and the liberal contributions made in England and in America enabled him to extend his cares to the education of the youth of his own country, no change was wrought in his own character, or in the nature of his duties. Had he employed assistant tutors with the funds contributed by others, or had the trustees in England established a school with Dr. Wheelock at its head, and paid salaries to him and his assistants, they would still have been private tutors; and the fact, that they were employed in the education of youth, could not have converted them into publick officers, concerned in the administration of publick duties, or have given the legislature a right to interfere in the management of the fund. The trustees, in whose care that fund was placed by the contributors, would have been permitted to execute their trust uncontrouled by legislative authority.

Whence, then, can be derived the idea, that Dartmouth College has become a publick institution, and its trustees publick officers, exercising powers conferred by the publick for publick objects? Not from the source, whence its funds were drawn, for its foundation is purely private and eleemosynary. Not from the application of those funds, for money may be given for education, and the persons receiving it do not by being employed in the education of youth, become members of the civil government. Is it from the act of incorporation? Let this subject be considered.

A corporation is an artificial being, invisible, intangible, and existing only in contemplation of law. Being the mere creature of law, it possesses only those properties, which the charter of its creation confers upon it, either expressly, or as incidental to its very existence. These are such as are supposed best calculated to effect the object, for which it was created. Among the most important are immortality, and, if the expression may be allowed, individuality; properties, by which a perpetual succession of many persons are considered as the same, and may act as a single individual. They enable a corporation to manage its own affairs, and to hold property without the perplexing intri-

cacies, the hazardous and endless necessity of perpetual conveyances for the purpose of transmitting it from hand to hand.
It is chiefly for the purpose of clothing bodies of men, in succession, with these qualities and capacities, that corporations
were invented, and are in use. By these means, a perpetual succession of individuals are capable of acting for the promotion
of the particular object, like one immortal being. But this
being does not share in the civil government of the country,
unless that be for the purpose, for which it was created. Its immortality no more confers on it political power, or a political
character than immortality would confer such power or character on a natural person. It is no more a state instrument,
than a natural person exercising the same powers would be. If
then a natural person employed by individuals in the education
of youth, or for the government of a seminary, in which youth
is educated, would not become a publick officer, or be considered as a member of the civil government, how is it, that this
artificial being, created by law, for the purpose of being employed by the same individuals for the same purposes, should
become a part of the civil government of the country? Is it
because its existence, its capacities, its powers are given by law?
Because the government has given it the power to take and to
hold property in a particular form, and for particular purposes,
has the government a consequent right substantially to change
that form, or to vary the purposes, to which the property is to
be applied? This principle has never been asserted, or recognized, and is supported by no authority. Can it derive aid from
reason?

The objects for which a corporation is created, are universally such, as the government wishes to promote. They are
deemed beneficial to the country; and this benefit constitutes
the consideration, and in most cases, the sole consideration of
the grant. In most eleemosynary institutions, the object would
be difficult, perhaps unattainable, without the aid of a charter
of incorporation. Charitable, or publick spirited individuals,
desirous of making permanent appropriations for charitable or
other useful purposes, find it impossible to effect their design
securely, and certainly, without an incorporating act. They apply to the government, state their beneficent object and offer to
advance the money necessary for its accomplishment, provided

the government will confer on the instrument, which is to execute their designs, the capacity to execute them. The proposition is considered and approved. The benefit to the publick is considered as an ample compensation for the faculty it confers, and the corporation is created. If the advantages to the publick constitute a full compensation for the faculty it gives, there can be no reason for exacting a further compensation by claiming a right to exercise over this artificial being, a power which changes its nature, and touches the fund, for the security and application of which it was created. There can be no reason for implying in a charter, given for a valuable consideration, a power, which is not only not expressed, but is in direct contradiction to its express stipulations.

From the fact then, that a charter of incorporation has been granted, nothing can be inferred, which changes the character of the institution or transfers to the government any new power over it. The character of civil institutions does not grow out of their incorporation, but out of the manner in which they are formed, and the objects for which they are created. The right to change them, is not founded on their being incorporated, but on their being the instruments of government, created for its purposes. The same institutions, created for the same objects, though not incorporated, would be publick institutions and, of course, be controulable by the legislature. The incorporating act, neither gives, nor prevents, this controul. Neither, in reason can the incorporating act change the character of a private eleemosynary institution.

We are next led to the enquiry, for whose benefit the property given to Dartmouth College was secured? The counsel for the defendant have insisted, that the beneficial interest is in the people of New-Hampshire. The charter, after reciting the preliminary measures, which had been taken, and the application for an act of incorporation, proceeds thus. "Know ye therefore, that we, considering the premises, and being willing to encourage the laudable and charitable design of spreading christian knowledge, among the savages of our American wilderness, and also that the best means of education be established, in our province of New-Hampshire, for the benefit of said province, do of our special grace, &c." Do these expressions bestow on New-Hampshire any exclusive right to the property of the college, any exclusive interest in the labours of the professors? Or do they merely indicate a willingness, that New-Hampshire should enjoy those advantages, which result to all from the establishment of a seminary of learning in the neighbourhood? On this point we think it impossible to entertain a serious doubt. The words themselves, unexplained by the context, indicate, that the "benefit intended for the province" is that, which is derived from "establishing the best means of education therein;" that is, from establishing in the province Dartmouth College, as constituted by the charter. But, if these words considered alone, could admit of doubt, that doubt is completely removed by an inspection of the entire instrument.

The particular interests of New-Hampshire never entered into the mind of the donors, never constituted a motive for their donation. The propagation of the christian religion among the savages, and the dissemination of useful knowledge among the youth of the country, were the avowed and the sole objects of their contributions. In these New-Hampshire would participate; but nothing particular or exclusive, was intended for her. Even the site of the college was selected, not for the sake of New-Hampshire, but because it was "most subservient to the great ends in view," and because liberal donations of land were offered by the proprietors, on condition, that the institution should be there established. The real advantages from the location of the college, are, perhaps, not less considerable to those on the west, than to those on the east side of Connecticut river. The clause which constitutes the incorporation, and expresses the objects, for which it was made, declares those objects to be the instruction of the Indians, "and also of English youth, and any others." So that the objects of the contributors, and the incorporating act were the same; the promotion of christianity, and of education generally, not the interests of New-Hampshire particularly.

From this review of the charter, it appears that Dartmouth College is an eleemosynary institution, incorporated for the purpose of perpetuating the application of the bounty of the donors to the specified objects of that bounty; that its trustees or governours, were originally named by the founder, and invested with the power of perpetuating themselves; that they are not publick officers, nor is it a civil institution, participating in the administration of government; but a charity school, or a seminary of education, incorporated for the preservation of its property and the perpetual application of that, property to the objects of its creation.

Yet a question remains to be considered, of more real difficulty on which more doubt has been entertained, than on all that have been discussed. The founders of the college, at least those, whose contributions were in money, have parted with the property bestowed upon it, and their representatives have no interest in that property. The donors of land are equally without interest, so long as the corporation shall exist. Could they be found, they are unaffected by any alteration in its constitution, and probably regardless of its form, or even of its existence. The students are fluctuating and no individual among our youth has a vested interest in the institution, which can be asserted in a court of justice. Neither the founders of the college, nor the youth, for whose benefit it was founded, complain of the alteration made in its charter, or think themselves injured by it. The trustees alone complain, and the trustees have no beneficial interest to be protected. Can this be such a contract, as the constitution intended to withdraw from the power of state legislation? Contracts, the parties to which have a vested beneficial interest, and those only, it has been said, are the objects about which the constitution is solicitous, and to which its protection is extended.

The court has bestowed on this argument the most deliberate consideration, and the result will be stated. Dr. Wheelock acting for himself, and for those, who at his solicitation, had made contributions to his school, applied for this charter, as the instrument which should enable him, and them to perpetuate their beneficent intention. It was granted. An artificial, immortal being, was created by the crown, capable of receiving and distributing forever, according to the will of the donors, the donations, which should be made to it. On this being, the contributions, which had been collected, were immediately bestowed. These gifts were made not indeed to make a profit for the donors or their posterity, but for something in their opinion of inestimable value; for something which they deemed a full equivalent for the money, with which it was purchased. The consideration for which they stipulated, is the perpetual application of the fund to its object, in the mode prescribed by themselves. Their descendants may take no interest in the preservation of this consideration. But in this respect their descendants are not their representatives. They are represented by the corporation. The corporation is the assignee of their rights, stands in their place and distributes their bounty, as they would themselves have distributed it, had they been immortal. So with respect to the students, who are to derive learning from this source. The corporation is a trustee for them also. Their potential rights, which taken distributively, are imperceptible, amount collectively to a most important interest. These are in the aggregate, to be exercised, asserted and protected, by the corporation. They were as completely out of the donors, at the instant of their being vested in the corporation, and as incapable of being asserted by the students as at present.

According to the theory of the British constitution, their parliament is omnipotent. To annul corporate rights might give a shock to publick opinion, which that government has chosen to avoid; but its power is not questioned. Had parliament immediately after the emanation of this charter, and the execution of those conveyances, which followed it, annulled the instrument, so that the living donors would have witnessed the disappointment of their hopes, the perfidy of the transaction would have been universally acknowledged. Yet then as now, the donors would have had no interest in the property; then, as now, those, who might be students, would have had no rights to be violated; then as now, it might be said, that the trustees, in whom the rights of all were combined, possessed no private, individual, beneficial interest in the property confided to their protection. Yet the contract would at that time, have been deemed sacred by all. What has since occurred to strip it of its inviolability? Circumstances have not changed it. In reason, in justice, and in law, it is now what it was in 1769.

This is plainly a contract to which the donors, the trustees and the crown (to whose rights and obligations New-Hampshire succeeds) were the original parties. It is a contract made on a valuable consideration. It is a contract for the security and disposition of property. It is a contract, on the faith of which, real and personal estate has been conveyed to the corporation. It is then a contract within the letter of the constitution; and within its spirit also, unless the fact, that the property is invested by the donors in trustees for the promotion of religion and education, for the benefit of persons, who are perpetually changing, though the objects remain the same, shall create a particular exception, taking this case out of the prohibition contained in the constitution.

It is more than possible, that the preservation of rights of this description was not particularly in the view of the framers of the constitution, when the clause under consideration was introduced into that instrument. It is probable, that interferences of more frequent recurrence, to which the temptation was stronger, and of which the mischief was more extensive, constituted the great motive for imposing this restriction on the state legislatures. But although a particular, and a rare case may not, in itself, be of sufficient magnitude to induce a rule, yet it must be governed by the rule, when established, unless some plain and strong reason for excluding it can be given. It is not enough to say, that this particular case was not in the mind of the convention, when the article was framed, nor of the American people, when it was adopted. It is necessary to go farther, and to say that, had this particular case been suggested, the language would have been so varied, as to exclude it, or it would have been made a special exception. The case being within the words of the rule, must be within its operation likewise, unless there be something in the literal construction so obviously absurd, or mischievous, or repugnant to the general spirit of the instrument, as to justify those, who expound the constitution in making it an exception.

On what safe and intelligible ground can this exception stand. There is no expression in the constitution, no sentiment delivered by its contemporaneous expounders, which would justify us in making it. In the absence of all authority of this kind, is there in the nature and reason of the case itself that, which would sustain a construction of the constitution, not warranted by its words? Are contracts of this description of a character to excite so little interest, that we must exclude them from the provisions of the constitution, as being unworthy of the attention of those, who framed the instrument? Or does publick policy so imperiously demand their remaining exposed to legislative alteration, as to compel us, or rather permit us to say, that these words, which were introduced to give stability to contracts, and which in their plain import comprehend this, must yet be so construed, as to exclude it?

Almost all eleemosynary corporations, those which are created for the promotion of religion, of charity or of education, are of the same character. The law of this case is the law of all. In every literary or charitable institution, unless the objects of the bounty be themselves incorporated, the whole legal interest is in trustees, and can be asserted only by them. The donors, or claimants of the bounty, if they can appear in court at all, can appear only to complain of the trustees. In all other situations, they are identified with, and personated by the trustees; and their rights, are to be defended and maintained by them. Religion, charity, and education, are in the law of England legatees, or donees, capable of receiving bequests, or donations in this form. They appear in court, and claim or defend by the corporation. Are they of so little estimation in the United States, that contracts for their benefit must be excluded from the protection of words, which in their natural import include them? Or do such contracts so necessarily require new modelling by the authority of the legislature, that the ordinary rules of construction must be disregarded in order to leave them exposed to legislative alteration?

All feel, that these objects are not deemed unimportant in the United States. The interest, which this case has excited proves, that they are not. The framers of the constitution did not deem them unworthy of its care and protection. They have, though in a different mode, manifested their respect for science, by reserving to the government of the Union the power, "to promote the progress of science and useful arts, by securing for limited times to authors and inventors, the exclusive right to their respective writings and discoveries." They have so far withdrawn science, and the useful arts, from the action of the state governments. Why then should they be supposed so regardless of contracts made for the advancement of literature, as to intend to exclude them from provisions, made for the security of ordinary contracts between man and man? No reason for making this supposition is perceived.

If the insignificance of the object does not require, that we should exclude contracts respecting it from the protection of the constitution; neither, as we conceive, is the policy of leaving them subject to legislative alteration so apparent, as to require a forced construction of that instrument in order to effect it. These eleemosynary institutions do not fill the place, which would otherwise be occupied by government, but that which would otherwise remain vacant. They are complete acquisitions to literature. They are donations to education; donations, which any government must be disposed rather to encourage than to discountenance. It requires no very critical examination of the human mind to enable us to determine, that one great inducement to these gifts is the conviction felt by the giver, that the disposition he makes of them is immutable. It is probable, that no man ever was, and that no man ever will be, the founder of a college, believing at the time, that an act of incorporation constitutes no security for the institution; believing, that it is immediately to be deemed a publick institution, whose funds are to be governed, and applied, not by the will of the donor, but by the will of the legislature. All such gifts are made in the pleasing, perhaps, delusive, hope, that the charity will flow forever in the channel, which the givers have marked out for it. If every man finds in his own bosom strong evidence of the universality of this sentiment, there can be but little reason to imagine, that the framers of our constitution were strangers to it, and that, feeling the necessity and policy of giving permanence and security to contracts, of withdrawing them from the influence of legislative bodies, whose fluctuating policy, and repeated interferences produced the most perplexing and injurious embarrassments, they still deemed it necessary to leave these contracts subject to those interferences. The motives for such an exception must be very powerful to justify the construction, which makes it.

The motives suggested at the bar grow out of the original appointment of the trustees, which is supposed to have been in a spirit hostile to the genius of our government, and the presumption, that if allowed to continue themselves, they now are, and must remain forever, what they originally were. Hence is inferred the necessity of applying to this corporation, and to other similar corporations, the correcting, and improving hand of the legislature.

It has been urged repeatedly, and certainly with a degree of earnestness, which attracted attention, that the trustees deriving their power from a regal source, must, necessarily partake of the spirit of their origin; and that their first principles, unimproved by that resplendent light, which has been shed around them, must continue to govern the college, and to guide the students. Before we enquire into the influence which this argument ought to have on the constitutional question, it may not be amiss to examine the fact, on which it rests. The first trustees were undoubtedly named in the charter by the crown; but at whose suggestion were they named? By whom were they selected? The charter informs us. Dr. Wheelock had represented, "that for many weighty reasons it would be expedient, that the gentlemen whom he had already nominated in his last will to be trustees in America, should be of the corporation now proposed." When afterwards, the trustees are named in the charter, can it be doubted, that the persons mentioned by Dr. Wheelock in his will were appointed? Some were probably added by the crown with the approbation of Dr. Wheelock. Among these is the Dr. himself. If any others were appointed at the instance of the crown, they are the governour, three members of the council, and the speaker of the house of representatives of the colony of New-Hampshire. The stations filled by these persons ought to rescue them from any other imputation, than too great a dependence on the crown. If in the revolution, that followed, they acted under the influence of this sentiment, they must have ceased to be trustees; if they took part with their countrymen, the imputation, which suspicion might excite, would no longer attach to them. The original trustees then, or most of them, were named by Dr. Wheelock, and those, who were added to his nomination, most probably with his approbation, were among the most eminent, and respectable individuals in New-Hampshire.

The only evidence, which we possess of the character of Dr. Wheelock, is furnished by this charter. The judicious means employed for the accomplishment of his object, and the success, which attended his endeavours, would lead to the opinion, that he united a sound understanding to that humanity and benevolence, which suggested his undertaking. It surely cannot be assumed, that his trustees were selected without judgment. With as little probability can it be assumed, that while the light of science and of liberal principles pervades the whole community, these originally benighted trustees remain in utter darkness, incapable of participating in the general improvement; that while the human race is rapidly advancing, they are stationary. Reasoning *a priori*, we should believe, that learned, and intelligent men selected by its patrons for the government of a literary institution, would select learned and intelligent men for their successors; men as well fitted for the government of a college, as those, who might be chosen by other means. Should this reasoning ever prove erroneous in a particular case, publick opinion, as has been stated at the bar, would correct the institution. The mere possibility of the contrary would not justify a construction of the constitution, which should exclude these contracts from the protection of a provision, whose terms comprehend them.

The opinion of the court after mature deliberation, is, that this is a contract, the obligation of which cannot be impaired without violating the constitution of the United States. This opinion appears to us to be equally supported by reason, and by the former decisions of this court.

2d. We next proceed to the enquiry—whether its obligation has been impaired by those acts of the legislature of New-Hampshire, to which the special verdict refers.

From the review of this charter, which has been taken, it appears, that the whole power of governing the college, of appointing and removing tutors, of fixing their salaries, of directing the course of study to be pursued by the students, and of filling up vacancies created in their own body, was vested in the trustees. On the part of the crown it was expressly stipulated, that this corporation, thus constituted should continue forever; and that the number of trustees should forever consist of twelve, and no more. By this contract the crown was bound, and could have made no violent alteration in its essential terms, without impairing its obligation.

By the revolution the duties, as well as the powers, of government devolved on the people of New-Hampshire. It is admitted, that among the latter, was comprehended the transcendent power of parliament, as well as that of the executive department. It is too clear to require the support of argument,

that all contracts and rights respecting property remained un-
changed by the revolution. The obligations then, which were
created by the charter to Dartmouth College, were the same
in the new, that they had been in the old government. The
power of the government was also the same. A repeal of this
charter at any time prior to the adoption of the present constitution of the United States, would have been an extraordinary
and unprecedented act of power, but one, which could have
been contested only by the restrictions upon the legislature, to
be found in the constitution of the state. But the constitution
of the United States has imposed this additional limitation,
that the legislature of a state, shall pass no act "impairing the
obligation of contracts."

It has been already stated, that the act "to amend the charter, and enlarge and improve the corporation of Dartmouth
College," increases the number of trustees to twenty-one,
gives the appointment of the additional numbers to the executive of the state, and creates a board of overseers, to consist of
twenty-five persons, of whom twenty-one are also appointed
by the executive of New-Hampshire, who have power to inspect and controul the most important acts of the trustees.

On the effect of this law, two opinions cannot be entertained. Between acting directly, and acting through the agency
of trustees and overseers, no essential difference is perceived.
The whole power of governing the college is transferred from
trustees appointed according to the will of the founder, expressed in the charter, to the executive of New-Hampshire.
The management and application of the funds of this eleemosynary institution, which are placed by the donors, in the hands
of trustees named in the charter, and empowered to perpetuate themselves, are placed by this act under the controul of the
government of the state. The will of the state is substituted for
the will of the donors, in every essential operation of the college. This is not an immaterial change. The founders of the
college contracted not merely for the perpetual application of
the funds which they gave to the objects, for which those
funds were given; they contracted also to secure that application by the constitution of the corporation. They contracted
for a system, which should, as far as human foresight can provide, retain forever the government of the literary institution,

they had formed, in the hands of persons approved by themselves. This system is totally changed. The charter of 1769 exists no longer. It is reorganized; and reorganized in such a manner, as to convert a literary institution, moulded according to the will of its founders, and placed under the controul of private literary men, into a machine entirely subservient to the will of government. This may be for the advantage of this college in particular, and may be for the advantage of literature in general; but it is not according to the will of the donors, and is subversive of that contract on the faith of which their property was given.

In the view which has been taken of this interesting case, the court has confined itself to the rights possessed by the trustees, as the assignees and representatives of the donors and founders, for the benefit of religion and literature. Yet it is not clear, that the trustees ought to be considered as destitute of such beneficial interest in themselves, as the law may respect. In addition to their being the legal owners of the property and to their having a freehold right in the powers confided to them, the charter itself countenances the idea, that trustees may also be tutors with salaries. The first president was one of the original trustees; and the charter provides that in case of vacancy, in that office "the senior professor or tutor, *being one of the trustees,* shall exercise the office of president, until the trustees shall make choice of, and appoint a president." According to the tenor of the charter, then, the trustees might without impropriety appoint a president and other professors from their own body. This is a power not entirely unconnected with an interest. If the proposition of the counsel for the defendant were sustained, if it were admitted, that those contracts only are protected by the constitution, a beneficial interest in which is vested in the party, who appears in court to assert that interest; yet it is by no means clear, that the trustees of Dartmouth College, have no beneficial interest in themselves.

But the court has deemed it unnecessary to investigate this particular point, being of opinion on general principles that in these private eleemosynary institutions, the body corporate, as possessing the whole legal and equitable interest, and completely representing the donors, for the purpose of executing the trust, has rights which are protected by the constitution.

It results from this opinion, that the acts of the legislature of New-Hampshire, which are stated in the special verdict found in this cause, are repugnant to the constitution of the United States; and that the judgment on this special verdict ought to have been for the plaintiffs. The judgment of the state court must therefore be reversed.

February 2, 1819

Opinion in McCulloch v. Maryland

In the case now to be determined, the defendant, a sovereign state, denies the obligation of a law enacted by the Legislature of the Union, and the plaintiff, on his part, contests the validity of an act which has been passed by the Legislature of that state. The Constitution of our country, in its most interesting and vital parts, is to be considered; the conflicting powers of the government of the Union and of its members, as marked in that Constitution, are to be discussed; and an opinion given, which may essentially influence the great operations of the government. No tribunal can approach such a question without a deep sense of its importance, and of the awful responsibility involved in its decision. But it must be decided peacefully, or remain a source of hostile legislation, perhaps of hostility of a still more serious nature; and if it is to be so decided, by this tribunal alone can the decision be made. On the Supreme Court of the United States has the Constitution of our country devolved this important duty.

The first question made in the cause is, Has Congress power to incorporate a Bank?

It has been truly said, that this can scarcely be considered as an open question, entirely unprejudiced by the former proceedings of the nation respecting it. The principle now contested was introduced at a very early period of our history, has been recognized by many successive legislatures, and has been acted upon by the judicial department, in cases of peculiar delicacy, as a law of undoubted obligation.

It will not be denied, that a bold and daring usurpation might be resisted, after an acquiescence still longer and more complete than this. But it is conceived that a doubtful question, one on which human reason may pause and the human judgment be suspended, in the decision of which the great principles of liberty are not concerned, but the respective powers of those who are equally the representatives of the people, to be adjusted, if not put at rest by the practice of the government, ought to receive a considerable impression from that practice. An exposition of the Constitution, deliberately established by legislative acts, on the faith of which an immense property has been advanced, ought not to be lightly disregarded.

The power now contested was exercised by the first Congress elected under the present Constitution. The bill for incorporating the Bank of the United States did not steal upon an unsuspecting legislature and pass unobserved. Its principle was completely understood, and was opposed with equal zeal and ability. After being resisted first in the fair and open field of debate, and afterwards in the executive cabinet, with as much persevering talent as any measure has ever experienced, and being supported by arguments which convinced minds as pure and as intelligent as this country can boast, it became a law. The original act was permitted to expire, but a short experience of the embarrassments to which the refusal to revive it exposed the government, convinced those who were most prejudiced against the measure of its necessity, and induced the passage of the present law. It would require no ordinary share of intrepidity to assert that a measure adopted under these circumstances was a bold and plain usurpation, to which the Constitution gave no countenance.

These observations belong to the cause; but they are not made under the impression that, were the question entirely new, the law would be found irreconcileable with the Constitution.

In discussing this question, the counsel for the State of Maryland have deemed it of some importance in the construction of the Constitution, to consider that instrument not as emanating from the people, but as the act of sovereign and independent states. The powers of the general government, it has been said, are delegated by the states, who alone are truly sovereign, and must be exercised in subordination to the states, who alone possess supreme dominion.

It would be difficult to sustain this proposition. The Convention which framed the Constitution was indeed elected by the state legislatures. But the instrument, when it came from their hands, was a mere proposal, without obligation, or pretensions to it. It was reported to the then existing Congress of the United States, with a request that it might "be submitted to a Convention of Delegates, chosen in each state by the people thereof, under the recommendation of its Legislature, for their assent and ratification." This mode of proceeding was adopted; and by the Convention, by Congress, and by the State Legislatures, the instrument was submitted to the people. They acted upon it in the only manner in which they can act safely, effectively, and wisely on such a subject, by assembling in Convention. It is true, they assembled in their several states—and where else should they have assembled? No political dreamer was ever wild enough to think of breaking down the lines which separate states, and of compounding the American people into one common mass. Of consequence, when they act they act in their states. But the measures they adopt do not, on that account, cease to be the measures of the people themselves, or become the measures of the state governments.

From these Conventions the Constitution derives its whole authority. The government proceeds directly from the people; is "ordained and established" in the name of the people; and is declared to be ordained "in order to form a more perfect union, establish justice, ensure domestic tranquility, and secure the blessings of liberty to themselves and to their posterity." The assent of the states, in their sovereign capacity is implied in calling a Convention, and thus submitting that instrument to the people. But the people were at perfect liberty to accept or reject it; and their act was final. It required not the affirmance, and could not be negatived, by the state governments. The Constitution, when thus adopted, was of complete obligation, and bound the state sovereignties.

It has been said, that the people had already surrendered all their powers to the state sovereignties, and had nothing more to give. But surely the question whether they may resume and modify the powers granted to government does not remain to be settled in this country. Much more might the legitimacy of the general government be doubted, had it been created by the states. The powers delegated to the state sovereignties were to be exercised by themselves, not by a distinct and independent sovereignty, created by themselves. To the formation of a league such as was the confederation, the state sovereignties were certainly competent. But when "in order to form a more perfect union," it was deemed necessary to change this alliance into an effective government, possessing great and sovereign power and acting directly on the people, the necessity of referring it to the people, and of deriving its powers directly from them, was felt and acknowledged by all.

The government of the Union, then, whatever may be the influence of this fact on the case, is, emphatically and truly, a government of the people. In form and in substance it emanates from them. Its powers are granted by them, and are to be exercised directly on them, and for their benefit.

This government is acknowledged by all to be one of enumerated powers. The principle that it can exercise only the powers granted to it, would seem too apparent to have required to be enforced by all those arguments which its enlightened friends, while it was depending before the people, found it necessary to urge. That principle is now universally admitted. But the question respecting the extent of the powers actually granted, is perpetually arising, and will probably continue to arise as long as our system shall exist.

In discussing these questions, the conflicting powers of the general and state governments must be brought into view, and the supremacy of their respective laws, when they are in opposition, must be settled.

If any one proposition could command the universal assent of mankind, we might expect it would be this—that the government of the Union, though limited in its powers, is supreme within its sphere of action. This would seem to result necessarily from its nature. It is the government of all; its powers are delegated by all; it represents all, and acts for all. Though any one state may be willing to control its operations, no state is willing to allow others to control them. The nation, on those subjects on which it can act, must necessarily bind its component parts. But this question is not left to mere reason: the people have, in express terms, decided it, by saying, "this constitution, and the laws of the United States, which shall be made in pursuance thereof," "shall be the supreme law of the land," and by requiring that the members of the state legislatures, and the officers of the executive and judicial departments of the states shall take the oath of fidelity to it.

The government of the United States, then, though limited in its powers, is supreme; and its laws, when made in pursuance of the constitution, form the supreme law of the land, "any thing in the constitution or laws of any state to the contrary notwithstanding."

Among the enumerated powers, we do not find that of establishing a bank or creating a corporation. But there is no phrase in the instrument which, like the articles of confederation, excludes incidental or implied powers; and requires that every thing granted shall be expressly and minutely described. Even the 10th amendment, which was framed for the purpose of quieting the excessive jealousies which had been excited, omits the word "expressly," and declares only that the powers "not delegated to the United States, nor prohibited to the states, are reserved to the states or to the people"; thus leaving the question, whether the particular power which may become the subject of contest has been delegated to the one government, or prohibited to the other, to depend on a fair construction of the whole instrument. The men who drew and adopted this amendment had experienced the embarrassments resulting from the insertion of this word in the articles of confederation, and probably omitted it to avoid those embarrassments. A constitution, to contain an accurate detail of all the subdivisions of which its great powers will admit, and of all the means by which they may be carried into execution, would partake of the prolixity of a legal code, and could scarcely be embraced by the human mind. It would probably never be understood by the public. Its nature, therefore, requires that only its great outlines should be marked, its important objects designated, and the minor ingredients which compose those objects be deduced from the nature of the objects themselves. That this idea was entertained by the framers of the American constitution, is not only to be inferred from the nature of the instrument, but from the language. Why else were some of the limitations, found in the ninth section of the 1st article, introduced? It is also, in some degree, warranted by their having omitted to use any restrictive term which might prevent its receiving a fair and just interpretation. In considering this question, then, we must never forget that it is *a constitution* we are expounding.

Although, among the enumerated powers of government, we do not find the word "bank" or "corporation," we find the great powers to lay and collect taxes, to borrow money, to regulate commerce, to declare and conduct a war, and to raise and support armies and navies. The sword and the purse, all the external relations, and no inconsiderable portion of the industry of the nation, are entrusted to its government. It can never be pretended that these vast powers draw after them others of inferior importance, merely because they are inferior. Such an idea can never be advanced. But it may with great reason be contended, that a government, entrusted with such ample powers, on the due execution of which the happiness and prosperity of the nation so vitally depends, must also be entrusted with ample means for their execution. The power being given, it is the interest of the nation to facilitate its execution. It can never be their interest, and cannot be presumed to have been their intention, to clog and embarrass its execution by withholding the most appropriate means. Throughout this vast republic, from the St. Croix to the Gulph of Mexico, from the Atlantic to the Pacific, revenue is to be collected and expended, armies are to be marched and supported. The exigencies of the nation may require that the treasure raised in the north should be transported to the south, *that* raised in the east conveyed to the west, or that this order should be reversed. Is that construction of the constitution to be preferred which would render these operations difficult, hazardous, and expensive? Can we adopt that construction, unless the words imperiously require it, which would impute to the framers of that instrument, when granting these powers for the public good, the intention of impeding their exercise by withholding a choice of means? If, indeed such be the mandate of the constitution, we have only to obey; but that instrument does not profess to enumerate the means by which the powers it confers may be executed, nor does it prohibit the creation of a corporation, if the existence of such a being be essential to the beneficial exercise of those powers. It is, then, the subject of fair enquiry, how far such means may be employed.

It is not denied, that the powers given to the government imply the ordinary means of execution. That, for example, of raising revenue and applying it to national purposes, is admitted to imply the power of conveying money from place to place, as the exigencies of the nation may require, and of employing the usual means of conveyance. But it is denied that the government has its choice of means; or that it may employ the most convenient means, if, to employ them, it be necessary to erect a corporation.

On what foundation does this argument rest? On this alone: The power of creating a corporation is one appertaining to sovereignty, and is not expressly conferred on Congress. This is true. But all legislative powers appertain to sovereignty. The original power of giving the law on any subject whatever, is a sovereign power; and if the government of the Union is restrained from creating a corporation as a means for performing its functions, on the single reason, that the creation of a corporation is an act of sovereignty; if the sufficiency of this reason be acknowledged, there would be some difficulty in sustaining the authority of Congress to pass other laws for the accomplishment of the same objects.

The government which has a right to do an act, and has imposed on it the duty of performing that act, must, according to the dictates of reason, be allowed to select the means; and those who contend that it may not select any appropriate means, that one particular mode of effecting the subject is excepted, take upon themselves the burden of establishing that exception.

The creation of a corporation, it is said, appertains to sovereignty. This is admitted. But to what portion of sovereignty does it appertain? Does it belong to one more than to another? In America, the powers of sovereignty are divided between the government of the Union and those of the states. They are each sovereign, with respect to the objects committed to it, and neither sovereign with respect to the objects committed to the other. We cannot comprehend that train of reasoning which would maintain that the extent of power granted by the people is to be ascertained, not by the nature and terms of the grant, but by its date. Some state constitutions were formed before, some since that of the United States. We cannot believe that their relation to each other is in any degree dependent upon this circumstance. Their respective powers must, we think, be precisely the same as if they had been formed at the same time. Had they been formed at the same time, and had the people conferred on the general government the power contained in the constitution, and on the states the whole residuum of power, would it have been asserted that the government of the

Union was not sovereign with respect to those objects which were entrusted to it, in relation to which its laws were declared to be supreme? If this could not have been asserted, we cannot well comprehend the process of reasoning which maintains, that a power appertaining to sovereignty cannot be connected with that vast portion of it which is granted to the general government, so far as it is calculated to subserve the legitimate objects of that government. The power of creating a corporation, though appertaining to sovereignty, is not, like the power of making war, of levying taxes, or of regulating commerce, a great substantive and independent power, which cannot be implied as incidental to other powers, or used as a means of executing them. It is never the end for which other powers are exercised, but a means by which other objects are accomplished. No contributions are made to charity for the sake of an incorporation, but a corporation is created to administer the charity; no seminary of learning is instituted in order to be incorporated, but the corporate character is conferred to subserve the purposes of education. No city was ever built with the sole object of being incorporated, but is incorporated as affording the best means of being well governed. The power of creating a corporation is never used for its own sake, but for the purpose of effecting something else. No sufficient reason is, therefore, perceived why it may not pass as incidental to those powers which are expressly given, if it be a direct mode of executing them.

But the constitution of the United States has not left the right of Congress to employ the necessary means for the execution of the powers conferred on the government, to general reasoning. To its enumeration of powers is added that of making "all laws which shall be necessary and proper for carrying into execution the foregoing powers, and all other powers vested by this constitution, in the government of the United States, or in any department thereof."

The Counsel of the State of Maryland have urged various arguments, to prove that this clause, though in terms a grant of power, is not so in effect; but is, really, restrictive of the general right, which might otherwise be implied, of selecting means for executing the enumerated powers.

They have found it necessary to contend that this clause was inserted for the purpose of conferring on Congress the power of making laws. That, without it, doubts might be entertained, whether Congress could exercise its powers in the form of legislation.

But could this be the object for which it was inserted? A government is created by the people, having legislative, executive, and judicial powers. Its legislative powers are vested in a Congress, which is to consist of a Senate and House of Representatives. Each House may determine the rules of its proceedings; and it is declared that every bill which shall have passed both houses, shall, before it become a law, be presented to the President of the United States. The 7th section describes the course of proceedings, by which a bill shall become a law, and, then, the 8th section enumerates the powers of Congress. Could it be necessary to say, that a legislature should exercise legislative powers, in the shape of legislation? After allowing each house to prescribe its own course of proceeding, after describing the manner in which a bill should become a law, would it have entered into the mind of a single member of the convention, that an express power to make laws was necessary, to enable the legislature to make them? That a legislature, endowed with legislative powers, can legislate, is a proposition too self-evident to have been questioned.

But the argument on which most reliance is placed, is drawn from the peculiar language of this clause. Congress is not empowered by it to make all laws which may have relation to the powers conferred on the government, but such only as may be "*necessary and proper*" for carrying them into execution. The word "*necessary*" is considered as controlling the whole sentence, and as limiting the right to pass laws for the execution of the granted powers, to such as are indispensable, and without which the power would be nugatory. That it excludes the choice of means, and leaves to Congress, in each case, that only which is most direct and simple.

Is it true, that this is the sense in which the word "necessary" is always used? Does it always import an absolute physical necessity, so strong, that one thing, to which another may be termed necessary, cannot exist without that other? We think it does not. If reference be had to its use, in the common affairs of the world, or in approved authors, we find that it frequently imports no more than that one thing is convenient, or useful, or essential to another. To employ the means necessary to an end, is generally understood as employing any means calculated to produce the end, and not as being confined to those single means, without which the end would be entirely unattainable. Such is the character of human language, that no word conveys to the mind, in all situations, one single definite idea; and nothing is more common than to use words in a figurative sense. Almost all compositions contain words, which, taken in their rigorous sense, would convey a meaning different from that which is obviously intended. It is essential to just construction that many words which import something excessive, should be understood in a more mitigated sense—in that sense which common usage justifies. The word 'necessary' is of this description. It has not a fixed character peculiar to itself. It admits of all degrees of comparison, and is often connected with other words which increase or diminish the impression the mind receives of the urgency it imports. A thing may be necessary, very necessary, absolutely or indispensably necessary. To no mind would the same idea be conveyed by these several phrazes. This comment on the word is well illustrated by the passage cited at the bar, from the 10th section of the 1st article of the constitution. It is, we think, impossible to compare the sentence which prohibits a state from laying "imposts, or duties on imports or exports, except what may be *absolutely* necessary for executing its inspection laws," with that which authorises Congress "to make all laws which shall be necessary and proper for carrying into execution" the powers of the general government, without feeling a conviction that the convention understood itself to change materially the meaning of the word "necessary" by prefixing the word "absolutely." This word, then, like others, is used in various senses, and, in its construction, the subject, the context, the intention of the person using them, are all to be taken into view.

Let this be done in the case under consideration. The subject is the execution of those great powers, on which the welfare of a nation essentially depends. It must have been the intention of those who gave these powers, to ensure, as far as human prudence could ensure, their beneficial execution. This could not be done by confiding the choice of means to such narrow limits as not to leave it in the power of Congress to adopt any which might be appropriate, & which were conducive to the end. This provision is made in a constitution intended to endure for ages to come, and, consequently, to be adapted to the various *crises* of human affairs. To have prescribed the means by which government should, in all future time, execute its powers, would have been to change, entirely, the character of the instrument, and give it the properties of a legal code. It would have been an unwise attempt to provide, by immutable rules, for exigencies which, if foreseen at all, must have been seen dimly, and which can be best provided for as they occur. To have declared that the best means shall not be used, but those alone without which the power given would be nugatory, would have been to deprive the legislature of the capacity to avail itself of experience, to exercise its reason, and to accommodate its legislation to circumstances. If we apply this principle of construction to any of the powers of the government, we shall find it so pernicious in its operation that we shall be compelled to discard it. The powers vested in Congress may certainly be carried into execution, without prescribing an oath of office. The power to exact this security for the faithful performance of duty, is not given, nor is it indispensably necessary. The different departments may be established, taxes may be imposed and collected, armies and navies may be raised and maintained, and money may be borrowed, without requiring an oath of office. It might be argued, with as much plausibility as other incidental powers have been assailed, that the convention was not unmindful of this subject. The oath which might be exacted—that of fidelity to the constitution, is prescribed, and no other can be required. Yet, he would be charged with insanity who should contend, that the legislature might not superadd, to the oath directed by the constitution, such other oath of office as its wisdom might suggest.

So, with respect to the whole penal code of the United States; whence arises the power to punish in cases not prescribed by the constitution? All admit that the government may, legitimately, punish any violation of its laws; and yet, this is not among the enumerated powers of Congress. The right to enforce the observance of law, by punishing its infraction, might be denied with the more plausibility, because it is expressly given in some cases.

Congress is empowered "to provide for the punishment of counterfeiting the securities and current coin of the United States," and "to define and punish piracies and felonies committed on the high seas, and offences against the laws of nations." The several powers of Congress may exist, in a very imperfect state to be sure, but they may exist, and be carried into execution, although no punishment should be inflicted in cases where the right to punish is not expressly given.

Take, for example, the power "to establish post offices and post roads." This power is executed by the single act of making the establishment. But, from this has been inferred the power and duty of carrying the mail, along the post road, from one post office to another. And, from this implied power, has again been inferred the right to punish those who steal letters from the post office, or rob the mail. It may be said, with some plausibility, that the right to carry the mail, and to punish those who rob it, is not indispensably necessary to the establishment of a post office and post road. This right is indeed essential to the beneficial exercise of the power, but not indispensably necessary to its existence. So, in the punishment of the crimes of stealing or falsifying a record or process of a court of the United States, or of perjury in such court. To punish these offences is certainly conducive to the due administration of justice. But courts may exist, and may decide the causes brought before them, though such crimes escape punishment.

The baneful influence of this narrow construction on all the operations of the government, and the absolute impracticability of maintaining it without rendering the government incompetent to its great objects, might be illustrated by numerous examples drawn from the constitution and from our laws. The good sense of the public has pronounced, without hesitation, that the power of punishment appertains to sovereignty, and may be exercised whenever the sovereign has a right to act, as incidental to his constitutional powers. It is a means for carrying into execution all sovereign powers, and may be used, although not indispensably necessary. It is a right incidental to the powers, and conducive to its beneficial exercise.

If this limited construction of the word "necessary" must be abandoned in order to punish, whence is derived the rule which would reinstate it, when the government would carry its powers into execution by means not vindictive in their nature? If the word "necessary" means "needful," "requisite," "essential," "conducive to," in order to let in the power of punishment for the infraction of law, why is it not equally comprehensive when required to authorise the use of means which facilitate the execution of the powers of government without the infliction of punishment?

In ascertaining the sense in which the word "necessary" is used in this clause of the constitution, we may derive some aid from that with which it is associated. Congress shall have power "to make all laws which shall be necessary and *proper* to carry into execution" the powers of the government. If the word "necessary" was used in that strict and rigorous sense for which the counsel for the State of Maryland contend, it would be an extraordinary departure from the usual course of the human mind, as exhibited in composition, to add a word, the only possible effect of which is to qualify that strict and rigorous meaning; to present to the mind the idea of some choice of means of legislation not straightened and compressed within the narrow limits for which gentlemen contend.

But the argument which most conclusively demonstrates the error of the construction contended for by the Counsel of Maryland, is founded on the intention of the convention, as manifested in the whole clause. To waste time and argument in proving that, without it, Congress might carry its powers into execution, would be not much less idle than to hold a lighted taper to the sun. As little can it be required to prove that, in the absence of this clause, Congress would have some choice of means. That it might employ those which in its judgment, would most advantageously effect the object to be accomplished. That any means adapted to the end, any means which tended directly to the execution of the constitutional powers of the government, were in themselves constitutional. This clause, as construed by the State of Maryland, would abridge and almost annihilate this useful and necessary right of the Legislature to select its means. That this could not be intended is, we should think, had it not been already controverted, too apparent for controversy. We think so for the following reasons.

1. The clause is placed among the powers of Congress, not among the limitations in those powers.

2nd. Its terms purport to enlarge, not to diminish the powers vested in the government, it purports to be an additional power, not a restriction on those already granted. No reason has been or can be assigned for thus concealing an intention to narrow the discretion of the national legislature under words which purport to enlarge it. The framers of the constitution wished its adoption, and well knew that it would be endangered by its strength, not by its weakness. Had they been capable of using language which would convey to the eye one idea, and, after deep reflection, impress on the mind another, they would rather have disguised the grant of power, than its limitation. If then their intention had been, by this clause, to restrain the free use of means which might otherwise have been implied, that intention would have been inserted in another place, and would have been expressed in terms resembling these. "In carrying into execution the foregoing powers and all others," &c. "no laws shall be passed but such as are necessary and proper." Had the intention been to make this clause restrictive, it would unquestionably have been so in form as well as in effect.

The result of the most careful and attentive consideration bestowed upon this clause is that, if it does not enlarge, it cannot be construed to restrain the powers of Congress, or to impair the right of the legislature to exercise its best judgment in the selection of measures to carry into execution the constitutional powers of the government. If no other motive for its insertion can be suggested, a sufficient one is found in the desire to remove all doubts respecting the right to legislate on that vast mass of incidental power which must be involved in the constitution, if that instrument be not a splendid bauble.

We admit, as all must admit, that the powers of the government are limited, and that its limits are not to be transcended. But we think the sound construction of the constitution must allow to the national legislature that discretion, with respect to the means by which the powers it confers are to be carried into execution, which will enable that body to perform the high duties assigned to it, in the manner most beneficial to the people. Let the end be legitimate, let it be within the scope of the constitution, and all means which are appropriate, which are plainly adapted to that end, which are not prohibited, but consist with the letter and spirit of the constitution, are constitutional.

That a corporation must be considered as a means not less usual, not of higher dignity, not more requiring a particular specification than other means, has been sufficiently proved. If we look to the origin of corporations, to the manner in which they have been framed in that government from which we have derived most of our legal principles and ideas, or to the uses to which they have been applied, we find no reason to suppose that a constitution, omitting, and wisely omitting, to enumerate all the means for carrying into execution the great powers vested in government, ought to have specified this. Had it been intended to grant this power as one which should be distinct and independent, to be exercised in any case whatever, it would have found a place among the enumerated powers of the government. But being considered merely as a means, to be employed only for the purpose of carrying into execution the given powers, there could be no motive for particularly mentioning it.

The propriety of this remark would seem to be generally acknowledged by the universal acquiescence in the construction which has been uniformly put on the 3rd sec. of the 4th article of the constitution. The power to "make all needful rules and regulations respecting the territory or other property belonging to the United States" is not more comprehensive, than the power "to make all laws which shall be necessary and proper for carrying into execution" the powers of the government. Yet all admit the constitutionality of a territorial government, which is a corporate body.

If a corporation may be employed indiscriminately with other means to carry into execution the powers of the government, no particular reason can be assigned for excluding the use of a bank if required for its fiscal operations. To use one, must be within the discretion of Congress, if it be an appropriate mode of executing the powers of government. That it is a convenient, a useful, and essential instrument in the prosecution of its fiscal operations, is not now a subject of controversy. All those who have been concerned in the administration of our finances, have concurred in representing its importance and necessity; and so strongly have they been felt, that statesmen of the first class, whose previous opinions against it had been confirmed by every circumstance which can fix the human judgment, have yielded those opinions to the exigencies of the nation. Under the confederation, Congress, justifying the measure by its necessity, transcended perhaps its powers to obtain the advantage of a bank; and our own legislation attests the universal conviction of the utility of this measure. The time has passed away when it can be necessary to enter into any discussion in order to prove the importance of this instrument as a means to effect the legitimate objects of the government.

But were its necessity less apparent, none can deny its being an appropriate measure; and if it is, the degree of its necessity, as has been very justly observed, is to be discussed in another place. Should Congress, in the execution of its powers, adopt measures which are prohibited by the constitution; or should Congress under the pretext of executing its powers, pass laws for the accomplishment of objects not entrusted to the government; it would become the painful duty of this tribunal, should a case requiring such a decision come before it, to say that such an act was not the law of the land. But where the law is not prohibited, and is really calculated to effect any of the objects entrusted to the government, to undertake here to enquire into the degree of its necessity, would be to pass the line which circumscribes the judicial department, and to tread on legislative ground. This court disclaims all pretensions to such a power.

After this declaration it can scarcely be necessary to say that the existence of state banks can have no possible influence on the question. No trace is to be found in the constitution of an intention to create a dependence of the government of the union on those of the states, for the execution of the great powers assigned to it. Its means are adequate to its ends; and on those means alone was it expected to rely for the accomplishment of its ends. To impose on it the necessity of resorting to means which it cannot controul, which another government may furnish or, withold, would render its course precarious, the result of its measures uncertain, and create a dependence on other governments which might disappoint its most important designs, and is incompatible with the language of that constitution. But were it otherwise, the choice of means implies a right to choose a national bank in preference to state banks, and Congress alone can make the election.

After the most deliberate consideration it is the unanimous and decided opinion of this court that the act to incorporate the Bank of the United States, is a law made in pursuance of the constitution, and is a part of the supreme law of the land.

The branches proceeding from the same stock, and being conducive to the complete accomplishment of the object, are equally constitutional. It would have been unwise to locate them in the charter, and it would be unnecessarily inconvenient to employ the legislative power in making those subordinate arrangements. The great duties of the bank are prescribed; those duties require branches: and the bank itself may, we think, be safely trusted with the selection of places where those branches shall be fixed; reserving always to the government the right to require that a branch shall be located where it may be deemed necessary. It being the opinion of the court that the act incorporating the bank is constitutional; and that the power of establishing a branch in the State of Maryland might be properly exercised by the bank itself we proceed to enquire.

2. Whether the State of Maryland may, without violating the constitution, tax that branch?

That the power of taxation is one of vital importance; that it is retained by the states; that it is not abridged by the grant of a similar power to the government of the union; that it is to be concurrently exercised by the two governments; are truths which have never been denied. But, such is the paramount character of the constitution, that its capacity to withdraw any subject from the action of even this power, is admitted. The states are expressly forbidden to lay any duties on imports or exports, except what may be absolutely necessary for executing their inspection laws. If the obligation of this prohibition must be conceded—if it may restrain a state from the exercise of its taxing power on imports and exports, the same paramount character would seem to restrain, as it certainly may restrain, a state from such other exercise of this power as is in its nature incompatible with, and repugnant to the constitutional laws of the Union. A law absolutely repugnant to another as entirely repeals that other, as if express terms of repeal were used.

On this ground the counsel for the bank place its claim to be exempted from the power of a state to tax its operations. There is no express provision for the case, but the claim has been sustained on a principle which so entirely pervades the constitution, is so intermixed with the materials which compose it, so interwoven with its web, so blended with its texture, as to be incapable of being separated from it, without rending it into shreds.

This great principle is, that the constitution and the laws made in pursuance thereof, are supreme; that they control the constitution and laws of the respective states, and cannot be controlled by them. From this, which may be almost termed an axiom, other propositions are deduced as corrollaries, on the truth or error of which, and on their application to this case, the cause has been supposed to depend. These are—1st. that a power to create implies a power to preserve. 2nd. that a power to destroy, if wielded by a different hand, is hostile to, and incompatible with these powers to create and to preserve. 3d. that where the repugnancy exists, that authority which is supreme must control, not yield to that over which it is supreme.

These propositions, as abstract truths, would, perhaps, never be controverted. Their application to this case, however, has been denied; and, both in maintaining the affirmative and the negative, a splendor of eloquence, and strength of argument, seldom, if ever, surpassed, have been displayed.

The power of Congress to create, and of course to continue, the bank, was the subject of the preceding part of this opinion, and is no longer to be considered as questionable.

That the power of taxing it by the States may be exercised so as to destroy it, is too obvious to be denied. But taxation is said to be an absolute power which acknowledges no other limits than those expressly prescribed in the constitution, and like sovereign power of every other description, is trusted to the discretion of those who use it. But the very terms of this argument admit that the sovereignty of the state, in the article of taxation itself, is subordinate to, and may be controlled by, the constitution of the United States. How far it has been controlled by that instrument must be a question of construction. In making this construction, no principle not declared, can be admissable, which would defeat the legitimate operations of a supreme government. It is of the very essence of supremacy to remove all obstacles to its action within its own sphere, and so to modify every power vested in subordinate governments, as to exempt its own operations from their own influence. This effect need not be stated in terms. It is so involved in the declaration of supremacy, so necessarily implied in it, that the expression of it could not make it more certain. We must, therefore, keep it in view while construing the constitution.

The argument on the part of the State of Maryland is not that the states may directly resist a law of Congress, but that they may exercise their acknowledged powers upon it, and that the constitution leaves them this right in the confidence that they will not abuse it.

Before we proceed to examine this argument, and to subject it to the test of the constitution, we must be permitted to bestow a few considerations on the nature and extent of this original right of taxation, which is acknowledged to remain with the states. It is admitted that the power of taxing the people and their property is essential to the very existence of government, and may be legitimately exercised on the objects to which it is applicable, to the utmost extent to which the government may chuse to carry it. The only security against the abuse of this power, is found in the structure of the government itself. In imposing a tax the legislature acts upon itself and upon its constituents. This is in general a sufficient security against erroneous and oppressive taxation.

The people of a state, therefore, give to their government a right of taxing themselves and their property, and as the exigencies of government cannot be limited, they prescribe no limits to the exercise of this right, resting confidently on the interest of the legislator, and on the influence of the constituents over their representative, to guard them against its abuse. But the means employed by the government of the union have no such security, nor is the right of a state to tax them sustained by the same theory. Those means are not given by the people of a particular state, not given by the constituents of the legislature which claim the right to tax them, but by the people of all the states. They are given by all, for the benefit of all—and upon theory, should be subjected to that government only which belongs to all.

It may be objected to this definition that the power of taxation is not confined to the people and property of a state. It may be exercised upon every object brought within its jurisdiction.

This is true. But to what source do we trace this right? It is obvious that it is an incident of sovereignty, and is co-extensive with that to which it is an incident. All subjects over which the sovereign power of a state extends are objects of taxation; but those over which it does not extend, are, upon the soundest principles, exempt from taxation. This proposition may almost be pronounced self-evident.

The sovereignty of a state extends to every thing which exists by its own authority, or is introduced by its permission, but does it extend to those means which are employed by Congress to carry into execution powers conferred on that body by the people of the U. States? We think it demonstrable that it does not. Those powers are not given by the people of a single state. They are given by the people of the United States to a government whose laws made in pursuance of the constitution are declared to be supreme—consequently, the people of a single state cannot confer a sovereignty which will extend over them.

If we measure the power of taxation residing in a state, by the extent of sovereignty which the people of a single state possess, and can confer on its government, we have an intelligible standard applicable to every case to which the power may be applied. We have a principle which leaves the power of taxing the people and property of a state unimpaired: which leaves to a state the command of all its resources: and which places beyond its reach, all those powers which are conferred by the people of the United States on the government of the Union, and all those means which are given for the purpose of carrying those powers into execution. We have a principle which is safe for the states, and safe for the Union. We are relieved, as we ought to be, from clashing sovereignty, from interfering powers: from a repugnancy between a right in one government to pull down, what there is an acknowledged right in another to build up; from the incompatibility of a right in one government to destroy what there is a right in another to preserve. We are not driven to the perplexing enquiry, so unfit for the judicial department, what degree of taxation is the legitimate use, and what degree may amount to the abuse, of the power. The attempt to use it on the means employed by the governments of the Union, in pursuance of the Constitution, is itself an abuse, because it is the usurpation of a power which the people of a single state cannot give.

We find then, on just theory, a total failure of this original right to tax the means employed by the government of the Union for the execution of its powers. The right never existed, and the question whether it has been surrendered, cannot arise.

But, waving this theory for the present, let us resume the enquiry whether this power can be exercised by the respective states, consistently with a fair construction of the constitution?

That the power to tax involves the power to destroy; that the power to destroy may defeat and render useless the power to create; that there is a plain repugnance in conferring on one government a power to controul the constitutional measures of another, which other, with respect to those very measures, is declared to be supreme over that which exerts the controul, are propositions not to be denied. But all inconsistencies are to be reconciled by the magic word *confidence*. Taxation, it is said, does not necessarily and unavoidably destroy. To carry it to the excess of destruction, would be an abuse, to presume which would banish that confidence which is essential to all government. But is this a case of confidence? Would the people of any one state trust those of another with a power to controul the most insignificant operations of their state government? We know they would not. Why then should we suppose that the people of any one state should be willing to trust those of another with a power to controul the operations of a government to which they have confided their most important and most valuable interests? In the Legislature of the Union alone, are all represented. The Legislature of the Union alone, therefore, can be trusted by the people with the power of controuling measures which concern all, in the confidence that it will not be abused. This, then, is not a case of confidence, and we must consider it as it really is.

If we apply the principle for which the state of Maryland contends, to the constitution generally, we shall find it capable of changing totally the character of that instrument. We shall find it capable of arresting all the measures of the government, and of prostrating it at the foot of the states. The American people have declared their Constitution, and the laws made in pursuance thereof, to be supreme; but this principle would transfer the supremacy in fact to the states.

If the states may tax one instrument employed by the government in the execution of its powers, they may tax any and every other instrument. They may tax the mail, they may tax the mint, they may tax patent rights, they may tax the papers of the custom house, they may tax judicial process, they may tax all the means employed by the government, to an excess which would defeat all the ends of government. This was not intended by the American people. They did not design to make their government dependent on the states.

Gentlemen say, they do not claim the right to extend state taxations to these objects. They limit their pretentions to property. But on what principle is this distinction made? Those who make it have furnished no reason for it, and the principle for which they contend denies it. They contend that the power of taxation has no other limit than is found in the 10th section of the 1st article of the constitution; that, with respect to every thing else, the power of the state is supreme, and admits of no control. If this be true, the distinction between property and other subjects to which the power of taxation is applicable, is merely arbitrary, and can never be sustained. This is not all. If the controling power of the states be established, if their supremacy as to taxation be acknowledged, what is to restrain their exercising this control in any shape they may please to give it? Their sovereignty is not confined to taxation. That is not the only mode in which it might be displayed. The question is, in truth, a question of supremacy; and if the right of the states to tax the means employed by the general government be conceded, the declaration that the constitution, and the laws made in pursuance thereof, shall be the supreme law of the land, is empty and unmeaning declamation.

In the course of the argument, the Federalist has been quoted; and the opinions expressed by the authors of that work have been justly supposed to be entitled to great respect in expounding the constitution. No tribute can be paid to their worth which exceeds their merit; but in applying their opinions to the cases which may arise in the progress of our government, a right to judge of their correctness must be retained; and, to understand the argument, we must examine the proposition it maintains and the objections against which it is directed. The subject of those numbers, from which passages have been cited, is the unlimited power of taxation which is vested in the general government.

The objection to this unlimited power, which the argument seeks to remove, is stated with fullness and clearness. It is, "that an indefinite power of taxation in the latter (the government of the Union) might, and probably would, in time, deprive the former (the government of the states) of the means of providing for their own necessities; and would subject them entirely to the mercy of the national legislature. As the laws of the Union are to become the supreme laws of the land; as it is to have power to pass all laws that may be necessary for carrying into execution the authorities with which it is proposed to vest it; the national government might at any time abolish the taxes imposed for state objects, upon the pretence of an interference with its own. It might allege a necessity for doing this, in order to give efficacy to the national revenues; and thus all the resources of taxation might, by degrees, become the subjects of federal monopoly, to the entire exclusion and destruction of the state governments."

The objections to the constitution which are noticed in these numbers, were to the undefined power of the government to tax, not to the incidental privilege of exempting its own measures from state taxation. The consequences apprehended from this undefined power, were: that it would absorb all the objects of taxation, "to the exclusion and destruction of the state governments." The arguments of the Federalist are intended to prove the fallacy of these apprehensions; not to prove that the government was incapable of executing any of its powers, without exposing the means it employed to the embarrassments of state taxation.

Arguments urged against these objections, and these apprehensions, are to be understood as relating to the points they mean to prove. Had the authors of those excellent essays been asked, whether they contended for that construction of the constitution, which would place within the reach of the states those measures which the government might adopt for the execution of its powers; no man, who has read their instructive pages, will hesitate to admit, that their answer must have been in the negative.

It has also been insisted, that, as the power of taxation in the general and state governments is acknowledged to be concurrent, every argument which would sustain the right of the general government to tax banks chartered by states, will equally sustain the right of the states to tax banks chartered by the general government.

But the two cases are not on the same reason. The people of all the States have created the general government; and have conferred upon it the general power of taxation. The people of all the States, and the States themselves, are represented in Congress, and by their Representatives exercise this power. When they tax the chartered institutions of the States, they tax their constituents; and these taxes must be uniform. But, when a state taxes the operations of the government of the United States, it acts upon institutions created, not by their own constituents, but by people, over whom they claim no control. It acts upon the measures of a government created by others, as well as themselves, for the benefit of others in common with themselves. The difference is that which always exists, and always must exist, between the action of the whole, or a part, and the action of a part and the whole—between the laws of a government declared to be supreme, and those of a government which, when in opposition to those laws, is not supreme.

But if the full application of this argument could be admitted, it might bring into question the right of Congress to tax the State Banks, and could not prove the right of the States to tax the Bank of the United States.

The court has bestowed on this subject its most deliberate

consideration. The result is a conviction that the States have no power, by taxation, or otherwise, to retard, impede, burden, or in any manner control the operations of the constitutional laws enacted by Congress to carry into execution the powers vested in the general government. This is, we think, the unavoidable consequence of that supremacy, which the Constitution has declared.

We are unanimously of opinion, that the law passed by the Legislature of Maryland, imposing a tax on the Bank of the United States, is unconstitutional, and void.

This opinion does not deprive the states of any resources which they originally possessed. It does not extend to a tax paid by the real property of the bank, in common with the other real property within the state, nor to a tax imposed on the interest which the citizens of Maryland may hold in this institution, in common with other property of the same description throughout the state. But this is a tax on the operations of the bank, and is consequently a tax on the operation of an instrument employed by the government of the Union, to carry its powers into execution. Such a tax must be unconstitutional.

The judgment of the court of appeals of the state of Maryland, is therefore erroneous, and must be reversed; and a mandate be issued to that court, directing a judgment to be entered for the plaintiff in error.

March 6, 1819

"OUR HERETICAL REASONING"

To Bushrod Washington

My dear Sir   Richmond March 27th.

I have a nephew a son of Major Taylor who is at school in Kentucky under the direction of my brother Doctor Marshall. He has written to me for some books which I cannot procure here, & which if I had them could not without much difficulty be conveyed from this place. I take the liberty to ask the favor of you to purchase them for me in Philadelphia & leave them with the bookseller packed up to be delivered to the order of

Doctor Marshall. The books I wish to purchase are Terence & Livy in latin, Longinus Thucydides & Demosthenes in Greek, also Xenophons retreat of the 10,000.

Be so good as to send the booksellers receipt for the money as it is to be inserted in an executors account. Should the inclosed be insufficient I will immediately remit the residue. I will thank you also to pay Delaplaine four dollars for me & take his receipt for that sum for the last half volume, I beleive it is the third.

Great dissatisfaction has been given to the politicians of Virginia by our opinion on the bank question. They have no objection to a decision in favor of the bank, since the good patriots who administer the government wished it, & would probably have been seriously offended with us had we dared to have decided otherwise, but they required an obsequious, silent opinion without reasons. That would have been satisfactory, but our heretical reasoning is pronounced most damnable. We shall be denounced bitterly in the papers & as not a word will be said on the other side we shall undoubtedly be condemned as a pack of consolidating aristocratics. The legislature & executive who have enacted the law but who have power & places to bestow will escape with impunity, while the poor court who have nothing to give & of whom nobody is afraid, bears all the obloquy of the measure.

We are in great distress here for money. Many of our merchants stop—a thing which was long unknown & was totally unexpected in Richmond. Farewell, I am dear Sir your

1819

A Friend to the Union No. I

MR. EDITOR,

My attention has been a good deal attracted by some essays which have appeared lately in one of the Virginia papers which seem to have for their object the infliction of deep wounds on the constitution through a misrepresentation of the opinion lately delivered by the Supreme Court on the constitutionality of the act incorporating the bank of the United States. I have bestowed a few leisure moments on the refutation of some of the mischievous errours contained in these essays; and, if you think what I have written worth publishing you will give this answer to Amphyction a place in your useful paper.

A spirit which was supposed to have been tranquillized by a long possession of the government, appears to be resuming its original activity in Virginia. The decision of the Supreme Court in the case of McCullough against the state of Maryland has been seized as a fair occasion for once more agitating the publick mind, and reviving those unfounded jealousies by whose blind aid ambition climbs the ladder of power.

The bill for incorporating the bank of the United States had become a law, without exciting a single murmur. The reason is obvious. Those who fill the legislative and executive departments are elected by the people, and are of course popular. In addition, they possess great power and great patronage. Had they been unjustly attacked, champions would have arisen on every side, who would with equal zeal and ability have presented the truth to a publick not unwilling to perceive it. But the Judges of the Supreme Court, separated from the people by the tenure of office, by age, and by the nature of their duties, are viewed with respect, unmingled with affection, or interest. They possess neither power nor patronage. They have no sops to give; and every coffeehouse furnishes a Cerberus, hoping some reward for that watchfulness which his bark proclaims; and restrained by no apprehension that any can be stimulated by personal considerations to expose the injustice of his attacks. We ought not, therefore, to be surprised if it should be deemed criminal in the judicial department to sustain a measure, which was adopted by the legislature, and by the executive with impunity. Hostility to the Union, must cease to be guided by its usual skill, when it fails to select the weakest department as that through which a breach may be effected.

The Inquirer, the leading paper of Virginia, abounds with hostile attacks on this opinion. That which is written with most talent, most system, and most design, appears under the signature of Amphyction. The Editor assures his readers that it contains "a most satisfactory exposition" "of the alarming errours of the Supreme Court of the United States" in their interpretation of the constitution; and Amphyction himself does not leave his object to conjecture. "Most ardently" does he "hope that this decision of the Supreme Court will attract the attention of the state legislatures, and that Virginia will, as heretofore, do her duty."

The avowed object being of so serious a nature, it behoves not only the friends of the Bank, but the friends of the constitution, the friends of Union, to examine well the principles which are denounced as heretical, and those which are supported as orthodox.

The objections of Amphyction are to that part of the opinion which declares the act incorporating the bank to be constitutional. He introduces them with expressing his disapprobation of that mode of transacting their official duties which the Supreme Court has adopted. He would prefer *seriatim* opinions, to the combined opinion of the bench delivered by a single Judge.

On the justness of this criticism in general, or on its peculiar application to this particular case, I shall make no observation; because the principles expressed in this single opinion are neither more nor less vulnerable than they would have been if expressed in six separate opinions. But the criticism was made for the purpose of conveying an insinuation which marks the spirit in which the discussion is conducted. "We are not," says Amphyction, "informed whether the whole court united in the course of reasoning adopted by the Chief Justice, nor whether they all accorded in the various positions and principles he advanced."

Now I humbly conceive this is a subject on which we are informed. The opinion is delivered, not in the name of the chief justice, but in the name of the whole court. This observation applies to the "reasoning adopted," and "to the various positions and principles which were advanced" as entirely as to the conclusions drawn from "those positions and principles." Throughout the whole opinion, the chief justice never speaks in the singular number, or in his own person, but as the mere organ of the court. In the presence of all the judges, and in their names he advances certain propositions as their propositions, and certain reasoning as their reasoning. I appeal to Amphyction himself, I appeal to every man accustomed to judicial proceedings, to determine whether the judges of the Supreme Court, men of high & respectable character, would sit by in silence, while great constitutional principles of which they disapproved, were advanced in their name, and as their principles. I appeal to the usage of the Supreme Court itself. Their decisions are reported, and are in possession of the publick. It has often happened that a judge concurring in the opinion of the court, but on reasons peculiar to himself, has stated his own reasoning. The great case of the Nereid is one among many examples, of this course of proceeding. In some instances too it has occurred, that the judge delivering the opinion of the court has stated the contrariety of reasoning on which the opinion was formed. Of this, the case of Olivera v. the Union Ensurance Co. is an example. The course of every tribunal must necessarily be, that the opinion which is to be delivered as the opinion of the court, is previously submitted to the consideration of all the judges; and, if any part of the reasoning be disapproved, it must be so modified as to receive the approbation of all, before it can he delivered as the opinion of all. Amphyction himself thinks so; for he says: "We are driven, however reluctantly, to the conclusion that each judge approves of each argument and position advanced by the chief justice."

Why then has he suggested a contrary idea? He leaves us in no uncertainty for the answer to this question.

After stating that the subject is one "which has employed his (the chief justice's) thoughts, his tongue, and his pen, as a politician and as an historian for more than thirty years," he adds that it "is one which has, perhaps more than any other, heretofore drawn a broad line of distinction between the two great parties in this country, in which line no one has taken a more distinguished and decided rank than the judge who has thus expounded the supreme law of the land."

The chief justice then is a federalist; who was a politician of some note before he was a judge; and who with his tongue and his pen, supported the opinions he avowed. To expose the reasoning of the court to still greater odium, if it be possible, we are told that "the liberal and latitudinous construction" he has attached to a term in the constitution, had been "attached to it" before him, "by Mr. Secretary Hamilton." The reasoning, then, of the court is, dexterously enough, ascribed to Mr. Secretary Hamilton and the chief justice, two inveterate federalists. This question cannot be trusted, by Amphyction, to his exposition of the constitution, unless the spirit of party be introduced into the cause, and made its judge. How favourable this spirit is to truth, and to a fair exercise of the human judgement, Amphyction well knows. Had he admitted his opinion, including the reasoning, to be what it professes to be—what it must be—the opinion and reasoning of all the judges—four of whom have no political sin upon their heads—who in addition to being eminent lawyers, have the still greater advantage of being sound republicans; of having been selected certainly not for their federalism, by Mr. Jefferson, and Mr. Madison, for the high stations they so properly fill, his argument would have been stripped of one powerful recommendation, and must have depended rather more on its intrinsick merit. We need not then be surprised that this improbable suggestion is made, although a sense of propriety has compelled the writer to abandon it as soon as its effect was produced.

Having thus prepared his readers for the dangerous errours contained in the opinion of the Supreme Court, Amphyction proceeds to inform them what those errours are.

"The first is the denial that the powers of the federal government were delegated by the states; and the second is that the grant of powers to that government, and particularly the grant of powers *necessary and proper* to carry the other powers into effect, ought to be construed in a liberal rather than a restricted sense."

But before Amphyction can permit himself to enter on his first point, he deems it necessary to cast a little more odium on the opinion he is about to examine. "For what purpose" he asks, "did the federal court decide that question?" After stating that it was totally unnecessary, that the opinion on it "is obiter and extrajudicial"; he adds that "whether the powers of the federal government were delegated to it by the states in their sovereign capacity, or by the people, can make but little difference in the extent of those powers. In either case it is still true that the powers of that government are limited by the charter that called it into existence" &c.

I shall not controvert the proposition that the constitution ought to receive the same construction, whether its powers were delegated by the people or the states. That Amphyction entertains the same opinion, is brought into some doubt by the extreme importance he attaches to his theory.

If the powers of the general government were to be in no degree affected by the source from which they were derived, it is not easy to comprehend how the liberty of the American people can depend on the adoption of the one opinion or of the other. The origin of the government would seem to be a mere historical fact, which it would be desirable to settle correctly, but for the settlement of which it could scarcely be necessary to call on the legislatures of the respective states or to express so earnest a hope that "Virginia would, as usual, do her duty." If it be possible for Amphyction to persuade himself that the right of the state legislatures "to canvass" or "remonstrate against the publick measures of the Congress or of the President," depended on their having delegated to the general government all its powers, it would prove only with what facility the most intelligent mind may impose on itself, when pursuing a favourite and dominant idea. Surely nothing can be more obvious, nothing better established, than that the right to canvass the measures of government, or to remonstrate against the abuse of power, must reside in all who are affected by those measures, or over whom that power is exercised, whether it was delegated by them or not. Were this allegation of Amphyction true, it would follow that the people have no right to canvass the measures of government, or to remonstrate against them. The right to canvass and remonstrate resides, according to his argument, in those only who have delegated the powers of the government. Those powers were delegated, not by the people, but by the states in their sovereign capacity. It follows that the states in their sovereign capacity, not the people, have the right to canvass publick measures. If this conclusion be false, as it must be, the premises are false also; and that a man of Amphyction's intelligence should have advanced them, only proves that he is too little accustomed to political opposition, and is too confident of the prejudices he addresses, to be very attentive to the correctness of his positions, or to the accuracy of his reasoning.

But if Amphyction had not been more anxious to throw

obloquy on the court than to ascertain its justice, he might have spared this unnecessary charge of travelling out of the case for the purpose of delivering, extrajudicially, a doctrine so dangerous as he represents this to be. The principles he now maintains, appear to have been advanced, and relied on at the bar. "The counsel for the state of Maryland," we are told in the opinion, "have deemed it of some importance in the construction of the constitution to consider that instrument, not as emanating from the people; but, as the act of sovereign and independent states. The powers of the general government, it has been said, are delegated by the states who alone are truly sovereign, and must be exercised in subordination to the states, who alone possess supreme dominion." It is in consequence of this argument that the subject is introduced into the opinion.

His eagerness to censure must be much stronger than his sense of justice, who will criminate a court for noticing an argument advanced by eminent counsel, as one of leading importance in the cause.

But waving any further discussion of these incidental observations, I will proceed to consider the first objection made to the opinion of the Supreme Court. It is stated to be "the denial that the powers of the federal government were delegated by the states."

This assertion is not literally true. The court has not, in terms, denied "that the powers of the federal government were delegated by the states," but has asserted affirmatively that it "is emphatically and truly a government of the people," that it, "in form and in substance emanates from them."

If Amphyction chuses to construe the affirmative assertion made by the court into a negative assertion that "the powers of the government were not delegated by the states," I shall not contest the point with him unless he uses the word "states" in a different sense from that which great part of his argument imports. In what sense, let me ask, does he use the word? Does he mean the people inhabiting that territory which constitutes a state? Or does he mean the government of that territory? If the former, the controversy is at an end. He concurs with the opinion he arraigns. The Supreme Court cannot be mistaken. It has said, not indeed in the same words, but in substance precisely what he says. The powers of the government were delegated, according to that opinion, by the people assembled in convention in their respective states, and deciding, as all admit, for their respective states.

If Amphyction means to assert, as I suppose he does, that the powers of the general government were delegated by the state legislatures, then I say that his assertion is contradicted by the words of the constitution, and by the fact; and is not supported even by that report, on which he so confidently relies.

The words of an instrument, unless there be some sinister design which shuns the light, will always represent the intention of those who frame it. An instrument intended to be the act of the people, will purport to be the act of the people. An instrument intended to be the act of the states, will purport to be the act of the states. Let us then examine those words of the constitution, which designate the source whence its powers are derived. They are: "We the people of the United States, in order to form a more perfect union, &c. do ordain and establish this constitution for the United States of America."

The constitution then proceeds in the name of the people to define the powers of that government which they were about to create.

This language cannot be misunderstood. It cannot be construed to mean, "We the states, &c."

If still more complete demonstration on this point could be required, it will be furnished by a comparison of the words just recited from the constitution, with those used in the articles of confederation.

The confederation was intended to be the act of the states, and was drawn in language comporting with that intention. The style is: "Articles of confederation and perpetual union between the states of New Hampshire, Massachusetts Bay, &c." The 3d article is completely descriptive of the character of the instrument. It is in these words: "The said states hereby severally enter into a firm league of friendship with each other for their common defence, the security of their liberties, and their mutual and general welfare; binding themselves to assist each other against all force offered to, or attacks made upon them, or any of them, on account of religion, sovereignty, trade, or any other pretence whatever."

The confederation was a mere alliance offensive and defensive, and purports to be, what it was intended to be, the act of sovereign states. The constitution is a government acting on the people, and purports to be, what it was intended to be, the act of the people.

The fact itself is in perfect consonance with the language of the instrument. It was not intended to submit the constitution to the decision of the state legislatures, nor was it submitted to their decision. It was referred to conventions of the people "for their assent or ratification," whose decision thereon was not to be reported to the state legislatures but to Congress. Had the legislature of every state in the Union been hostile to the constitution, it would still have gone into operation, if assented to and ratified by the conventions of the people. With what propriety, then, can it be denied to be the act of the people?

On this part of the question also, a comparison with the mode of proceeding for the adoption of the constitution, which was the act of the people, with that observed in adopting the confederation, which was the act of the states, may not be altogether useless.

We have seen that the constitution was submitted to the people themselves, assembled in convention.

The confederation was submitted to the state legislatures, who adopted or rejected it; and who expressed their adoption by empowering their members in Congress, who were their ministers plenipotentiary, to subscribe it in their behalf.

I cannot be mistaken when I say that no political proposition was ever more fully demonstrated than that maintained by the Supreme Court of the United States, respecting the source from which the government of the Union derives its powers.

I will now show that the very report cited by Amphyction, admits the proposition contained in the opinion he reprobates.

Certain resolutions he informs us had been adopted by the legislature of Virginia in 1798, one of which contained the assertion that the assembly viewed "the powers of the federal government as resulting from the compact to which the states are parties." "Those resolutions" he says "having been disapproved of by most of the other state legislatures, became the subject of examination at the succeeding session, and produced that

remarkable commentary which has generally been known by
the name of Madison's report." The language of this commentary on this part of that resolution is; "It is indeed true that the
term 'states,' is sometimes used in a vague sense and sometimes in different senses, according to the subject to which it is
applied. Thus it sometimes means the separate sections of territory occupied by the political societies within each; sometimes the particular governments established by those societies;
sometimes those societies as organized into those particular
governments; and lastly, it means the people in their highest
sovereign capacity."

In which of these senses does the committee assert that the
states are parties to the constitution or compact? In that sense
in which the term is used to designate the government established by the particular society within the territory? No. The
chairman of that committee had too much self respect, too much
respect for the opinions of intelligent men out of Virginia as
well as in it, to advance a proposition so totally untrue. The report continues: "Whatever different constructions of the term
'states' in the resolution may have been entertained, all will at
least concur in that last mentioned" (the people composing
those political societies in their highest sovereign capacity)
"because," the report proceeds, "in that sense the constitution
was submitted to the 'states.' In that sense the states ratified it;
and in that sense they are consequently parties to the compact
from which the powers of the federal government result."

This celebrated report, then, concurs exactly with the Supreme court, in the opinion that the constitution is the act of
the people.

I will now examine the facts on which those arguments are
founded, with which Amphyction attempts to support his
most extraordinary dogma.

The first is that "the federal convention of 1787, was composed
of delegates appointed by the respective state legislatures."

This fact is stated in the opinion of the court; and the inference drawn from it is completely refuted by the observation that
the constitution, when it came from the hands of that convention, was a mere proposal without any obligation. Its whole
obligation is derived from the assent and ratification of the
people afterwards assembled in state conventions. Had Am-

phyction confined himself to the assertion that the constitution was proposed to the people by delegates appointed by the state legislatures, he would have accorded with the Supreme Court, and would have asserted a fact which I believe no person is disposed to deny.

His second proposition is: "That the constitution was submitted to conventions elected by the people of the several states; that is to say, to the states themselves in their highest political and sovereign authority; by those separate conventions, representing, not the whole mass of the people of the United States, but the people only within the limits of the respective sovereign states, the constitution was adopted and brought into existence. The individuality of the several states was still kept up, &c."

It surely cannot escape Amphyction himself, that these positions accord precisely with the opinion he pronounces so mischievously erroneous. He admits in terms the whole subject in controversy. He admits that the powers of the general government were not delegated by the state governments, but by the people of the several states. This is the very proposition advanced by the Supreme Court, and advanced in terms too plain to be mistaken. The argument on the part of the state of Maryland was, as we learn from the opinion, that the constitution did not emanate from the people, but was the act of sovereign and independent states: clearly using the term "states" in a sense distinct from the term "people." It is this argument which is denied by the court; and in discussing it, after stating that the constitution was submitted to conventions of the people in their respective states, the opinion adds: "From these conventions the constitution derives its whole authority."

Were it possible to render the views of the court on this subject more clear, it is done in that part of the opinion which controverts the proposition advanced by the counsel for the state of Maryland, "that the people had already surrendered all their power to the state sovereignties and had nothing more to give;" and which, in opposition to this doctrine, maintains that the legitimacy of the general government would be much more questionable had it been created by the states. It is impossible to read that paragraph and retain a single doubt, if indeed a doubt could ever have been created, of the clear understanding of the court that the term people was used as designating the people of the states, and the term "states" as designating their government.

Amphyction adds, that those conventions represented "not the whole mass of the people of the United States, but the people only within the limits of the respective sovereign states." "The individuality of the several states was still kept up, &c."

And who has ever advanced the contrary opinion? Who has ever said that the convention of Pennsylvania represented the people of any other state, or decided for any other state than itself? who has ever been so absurd as to deny that "the individuality of the several states was still kept up?" Not the Supreme Court certainly. Such opinions may be imputed to the judges, by those who, finding nothing to censure in what is actually said, and being predetermined to censure, create odious phantoms which may be very proper objects of detestation, but which bear no resemblance to any thing that has proceeded from the court.

Nothing can be more obvious than that in every part of the opinion, the terms "state" and "state sovereignties" are used in reference to the state governments, as contradistinguished from the people of the states. The words of the federal convention, requesting that the constitution might "be submitted to a convention of delegates chosen in each state by the people thereof," are quoted; and it is added, "This mode of proceeding was adopted; and by the convention, by congress, and by the states legislatures, the instrument was submitted to the people." That is, to the people of the respective states; for that is the mode of proceeding said to have been recommended by the convention, and to have been adopted. After noticing that they assembled in their respective states, the opinion adds: "And where else should they have assembled? No political dreamer was ever wild enough to think of breaking down the lines which separate the states, and of compounding the American people into one mass."

Yet Amphyction affects to be controverting the reasoning of the supreme court when he says that the convention of our state did not represent all the people of the United States, that "the individuality of the several states was still kept up." Disregarding altogether the language of the court, he ascribes to the judges an opinion which they "say no political dreamer was ever wild enough to think of."

The next proposition advanced by Amphyction is that "the President is elected by persons who are, as to numbers, partly chosen on the federal principle"; and that the senators are chosen by the states legislatures.

If these facts are alleged for the purpose of proving that the powers of the general government were delegated by the state legislatures, he has not shown us, and I confess I do not perceive, their bearing on that point. If they are alleged to prove the separate existence of the states, he has very gravely demonstrated what every body knows, and what no body denies. He would be about as usefully employed in convincing us that we see with our eyes and hear with our ears.

The last fact on which the argument of Amphyction is founded is, that the constitution is to be amended by the legislatures of three fourths of the states, or by conventions of the same number of states, in the manner provided by the 5th article.

It is not true that the legislatures of the states can of themselves amend the constitution. They can only decide on those amendments which have previously been recommended to them by Congress. Or they may require Congress to call a convention of the people to propose amendments, which shall, at the discretion of Congress, be submitted to the state legislatures, or to conventions to be assembled in the respective states.

Were it untrue that the constitution confers on the state legislatures the power of making amendments, that would not prove that this power was delegated to them by themselves. The amendments would indeed be the act of the states, but the original would still be the act of the people.

I have now reviewed the first number of Amphyction; and will only add my regrets that a gentleman whose claims to our respect appear to be by no means inconsiderable should manifest such excessive hostility to the powers necessary for the preservation of the Union, as to arraign with such bitterness the opinion of the supreme court on an interesting constitutional question, either for doctrines not to be found in it, or on principles totally repugnant to the words of the constitution, and to the recorded facts respecting its adoption.

A FRIEND TO THE UNION.

Philadelphia Union, April 24, 1819

A Friend to the Union No. II

MR. EDITOR,

The second errour supposed by Amphyction to be contained in the opinion of the Supreme Court is: "That the grant of powers to Congress which may be *necessary and proper* to carry into execution, the other powers granted to them or to any department of the government, ought to be construed in a liberal rather than a restricted sense."

For the sake of accuracy I will observe that the Supreme Court has not said that this grant ought to be construed in a "liberal sense"; although it has certainly denied that it ought to be construed in that "restricted sense" for which Amphyction contends. If by the term "liberal sense" is intended an extension of the grant beyond the fair and usual import of the words, the principle is not to be found in the opinion we are examining.

There is certainly a medium between that restricted sense which confines the meaning of words to narrower limits than the common understanding of the world affixes to them, and that extended sense which would stretch them beyond their obvious import. There is a fair construction which gives to language the sense in which it is used, and interprets an instrument according to its true intention. It is this medium, this fair construction that the Supreme Court has taken for its guide. No passage can, I think, be extracted from the opinion, which recognises a different rule; and the passages are numerous which recognise this. In commenting on the omission of the word "expressly" in the 10th amendment, the court says: "Thus leaving the question whether the particular power which may become the subject of contest, has been delegated to the one government or prohibited to the other, to depend on a fair construction of the whole instrument." So too, in all the reasoning on the word "necessary," the court does not, in a single instance, claim the aid of a "latitudinous," or "liberal" construction; but relies, decided and confidently, on its true meaning, "taking into view the subject, the context, and the intention of the framers of the constitution."

Ought any other rule to have been adopted?

Amphyction answers this question in the affirmative. This word, he contends, and indeed all the words of the constitution, ought to be understood in a restricted sense; and for not adopting his rule, the Supreme Court has drawn upon itself his heaviest censure.

The contest, then, so far as profession goes, is between the fair sense of the words used in the constitution, and a restricted sense. The opinion professes to found itself on the fair interpretation. Amphyction professes to condemn that opinion because it ought to have adopted the restricted interpretation.

The counsel for the state of Maryland had contended that the clause authorizing Congress "to pass all laws *necessary and proper* to carry into execution" the various powers vested in the government, restrained the power which Congress would otherwise have possessed; and the reasoning of Amphyction would seem to support the same proposition.

This question is of real importance to the people of the United States. If the rule contended for would not absolutely arrest the progress of the government, it would certainly deny to those who administer it the means of executing its acknowledged powers in the manner most advantageous to those for whose benefit they were conferred.

To determine whether the one course or the other be most consistent with the constitution, and with the public good, let the principles laid down by the counsel for the state of Maryland, as stated in the opinion of the court, and the principles of Amphyction as stated by himself, be examined, and compared with the reasoning which has been so bitterly execrated.

The counsel for the state of Maryland, as we are informed, contended that the word "necessary" limits the right of Congress to pass laws for the execution of the specifick powers granted by the constitution "to such as are indispensable, and without which the power would be nugatory, that it excludes the choice of means, and leaves to Congress in each case that only which is most direct and simple."

Amphyction contends that necessary means "are those means *without which* the end *could not* be obtained." "When a law is about to pass, the inquiry," he says, "which ought to be made by Congress is, does the constitution expressly grant the power? If not, then, is this law one *without which* some power *cannot* be executed? If it is not, then it is a power reserved to the states, or to the people, and we may not use the means, nor pass the law."

With some variety of expression, the position maintained in the argument of the cause, and that maintained by Amphyction, are the same. Both contend that Congress can pass no laws to carry into execution their specifick powers, but such as are *indispensably* necessary; that they can employ no means but those *without which* the end *could not* be obtained.

Let us apply this rule to some of the powers delegated to the government.

Congress has power to lay and collect taxes.

According to the opinion of the Supreme Court, Congress may exercise this power in the manner most beneficial to the people, and may adopt those regulations which are adapted to the object, and will best accomplish it. But according to Amphyction, the inquiry must always be, whether the particular regulation be one *without which* the power *could not* be executed. If the power could be executed in any other way, the law is, in his opinion, unconstitutional.

Look at our tax laws. Observe their complex and multifarious regulations. All of them, no doubt, useful and conducing directly to the end; all of them essential to the beneficial exercise of the power. But how many may be indispensably necessary; how many may be such that without them the tax *could not* be collected, it is probable that neither Amphyction nor myself can say. In some of the laws imposing internal taxes, the collector is directed to advertise certain places of meeting, at which certain acts are to be performed; and those who do not attend and perform those acts are subject to an increased tax. Is this regulation indispensable to the collection of the tax? It is certainly proper and convenient; but who will deny that the tax may be collected without it?

In almost every conceivable case, there is more than one mode of accomplishing the end. Which, or is either, indispensable to that end? Congress, for example, may raise armies; but we are told they can execute this power only by those means which are indispensably necessary; those without which the army could not be raised. Is a bounty proposed? Congress must inquire whether a bounty be absolutely necessary? Whether it be possible to raise an army without it? If it be possible, the bounty, on this theory, is unconstitutional.

Undoubtedly there are other means for raising an army. Men may enlist without a bounty; and if they will not, they may be drafted. A bounty, then, according to Amphyction, is unconstitutional, because the power may be executed by a draft; and a draft is unconstitutional, because the power may be executed by a bounty.

So too, Congress may provide for calling out the militia; and this power may be executed by requisitions on the governours, by direct requisitions on the militia, or, perhaps, by receiving volunteers. According to the reasoning of Amphyction, no one of these modes can be constitutional, because no one of them is indispensably necessary.

Every case presents a choice of means. Every end may be attained by different means. Of no one of these means can it be truly said, that, "*without it*, the end *could not* be attained."

The rule then laid down by Amphyction is an impracticable, and consequently an erroneous rule.

If we examine the example he has adduced for its illustration, we shall find that, instead of sustaining, it disproves his proposition. The example is this: "Where lands are let by one man to another at the will of the lessor, and the lessor sows the land, and the lessee, after it is sown and before the corn is ripe, put him out, yet the lessor shall have the corn, and shall have *free entry ingress, and regress, to cut, and carry away the corn.*"

The right to the crop growing on the land when the lessor determines the estate, is an incident which the law, with much justice, annexes to a tenancy at will, but is not indispensable to its existence. To this right is annexed as a necessary incident, the power of carrying away the crop. The transportation of the crop then becomes the end for which entry into the land is allowed, and the mode of transportation, the means by which that end is to be accomplished. Has the tenant the choice of means, or can he use that mode of conveyance only without which the crop cannot be carried away? A crop may be removed by employing men only, by employing men and horses, by employing horses and carts, or by employing wagons. In some instances it may be removed by land or by water. Has the person entitled to the crop, and exercising this power of conveyance, his choice of means? or may the landlord say to him, whatever mode of conveyance he may adopt, this is not indispensably necessary; you might have conveyed away the crop by other means? Undoubtedly the person allowed to carry away his crop, would not be permitted to throw down the fences, trample the enclosed fields, and trespass at will on the landholder. But he has the choice of "appropriate" means for the removal of his property, and may use that which he thinks best.

This example then might very well have been put by the court, as an apt illustration of the rule avowed in their opinion.

The rule which Amphyction gives us, for the construction of the constitution, being obviously erroneous, let us examine that which is laid down by the Supreme Court.

The Court concludes a long course of reasoning which completely demonstrates the falacy of the construction made by the counsel for the state of Maryland, and now adopted by Amphyction, by stating its own opinion in these words: "We think the sound construction of the constitution must allow to the national legislature that discretion with respect to the means by which the powers it confers are to be carried into execution, which will enable that body to perform the high duties assigned to it, in the manner most beneficial to the people. Let the end be legitimate, let it be within the scope of the constitution, and all means which are appropriate, which are plainly adapted to that end, which are not prohibited, but consistent with the letter and spirit of the constitution, are constitutional."

To this rule of construction, unless it be itself grossly misconstrued, I can perceive no objection. I think, as the Supreme Court has thought, that it would be the proper rule, were the grant which has been the subject of so much discussion, expunged from the constitution.

It is a palpable misrepresentation of the opinion of the court to say, or to insinuate that it considers the grant of a power "to pass all laws necessary and proper for carrying into execution" the powers vested in the government, as augmenting those powers, and as one which is to be construed "latitudinously," or even "liberally."

It is to be recollected that the counsel for the state of Maryland had contended that this clause was to be construed as restraining and limiting that choice of means which the national legislature would otherwise possess. The reasoning of the court is opposed to this argument, and is concluded with this observation: "The result of the most careful and attentive consideration bestowed upon this clause is, that, if it does not enlarge, it cannot be construed to restrain the powers of congress, or to impair the rights of the legislature to exercise its best judgement in the selection of measures to carry into execution the constitutional powers of the government. If no other motive for its insertion can be suggested, a sufficient one is found in the desire to remove all doubt respecting the right to legislate on that vast mass of incidental powers which must be involved in the constitution, if that instrument be not a splendid bauble."

The court then has not contended that this grant enlarges, but that it does not restrain the powers of Congress; and I believe every man who reads the opinion will admit that the demonstration of this proposition is complete. It is so complete that Amphyction himself does not venture directly to controvert the conclusion, although the whole course of his reasoning seems intended to weaken the principles from which it is drawn. His whole argument appears to be intended to prove that this clause does restrain congress in the execution of all the powers conferred by the constitution, to those "means *without which* the end *could not* be obtained." Thus converting an apparent grant of power into a limitation of power.

The court has said, and I repeat it, that the constitution and laws of the United States abound with evidence demonstrating the errour of this construction. I have already stated some instances in which this rule must be discarded; and I will now refer to others which were selected by the court, the aptness of which Amphyction denies.

I will pass over the acts requiring an oath of office, because Amphyction seems half disposed to admit there is something in that particular example, and will proceed to some of those which he pronounces totally inapplicable.

Congress possesses power "to establish post offices, and post roads." Amphyction says that the right to carry the mail, and to punish those who rob it, are necessary incidents to this power. I admit it. But who does not perceive that, in making this assertion, he abandons his own interpretation of the word "necessary" and adopts that of the supreme court? Let us apply his rule to the case. Let us suppose a bill before congress to punish those who rob the mail. The inquiry is, he says: "Does the constitution expressly grant the power?" The answer must be in the negative. There is no express power to carry the mail, nor to punish those who rob it. The member is next to ask: "Is this law one without which the power cannot be executed?" That is, can a post office and a post road be established, without an act of Congress for the punishment of those who rob the mail? The plain common sense of every man will answer this question in the affirmative. These powers were divided under the confederation. Then the conclusion of the member must be, this right to punish those who rob the mail "is a power reserved to the states, or to the people, and we may not use the means, nor pass the law. Then the state legislature may pass laws to punish those who rob the mail, but congress cannot. Post offices and post roads may be established without such a law, and therefore the power to pass it is reserved to the states." Adopt the construction of Amphyction, and this conclusion is inevitable.

Let the question be on the right of Congress to pass an act for the punishment of those who falsify a record.

The power is to ordain and establish inferior courts, the judges of which shall hold their offices during good behaviour, and receive as a compensation for their services, salaries which shall not be diminished during their continuance in office. The second section defines the extent of the judicial power.

Is a law to punish those who falsify a record, one without which a court cannot be established, or one without which a court cannot exercise its functions? We know that under the confederation Congress had the power to establish, and did establish certain courts, and, had not the power to pass laws for the punishment of those who should falsify its records. Unquestionably such a law is "needful," "requisite," "essential," "conducive to," the due administration of justice; but no man can say it is one without which courts cannot decide causes, or without which it is physically impossible for them to perform their functions. According to the rule of Amphyction then, such a law cannot be enacted by Congress, but may be enacted by the state legislatures.

It would be tedious to go through all the examples put by the supreme court. They are all of the same character, and show, conclusively, that the principles maintained by the counsel for the state of Maryland, and by Amphyction, would essentially change the constitution, render the government of the Union incompetent to the objects for which it was instituted, and place all its powers under the control of the state legislatures. It would, in a great measure, reinstate the old confederation.

It cannot escape any attentive observer that Amphyction's strictures on the opinion of the supreme court, are founded on a total and obvious perversion of the plain meaning of that opinion, as well as on a misconstruction of the constitution. He occasionally substitutes words not used by the court, and employs others, neither in the connexion, nor in the sense, in which they are employed by the court, so as to ascribe to the opinion sentiments which it does not merely not contain, but which it excludes. The court does not say that the word "necessary" means whatever may be 'convenient,' or 'useful.' And when it uses "conducive to," that word is associated with others plainly showing that no remote, no distant conduciveness to the object, is in the mind of the court.

With as little remorse as the Procrustes of ancient fable stretched and lopped limbs in order to fit travellers to his bed does Amphyction extend and contract the meaning of words in the constitution, and in the opinion of the court, in order, to accommodate those papers to his strictures. Thus, he says, if Congress should impose a tax on Land, "it would be extremely *convenient*, and a very *appropriate* measure, and very *conducive* to their purpose of collecting this tax speedily, and promptly, if the state governments could be prohibited during the same year from laying & collecting a land tax. Were they to pass such a law and thereby directly encroach on one of the most undoubted rights of the states, the present liberal and sweeping construction of the clause by the Supreme court would justify the measure."

Now I deny that a law prohibiting the state legislatures from imposing a land tax would be an "appropriate" means, or any means whatever, to be employed in collecting the tax of the United States. It is not an instrument to be so employed. It is not a means "plainly adapted," or "conducive to" the end. The passage of such an act would be an attempt on the part of Congress, "under the pretext of executing its powers, to pass laws for the accomplishment of objects not intrusted to the government." So far is the construction given to this clause by the supreme court from being so "liberal & sweeping" as to "justify the measure" that the opinion expressly rejects it. Let its language be quoted. "That the power of taxation is one of vital importance; that it is retained by the states; that it is to be concurrently exercised by the two governments, are truths, says the opinion, which have never been denied." The court afterwards quotes a passage from the Federalist in which this construction is urged vehemently as an objection to the constitution itself, and obviously approves the argument against it.

Many laborious criticisms would be avoided; if those who are disposed to condemn a paper, would take the trouble to read, with a disposition to understand, it.

I shall not notice the various imaginary and loose opinions which Amphyction has collected, or suggested, because they are not imputable to the supreme court. I content myself with exposing *some* of his errours in construing the constitution, and in ascribing to the opinion he condemns, doctrines which it does not contain.

I cannot however avoid remarking that Amphyction himself, as soon as he has closed his stricture on the supreme court, seems to desert his own construction and take up their's. "I think it clear," he says, "that the intention of the constitution was to confer on Congress the power of resorting to such means as are incidental to the express powers; to such means as directly and necessarily tend to produce the desired effect."

How much more, let me ask, has been said by the supreme court? That court has said: "Let the end be legitimate, let it be within the scope of the constitution, and all means which are appropriate, which are plainly adapted to that end, which are not prohibited," "are constitutional." The word "appropriate," if Johnson be authority, means "peculiar," "consigned to some particular use or person,"—"belonging peculiarly."

Let the constructive words used by the supreme court, in this their acknowledged sense, be applied to any of the powers of Congress. Take for example, that of raising armies. The court has said that "all means which are appropriate," that is "all means which are peculiar" to raising armies, which are "consigned to that particular use," which "belong peculiarly" to it, all means which are, "plainly adapted" to the end, are constitutional.

If Amphyction is better pleased with his own language, I shall not contest its right to the preference; but what essential difference is there between "means which directly and necessarily tend to produce the desired effect," and means which "belong peculiarly" to the production of that effect? I acknowledge that I perceive none. Means which are "appropriate," which are "plainly adapted" to the end, must "directly and necessarily tend to produce" it. The difference however between these means, and those *without which* the effect *cannot* be produced, must be discerned by the most careless observer.

Let us apply these different definitions of the words, to any the most common affairs of human life. A leases to B a mill for a number of years on a contract that A shall receive half the profits, and shall pay half the expenses of all the machinery which B may erect therein, and which shall be "*necessary and proper*" for the manufacture of flower. Pending this lease, the elevator and hopper boy are invented, and applied, with great advantage, to the manufacture of flower. B erects them in his mill. A is very well satisfied with receiving the increased profits, but is unwilling to pay half the expense of the machinery, because, as he alleges, it was not "*necessary*" to the manufacture of flower. All will admit that this machinery is "appropriate, and plainly adapted to the end"; or, in the words of

Amphyction, that it "directly and necessarily tends to produce
the desired effect." But none can think it so indispensably necessary that the end *cannot* be produced *without* it. The end
was produced, flower was manufactured, before the elevator
and hopper boy were invented.

The same may be observed of the cotton machine of the
south, of the use of Gypsum on a farm, of many things which
occur in the ordinary transactions of human life.

It will be readily perceived in every case, that this rule of construction, which seems to have escaped Amphyction in a moment when the particular object of his essay was out of view,
and that contained in the opinion he condemns, are precisely
the same; and are both in direct opposition to that other restricted rule by which he tries the reasoning of the supreme
court.

If, as I think all will admit, that construction of the words in
which Amphyction and the court concur, furnish the true rule
for construing the words "*necessary and proper*" in a contract
between man & man, how much more certainly must it be the
true rule for construing a constitution—an instrument the nature of which excludes the possibility of inserting in it an enumeration of the means of executing its specifick powers. If this
rule be applicable to the relations between individuals, how
much more applicable must it be to the relations between the
people and their representatives, who are elected for the very
purpose of selecting the best means of executing the powers of
the government they are chosen to administer.

I have confined my observations to the reasoning of the
Supreme Court, and have taken no notice of the conclusion
drawn from it, because the essays I am reviewing make no objections to the latter, but denounce the former as false and
dangerous. I think, on the contrary, I hazard nothing when I
assert that the reasoning is less doubtful than the conclusion. I
myself concur in the conclusion; but I do not fear contradiction from any fair minded and intelligent man when I say that
the principles laid down by the court for the construction of
the constitution may all be sound, and yet the act for incorporating the Bank be unconstitutional. But if the act, be constitutional, the principles laid down by the court must be sound.
I defy Amphyction, I defy any man, to furnish an argument

which shall, at the same time, prove the Bank to be constitutional, and the reasoning of the court to be erroneous. Why then is Amphyction so delicate on the constitutionality of the law, while he is vehement and strenuous in his exertions to rouse the nation against the court? If we do not account for this by saying that the court is less popular, and therefore more vulnerable, than the executive and the legislature, how shall we account for it?

Before I conclude let me ask this gentleman and those who think with him, what train of reasoning would have satisfied him and them? The court did not volunteer in this business. The question was brought before them, and they could not escape it. What course then does Amphyction think they ought to have adopted? Does he think they ought to have declared the law unconstitutional and void? He does not say so; and we are not permitted to draw this inference from what he does say. After lamenting that *seriatim* opinions were not delivered, he supposes what might have been the opinions of Judges concurring in the decision, but dissenting from the reasoning, delivered by the Chief Justice. "Some of them" he says, "may have believed that it was for Congress to have judged of that necessity and propriety, and having exercised their undoubted functions in so deciding, that it was not consistent with judicial modesty to say there was no such necessity, and thus to arrogate to themselves a right of putting their *veto* upon a law."

Again, he says: "It may however be asked, whether I can at this day pretend to argue against the constitutionality of a bank established by Congress? In answer, I reply that it is not my intention by these remarks to bring that subject into discussion. I am willing to acquiesce in this particular case, so long as the charter continues without being violated—because it has been repeatedly argued before Congress, and not only in 1791 but in 1815, was solemnly decided in favour of the measure."

Let us suppose that the court had supported its decision by the reasoning which Amphyction conjectures may have influenced some of the Judges whom he does not appear inclined to censure, or by that which he adopts for himself. Suppose the court had said: "Congress has judged of the necessity and propriety of this measure, and having exercised their undoubted functions in so deciding, it is not consistent with judicial modesty to say there is no such necessity, and thus to arrogate to ourselves the right of putting our *veto* upon a law."

Or suppose the court, after hearing a most elaborate and able argument on the constitutionality of the law, had said: "It is not our intention to bring that subject into discussion. We are willing to acquiesce in this particular case so long as the charter continues without being violated—because it has been repeatedly argued before Congress, and not only in 1791, but in 1815, was solemnly decided against the measure."

Would this reasoning have satisfied, or ought it to have satisfied the publick? Would Amphyction himself be content with the declaration of the Supreme Court that, on any question concerning the constitutionality of an act, it is enough to say, "it is not consistent with judicial modesty" to contradict the opinion of Congress, and "thus to arrogate to themselves the right of putting their *veto* upon a law" or that "they are willing to acquiesce" in the particular act, "because it has been repeatedly argued before Congress, and not only in 1791, but in 1815," or at some other time since 1801, "was solemnly decided in favour of the measure?"

But if, as we must believe was the fact in this case, because it was so stated by the Judges, the court should be "unanimously and decidedly of opinion that the law is constitutional," would it comport with their honour, with their duty, or with truth, to insinuate an opinion that Congress had violated the constitution? If it would not, then was it incumbent on the court in this case, to pursue, not the course marked out by Amphyction but that which he censures. It was incumbent on them to state their real opinion and their reasons for it. Those reasons, I am persuaded, require only to be read with fairness and with attention to be approved.

A FRIEND TO THE UNION.

Philadelphia Union, April 28, 1819

THE DARTMOUTH COLLEGE AND BANK CASES

To Joseph Story

My dear Sir   Richmond Apl. 28th. 1819.

To day on my return from a tour to our upper country I had the pleasure of receiving your favor of the 16th. inst. I thank you very sincerely for the attention you have paid to the opinion in the case of the Dartmouth College & shall be obliged by your making the correction you propose. I would myself prefer that it should stand as you suggest; but were it otherwise, your opinion in a case on which I felt no particular solicitude, would be decisive with me.

Although I entirely approve the erasure of the words you propose to omit I will state to you, meerly as an excuse for having inserted them the thought which passed over my mind at the time.

The expression that a legislature might perform some judicial functions was carelessly introduced, but was introduced with a view to the prohibitions on the states contained in the constitution of the United States, not with a view to the interior regulations made by state constitutions. My idea was that it was entirely a subject for state regulation with which the courts of the United States could have no concern. I had understood that in Rhode Island & Connecticut the legislature or some branch of it exercised certain judicial powers, & I knew that in New York their senate was like the House of Lords in England a court of Dernier resort. Be this as it may I am happy that you have adverted to the subject & hope it will not be too late to omit the words to which you object.

The opinion in the Bank case has brought into operation the whole antifederal spirit of Virginia. Some latent feelings which have been working ever since the decision of Martin & Hunter have found vent on this occasion, & are working most furiously. The sin of the court is thought much more hienous than that of Congress or the President. The offence would have been equally great had we pronounced the law unconstitutional. They would have been more merciful had we said simply that it was for the legislature to decide on the necessity & not for the court &c.

I condole with you sincerely on the severe affliction with which you have been visited. It is one of those wounds which time will heal & for which, while green, occupation furnishes the best salve. I speak from repeated experience.

Farewell. With much esteem & regard, I am dear Sir your obedt

REPRINTING "A FRIEND TO THE UNION"

To Bushrod Washington

My dear Sir   Richmond May 6th. 1819

I have given you a great deal of trouble to very little purpose, & am now about to add to it, perhaps to as little. Our friend Mr. Bronson has made a curious piece of work of the essays he was requested to publish. He has cut out the middle of the first number to be inserted into the middle of the second; & to show his perfect impartiality, has cut out the middle of the second number to be inserted in the first. He has thrown these disrupted parts together without the least regard to their fitness & made a curious mixture—a sort of Olla podrida, which, however good the ingredients may be, when compounded as he has compounded them, are rather nauseous to the intellectual palate.

It is understood that this subject is not to drop. A very serious effort is undoubtedly making to have it taken up in the next legislature. It is said that some other essays written by a very great man are now preparing & will soon appear. On this account I am desirous that the answer to Amphyction should appear in its true shape & will be obliged to you to have it republished in the Alexandria paper. I will give the instructions which I will thank you to copy & furnish with the papers I now send containing those essays marked—to the editor.

Without any remark on the errors committed in the original publication—state it as taken from the union. Omit the letter to the editors & begin where the essay No. 1 begins. Continue to the mark in the third column of the first page of No. 1 (paper of Apl. 28) to the words "would seem to be," inclusive, in about the 13th. line of that column. Then proceed with what is misplaced in the second number (paper May 1st.) at the mark in the first column in the 6th. paragraph with the words "a meer historical fact" &c. & continue to the mark in the third column & end of the 10th. paragraph at the words "states leg-islatures" inclusive. Then return to the paper of Apl. 28 to the mark in the second column of the second page the beginning of the fifth paragraph & proceed with the words "This fact is stated in the opinion" &c to the end of the essay. These pieces form the first number.

The second number begins properly in the paper of the first of May. Continue it to the mark in the sixth paragraph of the first column to the words "goes, is between," inclusive. Then return to the first number to the mark in the 3d. column of the first page the second paragraph & proceed with the words "the fair sense of the words used in the constitution" &c & continue to the word "administer" at the end of the 4th. para-graph, in the second column of the second page. Then go to the mark in the 3d. column of the second number & begin at that mark with the words "I have confined" &c which com-mence the 11th. paragraph of that column. Continue to the end. These disjointed parts form the second number.

These directions are formed from the country paper. Your

"PREJUDICE WILL SWALLOW ANYTHING"

To Joseph Story

My dear Sir   Richmond May 27th. 1819
    I had the pleasure of receiving a few days past your favour of the 15th. & thank you very sincerely for the information you have given respecting the nail machines in use in your country. The information will be valuable to my friend.
    I am much obliged by the alterations you have made in the opinion in the Dartmouth college case, & am highly gratified by what you say respecting it. The opinion in the Bank case

continues to be denounced by the democracy in Virginia. An effort is certainly making to induce the legislature which will meet in December to take up the subject & to pass resolutions not very unlike those which were called forth by the alien & sedition laws in 1799. Whether the effort will be successful or not may perhaps depend in some measure on the sentiments of our sister states. To excite this ferment the opinion has been grossly misrepresented; and where its argument has been truely stated it has been met by principles one would think too palpably absurd for inteligent men. But prejudice will swallow anything. If the principles which have been advanced on this occasion were to prevail, the constitution would be converted into the old confederation. The piece to which you allude was not published in Virginia. Our patriotic papers admit no such political heresies. It contained I think a complete demonstration of the fallacies & errors contained in those attacks on the opinion of the court which have most credit here & are supposed to proceed from a high source, but was so mangled in the publication that those only who had bestowed close attention to the subject could understand it. There were two numbers & the Editor of the Union in Philadelphia the paper in which it was published, had mixed the different numbers together so as in several instances to place the reasoning intended to demonstrate one proposition under another. The points & the arguments were so separated from each other & so strangely mixed as to constitute a labyrinth to which those only who understood the whole subject perfectly could find a clue.

I wish to consult you on a case which to me who am not versed in admiralty proceedings has some difficulty. The Little Charles was libelled for a violation of the first embargo act in 1808. She was acquitted in the District but condemned in the circuit court. After a thousand delays a question is now before the circuit court as a court of Admiralty for judgement on the bond given on the property being restored. Several objections are made, two of which deserve consideration. The first is that the order for restitution was made, not in court, but by the Judge out of court not at a called court and second that the bond was taken by the marshal to himself & not the U.S. Upon this order the vessel was delivered & this bond has been returned to court but has not been acted on, Nor is there any act of the court approving the proceeding. It is contended to be a meer act *in pais* not sanctioned by the court. That it is the unauthorized act of the marshal who might release the bond or sue upon it; and that the court cannot consider it as in the place of the vessel & so act upon it. With great regard & esteem I am dear Sir your Obedt

ANSWERING "HAMPDEN"

To Bushrod Washington

My dear Sir   Richmond June 17th 1819
   The storm which has been for some time threatening the Judges has at length burst on their heads & a most serious hurricane it is. The author is spoken of with as much confidence as if his name was subscribed to his essays. It is worth your while to read them. They are in the Enquirer under the signature of Hampden.
   I find myself more stimulated on this subject than on any other because I beleive the design to be to injure the Judges & inpair the constitution. I have therefore thought of answering these essays & sending my pieces to you for publication in the Alexandria paper. I shall send them on in successive numbers but do not wish the first to be published till I shall have seen the last of Hampden. I will then write to you & request you to have the publications made immediately. As the numbers will be marked I hope no mistake will be made by the printer & that the manuscript will be given to the flame. I wish two papers of each number to be directed to T. Marshall, Oak hill Fauquier. I do not wish them to come to me lest some suspicion of the author should be created.
   I send you a check for 30$ on account of my subscription to your society for colonization. I am not sure that Mr. Caldwell is in the city or I should send it to him. Your

A Friend of the Constitution No. I

If it be true that no rational friend of the constitution can wish to expunge from it the judicial department, it must be difficult for those who believe the prosperity of the American people to be inseparable from the preservation of this government, to view with indifference the systematic efforts which certain restless politicians of Virginia have been for some time making, to degrade that department in the estimation of the public. It is not easy to resist the conviction that those efforts must have other and more dangerous objects, than merely to impair the confidence of the nation in the present judges.

The zealous and persevering hostility with which the constitution was originally opposed, cannot be forgotten. The deep rooted and vindictive hate, which grew out of unfounded jealousies, and was aggravated by defeat, though suspended for a time, seems never to have been appeased. The desire to strip the government of those effective powers, which enable it to accomplish the objects for which it was created; and, by construction, essentially to reinstate that miserable confederation, whose incompetency to the preservation of our union, the short interval between the treaty of Paris and the meeting of the general convention at Philadelphia, was sufficient to demonstrate, seems to have recovered all its activity. The leaders of this plan, like skilful engineers, batter the weakest part of the citadel, knowing well, that if that can be beaten down, and a breach effected, it will be afterwards found very difficult, if not impracticable, to defend the place. The judicial department, being without power, without patronage, without the legitimate means of ingratiating itself with the people, forms this weakest part; and is, at the same time, necessary to the very existence of the government, and to the effectual execution of its laws. Great constitutional questions are unavoidably brought before this department, and its decisions must sometimes depend on a course of intricate and abstruse reasoning, which it requires no inconsiderable degree of mental exertion to comprehend, and which may, of course, be grossly misrepresented. One of these questions, the case of McCullough against the state of Maryland, presents the fairest occasion for wounding mortally, the vital powers of the government, thro' its judiciary. Against the decision of the court, on this question, weighty interests & deep rooted prejudices are combined. The opportunity for the assault was too favorable not to be seized.

A writer in the Richmond Enquirer, under the signature of "Hampden," who is introduced to us by the editor, as holding "a pen equal to the great subject he has undertaken to discuss," after bestowing upon Congress in general, and some of its most respectable members in particular, language not much more decorous than that reserved for the judges, says, "The warfare waged by the judicial body has been of a bolder tone and character. It was not enough for them to sanction, in former times, the detestable doctrines of Pickering & Co. as aforesaid; it was not enough for them to annihilate the freedom of the press, by incarcerating all those who dared, with a manly freedom, to canvass the conduct of their public agents; it was not enough for the predecessors of the present judges to preach political sermons from the bench of justice, and bolster up the most unconstitutional measures of the most abandoned of our rulers; it did not suffice to do the business in detail, and ratify, one by one, the legislative infractions of the constitution. That process would have been too slow, and perhaps too troublesome. It was possible also, that some *Hampden* might make a stand against some ship money measure of the government, and, although he would lose his cause with the court, might ultimately gain it with *people*. They resolved, therefore, to put down all discussions of the kind in future, by a judicial *coup de main*; to give a general letter of attorney to the future legislators of the union; and to tread under foot all those parts and articles of the constitution, which had been heretofore deemed to set limits to the power of the federal legislature."

Without stopping to enquire whether this ranting declamation, this rash impeachment of the integrity, as well as opinions of all those who have successively filled the judicial department, be intended to illustrate the diffidence with which this modest gentleman addresses his fellow citizens, and the just comparison he has made between "the smallness of his means and the greatness of his undertaking"; or to demonstrate his perfect possession of that temperate, chastened, and well disciplined mind, which is so favorable to the investigation of truth, and which so well fits him who instructs the public, for tasks in which he engages, I shall endeavor to follow him, and to notice the evidence and the arguments with which he attempts to justify this unqualified arraignment of all those who have been selected for the great duty of expounding our constitution and our laws.

But before I proceed to discuss the principles for which Hampden contends, I must be permitted to bestow a few moments on some other of his preliminary observations.

After representing the "legislative power" as "every where extending the sphere of its activity, and drawing all power into its impetuous vortex," he adds, "That judicial power, which, according to Montesqueiu, is, in some measure, next to nothing, &c." "That judiciary, which, in Rome, according to the same writer, was not entrusted to decide questions which concerned the interest of the state, in the relation which it bears to the citizens; and which, in England, has only invaded the constitution in the worst of times, and then always on the side of arbitrary power, has also deemed its interference necessary in our country."

I do not quote this passage for the purpose of noticing the hostility of Hampden to those American principles, which, in confiding to the courts, both of the union and of the states, the power, have imposed on them the duty, of preserving the constitution as the permanent law of the land, from even legislative infractions: nor for the purpose of enquiring why he has thought it necessary to inform us that "the judiciary in England has only invaded the constitution in the worst of times, and then always on the side of arbitrary power." I mean only to mark the unjust and insidious insinuation, that the court had thrust itself into the controversy between the United States and the state of Maryland, and had unnecessarily volunteered its services. "The judiciary" he says, "has also deemed its interference necessary in our country."

If Hampden does not know that the court proceeded in this business, not because "it deemed its interference necessary," but because the question was brought regularly before it by those who had a right to demand, and did demand, its decision, he would do well to suspend his censures until he acquires the information which belongs to the subject; if he does know it, I leave it to himself to assign the motives for this insinuation.

With as little regard to the real state of the transaction, he represents the judges as going out of the case, and giving opinions on extrinsic matter. "The supreme court of the United States," he says, "have not only granted this general power of attorney to congress, but they have gone out of the record to do it in the present question. It was only necessary in that case to decide whether or not the bank law was necessary and proper within the meaning of the constitution, for carrying into effect some of the granted powers; but the court have in effect expunged those words from the constitution."

It is scarcely necessary to say that this charge of "in effect expunging those words from the constitution," exists only in the imagination of Hampden. It is the creature of his own mind. But let us see how he makes good his assertion, that the court "has gone out of the record." "It was necessary," he admits, "to decide whether or not the bank law was necessary and proper, within the meaning of the constitution, for carrying into effect some of the granted powers." And, how, let me ask, was the court to decide this question? Does it not plainly involve an enquiry into the meaning of those words as used in the constitution? The court is required to decide whether a particular act is inhibited by certain words in an instrument: yet if the judges examine the meaning of the words, they are stopped by Hampden, and accused of travelling out of the record. Their construction may be erroneous. This is open to argument. But to say that in making the construction they go out of the record, may indeed show the spirit in which these strictures originate; but can impose on no intelligent man.

I must also be permitted to remark that, in discussing a question concerning the power of congress to pass a particular act, it is not allowable to assume as a postulate that the interests of the people are necessarily on the side of the state which contests that power, or that the cause of liberty must be promoted by deciding the question against the government of the union. When the right to call out the militia was solemnly denied, and the right to lay an unlimited embargo was seriously questioned, Hampden himself, perhaps, was not of opinion that the interest or liberty of the public required the decision of those points to be against the claims of the United States. In fact, the government of the union, as well as those of the states, is created by the people, who have bestowed upon it certain powers for their own benefit, and who administer it for their own good. The people are as much interested, their liberty is as deeply concerned, in preventing encroachments on that government, in arresting the hands which would tear from it the powers they have conferred upon it, as in restraining it within its constitutional limits. The constitution has defined the powers of the government, and has established that division of power which its framers, and the American people, believed to be most conducive to the public happiness and to public liberty. The equipoise thus established is as much disturbed by taking weights out of the scale containing the powers of the government, as by putting weights into it. His hand is unfit to hold the state balance who occupies himself entirely in giving a preponderance to one of the scales.

If it be possible that congress may succeed "in seeing the constitution expounded by the *abuses* committed under it"; if "a new mode of amending the constitution" may be "added to the ample ones provided in that instrument, and the strongest checks established in it" may be "made to yield to the force of precedents"; if the time may soon arrive "when the constitution may be expounded without even looking into it—by merely reading the acts of a renegado congress, or adopting the outrageous doctrines of Pickering, Lloyd, or Sheffy": It is not less possible that the constitution may be so expounded by its enemies as to become totally inoperative, that a new mode of amendment, by way of report of committees of a state legislature, and resolutions thereon, may pluck from it power after power in detail, or may sweep off the whole at once by declaring that it shall execute its acknowledged powers by those scanty and inconvenient means only which the states shall prescribe, and without which the power cannot exist. Thus, "by this new mode of amendment," may that government which the American "people have ordained and established," "in order to form a more perfect union, establish justice, ensure domestic tranquility, provide for the common defence, promote the general welfare, and secure the blessings of liberty to themselves and their posterity," become an inanimate corpse, incapable of effecting any of these objects.

The question is, and ought to be considered, as a question of fair construction. Does the constitution, according to its true sense and spirit, authorize Congress to enact the particular law which forms the subject of enquiry? If it does, the best interests of the people, as well as the duty of those who decide, require that the question should be determined in the affirmative. If it does not, the same motives require a determination in the negative.

A FRIEND OF THE CONSTITUTION.

Gazette and Alexandria Daily Advertiser, June 30, 1819

A Friend of the Constitution No. II

I gladly take leave of the bitter invectives which compose the first number of Hampden, and proceed to a less irksome task—the examination of his argument.

These are introduced by laying down these propositions which he declares to be incontrovertible in themselves, and which he seems to suppose, demonstrate the errors of the opinion he censures.

I do not hazard much when I say that these propositions, if admitted to be true, so far from demonstrating the error of that opinion, do not even draw it into question. They may be all true, and yet every principle laid down in the opinion be perfectly correct.

The first is that the constitution conveyed only a limited grant of powers to the general government, and reserved the residuary powers to the government of the states and to the people.

Instead of controverting this proposition, I beg leave to add to the numerous respectable authorities quoted by Hampden in support of it, one other which, in this controversy at least, is entitled to some consideration, because it is furnished by the opinion he condemns. The supreme court say, "The government (of the United States) is acknowledged by all to be one of enumerated powers. The principle that it can exercise only the powers granted to it, would seem too apparent to have required to be enforced by all those arguments which its enlightened friends, while it was depending before the people, found it necessary to urge. That principle is now universally admitted. But the question respecting the extent of the powers actually granted, is perpetually arising, and will probably continue to arise, as long as our system shall exist."

The supreme court then has affirmed this proposition in terms as positive as those used by Hampden. The judges did not indeed fortify it by authority, nor was the necessity of doing so very apparent, as mathematicians do not demonstrate axioms, neither do judges or lawyers always deem it necessary to prove propositions, the truth of which "is universally admitted."

2d. The second proposition is that the limited grant to congress of certain enumerated powers, only carried with it such additional powers as were *fairly incidental* to them; or in other words, were necessary and proper for their execution.

I will here remark, merely for the sake of perspicuity, that the second branch of this proposition, which seems to be intended as explanatory of the first, introduces I think a distinct idea. The power to do a thing, and the power to carry that thing into execution, are I humbly conceive, the same power, and the one cannot be termed with propriety "additional" or "incidental" to the other. Under the confederation congress could do scarcely any thing, that body could only make requisitions on the states. The passage of a resolution requiring the states to furnish certain specified sums of money, was not an "additional" or "incidental" power, but a mode of executing that which was granted. Under the constitution, the powers of government are given in terms which authorise and require congress to execute them. The execution is of the essence of the power. Thus congress can lay and collect taxes. A law to lay and collect taxes, and making all the provisions to bring the money into the treasury, is not the exercise of an "additional power" but the execution of one expressly granted. The laws which punish those who resist the collection of the revenue, or which subject the estates of collection in the first instance to the claim of the United States, or which make other collateral provisions, may be traced to incidental powers. Not to those laws which simply execute the granted power. They are a part of the original grant.

The proposition itself, I am perfectly willing to admit, and should pass it over without a comment as one in no degree controverting the principles contained in the opinion of the supreme court, did I not suppose that some attention to the quotation made by Hampden, might conduce to a more clear and distinct understanding of those quotations themselves, and of their application to the subject under consideration.

The object of making them is, I presume, to show that a general grant of a specific power or thing, does not carry with it those incidents, or those means for giving the grant full and complete effect, which the opinion of the supreme court contends for.

His first quotation from Vattel contains words which might easily mislead a careless reader. "Since" says that author, "a nation is obliged to preserve itself, it has a right to every thing necessary for its preservation. For the law of nature gives us a right to every thing, without which we could not fulfil our obligation; otherwise it would oblige us to do impossibilities, or rather would contradict itself, in prescribing a duty, and prohibiting at the same time the only means of fulfilling it."

Hampden has been caught by the words "necessary," "without which," and "only means," in the foregoing passage, which he has marked in italics or capitals, so as to give them a weight not given by the author, and has inferred from them, and other passages in the same book, that what he denominates the incidental power, is limited to things strictly "necessary," or "without which" the obligation could not be fulfilled; and in no case, he says, "is a latitude allowed, as extensive as that claimed by the supreme court."

The great and obvious error of Hampden consists in this. He converts an affirmative into a negative proposition. He converts a declaration of Vattel, that a nation has a natural right to do certain things, into a declaration that a nation has no natural right to do other things. But for this, I could not ask a stronger passage to show that the terms on which Hampden relies, are employed in a very different sense from that in which he understands them. "A nation" says Vattel, "has a right to every thing *necessary* for its preservation." Will any man seriously contend that the rights of a nation are limited to those acts which are necessary for its preservation, in the sense affixed by Hampden to the term "necessary"? May it not pass the bounds of strict necessity, in order to consult or provide for its happiness, its convenience, its interest, its power? "The law of nature," says Vattel, "gives a right to every thing without which we could not fulfil an obligation." But does it inhibit every thing else? If it does, then our obligations are sufficiently broad and latitudinous to cover the whole extent of human policy and human action.

"A nation," says Vattel, in the same page, speaking of the destruction of a state, "has a right to every thing which can secure it from such a threatening danger, and to keep at a distance whatever is capable of causing its ruin." There is plainly no difference between that which a nation may do for its preservation, and that which it may do to prevent its ruin. It is a continuation of the same subject; the author means to convey the same sentiment; the change of phraseology is merely casual; and it is obvious that the restrictive terms used in the passage quoted by Hampden, are employed in such a mitigated sense, as to have the same signification with the broader words subsequently used on the same subject. In the whole, the author plainly recognizes the right acknowledged and acted upon by all the world, of a nation to exercise all its foresight, its policy, and its means, for its own security; and of the necessity of resorting to those means, it is the sole judge.

I certainly do not perceive the application of these paragraphs, but they are pressed into the service by Hampden.

We are also referred to a passage in Vattel, which respects tacit or implied engagements. I shall quote it rather more at large than we find it in Hampden. "Tacit faith," says that author, "is founded on a tacit consent, and tacit consent is that which is deduced by a just consequence from the steps taken by any one. Thus all that is included, as Grotius says, in the nature of certain acts on which an argument is made, is tacitly comprehended in the convention; or, in other words, every thing without which what is agreed cannot take place, is tacitly granted." Several examples of the rule are then given; as, the allowance of provisions to an army which has stipulated for permission to return home in safety; and the security which is tacitly promised to an enemy who demands or accepts an interview.

I acquiesce implicitly in the rule as laid down by Vattel and by Grotius. I wish to extend tacit consent no farther than to that which is deduced by a just consequence from the steps taken by any one; nor to comprehend, by implication, more in a convention than "is included in the nature of certain acts on which an agreement is made." If the supreme court goes farther, I do not understand their opinion.

The case put by Vattel, and quoted by Hampden, of the grant of a free passage, is one on which I should particularly rely, as strongly supporting that liberal and just construction for which I contend.

The grant of a free passage seems, necessarily, to imply no more than that the sovereign who makes the grant shall remain passive, and to include only "every particular connected with the passage of troops," "such as the liberty of carrying whatever may be necessary to an army, that of exercising military discipline on the officers and soldiers, and that of buying at a reasonable rate every thing that an army may want." Yet it is construed to go much further, and to stipulate for something active on the part of the sovereign making it. "He who grants the passage," says Vattel, "is, as far as lies in his power, to take care that it should be safe." That is, he is not only not to injure, but to protect the army while in his territory.

This is certainly a reasonable construction of the grant; but if the implication be necessary, the necessity cannot be absolute or indispensable.

The case of a grant of a house to one man, and of a garden to another, which could be entered only through the house, is put by Vattel as an example of the *restrictive*, in opposition to the *extensive* interpretation. Hampden cannot mean to give this example as forming a general rule—that construction is always *restrictive*, and never *extensive*; and never even reasonable.

In truth, the only principle which can be extracted from Vattel, and safely laid down as a general independent rule is, that pacts are to be understood according to the intention of the parties, and shall be construed liberally, or restrictively, as may best promote the objects for which they were made. For this I refer to his whole chapters on the faith, and on the interpretation of treaties. "The uncertainty of the sense," he observes, (b. 2. sec. 282) "that ought to be given to a law or a treaty, does not proceed from the obscurity, or any other fault in the expression, but also from the narrow limits of the human mind, which cannot foresee all cases and circumstances, or include all the consequences of what is appointed or promised; and, in short, from the impossibility of entering into the immense detail. We can only make laws or treaties in a general manner, and the interpretation ought to apply them to particular cases conformably to the intention of the legislature and of the contracting powers." "Again," (sec. 283) he says, "we do not presume that sensible persons had nothing in view in treating together, or in forming any other serious agreement. *The interpretation which renders a treaty null, and without effect cannot then, be admitted. It ought to be interpreted in such a manner as that it may have its effect, and not be found vain and illusive.* It is necessary to give the words that sense which ought to be presumed most conformable to the intention of those who speak. If many different interpretations present themselves, proper to avoid the nullity or absurdity of a treaty, we ought to prefer that which appears most agreeable to the intention for which it was dictated."

I trust then Hampden will not charge me, as he has charged the supreme court, with using "*high sounding words*," when, in his own language, I say that "I take it to be a clear principle of universal law—of the law of nature, of nations, of war, and of reason," that all instruments are to be construed fairly, so as to give effect to their intention, and I appeal with confidence to the authority to which Hampden has introduced us, to support my proposition.

A Friend of the Constitution.

Gazette and Alexandria Daily Advertiser, July 1, 1819

A Friend of the Constitution No. III

I now proceed to enquire how the principles of the common law apply to the case. Although I might cite from that code, examples of the extended construction of the words of a grant for the purpose of implying what is not expressed. As that "by the grant of a house, an orchard, and curtilage, may pass"; (*a*) or might cite from it the most complete evidence that the *intention* is the most sacred rule of interpretation. I am content to limit my observations to the phrases quoted by Hampden.

I admit it to be a principle of common law, "that when a man grants any thing, he grants also that without which the grant cannot have its effect"; and, by this word "effect," I understand, not a stinted, halfway effect, but full and complete effect, according to the intention of the parties, and to their mutual accommodation. Thus, a right of way over the land of another for a particular purpose, whether given expressly or by implication, is to be so exercised as to effect that purpose completely, with convenience to the grantee, and with as little injury to the landholder as is compatible with the full enjoyment of the right. The same principle is laid down by Lord Coke in the passage also quoted by Hampden. "For," says that great lawyer, "when the law doth give any thing, it giveth, impliedly whatsoever is necessary for the taking and enjoying of the same. And, therefore, the law giveth all that which is convenient; viz. free entry, egress, and regress, as much as is necessary." Hampden says the word "convenient" is here convertible with "necessary." This is true. But it is not less true that the word "necessary" is here convertible with "convenient." Lord Coke uses both words, as they are often used, in nearly the same sense. When so used, they signify neither a feigned convenience, nor a strict necessity; but a reasonable convenience, and a qualified necessity; both to be regulated by the state of the parties, and the nature of the act to be done. In this case, according to Lord Coke, the party having ingress, egress, and regress, in order to bring away his own, is not obliged to take it away at once; or before it is ready; he may use a reasonable convenience.

I admit also, "that the incident is to be taken *in reasonable and easy sense,* and not strained to comprehend things remote, unlikely, or unusual." By which I understand, that no strained construction, either to include or exclude the incident, is admissible; but that the natural construction is the true one. This is "taking the incident in a reasonable and easy sense."

(*a*) Ch. 5. b. 3 Ba. abr. 396 c. b. 6 Ba. abr. 384 title statute.

The doctrines of the common law then on this subject, are not at variance with those more general principles which are found in the laws of nature and nations. The rules prescribed by each are subjected to that great paramount law of reason, which pervades and regulates all human systems.

The object of language is to communicate the intention of him who speaks, and the great duty of a judge who construes an instrument, is to find the intention of its makers. There is no technical rule applicable to every case, which enjoins us to interpret instruments in a more restricted sense than their words import. The nature of the instrument, the words that are employed, the object to be effected, are all to be taken into consideration, and to have their due weight.

Although I have demonstrated, as I trust, that the quotations of Hampden contradict, instead of proving the principle he would extract from them, I should not do justice to the subject, were I to dismiss it without further comment.

The difference between the instruments in the examples taken from Vattel, or from the books of the common law, and the constitution of a nation, is, I think, too apparent to escape the observation of any reflecting man.

Take that of an invading army, which, after advancing far into the country of its enemy, stipulates for a safe return home.

The parties to this contract are enemies endeavoring to accomplish the ruin of each other. The contract relates to a single operation, the material circumstances connected with which may be, and therefore ought to be, foreseen, and minutely provided for. There is no reason for including in this stipulation, things which it does not clearly reach. Yet even in this case, the words are so construed as to comprehend more than is clearly expressed, in order to give full effect to the manifest intention of the parties. The same observations apply to the case of an interview between enemies.

So, the cases put in the books of the common law, are, all of them, cases of contract between individuals. Having only a single object to provide for, the provisions respecting that object might be explicit and full. It is not to be supposed that any essential circumstance will be omitted, which the parties intended to include in the grant, and there is consequently the less propriety in implying such circumstance. They are all likewise cases of property; and the terms of the grant cannot be enlarged in favor of one man, without impairing the rights of another. Yet, even in these cases, we have seen that every thing necessary to give full effect to the grant, every thing essential to the perfect enjoyment of the thing granted, passes by implication. Hampden himself is compelled to admit it to be "a clear principle of universal law"—"That the general grant of a thing, or power, carries with it all those means (and those only) which are necessary to the perfection of the grant, or the execution of the power." And he admits also, that by necessary means, he does not intend "in all cases, a sheer necessity"; which I understand to be equivalent to *an absolute or indispensable* necessity.

It can scarcely be necessary to say, that no one of the circumstances which might seem to justify rather a strict construction in the particular cases quoted by Hampden, apply to a constitution. It is not a contract between enemies seeking each other's destruction, and anxious to insert every particular, lest a watchful adversary should take advantage of the omission. Nor is it a case where implications in favor of one man impair the vested rights of another. Nor is it a contract for a single object, every thing relating to which, might be recollected and inserted. It is the act of a people, creating a government, without which they cannot exist as a people. The powers of this government are conferred for their own benefit, are essential to their own prosperity, and are to be exercised for their good, by persons chosen for that purpose by themselves. The object of the instrument is not a single one which can be minutely described, with all its circumstances. The attempt to do so, would totally change its nature, and defeat its purpose. It is intended to be a general system for all future times, to be adapted by those who administer it, to all future occasions that may come within its own view. From its nature, such an instrument can describe only the great objects it is intended to accomplish, and state in general terms, the specific powers which are deemed necessary for those objects. To direct the manner in which these powers are to be exercised, the means by which the objects of the government are to be effected, a legislature is granted. This would be totally useless, if its office and duty were performed in the constitution. This legislature is an emanation from the people themselves. It is a part chosen to represent the whole, and to mark, according to the judgement of the nation, its course, within those great outlines which are given in the constitution. It is impossible to construe such an instrument rightly, without adverting to its nature, and marking the points of difference which distinguish it from ordinary contracts.

The case which comes nearest to it, is a treaty regulating the future intercourse between two nations. If in such a treaty "it is impossible from the narrow limits of the human mind," to foresee all cases and circumstances, or include all consequences of what is appointed or promised, if, "from the impossibility of entering into this immense detail," the terms of a treaty must be general, and must be applied by interpretation to particular cases, so as to effect the intention of the parties; how much more impossible is it for a constitution to enter into this immense detail, and how much more necessary is it that its principles be applied to particulars by the legislature.

A still more decisive objection to the exact application of the cases put by Hampden, is, that a rule applicable to powers, which may, strictly speaking, be denominated incidental, is not equally applicable to all the means of executing enumerated powers.

An "incident," Hampden tells us, "is defined, in the common law, to be a thing appertaining to, or following another, as being more worthy or principal"; and is defined by Johnson, to be means falling in beside the main design. In his second proposition, he considers "an incident as an additional power."

I am content with these definitions. In applying them to the subject under consideration, I shall show conclusively that the means by which a power expressly granted is to be executed, would, most generally, be improperly classed with incidental powers.

Congress has power "to raise and support armies." Will any man contend that an act for raising an army of ten thousand men, for appointing the proper officers, for enlisting the troops, for allowing them pay and rations, proceeds from a power *appertaining to or following* the principal power to raise and support armies? Can such an act, with any propriety, be denominated, "means falling in beside the main design"? or "an additional power"?

Is it not too clear for controversy that such an act would be the direct execution of the principal power, and not of one appertaining to or following it? That it would be the main design itself, and not "means falling in beside it"? That it would be the primary, and not "an additional power"?

Had the right "to make rules for the government of the land and naval forces" not been expressly granted, a law made for that purpose would have rested, for its support, on the incidental or implied powers of congress, and to a question respecting its constitutionality, the doctrines of implication would have applied. But, the constitution having expressly given this power, the law enacting the articles of war is the instrument, or the means by which congress has chosen to execute it. With these means the doctrine of incidents has nothing to do. No court has a right to enquire whether the punishments inflicted by the articles of war are necessary or unnecessary. The means are appropriate, and congress may, constitutionally, select and vary them at will.

So congress has power "to establish post offices and post roads."

The law designating post offices and post roads, with all the provisions relating to that subject, is made in execution of this power. Such laws are the means which congress chuses to employ. But the right to punish those who rob the mail is an incidental power, and the question whether it is fairly deducible from the grant is open for argument. Under the confederation, congress possessed no implied powers, and was therefore unable to punish those who robbed the mail, but was capable of regulating the post office. These regulations were means, not incidents.

Thus too congress has power "to constitute tribunals inferior to the supreme court."

An act constituting these tribunals, defining their jurisdiction, regulating their proceedings, &c. is not an incident to the power, but the means of executing it. The legislature may multiply or diminish these tribunals, may vary their jurisdiction at will. These laws are means, and the constitution creates no question respecting their necessity. But a law to punish those who falsify a record, or who commit perjury or subornation of perjury, is an execution of an incidental power; and the question whether that incident is fairly deduced from the principal, is open to argument. Under the confederation congress could establish certain courts; but, having no incidental powers, was incapable of punishing those who falsified the records, or committed perjury within those courts.

In the exercise of an incidental power, we are always to enquire whether "it appertains to or follows the principal"; for the power itself may be questioned; but in exercising one that is granted, there is no question about the power, and the very business of a legislature is to select the means. It is not pretended that this right of selection may be fraudulently used to the destruction of the fair land marks of the constitution. Congress certainly may not, under the pretext of collecting taxes, or of guaranteeing to each state a republican form of government, alter the law of descents; but if the means have a plain relation to the end—if they be direct, natural and appropriate, who, but the people at the elections, shall, under the pretext of their being unnecessary, control the legislative will, and direct its understanding?

The distinction then between a power which is "incidental" or "additional" to another, and the means which may be employed to carry a given power into execution, though not perceived by Hampden, is most obvious. I have been the more particular in stating it, not only because his attention to it produces errors which pervade his whole argument, but because also it has led him to the application of language of the most unbecoming as well as unmerited asperity, to the judges of the supreme court. He is excessively displeased with them for not having used the word "incident" when speaking of "means." The term "means," he says, "started up on the present occasion, is not only undefined, but is general; and *guile*," he has permitted himself to add, "*covers itself under general expressions. Why should the supreme court*," he continues, "trump up a term on this occasion, which is equally novel, undefined, and general? Why should they select a term which is broad enough to demolish the limits prescribed to the general government by the constitution?"

All this irritation is excited by the heinous offence of using, when, speaking on one subject, words directly applicable to that subject, instead of employing those Hampden chuses to prescribe, but which belong to another, and a totally different subject. All must admit that there are *means* by which a legislature may carry its powers into execution; and Hampden is, I believe, the only man in the United States who will deny that the word *means* expresses that idea more accurately, and with more precision, than the word *incidents*.

It is certainly a piece of information which must surprise if it does not instruct us, that the word *means* has been "trumped up on this occasion" by the supreme court, that it is "equally novel, undefined and general," and that it is "broad enough to demolish the limits prescribed to the general government."

These strange positions are not in themselves more curious than the manner in which they are supported. We might reasonably expect to find that this favorite term "incidental," which must be dragged into use, not only where it is appropriate, but where it is inappropriate also, was employed in the constitution, and might thence derive some pretensions to this preference over every other word. It is not however to be found in that instrument—and one would therefore suppose, might be used or rejected with impunity, according to its fitness to the subject discussed.

But Hampden tells us that the terms "necessary" and "incidental" powers "were those uniformly used at the outset of the constitution; while the term means is entirely of modern origin." In support of this assertion he immediately quotes a passage from the Federalist, which contains the word *means*, and does not contain the word *incidental*. "A power," says the Federalist in the passage referred to, "is nothing but the ability or faculty of doing a thing, and that ability includes the means necessary for its execution."

If, instead of this general reference to the terms "uniformly used at the outset of the constitution" we go to particulars, we find the words *incidental* and *means*, employed equally, as either in the opinion of the speaker or writer was best adapted to the occasion.

In the debates in the first congress on the bank bill, we find the opponents of that measure continually using the word *means*—and some gentlemen said "the true exposition of a necessary mean to produce a given end, was that mean without which the end could not be produced.

The friends of the bill also employed the same term. They maintained the sound construction of the clause granting to congress the right "to make all laws necessary and proper" for carrying into execution the powers vested in the government, to be a recognition of an authority in the national legislature to employ all the known usual *means* for executing those powers. They farther contended that a bank was a known and usual instrument by which several of them were exercised.

In the opinions afterwards given on this subject by the cabinet ministers, as stated to us in the life of Washington, this term is repeatedly used. The secretary of state and the attorney general, observe in substance, that "the constitution allows only the means which are necessary, not those which are convenient." And, after stating the dangerous consequences of such a latitudinous construction as they suppose was contended for by the friends of the bill, these gentlemen add "therefore it was that the constitution restrained them to *necessary means*, that is to say, to those *means* without which the grant of power must be nugatory."

The secretary of the treasury commences his argument with the general proposition. "That every power vested in a government, is, in its nature, *sovereign*, and includes, by *force* of the *term* a right to employ all the *means* requisite and *fairly applicable* to the attainment of the *ends* of such power."

It would be tedious to cite from this masterly argument, every passage in which we find this word *means*. It is used whenever the occasion requires it. It is used too in all the papers of the day which have fallen within my observation. How then can Hampden justify his assertion that this word is "trumped up" by the supreme court, that it is "novel, undefined, and general"?

The third & last proposition of Hampden is, "that the insertion of the words *necessary and proper* in the last part of the 8th section of the 1st article, did not enlarge powers previously given, but were inserted only through abundant caution."

To the declaration that I do not mean to controvert this proposition, I will only add the following extract from the opinion of the supreme court. "The result of the most careful and attentive consideration bestowed upon this clause is that, if it does not enlarge, it cannot be construed to restrain the powers of congress, or to impair the rights of the legislature to exercise its best judgement in the selection of measures to carry into execution the constitutional powers of the government. If no other motive for its insertion can be suggested, a sufficient one is found in the desire to remove all doubts respecting the right to legislate on that vast mass of incidental powers which must be involved in the constitution, if that instrument be not a splendid bauble."

The court then does not give to these words any greater extension than is allowed to them by Hampden.

The three general propositions laid down by this writer as containing those great and fundamental truths which are to convict the supreme court of error, have now been examined. The first is directly affirmed, & the last admitted, in the opinion so much reprobated. The second contains in itself, no principle, which that opinion controverts. Yet the quotations arranged under it, and the aspersions, alike unjust and injurious on the supreme court of our country, which are intermingled with those quotations, have been noticed in some detail, because this was necessary to the correct understanding of this application to the subject under discussion.

A FRIEND OF THE CONSTITUTION.

Gazette and Alexandria Daily Advertiser, July 2, 1819

A Friend of the Constitution No. IV

In his third number, Hampden states those specific objections to the opinion of the supreme court, which are to justify the virulent invectives he has, so unsparingly bestowed on the judicial department.

Before noticing these objections, I must be allowed to observe that, in recapitulating what he supposes himself to have established in his preceeding numbers, he entirely misrepresents what he has himself attempted to prove.

After stating that the clause containing the words necessary and proper was "tautologous and redundant," he adds, "I have also shown that, in that case, such means were implied, and such only, as were essential to effectuate the power; and that this is the case in all the codes of the law of nature, of nations, of war, of reason, and the common law. The means, and the only means, admitted by them all, and especially by the common law, are laid down emphatically to be such, *without which*, the grant cannot have its effect."

Can Hampden possibly believe that he has even attempted to show these things? Can he possibly have so far misunderstood himself? Or does he shift his ground to impose on his readers? Can he already have forgotten that all his quotations and all his arguments apply to "incidental" or "additional" powers, not to the *means* by which powers are to be executed? Can it have escaped his recollection that, so far from even making an effort to show that by any law whatever, it is "laid down emphatically" that those means only may be used in the execution of the power "*without which* the grant cannot have its effect," he has proscribed the term itself as one "broad enough to demolish the limits prescribed to the general government by the constitution"? "As one which might cover the latent designs of ambition and change the nature of the general government"? Does he not remember, or does he suppose his readers will not remember, the motives he ascribes to the supreme court for "trumping up this equally novel, undefined, and general term"? I will not retort on Hampden the charge of "*guile*" on this occasion, but I cannot leave him the advantage he claims, of having proved that which he has not even suggested. I have not controverted his real proposition "that the limited grant to congress of certain enumerated powers, only carried with it such additional powers as were *fairly incidental* to them." But I utterly deny that when a power is granted, "those means *only* may be used in its execution, *without which* the grant cannot have its effect." I utterly deny that this proposition is maintained in any code whatever. When the attempt to establish it shall be made it will be time enough to show that it is totally unsustainable.

I now proceed to the errors ascribed by Hampden, to the opinion of the supreme court.

The first is that the court has agreed in favor of an enlarged construction of the clause authorizing congress "to make all laws necessary and proper for carrying into execution" the powers vested in the government.

Hampden does not venture to assert in express terms that the court has ascribed to that clause the quality of enlarging the powers of congress, or of enabling the legislature to do that which it might not have done had the clause been omitted. He knows well that such an assertion would have been unfounded, for he says "the supreme court itself admits that these terms were used & *only used*, to remove all doubts of the implied powers of the national legislature in relation to the great mass of concerns entrusted to it. This is an admission by the court that they were not used for the purpose of enlargement."

Why then does he seek indirectly to impress on the minds of his readers this idea known to himself to be incorrect?

But I will advert to the particular instances of this error, which he has selected in support of his charge.

The first is that the supreme court has said that this clause "is placed among the powers of the government, and not among the limitations on those powers."

That it is so placed, is acknowledged. But the court is supposed to be highly culpable for stating this truth, because it was stated for a purpose which this writer condemns.

To demonstrate that this argument was not used for the purpose, or in the manner alleged by Hampden, it is only necessary to advert to the opinion itself.

The court has laid down the proposition that "the government which has a right to do an act, and has imposed upon it the duty of performing that act must, according to the dictates of reason, have a right to select the means." Having reasoned on this proposition, the court adds, but the constitution of the United States has not left the right of congress to employ the necessary means for the execution of the powers conferred on the government to general reasoning. To its enumeration of powers is added that of making "all laws which shall be necessary and proper."

The meaning of the court cannot be mistaken. It is that this clause expresses what the preceding reasoning shewed must be implied.

The court then proceeds, "The counsel for the state of Maryland have urged various arguments to prove that this clause, tho' in terms a grant of power, is not so in effect; but is really restrictive of the general right, which might otherwise be implied, of selecting means for executing the enumerated powers."

The court then proceeds to combat these arguments of counsel—and combats them so successfully as to draw from Hampden himself the acknowledgement that "the words prohibit nothing to the general government." "It is only contended," he says, "That they create no enlargement of the powers previously given." Yet after thus explicitly yielding the point which was really in contest, he attempts to turn this total defeat into a victory, by contending that those arguments which were urged to prove that this clause did not restrain the powers of congress were brought forward to prove that it enlarges them, and fails of doing so.

No man, I think, who will even glance at the opinion, will fall into the error into which Hampden would lead him. The court, after reasoning at some length upon the clause, says, "To waste time and argument to prove that, without it, congress might carry its powers into execution, would be not much less idle than to hold a lighted taper to the sun. As little can it be required to prove that, in the absence of this clause, congress would have some choice of means," &c. "This clause," the court adds, "as construed by the state of Maryland, would abridge, and almost annihilate this useful and necessary right of the legislature to select its means. That this could not be intended, is, we should think, had it not been already controverted, too apparent for controversy. We think so for the following reasons: The clause is placed among the powers of congress, and not among the limitations on those powers."

The court proceeds to state several other reasons, to show that the clause could not have been intended by the convention to abridge those powers which congress would otherwise have possessed, and concludes with expressing the entire conviction that it could not be construed "to impair the right of the legislature to exercise its best judgement in the selection of measures to carry into execution the constitutional powers of the government." Hampden himself refers to that part of this conclusion which assigns to the clause the office of removing all doubt respecting the right "to legislate on that vast mass of incidental powers, which must be involved in the constitution," and approves it. Yet he has mentioned this argument, "that the clause is placed among the powers of congress, and not among the limitations on those powers," as his first objection to the opinion of the court; and he objects to it, not because the statement is untrue, but because the court urged it to establish an enlarged construction, an "extension" of the powers of congress.

I appeal to any man of the most ordinary understanding, when I ask if Hampden can possibly have misunderstood the opinion of the supreme court on this point? If he has not, why has he misrepresented it?

The second reason assigned by the court to prove that this clause could not be intended to abridge the powers of congress, is, "That its terms purport to enlarge, not to diminish the powers vested in the government."

Its terms are, "Congress shall have power to make all laws which may be necessary and proper for carrying into execution the foregoing powers."

I ask, with much confidence, whether these words *purport* to be words of grant, or of limitation? If the answer must be that they are words of grant, then the court stated them correctly. Hampden cannot controvert this; but he censures the argument, because it was urged to prove an extension of the powers of government. It was not so urged. The court states it explicitly as the second reason for believing that this clause did not *abridge* the powers of congress; and adds "no reason has been, or can be assigned, for thus concealing an intention to narrow the discretion of the national legislature, under words which purport to enlarge it."

Why, again let me ask, why has Hampden thus plainly misrepresented the opinion he condemns?

"The supreme court," he says, "has also claimed such an enlargement, on the ground that our constitution is one of a vast republic, whose limits they have pompously swelled, and vastly exaggerated."

The supreme court has not *claimed* "such enlargement" on

the ground stated by this very inaccurate writer, or on any other ground.

After stating truly the extent of our great republic, the court says, "The exigencies of the nation may require that the treasure raised in the north should be transported to the south, *that* raised in the east conveyed to the west, or that this order should be reversed. Is that construction of the constitution to be preferred which would render these operations difficult, hazardous, and expensive?" &c.

I refer to this whole paragraph in the opinion; and aver that not a syllable uttered by the court, applies to an enlargement of the powers of congress. The reasoning of the judges is opposed to that restricted construction which would embarrass congress, in the execution of its acknowledged powers; and maintains that such construction, if not required by the words of the instrument, ought not to be adopted of choice; but make no allusion to a construction enlarging the grant beyond the meaning of its ends. The charge of having "pompously swelled, and greatly exaggerated" the limits of the United States, would be too paltry for notice, were it not to remark, that, even in the most unimportant circumstances, Hampden delights to cast unmerited censure. The court had said, "From the St. Croix to the Gulph of Mexico, from the Atlantic to the Pacific, revenue is to be collected and expended, armies are to be marched and supported." And is not the St. Croix our north-eastern boundary? Is not Louisiana bounded by the Gulph of Mexico on the south? Does not our late treaty with England establish a line between the territory of the two governments, to the Pacific? And do we not, independent of our unratified treaty with Spain, claim the mouth of the Columbia, which empties into that ocean?

"The supreme court," says Hampden, "also claimed favor in this particular, on account of the magnitude of the trust confided to the general government."

This charge, like every other, is totally unfounded. The language of the court is, "the sword and the purse, all the external relations, and no inconsiderable portion of the industry of the nation, are entrusted to its government. It can never be pretended that such vast powers draw after them others which are inferior, merely because they are inferior. Such an idea can never be advanced. But it may with great reason be contended that a government entrusted with such ample powers, on the due execution of which the happiness and prosperity of the nation so vitally depend, must also be entrusted with ample means for their execution. The power being given, it is the interest of the nation to facilitate its execution. It can never be their interest, and cannot be presumed to have been their intention, to clog and embarass its execution."

And I ask if every sentiment here advanced be not strictly true? Congress has power to raise armies. Whatever doubts Hampden may entertain of the propriety of granting this power, can he seriously contend that its execution should be so clogged and embarrassed as that the troops cannot be raised in the manner most economical and most convenient to the people? So congress has power to levy taxes, with this only limitation, that direct taxes shall be proportioned to numbers, and indirect taxes shall be uniform. Does he so construe the constitution as to impose other limitations, or to inhibit congress from raising taxes by the means least burthensome to the people?

But be this as it may, it is most obvious that the opinion does not even hint the idea ascribed to it by Hampden. So far from suggesting that an enlarged construction is to be inferred from the magnitude of the trust, it expressly rejects this inference by saying, "It can never be pretended that such vast powers draw after them others which are inferior, merely because they are inferior." The argument is plainly advanced by the court in opposition to that unnaturally restrained construction which had been pressed by the counsel for the state of Maryland; and contends only that the government should be allowed, for the execution of its powers, means co-extensive with them.

I ask if Hampden himself can deny the correctness of this reasoning? I ask if he can discern any thing in the proposition that means for the execution of powers should be proportioned to the powers themselves, which contends that those powers ought to be enlarged by construction or otherwise?

A FRIEND OF THE CONSTITUTION.

Gazette and Alexandria Daily Advertiser, July 3, 1819

A Friend of the Constitution No. V

With as little regard to the text on which he comments as was shown in the instances mentioned in the preceding number, Hampden says, "The court is pleased to remind us with the same view" (that is with a view to a construction that shall extend the powers of congress) "that it is a constitution we are expounding."

He is so very reasonable as not to deny that it is a constitution. Consequently he does not, on this occasion, charge the court with using an inaccurate expression. Its offensiveness consists only in the intention with which it is used. This criminal intention exists only in the fertile imagination of Hampden. The court makes no allusion whatever to that enlarged construction which he ascribes to it.

In answer to the argument that the clause under consideration so narrowed the powers of congress as to prohibit, the passage of any law *without which* any given power could be executed, the court, after showing that the word *necessary* did not always import the last degree of necessity, or that "*sheer* necessity" of which Hampden speaks, adds, "in its construction, the subject, the context, the intention of the person using it, are all to be taken into view." And I stop to ask if any fair mind can reject this rule of exposition? This "provision," continues the court, "is made in a constitution intended to endure for ages to come—and, consequently, to be adapted to the various crises of human affairs. To have prescribed the means by which government should, in all future time, execute its powers, would have been to change entirely the character of the instrument, and to give it the properties of a legal code."

The passage is too long to be quoted entire, but I say with confidence that it does not contain the most distant allusion to any extension, by construction of the powers of congress. Its sole object is to remind us that a constitution cannot possibly enumerate the means by which the powers of government are to be carried into execution.

The correctness of this position, Hampden does not venture to deny. He distinctly admits it; but thinks it necessary to add, (as if the contrary had been insinuated by the supreme court) "that the constitution establishes a *criterion* in relation to them, and that criterion should be the *law* to the several departments in making the selection."

The whole opinion of the court proceeds upon this basis, as on a truth not to be controverted. The principle it labors to establish is, not that congress may select means beyond the limits of the constitution, but means within those limits.

The grand objection made to the opinion so bitterly inculpated is, that it construes the clause which has been so frequently repeated, as an enlargement of the enumerated powers of congress, and contends, throughout, for an extension of these powers beyond the import of the words. To support this objection, various passages are selected from it. I have reviewed them all; and have, I think demonstrated that no one of them will bear the construction for which Hampden contends. I do not fear to be contradicted by any rational man who will read the opinion with a real desire to understand it, when I say that it contains not a single sentence in support of these doctrines. In form and in substance, it is a refutation of the argument that this clause narrows the right of congress to execute its powers; and it claims only that, in ascertaining the true extent of those powers, the constitution should be fairly construed.

Why has Hampden attempted thus plainly to pervert this opinion, and to ascribe to it doctrines which it clearly rejects? He knows well that prejudices once impressed on the public mind, are not easily removed; and that the progress of truth and reason is slow.

I should perhaps trespass too much on the patience of the public, were I to advert with the same minuteness to every thing said by Hampden on the subject of the means by which congress may constitutionally exercise its enumerated powers, or to cite from the opinion of the court the several passages to which he alludes with disapprobation, and which he mistates either directly or by insinuation. I have examined them all with attention, and I say, without fear of contradiction, that the general principles maintained by the supreme court are, that the constitution may be construed as if the clause which has been so much discussed, had been entirely omitted. That the powers of congress are expressed in terms which, without its aid, enable and require the legislature to execute them, and of course, to take means for their execution. That the choice of these means devolve on the legislature, whose right, and whose duty it is, to adopt those which are most advantageous to the people, provided they be within the limits of the constitution. Their constitutionality depends on their being the natural, direct, and appropriate means, or the known and usual means, for the execution of the given power.

In no single instance does the court admit the unlimited power of congress to adopt any means whatever, and thus to pass the limits prescribed by the constitution. Not only is the discretion claimed for the legislature in the selection of its means, always limited in terms, to such as are appropriate, but the court expressly says, "should congress under the pretext of executing its powers, pass laws for the accomplishment of objects, not entrusted to the government, it would become the painful duty of this tribunal, should a case requiring such a decision come before it, to say that such an act was not the law of the land."

How then can Hampden justify to his country, or even to himself, the declarations "that the court had resolved to put down all discussions respecting the powers of the government in future, by a judicial *coup de main*; to give a general letter of attorney to the future legislators of the union; and to tread under foot all those parts and articles of the constitution which had been heretofore deemed to set limits to the power of the federal legislature." That in fact "the court had granted to congress unlimited powers under the pretext of a discretion in selecting means"?

In a grand effort to impair the constitution of our country by construction, the doctrine "that the end will justify the means," seems not to be entirely exploded.

Hampden is much dissatisfied with the declaration of the court "that the general government, though limited in its powers, is supreme within the sphere of its action." He "does not understand this jargon. This word supreme," he says, "does not sound well in a government which acts under a limited constitution."

This writer, the least of whose charges against the supreme court is inaccuracy of language, would seem to have confounded *supremacy* with *despotism*. The word "supreme" means "highest in authority"; and there must be a highest in authority under a limited, as well as under an unlimited constitution. Is not the government of the union, "within its sphere of action," "supreme," or "highest in authority"? This is certainly the fact, and is as certainly the language of the constitution. That instrument declares, that "This constitution and the laws of the United States, made in pursuance thereof," &c. "shall be the supreme law of the land." The states, the state judges, and the people, are bound by it, "any thing in the constitution or laws of any state to the contrary notwithstanding." Is not that power supreme which can give the supreme law?

The constitution may be changed, any constitution may be changed. But while it remains what it is, the government "while moving within its proper sphere," is supreme. What authority is above it?

This "jargon" may grate harshly on the ears of Hampden, and he may be unaccustomed to it; but it is the language of truth, and of the constitution, and his displeasure will not banish it. The language of nature and of truth would grate harshly on the ears of an Eastern despot, unaccustomed to its words. He would not like "such jargon." But it would not be, on that account, inaccurate or improper.

In the continued spirit of misrepresentation, Hampden says, "The court is of opinion, that the right to establish a bank stands on the same foundation with that to exact oaths of office"; and also, that "the denial of a right to establish banks" "carries with it the denial of that of annexing punishments to crimes."

I do not deny that the cases bear a strong analogy to each other; but I do deny that the court has made the statement ascribed to it; and therefore, I do not deem it incumbent on me, in this mere justification of a judicial opinion, to show the fallacy of Hampden's distinctions between them, or to prove propositions, however true they may be, which that opinion does not assert.

The counsel for the state of Maryland, we are told, had contended that the clause which Hampden asserts to be "tautologous and redundant," "limits the right of congress to make laws for the execution of the powers granted by the constitution, to such as are indispensable, and *without which* the power would be nugatory."

The court rejects this construction, and in reasoning against it, says, "If we apply this principle to any of the powers of the government, we shall find it so pernicious in its operation, that we shall be compelled to discard it." The court then proceeds to show that this principle, if recognized, would prove many of those acts, the constitutionality of which, are universally acknowledged, such as the act prescribing the oaths of office, &c. to be usurpations. The argument is, avowedly, urged to disprove a proposition supported by counsel in the cause, as all essential in the construction of the constitution, but which Hampden expressly abandons as unsustainable.

He is equally incorrect when he says, "The supreme court is farther of opinion, that the power of incorporating banks is justified by the admitted right of congress to establish governments for the vacant territories of the United States."

The court had shown by a long, and, I think, an accurate course of reasoning, that, "if the end be within the scope of the constitution, all means which are appropriate, which are plainly adapted to that end, which are not prohibited, but consist with the letter and the spirit of the constitution, are constitutional."

But it had been urged that a bank, should it even be a measure of this description, is placed beyond the reach of congress, because the legislature of the union has no power to erect a corporation.

The court proceeds to consider this argument; and, in order to show its fallacy, proves incontestably, that the act of incorporation is the mere annexation of a quality to a measure, to the doing which, if the measure itself be proper, the constitution creates no objection. In illustration of this argument, reference is made to the territorial governments which are corporations. This reference is not made for the purpose of showing that a bank is as absolutely necessary to the union, as a government to a territory; but of showing that if an instrument be proper in itself, the circumstance that an act of incorporation is essential to its efficacy, creates no constitutional objection to it.

After a long and perspicuous review of the arguments which had been urged against the act of congress which was under consideration, the court proceeds to the act itself, and places its constitutionality simply on the ground, that a bank is "a convenient, a useful, and an essential instrument in the prosecution of the fiscal operations of the government." "That all those who have been concerned in the administration of the finances, have concurred in representing its importance and necessity."

The court may be mistaken in the "propriety and necessity" of this instrument. I do not think so; but others may honestly entertain this opinion. Be this as it may, the grand objection to the opinion, the reason assigned for all the malignant calumnies which have been heaped upon the judicial department, is, not that the court has decided erroneously, but that its decision is placed on principles which prostrate all the barriers to the unlimited power of the general government. That it "has made a declaratory decision that congress has power to bind us in all cases whatsoever."

We had before seen how totally untrue this allegation is, so far as it relies for support on the general reasoning of the court; and we now see how untrue it is, so far as it relies on the particular reason expressly given for the decision. That particular reason is, that a bank "is a convenient, a useful, an essential instrument in the prosecution of the fiscal operations of the government, the importance and necessity of which" is so strong that the best judges of that importance and necessity have concurred in representing; and the most intelligent original enemies of the measure have admitted it.

Hampden himself seems half inclined to make this admission. He says, "there is no doubt but many of those who voted for the bank, did it under what was supposed the peculiar pressure of the times. It was not adopted in relation to ordinary times, nor on the ground of its being a constitutional measure."

If "the pressure of the times" when this bill passed, rendered it necessary, I am at a loss to conceive how it can be repugnant to that constitution which was made for all times. The peculiar circumstances of the moment may render a measure more or less wise, but cannot render it more or less constitutional.

I have claimed too much of the public attention already, to be equally minute on the remaining observations of Hampden. On his argument therefore respecting the necessity of the bank, I will make only one remark, the correctness of which will be perceived by all who read that argument. He requires that a measure, to be constitutional, must be so indispensable that without it the power cannot be executed. This principle, if at all sustainable, can only be sustained by contending that the clause in which the word "necessary" is found, abridges the powers congress would otherwise have possessed. This construction he has expressly surrendered. He cannot be permitted to avail himself of a construction which he, in terms, abandons.

A FRIEND OF THE CONSTITUTION.

Gazette and Alexandria Daily Advertiser, July 5, 1819

A Friend of the Constitution No. VI

Hampden has deemed it proper to introduce his objections to the jurisdiction of the court, in the case of McCulloch against the state of Maryland, with a long dissertation on the nature of our government. On so much of this dissertation as labors to prove that it is not a consolidated one, I will only remark, that it is a truth universally known and universally admitted. No person in his senses ever has, ever will, or ever can controvert it. Any writer who pleases, may certainly amuse himself with the demonstration of this political axiom but he adds just as much to our political knowledge, as he would to our geographical, were he to tell us, and produce a long train of authorities to prove it, that the United States lie on the western, and not on the eastern side of the atlantic.

But when Hampden says that however "indistinct" may be the language of the court, on this point, "their doctrines admit of no controversy. They show the government to be, in the opinion of the court, a consolidated, and not a federal government." His assertion is neither equally true, nor equally innocent.

The question whether our government is consolidated or federal, does not appear to have been stirred in the argument of the cause. It does not appear to have occurred to counsel on either side, that any question respecting the existence of the state governments, as a part of the American system, could any where be made. The motion of such a point would probably have excited not much less surprize, than if any gentleman had thought proper seriously to maintain that there was a bench and a bar, and judges on the one, and lawyers at the other. It is not wonderful then, that the court should have omitted to state such a question in terms, or formally to decide it. But the principles laid down, and the language used, presuppose the existence of states as a part of our system, too clearly to be misunderstood by any person.

The court says, that "the defendant is a sovereign state"; that "the conflicting powers of the government of the union, and of its members, as marked in the constitution, are to be discussed"; "that the government of the union is one of enumerated powers"; "that it can exercise only the powers which are granted to it"; that "no political dreamer was ever wild enough to think of breaking down the lines which separate states, and of compounding the American people into one mass"; "that the assent of the states in their sovereign capacity" to the constitution, "is implied in calling a convention, and thus submitting that instrument to the people"; "that in discussing the questions" "respecting the extent of the powers actually granted", "the conflicting powers of the general and state governments, must be brought into view"; "that the constitution requires" that "the members of the state legislatures, and the officers of the executive and judicial departments of the states, shall take the oath of fidelity to it."

If Hampden can reconcile these passages with his assertion, he will, I doubt not, also reconcile the following, as preliminary to discussing the right of a state to tax the bank; the court says, "That the power of taxation is one of vital importance; that it is retained by the states; that it is not abridged by the grant of a similar power to the government of the union; that it is to be concurrently exercised by the two governments; are truths which have never been denied."

The whole opinion is replete with passages such as these. They demonstrate, as conclusively as words can demonstrate, the incorrectness of the assertion, imputing to it the doctrine that the government of the United States is a consolidated one.

Without making, at this time, farther quotations from that opinion, I will proceed to examine the reasons given for the assertions, that this plain language is "indistinct"; & that it conveys "*doctrines*" directly the reverse of what the words import.

I shall do so the more readily, because, in treating this part of the subject, this gentleman, though he rarely states correctly the opinion he professes to quote, discloses still more clearly than heretofore, his real sentiments, and real objects; and because those sentiments and that object ought, I think, to receive the most serious attention of the people.

Hampden frequently uses, for what purpose let him say, the word "national" as synonimous with "consolidated." Thus he says, "It is not easy to discern how a government whose members are sovereign states, and whose powers conflict with those of such states, can be a national or consolidated government."

I deny that these terms are convertible. The government of the United States is almost universally denominated the national government, or the government of the nation. It is repeatedly so termed in the Federalist, and in other political treatises, and has never been termed a consolidated government.

Hampden defines a consolidated government to be "one which acts only on individuals, and in which other states and governments are not known." What name will he give us for a government "which acts only on individuals," but "in which other states and governments are known"? Such is the government of the United States; and, in a work (*a*) now acknowledged by all to be a clear and a just exposition of the constitution, we are told, that, according to the definitions of those terms given by its opponents, "it is neither a national, nor a federal constitution; but a composition of both."

But waving, for the present, any controversy about terms, I will proceed to the evidence adduced in support of the charge that the language of the court, on the question of consolidation, is indistinct.

The first is, that "They use the word *people* in a sense seeming clearly to import the people of the United States, as contradistinguished from the people of the several states; from which the inference would arise, that the states were not known in the establishment of the constitution." As no particular passage in the opinion is referred to, it is not in my power, by quoting the words of the court, to give a precise refutation to this alle-

(*a*) Federalist, No. 39.

gation. I must content myself with the more general, and less pointed observations.

The counsel for the state of Maryland, we are told, contended that the constitution was the act of sovereign states, as contradistinguished from the people. In opposition to this proposition, the court maintained that the constitution is not the act of the state governments, but of the people of the states. In the course of this argument, the term—*the people*—without any annexation, is frequently used; but never in a sense excluding the idea that the people were divided into distinct societies, or indicating the non-existence of states. It is positively denied that this use of the term, even unaccompanied by those passages with which the opinion abounds, would afford any countenance to the inference "that the states were not known in the establishment of the constitution." Still less can such an inference arise in opposition to the express and repeated declarations of the court.

If instead of using the word "*people*" generally, and in a sense avowedly contradistinguished from their governments, the court had used the words "*people of the United States*," not even this language would have had any tendency to warrant the inference which is said to arise.

Will Hampden deny that there is such a people as the people of the United States? Have we no national existence? We were charged by the late emperor of France with having no national character, or actual existence as a nation; but not even he denied our theoretical or constitutional existence. If congress declares war, are we not at war as a nation? Are not war and peace national acts? Are not all the measures of the government national measures? The United States is a nation; but a nation composed of states in many, though not in all, respects, sovereign. The people of these states are also the people of the United States. The two characters, so far from being incompatible with each other, are identified. This is the language of the constitution. In that instrument, the people of the states term themselves "the people of the United States." A senator must have been nine, a representative seven years "a citizen of the United States." "No person except a natural born citizen, or a citizen of the United States at the time of the adoption of the constitution," is eligible to the office of president. The oath taken by every adopted citizen, is as a citizen of the United States; and we are all citizens, not only of our particular states, but also of this great republic.

The constitution then does not recognize, but rejects, this incompatibility of our existence and character as a nation, with the existence of the several states. Hampden himself says that the words, "we the people of the United States," in the constitution, do "not necessarily import the people of *America,* in exclusion of those of the *several states.*" And I insist that, so far from excluding, they include, "those of the several states." Surely then the term "the people," used generally by the supreme court, and expressly applied to the people acting in their several states, cannot justify the inference "that the states were not known in the establishment of the constitution."

"The opinion of the supreme court," says Hampden, "seems farther to incline to the side of consolidation, from their considering the government as no alliance or league, and from their seeming to say that a federal government must be the offspring of state governments."

I admit explicitly that the court considers the constitution as a government, and not "a league." On this point I shall make some farther observations hereafter. But I deny "their seeming to say that a federal government must be the offspring of state governments." They have expressly said the very reverse. In answer to the argument, that the people had already conferred all the powers of government on the state authorities, "and had nothing left to give," the court says, "much more might the legitimacy of the general government be doubted, had it been created by the states." When Hampden contends that state governments had no power to change the constitution, and represents himself as opposing, in this respect, the opinion he condemns, he is in fact reurging the very argument which had been previously advanced in that opinion. "The powers delegated to the state sovereignties," says the court, "were to be exercised by themselves, not by a distinct independent sovereignty created by themselves."

A FRIEND OF THE CONSTITUTION.

Gazette and Alexandria Daily Advertiser, July 6, 1819

A Friend of the Constitution No. VII

I proceed now to those doctrines, which, according to Hampden, "show the government to be, in the opinion of the court, a consolidated, and not a federal government."

"Differing from the court entirely," he says, "on this subject, he will give his own view of it."

We must, of course, suppose his view to be in proportion to that from which he differs.

In stating this difference, he tells us, "The constitution of the United States was not adopted by the people of the United States as one people, it was adopted by the several states," &c. And he then proceeds to show that the constitution was adopted by the people of the several states acting in separate conventions.

This is precisely what the court had previously said. It is to be recollected that the question discussed by the court, was, not whether the constitution was the act of the people in mass, or in states; but whether it was the act of the people, or of the state governments? In discussing this question, the court says, "The constitution was reported to the then existing congress of the United States, with a request that it might be submitted to a convention of delegates, chosen in each state by the people thereof, under the recommendation of its legislature, for their assent and ratification. This mode of proceeding was adopted."

Language, I think, cannot be more explicit than this; nor more entirely repugnant to the idea that the people acted in one body, and not by states.

Hampden also alleges in support of this plain perversion of the language and meaning of the court, the stress laid on the words "We, the people of the United States," in the preamble of the constitution.

The opinion cannot be inspected without perceiving that these words are not quoted, as "importing" in the constitution, "the people of America in exclusion of those of the *several* states," but as importing the people, in exclusion of their governments.

The court then has not denied, but has affirmed, that the constitution was adopted by the people acting as states.

Were it even otherwise, this error respecting the origin of

the government, would not have proved it "to be in the opinion of the court, a consolidated, and not a federal government."

The character of a government depends on its constitution; not on its being adopted by the people acting in a single body, or in single bodies. The kingdom of Great Britain and Ireland is a consolidated kingdom. Yet it formerly consisted of three distinct kingdoms—England, Scotland, & Ireland; and this union was effected by their several parliaments, acting separately in each kingdom.

The convention of France, which was assembled in 1792, consisted of a single body elected by the people of the whole nation. Had the faction of the Gironde prevailed, and a federal republic been established, it would not have been the less a federal republic, because it was adopted by the representatives of the whole people, acting in mass.

If then the judges had made the assertion ascribed to them, they would have advanced a doctrine equally untrue and absurd, but not one which would "show that, in their opinion, our government is consolidated, and not federal."

The fact alleged then, and the conclusion drawn from it, are equally erroneous.

Hampden states many arguments which he supposes the court might urge in favor of consolidation, all of which he ingeniously refutes; but as the court has not itself urged one of these arguments, and has not, in the most distant manner, suggested a single idea in favor of consolidation, I shall be excused for passing them over without a comment.

I cannot, however, pass over, in like manner, his idea that the ligament which binds the states together, is "an alliance, or a league."

This is the point to which all his arguments tend. To establish this fundamental principle, an unnatural or restricted construction of the constitution is pressed upon us, and a fair exercise of the powers it confers, is reviled as an infraction of state rights. We need no longer be surprized at finding principles supported which would reduce the constitution to a dead letter, at the irritation excited by a course of reasoning which puts down those principles, at the effort to render the terms *American people* and *national government*, odious; at hearing that the supremacy of the whole within its sphere of action, over the parts is "jargon"; or at the exaggerated description of the power of the states to make amendments. All this is the necessary consequence of the doctrine that the constitution is not a national government, but a league, or a contract of alliance between the states, sovereign and independent.

But our constitution is not a league. It is a government; and has all the constituent parts of a government. It has established legislative, executive, and judicial departments, all of which act directly on the people, not through the medium of the state governments.

The confederation was, essentially, a league; and congress was a corps of ambassadors, to be recalled at the will of their masters. This corps could do nothing but declare war or make peace. They could neither carry on a war nor execute the articles of peace. They had a right to propose certain things to their sovereigns, and to require a compliance with their resolution; but they could, by their own power, execute nothing. A government, on the contrary, carries its resolutions into execution by its own means, and ours is a government. Who ever heard of sovereigns in league with each other, whose agents assembled in congress, were authorized to levy or collect taxes on their people, to shut up and open ports at will, or to make any laws and carry them into execution? Who ever heard of sovereigns taking the oath of fidelity to their agents? Who ever heard of sovereigns in league with each other, stripping themselves of all the important attributes of sovereignty, and transferring those attributes to their ambassadors?

The people of the United States have certainly a right, if they choose to exercise it, to reduce their government to a league. But let them act understandingly. Let them not be impelled to destroy the constitution, under the pretext of defending state rights from invasion. Let them, before they proceed too far in the course they are invited to take, look back to that awful and instructive period of our history which preceded the adoption of our constitution. These states were then truly sovereign, and were bound together only by a league. Examine with attention, for the subject deserves all your attention, the consequences of such a system. They are truly depicted in the Federalist, especially in the 15th No. of that work. The author thus commences his catalogue of the ills it had brought upon us. "We may indeed, with propriety, be said to have reached almost the last stage of national humiliation. There is scarcely any thing that can wound the pride, or degrade the character, of an independent people, which we do not experience." And he concludes his long and dark detail of those ills with saying, "To shorten an enumeration of particulars which can afford neither pleasure nor instruction, it may in general be demanded, what indication is there of national disorder, poverty, and insignificance, that could befal a community so peculiarly blessed with natural advantages as we are, which does not form a part of the dark catalogue of our public misfortunes."

Such was the situation to which these states were brought, in four years of peace, by their league. To change it into an effective government, or to fall to pieces from the weight of its constituent parts, & the weakness of its cement, was the alternative presented to the people of the United States. The wisdom and patriotism of our country chose the former. Let us not blindly and inconsiderately replunge into the difficulties from which that wisdom and that patriotism have extricated us.

A FRIEND OF THE CONSTITUTION.

Gazette and Alexandria Daily Advertiser, July 9, 1819

A Friend of the Constitution No. VIII

The last accusation brought against the supreme court, is, a violation of the constitution, by deciding a cause not within its jurisdiction.

Grave as is this charge, the question is still more important to the people than to the judges. It more deeply concerns the prosperity of the union, the due execution of its laws, and even its preservation, that its courts should possess the jurisdiction Hampden denies them, than it does the character of the judges, to stand acquitted of usurpation.

Before I proceed to examine this question, I must be allowed to express some surprize at its not having occurred to the counsel for the state of Maryland. The talents of those gentlemen are universally acknowledged; and, if we may judge of their zeal by the specimens of their arguments given in the opinion of the court, they made every point which judgment, ingenuity, or imagination could suggest, on which a decent self respect would permit them to insist. How happened it, then, that this point of jurisdiction escaped them?

A brief consideration of the subject will, I am persuaded, solve this difficulty.

The reasoning on which this objection seems to be founded, proceeds from the fundamental error, that our constitution is a mere league, or a compact, between the several state governments, and the general government. Under the influence of this unaccountable delusion, he makes some quotations from Vattel, favorable to the choice of a foreign government as an umpire to decide controversies which may arise between the government of the union and those of the states. "The princes of Neufchatel" we are informed, "established in 1406, the canton of Berne, the judge and perpetual arbitrator of their disputes."

Were the petty princes of Neufchatel united under one paramount government having a constitutional power to adjust their differences, or were they only in alliance with each other? Was there any analogy between their situation and that of the United States? This at least ought to be shown by him who holds up to us their example for imitation.

He tells us also, on the same authority, "that among sovereigns who acknowledge no superior, treaties form the only mode of adjusting their several pretensions"; and "that *neither* of the contracting parties has a right to interpret the *pact* or treaty, at his pleasure."

There is no difficulty in admitting this doctrine. The only difficulty consists in discerning its application to the United States. It applies to independent sovereigns, who stand in no relation to each other, but that which is created by the general law of nations, and by treaty. Has Hampden succeeded in convincing his fellow citizens that this is the condition of the American states?

Without pressing further the total inapplicability of these historical facts, and general principles, to our situation; or urging the weakness and danger of introducing into our system, a foreign potentate as the arbiter of our domestic disputes, I will proceed to examine the question of jurisdiction on its real grounds.

I will premise that the constitution of the United States is not an alliance, or a league, between independent sovereigns; nor a compact between the government of the union, and those of the states; but is itself a government, created for the nation by the whole American people, acting by convention assembled in and for their respective states. It does not possess a single feature belonging to a league, as contradistinguished from a government. A league is formed by the sovereigns who become members of it; our constitution is formed by the people themselves, who have adopted it without employing, in that act, the agency of the state legislatures. The measures of a league are carried into execution by the sovereigns who compose it; the measures of our national government are carried into execution by itself, without requiring the agency of the states. The representatives of sovereigns in league with each other, act in subordination to those sovereigns, and under their particular instruction; the government of the union, "within its sphere of action," is "supreme"; and, although its laws should be in direct opposition to the instructions of every state legislature in the union, they are "the supreme law of the land, any thing in the constitution or laws of any state to the contrary notwithstanding." This government has all the departments, and all the capacities for performing its various functions, which a free people is accustomed to bestow on its government. It is not then, in any point of view a league.

As little does it resemble a compact between itself and its members.

A contract is "an agreement on sufficient consideration to do or not to do a particular thing."

There must be parties. These parties must make an agreement, and something must proceed to and from each.

The government of the United States can certainly not be a party to the instrument by which it was created. It cannot have been concerned in making that by which it was brought into existence.

Neither have the state governments made this instrument. It is the act of the people themselves, and not the act of their governments.

There is then no agreement formed between the government of the United States and those of the states. Our constitution is not a compact. It is the act of a single party. It is the act of people of the United States, assembling in their respective states, and adopting a government for the whole nation. Their motives for this act are assigned by themselves. They have specified the objects they intended to accomplish, and have enumerated the powers with which those objects were to be accomplished.

All arguments founded on leagues and compacts, must be fallacious when applied to a government like this. We are to examine the powers actually conferred by the people on their government; and the capacities bestowed upon it for the execution of those powers.

This government possesses a judicial department; which, like the others, is erected by the people of the United States. It is not a partial, local tribunal, but, one which is national.

For what purpose was this department created?

Before we look into the constitution for an answer to this question, let any reasonable man ask himself what must have been the primary motive of a people forming a national government for endowing it with a judicial department? Must it not have been the desire of having a tribunal for the decision of all national questions? If questions which concern the nation might be submitted to the local tribunals no motive could exist for establishing this national tribunal. Such is the language of reason. What is the language of the constitution?

"The judicial power shall extend to all cases in law and equity, arising under this constitution, the laws of the United States & treaties made or to be made under their authority."

Cases then arising under the constitution, and under the laws and treaties of the U. States, are, as was to be expected, the objects which stood first, in the mind of the framers of the constitution.

Is the case of M'Cullough against the state of Maryland of this description?

Only two points appear to have been made by the defendant in the argument.

1st. That the act of congress establishing the bank is unconstitutional and void.

2d. That the act of the legislature of Maryland is constitutional, and consequently obligatory.

It was then a case arising under the constitution. Let us hear how Hampden contrives to withdraw it from the jurisdiction of the court.

He relies first on certain authorities which he quotes as being favorable to his opinion. In the Federalist, he says, "the supremacy of either party in such cases" ("these clashings between the respective governments") "seems to be denied."

If he seems to say no more than that the positive supremacy of an act of Congress, until it shall be tried by the standard of the constitution, is denied, he is undoubtedly correct. But the application of this opinion to the jurisdiction of the court cannot readily be perceived.

If he means to say that, the jurisdiction of the supremacy of the judicial department, in cases of this description, "seems to be denied" by the Federalist, he is as certainly incorrect.

The writers of that valuable treatise allow a concurrent jurisdiction in such cases, except so far as that of the state courts may be restrained by congress; but the supremacy of the courts of the United States, is expressly recognized. In the 80th No. they are full and explicit to the point, that the courts of the Union have, and ought to have jurisdiction, in all cases, arising under the constitution and laws of the United States. After laying down as political axioms, the propositions that the judicial department should be co-extensive with the legislative, and with the provisions of the constitution, the Federalist says "thirteen independent courts of final jurisdiction over the same causes, arising upon the same laws, is a hydra in government from which nothing but contradiction and confusion can proceed."

"Still less may be said in regard to the third point. Controversies between the nation and its members, or citizens, can only be properly referred to the national tribunals."

In the 82d No. speaking of the concurrent jurisdiction of the different courts, he adds, "here another question occurs—what relation would subsist between the national and state courts, in these instances of concurrent jurisdiction? I answer that an appeal would certainly lie to the supreme court of the United

States." The writer then proceeds to give his reasons for this opinion.

It is then most certain that the Federalist, does not "seem to deny," but does expressly affirm, that the jurisdiction and supremacy of the courts of the United States, in "all cases arising under the constitution"; which jurisdiction may be applied in the appellate form to those decided in the state courts.

Hampden refers also to two judicial decisions, which, he says, "are in full accordance with his principles." These are the case of Hunter *v.* Fairfax, and the case of the commonwealth of Pennsylvania *v.* Cobbett. In the first case he says the court of appeals of Virginia declared "an act of congress unconstitutional, although it had been sanctioned by the opinion of the supreme court of the United States."

This is true; and it is the only example furnished by any court in the union of a sentiment favorable to that "hydra in government, from which," says the Federalist, "nothing but contradiction and confusion can proceed." But it is also true that this decision was reversed by the unanimous opinion of the supreme court, and has, notwithstanding the acknowledged respectability of the court of appeals of Virginia, been disapproved by every state court, and they are not a few, which has had occasion to act on the subject. The supreme court, as we perceive in the reports, has reversed the decisions of many state courts founded on laws supported by a good deal of state feeling. In every instance, except that of Hunter and Fairfax, the judgment of reversal has been acquiesced in, and the jurisdiction of the court has been recognized. If the most unequivocal indications of the public sentiment may be trusted, it is not hazarding much to say, that, out of Virginia, there is probably not a single judge, nor a single lawyer of eminence, who does not dissent from the principles laid down by the court of appeals in Hunter and Fairfax.

Hampden's representation of the case of the commonwealth and Cobbett is entirely inaccurate. In that case, the supreme court of Pennsylvania did not come to the resolutions he recapitulates, nor, "go on to render a judgment bottomed on those principles, and in opposition to the provisions of an act of congress."

The case, as reported in the 3d Dal. is this: Cobbett had been guilty of an offence against the criminal code of Pennsylvania, and had been bound in a recognizance to be of good behaviour. His recognizance having been put in suit, he endeavored to remove the cause into the federal court on an affidavit that he was an alien. This motion was opposed, not on the unconstitutionality of the act of congress, but on its construction. The counsel for the commonwealth contended that the case was not within the act, 1st because it gave the circuit court no jurisdiction in a cause where a state was a party; and 2dly because it was not, properly speaking, "a civil suit"; but was incidental to, and in the nature of, a criminal action.

On these grounds the court decided that the act of congress did not embrace the case.

When the decision was about to be made, chief justice McKean, who was, not long afterwards, elected governor of Pennsylvania, whether in his character as a candidate or a judge, I submit to every intelligent reader, thought proper to deliver a political disquisition on the constitution of the United States. "Previous to the delivery of my opinion," he says, "in a cause of so much importance, as to the consequences of the decision, I will make a few preliminary observations on the constitution and laws of the United States of America." He then proceeds with the political disquisition stated by Hampden. But this is so far from being a part of the opinion of the court, that it was neither understood, nor stated, even by himself, as belonging in any manner to the cause. After having finished this dissertation, he says, "I shall now consider the case before us." The opinion of the court is then delivered, in which not one syllable indicating the unconstitutionality of the act of congress is to be found. It was held not to comprehend the case.

This decision then, so far from questioning the validity of an act of congress, clearly recognizes its authority. The construction given to the act was, I presume, tho't correct by Mr. Cobbett's counsel, or he would have brought the question before the Federal courts.

A FRIEND OF THE CONSTITUTION.

Gazette and Alexandria Daily Advertiser, July 14, 1819

A Friend of the Constitution No. IX

Hampden is not more successful in his reasoning against the jurisdiction of the court, than in his authorities.

Having finished his quotations, he exclaims—How after all this, in this contest between the head, and one of the members of our confederacy, in this vital contest for power between them, can the supreme court assert its exclusive right to determine the controversy?

The court has itself answered this question. It has said— "On the supreme court of the United States, has the constitution of our country devolved this important duty."

Such a question cannot assume a form for judicial investigation, without being "a case arising under the constitution"; and to "all" such cases "the *judicial power*" is expressly extended. The right asserted by the court, is then, expressly given by the great fundamental law which unites us as a nation.

If we were now making, instead of controversy, a constitution, where else could this important duty of deciding questions which grow out of the constitution, and the laws of the union, be safely or wisely placed? Would any sane mind prefer to the peaceful and quiet mode of carrying the laws of the union into execution by the judicial arm, that they should be trampled under foot, or enforced by the sword? That every law of the United States should be resisted with impunity, or produce a civil war? If not, what other alternative presents itself? Hampden suggests the arbitration of some foreign potentate —Britain, France, or Russia, for example. Is he sure that the parties could agree on an arbiter? Is he sure that such arbiter would be influenced entirely by the principles of right and not at all by those of policy? Is he sure that such arbiter would understand the constitution and laws of the United States? Is he sure that this intrusion of a foreign potentate into our domestic "vital contests for power" would not give that potentate an undue influence over the weaker party, and lead to intrigues which might foment divisions, animate discord, and finally produce dismemberment? If he is not certain on these and many other points which suggest themselves, and ought to be considered, how can he think the submission of these controversies to such an arbiter, preferable to the submission of them to a domestic tribunal, composed of American citizens, selected by the man in whom the American people have reposed their highest confidence, approved by the representatives of the state sovereignties, and placed by the people themselves in a situation which exempts them from all undue influence?

But this is not now a question open for consideration. The constitution has decided it.

After expressing some doubts respecting the propriety of that great American principle, the judicial right to decide on the supremacy of the constitution, a right which is inseparable from the idea of a paramount law, a written constitution, he adds, "but the present claim on the part of the judiciary is to give unlimited powers to a government only clothed by the people with those which are limited. It claims the right, in effect, to change the government, to convert a federal into a consolidated government."

Hampden leaves us to search for that part of the opinion in which this claim is asserted. Is it in the following? "This government is acknowledged by all to be one of enumerated powers. The principle that it can exercise only the powers granted to it, would seem too apparent," &c.

If not in this, or in such as this, for the opinion abounds with them, is it inseparable from the power of deciding in the last resort, all questions "arising under the constitution and laws" of the United States? If he contends that it is, I answer that the constitution has expressly given the power, and the exercise of it, cannot be the assertion of a right to change that instrument.

Hampden again demands the clause in the constitution which grants this jurisdiction, "The necessity," he says, "of showing an express provision for a right claimed by one of the contracting parties to pass finally on the rights or powers of another" "is increased when the right is claimed for a deputy or department of such contracting party. The supreme court is but a department of the general government."

I am not sure that I comprehend the meaning of these sentences. The words "one of the contracting parties" and "general government," appear to be used in the same sense, as designating the same object. So the words "deputy" and "department of such contracting party." If they are not to be understood so, I am unable to construe them. If they are, then let me ask what is meant by the word "general government"? Is it Congress? Is it the whole government? If the former, whence does he derive his authority for saying that the judicial department is the "deputy" of congress? Certainly, not from the constitution. According to that instrument, the judicial, is a co-ordinate department, created at the same time, and proceeding from the same source, with the legislative and executive departments.

If the latter, the whole government consists of departments. Neither of these is the deputy of the whole, or of the other two. Neither can perform the duties, or exercise the powers assigned to another; nor can all of them together participate in those duties and powers, or perform them jointly. Each is confined to the sphere of action prescribed to it by the people of the United States, and within that sphere, performs its functions alone. The legislature and executive can no more unite with the judiciary in deciding a cause, than the judiciary can unite with them in making a law, or appointing a foreign minister. On a judicial question then, the judicial department is the government, and can alone exercise the judicial power of the United States.

Can Hampden have been so inattentive to the constitution of his country as not to have made these observations; or does his hostility to this department lead him to indulge in expressions which his sober judgement must tell him are totally misapplied?

But he denies that there exists in the government a power to decide this controversy. He says—"They cannot do it unless we tread under foot the principle which forbids a party to decide his own cause."

Let us temperately examine how far this principle applies to the case.

The government of the Union was created by, and for, the people of the United States. It has a department in which is vested its whole legislative power, and a department in which is vested its whole judicial power. These departments are filled by citizens of the several states.

The propriety and power of making any law which is proposed must be discussed in the legislature before it is enacted. If any person to whom the law may apply, contests its validity, the case is brought before the court. The power of Congress to pass the law is drawn into question. But the courts of the union, Hampden says, cannot decide this question "without treading under foot the principle that forbids a man to decide his own cause."

What would be the condition of the world should this principle be deemed applicable to the exercise of the judicial authority by the regular tribunals of the country?

Any individual of Virginia, for example, chooses to deny the validity of a law, and proceedings for its enforcement are instituted. But, according to this new doctrine the court of the state is incapable of deciding a question involving the power of the legislature, without treading under foot this sacred principle. Let the state itself be a nominal party as in prosecutions for crimes, or suits against its debtors, and the violation of the sacred principle would be still more apparent. How are these questions to be settled without the intervention of a court? Or are they to remain for ever suspended?

It is the plain dictate of common sense, and the whole political system is founded on the idea, that the departments of government are the agents of the nation, and will perform, within their respective spheres, the duties assigned to them. The whole owes to its parts the peaceful decision of every controversy which may arise among its members. It is one of the great duties of government, one of the great objects for which it is instituted. Agents for the performance of this duty must be furnished, or the government fails in one of the great ends of its creation.

To whom more safely than to the judges are judicial questions to be referred? They are selected from the great body of the people for the purpose of deciding them. To secure impartiality, they are made perfectly independent. They have no personal interest in aggrandizing the legislative power. Their paramount interest is the public prosperity, in which is involved their own and that of their families. No tribunal can be less liable to be swayed by unworthy motives from a conscientious performance of duty. It is not then the party sitting in his own cause. It is the application to individuals by one department of the acts of another department of the government. The people are the authors of all; the departments are their agents; and if the judge be personally disinterested, he is as exempt from any political interest that might influence his opinion, as imperfect human institutions can make him.

To the demand that the words which give the jurisdiction should be stated, I answer—they have already been stated. The jurisdiction is expressly given in the words "the judicial power shall extend to all cases arising under this constitution." How does Hampden elude this provision? Not by denying that the case "arises under the constitution." That, not even he can venture to deny. How then does he elude it? He says that "these words may be otherwise abundantly satisfied." But how "otherwise satisfied," he has not told us; nor can he. I admit there are other cases arising under the constitution. But the words are "all cases" and I deny that the word "some," can be substituted for "all," or that the word "all," can be satisfied if any one case can be withdrawn from the jurisdiction of the court. But the same reason may be assigned for withdrawing any or every other case. As each occurs, Hampden may say "these words may be otherwise abundantly satisfied." What peculiar reason has he assigned for this case which is not equally applicable to any and every other? His reason is that the case involves an enquiry, into the extent of the powers of the general government, and of a state government. And I ask what case can arise under the constitution which does not involve one or both of these enquiries? Let Hampden, if he can, state the case.

These words then cannot be otherwise satisfied. Hampden does not merely contract, he annihilates them.

But suppose him to succeed in excluding from the federal courts, all cases in which a question respecting the powers of the government of the union, or of a state can arise, are they to remain for ever undecided? Hampden does not say so. They must of course be decided in the state courts. He quotes, as sustaining his principles, a decision of the court of appeals in Virginia overruling an act of congress; and a decision of the supreme court of Pennsylvania, (though in this he is mistaken) to the same effect. It follows then that great national questions are to be decided, not by the tribunal created for their decision by the people of the United States, but by the tribunal created by the state which contests the validity of the act of congress, or asserts the validity of its own act. Thus, in the language of the Federalist, (No. 45) presenting to the world "for the first time, a system of government founded on an inversion of the fundamental principles of all government"; "the authority of the whole society every where subordinate to the authority of the parts"; "a monster in which the head is under the direction of the members."

Hampden is not more fortunate in the second principle with which he attempts to sustain this strange construction of the constitution, although he is pleased to term it "conclusive." "The rank of this controversy," he says, "between the head and one of the members of the confederacy, may be said to be superior to those depending between two of the members; and the lawyers well know that a specification beginning with a person or thing of an inferior grade, excludes those of a superior."

If I could be surprized at any argument found in the essays of Hampden, I should be surprised at this.

The jurisdiction of the federal courts, as described in the constitution, is dependent on two distinct considerations. The first is the character of the cause; the second, the character of the parties. All cases arising under the constitution, laws, and treaties of the United States; all cases affecting public ministers; and all cases of admiralty and maritime jurisdiction; are cognizable in those courts, whoever may be the parties. The cases of the second class depend entirely on the character of the parties, without regard to the nature of the cause. It is not necessary that these two properties should be combined in the same cause, in order to give the court jurisdiction. If a case arise under the constitution, it is immaterial who are the parties; and if an alien be a party, it is not requisite that the case should arise under the constitution.

But McCullough, not the United States, is the party on the record; and were it otherwise, that circumstance would bring the case within, not exclude it from, the jurisdiction of the court. The constitution expressly gives jurisdiction to the courts of the union in "cases to which the United States shall be a party."

There is then no one objection made to the opinion of the supreme court which fails more entirely than this to its jurisdiction.

I have been induced to review these essays the more in detail, because they are intended to produce a very serious effect; and because they advance principles which go, in my judgment, to the utter subversion of the constitution. Let Hampden succeed, and that instrument will be radically changed. The government of the whole will be prostrated at the feet of its members; and that grand effort of wisdom, virtue, and patriotism, which produced it, will be totally defeated.

A FRIEND OF THE CONSTITUTION.

Gazette and Alexandria Daily Advertiser, July 15, 1819

AMPHYCTION, HAMPDEN, AND HORTENSIUS

To Bushrod Washington

My dear Sir   Richmond Aug. 3d. 1819

You will receive with this some printed reports which are all that I can get on the subject of your enquiries. I learn that the affairs of the society, so far as respects the country, are in a very deranged state; but I have no personal knowledge from which I can speak. The fact however is generally beleived, & is supposed to be notorious. I have heard that applications on account of losses have been made without success, but I know of no particular case.

In the enquirer you have probably seen before this, a full & fair statement of the case of the pirates. It is adjourned to the supreme court. I have serious doubts of the sufficiency of the law to authorize the infliction of punishment in a case of as notorious piracy as ever occurred.

If you have an opportunity of sending the reserved sets of "a friend to the constitution" to oak hill in Fauquier during the month of August by any waggon, I shall receive them. Perhaps I may direct a waggoner to call on you. Should there be no opportunity to oak hill, perhaps you may send them by some opportunity to this place. My object is to put them in the hands of some member of assembly should an attempt be made to move the subject in the legislature. Keep them till they may be sent without any very considerable expence.

Amphyction is Judge Brockenbrough.

Hampden is Judge Roane.

Hortensius is G. Hay.

CHIEF JUSTICE OF
THE SUPREME COURT
1820–1835

To John Marshall, Jr.

My dear Son   Richmond July 10th. 1820

I received two or three days past your letter of the 30th. of June & am very glad to hear both of the health of your family & of your prospects for a crop. This gladness however has no inconsiderable portion of alloy. I consider the smut in your wheat as a much more serious mischief than you seem to apprehend. It injures the grain very much & it is to be feared will so darken your flour as to prevent its being passed as superfine however well it may be ground. This is not the sole nor the greatest mischief. There is serious danger of its growing upon you. If you continue to sow the same seed, it will encrease rapidly on you, unless you take great precautions; & I am not sure that any precautions will secure you. The common opinion is that rolling the seed well in quick lime is of great service & I beleive it is; but I am not certain that absolute dependence can be placed on it. My own experience is that there will still remain some smut. I think also that there is considerable advantage in allowing your wheat, especially that intended for seed, to get very ripe. By allowing it to stand to the very last much of the smut will waste away, in addition to which the grain is I am inclined to beleive less liable to the disease when sown for the next years crop.

Your mothers health is a little improved. She has slept for several nights without opium. She desires me to tell you that she was much gratified with your letter to her. She is peculiarly pleased with having a full account of your plantation & domestic affairs. Although deprived of the hope of ever visiting her children she takes a deep interest in all their affairs & complains that you have not given her an account of your house, or told her how Elizabeth likes it. She was amused at your returns for your butter & requests Elizabeth not to be discouraged. Tho butter at 12 p cents per pound is certainly but a slow way of making a fortune yet it has this advantage—it shows how highly a Farmer & Farmer's wife must value a small sum

of money. Your mother joins me in love to Elizabeth & yourself. I am my dear Son your affectionate Father.

UPCOMING SUPREME COURT CASES

To Bushrod Washington

My dear Sir   Washington Feby. 8th. 1821
    I reached this place yesterday after a very fatiguing journey,
& found all our brethren well, & all of them joining me in sincere regrets for your indisposition. However unwilling we may
be to lose your aid, we all think that it would be madness to
encounter the hazard of joining us, unless your health should
be entirely restored. We hope, however, that you are improving,
& will continue to improve, so that you may, after the earth &
Atmosphere shall become dry, favor us with a short visit. Should
you be well enough to remain with us a few days towards the
end of the month we would avail ourselves of that time to deliver the opinion in the case of the Isabella & in the case of the
outstanding titles. If your health should enable you to hear an
argument, we might also hear one in the case of the statute of
limitations from New Hampshire, upon which the court was
divided & which is to be reargued in the presence of Judge
Todd. It is probable too that the case from Virginia, which has
excited so much commotion in our legislature, will be set to
some late day & it certainly is desirable that the court should
be as full as possible when it is decided. I mention these things
as eventually to be wished, but as depending altogether on
your being enabled to pass a few days in Washington with perfect safety to your self; for we all concur in advising you not to
encounter the slightest hazard to your health from any consideration whatever. In the progress of the term you will be enabled to form a better judgement of what you may do without
danger; and more we all request that you will not think of
attempting.
    The wine is in fine order & we shall at dinner give a bumper
to your better health.
    I have brought with me the letters copied in Richmond, &

hope I may see you & have some conversation on this subject before my return to Richmond.

My brethren all join me in sincere wishes for your better health. I am my dear Sir with esteem & affection, Your

"WE DINE OUT TOO FREQUENTLY"

To Mary W. Marshall

My dearest Polly   Washington March 26th. 1821

I had the pleasure to day of receiving a letter from James of the 24th. informing me of your return from Chiccahominy. I am very glad to hear that you have passed safely through the noisy rejoicings of the 22d & are as well as usual. I hope care was taken to keep every thing quiet while you were at the plantation & that you slept better than you did at christmass. James informs me that you heard the drum distinctly & that the Cannon shook the house. Of course your mornings nap was interrupted but I hope you slept through the night.

Judge Washington still continues unwell at Alexandria & I have no hope of his joining us during the court. We continue very busy & have as much rain as heart could wish. We dine out too frequently & I think eating such late & hearty dinners disagrees with me. I watch myself, & resolve every day that I will be moderate but I cannot keep my resolution.

Washington is still very gay. There are continual parties but I make a point not to go to them. Farewell my dearest Polly, I am your ever affectionate

February 26, 1821

Opinion in Cohens v. Virginia

THIS is a writ of error to a judgment rendered in the Court of Hustings for the Borough of Norfolk, on an information for selling lottery tickets contrary to an act of the Legislature of Virginia. In the state court, the defendant claimed the protection of an act of Congress. A case was agreed between the parties, which states the act of Assembly on which the prosecution was founded, and the act of Congress on which the defendant relied, and concludes in these words: "If upon this case the court shall be of opinion that the acts of Congress before mentioned were valid, and, on the true construction of those acts, the lottery tickets sold by the defendants as aforesaid might lawfully be sold within the state of Virginia, notwithstanding the act or statute of the general assembly of Virginia prohibiting such sale, then judgment to be entered for the defendants: And if the court should be of opinion that the statute or act of the general assembly of the state of Virginia, prohibiting such sale, is valid, notwithstanding the said acts of Congress, then judgment to be entered that the defendants are guilty, and that the commonwealth recover against them one hundred dollars and costs."

Judgment was rendered against the defendants; and the court in which it was rendered being the highest court of the state in which the cause was cognizable, the record has been brought into this court by writ of error.

The defendant in error moves to dismiss this writ, for want of jurisdiction.

In support of this motion, three points have been made, and argued with the ability which the importance of the question merits. These points are—

1st. That a state is a defendant.

2d. That no writ of error lies from this court to a state court.

3d. The third point has been presented in different forms by the gentlemen who have argued it. The counsel who opened the cause, said that the want of jurisdiction was shown by the subject matter of the case. The counsel who followed him, said that jurisdiction was not given by the judicial act. The court has bestowed all its attention on the arguments of both gentlemen, and supposes that their tendency is to show that this court has no jurisdiction of the case, or, in other words, has no right to review the judgment of the state court, because neither the constitution nor any law of the United States has been violated by that judgment.

The questions presented to the court by the two first points made at the bar are of great magnitude, and may be truly said vitally to affect the Union. They exclude the inquiry whether the constitution and laws of the United States have been violated by the judgment which the plaintiffs in error seek to review; and maintain that, admitting such violation, it is not in the power of the government to apply a corrective. They maintain that the nation does not possess a department capable of restraining peaceably, and by authority of law, any attempts which may be made, either intentionally or inadvertently, by a part, against the legitimate powers of the whole; and that the government is reduced to the alternative of submitting to such attempts, or of resisting them by force. They maintain that the constitution of the United States has provided no tribunal for the final construction of itself, or of the laws or treaties of the nation; but that this power may be exercised in the last resort by the courts of every state in the Union. That the constitution, laws, and treaties, may receive as many constructions as there are states; and that this is not a mischief, or, if a mischief, is irremediable. These abstract propositions are to be determined; for he who demands decision without permitting inquiry affirms that the decision he asks does not depend on inquiry.

If such be the constitution, it is the duty of the court to bow with respectful submission to its provisions. If such be not the constitution, it is equally the duty of this court to say so; and to perform that task which the American people have assigned to the judicial department.

1st. The first question to be considered is, whether the jurisdiction of this court is excluded by the character of the parties, one of them being a state, and the other a citizen of that State?

The second section of the third article of the constitution defines the extent of the judicial power of the United States. Jurisdiction is given to the courts of the Union in two classes of cases. In the first, their jurisdiction depends on the character of the cause, whoever may be the parties. This class comprehends "all cases in law and equity arising under this constitution, the laws of the United States, and treaties made, or which shall be made, under their authority." This clause extends the jurisdiction of the court to all the cases described, without making in its terms any exception whatever, and without any regard to the condition of the party. If there be any exception, it is to be implied against the express words of the article.

In the second class, the jurisdiction depends entirely on the character of the parties. In this are comprehended "controversies between two or more states, between a state and citizens of another state," "and between a state and foreign states, citizens, or subjects." If these be the parties, it is entirely unimportant what may be the subject of controversy. Be it what it may, these parties have a constitutional right to come into the courts of the Union.

The counsel for the defendant in error have stated that the cases which arise under the constitution must grow out of those provisions which are capable of self-execution; examples of which are to be found in the 2d section of the 4th article, and in the 10th section of the 1st article.

A case which arises under a law of the United States must, we are likewise told be a right given by some act which becomes necessary to execute the powers given in the constitution, of which the law of naturalization is mentioned as an example.

The use intended to be made of this exposition of the first part of the section defining the extent of the judicial power, is not clearly understood. If the intention be merely to distinguish cases arising under the constitution from those arising under a law, for the sake of precision in the application of this argument, these propositions will not be controverted. If it be to maintain that a case arising under the constitution, or a law, must be one in which a party comes into court to demand something conferred on him by the constitution or a law, we think the construction too narrow. A case in law or equity consists of the right of the one party, as well as of the other, and may truly be said to arise under the constitution or a law of the United States, whenever its correct decision depends on the construction of either. Congress seems to have intended to give its own construction of this part of the constitution in the

25th section of the judicial act; and we perceive no reason to depart from that construction.

The jurisdiction of the court, then, being extended by the letter of the constitution to all cases arising under it, or under the laws of the United States, it follows that those who would withdraw any case of this description from that jurisdiction, must sustain the exemption they claim on the spirit and true meaning of the constitution, which spirit and true meaning must be so apparent as to overrule the words which its framers have employed.

The counsel for the defendant in error have undertaken to do this; and have laid down the general proposition, that a sovereign independent state is not suable, except by its own consent.

This general proposition will not be controverted. But its consent is not requisite in each particular case. It may be given in a general law. And if a state has surrendered any portion of its sovereignty, the question whether a liability to suit be a part of this portion depends on the instrument by which the surrender is made. If, upon a just construction of that instrument, it shall appear that the state has submitted to be sued, then it has parted with this sovereign right of judging in every case on the justice of its own pretensions, and has entrusted that power to a tribunal in whose impartiality it confides.

The American states as well as the American people, have believed a close and firm Union to be essential to their liberty and to their happiness. They have been taught by experience, that this Union cannot exist without a government for the whole; and they have been taught by the same experience that this government would be a mere shadow, that must disappoint all their hopes, unless invested with large portions of that sovereignty which belongs to independent states. Under the influence of this opinion, and thus instructed by experience, the American people, in the conventions of their respective states, adopted the present constitution.

If it could be doubted whether from its nature, it were not supreme in all cases where it is empowered to act, that doubt would be removed by the declaration that "this constitution, and the laws of the United States which shall be made in pursuance thereof, and all treaties made, or which shall be made, under the authority of the United States, shall be the supreme law of the land; and the judges in every state shall be bound thereby; any thing in the constitution or laws of any state to the contrary notwithstanding."

This is the authoritative language of the American people; and, if gentlemen please, of the American states. It marks, with lines too strong to be mistaken, the characteristic distinction between the government of the Union, and those of the states. The General Government, though limited as to its objects, is supreme with respect to those objects. This principle is a part of the constitution; and if there be any who deny its necessity, none can deny its authority.

To this supreme government ample powers are confided; and, if it were possible to doubt the great purposes for which they were so confided, the people of the United States have declared that they are given "in order to form a more perfect union, establish justice, ensure domestic tranquillity, provide for the common defence, promote the general welfare, and secure the blessings of liberty to themselves and their posterity."

With the ample powers confided to this supreme government, for these interesting purposes, are connected many express and important limitations on the sovereignty of the states, which are made for the same purposes. The powers of the Union on the great subjects of war, peace, and commerce, and on many others, are in themselves limitations of the sovereignty of the states; but in addition to these, the sovereignty of the states is surrendered in many instances where the surrender can only operate to the benefit of the people, and where, perhaps, no other power is conferred on Congress than a conservative power to maintain the principles established in the constitution. The maintenance of these principles in their purity, is certainly among the great duties of the government. One of the instruments by which this duty may be peaceably performed, is the judicial department. It is authorized to decide all cases of every description, arising under the constitution or laws of the United States. From this general grant of jurisdiction, no exception is made of those cases in which a state may be a party. When we consider the situation of the government of the Union and of a State, in relation to each other, the nature of our constitution, the subordination of the state governments to that constitution, the great purpose for which jurisdiction over all cases arising under the constitution and laws of the United States, is confided to the judicial department, are we at liberty to insert in this general grant, an exception of those cases in which a state may be a party? Will the spirit of the constitution justify this attempt to control its words? We think it will not. We think a case arising under the constitution or laws of the United States, is cognizable in the courts of the Union, whoever may be the parties to that case.

Had any doubt existed with respect to the just construction of this part of the section, that doubt would have been removed by the enumeration of those cases to which the jurisdiction of the federal courts is extended, in consequence of the character of the parties. In that enumeration we find "controversies between two or more states, between a state and citizens of another state," "and between a state and foreign states, citizens, or subjects."

One of the express objects, then, for which the judicial department was established, is the decision of controversies between states, and between a state and individuals. The mere circumstance that a state is a party gives jurisdiction to the court. How, then, can it be contended that the very same instrument, in the very same section, should be so construed as that this same circumstance should withdraw a case from the jurisdiction of the court, where the constitution or laws of the United States are supposed to have been violated? The constitution gave to every person having a claim upon a state, a right to submit his case to the court of the nation. However unimportant his claim might be, however little the community might be interested in its decision, the framers of our constitution thought it necessary for the purposes of justice, to provide a tribunal as superior to influence as possible, in which that claim might be decided. Can it be imagined that the same persons considered a case involving the constitution of our country and the majesty of the laws, questions in which every American citizen must be deeply interested, as withdrawn from this tribunal, because a state is a party?

While weighing arguments drawn from the nature of government, and from the general spirit of an instrument, and urged for the purpose of narrowing the construction which the words of that instrument seem to require, it is proper to place in the opposite scale those principles, drawn from the same sources, which go to sustain the words in their full operation and natural import. One of these, which has been pressed with great force by the counsel for the plaintiff in error, is, that the judicial power of every well constituted government must be co-extensive with the legislative, and must be capable of deciding every judicial question which grows out of the constitution and laws.

If any proposition may be considered as a political axiom, this, we think, maybe so considered. In reasoning upon it as an abstract question, there would probably exist no contrariety of opinion respecting it. Every argument, proving the necessity of the department, proves also the propriety of giving this extent to it. We do not mean to say that the jurisdiction of the courts of the Union should be construed to be co-extensive with the legislative, merely because it is fit that it should be so; but we mean to say that this fitness furnishes an argument in construing the constitution which ought never to be overlooked, and which is most especially entitled to consideration when we are enquiring whether the words of the instrument which purport to establish this principle, shall be contracted for the purpose of destroying it.

The mischievous consequences of the construction contended for on the part of Virginia are also entitled to great consideration. It would prostrate, it has been said, the government and its laws at the feet of every state in the Union. And would not this be its effect? What power of the government could be executed by its own means, in any state disposed to resist its execution by a course of legislation? The laws must be executed by individuals acting within the several states. If these individuals may be exposed to penalties, and if the courts of the Union cannot correct the judgments by which these penalties may be enforced, the course of the government may be, at any time, arrested by the will of one of its members. Each member will possess a *veto* on the will of the whole.

The answer which has been given to this argument does not deny its truth, but insists that confidence is reposed, and may be safely reposed, in the state institutions; and that, if they shall ever become so insane or so wicked as to seek the destruction of the government, they may accomplish their object by refusing to perform the functions assigned to them.

We readily concur with the counsel for the defendant in the declaration that the cases which have been put of direct legislative resistance for the purpose of opposing the acknowledged powers of the government, are extreme cases, and in the hope that they will never occur; but we cannot help believing, that a general conviction of the total incapacity of the government to protect itself and its laws in such cases, would contribute in no inconsiderable degree to their occurrence.

Let it be admitted, that the cases which have been put are extreme and improbable, yet there are gradations of opposition to the laws, far short of those cases, which might have a baneful influence on the affairs of the nation. Different states may entertain different opinions on the true construction of the constitutional powers of Congress. We know that, at one time, the assumption of the debts contracted by the several states, during the war of our revolution, was deemed unconstitutional by some of them. We know too that, at other times, certain taxes, imposed by Congress, have been pronounced unconstitutional. Other laws have been questioned partially, while they were supported by the great majority of the American people. We have no assurance that we shall be less divided than we have been. States may legislate in conformity to their opinions, and may enforce those opinions by penalties. It would be hazarding too much to assert that the judicatures of the states will be exempt from the prejudices by which the legislatures and people are influenced, and will constitute perfectly impartial tribunals. In many states the judges are dependent for office and for salary on the will of the legislature. The constitution of the United States furnishes no security against the universal adoption of this principle. When we observe the importance which that constitution attaches to the independence of judges, we are the less inclined to suppose that it can have intended to leave these constitutional questions to tribunals where this independence may not exist, in all cases where a state shall prosecute an individual who claims the protection of an act of Congress. These prosecutions may take place even without a legislative act. A person making a seizure under an act of Congress, may be indicted as a trespasser, if force has been employed, and of this a jury may judge. How extensive may be the mischief if the first decisions in such cases should be final!

These collisions may take place in times of no extraordinary commotion. But a constitution is framed for ages to come, and is designed to approach immortality as nearly as human institutions can approach it. Its course cannot always be tranquil. It is exposed to storms and tempests, and its framers must be unwise statesmen, indeed, if they have not provided it, as far as its nature will permit, with the means of self-preservation from the perils it may be destined to encounter. No government ought to be so defective in its organization as not to contain within itself the means of securing the execution of its own laws against other dangers than those which occur every day. Courts of justice are the means most usually employed; and it is reasonable to expect that a government should repose on its own courts rather than on others. There is certainly nothing in the circumstances under which our constitution was formed; nothing in the history of the times, which would justify the opinion that the confidence reposed in the states was so implicit as to leave in them and their tribunals the power of resisting or defeating, in the form of law, the legitimate measures of the Union. The requisitions of Congress, under the confederation, were as constitutionally obligatory as the laws enacted by the present Congress. That they were habitually disregarded, is a fact of universal notoriety. With the knowledge of this fact, and under its full pressure, a convention was assembled to change the system. Is it so improbable that they should confer on the judicial department the power of construing the constitution and laws of the Union in every case, in the last resort, and of preserving them from all violation from every quarter, so far as judicial decisions can preserve them, that this improbability should essentially affect the construction of the new system? We are told, and we are truly told, that the great change which is to give efficacy to the present system, is its ability to act on individuals directly, instead of acting through the instrumentality of state governments. But ought not this ability, in reason and sound policy, to be applied directly to the protection of individuals employed in the execution of the laws, as well as to their coercion. Your laws reach the individual without the aid of any other power; why may they not protect him from punishment for performing his duty in executing them?

The counsel for Virginia endeavor to obviate the force of these arguments by saying that the dangers they suggest, if not imaginary, are inevitable; that the constitution can make no provision against them; and that, therefore, in construing that instrument, they ought to be excluded from our consideration. This state of things, they say, cannot arise until there shall be a disposition so hostile to the present political system as to produce a determination to destroy it, and, when that determination shall be produced, its effects will not be restrained by parchment stipulations. The fate of the constitution will not then depend on judicial decisions. But, should no appeal be made to force, the states can put an end to the government by refusing to act. They have only not to elect Senators, and it expires without a struggle.

It is very true that, whenever hostility to the existing system shall become universal, it will be also irresistible. The people made the constitution, and the people can unmake it. It is the creature of their will, and lives only by their will. But this supreme and irresistible power to make or to unmake, resides only in the whole body of the people; not in any subdivision of them. The attempt of any of the parts to exercise it is usurpation, and ought to be repelled by those to whom the people have delegated their power of repelling it.

The acknowledged inability of the government, then, to sustain itself against the public will, and, by force or otherwise, to control the whole nation, is no sound argument in support of its constitutional inability to preserve itself against a section of the nation acting in opposition to the general will.

It is true, that if all the states, or a majority of them, refuse to elect Senators, the legislative powers of the Union will be suspended. But if any one state shall refuse to elect them, the Senate will not, on that account, be the less capable of performing all its functions. The argument founded on this fact would seem rather to prove the subordination of the parts to the whole, than the complete independence of any one of them. The framers of the constitution were indeed, unable to make any provisions which should protect that instrument against a general combination of the states, or of the people, for its destruction; and, conscious of this inability, they have not made the attempt. But they were able to provide against the operation of measures adopted in any one state, whose tendency might be to arrest the execution of the laws, and this it was the part of true wisdom to attempt. We think they have attempted it.

It has been also urged, as an additional objection to the jurisdiction of the court, that cases between a state and one of its own citizens, do not come within the general scope of the constitution, and were obviously never intended to be made cognizable in the federal courts. The state tribunals might be suspected of partiality in cases between itself or its citizens and aliens, or the citizens of another state, but not in proceedings by a state against its own citizens. That jealousy which might exist in the first case, could not exist in the last, and therefore the judicial power is not extended to the last.

This is very true, so far as jurisdiction depends on the character of the parties; and the argument would have great force if urged to prove that this court could not establish the demand of a citizen upon his state, but is not entitled to the same force when urged to prove that this court cannot enquire whether the constitution or laws of the United States protect a citizen from a prosecution instituted against him by a state. If jurisdiction depended entirely on the character of the parties, and was not given where the parties have not an original right to come into court, that part of the 2d section of the 3d article which extends the judicial power to all cases arising under the constitution and laws of the United States, would be mere surplusage. It is to give jurisdiction where the character of the parties would not give it, that this very important part of the clause was inserted. It may be true, that the partiality of the state tribunals, in ordinary controversies between a state and its citizens, was not apprehended, and therefore the judicial power of the Union was not extended to such cases; but this was not the sole, nor the greatest, object for which this department was created. A more important, a much more interesting, object was the preservation of the constitution and laws of the United States, so far as they can be preserved by judicial authority, and therefore the jurisdiction of the courts of the union was expressly extended to all cases arising under that constitution and those laws. If the constitution or laws may be violated by proceedings instituted by a state against its own citizens, and if that violation may be such as essentially to affect the constitution and the laws, such as to arrest the progress of government in its constitutional course, why should these cases be excepted from that provision which expressly extends the judicial power of the Union to *all* cases arising under the constitution and laws?

After bestowing on this subject the most attentive consideration, the court can perceive no reason founded on the character of the parties for introducing an exception which the constitution has not made; and we think that the judicial power, as originally given, extends to all cases arising under the constitution or a law of the United States whoever may be the parties.

It has been also contended that this jurisdiction, if given, is original, and cannot be exercised in the appellate form.

The words of the constitution are, "in all cases affecting ambassadors, other public ministers, and consuls, and those in which a state shall be party, the supreme court shall have original jurisdiction." In all the other cases before mentioned the supreme court shall have appellate jurisdiction.

This distinction between original and appellate jurisdiction excludes, we are told, in all cases, the exercise of the one where the other is given.

The constitution gives the supreme court original jurisdiction in certain enumerated cases, and gives it appellate jurisdiction in all others. Among those in which jurisdiction must be exercised in the appellate form are cases arising under the constitution and laws of the United States. These provisions of the constitution are equally obligatory and are to be equally respected. If a state be a party the jurisdiction of this court is original; if the case arise under a constitution or a law the jurisdiction is appellate. But a case to which a state is a party may arise under the constitution or a law of the United States. What rule is applicable to such a case? What then becomes the duty of the court? Certainly, we think, so to construe the constitution as to give effect to both provisions as far as it is possible to reconcile them, and not to permit their seeming repugnancy to destroy each other. We must endeavour so to construe them as to preserve the true intent and meaning of the instrument.

In one description of cases the jurisdiction of the court is founded entirely on the character of the parties; and the nature of the controversy is not contemplated by the constitution. The character of the parties is every thing, the nature of the case nothing. In the other description of cases, the jurisdiction is founded entirely on the character of the case, and the parties are not contemplated by the constitution. In these the nature of the case is every thing, the character of the parties nothing. When then the constitution declares the jurisdiction, in cases where a state shall be a party, to be original; and in all cases arising under the constitution or a law to be appellate; the conclusion seems irresistible, that its framers designed to include in the first class those cases in which jurisdiction is given because a state is a party; and to include in the second those in which jurisdiction is given because the case arises under the constitution or a law.

This reasonable construction is rendered necessary by other considerations.

That the constitution or a law of the United States is involved in a case, and makes a part of it, may appear in the progress of a cause, in which the courts of the Union, but for that circumstance, would have no jurisdiction, and which of consequence could not originate in the supreme court. In such a case the jurisdiction can be exercised only in its appellate form. To deny its exercise in this form is to deny its existence, and would be to construe a clause dividing the power of the supreme court in such manner as in a considerable degree to defeat the power itself. All must perceive that this construction can be justified only where it is absolutely necessary. We do not think the article under consideration presents that necessity.

It is observable that in this distributive clause no negative words are introduced. This observation is not made for the purpose of contending that the legislature may "apportion the judicial power between the Supreme and inferior courts according to its will." That would be, as was said by this court in the case of Marbury vs. Madison, to render the distributive clause "mere surplusage," to make it "form without substance." This cannot, therefore, be the true construction of the article.

But, although the absence of negative words will not authorize the legislature to disregard the distribution of the power previously granted, their absence will justify a sound construction of the whole article, so as to give every part its intended effect. It is admitted that "affirmative words are often, in their operation, negative of other objects than those affirmed"; and that where "a negative or exclusive sense must be given to them, or they have no operation at all," they must receive that negative or exclusive sense. But where they have full operation without it, where it would destroy some of the most important objects for which the power was created, then, we think, affirmative words ought not to be construed negatively.

The constitution declares that, in cases where a state is a party, the Supreme court shall have original jurisdiction, but does not say that its appellate jurisdiction shall not be exercised in cases where, from their nature, appellate jurisdiction is given, whether a state be or be not a party. It may be conceded that, where the case is of such a nature as to admit of its originating in the Supreme Court, it ought to originate there; but where, from its nature, it cannot originate in that court, these words ought not to be so construed as to require it. There are many cases in which it would be found extremely difficult, and subversive of the spirit of the constitution, to maintain the construction that appellate jurisdiction cannot be exercised where one of the parties might sue or be sued in this court.

The constitution defines the jurisdiction of the Supreme Court, but does not define that of the inferior courts. Can it be affirmed that a state might not sue the citizen of another state in a circuit court? Should the circuit court decide for or against its jurisdiction, should it dismiss the suit, or give judgment against the state, might not its decision be revised in the Supreme Court? The argument is, that it could not; and the very clause which is urged to prove that the circuit court could give no judgment in the case, is also urged to prove that its judgment is irreversible. A supervising court, whose peculiar province it is to correct the errors of an inferior court, has no power to correct a judgment given without jurisdiction, because, in the same case that supervising Court has original jurisdiction. Had negative words been employed, it would be difficult to give them this construction if they would admit of any other. But, without negative words, this irrational construction can never be maintained.

So, too, in the same clause, the jurisdiction of the court is declared to be original, "in cases affecting ambassadors, other public ministers, and consuls." There is, perhaps, no part of the article under consideration so much required by national policy as this; unless it be that part which extends the judicial power "to all cases arising under the constitution, laws, and treaties, of the United States." It has been generally held that the state courts have a concurrent jurisdiction with the federal courts, in cases to which the judicial power is extended, unless the jurisdiction of the federal courts be rendered exclusive by the words of the 3d article. If the words "to all cases" give exclusive jurisdiction in cases affecting foreign ministers, they may also give exclusive jurisdiction, if such be the will of Congress, in cases arising under the constitution, laws, and treaties, of the United States. Now, suppose an individual were to sue a foreign minister in a state court, and that court were to maintain its jurisdiction, and render judgment against the minister, could it be contended that this court would be incapable of revising such judgment, because the constitution had given it original jurisdiction in the case? If this could be maintained, then a clause inserted for the purpose of excluding the jurisdiction of all other courts than this, in a particular case, would have the effect of excluding the jurisdiction of this court in that very case, if the suit were to be brought in another court, and that court were to assert jurisdiction. This tribunal, according to the argument which has been urged, could neither revise the judgment of such other court, nor suspend its proceedings: for a writ of prohibition, or any other similar writ, is in the nature of appellate process.

Foreign consuls frequently assert, in our prize courts, the claims of their fellow subjects. These suits are maintained by them as consuls. The appellate power of this court has been frequently exercised in such cases, and has never been questioned. It would be extremely mischievous to withhold its exercise. Yet the consul is a party on the record. The truth is, that where the words confer only appellate jurisdiction, original jurisdiction is most clearly not given; but, where the words admit of appellate jurisdiction, the power to take cognizance of the suit originally does not necessarily negative the power to decide upon it on an appeal, if it may originate in a different court.

It is, we think, apparent that, to give this distributive clause the interpretation contended for, to give to its affirmative words a negative operation, in every possible case, would, in some instances, defeat the obvious intention of the article. Such an interpretation would not consist with those rules which, from time immemorial, have guided courts, in their construction of instruments brought under their consideration. It must, therefore, be discarded. Every part of the article must be taken into view, and that construction adopted which will consist with its words, and promote its general intention. The court may imply a negative from affirmative words, where the implication promotes, not where it defeats the intention.

If we apply this principle, the correctness of which we believe will not be controverted, to the distributive clause under consideration, the result, we think, would be this: The original jurisdiction of the Supreme Court, in cases where a state is a party, refers to those cases in which, according to the grant of power made in the preceding clause, jurisdiction might be exercised in consequence of the character of the party, and an original suit, might be instituted in any of the federal courts; not to those cases in which an original suit might not be instituted in a federal court. Of the last description, is every case between a state and its citizens, and perhaps every case in which a state is enforcing its penal laws. In such cases, therefore, the Supreme Court cannot take original jurisdiction. In every other case, that is, in every case to which the judicial power extends, and in which original jurisdiction is not expressly given, that judicial power shall be exercised in the appellate, and only in the appellate form. The original jurisdiction of this court cannot be enlarged, but its appellate jurisdiction may be exercised in every case cognizable under the 3d article of the constitution, in the federal courts, in which original jurisdiction cannot be exercised; and the extent of this judicial power is to be measured, not by giving the affirmative words of the distributive clause a negative operation in every possible case, but by giving their true meaning to the words which define its extent.

The counsel for the defendant in error urge, in opposition to this rule of construction, some dicta of the court in the case of Marbury vs. Madison.

It is a maxim not to be disregarded, that general expressions, in every opinion, are to be taken in connection with the case in which those expressions are used. If they go beyond the case, they may be respected, but ought not to control the judgment in a subsequent suit when the very point is presented for decision. The reason of this maxim is obvious. The question actually before the court is investigated with care, and considered in its full extent. Other principles which may serve to illustrate it, are considered in their relation to the case decided, but their possible bearing on all other cases is seldom completely investigated.

In the case of Marbury vs. Madison, the single question before the court, so far as that case can be applied to this, was, whether the legislature could give this court original jurisdiction in a case in which the constitution had clearly not given it, and in which no doubt respecting the construction of the article could possibly be raised. The court decided, and we think very properly, that the legislature could not give original jurisdiction in such a case. But, in the reasoning of the court in support of this decision, some expressions are used which go far beyond it. The counsel for Marbury had insisted on the unlimited discretion of the legislature in the apportionment of the judicial power; and it is against this argument that the reasoning of the court is directed. They say that, if such had been the intention of the article, "it would certainly have been useless to proceed farther than to define the judicial power, and the tribunals in which it should be vested." The court says that such a construction would render the clause dividing the jurisdiction of the court into original and appellate, totally useless; that "affirmative words are often, in their operation, negative of other objects than those which are affirmed; and, in this case, (in the case of Marbury vs. Madison,) a negative or exclusive sense must be given to them, or they have no operation at all." "It cannot be presumed," adds the Court, "that any clause in the constitution is intended to be without effect; and, therefore, such a construction is inadmissible unless the words require it."

The whole reasoning of the court proceeds upon the idea that the affirmative words of the clause giving one sort of jurisdiction, must imply a negative of any other sort of jurisdiction, because otherwise the words would be totally inoperative, and this reasoning is advanced in a case to which it was strictly applicable. If in that case original jurisdiction could have been exercised, the clause under consideration would have been entirely useless. Having such cases only in its view, the court lays down a principle which is generally correct, in terms much broader than the decision, and not only much broader than the reasoning with which that decision is supported, but in some instances contradictory to its principle. The reasoning sustains the negative operation of the words in that case, because otherwise the clause would have no meaning whatever, and because such operation was necessary to give effect to the intention of the article. The effort now made is, to apply the conclusion to which the court was conducted by that reasoning in the particular case, to one in which the words have their full operation when understood affirmatively, and in which the negative, or exclusive sense is to be so used as to defeat some of the great objects of the article.

To this construction the court cannot give its assent. The general expressions in the case of Marbury vs. Madison must be understood with the limitations which are given to them in this opinion; limitations which in no degree affect the decision in that case, or the tenor of its reasoning.

The counsel who closed the argument, put several cases for the purpose of illustration, which he supposed to arise under the Constitution, and yet to be, apparently, without the jurisdiction of the court.

Were a state to lay a duty on exports, to collect the money and place it in her treasury, could the citizen who paid it, he asks, maintain a suit in this court against such state, to recover back the money?

Perhaps not. Without, however, deciding such supposed case, we may say that it is entirely unlike that under consideration.

The citizen who has paid his money to his state, under a law that is void, is in the same situation with every other person who has paid money by mistake. The law raises an assumpsit to return the money, and it is upon that assumpsit that the action is to be maintained. To refuse to comply with this assumpsit may be no more a violation of the constitution, than to refuse to comply with any other; and as the federal courts never had jurisdiction over contracts between a state and its citizens, they may have none over this. But let us so vary the supposed case, as to give it a real resemblance to that under consideration. Suppose a citizen to refuse to pay this export duty, and a suit to be instituted for the purpose of compelling him to pay it. He pleads the constitution of the United States in bar of the action, notwithstanding which the court gives judgment against him. This would be a case arising under the constitution, and would be the very case now before the court.

We are also asked, if a state should confiscate property secured by a treaty, whether the individual could maintain an action for that property?

If the property confiscated be debts, our own experience informs us that the remedy of the creditor against his debtor remains. If it be land, which is secured by a treaty, and afterwards confiscated by a state, the argument does not assume that this title, thus secured, could be extinguished by an act of confiscation. The injured party, therefore, has his remedy against the occupant of the land for that which the treaty secures to him, not against the state for money which is not secured to him.

The case of a state which pays off its own debts with paper money, no more resembles this than do those to which we have already adverted. The courts have no jurisdiction over the contract. They cannot enforce it, nor judge of its violation. Let it be that the act discharging the debt is a mere nullity, and that it is still due. Yet the federal courts have no cognizance of the case. But suppose a state to institute proceedings against an individual, which depended on the validity of an act emitting bills of credit: suppose a state to prosecute one of its citizens for refusing paper money, who should plead the constitution in bar of such prosecution. If his plea should be overruled and judgment rendered against him, his case would resemble this; and, unless the jurisdiction of this court might be exercised over it, the constitution would be violated, and the injured party be unable to bring his case before that tribunal to which the people of the United States have assigned all such cases.

It is most true that this court will not take jurisdiction if it should not; but it is equally true, that it must take jurisdiction if it should. The judiciary cannot, as the legislature may, avoid a measure because it approaches the confines of the constitution. We cannot pass it by because it is doubtful. With whatever doubts, with whatever difficulties, a case may be attended, we must decide it, if it be brought before us. We have no more right to decline the exercise of jurisdiction which is given, than to usurp that which is not given. The one or the other would be treason to the constitution. Questions may occur which we would gladly avoid; but we cannot avoid them. All we can do is to exercise our best judgment, and conscientiously to perform our duty. In doing this, on the present occasion, we find this tribunal invested with appellate jurisdiction in *all* cases arising under the constitution and laws of the United States. We find no exception to this grant, and we cannot insert one.

To escape the operation of these comprehensive words, the counsel for the defendant has mentioned instances in which the constitution might be violated without giving jurisdiction to this court. These words, therefore, however universal in their expression, must, he contends, be limited and controlled in their construction by circumstances. One of these instances is the grant by a state of a patent of nobility. The court, he says, cannot annul this grant.

This may be very true, but by no means justifies the inference drawn from it. The article does not extend the judicial power to every violation of the constitution which may possibly take place, but to "a case in law or equity," in which a right, under such law, is asserted in a court of justice. If the question cannot be brought into a court, then there is no case in law or equity, and no jurisdiction is given by the words of the article. But if, in any controversy depending in a court, the cause should depend on the validity of such a law, that would be a case arising under the constitution, to which the judicial power of the United States would extend. The same observation applies to the other instances with which the counsel who opened the cause has illustrated this argument. Although they show that there may be violations of the constitution of which the courts can take no cognizance, they do not show that an interpretation more restrictive than the words themselves import ought to be given to this article. They do not show that there can be "a *case* in law or equity," arising under the constitution, to which the judicial power does not extend.

We think, then, that, as the constitution originally stood, the appellate jurisdiction of this court, in all cases arising under the constitution, laws, or treaties, of the United States, was not arrested by the circumstance that a state was a party.

This leads to a consideration of the 11th amendment.

It is in these words: "The judicial power of the United States shall not be construed to extend to any suit in law or equity commenced or prosecuted against one of the United States by citizens of another state, or by citizens or subjects of any foreign state."

It is a part of our history, that, at the adoption of the constitution, all the states were greatly indebted; and the apprehension that these debts might be prosecuted in the federal courts formed a very serious objection to that instrument. Suits were instituted; and the court maintained its jurisdiction. The alarm was general; and, to quiet the apprehensions that were so extensively entertained, this amendment was proposed in Congress, and adopted by the state legislatures. That its motive was not to maintain the sovereignty of a state from the degradation supposed to attend a compulsory appearance before the tribunal of the nation may be inferred from the terms of the amendment. It does not comprehend controversies between two or more states, or between a state and a foreign state. The jurisdiction of the court still extends to these cases; and in these a state may still be sued. We must ascribe the amendment, then, to some other cause than the dignity of a state. There is no difficulty in finding this cause. Those who were inhibited from commencing a suit against a state, or from prosecuting one which might be commenced before the adoption of the amendment, were persons who might probably be its creditors. There was not much reason to fear that foreign or sister states would be creditors to any considerable amount, and there was reason to retain the jurisdiction of the court in those cases, because it might be essential to the preservation of peace. The amendment therefore extended to suits commenced or prosecuted by individuals, but not to those brought by states.

The first impression made on the mind by this amendment

is, that it was intended for those cases, and for those only, in which some demand against a state is made by an individual in the courts of the Union. If we consider the causes to which it is to be traced, we are conducted to the same conclusion. A general interest might well be felt in leaving to a state the full power of consulting its convenience in the adjustment of its debts, or of other claims upon it; but no interest could be felt in so changing the relations between the whole and its parts as to strip the government of the means of protecting, by the instrumentality of its courts, the constitution and laws from active violation.

The words of the amendment appear to the court to justify and require this construction. The judicial power is not "to extend to any suit in law or equity commenced or prosecuted against one of the United States by citizens of another state," &c.

What is a suit? We understand it to be the prosecution, or pursuit, of some claim, demand, or request. In law language, it is the prosecution of some demand in a court of justice. The remedy for every species of wrong is, says Judge Blackstone, "the being put in possession of that right whereof the party injured is deprived." "The instruments whereby this remedy is obtained are a diversity of suits and actions, which are defined by the Mirror to be 'the lawful demand of one's right.' Or, as Bracton and Fleta express it, in the words of Justinian, '*jus prosequendi in judicio quod aliqui debetur.*'" The right of prosecuting &c. Blackstone then proceeds to describe every species of remedy by suit; and they are all cases where the party suing claims to obtain something to which he has a right.

To commence a suit, is to demand something by the institution of process in a court of justice, and to prosecute the suit, is, according to the common acceptation of language, to continue that demand. By a suit commenced by an individual against a state, we should understand process sued out by that individual against the state, for the purpose of establishing some claim against it by the judgment of a court; and the prosecution of that suit is its continuance. Whatever may be the stages of its progress, the actor is still the same. Suits had been commenced in the supreme court against some of the states before this amendment was introduced into Congress, and others might be commenced before it should be adopted by the state legislatures, and might be depending at the time of its adoption. The object of the amendment was not only to prevent the commencement of future suits, but to arrest the prosecution of those which might be commenced when this article should form a part of the constitution. It therefore embraces both objects; and its meaning is, that the judicial power shall not be construed to extend to any suit which may be commenced, or which, if already commenced, may be prosecuted against a state by the citizen of another state. If a suit, brought in one court, and carried by legal process to a supervising court, be a continuation of the same suit, then this suit is not commenced nor, prosecuted against a state. It is clearly in its commencement the suit of a state against an individual, which suit is transferred to this court, not for the purpose of asserting any claim against the state, but for the purpose of asserting a constitutional defence against a claim made by a state.

A writ of error is defined to be, a commission by which the judges of one court are authorized to examine a record upon which a judgment was given in another court, and, on such examination, to affirm or reverse the same according to law. If, says my Lord Coke, by the writ of error, the plaintiff may recover, or be restored to any thing, it may be released by the name of an action. In Bacon's Abridgement, title Error, letter L, it is laid down that "where by a writ of error, the plaintiff shall recover, or be restored to any personal thing, as debt, damage, or the like, a release of all actions personal is a good plea; and when land is to be recovered or restored in a writ of error, a release of actions real is a good bar; but where by a writ of error the plaintiff shall not be restored to any personal or real thing, a release of all actions, real or personal, is no bar." And for this we have the authority of Lord Coke, both in his Commentary on Littleton and in his Reports. A writ of error, then, is in the nature of a suit or action when it is to restore the party who obtains it to the possession of any thing which is withheld from him, not when its operation is entirely defensive.

This rule will apply to writs of error from the courts of the United States, as well as to those writs in England.

Under the judicial act the effect of a writ of error is simply to bring the record into court and submit the judgment of the inferior tribunal to re-examination. It does not in any manner act upon the parties, it acts only on the record. It removes the record into the supervising tribunal. Where then a state obtains a judgment against an individual, and the court rendering such judgment overrules a defence set up under the constitution or laws of the United States, the transfer of this record into the supreme court for the sole purpose of enquiring whether the judgment violates the constitution or laws of the United States can, with no propriety, we think, be denominated a suit commenced or prosecuted against the state whose judgment is so far re-examined. Nothing is demanded from the state. No claim against it of any description is asserted or prosecuted. The party is not to be restored to the possession of any thing. Essentially it is an appeal on a single point; and the defendant who appeals from a judgment rendered against him, is never said to commence or prosecute a suit against the plaintiff who has obtained the judgment. The writ of error is given rather than an appeal, because it is the more usual mode of removing suits at common law; and because perhaps it is more technically proper where a single point of law, and not the whole case, is to be re-examined. But an appeal might be given, and might be so regulated as to effect every purpose of a writ of error. The mode of removal is form, and not substance. Whether it be by writ of error or appeal, no claim is asserted, no demand is made by the original defendant; he only asserts the constitutional right to have his defence examined by that tribunal whose province it is to construe the constitution and laws of the Union.

The only part of the proceeding which is in any manner personal is the citation. And what is the citation? It is simply notice to the opposite party that the record is transferred into another court where he may appear, or decline to appear, as his judgment or inclination may determine. As the party who has obtained a judgment is out of court, and may therefore not know that his cause is removed, common justice requires that notice of the fact should be given him. But this notice is not a suit, nor has it the effect of process. If the party does not choose to appear, he cannot be brought into court, nor is his failure to appear considered as a default. Judgment cannot be given against him for his nonappearance, but the judgment is to be re-examined and reversed, or affirmed in like manner as if the party had appeared and argued his cause.

The point of view in which this writ of error with its citation has been considered uniformly in the courts of the Union, has been well illustrated by a reference to the course of this court in suits instituted by the United States. The universally received opinion is that no suit can be commenced or prosecuted against the United States. That the judicial act does not authorize such suits. Yet writs of error, accompanied with citations, have uniformly issued for the removal of judgments in favor of the United States into a superior court where they have, like those in favor of an individual, been re-examined and affirmed, or reversed. It has never been suggested that such writ of error was a suit against the United States, and therefore not within the jurisdiction of the appellate Court.

It is then the opinion of the court that the defendant who removes a judgment rendered against him by a state court into this court, for the purpose of re-examining the question whether that judgment be in violation of the constitution or laws of the United States, does not commence or prosecute a suit against the state, whatever may be its opinion where the effect of the writ may be to restore the party to the possession of a thing which he demands.

But, should we in this be mistaken, the error does not affect the case now before the court. If this writ of error be a suit in the sense of the 11th amendment, it is not a suit commenced or prosecuted "by a citizen of another state, or by a citizen, or subject of any foreign state." It is not then within the amendment, but is governed entirely by the constitution as originally framed, and we have already seen that in its origin, the judicial power was extended to all cases arising under the constitution or laws of the United States, without respect to parties.

2d. The second objection to the jurisdiction of the court is, that its appellate power cannot be exercised, in any case, over the judgment of a state court.

This objection is sustained chiefly by arguments drawn from the supposed total separation of the judiciary of a state from that of the Union, and their entire independence of each other. The argument considers the federal judiciary as completely foreign to that of a state; and as being no more connected with it in any respect whatever, than the court of a foreign state. If this hypothesis be just, the argument founded on it is equally so; but if the hypothesis be not supported by the constitution, the argument fails with it.

This hypothesis is not founded on any words in the constitution, which might seem to countenance it, but on the unreasonableness of giving a contrary construction to words which seem to require it; and on the incompatibility of the application of the appellate jurisdiction to the judgments of state courts, with that constitutional relation which subsists between the government of the Union and the governments of those states which compose it.

Let this unreasonableness, this total incompatibility, be examined.

That the United States form, for many and for most important purposes, a single nation, has not yet been denied. In war, we are one people. In making peace, we are one people. In all commercial regulations, we are one and the same people. In many other respects, the American people are one, and the government which is alone capable of controling and managing their interests in all these respects, is the government of the Union. It is their government, and in that character they have no other. America has chosen to be, in many respects, and to many purposes, a nation; and for all these purposes, her government is complete; to all these objects, it is competent. They have declared, that, in the exercise of all powers given for these objects, it is supreme. It can, then, in effecting these objects, legitimately control all individuals or governments within the American territory. The constitution and laws of a state, so far as they are repugnant to the constitution and laws of the United States, are absolutely void. These states are constituent parts of the United States. They are members of one great empire—for some purposes sovereign: for some purposes subordinate.

In a government so constituted, is it unreasonable that the judicial power should be competent to give efficacy to the constitutional laws of the legislature? That department can decide on the validity of the constitution or law of a state, if it be repugnant to the constitution or to a law of the United States. Is it unreasonable that it should also be empowered to decide on the judgment of a state tribunal enforcing such unconstitutional law? Is it so very unreasonable as to furnish a justification for controling the words of the constitution?

We think it is not. We think that in a government acknowledgedly supreme with respect to objects of vital interest to the nation, there is nothing inconsistent with sound reason, nothing incompatible with the nature of government, in making all its departments supreme, so far as respects those objects, and so far as is necessary to their attainment. The exercise of the appellate power over those judgments of the state tribunals which may contravene the constitution or laws of the United States, is, we believe, essential to the attainment of those objects.

The propriety of entrusting the construction of the constitution, and laws made in pursuance thereof, to the judiciary of the Union, has not, we believe, as yet been drawn into question. It seems to be a corollary from this political axiom, that the federal courts should either possess exclusive jurisdiction in such cases, or a power to revise the judgments rendered in them, by the state tribunals. If the federal and state courts have concurrent jurisdiction in all cases arising under the constitution, laws, and treaties, of the United States; and if a case of this description brought in a state court cannot be removed before judgment, nor revised after judgment, then the construction of the constitution, laws, and treaties of the United States, is not confided particularly to their judicial department, but is confided equally to that department and to the state courts, however they may be constituted. "Thirteen independent courts," says a very celebrated statesman, and we have now more than twenty, "of final jurisdiction over the same causes, arising upon the same laws, is a hydra in government, from which nothing but contradiction and confusion can proceed."

Dismissing the unpleasant suggestion that any motives which may not be fairly avowed, or which ought not to exist, can ever influence a state or its courts, the necessity of uniformity as well as correctness in expounding the constitution and laws of the United States, would itself suggest the propriety of vesting in some single tribunal the power of deciding, in the last resort, all cases in which they are involved.

We are not restrained, then, by the political relations

between the general and state governments, from construing the words of the constitution defining the judicial power in their true sense. We are not bound to construe them more restrictively than they naturally import.

They give to the supreme court appellate jurisdiction in all cases arising under the constitution, laws, and treaties, of the United States. The words are broad enough to comprehend all cases of this description, in whatever court they may be decided. In expounding them, we may be permitted to take into view those considerations to which courts have always allowed great weight in the exposition of laws.

The framers of the constitution would naturally examine the state of things existing at the time; and their work sufficiently attests that they did so. All acknowledge that they were convened for the purpose of strengthening the confederation by enlarging the powers of the government, and by giving efficacy to those which it before possessed, but could not exercise. They inform us themselves, in the instrument they presented to the American public, that one of its objects was to form a more perfect union. Under such circumstances, we certainly should not expect to find, in that instrument, a diminution of the powers of the actual government.

Previous to the adoption of the confederation, Congress established courts which received appeals in prize causes decided in the courts of the respective states. This power of the government, to establish tribunals for these appeals, was thought consistent with, and was founded on, its political relations with the states. These courts did exercise appellate jurisdiction over those cases decided in the state courts, to which the judicial power of the federal government extended.

The confederation gave to Congress the power "of establishing courts for receiving and determining finally appeals in all cases of captures."

This power was uniformly construed to authorize those courts to receive appeals from the sentences of state courts, and to affirm or reverse them. State tribunals are not mentioned; but this clause in the confederation necessarily comprises them. Yet the relation between the general and state governments was much weaker, much more lax, under the confederation than under the present constitution; and the states being much more completely sovereign, their institutions were much more independent.

The convention which framed the constitution, on turning their attention to the judicial power, found it limited to a few objects, but exercised, with respect to some of those objects, in its appellate form, over the judgments of the state courts. They extend it, among other objects, to all cases arising under the constitution, laws, and treaties, of the United States; and, in a subsequent clause, declare that, in such cases, the supreme court shall exercise appellate jurisdiction. Nothing seems to be given which would justify the withdrawal of a judgment rendered in a state court, on the constitution, laws, or treaties, of the United States, from this appellate jurisdiction.

Great weight has always been attached, and very rightly attached, to contemporaneous exposition. No question, it is believed, has arisen to which this principle applies more unequivocally than to that now under consideration.

The opinion of the Federalist has always been considered as of great authority. It is a complete commentary on our constitution; and is appealed to by all parties in the questions to which that instrument has given birth. Its intrinsic merit entitles it to this high rank; and the part two of its authors performed in framing the constitution put it very much in their power to explain the views with which it was framed. These essays having been published while the constitution was before the nation for adoption or rejection, and having been written in answer to objections founded entirely on the extent of its powers, and on its diminution of state sovereignty, are entitled to the more consideration where they frankly avow that the power objected to is given, and defend it.

In discussing the extent of the judicial power, the Federalist says, "Here another question occurs: what relation would subsist between the national and state courts in these instances of concurrent jurisdiction? I answer, that an appeal would certainly lie from the latter, to the supreme court of the United States. The constitution in direct terms gives an appellate jurisdiction to the supreme court in all the enumerated cases of federal cognizance in which it is not to have an original one, without a single expression to confine its operation to the inferior federal courts. The objects of appeal, not the tribunals from which it is to be made, are alone contemplated. From this circumstance, and from the reason of the thing, it ought to be construed to extend to the state tribunals. Either this must be the case, or the local courts must be excluded from a concurrent jurisdiction in matters of national concern, else the judiciary authority of the Union maybe eluded at the pleasure of every plaintiff or prosecutor. Neither of these consequences ought, without evident necessity, to be involved; the latter would be entirely inadmissible, as it would defeat some of the most important and avowed purposes of the proposed government, and would essentially embarrass its measures. Nor do I perceive any foundation for such a supposition. Agreeably to the remark already made, the national and state systems are to be regarded as ONE WHOLE. The courts of the latter will of course be natural auxiliaries to the execution of the laws of the Union, and an appeal from them will as naturally lie to that tribunal which is destined to unite and assimilate the principles of natural justice and the rules of national decision. The evident aim of the plan of the national convention is, that all the causes of the specified classes shall, for weighty public reasons, receive their original or final determination in the courts of the Union. To confine, therefore, the general expressions which give appellate jurisdiction to the supreme court, to appeals from the subordinate federal courts, instead of allowing their extension to the state courts, would be to abridge the latitude of the terms, in subversion of the intent, contrary to every sound rule of interpretation."

A contemporaneous exposition of the constitution, certainly of not less authority than that which has been just cited, is the judicial act itself. We know that in the Congress which passed that act were many eminent members of the convention which formed the constitution. Not a single individual, so far as is known, supposed that part of the act which gives the supreme court appellate jurisdiction over the judgments of the state courts in the cases therein specified, to be unauthorized by the constitution.

While on this part of the argument, it may be also material to observe that the uniform decisions of this court on the point now under consideration, have been assented to, with a single exception, by the courts of every state in the Union whose judgments have been revised. It has been the unwelcome duty of this tribunal to reverse the judgments of many state courts in cases in which the strongest state feelings were engaged. Judges, whose talents and character would grace any bench, to whom a disposition to submit to jurisdiction that is usurped, or to surrender their legitimate powers, will certainly not be imputed, have yielded without hesitation to the authority by which their judgments were reversed, while they, perhaps, disapproved the judgment of reversal.

This concurrence of statesmen, of legislators, and of judges, in the same construction of the constitution, may justly inspire some confidence in that construction.

In opposition to it, the counsel who made this point has presented in a great variety of forms, the idea already noticed, that the federal and state courts must, of necessity, and from the nature of the constitution, be in all things totally distinct and independent of each other. If this court can correct the errors of the courts of Virginia, he says it makes them courts of the United States, or becomes itself a part of the judiciary of Virginia.

But, it has been already shown that neither of these consequences necessarily follows: The American people may certainly give to a national tribunal a supervising power over those judgments of the state courts which may conflict with the constitution, laws, or treaties, of the United States, without converting them into federal courts, or converting the national into a state tribunal. The one court still derives its authority from the state, the other still derives its authority from the nation.

If it shall be established, he says, that this court has appellate jurisdiction over the state courts in all cases enumerated in the 3d article of the constitution, a complete consolidation of the states, so far as respects judicial power is produced.

But, certainly the mind of the gentleman who urged this argument is too accurate not to perceive that he has carried it too far; that the premises by no means justify the conclusion. "A complete consolidation of the states, so far as respects the judicial power," would authorize the legislature to confer on the federal courts appellate jurisdiction from the state courts in all cases whatsoever. The distinction between such a power, and that of giving appellate jurisdiction in a few specified cases in the decision of which the nation takes an interest, is too obvious not to be perceived by all.

This opinion has been already drawn out to too great a length to admit of entering into a particular consideration of the various forms in which the counsel who made this point has, with much ingenuity, presented his argument to the court. The argument in all its forms is essentially the same. It is founded, not on the words of the constitution, but on its spirit, a spirit extracted, not from the words of the instrument, but from his view of the nature of our union and of the great fundamental principles on which the fabric stands.

To this argument, in all its forms, the same answer may be given. Let the nature and objects of our union be considered; let the great fundamental principles on which the fabric stands be examined, and we think the result must be, that there is nothing so extravagantly absurd in giving to the court of the nation the power of revising the decisions of local tribunals on questions which affect the nation, as to require that words which import this power should be restricted by a forced construction. The question then must depend on the words themselves; and on their construction we shall be the more readily excused for not adding to the observations already made, because the subject was fully discussed and exhausted in the case of Martin vs. Hunter.

3d. We come now to the third objection, which, though differently stated by the counsel, is substantially the same. One gentleman has said that the judicial act does not give jurisdiction in the case.

The cause was argued in the state court, on a case agreed by the parties, which states the prosecution under a law for selling lottery tickets, which is set forth, and further states the act of Congress by which the city of Washington was authorized to establish the lottery. It then states that the lottery was regularly established by virtue of the act, and concludes with referring to the court the questions, whether the act of Congress be valid? whether, on its just construction, it constitutes a bar to the prosecution? and, whether the act of Assembly, on which the prosecution is founded, be not itself invalid? These questions were decided against the operation of the act of Congress, and in favor of the operation of the act of the state.

If the 25th section of the judicial act be inspected, it will at once be perceived that it comprehends expressly the case under consideration.

But it is not upon the letter of the act that the gentleman who stated this point in this form, founds his argument. Both gentlemen concur substantially in their views of this part of the case. They deny that the act of Congress, on which the plaintiff in error relies, is a law of the United States; or, if a law of the United States, is within the second clause of the sixth article.

In the enumeration of the powers of Congress, which is made in the 8th section of the first article, we find that of exercising exclusive legislation over such district as shall become the seat of government. This power, like all others which are specified, is conferred on Congress as the legislature of the Union; for, strip them of that character, and they would not possess it. In no other character can it be exercised. In legislating for the district, they necessarily preserve the character of the legislature of the Union; for, it is in that character alone that the constitution confers on them this power of exclusive legislation. This proposition need not be enforced.

The 2d clause of the 6th article declares, that "This constitution, and the laws of the United States, which shall be made in pursuance thereof, shall be the supreme law of the land."

The clause which gives exclusive jurisdiction is, unquestionably, a part of the constitution, and, as such, binds all the United States. Those who contend that acts of Congress, made in pursuance of this power, do not, like acts made in pursuance of other powers, bind the nation, ought to show some safe and clear rule which shall support this construction, and prove that an act of Congress, clothed in all the forms which attend other legislative acts, and passed in virtue of a power conferred on, and exercised by, Congress, as the legislature of the Union, is not a law of the United States, and does not bind them.

One of the gentlemen sought to illustrate his proposition that Congress, when legislating for the District, assumed a distinct character, and was reduced to a mere local legislature, whose laws could possess no obligation out of the 10 miles square, by a reference to the complex character of this court. It is, they say, a court of common law and a court of equity. Its character, when sitting as a court of common law, is as distinct from its character when sitting as a court of equity, as if the powers belonging to those departments were vested in different tribunals. Though united in the same tribunal, they are never confounded with each other.

Without enquiring how far the union of different characters in one court, may be applicable, in principle, to the union in Congress of the power of exclusive legislation in some places, and of limited legislation in others, it may be observed, that the forms of proceedings in a court of law are so totally unlike the forms of proceedings in a court of equity, that a mere inspection of the record gives decisive information of the character in which the court sits, and consequently of the extent of its powers. But if the forms of proceeding were precisely the same, and the Court the same, the distinction would disappear.

Since Congress legislates in the same forms, and in the same character, in virtue of powers of equal obligation, conferred in the same instrument, when exercising its exclusive powers of legislation, as well as when exercising those which are limited, we must enquire whether there be any thing in the nature of this exclusive legislation which necessarily confines the operation of the laws made in virtue of this power to the place with a view to which they are made.

Connected with the power to legislate within this district, is a similar power in forts, arsenals, dock yards, &c. Congress has a right to punish murder in a fort, or other place within its exclusive jurisdiction; but no general right to punish murder committed within any of the states. In the act for the punishment of crimes against the United States, murder committed within a fort, or any other place or district of country, under the sole and exclusive jurisdiction of the United States, is punished with death. Thus Congress legislates in the same act, under its exclusive and its limited powers.

The act proceeds to direct that the body of the criminal, after execution, may be delivered to a surgeon for dissection, and punishes any person who shall rescue such body during its conveyance from the place of execution to the surgeon to whom it is to be delivered.

Let these actual provisions of the law, or any other provisions which can be made on the subject, be considered with a view to the character in which Congress acts when exercising its powers of exclusive legislation.

If Congress is to be considered merely as a local legislature, invested, as to this object, with powers limited to the fort, or other place, in which the murder may be committed, if its general powers cannot come in aid of these local powers, how can the offence be tried in any other court than that of the place in which it has been committed? How can the offender be conveyed to, or tried in, any other place? How can he be executed elsewhere? How can his body be conveyed through a country under the jurisdiction of another sovereign, and the individual punished who, within that jurisdiction, shall rescue the body.

Were any one state of the Union to pass a law for trying a criminal in a court not created by itself, in a place not within its jurisdiction and direct the sentence to be executed without its territory, we should all perceive and acknowledge its incompetency to such a course of legislation. If Congress be not equally incompetent, it is because that body unites the powers of local legislation with those which are to operate through the Union, and may use the last in aid of the first, or because the power of exercising exclusive legislation draws after it, as an incident, the power of making that legislation effectual, and the incidental power may be exercised throughout the Union, because the principal power is given to that body as the legislature of the Union.

So, in the same act, a person who, having knowledge of the commission of murder or other felony on the high seas, or within any fort, arsenal, dock-yard, magazine, or other place or district of country within the sole and exclusive jurisdiction of the United States, shall conceal the same, &c. he shall be adjudged guilty of misprision of felony, and shall be adjudged to be imprisoned, &c.

It is clear that Congress cannot punish felonies generally; and, of consequence, cannot punish misprision of felony. It is equally clear that a state legislature, the state of Maryland for example, cannot punish those who, in another state, conceal a felony committed in Maryland. How, then, is it that Congress, legislating exclusively for a fort, punishes those who, out of that fort, conceal a felony committed within it?

The solution, and the only solution of the difficulty is, that the power vested, in Congress, as the legislature of the U. States, to legislate exclusively within any place ceded by a state, carries with it, as an incident, the right to make that power effectual. If a felon escape out of the state in which the act has been committed, the government cannot pursue him into another state, and apprehend him there, but must demand him from the Executive power of that other state. If Congress were to be considered merely as the local legislature for the fort or other place in which the offence might be committed, then, this principle would apply to them as to other local legislatures, and the felon who should escape out of the fort or other place, in which the felony may have been committed, could not be apprehended by the marshal, but must be demanded from the Executive of the state. But we know that the principle does not apply and the reason is, that Congress is not a local legislature, but exercises this particular power, like all its other powers in its high character, as the legislature of the Union. The American people thought it a necessary power, and they conferred it for their own benefit. Being so conferred, it carries with it all those incidental powers which are necessary to its complete and effectual execution.

Whether any particular law be designed to operate without the district or not, depends on the words of that law. If it be designed so to operate, then the question whether the power so exercised be incidental to the power of exclusive legislation, and be warranted by the constitution, requires a consideration of that instrument. In such cases the constitution and the law must be compared and construed. This is the exercise of jurisdiction. It is the only exercise of it which is allowed in such a case. For the act of Congress directs that "no other error shall be assigned or regarded as a ground of reversal, in any such case as aforesaid, than such as appears on the face of the record, and immediately respects the before mentioned questions of validity or construction of the said constitution, treaties," &c.

The whole merits of this case, then, consist in the construction of the constitution and the act of Congress. The jurisdiction of the court, if acknowledged, goes no farther. This we are required to do without the exercise of jurisdiction.

The counsel for the state of Virginia have, in support of this motion, urged many arguments of great weight against the application of the act of Congress to such a case as this; but those arguments go to the construction of the constitution or of the law, or both; and seem therefore rather calculated to sustain their cause upon its merits, than to prove a failure of jurisdiction in the court.

After having bestowed upon this question the most deliberate consideration of which we are capable, the Court is unanimously of opinion that the objections to its jurisdiction are not sustained, and that the motion ought to be overruled.

March 3, 1821

"THE CHAMPION OF DISMEMBERMENT"

To Joseph Story

Dear Sir   Richmond June 15th. 1821

A question has occurred in the course of this term which I have taken under advisement for the purpose of enquiring whether it has been decided by my brethren. It is this. **A** & **B** trading under the firm of A B & Co. were indebted to the U.S. on bonds for duties. They made an assignment of all their social effects to secure certain creditors of the firm. **A** had private property to a considerable amount which he afterwards conveyed to secure his individual creditors. The question is whether the first conveyance was an act of insolvency within the act of Congress so that the priority of the U.S. attached on the social effects, or whether the act of insolvency was not committed until the execution of the second deed. The case arises on a contest between the creditors secured by the two deeds, each contending that the claim of the U.S. should be satisfied by the other. Had the second deed never been executed would the first have amounted to an act of insolvency on the part of the firm? If the case has ever occurred in your circuit I shall be glad to know how it has been decided. If it has never occurred you will oblige me by stating your opinion on it if you have one.

The opinion of the supreme court in the lottery case has been assaulted with a degree of virulence transcending what has appeared on any former occasion. Algernon Sydney is written by the gentleman who is so much distinguished for his feelings towards the supreme court, & if you have not an opportunity of seeing the Enquirer I will send it to you. There are other minor gentry who seek to curry favor & get into office by adding their mite of abuse, but I think for coarseness & malignity of invective Algernon Sidney surpasses all party writers who have ever made pretensions to any decency of character. There is on this subject no such thing as a free press in Virginia; and of consequence the calumnies & misrepresentations of this gentleman will remain uncontradicted & will by many be beleived to be true. He will be supposed to be the champion of state rights instead of being what he really is the champion of dismemberment. With great regard & esteem, I am dear Sir yours &c

I am anxious to know whether that amendment to the constitution on which Mr. Webster & yourself were so distinguished has been approved or rejected by your sapient people.

A SON'S NEED FOR SHIRTS

To Edward C. Marshall

My dear Son   Richmond June 24th. 1821

I received to day your letter of the 12th. or 14th. I do not know which.

I am glad to hear that Doctor Peyton has a prospect of obtaining a gentleman of abilities for his school & am entirely willing that you should remain with him another year. If you employ your time to the best advantage I am persuaded that you may derive great benefit from devoting to the earlier studies another year; & think it probable that your education may be more complete than it would be should you enter the sophomore class this autumn.

Had you expressed to your mother a month or two past your want of shirts, she would have got them ready to send up by Mr. Page or Miss Pickett, but they are gone & it is not probable that another opportunity will offer till I come up in August. You ought to recollect that making of shirts like every thing else requires some thing more than a mere order for their production. Had you given your mother notice in March or April of your wants she would have procured the linnen & have endeavoured at least to have them made up; but if she were now to purchase the linnen it would take three or four weeks to make the shirts & then we should have to wait for an opportunity to send them. You may be assured that the way to have your wants supplied is to foresee them. It is probable that I may bring you shirts in August.

You wrote to your mother for a straw hat & I procured one which I have sent by Miss M. Pickett. She promises to leave it at the court house either at Mr. Picketts or Mr. Colstons. You would perhaps do well to go for it.

If you can get the books you want at alexandria, it will be well to do so. If you cannot let me know it in time that I may endeavor to carry them up with me.

I am very sorry to hear that you are afflicted with sore eyes. Your mother recommends it to you to get the small twigs of sassafras which have young pith, to strip off the outer bark & then split the twigs & cut them into tolerably short pieces & put them in a cup of water & stand there for an hour or so when the water will become a jelly. Bath your eyes in this jelly & she thinks it will be of great service to them. I am my dear Son your affectionate Father

Your mother who is now very unwell complains of your writing to her so seldom.

JEFFERSON'S CRITICISM OF THE COURT

To Joseph Story

My dear Sir   Richmond July 13th. 1821

I had yesterday the pleasure of receiving your letter of the 27th. of June by which I am greatly obliged. I shall decide the case concerning which I enquired in conformity with your opinion. The law of the case I have thought very doubtful, the equity of it is I think pretty clear.

Your kind expressions respecting myself gratify me very much. Entertaining the truest affection & esteem for my brethren generally, & for yourself particularly, it is extremely gratiful to believe that it is reciprocated. The harmony of the bench will, I hope & pray, never be disturbed. We have external & political enemies enough to preserve internal peace.

What you say of Mr. Jeffersons letter rather grieves than surprizes me. It grieves me because his influence is still so great that many—very many will adopt his opinions however unsound they may be, & however contradictory to their own reason. I cannot describe the surprize & mortification I have felt at hearing that Mr. Madison has embraced them with respect to the judicial department.

For Mr. Jeffersons opinion as respects this department it is not difficult to assign the cause. He is among the most ambitious, & I suspect among the most unforgiving of men. His great power is over the mass of the people & this power is chiefly acquired by professions of democracy. Every check on the wild impulse of the moment is a check on his own power, & he is unfriendly to the source from which it flows. He looks, of course, with ill will at an independent judiciary.

That in a free country with a written constitution, any inteligent man should wish a dependent judiciary, or should think that the constitution is not a law for the court as well as the legislature, would astonish me if I had not learnt from observation that, with many men, the judgement is completely controuled by the passions. The case of the mandamus may be the cloak, but the batture is recollected with still more resentment.

I send you the papers containing the essays of Algernon

Sidney. Their coarseness & malignity would designate the author if he was not avowed. The argument, if it may be called one, is I think as weak as its language is violent & prolix. Two other gentlemen have appeared in the papers on this subject. One of them is deeply concerned in pillaging the purchasers of the Fairfax estate in which goodly work he fears no other obstruction than what arises from the appellate power of the supreme court, & the other is a hunter after office who hopes by his violent hostility to the Union which in Virginia assumes the name of regard for State rights; & by his devotion to Algernon Sidney, to obtain one. In support of the sound principles of the constitution, & of the Union of the States, not a pen is drawn. In Virginia the tendency of things verges rapidly to the destruction of the government & the reestablishment of a league of Sovereign States. I look elsewhere for safety. With very much esteem & affection, I am dear Sir your

I will thank you for the copy of the debates

"AN ATTACK UPON THE UNION"

To Joseph Story

My dear Sir   Richmond Septr. 18th. 1821

I had yesterday the pleasure of receiving your favor of the 9th. I thank you for your Quintal of fish & shall try my possibles to observe your instructions in the cooking department. I hope to succeed; but be this as it may I promise to feed on the fish with an appetite which would not disgrace a genuine descendant of one of the Pilgrims.

I am a little surprized at the request which you say has been made to Mr. Hall, although there is no reason for my being so. The settled hostility of the gentleman who has made that request to the judicial department will show itself in that & in every other form which he beleives will conduce to its object. For this he has several motives; & it is not among the weakest that the department could never lend itself as a tool to work for his political power. The Batture will never be forgotten.

Indeed there is some reason to beleive that the essays written against the Supreme court were, in a degree at least, stimulated by this gentleman; and that, although the coarseness of the language belongs exclusively to the Author, its acerbity has been increased by his communications with the great Lama of the mountains. He may therefore feel himself in some measure required to obtain its republication in some place of distinction. But what does Mr. Hall purpose to do? I do not suppose you would willingly interfere so as to prevent his making the publication although I really think it is in form & substance totally unfit to be placed in his law journal. I really think a proper reply to the request would be to say that no objection existed to the publication of any law argument against the opinion of the Supreme court, but that the coarseness of its language, its personal & official abuse & its tedious prolixity constituted objections to the insertion of Algernon Sidney which were insuperable. If however Mr. Hall determines to comply with this request, I think he ought, unless he means to make himself a party militant, to say that he publishes that piece by particular request; & ought to subjoin the masterly answer of Mr. Wheaton. I shall wish to know what course Mr. Hall will pursue.

I have not yet received the debates in your convention. Mr. Caldwell I presume has not met with an opportunity to send the volume. I shall read it with much pleasure.

I have seen a sketch of your address to the Suffolk bar & shall be very glad to have it at large. I have no doubt of being much gratified by the manner in which the subjects you mention are treated.

A deep design to convert our government into a meer league of States has taken strong hold of a powerful & violent party in Virginia. The attack upon the judiciary is in fact an attack upon the union. The judicial department is well understood to be that through which the government may be attacked most successfully, because it is without patronage, & of course without power, and it is equally well understood that every subtraction from its jurisdiction is a vital wound to the government itself. The attack upon it therefore is a marked battery aimed at the government itself. The whole attack, if not originating with Mr. Jefferson, is obviously approved & guided by him. It is therefore formidable in other states as well as in this; & it behoves the friends of the union to be more on the alert than they have been. An effort will certainly be made to repeal the 25th. Sec. of the judicial act.

I have a case before me which cannot be carried up to the supreme court & which presents difficulties which appear to me to be considerable. It is an action of debt brought by the U.S. for a forfeiture incurred by rescuing some distilled Spirits which had not been proceeded on by the Distiller according to law.

The declaration charges in the alternative that the defendants or one of them rescued or caused to be rescued &c.

It is clear enough that this would be ill in an indictment or information, but I am inclined to think it is cured by our statute of jeofails. The defendents insist that this statute does not apply to suits brought by the U.S.—but I think it does.

Another difficulty has puzzled me so much that I have taken the case under advisement with the intention of consulting some of my more experienced brethren.

The difficulty is this: At the trial the rescue was proved only by two depositions. Each contains the following expressions. "On Novr. 17th. 1815, *agreeable to written & verbal instructions from Mr. William McKinly collector*, I" &c.

The defendants demurred to the testimony & the District court gave judgement for the plaintiffs.

It is contended 1st. That there is no sufficient evidence that McKinly is collector. His commission ought to be produced & its absence cannot be supplied—but here is not even a direct averment that he is collector.

2d. The written instructions of the collector ought to be produced to show that the seizure was made under his authority.

You are accustomed to these cases. Will you aid me with your advice? Yours truely & sincerely

THE SUPREME COURT AND TREATIES

To James M. Marshall

My dear brother   Richmond July 9th. 1822

I have searched the journals of the house of Delegates & find that the bill for confiscating the estate of Lord Fairfax passed that house in January 1786. It was lost in the Senate. Whether it was negatived or lost meerely from the multiplicity of business, it being sent up at the close of the session, I am unable to say, as the journals of the senate are not here, but in the custody of Mr. Hansford, the Clerk, who resides in King George. If you wish to make any enquiries into this subject, Charles Marshall will probably pass near Mr. Hansford on some visit to his Father in law & may make them for you. The bill was sent up to the senate on the 11th. of Jany. 1786. I presume however your object cannot be effected as the bill passed the house of Delegates. The act of compromise itself is an act of disclaimer on the part of the State.

I have wished to impress on your son before the argument of this cause one consideration which appears to me to be of great weight.

Although Judge White will, of course, conform to the decision of the court of appeals against the appellate jurisdiction of the Supreme court, & therefore deny that the opinion in the case of Fairfax & Hunter is binding, yet he must admit that the supreme court is the proper tribunal for expounding the treaties of the United States, & that its decisions on a treaty are binding on the state courts, whether they possess the appellate jurisdiction or not. Thus the exposition of a british court of an act of Parliament, or of any foreign court of a foreign edict, are considered as conclusive. No court in any case will controvert it. Thus the exposition of any state law by the courts of that state, are considered in the courts of all the other states, and in those of the United states, as a correct exposition, not to be reexamined. The only exception to this rule is where the statute of a state is supposed to violate the constitution of the United States, in which case the courts of the Union claim a controuling & supervising power. Thus any construction made by the courts of Virginia on the statute of descents or of distribution, or on any other subject, is admitted as conclusive in the federal courts, although those courts might have decided differently on the statute itself. The principle is that the courts of every government are the proper tribunals for construing the legislative acts of that government. Upon this principle the Supreme court of the United States, independent of its appellate jurisdiction, is the proper tribunal for construing the laws & treaties of the United States; and the construction of that court ought to be received every where as the right construction.

The Supreme court of the United States has settled the construction of the treaty of peace to be that lands at that time held by British subjects were not escheatable or grantable by a state. The case of Hunter & Fairfax is very absurdly put on the treaty of 94 but other cases have put the same construction on the treaty of peace. I refer particularly to Smith v The State of Maryland 6th. Cranch Jackson v Clarke 3 Wheaton & Orr v Hodgson 4 Wheaton. The last case is explicit & was decided unanimously, Judge Johnson assenting. This being the construction of the highest court of the government which is a party to the treaty is to be considered by all the world as its true construction unless Great Britain, the other party, should controvert it. The court of appeals has not denied this principle. The dicta of Judge Roane respecting the treaty were anterior to this constitutional construction of it.

I fear it will not be in my power to be at Happy creek before the 6th. of August. I shall probably reach Fauquier about that time. If I can get up sooner I will see you. I shall make another visit to Cumberland & purpose returning by Mr. Colstons. It is not impossible that I may pass a night at Bath. I am my dear brother your affectionate

The effect of the principle I have stated is that we hold not under the compromise but under the treaty, and the question is what does the compromise take from us?

A WINTER JOURNEY TO WASHINGTON

To Mary W. Marshall

My dearest Polly   Washington, February 4th. 1823
   I arrived at this place yesterday between ten & eleven & am now sitting by a fine wood fire in one of the best rooms in the city about to tell my beloved wife what a comfortable Journey I have had & how well I am now situated. The roads were better than I have ever found them at this season of the year, & we accomplished our Journey each day a very little after dark. Last winter I got into Alexandria after eleven at night, & this winter about seven. One stage sooner & the roads would not have been nearly so good; one stage later & they would have been bad, for on Monday morning we found the ground covered with a wet snow which dissolved rapidly & will make them very deep. It is the first time that I have been fortunate in my day of setting out.
   When I reached Fredericksburg I found that James had left no instructions at the stage office respecting the trunk, & I brought it with me to Alexandria, &, as Mr. Ashby is not now in the town or in business, I left it with Mr. Massie. I found my unkle Keith in his bed very unwell, though rather getting better. I was very glad that I went to see him though it was early in the morning & in a wet snow because he had been en-quiring for me & seemed much gratified at the call. My aunt is much better but was not up.
   We paid our visit yesterday to the President whom we found in good health but a year older I think than he was last winter, & looking very serious.
   Mr. Washington has been very unwell. I have not yet asked him how it happens that he did not write to me, but I have no doubt it is to be ascribed to his apprehension respecting his health.
   I have not yet seen or heard anything concerning Richard Martyr.
   Soon after dinner yesterday the French Chargé d'affaires called upon us with a pressing invitation to be present at a party given to the young couple, a gentleman of the French

legation & the daughter of the secretary of the navy who are lately married. There was a most briliant illumination which we saw and admired, & then we returned.

Mr. Johnson is not arrived & Mr. Todd is too sick to come. I very much fear that we shall lose him. Today we should set in to close business were it not that Mr. Wirt is unfortunately very sick. This I regret very much for his own sake, & some thing on a public account. Farewell my dearest Polly. I am ever your affectionate

Opinion in Johnson v. McIntosh

THE plaintiffs in this cause claim the land, in their declaration mentioned, under two grants, purporting to be made, the first in 1773, and the last in 1775, by the chiefs of certain Indian tribes, constituting the Illinois and the Piankeshaw nations; and the question is whether this title can be recognised in the Courts of the United States?

The facts, as stated in the case agreed, show the authority of the chiefs who executed this conveyance, so far as it could be given by their own people; and likewise show, that the particular tribes for whom these chiefs acted were in rightful possession of the land they sold. The inquiry, therefore, is, in a great measure, confined to the power of Indians to give, and of private individuals to receive, a title which can be sustained in the Courts of this country.

As the right of society, to prescribe those rules by which property may be acquired and preserved is not, and cannot be drawn into question; as the title to lands, especially, is and must be admitted to depend entirely on the law of the nation in which they lie; it will be necessary, in pursuing this inquiry, to examine, not singly those principles of abstract justice, which the Creator of all things has impressed on the mind of his creature man, and which are admitted to regulate, in a great degree, the rights of civilized nations, whose perfect independence is acknowledged; but those principles also which our own government has adopted in the particular case, and given us as the rule for our decision.

On the discovery of this immense continent, the great nations of Europe were eager to appropriate to themselves so much of it as they could respectively acquire. Its vast extent offered an ample field to the ambition and enterprise of all; and the character and religion of its inhabitants afforded an apology for considering them as a people over whom the superior genius of Europe might claim an ascendency. The potentates of the old world found no difficulty in convincing themselves that they made ample compensation to the inhabitants of the new, by bestowing on them civilization and Christianity, in exchange for unlimited independence. But, as they were all in pursuit of nearly the same object, it was necessary, in order to avoid conflicting settlements, and consequent war with each other, to establish a principle, which all should acknowledge as the law by which the right of acquisition, which they all asserted, should be regulated as between themselves. This principle was, that discovery gave title to the government by whose subjects, or by whose authority, it was made, against all other European governments, which title might be consummated by possession.

The exclusion of all other Europeans, necessarily gave to the nation making the discovery the sole right of acquiring the soil from the natives, and establishing settlements upon it. It was a right with which no Europeans could interfere. It was a right which all asserted for themselves, and to the assertion of which, by others, all assented.

Those relations which were to exist between the discoverer and the natives, were to be regulated by themselves. The rights thus acquired being exclusive, no other power could interpose between them.

In the establishment of these relations, the rights of the original inhabitants were, in no instance, entirely disregarded; but were necessarily, to a considerable extent, impaired. They were admitted to be the rightful occupants of the soil, with a legal as well as just claim to retain possession of it, and to use it according to their own discretion; but their rights to complete sovereignty, as independent nations, were necessarily diminished, and their power to dispose of the soil at their own will, to whomsoever they pleased, was denied by the original fundamental principle, that discovery gave exclusive title to those who made it.

While the different nations of Europe respected the right of the natives, as occupants, they asserted the ultimate dominion to be in themselves; and claimed and exercised, as a consequence of this ultimate dominion, a power to grant the soil, while yet in possession of the natives. These grants have been understood by all, to convey a title to the grantees, subject only to the Indian right of occupancy.

The history of America, from its discovery to the present day, proves, we think, the universal recognition of these principles.

Spain did not rest her title solely on the grant of the Pope. Her discussions respecting boundary, with France, with Great Britain, and with the United States, all show that she placed it on the rights given by discovery. Portugal sustained her claim to the Brazils by the same title.

France, also, founded her title to the vast territories she claimed in America on discovery. However conciliatory her conduct to the natives may have been, she still asserted her right of dominion over a great extent of country not actually settled by Frenchmen, and her exclusive right to acquire and dispose of the soil which remained in the occupation of Indians. Her monarch claimed all Canada and Acadie, as colonies of France, at a time when the French population was very inconsiderable, and the Indians occupied almost the whole country. He also claimed Louisiana, comprehending the immense territories watered by the Mississippi, and the rivers which empty into it, by the title of discovery. The letters patent granted to the Sieur Demons, in 1603, constitute him Lieutenant General, and the representative of the King in Acadie, which is described as stretching from the 40th to the 46th degree of north latitude; with authority to extend the power of the French over that country, and its inhabitants, to give laws to the people, to treat with the natives, and enforce the observance of treaties, and to parcel out, and give title to lands, according to his own judgment.

The States of Holland also made acquisitions in America, and sustained their right on the common principle adopted by all Europe. They allege, as we are told by Smith, in his History of New-York, that Henry Hudson, who sailed, as they say, under the orders of their East India Company, discovered the country from the Delaware to the Hudson, up which he sailed to the 43d degree of north latitude; and this country they claimed under the title acquired by this voyage. Their first object was commercial, as appears by a grant made to a company of merchants in 1614; but in 1621, the States General made, as we are told by Mr. Smith, a grant of the country to the West India Company, by the name of New Netherlands.

The claim of the Dutch was always contested by the English; not because they questioned the title given by discovery, but because they insisted on being themselves the rightful claimants under that title. Their pretensions were finally decided by the sword.

No one of the powers of Europe gave its full assent to this principle, more unequivocally than England. The documents upon this subject are ample and complete. So early as the year 1496, her monarch granted a commission to the Cabots, to discover countries then unknown to *Christian people*, and to take possession of them in the name of the king of England. Two years afterwards, Cabot proceeded on this voyage, and discovered the continent of North America, along which he sailed as far south as Virginia. To this discovery the English trace their title.

In this first effort made by the English government to acquire territory on this continent, we perceive a complete recognition of the principle which has been mentioned. The right of discovery given by this commission, is confined to countries "then unknown to all Christian people"; and of these countries Cabot was empowered to take possession in the name of the king of England. Thus asserting a right to take possession, notwithstanding the occupancy of the natives, who were heathens, and, at the same time, admitting the prior title of any Christian people who may have made a previous discovery.

The same principle continued to be recognised. The charter granted to Sir Humphrey Gilbert, in 1578, authorizes him to discover and take possession of such remote, heathen, and barbarous lands, as were not actually possessed by any Christian prince or people. This charter was afterwards renewed to Sir Walter Raleigh, in nearly the same terms.

By the charter of 1606, under which the first permanent English settlement on this continent was made, James I. granted to Sir Thomas Gates and others, those territories in America lying on the seacoast, between the 34th and 45th degrees of north latitude, and which either belonged to that monarch, or were not then possessed by any other Christian prince or people. The grantees were divided into two companies at their own request. The first, or southern colony, was directed to settle between the 34th and 41st degrees of north latitude; and the second, or northern colony, between the 38th and 45th degrees.

In 1609, after some expensive and not very successful attempts at settlement had been made, a new and more enlarged charter was given by the crown to the first colony, in which the king granted to the "Treasurer and Company of Adventurers of the city of London for the first colony in Virginia," in absolute property, the lands extending along the seacoast four hundred miles, and into the land throughout from sea to sea. This charter, which is a part of the special verdict in this cause, was annulled, so far as respected the rights of the company, by the judgment of the Court of King's Bench on a writ of *quo warranto*; but the whole effect allowed to this judgment was, to revest in the crown the powers of government, and the title to the lands within its limits.

At the solicitation of those who held under the grant to the second or northern colony, a new and more enlarged charter was granted to the Duke of Lenox and others, in 1620, who were denominated the Plymouth Company, conveying to them in absolute property all the lands between the 40th and 48th degrees of north latitude.

Under this patent, New-England has been in a great measure settled. The company conveyed to Henry Rosewell and others, in 1627, that territory which is now Massachusetts; and in 1628, a charter of incorporation, comprehending the powers of government, was granted to the purchasers.

Great part of New-England was granted by this company, which, at length, divided their remaining lands among themselves; and, in 1635, surrendered their charter to the crown. A patent was granted to Gorges for Maine, which was allotted to him in the division of property.

All the grants made by the Plymouth Company, so far as we can learn, have been respected. In pursuance of the same principle, the king, in 1664, granted to the Duke of York the country of New-England as far south as the Delaware bay. His royal highness transferred New-Jersey to Lord Berkeley and Sir George Carteret.

In 1663, the crown granted to Lord Clarendon and others, the country lying between the 36th degree of north latitude and the river St. Mathes; and, in 1666, the proprietors obtained from the crown a new charter, granting to them that province in the king's dominions in North America which lies from 36 degrees 30 minutes north latitude to the 29th degree, and from the Atlantic ocean to the South sea.

Thus has our whole country been granted by the crown while in the occupation of the Indians. These grants purport to convey the soil as well as the right of dominion to the grantees. In those governments which were denominated royal, where the right to the soil was not vested in individuals, but remained in the crown, or was vested in the colonial government, the king claimed and exercised the right of granting lands, and of dismembering the government at his will. The grants made out of the two original colonies, after the resumption of their charters by the crown, are examples of this. The governments of New-England, New-York, New-Jersey, Pennsylvania, Maryland, and a part of Carolina, were thus created. In all of them, the soil, at the time the grants were made, was occupied by the Indians. Yet almost every title within those governments is dependent on these grants. In some instances, the soil was conveyed by the crown unaccompanied by the powers of government, as in the case of the northern neck of Virginia. It has never been objected to this, or to any other similar grant, that the title as well as possession was in the Indians when it was made, and that it passed nothing on that account.

These various patents cannot be considered as nullities; nor can they be limited to a mere grant of the powers of government. A charter intended to convey political power only, would never contain words expressly granting the land, the soil, and the waters. Some of them purport to convey the soil alone; and in those cases in which the powers of government, as well as the soil, are conveyed to individuals, the crown has always acknowledged itself to be bound by the grant. Though the power to dismember regal governments was asserted and exercised, the power to dismember proprietary governments was not claimed; and, in some instances, even after the powers of government were revested in the crown, the title of the proprietors to the soil was respected.

Charles II. was extremely anxious to acquire the property of Maine, but the grantees sold it to Massachusetts, and he did not venture to contest the right of that colony to the soil. The Carolinas were originally proprietary governments. In 1721 a revolution was effected by the people, who shook off their obedience to the proprietors, and declared their dependence immediately on the crown. The king, however, purchased the title of those who were disposed to sell. One of them, Lord Carteret, surrendered his interest in the government, but retained his title to the soil. That title was respected till the revolution, when it was forfeited by the laws of war.

Further proof of the extent to which this principle has been recognised, will be found in the history of the wars, negotiations, and treaties, which the different nations, claiming territory in America, have carried on, and held with each other.

The contests between the cabinets of Versailles and Madrid, respecting the territory on the northern coast of the gulf of Mexico, were fierce and bloody; and continued, until the establishment of a Bourbon on the throne of Spain, produced such amicable dispositions in the two crowns, as to suspend or terminate them.

Between France and Great Britain, whose discoveries as well as settlements were nearly contemporaneous, contests for the country, actually covered by the Indians, began as soon as their settlements approached each other, and were continued until finally settled in the year 1763, by the treaty of Paris.

Each nation had granted and partially settled the country, denominated by the French, Acadie, and by the English, Nova Scotia. By the 12th article of the treaty of Utrecht, made in 1713, his most Christian Majesty ceded to the Queen of Great Britain, "all Nova Scotia or Acadie, with its ancient boundaries." A great part of the ceded territory was in the possession of the Indians, and the extent of the cession could not be adjusted by the commissioners to whom it was to be referred.

The treaty of Aix la Chapelle, which was made on the principle of the *status ante bellum,* did not remove this subject of controversy. Commissioners for its adjustment were appointed, whose very able and elaborate, though unsuccessful arguments, in favour of the title of their respective sovereigns, show how entirely each relied on the title given by discovery to lands remaining in the possession of Indians.

After the termination of this fruitless discussion, the subject was transferred to Europe, and taken up by the cabinets of Versailles and London. This controversy embraced not only the boundaries of New-England, Nova Scotia, and that part of Canada which adjoined those colonies, but embraced our whole western country also. France contended not only that the St. Lawrence was to be considered as the centre of Canada, but that the Ohio was within that colony. She founded this claim on discovery, and on having used that river for the transportation of troops, in a war with some southern Indians.

This river was comprehended in the chartered limits of Virginia; but, though the right of England to a reasonable extent of country, in virtue of her discovery of the seacoast, and of the settlements she made on it, was not to be questioned; her claim of all the lands to the Pacific ocean, because she had discovered the country washed by the Atlantic, might, without derogating from the principle recognised by all, be deemed extravagant. It interfered, too, with the claims of France, founded on the same principle. She therefore sought to strengthen her original title to the lands in controversy, by insisting that it had been acknowledged by France in the 15th article of the treaty of Utrecht. The dispute respecting the construction of that article, has no tendency to impair the principle, that discovery gave a title to lands still remaining in the possession of the Indians. Whichever title prevailed, it was still a title to lands occupied by the Indians, whose right of occupancy neither controverted, and neither had then extinguished.

These conflicting claims produced a long and bloody war, which was terminated by the conquest of the whole country east of the Mississippi. In the treaty of 1763, France ceded and guaranteed to Great Britain, all Nova Scotia, or Acadie, and Canada, with their dependencies; and it was agreed, that the boundaries between the territories of the two nations, in America, should be irrevocably fixed by a line drawn from the source of the Mississippi, through the middle of that river and the lakes Maurepas and Ponchartrain, to the sea. This treaty expressly cedes, and has always been understood to cede, the whole country, on the English side of the dividing line, between the two nations, although a great and valuable part of it was occupied by the Indians. Great Britain, on her part, surrendered to France all her pretensions to the country west of the Mississippi. It has never been supposed that she surrendered nothing, although she was not in actual possession of a foot of land. She surrendered all right to acquire the country; and any after attempt to purchase it from the Indians, would have been considered and treated as an invasion of the territories of France.

By the 20th article of the same treaty, Spain ceded Florida, with its dependencies, and all the country she claimed east or southeast of the Mississippi, to Great Britain. Great part of this territory also was in possession of the Indians.

By a secret treaty, which was executed about the same time, France ceded Louisiana to Spain; and Spain has since retroceded the same country to France. At the time both of its cession and retrocession, it was occupied, chiefly, by the Indians.

Thus, all the nations of Europe, who have acquired territory on this continent, have asserted in themselves, and have recognised in others, the exclusive right of the discoverer to appropriate the lands occupied by the Indians. Have the American States rejected or adopted this principle?

By the treaty which concluded the war of our revolution, Great Britain relinquished all claim, not only to the government, but to the "propriety and territorial rights of the United States," whose boundaries were fixed in the second article. By this treaty, the powers of government, and the right to soil, which had previously been in Great Britain, passed definitively to these States. We had before taken possession of them, by declaring independence; but neither the declaration of independence, nor the treaty confirming it, could give us more than that which we before possessed, or to which Great Britain was before entitled. It has never been doubted, that either the United States, or the several States, had a clear title to all the lands within the boundary lines described in the treaty, subject only to the Indian right of occupancy, and that the exclusive power to extinguish that right, was vested in that government which might constitutionally exercise it.

Virginia, particularly, within whose chartered limits the land in controversy lay, passed an act, in the year 1779, declaring her "exclusive right of pre-emption from the Indians, of all the lands within the limits of her own chartered territory, and that no person or persons whatsoever, have, or ever had, a right to purchase any lands within the same, from any Indian nation, except only persons duly authorized to make such purchase; formerly for the use and benefit of the colony, and lately for the Commonwealth." The act then proceeds to annul all deeds made by Indians to individuals, for the private use of the purchasers.

Without ascribing to this act the power of annulling vested rights, or admitting it to countervail the testimony furnished by the marginal note opposite to the title of the law, forbidding purchases from the Indians, in the revisals of the Virginia statutes, stating that law to be repealed, it may safely be considered as an unequivocal affirmance, on the part of Virginia, of the broad principle which had always been maintained, that the exclusive right to purchase from the Indians resided in the government.

In pursuance of the same idea, Virginia proceeded, at the same session, to open her land office, for the sale of that country which now constitutes Kentucky, a country, every acre of which was then claimed and possessed by Indians, who maintained their title with as much persevering courage as was ever manifested by any people.

The States, having within their chartered limits different portions of territory covered by Indians, ceded that territory, generally, to the United States, on conditions expressed in their deeds of cession, which demonstrate the opinion, that they ceded the soil as well as jurisdiction, and that in doing so, they granted a productive fund to the government of the Union. The lands in controversy lay within the chartered limits of Virginia, and were ceded with the whole country northwest of the river Ohio. This grant contained reservations and stipulations, which could only be made by the owners of the soil; and concluded with a stipulation, that "all the lands in the ceded territory, not reserved, should be considered as a common fund, for the use and benefit of such of the United States as have become, or shall become, members of the confederation," &c. "according to their usual respective proportions in the general charge and expenditure, and shall be faithfully and *bona fide* disposed of for that purpose, and for no other use or purpose whatsoever."

The ceded territory was occupied by numerous and warlike tribes of Indians; but the exclusive right of the United States to extinguish their title, and to grant the soil, has never, we believe, been doubted.

After these States became independent, a controversy subsisted between them and Spain respecting boundary. By the treaty of 1795, this controversy was adjusted, and Spain ceded to the United States the territory in question. This territory, though claimed by both nations, was chiefly in the actual occupation of Indians.

The magnificent purchase of Louisiana, was the purchase from France of a country almost entirely occupied by numerous tribes of Indians, who are in fact independent. Yet, any attempt of others to intrude into that country, would be considered as an aggression which would justify war.

Our late acquisitions from Spain are of the same character; and the negotiations which preceded those acquisitions, recognise and elucidate the principle which has been received as the foundation of all European title in America.

The United States, then, have unequivocally acceded to that great and broad rule by which its civilized inhabitants now hold this country. They hold, and assert in themselves, the title by which it was acquired. They maintain, as all others have maintained, that discovery gave an exclusive right to extinguish the Indian title of occupancy, either by purchase or by conquest; and gave also a right to such a degree of sovereignty, as the circumstances of the people would allow them to exercise.

The power now possessed by the government of the United States to grant lands, resided, while we were colonies, in the crown, or its grantees. The validity of the titles given by either has never been questioned in our Courts. It has been exercised uniformly over territory in possession of the Indians. The existence of this power must negative the existence of any right which may conflict with, and control it. An absolute title to lands cannot exist, at the same time, in different persons, or in different governments. An absolute, must be an exclusive title, or at least a title which excludes all others not compatible with it. All our institutions recognise the absolute title of the crown, subject only to the Indian right of occupancy, and recognise the absolute title of the crown to extinguish that right. This is incompatible with an absolute and complete title in the Indians.

We will not enter into the controversy, whether agriculturists, merchants, and manufacturers, have a right, on abstract principles, to expel hunters from the territory they possess, or to contract their limits. Conquest gives a title which the Courts of the conqueror cannot deny, whatever the private and speculative opinions of individuals may be, respecting the original justice of the claim which has been successfully asserted. The British government, which was then our government, and whose rights have passed to the United States, asserted a title to all the lands occupied by Indians, within the chartered limits of the British colonies. It asserted also a limited sovereignty over them, and the exclusive right of extinguishing the title which occupancy gave to them. These claims have been maintained and established as far west as the river Mississippi, by the sword. The title to a vast portion of the lands we now hold, originates in them. It is not for the Courts of this country to question the validity of this title, or to sustain one which is incompatible with it.

Although we do not mean to engage in the defence of those principles which Europeans have applied to Indian title, they may, we think, find some excuse, if not justification, in the character and habits of the people whose rights have been wrested from them.

The title by conquest is acquired and maintained by force. The conqueror prescribes its limits. Humanity, however, acting on public opinion, has established, as a general rule, that the conquered shall not be wantonly oppressed, and that their condition shall remain as eligible as is compatible with the objects of the conquest. Most usually, they are incorporated with the victorious nation, and become subjects or citizens of the government with which they are connected. The new and old members of the society mingle with each other; the distinction between them is gradually lost, and they make one people. Where this incorporation is practicable, humanity demands, and a wise policy requires, that the rights of the conquered to property should remain unimpaired; that the new subjects should be governed as equitably as the old, and that confidence in their security should gradually banish the painful sense of being separated from their ancient connexions, and united by force to strangers.

When the conquest is complete, and the conquered inhabitants can be blended with the conquerors, or safely governed as a distinct people, public opinion, which not even the conqueror can disregard, imposes these restraints upon him; and he cannot neglect them without injury to his fame, and hazard to his power.

But the tribes of Indians inhabiting this country were fierce savages, whose occupation was war, and whose subsistence was drawn chiefly from the forest. To leave them in possession of their country, was to leave the country a wilderness; to govern them as a distinct people, was impossible, because they were as brave and as high spirited as they were fierce, and were ready to repel by arms every attempt on their independence.

What was the inevitable consequence of this state of things? The Europeans were under the necessity either of abandoning the country, and relinquishing their pompous claims to it, or of enforcing those claims by the sword, and by the adoption of principles adapted to the condition of a people with whom it was impossible to mix, and who could not be governed as a distinct society, or of remaining in their neighbourhood, and exposing themselves and their families to the perpetual hazard of being massacred.

Frequent and bloody wars, in which the whites were not always the aggressors, unavoidably ensued. European policy, numbers, and skill, prevailed. As the white population advanced, that of the Indians necessarily receded. The country in the immediate neighbourhood of agriculturists became unfit for them. The game fled into thicker and more unbroken forests, and the Indians followed. The soil, to which the crown originally claimed title, being no longer occupied by its ancient inhabitants, was parcelled out according to the will of the sovereign power, and taken possession of by persons who claimed immediately from the crown, or mediately, through its grantees or deputies.

That law which regulates, and ought to regulate in general, the relations between the conqueror and conquered, was incapable of application to a people under such circumstances. The resort to some new and different rule, better adapted to the actual state of things, was unavoidable. Every rule which can be suggested will be found to be attended with great difficulty.

However extravagant the pretension of converting the discovery of an inhabited country into conquest may appear; if the principle has been asserted in the first instance, and afterwards sustained; if a country has been acquired and held under it; if the property of the great mass of the community originates in it, it becomes the law of the land, and cannot be questioned. So, too, with respect to the concomitant principle, that the Indian inhabitants are to be considered merely as occupants, to be protected, indeed, while in peace, in the possession of their lands, but to be deemed incapable of transferring the absolute title to others. However this restriction may be opposed to natural right, and to the usages of civilized nations, yet, if it be indispensable to that system under which the country has been settled, and be adapted to the actual condition of the two people, it may, perhaps, be supported by reason, and certainly cannot be rejected by Courts of justice.

This question is not entirely new in this Court. The case of *Fletcher* v. *Peck*, grew out of a sale made by the State of Georgia of a large tract of country within the limits of that State, the grant of which was afterwards resumed. The action was brought by a sub-purchaser, on the contract of sale, and one of the covenants in the deed was, that the State of Georgia was, at the time of sale, seised in fee of the premises. The real question presented by the issue was, whether the seisin in fee was in the State of Georgia, or in the United States. After stating, that this controversy between the several States and the United States, had been compromised, the Court thought it necessary to notice the Indian title, which, although entitled to the respect of all Courts until it should be legitimately extinguished, was declared not to be such as to be absolutely repugnant to a seisin in fee on the part of the State.

This opinion conforms precisely to the principle which has been supposed to be recognised by all European governments, from the first settlement of America. The absolute ultimate title has been considered as acquired by discovery, subject only to the Indian title of occupancy, which title the discoverers possessed the exclusive right of acquiring. Such a right is no more incompatible with a seisin in fee, than a lease for years, and might as effectually bar an ejectment.

Another view has been taken of this question, which deserves to be considered. The title of the crown, whatever it might be, could be acquired only by a conveyance from the crown. If an individual might extinguish the Indian title for his own benefit, or, in other words, might purchase it, still he could acquire only that title. Admitting their power to change their laws or usages, so far as to allow an individual to separate a portion of their lands from the common stock, and hold it in severalty, still it is a part of their territory, and is held under them, by a title dependent on their laws. The grant derives its efficacy from their will; and, if they choose to resume it, and make a different disposition of the land, the Courts of the United States cannot interpose for the protection of the title. The person who purchases lands from the Indians, within their territory, incorporates himself with them, so far as respects the property purchased; holds their title under their protection, and subject to their laws. If they annul the grant, we know of no tribunal which can revise and set aside the proceeding. We know of no principle which can distinguish this case from a grant made to a native Indian, authorizing him to hold a particular tract of land in severalty.

As such a grant could not separate the Indian from his nation, nor give a title which our Courts could distinguish from the title of his tribe, as it might still be conquered from, or ceded by his tribe, we can perceive no legal principle which will authorize a Court to say, that different consequences are attached to this purchase, because it was made by a stranger. By the treaties concluded between the United States and the Indian nations, whose title the plaintiffs claim, the country comprehending the lands in controversy has been ceded to the United States, without any reservation of their title. These nations had been at war with the United States, and had an unquestionable right to annul any grant they had made to American citizens. Their cession of the country, without a reservation of this land, affords a fair presumption, that they considered it as of no validity. They ceded to the United States this very property, after having used it in common with other lands, as their own, from the date of their deeds to the time of cession; and the attempt now made, is to set up their title against that of the United States.

The proclamation issued by the King of Great Britain, in 1763, has been considered, and, we think, with reason, as constituting an additional objection to the title of the plaintiffs.

By that proclamation, the crown reserved under its own

dominion and protection, for the use of the Indians, "all the land and territories lying to the westward of the sources of the rivers which fall into the sea from the west and northwest," and strictly forbade all British subjects from making any purchases or settlements whatever, or taking possession of the reserved lands.

It has been contended, that, in this proclamation, the king transcended his constitutional powers; and the case of *Campbell* v. *Hall*, (reported by *Cowper*,) is relied on to support this position.

It is supposed to be a principle of universal law, that, if an uninhabited country be discovered by a number of individuals, who acknowledge no connexion with, and owe no allegiance to, any government whatever, the country becomes the property of the discoverers, so far at least as they can use it. They acquire a title in common. The title of the whole land is in the whole society. It is to be divided and parcelled out according to the will of the society, expressed by the whole body, or by that organ which is authorized by the whole to express it.

If the discovery be made, and possession of the country be taken, under the authority of an existing government, which is acknowledged by the emigrants, it is supposed to be equally well settled, that the discovery is made for the whole nation, that the country becomes a part of the nation, and that the vacant soil is to be disposed of by that organ of the government which has the constitutional power to dispose of the national domains, by that organ in which all vacant territory is vested by law.

According to the theory of the British constitution, all vacant lands are vested in the crown, as representing the nation; and the exclusive power to grant them is admitted to reside in the crown, as a branch of the royal prerogative. It has been already shown, that this principle was as fully recognised in America as in the island of Great Britain. All the lands we hold were originally granted by the crown; and the establishment of a regal government has never been considered as impairing its right to grant lands within the chartered limits of such colony. In addition to the proof of this principle, furnished by the immense grants, already mentioned, of lands lying within the chartered limits of Virginia, the continuing right of the crown to grant lands lying within that colony was always admitted. A title might be obtained, either by making an entry with the surveyor of a county, in pursuance of law, or by an order of the governor in council, who was the deputy of the king, or by an immediate grant from the crown. In Virginia, therefore, as well as elsewhere in the British dominions, the complete title of the crown to vacant lands was acknowledged.

So far as respected the authority of the crown, no distinction was taken between vacant lands and lands occupied by the Indians. The title, subject only to the right of occupancy by the Indians, was admitted to be in the king, as was his right to grant that title. The lands, then, to which this proclamation referred, were lands which the king had a right to grant, or to reserve for the Indians.

According to the theory of the British constitution, the royal prerogative is very extensive, so far as respects the political relations between Great Britain and foreign nations. The peculiar situation of the Indians, necessarily considered, in some respects, as a dependent, and in some respects as a distinct people, occupying a country claimed by Great Britain, and yet too powerful and brave not to be dreaded as formidable enemies, required, that means should be adopted for the preservation of peace; and that their friendship should be secured by quieting their alarms for their property. This was to be effected by restraining the encroachments of the whites; and the power to do this was never, we believe, denied by the colonies to the crown.

In the case of *Campbell* against *Hall*, that part of the proclamation was determined to be illegal, which imposed a tax on a conquered province, after a government had been bestowed upon it. The correctness of this decision cannot be questioned, but its application to the case at bar cannot be admitted. Since the expulsion of the Stuart family, the power of imposing taxes, by proclamation, has never been claimed as a branch of regal prerogative; but the powers of granting, or refusing to grant, vacant lands, and of restraining encroachments on the Indians, have always been asserted and admitted.

The authority of this proclamation, so far as it respected this continent, has never been denied, and the titles it gave to lands have always been sustained in our Courts.

In the argument of this cause, the counsel for the plaintiffs have relied very much on the opinions expressed by men holding offices of trust, and on various proceedings in America, to sustain titles to land derived from the Indians.

The collection of claims to lands lying in the western country, made in the 1st volume of the Laws of the United States, has been referred to; but we find nothing in that collection to support the argument. Most of the titles were derived from persons professing to act under the authority of the government existing at the time; and the two grants under which the plaintiffs claim, are supposed, by the person under whose inspection the collection was made, to be void, because forbidden by the royal proclamation of 1763. It is not unworthy of remark, that the usual mode adopted by the Indians for granting lands to individuals, has been to reserve them in a treaty, or to grant them under the sanction of the commissioners with whom the treaty was negotiated. The practice, in such case, to grant to the crown, for the use of the individual, is some evidence of a general understanding, that the validity even of such a grant depended on its receiving the royal sanction.

The controversy between the colony of Connecticut and the Mohegan Indians, depended on the nature and extent of a grant made by those Indians to the colony; on the nature and extent of the reservations made by the Indians, in their several deeds and treaties, which were alleged to be recognised by the legitimate authority; and on the violation by the colony of rights thus reserved and secured. We do not perceive, in that case, any assertion of the principle, that individuals might obtain a complete and valid title from the Indians.

It has been stated, that in the memorial transmitted from the Cabinet of London to that of Versailles, during the controversy between the two nations, respecting boundary, which took place in 1755, the Indian right to the soil is recognised. But this recognition was made with reference to their character as Indians, and for the purpose of showing that they were fixed to a particular territory. It was made for the purpose of sustaining the claim of his Britannic majesty to dominion over them.

The opinion of the Attorney and Solicitor General, Pratt and Yorke, have been adduced to prove, that, in the opinion of those great law officers, the Indian grant could convey a title to the soil without a patent emanating from the crown. The opinion of those persons would certainly be of great authority on such a question, and we were not a little surprised, when it was read, at the doctrine it seemed to advance. An opinion so contrary to the whole practice of the crown, and to the uniform opinions given on all other occasions by its great law officers, ought to be very explicit, and accompanied by the circumstances under which it was given, and to which it was applied, before we can be assured that it is properly understood. In a pamphlet, written for the purpose of asserting the Indian title, styled "*Plain Facts*," the same opinion is quoted, and is said to relate to purchases made in the East Indies. It is, of course, entirely inapplicable to purchases made in America. Chalmers, in whose collection this opinion is found, does not say to whom it applies; but there is reason to believe, that the author of *Plain Facts* is, in this respect, correct. The opinion commences thus: "In respect to such places as have been, or shall be acquired, by treaty or grant, from any of the Indian princes or governments, your majesty's letters patent are not necessary." The words "princes or governments," are usually applied to the East Indians, but not to those of North America. We speak of their sachems, their warriors, their chiefmen, their nations or tribes, not of their "princes or governments." The question on which the opinion was given, too, and to which it relates, was, whether the king's subjects carry with them the common law wherever they may form settlements. The opinion is given with a view to this point, and its object must be kept in mind while construing its expressions.

Much reliance is also placed on the fact, that many tracts are now held in the United States under the Indian title, the validity of which is not questioned.

Before the importance attached to this fact is conceded, the circumstances under which such grants were obtained, and such titles are supported, ought to be considered. These lands lie chiefly in the eastern States. It is known that the Plymouth Company made many extensive grants, which, from their ignorance of the country, interfered with each other. It is also known that Mason, to whom New-Hampshire, and Gorges, to whom Maine was granted, found great difficulty in managing such unwieldy property. The country was settled by emigrants, some from Europe, but chiefly from Massachusetts, who took possession of lands they found unoccupied, and secured themselves in that possession by the best means in their power. The disturbances in England, and the civil war and revolution which followed those disturbances, prevented any interference on the part of the mother country, and the proprietors were unable to maintain their title. In the mean time, Massachusetts claimed the country, and governed it. As her claim was adversary to that of the proprietors, she encouraged the settlement of persons made under her authority, and encouraged, likewise, their securing themselves in possession, by purchasing the acquiescence and forbearance of the Indians.

After the restoration of Charles II., Gorges and Mason, when they attempted to establish their title, found themselves opposed by men, who held under Massachusetts, and under the Indians. The title of the proprietors was resisted; and though, in some cases, compromises were made and in some, the opinion of a Court was given ultimately in their favour, the juries found uniformly against them. They became wearied with the struggle, and sold their property. The titles held under the Indians, were sanctioned by length of possession; but there is no case, so far as we are informed, of a judicial decision in their favour.

Much reliance has also been placed on a recital contained in the charter of Rhode-Island, and on a letter addressed to the governors of the neighbouring colonies, by the king's command, in which some expressions are inserted, indicating the royal approbation of titles acquired from the Indians.

The charter to Rhode-Island recites, "that the said John Clark, and others, had transplanted themselves into the midst of the Indian nations, and were seised and possessed, by purchase and consent of the said natives, to their full content, of such lands," &c. And the letter recites, that "Thomas Chifflinch, and others, having, in the right of Major Asperton, a just propriety in the Narraghanset country, in New-England, by grants from the native princes of that country, and being desirous to improve it into an English colony," &c. "are yet daily disturbed."

The impression this language might make, if viewed apart from the circumstances under which it was employed, will be effaced, when considered in connexion with those circumstances.

In the year 1635, the Plymouth Company surrendered their charter to the crown. About the same time, the religious dissentions of Massachusetts expelled from that colony several societies of individuals, one of which settled in Rhode-Island, on lands purchased from the Indians. They were not within the chartered limits of Massachusetts, and the English government was too much occupied at home to bestow its attention on this subject. There existed no authority to arrest their settlement of the country. If they obtained the Indian title, there were none to assert the title of the crown. Under these circumstances, the settlement became considerable. Individuals acquired separate property in lands which they cultivated and improved; a government was established among themselves; and no power existed in America which could rightfully interfere with it.

On the restoration of Charles II., this small society hastened to acknowledge his authority, and to solicit his confirmation of their title to the soil, and to jurisdiction over the country. Their solicitations were successful, and a charter was granted to them, containing the recital which has been mentioned.

It is obvious, that this transaction can amount to no acknowledgment, that the Indian grant could convey a title paramount to that of the crown, or could, in itself, constitute a complete title. On the contrary, the charter of the crown was considered as indispensable to its completion.

It has never been contended, that the Indian title amounted to nothing. Their right of possession has never been questioned. The claim of government extends to the complete ultimate title, charged with the right of possession, and to the exclusive power of acquiring that right. The object of the crown was to settle the seacoast of America; and when a portion of it was settled, without violating the rights of others, by persons professing their loyalty, and soliciting the royal sanction of an act, the consequences of which were ascertained to be beneficial, it would have been as unwise as ungracious to expel them from their habitations, because they had obtained the Indian title otherwise than through the agency of government. The very grant of a charter is an assertion of the title of the crown, and its words convey the same idea. The country granted, is said to be "our island called Rhode-Island"; and the charter contains an actual grant of the soil, as well as of the powers of government.

The letter was written a few months before the charter was issued, apparently at the request of the agents of the intended colony, for the sole purpose of preventing the trespasses of neighbours, who were disposed to claim some authority over them. The king, being willing himself to ratify and confirm their title, was, of course, inclined to quiet them in their possession.

This charter, and this letter, certainly sanction a previous unauthorized purchase from Indians, under the circumstances attending that particular purchase, but are far from supporting the general proposition, that a title acquired from the Indians would be valid against a title acquired from the crown, or without the confirmation of the crown.

The acts of several colonial assemblies, prohibiting purchases from the Indians, have also been relied on, as proving, that, independent of such prohibitions, Indian deeds would be valid. But, we think this fact, at most, equivocal. While the existence of such purchases would justify their prohibition, even by colonies which considered Indian deeds as previously invalid, the fact that such acts have been generally passed, is strong evidence of the general opinion, that such purchases are opposed by the soundest principles of wisdom and national policy.

After bestowing on this subject a degree of attention which was more required by the magnitude of the interest in litigation, and the able and elaborate arguments of the bar, than by its intrinsic difficulty, the Court is decidedly of opinion, that the plaintiffs do not exhibit a title which can be sustained in the Court of the United States; and that there is no error in the judgment which was rendered against them in the District Court of Illinois.

Judgment affirmed, with costs.

February 28, 1823

PREPARING A SECOND EDITION OF "THE LIFE"

To Bushrod Washington

My dear Sir   Richmond May 3d. 1823
    Yesterday on my return from the upper country I found your letter of the 8th. of April & immediately deposited with the clerk of the district court the copy of the title of your reports.

    I am very glad to hear that Mr. Small will undertake the printing you wished to put into his hands & think the terms you mention quite satisfactory.

    I had gone through the corrections of the life of Washington & arranged the work into four volumes; the first to contain a history of all which precedes the appointment of General Washington to the command of the army; the 2d. & 3d. to comprehend his birth his part in the French war, & the history of the war of the Revolution after his appointment to the command of the American army. The 4th. to comprehend the matter now contained in the 5th. but somewhat abridged. The volumes will be about the present size if printed in the same type, if in a smaller the editor can calculate much better than myself at the reduction which will take place. I should be unwilling to reduce the type so much as to make the reading irksome. Mr. Small however will decide on this point. The last volume will be somewhat reduced, but not in proportion to the other parts of the work. I am quite willing as I told you to take on myself the risk of the first volume & shall be glad to know what the expense will be.

    I did not recover my health sufficiently to set in to close reading till I went to the upper country & shall in a few days set out for North Carolina, after which comes the long term in Richmond. I shall however proceed with as much dispatch as is in my power in reading the letters. I will let you know what progress I make & shall be glad to hear from you again, if this reaches you in Philadelphia respecting the publishing the 2d. ed. of the Life. I am dear Sir sincerely & affectionately, your

CONCERN ABOUT A RUMORED APPOINTMENT

To Joseph Story

My dear Sir   Richmond July 2d. 1823

I had the pleasure a few days past of receiving your letter of the 22d. of June & am greatly obliged by your friendly attention to my son. I am sorry that he misunderstood me so far as to request an advance of money from you when you could not have funds of mine in your hands. I gave him what I hoped would be sufficient for all his purposes until he should enter college but told him, should I be mistaken respecting the amount of his expenditures to apply to you. I did not suspect that his application would be made till the month of August.

The case concerning the securities of the cashier of the Bank goes to the Supreme court & will probably be reversed. I suppose so because I conjecture that the practice of banks has not conformed to my construction of the law. The Judge however who draws the opinion must have more ingenuity than I have if he draws a good one.

The main question respects the validity of the bond on which the suit was instituted. It was signed at different times and left in possession of the cashier, certainly I suppose in the expectation that he would forward it to the proper place. The plea of non est factum was put in among other pleas & the plaintiff proved the signature of the obligors, & relied on the possession of the bond & the suit on it as evidence to be left to the jury of its delivery & acceptance.

The cause was argued with very great ability, and it was contended that this would not be sufficient in any case—but if in general—not in this case.

I held very clearly that in the case of an individual obligee the evidence would authorize the jury to infer delivery, but not in the case of the bank of the United States.

The incorporating act requires that before the cashier shall be permitted to enter on the duties of his office he shall give bond with security to be approved by the board of directors for the faithful performance of its duties. I had no doubt that the suit upon the bond was evidence of its acceptance, & consequently of its being approved, if that fact could be established by parol evidence; but I was of opinion that it could not be so established. The board of directors, I thought, could only speak by their record. They cannot speak or act as individuals speak or act. They speak & act by their minutes. Their approbation & acceptance of the bond could not be expressed otherwise than officially on their minutes, & no other evidence than the minutes could establish the fact. I therefore did not permit the bond to go to the jury.

The question was entirely new & I was at first rather in favour of the plaintiffs. But in so lax a manner was this business conducted as to show very clearly that the cashier was in the full performance of his duty before the bond was executed, & to leave it very doubtful whether the breaches assigned were not committed before the bond passed out of the possession of the cashier. There was reason to believe that it had never been seen by the board of directors till he was removed from office, if then. It was impossible not to foresee that if the bond went to the jury questions would immediately arise on the time of its commencing obligation. The date could not be the guide because it was not executed at its date. If the time when it was signed by the last obligor should be insisted on, it was obvious that it had not then been seen or approved by the directors nor was it accepted by them. The delivery therefore could not be complete. If the time when it came to the possession of the directors were to be taken, it probably never came to their possession. These difficulties produced a close examination of the point, the result of which was a perfect conviction that the minutes of the board could alone prove the acceptance of the bond. I did not doubt that the board of Philadelphia might have authorized the board at Richmond to accept the bond, but such authority ought to appear by the minutes of the board at Philadelphia.

I shall bow with respect to the judgement of reversal but till it is given I shall retain the opinion I have expressed. With great & affectionate esteem, I am your

You alarm me respecting the successor of our much lamented friend. I too had heard a rumour which I hoped was impossible. Our Presidents I fear will never again seek to make our department respectable.

LAWS AGAINST FREE BLACK SAILORS

To Joseph Story

My dear Sir

Being entirely uncertain at what time & to what amount advances for my son may be expected, I have taken the liberty once more to trespass on your goodness so far as to send you a check on the branch of the Bank at Washington for $150. I hope it may be passed without difficulty or trouble through the branch at Boston, or through your bank at Salem, in the same manner as your drafts for your own salary are passed. Should there be any discount upon it, that of course is chargeable on the draft. I could have remitted this draft or a bill directly to my son, but I sent him a bill in August for $100, & my sons, in the north, have such an aptitude for spending money, that I am unwilling to tempt Edward by placing too much in his hands.

Our brother Johnson, I percieve, has hung himself on a democratic snag in a hedge composed entirely of thorny state rights in South Carolina, and will find some difficulty, I fear, in getting off into smooth open ground.

You have I presume seen his opinion in the national Intelligencer, & could scarcely have supposed that it would have excited so much irritation as it seems to have produced. The subject is one of much feeling in the south. Of this I was apprized, but did not think it would have shown itself in such strength as it has. The decision has been considered as another act of judicial usurpation; but the sentiment has been avowed that if this be the constitution, it is better to break that instrument than submit to the principle. Reference has been made to the Massacres of St. Domingo, and the people have been reminded that those massacres also originated in the theories of a distant government, insensible of, & not participating in the dangers their systems produced. It is suggested that the point will be brought before the Supreme court, but the writer seems to despair of a more favorable decision from that tribunal since they are deserted by the friend in whom their confidence was placed.

Thus you see fuel is continually adding to the fire at which the *exaltées* are about to roast the judicial department. You have, it is said, some law in Massachusetts not very unlike in principle to that which our brother has declared unconstitutional. We have its twin brother in Virginia, and a case was brought before me in which I might have considered its constitutionality had I chosen to do so; but it was not absolutely necessary, &, as I am not fond of butting against a wall in sport, I escaped on the construction of the act. Farewell. I am my dear Sir with affectionate esteem, your

September 26, 1823

"NON EST QUALIS ERAT"

To Joseph Story

My dear Sir   Richmond Decr. 9th. 1823
    I had the pleasure yesterday of receiving your letter of the 24th. ultimo & congratulate you on passing through your circuit in such good health & spirits. Our brother Washington was so unwell as to be under the necessity of adjournning the court at Philadelphia without going through the docket. I am still engaged at this place in a sort of dilatory way, doing very little, and still having something to do. A case was argued yesterday which I would send to the supreme court if I could, but I cannot. The Pilot, an american vessel was captured by Pirates & converted into a piratical cruizer. She was then recaptured by one of our squadron under Commodore Porter, after a sharp action. She was brought into Norfolk, libelled as prize, & claimed by the original owner. The attorney for the captors abandoned the claim as prize, and asked salvage. This claim was resisted on the ground that the capture was not within the act of 1800, because that applies only to recaptures from an enemy of the United States, not to recaptures from a Pirate. It was insisted too that the act of 1819 does not give salvage for a

recapture made by a national ship, because, although an american vessel recaptured by a merchantman or private vessel is to be brought in, yet such vessel recaptured by a national ship is not to be brought in. As there is no salvage given by statute, the claim it was said must rest upon general law. It was admitted that according to that law salvage is due for a vessel recaptured by a private ship, but not for a vessel recaptured by a national ship, because the nation owes protection to all its people, and it is a part of the duty of the national force to afford this protection. In the present case it was one of the objects of the expedition. It was said that the general dicta that salvage is due for recaptures made from Pirates must be limited to such as are made by private ships or by the public ships of some other nation than that of the recaptured vessel.

The council for the recaptors relied chiefly on the general principle that by the law of nations, or by the general Maritime law salvage is due for all vessels recaptured from pirates.

The District Judge gave salvage & the owners have appealed. I do not know that the question has ever arisen in any of the courts of the United States. Perhaps your information may be more extensive, and I will thank you to give it to me. If the case has not been decided you will greatly oblige me by your sentiments on it, as I know that you are more *au fait* on these questions than I am. The sooner I hear from you, provided you are satisfied in the case, the better.

I have read the correspondence to which you refer and regret its publication extremely. I feel great respect for Mr. Adams, and shall always feel it whatever he may do. The extreme bitterness with which he speaks of honourable men who were once his friends, is calculated to mortify and pain those who remain truely attached to him. A comparison of the language he applies to gentlemen of high character in Massachusetts with that which, in the early part of the correspondence, he applied to those who were always his enemies and gross calumniators, who cannot even now treat him with decency, inspires serious reflections. We can only say non est qualis erat.

I think I can *guess*, although not born north of the Hudson, what you hint at respecting the Presidential election; but I shall be as careful not to commit my *guess* to paper as you are respecting your scheme.

Farewell. Providence I hope will continue to take care of us. With affectionate esteem, I am dear Sir your obedt

PROPOSALS TO ALTER THE SUPREME COURT

To Henry Clay

Dear Sir   Richmond Decr. 22d. 1823
    Your favour of the 11th. reached me in due time and I can assure you that its perusal gave me no "trouble." With an abatement, which I dare say you are prepared to expect, that is —that few non residents of Kentucky will concur with the citizens of that state in opinion, either on their laws respecting the occupants of lands, or what is miscalled their "relief system," I had a sort of half way disposition to think with you on several points, till that section of my mind which was disposed to arrange itself with you was completely routed by Mr. Johnsons proposition in the senate. That gentleman, I percieve has moved a resolution requiring a concurrence of more than a majority of all the Judges of the supreme court to decide that a law is repugnant to the constitution.
    It is the privilege of age to utter *wise sayings* somewhat like proverbs, in the shape of counsel, as a substitute for that powerful and convincing argument which it has lost the faculty of making; but this privilege is more than countervailed by another which is possessed and generally exercised by the middle aged as well as the young—it is to disregard entirely the wise sayings of the old. When I exercise my privilege, I am not quite so old or so unreasonable as to suspect that you are not in perfect readiness to exercise yours also.
    But for the apothegm. If I do not come to it quickly you will think I waste more time in preparing for it than it is worth after being introduced. I will say then at once that it is among the most dangerous things in legislation to enact a general law of great and extensive influence to effect a particular object; or to legislate for a nation under a strong excitement which must be suspected to influence the judgement. If the mental eye be directed to a single object, it is not easy for the legislator,

intent only on that object, to look all around him, and to percieve and guard against the serious mischief with which his measure may burn. I am perhaps more alive to what concerns the judicial department, and attach more importance to its organization, than my fellow citizens in the legislature or executive, but let me ask if serious inconvenience is not to be apprehended from a very numerous supreme court? It ought not to be too small; but the one extreme is as much to be avoided as the other.

Let me ask too, and I put the question very seriously, if a regulation requiring a concurrence of more than a majority of all the Judges to decide any case, ought not to be well considered in all its bearings, before its adoption? To say nothing of the influence of such a rule on the business of the court, let me ask your attention to the enquiry whether it accords with the spirit of the constitution? If it goes to defeat an object which the constitution obviously designs to accomplish, I need not say to you that, although the judiciary may be bound by it, a conscientious legislator can never assent to it. It is I think difficult to read that instrument attentively without feeling the conviction that it intends to provide a tribunal for every case of collision between itself and a law, so far as such case can assume a form for judicial enquiry; and a law incapable of being placed in such form can rarely have very extensive or pernicious effects.

If this be the obvious intention of the constitution, can the legislature withdraw such cases from that tribunal without counteracting its views and defeating its objects? If congress should say explicitly that the courts of the union should never enter into the enquiry concerning the constitutionality of a law; or should dismiss for want of jurisdiction, every case depending on a law deemed by the court to be unconstitutional; could there be two opinions respecting such an act? And what substantial difference is there between such a law, if law it may be called, and one which makes the decision to depend on an event which will seldom happen? What substantial difference is there between withdrawing a question from a court, and disabling a court from deciding that question? Those only, I should think, who were capable of drawing the memorable distinction as to tenure of office, between removing the Judge from the office, and removing the office from the Judge, can take this distinction.

That the measure proposed in the senate has this tendency is not, I presume, doubted by any person; that it will very often have this effect practically is, I think, as little to be questioned. When we consider the remoteness, the numbers, and the age of the Judges, we cannot expect that the assemblage of all of them, when they shall amount to ten, will be of frequent recurrence. The difficulty of the questions, and other considerations, may often divide those who do attend. To require almost unanimity, is to require what cannot often happen, and consequently to disable the court from deciding constitutional questions.

A majority of the court is according to constant usage and the common understanding of mankind as much the court, as the majority of the legislature is the legislature; and it seems to me that a law requiring more than a majority to make a decision as much counteracts the views of the constitution as an act requiring more than a majority of the legislature to pass a law.

But I will detain you no longer with my prosing & will only add that I am with great respect & esteem, your obedt. Servt

RECALLING A COURTSHIP

To Mary W. Marshall

My dearest Polly   Washington Feby. 23d. 1824

I was made extremely uneasy to day by being informed that you had heard of my fall before my letter reached you and had supposed me to be hurt much worse than I was in reality. I had hoped that my letter would be the first communication you would receive on the subject.

I have been disappointed in being kept longer from court than I expected. Old men I find do not get over sprains and hurts quite as quickly as young ones. Although I feel no pain when perfectly still, yet I cannot get up and move about without difficulty, & cannot put on my coat. Of course I cannot go to court. I believe confidently however that I shall go the beginning of next week. Altho I do not get well as immediately as I expected myself, the doctors say I mend a great deal faster than they expected. Everything is certainly in the best possible train. The swelling has gone entirely down, and I have not the slightest appearance of fever.

I have been treated with a degree of kindness and attention which is very flattering. All my friends have called to see me. The President himself has visited me and has expressed his wish to serve me in any manner that may be in his power. I have however in reserve a still higher compliment which would very much surprize you and all others who know me. All the Ladies of the Secretaries have called on me, some more than once, and have brought me more jelly than I can eat, and have offered me a great many good things. I thank them but stick to my barly broth.

Notwithstanding these attentions I have a plenty of time on my hands in the night as well as in the day. How do you think I beguile it? I am almost tempted to leave you to guess till I write again. But as I suppose you will have rather more curiosity in my absence than you usually show to hear my stories when I am present, I will tell you without waiting to be asked. You must know then that l begin with the ball at York, and with the dinner on the fish at your house the next day: I then retrace my visit to York, our splendid assembly at the Palace in Williamsburg, my visit to Richmond where I acted Pa for a fortnight, my return the ensuing fall and the very welcome reception you gave me on your arrival from Dover, our little tiffs & makings up, my feelings while Major Dick was courting You, my trip to the cottage, the lock of hair, my visit again to Richmond the ensuing fall, and all the thousand indescribable but deeply affecting instances of your affection or coldness which constituted for a time the happiness or misery of my life and will always be recollected with a degree of interest which can never be lost while recollection remains.

Thus is it that I find amusement for those hours which I pass without company or books.

Farewell my dearest Polly. I beg you beleive that tho confined I am free from pain & shall soon be free from confinement. Yours ever

Opinion in Gibbons v. Ogden

This is a writ of error to a decree of the highest court of law or equity in the State of New York, affirming a decree pronounced by the Chancellor of that State.

The Legislature of New York has enacted several laws for the purpose of securing to Robert R. Livingston and Robert Fulton the exclusive navigation of all the waters within the jurisdiction of that State, with boats moved by fire or steam, for a term of years, which has not yet expired; and has authorized the Chancellor to award an injunction, restraining any person whatever from navigating those waters with boats of that description.

This bill was filed by Aaron Ogden, claiming as assignee of Livingston and Fulton, suggesting that Thomas Gibbon, the plaintiff in error, was in possession of two steam-boats, the Stoudinger and Bellona, which were actually employed in running between New York and Elizabethtown in New Jersey, in violation of the exclusive privilege conferred on the plaintiff, and praying an injunction to restrain the said Gibbon from using the said boats, or any others propelled by fire or steam, in navigating the waters within the territory of New York.

The injunction having been awarded, the answer of Gibbon was filed, in which he stated that the boats employed by him were duly enrolled and licensed, according to the act of Congress, to carry on the coasting trade of the United States; and insisted on his right, in virtue of that license, to navigate the waters between Elizabethtown and New York, the acts of the Legislature of New York notwithstanding.

The Chancellor perpetuated the injunction, being of opinion that the acts conferring the privilege were not repugnant to the Constitution and laws of the United States, and were valid. This decree was affirmed, in the Court for the trial of impeachments and correction of errors, which is the highest tribunal before which the cause could be carried in the State.

The plaintiff in error contends that this decree is erroneous, because the laws which purport to give the exclusive privilege it sustains, are repugnant to the Constitution and laws of the United States.

They are said to be repugnant—

1st. To that clause in the Constitution which authorizes Congress to regulate commerce.

2d. To that which authorizes Congress to promote the progress of science and useful arts.

The State of New York maintains the constitutionality of these laws; and their Legislature, their Council of Revision, and their Judges, have repeatedly concurred in this opinion. It is supported by great names—by names which have all the titles to consideration that virtue, intelligence, and office, can bestow. No tribunal can approach the decision of this question, without feeling a just and real respect for that opinion which is sustained by such authority; but it is the province of this Court, while it respects, not to bow to it implicitly; and the Judges must exercise, in the examination of the subject, that understanding which Providence has bestowed upon them, with that independence which the people of the United States expect from this department of the government.

As preliminary to the very able discussions of the Constitution, which we have heard from the bar, and as having some influence on its construction, reference has been made to the political situation of these States, anterior to its formation. It has been said, that they were sovereign; were completely independent, and were connected with each other only by a league. This is true. But, when these allied sovereigns converted their league into a government—when they converted their Congress of Ambassadors, deputed to deliberate on their common concerns, and to recommend measures of general utility, into a Legislature empowered to enact laws on the most interesting subjects, the whole character, in which the States appear, underwent a change, the extent of which must be determined by a fair consideration of the instrument by which that change was effected.

This instrument contains an enumeration of powers expressly granted by the people to their government. It has been said, that these powers ought to be construed strictly. But why ought they to be so construed? Is there one sentence in the Constitution which gives countenance to this rule? In the last of the enumerated powers, that which grants, expressly, the means for carrying all others into execution, Congress is authorized "to make all laws which shall be necessary and proper" for the purpose. But this limitation on the means which may be used, is not extended to the powers which are conferred; nor is there one sentence in the Constitution, which has been pointed out by the gentlemen of the bar, or which we have been able to discern, that prescribes this rule. We do not, therefore, think ourselves justified in adopting it. What do gentlemen mean by a strict construction? If they contend only against that enlarged construction which would extend words beyond their natural and obvious import, we might question the application of the term, but should not controvert the principle. If they contend for that narrow construction which, in support of some theory not to be found in the Constitution, would deny to the government those powers which the words of the grant, as usually understood, import, and which are consistent with the general views and objects of the instrument, for that narrow construction which would cripple the government, and render it unequal to the objects for which it is declared to be instituted, and to which the powers given, as fairly understood, render it competent, then we cannot perceive the propriety of this strict construction, nor adopt it as the rule by which the Constitution is to be expounded. As men, whose intentions require no concealment, generally employ the words which most directly and aptly express the ideas they intend to convey, the enlightened patriots who framed our Constitution, and the people who adopted it, must be understood to have employed words in their natural sense, and to have intended what they have said. If, from the imperfection of human language, there should be serious doubts respecting the extent of any given power, it is a well settled rule, that the objects for which it was given, especially when those objects are expressed in the instrument itself, should have great influence in the construction. We know of no reason for excluding this rule from the present case. The grant does not convey power which might be beneficial to the grantor if retained by himself, or, which can enure solely to the benefit of the grantee; but is an investment of power for the general advantage, in the hands of agents selected for that purpose, which power can never be exercised by the people themselves, but must be placed in the hands of agents or lie dormant. We know of no rule for construing the extent of such powers, other than is given by the language of the instrument which confers them, taken in connexion with the purposes for which they were conferred.

The words are—"Congress shall have power to regulate commerce with foreign nations, and among the several states, and with the Indian tribes."

The subject to be regulated is commerce; and our constitution being, as was aptly said at the bar, one of enumeration, and not of definition, to ascertain the extent of the power, it becomes necessary to settle the meaning of the word. The counsel for the appellee would limit it to traffic, to buying and selling, or the interchange of commodities, and do not admit that it comprehends navigation. This would restrict a general term, applicable to many objects, to one of its significations. Commerce undoubtedly is traffic, but it is something more: It is intercourse. It describes the commercial intercourse between nations, and parts of nations, in all its branches, and is regulated by prescribing rules for carrying on that intercourse. The mind can scarcely conceive a system for regulating commerce between nations which shall exclude all laws concerning navigation, which shall be silent on the admission of the vessels of the one nation into the ports of the other, and be confined to prescribing rules for the conduct of individuals in the actual employment of buying and selling, or of barter.

If commerce does not include navigation, the government of the Union has no direct power over that subject, and can make no law prescribing what shall constitute American vessels, or requiring that they shall be navigated by American seamen. Yet this power has been exercised from the commencement of the government, has been exercised with the consent of all, and has been understood by all to be a commercial regulation. All America understands, and has uniformly understood, the word "commerce" to comprehend navigation. It was so understood, and must have been so understood, when the Constitution was framed. The power over commerce, including navigation, was one of the primary objects for which the people of America adopted their government, and must have been contemplated in forming it. The convention must have used the word in that sense, because all have understood it in that sense; and the attempt to restrict it comes too late.

If the opinion that "commerce," as the word is used in the Constitution, comprehends navigation also, require any additional confirmation, that additional confirmation is, we think, furnished by the words of the instrument itself.

It is a rule of construction acknowledged by all, that the exceptions from a power mark its extent; for it would be absurd, as well as useless, to except from a granted power that which was not granted—that which the words of the grant could not comprehend. If, then, there are, in the constitution plain exceptions from the power over navigation, plain inhibitions to the exercise of that power in a particular way, it is proof that those who made these exceptions, and prescribed these inhibitions, understood the power to which they applied as being granted.

The 9th section of the 1st article declares, that "no preference shall be given by any regulation of commerce or revenue, to the ports of one state over those of another." This clause cannot be understood as applicable to those laws only which are passed for purposes of revenue, because it is expressly applied to commercial regulations; and the most obvious preference which can be given to one port over another, in regulating commerce, relates to navigation. But the subsequent part of the sentence is still more explicit. It is, "nor shall vessels bound to or from one state, be obliged to enter, clear, or pay duties, in another." These words have a direct reference to navigation.

The universally acknowledged power of the government to impose embargoes, must also be considered as showing that all America is united in that construction which comprehends navigation in the word commerce. Gentlemen have said, in argument, that this is a branch of the warmaking power, and that an embargo is an instrument of war, not a regulation of trade.

That it may be, and often is used as an instrument of war, cannot be denied. An embargo may be imposed for the purpose of facilitating the equipment or manning of a fleet, or for the purpose of concealing the progress of an expedition preparing to sail from a particular port. In these, and in similar cases, it is a military instrument, and partakes of the nature of war. But all embargoes are not of this description. They are, sometimes, resorted to without a view to war, and with a single view to commerce. In such case an embargo is no more a war-measure than a merchantman is a ship of war, because both are vessels which navigate the ocean with sails and seamen.

When Congress imposed that embargo, which, for a time, engaged the attention of every man in the United States, the avowed object of the law was the protection of commerce and the avoiding of war. By its friends and its enemies it was treated as a commercial, not as a war measure. The persevering earnestness and zeal with which it was opposed, in a part of our country which supposed its interests to be vitally affected by the act, cannot be forgotten. A want of astuteness in discovering objections to a measure to which they felt the most deep rooted hostility, will not be imputed to those who were arrayed in opposition to this. Yet they never suspected that navigation was no branch of trade, and was, therefore, not comprehended in the power to regulate commerce. They did, indeed, contest the constitutionality of the act, but on a principle which admits the construction for which the appellant contends. They denied that the particular law in question was made in pursuance of the constitution, not because the power could not act directly on vessels, but because a perpetual embargo was the annihilation, and not the regulation of commerce. In terms, they admitted the applicability of the words used in the Constitution to vessels; and that, in a case which produced a degree and an extent of excitement calculated to draw forth every principle on which legitimate resistance could be sustained. No example could more strongly illustrate the universal understanding of the American people on this subject.

The word used in the Constitution, then, comprehends, and has been always understood to comprehend, navigation within its meaning; and a power to regulate navigation is as expressly granted, as if that term had been added to the word "commerce."

To what commerce does this power extend? The Constitution informs us to commerce "with foreign nations, and among the several states, and with the Indian tribes."

It has, we believe, been universally admitted, that these words comprehend every species of commercial intercourse between the United States and foreign nations. No sort of trade can be carried on between this country and any other, to which this power does not extend. It has been truly said, that commerce, as the word is used in the constitution, is a unit, every part of which is indicated by the term.

If this be the admitted meaning of the word, in its application to foreign nations, it must carry the same meaning throughout the sentence, and remain a unit, unless there be some plain intelligible cause which alters it.

The subject to which the power is next applied, is to commerce "among the several states." The word "among" means intermingled with. A thing which is among others, is intermingled with them. Commerce among the states cannot stop at the external boundary line of each state, but may be introduced into the interior.

It is not intended to say that these words comprehend that commerce, which is completely internal, which is carried on between man and man in a state, or between different parts of the same state, and which does not extend to, or affect other states. Such a power would be inconvenient, and is certainly unnecessary.

Comprehensive as the word "among" is, it may very properly be restricted to that commerce which concerns more states than one. The phrase is not one which would probably have been selected to indicate the completely interior traffic of a state, because it is not an apt phrase for that purpose; and the enumeration of the particular classes of commerce to which the power was to be extended, would not have been made, had the intention been to extend the power to every description. The enumeration presupposes something not enumerated; and that something, if we regard the language or the subject of the sentence, must be the exclusively internal commerce of a state. The genius and character of the whole government seem to be, that its action is to be applied to all the external concerns of the nation, and to those internal concerns which affect the states generally; but not to those which are completely within a particular state, which do not affect other states, and with which it is not necessary to interfere for the purpose of executing some of the general powers of the government. The completely internal commerce of a state, then, may be considered as reserved for the state itself.

But, in regulating commerce with foreign nations, the power

of Congress does not stop at the jurisdictional lines of the several states. It would be a very useless power if it could not pass those lines. The commerce of the United States with foreign nations is that of the whole United States. Every district has a right to participate in it. The deep streams which penetrate our country in every direction, pass through the interior of almost every state in the Union, and furnish the means of exercising this right. If Congress has the power to regulate it, that power must be exercised wherever the subject exists. If it exists within the states, if a foreign voyage may commence or terminate at a port within a state, then the power of Congress may be exercised within a state.

This principle is, if possible, still more clear when applied to commerce "among the several states." They either join each other, in which case they are separated by a mathematical line; or they are remote from each other, in which case other states lie between them. What is commerce "among" them, and how is it to be conducted? Can a trading expedition between two adjoining states, commence and terminate outside of each? And if the trading intercourse be between two states remote from each other, must it not commence in one, terminate in the other, and probably pass through a third? Commerce among the states must, of necessity, be commerce within the states. In the regulation of trade with the Indian tribes, the action of the law, especially when the constitution was made, was chiefly within a state. The power of Congress, then, whatever it may be, must be exercised within the territorial jurisdiction of the several states. The sense of the nation on this subject is unequivocally manifested by the provisions made in the laws for transporting goods, by land, between Baltimore and Providence, between New York and Philadelphia, and between Philadelphia and Baltimore.

We are now arrived at the inquiry—What is this power?

It is the power to regulate, that is, to prescribe, the rule by which commerce is to be governed. This power, like all others vested in Congress, is complete in itself; may be exercised to its utmost extent; and acknowledges no limitations, other than are prescribed in the constitution. These are expressed in plain terms, and do not affect the questions which arise in this case, or which have been discussed at the bar. If, as has always been understood, the sovereignty of Congress, though limited to specified objects, is plenary as to those objects, the power over commerce with foreign nations and among the several states, is vested in Congress as absolutely as it would be in a single government, having in its constitution the same restrictions on the exercise of the power as are found in the constitution of the United States. The wisdom and the discretion of Congress, their identity with the people, and the influence which their constituents possess at elections, are, in this, as in many other instances, as that, for example, of declaring war, the sole restraints on which they have relied to secure them from its abuse. They are the restraints on which the people must often rely solely in all representative governments.

The power of Congress, then, comprehends navigation within the limits of every state in the Union; so far as that navigation may be, in any manner, connected with "commerce with foreign nations, or among the several states, or with the Indian tribes." It may, of consequence, pass the jurisdictional line of New York, and act upon the very waters to which the prohibition now under consideration applies.

But it has been urged with great earnestness that, altho' the power of Congress to regulate commerce with foreign nations and among the several states be co-extensive with the subject itself, & have no other limits than are prescribed in the constitution, yet the states may severally exercise the same power within their respective jurisdictions. In support of this argument, it is said, that they possessed it as an inseparable attribute of sovereignty before the formation of the constitution and still retain it, except so far as they have surrendered it by that instrument; that this principle results from the nature of the government, and is secured by the tenth amendment; that an affirmative grant of power is not exclusive, unless in its own nature it be such that the continued exercise of it by the former possessor is inconsistent with the grant, and that this is not of that description.

The plaintiff, conceding these postulates, except the last, contends, that full power to regulate a particular subject, implies the whole power, and leaves no residuum; that a grant of the whole is incompatible with the existence of a right in another to any part of it.

Both parties have appealed to the constitution, to legislative acts, and judicial decisions; and have drawn arguments from all these sources to support and illustrate the propositions they respectively maintain.

The grant of the power to lay and collect taxes is, like the power to regulate commerce, made in general terms, and has never been understood to interfere with the exercise of the same power by the states; and hence has been drawn an argument which has been applied to the question under consideration. But the two grants are not, it is conceived, similar in their terms or their nature. Although many of the powers formerly exercised by the states are transferred to the government of the Union, yet the state governments remain, and constitute a most important part of our system. The power of taxation is indispensable to their existence, and is a power which, in its own nature, is capable of residing in, and being exercised by, different authorities at the same time. We are accustomed to see it placed, for different purposes, in different hands. Taxation is the simple operation of taking small portions from a perpetually accumulating mass, susceptible of almost infinite division, and a power in one to take what is necessary for certain purposes is not, in its nature, incompatible with a power in another to take what is necessary for other purposes. Congress is authorized to lay and collect taxes, &c. to pay the debts and provide for the common defence and general welfare of the United States. This does not interfere with the power of the states to tax for the support of their own governments; nor is the exercise of that power by the states an exercise of any portion of the power that is granted to the United States. In imposing taxes for state purposes, they are not doing what Congress is empowered to do. Congress is not empowered to tax for those purposes which are within the exclusive province of the states. When, then, each government exercises the power of taxation, either is exercising the power of the other. But when a state proceeds to regulate commerce with foreign nations, or among the several states, it is exercising the very power that is granted to Congress, and is doing the very thing which Congress is authorized to do. There is no analogy, then, between the power of taxation and the power of regulating commerce.

In discussing the question whether this power is still in the states, in the case under consideration, we may dismiss from it the inquiry whether it is surrendered by the mere grant to Congress, or is retained until Congress shall exercise the power. We may dismiss that inquiry, because it has been exercised, and the regulations which Congress deemed it proper to make, are now in full operation. The sole question is, can a state regulate commerce with foreign nations and among the states, while Congress is regulating it?

The counsel for the appellee answered this question in the affirmative, and rely very much on the restrictions in the 10th section as supporting their opinion. They say, very truly, that limitations of a power furnish a strong argument in favour of the existence of that power, and that the section which prohibits the states from laying duties on imports or exports proves that this power might have been exercised had it not been expressly forbidden; and, consequently, that any other commercial regulation, not expressly forbidden, to which the original power of the state was competent, may still be made.

That this restriction shows the opinion of the Convention, that a state might impose duties on exports and imports, if not expressly forbidden, will be conceded; but that it follows as a consequence, from this concession, that a state may regulate commerce with foreign nations and among the states, cannot be admitted.

We must first determine, whether the act of laying "duties or imposts on imports or exports," is considered in the constitution as a branch of the taxing power, or of the power to regulate commerce. We think it very clear, that it is considered as a branch of the taxing power. It is so treated in the first clause of the 8th section: "Congress shall have power to lay and collect taxes, duties, imposts, and excises;" and before commerce is mentioned, the rule by which the exercise of this power must be governed, is declared. It is, that all duties, imposts, and excises, shall be uniform. In a separate clause of the enumeration, the power to regulate commerce is given, as being entirely distinct from the right to levy taxes and imposts, and as being a new power, not before conferred. The Constitution, then, considers these powers as substantive, and distinct from each other; and so places them in the enumeration it contains. The power of imposing duties on imports, is classed with the power to levy taxes, and that seems to be its natural place. But the power to levy taxes could never be considered as abridging the right of the states on that subject; and they might, consequently, have exercised it by levying duties on imports or exports, had the Constitution contained no prohibition on this subject. This prohibition, then, is an exception from the acknowledged power of the states to levy taxes, not from the questionable power to regulate commerce.

"A duty of tonnage," is as much a tax, as a duty on imports or exports; and the reason which induced the prohibition of those taxes, extends to this also. This tax may be imposed by a state, with the consent of Congress; and it may be admitted, that Congress cannot give a right to a state, in virtue of its own powers. But a duty of tonnage being part of the power of imposing taxes, its prohibition may certainly be made to depend on Congress, without affording any implication respecting a power to regulate commerce. It is true, that duties may often be, and in fact often are, imposed on tonnage, with a view to the regulation of commerce; but they may be also imposed with a view to revenue; and it was, therefore, a prudent precaution, to prohibit the states from exercising this power. The idea that the same measure might, according to circumstances, be arranged with different classes of power, was no novelty to the framers of our Constitution. Those illustrious statesmen and patriots had been, many of them, deeply engaged in the discussions which preceded the war of our Revolution, and all of them were well read in those discussions. The right to regulate commerce, even by the imposition of duties, was not controverted; but the right to impose a duty for the purpose of revenue, produced a war as important, perhaps, in its consequences to the human race, as any the world has ever witnessed.

These restrictions, then, are on the taxing power, not on that to regulate commerce; and presuppose the existence of that which they restrain, not of that which they do not purport to restrain.

But, the inspection laws are said to be regulations of commerce, and are certainly recognized in the Constitution, as being passed in the exercise of a power remaining with the states.

That inspection laws may have a remote and considerable influence on commerce, will not be denied; but that a power to regulate commerce is the source from which the right to pass them is derived cannot be admitted. The object of inspection laws is to improve the quality of articles produced by the labor of a country; to fit them for exportation, or, it may be, for domestic use. They act upon the subject before it becomes an article of foreign commerce, or of commerce among the states, and prepare it for that purpose. They form a portion of that immense mass of legislation which embraces every thing within the territory of a state, not surrendered to the general government: all which can be most advantageously exercised by the states themselves. Inspection laws, quarantine laws, health laws, of every description, as well as laws for regulating the internal commerce of a state, and those which respect turnpike roads, ferries, &c. are component parts of this mass.

No direct general power over these objects is granted to Congress; and, consequently, they remain subject to state legislation. If the legislative power of the Union can reach them, it must be for national purposes; it must be where the power is expressly given for a special purpose, or is clearly incidental to some power which is expressly given. It is obvious, that the government of the Union, in the exercise of its express powers —that, for example, of regulating commerce with foreign nations and among the states—may use means that may also be employed by a state, in the exercise of its acknowledged powers —that, for example, of regulating commerce within the state. If Congress license vessels to sail from one port to another, in the same state, the act is supposed to be necessarily incidental to the power expressly granted to Congress, and implies no claim of a direct power to regulate the purely internal commerce of a state, or to act directly on its system of police. So, if a state, in passing laws on subjects acknowledged to be within its control, and with a view to those subjects, which shall adopt a measure of the same character with one which Congress may adopt, it does not derive its authority from the particular power which has been granted, but from some other, which remains with the state, and may be executed by the same means. All experience shows, that the same measures, or measures scarcely distinguishable from each other, may flow from distinct powers; but this does not prove, that the powers themselves are identical. Although the means used in their execution may sometimes approach each other so nearly as to be confounded, there are other situations in which they are sufficiently distinct to establish their individuality.

In our complex system, presenting the rare and difficult scheme of one general government, whose action extends over the whole, but which possesses only certain enumerated powers; and of numerous state governments, which retain and exercise all powers not delegated to the Union, contests respecting power must arise. Were it even otherwise, the measures taken by the respective governments to execute their acknowledged powers, would often be of the same description, and might, sometimes, interfere. This, however, does not prove, that the one is exercising, or has a right to exercise, the powers of the other.

The acts of Congress, passed in 1796 & 1799, empowering and directing the officers of the general government to conform to, and assist in the execution of, the quarantine and health laws of a state, proceed, it is said, upon the idea that these laws are constitutional. It is undoubtedly true, that they do proceed upon that idea; and the constitutionality of such laws has never, so far as we are informed, been denied. But they do not imply an acknowledgement that a state may rightfully regulate commerce with foreign nations, or among the states; for they do not imply that such laws are an exercise of that power, or enacted with a view to it. On the contrary, they are treated as quarantine and health laws, are so denominated in the acts of Congress, and are considered as flowing from the acknowledged power of a state, to provide for the health of its citizens. But, as it was apparent that some of the provisions made for this purpose, and in virtue of this power, might interfere with, and be affected by the laws of the United States, made for the regulation of commerce, Congress, in that spirit of harmony and conciliation which ought always to characterize the conduct of governments standing in the relation which that of the Union and those of the States bear to each other, has directed its officers to aid in the execution of these laws; and has, in some measure, adapted its own legislation to this object, by making provisions in aid of those of the states. But, in making these provisions, the opinion is unequivocally manifested, that Congress may control the state laws, so far as it may be necessary to control them for the regulation of commerce.

The act passed in 1803, prohibiting the importation of slaves into any state which shall itself prohibit their importation, implies, it is said, an admission that the states possessed the power to exclude or admit them; from which it is inferred that they possess the same power with respect to all other articles.

If this inference were correct, if this power was exercised, not under any particular clause in the constitution, but in virtue of a general right over the subject of commerce, to exist as long as the constitution itself, it might now be exercised. Any state might now import African slaves into its own territory. But, it is obvious that the power of the states over this subject, previous to the year 1808, constitutes an exception to the power of Congress to regulate commerce, and the exception is expressed in such words as to manifest clearly the intention to continue the preexisting right of the states to admit or exclude for a limited period. The words are, "the migration or importation of such persons as any of the states now existing *shall* think proper to admit, shall not be prohibited by the Congress prior to the year 1808." The whole object of the exception is to preserve the power to those states which might be disposed to exercise it and its language seems to the court to convey this idea unequivocally. The possession of this particular power, then, during the time limited in the constitution, cannot be admitted to prove the possession of any other similar power.

It has been said that the act of August 7, 1789, acknowledges a concurrent power in the states to regulate the conduct of pilots, and hence is inferred an admission of their concurrent right with Congress to regulate commerce with foreign nations, and among the states. But, this inference is not, we think, justified by the fact.

Although Congress cannot enable a state to legislate, Congress may adopt the provisions of a state on any subject. When the government of the Union was brought into existence, it found a system for the regulation of its pilots in full force in every state. The act which has been mentioned adopts this system, and gives it the same validity as if its provisions had been specially made by Congress. But the act, it may be said, is prospective also, and the adoption of laws to be made in future presupposes the right in the maker to legislate on the subject.

The act unquestionably manifests an intention to leave this subject entirely to the states, until Congress should think proper to interpose; but the very enactment of such a law indicates an opinion that it was necessary; that the existing system would not be applicable to the new state of things unless expressly applied to it by Congress. But this section is confined to pilots within the "bays, inlets, rivers, harbours, and ports of the United States," which are, of course, in whole or in part, also within the limits of some particular state. The acknowledged power of a state to regulate its police, its domestic trade, and to govern its own citizens, may enable it to legislate on this subject to a considerable extent; and the adoption of its system by Congress, and the application of it to the whole subject of commerce, does not seem to the court to imply a right in the states so to apply it of their own authority. But, the adoption of the state system being temporary, being only "until further legislative provision shall be made by Congress," shews, conclusively an opinion that Congress could control the whole subject, and might adopt the system of the states, or provide one of its own.

A state, it is said, or even a private citizen, may construct light houses. But gentlemen must be aware, that, if this proves a power in a state to regulate commerce, it proves that the same power is in the citizen. States, or individuals, who own lands, may, if not forbidden by law, erect on those lands what buildings they please; but this power is entirely distinct from that of regulating commerce, and may, we presume, be restrained, if exercised so as to produce a public mischief.

These acts were cited at the bar for the purpose of shewing an opinion in Congress that the states possess, concurrently with the legislature of the Union, the power to regulate commerce with foreign nations and among the states. Upon reviewing them, we think they do not establish the proposition they were intended to prove. They shew the opinion that the states retain powers enabling them to pass the laws to which allusion has been made, not that those laws proceed from the particular power which has been delegated to Congress.

It has been contended by the counsel for the appellant, that, as the word "to regulate" implies in its nature full power over the thing to be regulated, it excludes necessarily the action of all others that would perform the same operation on the same thing. That regulation is designed for the entire result, applying to those parts which remain as they were, as well as to those which are altered. It produces a uniform whole, which is as much disturbed and deranged by changing what the regulating power designs to leave untouched, as that on which it has operated.

There is great force in this argument, and the court is not satisfied that it has been refuted.

Since, however, in exercising the power of regulating their own purely internal affairs, whether of trade or police, the states may sometimes enact laws, the validity of which depends on their interfering with, and being contrary to, an act of Congress passed in pursuance of the Constitution, the court will enter upon the inquiry, whether the laws of New York, as expounded by the highest tribunal of that state, have, in their application to this case, come into collision with an act of Congress, and deprived a citizen of a right to which that act entitles him. Should this collision exist, it will be immaterial whether those laws were passed in virtue of a concurrent power "to regulate commerce with foreign nations and among the several states," or in virtue of a power to regulate their domestic trade and police. In the one case and the other, the acts of New York must yield to the law of Congress; and the decision sustaining the privilege they confer, against a right given by a law of the Union, must be erroneous.

This opinion has been frequently expressed in this court, and is founded as well on the nature of the government as on the words of the Constitution. In argument, however, it has been contended that, if a law passed by a state, in the exercise of its acknowledged sovereignty, comes into conflict with a law passed by congress in pursuance of the Constitution, they affect the subject and each other like equal opposing powers.

But the framers of our Constitution foresaw this state of things, and provided for it, by declaring the supremacy not only of itself, but of the laws made in pursuance of it. The nullity of any act inconsistent with the Constitution, is produced by the declaration, that the Constitution is the supreme law. The appropriate application of that part of the clause which confers the same supremacy on laws and treaties, is to such acts of the state legislatures as do not transcend their powers, but, though enacted in the execution of acknowledged state powers, interfere with, or are contrary to, the laws of Congress, made in pursuance of the Constitution, or some treaty made under the authority of the United States. In every such case, the act of Congress, or the treaty, is supreme; and the law of the state, though enacted in the exercise of powers not controverted, must yield to it.

In pursuing this inquiry at the bar, it has been said that the Constitution does not confer the right of intercourse between state and state. That right derives its source from those laws whose authority is acknowledged by civilized man throughout the world. This is true. The Constitution found it an existing right, and give to Congress the power to regulate it. In the exercise of this power, Congress has passed "An act for enrolling or licensing ships or vessels to be employed in the coasting trade, and fisheries, and for regulating the same." The counsel for the appellee contend that this act does not give the right to sail from port to port, but confines itself to regulating a pre-existing right so far only as to confer certain privileges on enrolled and licensed vessels in its exercise.

It will at once occur, that, when a legislature attaches certain privileges and exemptions to the exercise of a right over which its control is absolute, the law must imply a power to exercise the right. The privileges are gone if the right itself be annihilated. It would be contrary to all reason, and to the course of human affairs, to say that a state is unable to strip a vessel of the particular privileges attendant on the exercise of a right, and yet may annul the right itself; that the State of New York cannot prevent an enrolled and licensed vessel, proceeding from Elizabeth town, in N. Jersey, to N. York, from enjoying, in her course, and, on her entrance into port, all the privileges conferred by the act of Congress, but can shut her up in her own port, and prohibit altogether her entering the waters and ports of another state. To the court it seems very clear, that the whole act on the subject of the coasting trade, according to those principles which govern the construction of statutes, implies unequivocally, an authority to licensed vessels to carry on the coasting trade.

But we will proceed briefly to notice those sections which bear more directly on the subject.

The first section declares, that vessels enrolled by virtue of a previous law, and certain other vessels enrolled as described in that act, and having a license in force as is by the act required, "and no others, shall be deemed ships or vessels of the United States, entitled to the privileges of ships or vessels employed in the coasting trade."

This section seems to the court to contain a positive enactment that the vessels it describes shall be entitled to the privileges of ships or vessels employed in the coasting trade. These privileges cannot be separated from the trade, and cannot be enjoyed unless the trade may be prosecuted. The grant of the privilege is an idle, empty form, conveying nothing, unless it convey the right to which the privilege is attached, and in the exercise of which its whole value consists. To construe these words otherwise than as entitling the ships or vessels described to carry on the coasting trade, would be, we think, to disregard the apparent intent of the act.

The fourth section directs the proper officer to grant to a vessel qualified to receive it, "a license for carrying on the coasting trade;" and prescribes its form. After reciting the compliance of the applicant with the previous requisites of the law, the operative words of the instrument are, "license is hereby granted for the said steam boat Bellona, to be employed in carrying on the coasting trade for one year from the date hereof, and no longer."

These are not the words of the officer—they are the words of the legislature; and convey as explicitly the authority the act intended to give, and operate as effectually, as if they had been inserted in any other part of the act than in the license itself.

The word "license" means permission or authority; and a license to do any particular thing is a permission or authority to do that thing; and if granted by a person having power to grant it, transfers to the grantee the right to do whatever it purports to authorize. It certainly transfers to him all the right which the grantor can transfer, to do what is within the terms of the license.

Would the validity or effect of such an instrument be questioned by the appellee, if executed by persons claiming regularly under the laws of New York?

The license must be understood to be what it purports to
be, a legislative authority to the steam boat Bellona "to be employed in carrying on the coasting trade for one year from its
date."

It has been denied that these words authorize a voyage from
New Jersey to New York. It is true that no ports are specified;
but it is equally true that the words used are perfectly intelligible, and do confer such authority as unquestionably as if the
ports had been mentioned. The coasting trade is a term well
understood. The law has defined it; and all know its meaning
perfectly. The act describes, with great minuteness, the various
operations of a vessel engaged in it; and it cannot, we think, be
doubted, that a voyage from New Jersey to New York is one of
those operations.

Notwithstanding the decided language of the license, it has
also been maintained, that it gives no right to trade, and that
its sole purpose is to confer the American character.

The answer given to this argument, that the American character is conferred by the enrolment, and not by the license, is,
we think, founded too clearly in the words of the law, to require the support of any additional observations. The enrolment of vessels designed for the coasting trade, corresponds
precisely with the registration of vessels designed for the foreign trade, and requires every circumstance which can constitute the American character. The licence can be granted only
to vessels already enrolled, if they be of the burthen of twenty
tons, and upwards; and requires no circumstance essential to
the American character. The object of the license, then, cannot
be to ascertain the character of the vessel, but to do what it
professes to do—that is, to give permission to a vessel already
proved by her enrolment to be American, to carry on the
coasting trade.

But, if the license be a permit to carry on the coasting trade,
the appellee denies that these boats were engaged in that
trade, or that the decree under consideration has restrained
them from prosecuting it. The boats of the appellant were, we

are told, employed in the transportation of passengers; and this is no part of that commerce which Congress may regulate.

If, as our whole course of legislation on this subject shows, the power of Congress has been universally understood in America, to comprehend navigation, it is a very persuasive, if not a conclusive argument, to prove that the construction is correct; and, if it be correct, no clear distinction is perceived between the power to regulate vessels employed in transporting men for hire, and property for hire. The subject is transferred to Congress and no exception to the grant can be admitted, which is not proved by the words or the nature of the thing. A coasting vessel employed in the transportation of passengers, is as much a portion of the American marine, as one employed in the transportation of a cargo: and no reason is perceived why such vessel should be withdrawn from the regulating power of that government which has been thought best fitted for the purpose generally. The provisions of the law respecting native seamen, and respecting ownership, are as applicable to vessels carrying men, as to vessels carrying manufactures; and no reason is perceived why the power over the subject should not be placed in the same hands. The argument urged at the bar, rests on the foundation that the power of Congress does not extend to navigation, as a branch of commerce; and can only be applied to that subject incidentally and occasionally. But if that foundation be removed, we must show some plain intelligible distinction, supported by the constitution, or by reason, for discriminating between the power of Congress over vessels employed in navigating the same seas. We can perceive no such distinction.

If we refer to the constitution, the inference to be drawn from it is rather against the distinction. The section which restrains Congress from prohibiting the migration or importation of such persons as any of the States may think proper to admit, until the year 1808, has always been considered as an exception from the power to regulate commerce, and certainly seems to class migration with importation. Migration applies as appropriately to voluntary, as importation does to involuntary, arrivals; and, so far as an exception from a power proves its existence, this section proves that the power to regulate commerce applies equally to the regulation of vessels employed in transporting men who pass from place to place voluntarily, and to those who pass involuntarily.

If the power reside in Congress, as a portion of the general grant to regulate commerce, then acts applying that power to vessels generally, must be construed as comprehending all vessels. If none appear to be excluded by the language of the act, none can be excluded by construction. Vessels have always been employed to a greater or less extent in the transportation of passengers, and have never been supposed to be, on that account, withdrawn from the control or protection of Congress. Packets which ply along the coast, as well as those which make voyages between Europe and America, consider the transportation of passengers as an important part of their business. Yet, it has never been suspected that the general laws of navigation did not apply to them.

The duty act, sections 23 and 46, contains provisions respecting passengers, and shows that vessels which transport them, have the same rights and must perform the same duties, with other vessels. They are governed by the general laws of navigation.

In the progress of things, this seems to have grown into a particular employment, and to have attracted the particular attention of government. Congress was no longer satisfied with comprehending vessels engaged specially in this business within those provisions which were intended for vessels generally, and, on the 2d of March, 1819, passed "An act regulating passenger ships and vessels." This wise and humane law provides for the safety and comfort of passengers, and for the communication of every thing concerning them, which may interest the Government, to the Department of State, but makes no provision concerning the entry of the vessel, or her conduct in the waters of the United States. This, we think, shows conclusively the sense of Congress, (if, indeed, any evidence to that point could be required,) that the pre-existing regulations comprehended passenger ships, among others; and, in prescribing the same duties, the Legislature must have considered them as possessing the same rights.

If, then, it were even true, that the Bellona and the Stoudinger were employed exclusively in the conveyance of passengers between New York and New Jersey, it would not follow, that this occupation did not constitute a part of the coasting trade of the United States, and was not protected by the license annexed to the answer. But we cannot perceive how the occupation of these vessels can be drawn into question, in the case before the court. The laws of New York, which grant the exclusive privilege set up by the appellee, take no notice of the employment of vessels, and relate only to the principle by which they are propelled. Those laws do not inquire, whether vessels are engaged in transporting men or merchandise, but whether they are moved by steam or wind. If by the former, the waters of New York are closed against them, though their cargoes be dutiable goods, which the laws of the United States permit them to enter and deliver in New York. If by the latter, those waters are free to them, though they should carry passengers only. In conformity with the law, is the bill of the plaintiff in the state court. The bill does not complain that the Bellona and the Stoudinger carry passengers, but that they are moved by steam. This is the injury of which he complains, and is the sole injury against the continuance of which he asks relief. The bill does not even allege, specially, that those vessels were employed in the transportation of passengers, but says, generally, that they were employed "in the transportation of passengers, or otherwise." The answer avers, only, that they were employed in the coasting trade, and insists on the right to carry on any trade authorized by the license. No testimony is taken, and the writ of injunction and decree restrain these licensed vessels, not from carrying passengers, but from being moved through the waters of New York by steam, for any purpose whatever.

The questions, then, whether the conveyance of passengers be a part of the coasting trade, and whether a vessel can be protected in that occupation by a coasting license, are not, and cannot be, raised in this case. The real and sole question seems to be, whether a steam machine, in actual use, deprives a vessel of the privileges conferred by a license.

In considering this question, the first idea which presents itself, is, that the laws of Congress for the regulation of commerce, do not look to the principle by which vessels are moved. That subject is left entirely to individual discretion; and, in that vast and complex system of legislative enactment concerning it, which embraces every thing that the Legislature thought it necessary to notice, there is not, we believe, one word respecting the peculiar principle by which vessels are propelled through the water, except what may be found in a single act, granting a particular privilege to steam boats. With this exception, every act, either prescribing duties, or granting privileges, applies to every vessel, whether navigated by the instrumentality of wind or fire, or sails or machinery. The whole weight of proof, then, is thrown upon him who would introduce a distinction to which the words of the law give no countenance.

If a real difference could be admitted to exist between vessels carrying passengers, and others, it has already been observed, that there is no fact in this case which can bring up that question. And, if the occupation of steam boats be a matter of such general notoriety, that the Court may be presumed to know it, although not specially informed by the record, then we deny that the transportation of passengers is their exclusive occupation. It is a matter of general history, that, in our Western waters, their principal employment is the transportation of merchandise; and all know that, in the waters of the Atlantic they are frequently so employed.

But all inquiry into this subject seems to the Court to be put completely at rest, by the act already mentioned, entitled "An act for the enrolling and licensing of steam boats."

This act authorizes a steam boat employed, or intended to be employed, only in a river or bay of the United States, owned wholly or in part by an alien, resident within the United States, to be enrolled and licensed as if the same belonged to a citizen of the United States.

This act demonstrates the opinion of Congress, that steam boats may be enrolled and licensed, in common with vessels using sails. They are, of course, entitled to the same privileges, and can no more be restrained from navigating waters and entering ports which are free to such vessels, than if they were wafted on their voyage by the winds, instead of being propelled by the agency of fire. The one element may be as legitimately used as the other, for every commercial purpose authorized by the laws of the Union, and the act of a State, inhibiting the use of either, to any vessel having a license under the act of Congress, comes, we think, in direct collision with that act.

As this decides the cause, it is unnecessary to enter into an examination of that part of the constitution which empowers Congress to promote the progress of science and the useful arts.

The Court is aware that, in stating the train of reasoning by which we have been conducted to this result, much time has been consumed in the attempt to demonstrate propositions which may have been thought axioms. It is felt that the tediousness inseparable from the endeavour to prove that which is already clear, is imputable to a considerable part of this opinion. But it was unavoidable. The conclusion to which we have come, depends on a chain of principles which it was necessary to preserve unbroken; and, although some of them were thought nearly self-evident, the magnitude of the question, the weight of character belonging to those from whose judgment we dissent, and the argument at the bar, demanded that we should assume nothing.

Powerful and ingenious minds, taking, as postulates, that the powers expressly granted to the Government of the Union, are to be contracted by construction into the narrowest possible compass, and that the original powers of the States are retained, if any possible construction will retain them, may, by a course of well-digested, but refined and metaphysical reasoning, founded on these premises, explain away the constitution of our country, and leave it, a magnificent structure, indeed, to look at, but totally unfit for use. They may so entangle and perplex the understanding, as to obscure principles which were before thought quite plain, and induce doubts where, if the mind were to pursue its own course, none would be perceived. In such a case, it is peculiarly necessary to recur to safe and fundamental principles, to sustain those principles, and, when sustained, to make them the test of the arguments to be examined.

Thomas Gibbons

v

Aaron Ogden

This cause came on to be heard on the transcript of the record of the court For the trial of Impeachments, and correction of Errors of the state of New York and was argued by counsel, on consideration whereof this court is of opinion that the several licenses to the steamboats The Stoudinger and The Bellona to carry on the coasting trade which are setup by the appellant Thomas Gibbons in his answer to the bill of the Appellee Aaron Ogden filed in the court of chancery for the state of New York which were granted under an act of Congress passed in pursuance of the constitution of the United States gave full authority to those vessels to navigate the waters of the United States by steam or otherwise for the purpose of carrying on the coasting trade any law of the state of New York to the contrary notwithstanding; and that so much of the several laws of the state of New York as prohibits vessels licensed according to the laws of the United States from navigating the waters of New York by means of fire or steam is repugnant to the constitution and void. This court is therefore of opinion that the decree of the court of the state of New York For the trial of Impeachments and the correction of Errors, affirming the decree of the chancellor of that state which perpetually injoins the said Thomas Gibbons the appellant from navigating the waters of the state of New York with the steam boats the Stoudinger and the Bellona by steam or fire is erroneous and ought to be reversed and the same is hereby reversed and annulled. And this court doth farther direct order and decree that the bill of the said Aaron Ogden be dismissed and the same is hereby dismissed accordingly.

March 2, 1824

"HEAVEN BLESS YOU MY DEAREST"

To Mary W. Marshall

My dearest Polly   Washington March 23d.
The time now approaches when I shall again see my beloved wife whom I hope to meet in tolerable health and spirits. I shall reach Richmond in the steamboat which comes up on friday night but suppose I shall not be at home till saturday morning. I imagine the boat will not be up before nine Oclock at night in which case I shall remain in it all night. If I do not come up till it is too late to come home I wish you would direct Oby to come down to Rockets very early in order to carry home my portmanteau.

I have not the use of my arm sufficiently to put it into the sleeves of my coat, but I am entirely free from pain.

I was very much surprized at the arrival of John and Elizabeth last tuesday evening. They came by this place in their way to Baltimore, in consequence of the Baltimore boat being stopped for repairs. They proceeded on wednesday in the stage & on thursday John returned on his way to Fauquier. All was well.

I am just called in to conference. Heaven bless you my dearest Polly, I am your ever affectionate

1824

Preface to
A History of the Colonies

So large a portion of the life of General Washington was devoted to the public, so elevated and important were the stations which he filled, that the history of his life is, at the same time, the history of his nation.

The part he took, while commander in chief, in the civil as well as military affairs of the United States, was so considerable, that few events of general interest occurred, which were not, in some degree, influenced by him. A detail of the transactions in which he was either immediately or remotely concerned, would comprehend so great a part of those which belong to general history, that the entire exclusion of the few in which he bore no part, while it would scarcely give to the work more of the peculiar character of biography, would expose it to the charge of being an incomplete history of the times.

His administration of the government while President of the United States, cannot be well understood without a full knowledge of the political measures of the day, and of the motives by which his own conduct was regulated.

These considerations appeared to require that his biography should present a general historical view of the transactions of the time, as well as a particular narrative of the part performed by himself.

Our ideas of America, of the character of our revolution, of those who engaged in it, and of the struggles by which it was accomplished, would be imperfect without some knowledge of our colonial history. No work had been published when this was undertaken, from which that knowledge could be collected. To have taken up the history of the United States when the command of the army was conferred on General Washington, would have been to introduce the reader abruptly into the midst of scenes and transactions, with the causes of which, and with the actors in them, he would naturally wish to be intimately acquainted. This was the apology of the author for the introductory volume to the Life of General Washington. Had the essays since written towards a general history of the English colonies been then in possession of the public, this volume would not have appeared. But, although they might have prevented its appearance, they ought not to prevent its being corrected and offered to the public in a form less exceptionable than that which it originally bore. From the extreme, I may add unpardonable, precipitation with which it was hurried to the press, many errors were overlooked which, on a perusal of the book, were as apparent to the author as to others. He was desirous of correcting these errors, and of making the work more worthy of the public to which it was offered, as well as more satisfactory to himself. For this purpose he has given it, since the impressions under which it was compiled have worn off, more than one attentive reading; has made several alterations in the language; and has expunged much of the less essential matter with which the narrative was burthened. He dares not flatter himself that he has succeeded completely in his attempt to entitle this work to the approbation of the literary public of America; but hopes that its claims to that approbation are stronger than in its original form.

Believing that motives no longer exist for connecting the History of the English Colonies in North America with the Life of Washington, the author has obtained the permission of the proprietor of the copy-right to separate the Introduction from the other volumes, and to publish it as a distinct work.

1824

THE IMPORTANCE OF FEMALE EDUCATION

To Thomas W. White

Sir   Richmond Novr. 29th. 1824

I have received the volume of Mr. Garnetts lectures with which you favored me, and have devoted the first liesure time I could well spare to its perusal. I had read this little work when first published, and was so well pleased with it as to place it in the hands of several of my young friends for whose improvement I was particularly sollicitous.

The subject is, in my opinion of the deepest interest. I have always believed that national character, as well as happiness, depends more on the female part of society than is generally imagined. Precepts from the lips of a beloved mother, inculcated in the amiable, graceful, and affectionate manner which belongs to the parent and the sex, sink deep in the heart, and make an impression which is seldom entirely effaced. These impressions have an influence on character which may contribute greatly to the happiness or misery, the eminence or insignificancy of the individual.

If the agency of the mother in forming the character of her children is, in truth, so considerable as I think it, if she does so much towards making her son what she would wish him to be, and her daughter to resemble herself, how essential is it that she should be fitted for the beneficial performance of these essential duties.

To accomplish this beneficial purpose is the object of Mr. Garnetts lectures; and he has done much towards its attainment. His precepts appear to be drawn from deep and accurate observation of human life and manners, and to be admirably well calculated to improve the understanding, and the heart. They form a sure and safe foundation for female character, and contain rules of conduct which cannot be too well considered or too generally applied. They are communicated too with a sprightliness of style and agreeableness of manner which cannot fail to ensure a favorable reception to the instruction they convey. I am Sir very respectfully, Your obedt

REMEMBERING A BALL

To Mary W. Marshall

My dearest Polly   Washington Feby. 8th. 1825

I reached this place yesterday & paid our accustomed visit to the President whom I found in good health & looking quite chearful. I am now sitting by a good fire in an excellent room, the same I occupied last year, scribling to my beloved wife. Neither Judge Johnson nor Story has arrived, and our brother Todd I am told is so very unwell that we have reason to fear we shall never see him again. Story too has been sick, but is on the way and we look for him today.

I have never found the roads so good before in the winter season. I reached Alexandria on saturday evening before five, and have never before got in by daylight, seldom earlier than nine, and once or twice as late as eleven. I rejoiced that I had not taken the steamboat.

I have seldom gone counter to your advice without repenting it; but as I came on friday & saturday, hugging myself up in my warm cloak, I could not help congratulating myself on the comfort I enjoyed compared to the suffering I should have felt had I come without it.

I rode from Hanover court house to Fredericksburg with a

Mrs. Stone, formerly Miss Booth, a niece of Mrs. Dandridge. She told me that the first ball at which she had ever been was in Richmond when she accompanied her aunt in Mrs. Amblers coach, and that both you and myself were in the same carriage, then unmarried. She said she had never seen me since, and that when I got into the stage she remembered the evening and all she saw as perfectly as if it had been yesterday.

I dined on sunday with my Aunt Keith. She was at first very much affected, but became chearful in a few minutes. I was visited on Saturday night by my nephew William Marshall, son of my brother Lewis, who is studying divinity at the Theological school in Alexandria. He is a very promising and a remarkably fine looking young man. He dined at my Aunt Keiths on sunday, & I was very much pleased with him.

I cannot help hoping that Mr. Picket has been able to fill the ice house on friday & saturday. If those two days have passed away without accomplishing the object I fear all the [   ] is over & that we must look else wher [   ] unless he should fill it with a cargo [   ] north. He spoke of this bef[   ]. Farewell my dearest Polly

"THE RIGHT SIDE OF SEVENTY"

To Mary W. Marshall

My dearest Polly   Washington Feb. 12th. 26
    I am settled down in my old habits as regularly as if I was still on the right side of seventy. I get up as early as ever, take my walk of three miles by seven, think of you, & then set down to business. I have had a pretty severe attack of the influenza, & the cough & confusion in the head still continue, though the soar throat has left me, & the inflammation of the stomack or lungs has entirely subsided. If you had no other reason to know how old I am you would be reminded of it by my dwelling thus on a trifling indisposition. Our brother Story just arrived today while we were at dinner. He was stopped a week at Philadelphia by the influenza which he has had pretty nearly as bad as myself. It only induced me to push forward &

not stay a day as usual in Alexandria in order to visit my old and good aunt.

I have not heard a word from Fauquier since leaving Richmond but expect soon to receive a letter from Tom as I have written to inform him that you will advance the 200$ he wants; or rather that l read your wishes so plainly that I had determined to furnish them myself.

I have received three invitations for evening parties this week. See how gay Washington is & how much Miss Jones has lost by her journey to Richmond. If you were here and would go with me I am not sure that my influenza or court business would keep me constantly within doors, but as it is I do not feast my eyes with gazing at the numerous belles who flock to this place during the winters. If Lucy Fisher could persuade [   ] to become a candidate for Congress, and persuade the people to elect him, she might come and have a charming time of it.

Farewell my dearest Polly. However I may jest about trifles I am always sincere and in earnest when I say that I am most affectionately, Your

"THOSE WHO FOLLOW US"

To Timothy Pickering

Dear Sir   Washington March 20th. 26

I had the pleasure of receiving your letters of the 17th & 23d. of Jany. by Mr. Story & congratulate you very sincerely on the vigorous health which your letters manifest. It is consoling to think that we may look forward to very advanced life with the hope of preserving with health & temperance so large a share of mental & bodily strength as to make life still desirable & agreeable.

I concur with you in thinking that nothing portends more calamity & mischief to the Southern states than their slave population; Yet they seem to cherish the evil and to view with immovable prejudice & dislike every thing which may tend to diminish it. I do not wonder that they should resist any attempt should one be made to interfere with the rights of property, but they have a feverish jealousy of measures which may do good without the hazard of harm that is I think very unwise.

All America I believe will join you in opinion respecting the late intemperate course of the Governour of Georgia. I very much fear that the embarassment into which the purchase from the Creeks has thrown us will be prolonged by a rejection of the last treaty.

You are undoubtedly right in supposing Mr. Giles to be a discontented man. He was unquestionably a very powerful debater on the floor of either branch of the legislature & has seen men placed before him by the party which he has served very effectually to whom he gave precedence very reluctantly. He fell out with Virginia too but seems now determined to write himself again into favour. His health has been for some years very bad, but he is now getting rather better and would be very glad to come forward once more in political life. He is undoubtedly desirous of recommencing his career as a public man. He may probably be successful as he undoubtedly possesses & is beleived to possess considerable talents, and avows opinions which are very popular in Virginia.

Your recollection of events which took place for the last twenty years is very accurate and you replace in my memory many things which I had almost forgotten. There are not many who retain them as fresh as you do, and I am persuaded that they will soon be entirely lost. Those who follow us will know very little of the real transactions of our day, and will have very untrue impressions respecting men & things. Such is the lot of humanity.

Farewell. With sincere wishes for your health & happiness and with great and respectful esteem, I am dear Sir Your Obedt

Memorandum by Jared Sparks on a Conversation with Marshall

Called on Chief Justice Marshall; entered his yard through a broken wooden gate, fastened by a leather strap and opened with some difficulty, rang, and an old lady came to the door. I asked if Judge Marshall was at home. "No," said she, "he is not in the house; he may be in the office," and pointed to a small brick building in one corner of the yard. I knocked at the door, and it was opened by a tall, venerable-looking man, dressed with extreme plainness, and having an air of affability in his manners. I introduced myself as the person who had just received a letter from him concerning General Washington's letters, and he immediately entered into conversation on that subject. He appeared to think favorably of my project, but intimated that all the papers were entirely at the disposal of Judge Washington. He said that he had read with care all General Washington's letters in the copies left by him, and intimated that a selection only could with propriety be printed, as there was in many of them a repetition, not only of ideas, but of language. This was a necessary consequence of his writing to so many persons on the same subjects, and nearly at the same time. He spoke to me of the history of Virginia; said Stith's History and Beverly's were of the highest authority, and might be relied on. Of Burk he only remarked that the author was fond of indulging his imagination, "but," he added in a good-natured way, "there is no harm in a little ornament, I suppose." He neither censured nor commended the work. He conversed some time on what he calls an error in the history of Virginia as generally received. Robertson states that Virginia recognized King Charles II. before he was proclaimed in England. Henning, it seems, in his voluminous compilation of Virginia statutes, has denied the fact. Judge Marshall says that Henning is right in stating that no such act was ever passed formally by the legislature or assembly of the colony, but yet he is mistaken in affirming that such was not the state of feeling among the leading people. Beverly affirms it was, and as he was connected with the leading families of the colony, and acquainted with the circumstances, his testimony ought to be re-

ceived implicitly. Such and other things were the topics of conversation, till the short hour of a ceremonious visit had run
out. I retired much pleased with the urbanity and kindly manners of the Chief Justice. There is consistency in all things
about him, his house, grounds, office, himself, bear marks of a
primitive simplicity and plainness rarely to be seen combined.

April 1, 1826

A LIBEL CASE

To Joseph Story

My dear Sir   Richmond May 31st. 1826
  I send you by the General Jackson (because the name must
render every part of its cargo valuable in your estimation) a
small cask of hams which I hope you will find tolerably good in
themselves. They are packed in hiccory ashes; and our Ladies,
who are skilful in the management of their Hams, say that they
must be taken out on their arrival & put in a cool dry place as
the hiccory ashes may probably become lye on the voyage. They
will be deposited with Henry Hovey & Co No. 23 Central
Wharf, Boston.
  I am now engaged in my circuit duties at this place, & shall
finish today an issue out of chancery to try the legitimacy of
two children of a woman residing in North Carolina in the free
indulgence of her natural appetites, whose husband resided in
Virginia with another woman whom he married between the
two births. Our best lawyers are engaged in it, and yesterday
was employed by Stannard in continuation & Johnson. Wickham closes today. Leigh occupied so much of the preceding
day as remained after reading the testimony.
  I counted on a longer term in North Carolina than I actually
had. A cause was for trial between two New England clergymen
in which one had charged the other with very serious crimes;
and on being sued, had pleaded that the words written, for it is
a libel, were true. They have taken the depositions of almost all
New England; & I am told by the lawyers that the testimony is
very contradictory. All was ready; but the combatants seemed

to fear each other, and the cause was continued in the hope that one more effort might produce a reference, if not a compromise. All their former attempts had failed. Notwithstanding my knowledge of the persevering firmness with which gentlemen of the sacred profession pursue their objects, I was surprized at this—obstinacy may I call it—till I was informed that it was Presbyterian vs. Unitarian.

I find the bill for multiplying our numbers has failed, although a majority of both houses was in its favour. It will probably pass next session. The chance of such a bill is better the second session of any Congress than the first. I hope the seven judges will convene at our next term & that the constitutional questions depending before us may be argued and decided. I am glad that our brother Tremble has passed the senate *Maugre* Mr. Rowan.

Our friend & brother Washington seems to have been involved by his respect for the Sabbath in a very unpleasant affair with about thirty members of Congress. I am truely sorry for this casualty. The circumstance I presume could not have occurred had his previous notice & letter to the Captain of the Steamboat been communicated to them.

Edward, who has run away from Cambridge, left us yesterday on an expedition to the mountains, to take possession of his farm & acquire, if he can, a different science from what is taught at college. A drought such as has never been known at this season has affected our crops considerably, but we shall make too much for the demand unless our northern brethren will double their number of manufacturers, or double their appetites. Farewell. I am my dear Sir your affectionate

ANTICIPATING A SON'S ENGAGEMENT

To Samuel Fay

Dear Sir   Richmond Septr. 15th. 1826
I received a letter from my son Edward, soon after his last arrival in Cambridge, informing me that his addresses to your daughter had been favorably received by her, and that he had

been so fortunate as to obtain the approbation of her parents. A second letter written immediately on his return to Virginia repeats this information.

I had feared that the almost entire separation of miss Fay from her natural friends and all the companions of her youth, wou'd be too great a sacrifice to be made; and, if made, would produce permanent unhappiness. That she has been induced to make it chearfully is the best proof of that sincere affection which is I am persuaded, when mutual, the never failing source of felicity to those who are united under its influence.

My sons situation is far from being splendid, but I hope to make it comfortable with proper exertions on his part; and though he will reside in the country, the neighborhood is far from being ineligible. His wife must be an economist, & will I trust find her truest happiness at home!

I write to assure you of the satisfaction with which I look forward to my sons connexion with a young lady whom he describes as entitled to the strongest sentiments of love and esteem; and that she will be received by his mother and myself as our own daughter, and with that parental affection which is the best though an inadequate substitute for the deep loss she will sustain in parting from Mrs. Fay & yourself. I can promise too for my other sons in the midst of whom Edward will be settled, and for their wives, that she will receive the most affectionate and cordial welcome.

Have the goodness to present Mrs. Marshall's compliments & my own to Mrs. Fay & our future daughter, and to believe that I am with great respect, your obedt

APOLOGIZING FOR A MISUNDERSTANDING

To Samuel Fay

Dear Sir   Richmond Oct. 15th. 1826

Your letter reached me yesterday. As it conveys a positive and deliberate rejection of my son it would of course terminate our correspondence did I not feel that my letter requires an apology.

It must have appeared very strange to you sir that, while your objections to a connexion between our families remained immoveable, I should treat it—[   ] to yourself, as an affair already arranged. I entreat you to believe that I am incapable of knowingly committing such an impropriety, and that I wrote under a total misunderstanding of the actual state of things. I have not seen Edward since May; but his letters to his mother & myself from Cambridge, and one from Alexandria on his return, state his reception with delight, and dwell on his expected union with the lady of his choice, in the language of a young man who sees nothing but felicity before him. He did not indeed say in terms that he had conversed with you and received expressly your consent to his marriage with your daughter, but every thing he said implied that all obstacles were removed, and that the event itself was certain, though the time was not fixed. I could not suppose it possible that he had left Cambridge under these impressions without full explanations with the Father of the lady he was addressing. Not doubting that you had viewed the attachment, which I then supposed to be mutual, between our children, with as much indulgence as myself, my heart told me that, as no direct communication had ever been made by me, it could not be displeasing to a Father totally unacquainted with the connexions of the gentleman who was to marry his daughter, and to remove her to a great distance from her friends, to be assured that she would be received with cordial & tender affection by the family into which she was about to enter.

I hope Edward has received notice of your decision, and that it is made with the approbation of Mrs. & Miss Fay. It is kindness to awaken him as soon as possible from the dream of happiness in which he has been too long indulging.

I am far from imputing blame to you or to Mrs. Fay for this misapprehension into which I have been led or for the pain my son will experience at the disappointment of his hopes. That tender solicitude which Parents must feel for their daughter gives them a right to reject the addresses of any man to whom they are unwilling to entrust her, and it is their duty to exercise this right whenever they believe its exercise necessary to her happiness. It is for themselves alone to judge of the correctness of the reasoning by which their minds are led to the conclusion; it is enough for others to know that such is their conclusion. But your objections have intrinsic weight and will be respected independent of their authority. They are such as I anticipated when first informed by my son that he meditated addressing a young lady in Cambridge. I felt the immense sacrifice she would make in leaving her friends to come with him to a land of strangers, and was convinced that misery would follow their marriage unless warded off by deep rooted love for the person for whom it was made. Under this conviction, when I stated the repinings which this vast change of situation would probably produce, I required Edward should he prosecute his intentions, to disclose his real circumstances that the decision of the family might be made under no mistaken view of the situation in which their daughter would be placed. I wished it to be known that she would live in the country, not even in the neighbourhood of a town, and upon a farm which required industry & economy in its master.

It is not an empty compliment when I say that I am grieved to hear of the feeble state of health in which Miss Fay finds herself. I have accustomed myself to take an interest in what concerns her which I cannot instantly dismiss, and shall enquire respecting her health with the sincere wish to hear that the threatening and obstinate symptoms of which you speak have yielded to medicine & exercise. With compliments to Mrs. Fay and With great respect for yourself, I am Sir your Obedt

READING JANE AUSTEN

To Joseph Story

My Dear Sir: Richmond, November 26th, 1826.
I have deferred thanking you for the copy of your Discourse before the Society of Phi Beta Kappa, until there was some probability that my letter might find you at Salem. . . .

But it is time to return to your discourse. I have read it with real pleasure, and am particularly gratified with your eulogy on the ladies. It is matter of great satisfaction to me to find another Judge, who, though not as old as myself, thinks justly of the fair sex, and commits his sentiments to print. I was a little mortified, however, to find that you had not admitted the name of Miss Austen into your list of favorites. I had just finished reading her novels when I received your discourse, and was so much pleased with them that I looked in it for her name, and was rather disappointed at not finding it. Her flights are not lofty, she does not soar on eagle's wings, but she is pleasing, interesting, equable, and yet amusing. I count on your making some apology for this omission. . . . Farewell. With esteem and affection, I am yours,

Opinion in Ogden v. Saunders

I<small>T</small> is well known that the Court has been divided in opinion on this case. Three Judges, Mr. Justice D<small>UVALL</small>, Mr. Justice S<small>TORY</small>, and myself, do not concur in the judgment which has been pronounced. We have taken a different view of the very interesting question which has been discussed with so much talent, as well as labour, at the bar, and I am directed to state the course of reasoning on which we have formed the opinion that the discharge pleaded by the defendant is no bar to the action.

The single question for consideration, is, whether the act of the State of New-York is consistent with or repugnant to the constitution of the United States?

This Court has so often expressed the sentiments of profound and respectful reverence with which it approaches questions of this character, as to make it unnecessary now to say more than that, if it be right that the power of preserving the constitution from legislative infraction, should reside any where, it cannot be wrong, it must be right, that those on whom the delicate and important duty is conferred should perform it according to their best judgment.

Much, too, has been said concerning the principles of construction which ought to be applied to the constitution of the United States.

On this subject, also, the Court has taken such frequent occasion to declare its opinion, as to make it unnecessary, at least, to enter again into an elaborate discussion of it. To say that the intention of the instrument must prevail; that this intention must be collected from its words; that its words are to be understood in that sense in which they are generally used by those for whom the instrument was intended; that its provisions are neither to be restricted into insignificance, nor extended to objects not comprehended in them, nor contemplated by its framers—is to repeat what has been already said more at large, and is all that can be necessary.

As preliminary to a more particular investigation of the clause in the constitution, on which the case now under consideration is supposed to depend, it may be proper to inquire how far it is affected by the former decisions of this Court.

In *Sturges* v. *Crowninshield*, it was determined, that an act which discharged the debtor from a contract entered into previous to its passage, was repugnant to the constitution. The reasoning which conducted the Court to that conclusion might, perhaps, conduct it farther; and with that reasoning, (for myself alone this expression is used,) I have never yet seen cause to be dissatisfied. But that decision is not supposed to be a precedent for *Ogden* v. *Saunders*, because the two cases differ from each other in a material fact; and it is a general rule, expressly recognised by the Court in *Sturges* v. *Crowninshield*, that the positive authority of a decision is co-extensive only with the facts on which it is made. In *Sturges* v. *Crowninshield*, the law acted on a contract which was made before its passage; in this case, the contract was entered into after the passage of the law.

In *M'Neil* v. *M'Millan*, the contract, though subsequent to the passage of the act, was made in a different State, by persons residing in that State, and, consequently, without any view to the law, the benefit of which was claimed by the debtor.

The *Farmers' and Mechanics' Bank of Pennsylvania* v. *Smith* differed from *Sturges* v. *Crowninshield* only in this, that the plaintiff and defendant were both residents of the State in which the law was enacted, and in which it was applied. The Court was of opinion that this difference was unimportant.

It has then been decided, that an act which discharges the debtor from pre-existing contracts is void; and that an act which operates on future contracts is inapplicable to a contract made in a different State, at whatever time it may have been entered into.

Neither of these decisions comprehends the question now presented to the Court. It is, consequently, open for discussion.

The provision of the constitution is, that "no State shall pass any law" "impairing the obligation of contracts." The plaintiff in error contends that this provision inhibits the passage of retrospective laws only—of such as act on contracts in existence at their passage. The defendant in error maintains that it comprehends all future laws, whether prospective or retrospective, and withdraws every contract from State legislation, the obligation of which has become complete.

That there is an essential difference in principle between

laws which act on past, and those which act on future contracts; that those of the first description can seldom be justified, while those of the last are proper subjects of ordinary legislative discretion, must be admitted. A constitutional restriction, therefore, on the power to pass laws of the one class, may very well consist with entire legislative freedom respecting those of the other. Yet, when we consider the nature of our Union; that it is intended to make us, in a great measure, one people, as to commercial objects; that, so far as respects the intercommunication of individuals, the lines of separation between States are, in many respects, obliterated; it would not be matter of surprise, if, on the delicate subject of contracts once formed, the interference of State legislation should he greatly abridged, or entirely forbidden. In the nature of the provision, then, there seems to be nothing which ought to influence our construction of the words; and, in making that construction, the whole clause, which consists of a single sentence, is to be taken together, and the intention is to be collected from the whole.

The first paragraph of the tenth section of the first article, which comprehends the provision under consideration, contains an enumeration of those cases in which the action of the State legislature is entirely prohibited. The second enumerates those in which the prohibition is modified. The first paragraph, consisting of total prohibitions, comprehends two classes of powers. Those of the first are political and general in their nature, being an exercise of sovereignty without affecting the rights of individuals. These are, the powers "to enter into any treaty, alliance, or confederation; grant letters of marque or reprisal, coin money, emit bills of credit."

The second class of prohibited laws comprehends those whose operation consists in their action on individuals. These are, laws which make any thing but gold and silver coin a tender in payment of debts, bills of attainder, *ex post facto* laws, or laws impairing the obligation of contracts, or which grant any title of nobility.

In all these cases, whether the thing prohibited be the exercise of mere political power, or legislative action on individuals, the prohibition is complete and total. There is no exception from it. Legislation of every description is comprehended within it. A State is as entirely forbidden to pass laws impairing the obligation of contracts, as to make treaties, or coin money. The question recurs, what is a law impairing the obligation of contracts?

In solving this question, all the acumen which controversy can give to the human mind, has been employed in scanning the whole sentence, and every word of it. Arguments have been drawn from the context, and from the particular terms in which the prohibition is expressed, for the purpose, on the one part, of showing its application to all laws which act upon contracts, whether prospectively or retrospectively; and, on the other, of limiting it to laws which act on contracts previously formed.

The first impression which the words make on the mind, would probably be, that the prohibition was intended to be general. A contract is commonly understood to be the agreement of the parties; and, if it be not illegal, to bind them to the extent of their stipulations. It requires reflection, it requires some intellectual effort, to efface this impression, and to come to the conclusion, that the words contract and obligation, as used in the constitution, are not used in this sense. If, however, the result of this mental effort, fairly made, be the correction of this impression, it ought to be corrected.

So much of this prohibition as restrains the power of the States to punish offenders in criminal cases, the prohibition to pass bills of attainder and *ex post facto* laws, is, in its very terms, confined to pre-existing cases. A bill of attainder can be only for crimes already committed; and a law is not *ex post facto*, unless it looks back to an act done before its passage. Language is incapable of expressing, in plainer terms, that the mind of the Convention was directed to retroactive legislation. The thing forbidden is retroaction. But that part of the clause which relates to the civil transactions of individuals, is expressed in more general terms; in terms which comprehend, in their ordinary signification, cases which occur after, as well as those which occur before, the passage of the act. It forbids a State to make any thing but gold and silver coin a tender in payment of debts, or to pass any law impairing the obligation of contracts. These prohibitions relate to kindred subjects. They contemplate legislative interference with private rights, and restrain that interference. In construing that part of the clause which respects tender laws, a distinction has never been attempted between debts existing at the time the law may be passed, and debts afterwards created. The prohibition has been considered as total; and yet the difference in principle between making property a tender in payment of debts, contracted after the passage of the act, and discharging those debts without payment, or by the surrender of property, between an absolute right to tender in payment, and a contingent right to tender in payment, or in discharge of the debt, is not clearly discernible. Nor is the difference in language so obvious, as to denote plainly a difference of intention in the framers of the instrument. "No State shall make any thing but gold and silver coin a tender in payment of debts." Does the word "debts" mean, generally, those due when the law applies to the case, or is it limited to debts due at the passage of the act? The same train of reasoning which would confine the subsequent words to contracts existing at the passage of the law, would go far in confining these words to debts existing at that time. Yet, this distinction has never, we believe, occurred to any person. How soon it may occur is not for us to determine. We think it would, unquestionably, defeat the object of the clause.

The counsel for the plaintiff insist, that the word "impairing," in the present tense, limits the signification of the provision to the operation of the act at the time of its passage; that no law can be accurately said to impair the obligation of contracts, unless the contracts exist at the time. The law cannot impair what does not exist. It cannot act on nonentities.

There might be weight in this argument, if the prohibited laws were such only as operated of themselves, and immediately on the contract. But insolvent laws are to operate on a future, contingent, unforeseen event. The time to which the word "impairing" applies, is not the time of the passage of the act, but of its action on the contract. That is, the time present in contemplation of the prohibition. The law, at its passage, has no effect whatever on the contract. Thus, if a note be given in New-York for the payment of money, and the debtor removes out of that State into Connecticut, and becomes insolvent, it is not pretended that his debt can be discharged by the law of New-York. Consequently, that law did not operate on the contract at its formation. When, then, does its operation commence? We answer, when it is applied to the contract. Then, if ever, and not till then, it acts on the contract, and becomes a law impairing its obligation. Were its constitutionality, with respect to previous contracts, to be admitted, it would not impair their obligation until an insolvency should take place, and a certificate of discharge be granted. Till these events occur, its impairing faculty is suspended. A law, then, of this description, if it derogates from the obligation of a contract, when applied to it, is, grammatically speaking, as much a law impairing that obligation, though made previous to its formation, as if made subsequently.

A question of more difficulty has been pressed with great earnestness. It is, what is the original obligation of a contract, made after the passage of such an act as the insolvent law of New-York? Is it unconditional to perform the very thing stipulated, or is the condition implied, that, in the event of insolvency, the contract shall be satisfied by the surrender of property? The original obligation, whatever that may be, must be preserved by the constitution. Any law which lessens, must impair it.

All admit, that the constitution refers to, and preserves, the legal, not the moral obligation of a contract. Obligations purely moral, are to be enforced by the operation of internal and invisible agents, not by the agency of human laws. The restraints imposed on States by the constitution, are intended for those objects which would, if not restrained, be the subject of State legislation. What, then, was the original legal obligation of the contract now under the consideration of the Court?

The plaintiff insists, that the law enters into the contract so completely as to become a constituent part of it. That it is to be construed as if it contained an express stipulation to be discharged, should the debtor become insolvent, by the surrender of all his property for the benefit of his creditors, in pursuance of the act of the legislature.

This is, unquestionably, pressing the argument very far; and the establishment of the principle leads inevitably to consequences which would affect society deeply and seriously.

Had an express condition been inserted in the contract, declaring that the debtor might be discharged from it at any time by surrendering all his property to his creditors, this condition would have bound the creditor. It would have constituted the obligation of his contract; and a legislative act annulling the condition would impair the contract. Such an act would, as is admitted by all, be unconstitutional, because it operates on pre-existing agreements. If a law authorizing debtors to discharge themselves from their debts by surrendering their property, enters into the contract, and forms a part of it, if it is equivalent to a stipulation between the parties, no repeal of the law can affect contracts made during its existence. The effort to give it that effect would impair their obligation. The counsel for the plaintiff perceive, and avow this consequence, in effect, when they contend, that to deny the operation of the law on the contract under consideration, is to impair its obligation. Are gentlemen prepared to say, that an insolvent law, once enacted, must, to a considerable extent, be permanent? That the legislature is incapable of varying it so far as respects existing contracts?

So, too, if one of the conditions of an obligation for the payment of money be, that on the insolvency of the obligor, or on any event agreed on by the parties, he should be at liberty to discharge it by the tender of all, or part of his property, no question could exist respecting the validity of the contract, or respecting its security from legislative interference. If it should be determined, that a law authorizing the same tender, on the same contingency, enters into, and forms a part of the contract, then, a tender law, though expressly forbidden, with an obvious view to its prospective, as well as retrospective operation, would, by becoming the contract of the parties, subject all contracts made after its passage to its control. If it be said, that such a law would be obviously unconstitutional and void, and, therefore, could not be a constituent part of the contract, we answer, that if the insolvent law be unconstitutional, it is equally void, and equally incapable of becoming, by mere implication, a part of the contract. The plainness of the repugnancy does not change the question. That may be very clear to one intellect, which is far from being so to another. The law now under consideration is, in the opinion of one party, clearly consistent with the constitution, and, in the opinion of the other, as clearly repugnant to it. We do not admit the correctness of that reasoning which would settle this question by introducing into the contract a stipulation not admitted by the parties.

This idea admits of being pressed still farther. If one law enters into all subsequent contracts, so does every other law which relates to the subject. A legislative act, then, declaring that all contracts should be subject to legislative control, and should be discharged as the legislature might prescribe, would become a component part of every contract, and be one of its conditions. Thus, one of the most important features in the constitution of the United States, one which the state of the times most urgently required, one on which the good and the wise reposed confidently for securing the prosperity and harmony of our citizens, would lie prostrate, and be construed into an inanimate, inoperative, unmeaning clause.

Gentlemen are struck with the enormity of this result, and deny that their principle leads to it. They distinguish, or attempt to distinguish, between the incorporation of a general law, such as has been stated, and the incorporation of a particular law, such as the insolvent law of New-York, into the contract. But will reason sustain this distinction? They say, that men cannot be supposed to agree to so indefinite an article as such a general law would be, but may well be supposed to agree to an article, reasonable in itself, and the full extent of which is understood.

But the principle contended for does not make the insertion of this new term or condition into the contract, to depend upon its reasonableness. It is inserted because the legislature has so enacted. If the enactment of the legislature becomes a condition of the contract because it is an enactment, then it is a high prerogative, indeed, to decide, that one enactment shall enter the contract, while another, proceeding from the same authority, shall be excluded from it.

The counsel for the plaintiff illustrates and supports this position by several legal principles, and by some decisions of this Court, which have been relied on as being applicable to it.

The first case put is, interest on a bond payable on demand, which does not stipulate interest. This, he says, is not a part of the remedy, but a new term in the contract.

Let the correctness of this averment be tried by the course of proceeding in such cases.

The failure to pay, according to stipulation, is a breach of the contract, and the means used to enforce it constitute the remedy which society affords the injured party. If the obligation contains a penalty, this remedy is universally so regulated that the judgment shall be entered for the penalty, to be discharged by the payment of the principal and interest. But the case on which counsel has reasoned is a single bill. In this case, the party who has broken his contract is liable for damages. The proceeding to obtain those damages is as much a part of the remedy as the proceeding to obtain the debt. They are claimed in the same declaration, and as being distinct from each other. The damages must be assessed by a jury; whereas, if interest formed a part of the debt, it would be recovered as part of it. The declaration would claim it as a part of the debt; and yet, if a suitor were to declare on such a bond as containing this new term for the payment of interest, he would not be permitted to give a bond in evidence in which this supposed term was not written. Any law regulating the proceedings of Courts on this subject, would be a law regulating the remedy.

The liability of the drawer of a bill of exchange, stands upon the same principle with every other implied contract. He has received the money of the person in whose favour the bill is drawn, and promises that it shall be returned by the drawee. If the drawee fail to pay the bill, then the promise of the drawer is broken, and for this breach of contract he is liable. The same principle applies to the endorser. His contract is not written, but his name is evidence of his promise that the bill shall be paid, and of his having received value for it. He is, in effect, a new drawer, and has made a new contract. The law does not require that this contract shall be in writing; and, in determining what evidence shall be sufficient to prove it, does not introduce new conditions not actually made by the parties. The same reasoning applies to the principle which requires notice. The original contract is not written at large. It is founded on the acts of the parties, and its extent is measured by those acts. A. draws on B. in favour of C., for value received. The bill is evidence that he has received value, and has promised that it shall be paid. He has funds in the hands of the drawer, and has a right to expect that his promise will be performed. He has, also, a right to expect notice of its non-performance, because his conduct may be materially influenced by this failure of the drawee. He ought to have notice that *his* bill is disgraced, because this notice enables him to take measures for his own security. It is reasonable that he should stipulate for this notice, and the law presumes that he did stipulate for it.

A great mass of human transactions depends upon implied contracts; upon contracts which are not written, but which grow out of the acts of the parties. In such cases, the parties are supposed to have made those stipulations, which, as honest, fair, and just men, they ought to have made. When the law assumes that they have made these stipulations, it does not vary their contract, or introduce new terms into it, but declares that certain acts, unexplained by compact, impose certain duties, and that the parties had stipulated for their performance. The difference is obvious between this and the introduction of a new condition into a contract drawn out in writing, in which the parties have expressed every thing that is to be done by either.

The usage of banks, by which days of grace are allowed on notes payable and negotiable in bank, is of the same character. Days of grace, from their very term, originate partly in convenience, and partly in the indulgence of the creditor. By the terms of the note, the debtor has to the last hour of the day on which it becomes payable, to comply with it; and it would often be inconvenient to take any steps after the close of day. It is often convenient to postpone subsequent proceedings till the next day. Usage has extended this time of grace generally to three days, and in some banks to four. This usage is made a part of the contract, not by the interference of the legislature, but by the act of the parties. The case cited from 9 *Wheat. Rep.* 581. is a note discounted in bank. In all such cases the bank receives, and the maker of the note pays, interest for the days of grace. This would be illegal and usurious, if the money was not lent for these additional days. The extent of the loan, therefore, is regulated by the act of the parties, and this part of the contract is founded on their act. Since, by contract, the maker is not liable for his note until the days of grace are expired, he has not broken his contract until they expire. The duty of giving notice to the endorser of his failure, does not rise, until the failure has taken place; and, consequently, the promise of the bank to give such notice is performed, if it be given when the event has happened.

The case of the *Bank of Columbia* v. *Oakley*, (4 *Wheat. Rep.* 235.) was one in which the legislature had given a summary remedy to the bank for a broken contract, and had placed that remedy in the hands of the bank itself. The case did not turn on the question whether the law of Maryland was introduced into the contract, but whether a party might not, by his own conduct, renounce his claim to the trial by jury in a particular case. The Court likened it to submissions to arbitration, and to stipulation and forthcoming bonds. The principle settled in that case is, that a party may renounce a benefit, and that *Oakley* had exercised this right.

The cases from *Strange* and *East* turn upon a principle, which is generally recognised, but which is entirely distinct from that which they are cited to support. It is, that a man who is discharged by the tribunals of his own country, acting under its laws, may plead that discharge in any other country. The principle is, that laws act upon a contract, not that they enter into it, and become a stipulation of the parties. Society affords a remedy for breaches of contract. If that remedy has been applied, the claim to it is extinguished. The external action of law upon contracts, by administering the remedy for their breach, or otherwise, is the usual exercise of legislative power. The interference with those contracts, by introducing conditions into them not agreed to by the parties, would be a very unusual and a very extraordinary exercise of the legislative power, which ought not to be gratuitously attributed to laws that do not profess to claim it. If the law becomes a part of the contract, change of place would not expunge the condition. A contract made in New-York would be the same in any other State as in New-York, and would still retain the stipulation originally introduced into it, that the debtor should be discharged by the surrender of his estate.

It is not, we think, true, that contracts are entered into in contemplation of the insolvency of the obligor. They are framed with the expectation that they will be literally performed. Insolvency is undoubtedly a casualty which is possible, but is never expected. In the ordinary course of human transactions, if even suspected, provision is made for it, by taking security against it. When it comes unlooked for, it would be entirely contrary to reason to consider it as a part of the contract.

We have, then, no hesitation in saying that, however law may act upon contracts, it does not enter into them, and become a part of the agreement. The effect of such a principle would be a mischievous abridgment of legislative power over subjects within the proper jurisdiction of States, by arresting their power to repeal or modify such laws with respect to existing contracts.

But, although the argument is not sustainable in this form, it assumes another, in which it is more plausible. Contract, it is said, being the creature of society, derives its obligation from the law; and, although the law may not enter into the agreement so as to form a constituent part of it, still it acts externally upon the contract, and determines how far the principle of coercion shall be applied to it; and this being universally understood, no individual can complain justly of its application to himself, in a case where it was known when the contract was formed.

This argument has been illustrated by references to the statutes of frauds, of usury, and of limitations. The construction of the words in the constitution, respecting contracts, for which the defendants contend, would, it has been said, withdraw all these subjects from State legislation. The acknowledgment, that they remain within it, is urged as an admission, that contract is not withdrawn by the constitution, but remains under State control, subject to this restriction only, that no law shall be passed impairing the obligation of contracts in existence at its passage.

The defendants maintain that an error lies at the very foundation of this argument. It assumes that contract is the mere creature of society, and derives all its obligation from human legislation. That it is not the stipulation an individual makes which binds him, but some declaration of the supreme power of a State to which he belongs, that he shall perform what he has undertaken to perform. That though this original declaration may be lost in remote antiquity, it must be presumed as the origin of the obligation of contracts. This postulate the defendants deny, and, we think, with great reason.

It is an argument of no inconsiderable weight against it, that we find no trace of such an enactment. So far back as human research carries us, we find the judicial power as a part of the executive, administering justice by the application of remedies to violated rights, or broken contracts. We find that power applying these remedies on the idea of a pre-existing obligation on every man to do what he has promised on consideration to do; that the breach of this obligation is an injury for which the injured party has a just claim to compensation, and that society ought to afford him a remedy for that injury. We find allusions to the mode of acquiring property, but we find no allusion, from the earliest time, to any supposed act of the governing power giving obligation to contracts. On the contrary, the proceedings respecting them of which we know any thing, evince the idea of a pre-existing intrinsic obligation which human law enforces. If, on tracing the right to contract, and the obligations created by contract, to their source, we find them to exist anterior to, and independent of society, we may reasonably conclude that those original and pre-existing principles are, like many other natural rights, brought with man into society; and, although they may be controlled, are not given by human legislation.

In the rudest state of nature a man governs himself, and labours for his own purposes. That which he acquires is his own, at least while in his possession, and he may transfer it to another. This transfer passes his right to that other. Hence the right to barter. One man may have acquired more skins than are necessary for his protection from the cold; another more food than is necessary for his immediate use. They agree each to supply the wants of the other from his surplus. Is this contract without obligation? If one of them, having received and eaten the food he needed, refuses to deliver the skin, may not the other rightfully compel him to deliver it? Or two persons agree to unite their strength and skill to hunt together for their mutual advantage, engaging to divide the animal they shall master. Can one of them rightfully take the whole? or, should he attempt it, may not the other force him to a division? If the answer to these questions must affirm the duty of keeping faith between these parties, and the right to enforce it if violated, the answer admits the obligation of contracts, because, upon that obligation depends the right to enforce them. Superior strength may give the power, but cannot give the right. The rightfulness of coercion must depend on the pre-existing obligation to do that for which compulsion is used. It is no objection to the principle, that the injured party may be the weakest. In society, the wrong-doer may be too powerful for the law. He may deride its coercive power, yet his contracts are obligatory; and, if society acquire the power of coercion, that power will be applied without previously enacting that his contract is obligatory.

Independent nations are individuals in a state of nature. Whence is derived the obligation of their contracts? They admit the existence of no superior legislative power which is to give them validity, yet their validity is acknowledged by all. If one of these contracts be broken, all admit the right of the injured party to demand reparation for the injury, and to enforce that reparation of it be withheld. He may not have the power to enforce it, but the whole civilized world concurs in saying, that the power, if possessed, is rightfully used.

In a state of nature, these individuals may contract, their contracts are obligatory, and force may rightfully be employed to coerce the party who has broken his engagement.

What is the effect of society upon these rights? When men unite together and form a government, do they surrender their right to contract, as well as their right to enforce the observance of contracts? For what purpose should they make this surrender? Government cannot exercise this power for individuals. It is better that they should exercise it for themselves. For what purpose, then, should the surrender be made? It can only be, that government may give it back again. As we have no evidence of the surrender, or of the restoration of the right; as this operation of surrender and restoration would be an idle and useless ceremony, the rational inference seems to be, that neither has ever been made; that individuals do not derive from government their right to contract, but bring that right with them into society; that obligation is not conferred on contracts by positive law, but is intrinsic, and is conferred by the act of the parties. This results from the right which every man retains to acquire property, to dispose of that property according to his own judgment, and to pledge himself for a future act. These rights are not given by society but are brought into it. The right of coercion is necessarily surrendered to government, and this surrender imposes on government the correlative duty of furnishing a remedy. The right to regulate contracts, to prescribe rules by which they shall be evidenced, to prohibit such as may be deemed mischievous, is unquestionable, and has been universally exercised. So far as this power has restrained the original right of individuals to bind themselves by contract, it is restrained; but beyond these actual restraints the original power remains unimpaired.

This reasoning is, undoubtedly, much strengthened by the authority of those writers on natural and national law, whose opinions have been viewed with profound respect by the wisest men of the present, and of past ages.

Supposing the obligation of the contract to be derived from the agreement of the parties, we will inquire how far law acts externally on it, and may control that obligation. That law may have, on future contracts, all the effect which the counsel for the plaintiff in error claim, will not be denied. That it is capable of discharging the debtor under the circumstances, and on the conditions prescribed in the statute which has been pleaded in this case, will not be controverted. But as this is an operation which was not intended by the parties, nor contemplated by them, the particular act can be entitled to this operation only when it has the full force of law. A law may determine the obligation of a contract on the happening of a contingency, because it is the law. If it be not the law, it cannot have this effect. When its existence as law is denied, that existence cannot be proved by showing what are the qualities of a law. Law has been defined by a writer, whose definitions especially have been the theme of almost universal panegyric, "to be a rule of civil conduct prescribed by the supreme power in a State." In our system, the legislature of a State is the supreme power, in all cases where its action is not restrained by the constitution of the United States. Where it is so restrained, the legislature ceases to be the supreme power, and its acts are not law. It is, then, begging the question to say, that, because contracts may be discharged by a law previously enacted, this contract may be discharged by this act of the legislature of New-York; for the question returns upon us, is this act a law?

Is it consistent with, or repugnant to, the constitution of the United States? This question is to be solved only by the constitution itself.

In examining it, we readily admit, that the whole subject of contracts is under the control of society, and that all the power of society over it resides in the State legislatures, except in those special cases where restraint is imposed by the constitution of the United States. The particular restraint now under consideration is on the power to impair the obligation of contracts. The extent of this restraint cannot be ascertained by showing that the legislature may prescribe the circumstances, on which the original validity of a contract shall be made to depend. If the legislative will be, that certain agreements shall be in writing, that they shall be sealed, that they shall be attested by a certain number of witnesses, that they shall be recorded, or that they shall assume any prescribed form before they become obligatory, all these are regulations which society may rightfully make and which do not come within the restrictions of the constitution, because they do not *impair* the obligation of the contract. The obligation must exist before it can be impaired; and a prohibition to impair it, when made, does not imply an inability to prescribe those circumstances which shall create its obligation. The statutes of frauds, therefore, which have been enacted in the several States, and which are acknowledged to flow from the proper exercise of State sovereignty, prescribe regulations which must precede the obligation of the contract, and, consequently, cannot impair that obligation. Acts of this description, therefore, are most clearly not within the prohibition of the constitution.

The acts against usury are of the same character. They declare the contract to be void in the beginning. They deny that the instrument ever became a contract. They deny it all original obligation; and cannot impair that which never came into existence.

Acts of limitations approach more nearly to the subject of consideration, but are not identified with it. They defeat a contract once obligatory, and may, therefore, be supposed to partake of the character of laws which impair its obligation. But a practical view of the subject will show us that the two laws stand upon distinct principles.

In the case of *Sturges* v. *Crowninshield*, it was observed by the Court, that these statutes relate only to the remedies which are furnished in the Courts; and their language is generally confined to the remedy. They do not purport to dispense with the performance of a contract, but proceed on the presumption that a certain length of time, unexplained by circumstances, is reasonable evidence of a performance. It is on this idea alone that it is possible to sustain the decision, that a bare acknowledgment of the debt, unaccompanied with any new promise, shall remove that bar created by the act. It would be a mischief not to be tolerated, if contracts might be set up at any distance of time, when the evidence of payment might be lost, and the estates of the dead, or even of the living, be subjected to these stale obligations. The principle is, without the aid of a statute, adopted by the Courts as a rule of justice. The legislature has enacted no statute of limitations as a bar to suits on sealed instruments. Yet twenty years of unexplained silence on the part of the creditor is evidence of payment. On parol contracts, or on written contracts not under seal, which are considered in a less solemn point of view than sealed instruments, the legislature has supposed that a shorter time might amount to evidence of performance, and has so enacted. All have acquiesced in these enactments, but have never considered them as being of that class of laws which impair the obligation of contracts. In prescribing the evidence which shall be received in its Courts, and the effect of that evidence, the State is exercising its acknowledged powers. It is likewise in the exercise of its legitimate powers, when it is regulating the remedy and mode of proceeding in its Courts.

The counsel for the plaintiff in error insist, that the right to regulate the remedy and to modify the obligation of the contract are the same; that obligation and remedy are identical, that they are synonymous—two words conveying the same idea.

The answer given to this proposition by the defendant's counsel seems to be conclusive. They originate at different times. The obligation to perform is coeval with the undertaking to perform; it originates with the contract itself and operates anterior to the time of performance. The remedy acts upon a broken contract, and enforces a pre-existing obligation.

If there be any thing in the observations made in a preceding part of this opinion respecting the source from which contracts derive their obligation, the proposition we are now considering cannot be true. It was shown, we think satisfactorily, that the right to contract is the attribute of a free agent, and that he may rightfully coerce performance from another free agent who violates his faith. Contracts have, consequently, an intrinsic obligation. When men come into society, they can no longer exercise this original and natural right of coercion. It would be incompatible with general peace, and is, therefore, surrendered. Society prohibits the use of private individual coercion, and gives in its place a more safe and more certain remedy. But the right to contract is not surrendered with the right to coerce performance. It is still incident to that degree of free agency which the laws leave to every individual, and the obligation of the contract is a necessary consequence of the right to make it. Laws regulate this right, but, where not regulated, it is retained in its original extent. Obligation and remedy, then, are not identical; they originate at different times, and are derived from different sources.

But, although the identity of obligation and remedy be disproved, it may be, and has been urged, that they are precisely commensurate with each other, and are such sympathetic essences, if the expression may he allowed, that the action of law upon the remedy is immediately felt by the obligation—that they live, languish, and die together. The use made of this argument is to show the absurdity and self-contradiction of the construction which maintains the inviolability of obligation, while it leaves the remedy to the State governments.

We do not perceive this absurdity or self-contradiction.

Our country exhibits the extraordinary spectacle of distinct, and, in many respects, independent governments over the same territory and the same people. The local governments are restrained from impairing the obligation of contracts, but they furnish the remedy to enforce them, and administer that remedy in tribunals constituted by themselves. It has been shown that the obligation is distinct from the remedy, and, it would seem to follow, that law might act on the remedy without acting on the obligation. To afford a remedy is certainly the high duty of those who govern to those who are governed. A failure in the performance of this duty subjects the government to the just reproach of the world. But the constitution has not undertaken to enforce its performance. That instrument treats the States with the respect which is due to intelligent beings, understanding their duties, and willing to perform them; not as insane beings, who must be compelled to act for self-preservation. Its language is the language of restraint, not of coercion. It prohibits the States from passing any law impairing the obligation of contracts; it does not enjoin them to enforce contracts. Should a State be sufficiently insane to shut up or abolish its Courts, and thereby withhold all remedy, would this annihilation of remedy annihilate the obligation also of contracts? We know it would not. If the debtor should come within the jurisdiction of any Court of another State, the remedy would be immediately applied, and the inherent obligation of the contract enforced. This cannot be ascribed to a renewal of the obligation; for passing the line of a state cannot re-create an obligation which was extinguished. It must be the original obligation derived from the agreement of the parties, and which exists unimpaired though the remedy was withdrawn.

But, we are told, that the power of the State over the remedy may be used to the destruction of all beneficial results from the right; and hence it is inferred, that the construction which maintains the inviolability of the obligation, must be extended to the power of regulating the remedy.

The difficulty which this view of the subject presents, does not proceed from the identity or connexion of right and remedy, but from the existence of distinct governments acting on kindred subjects. The constitution contemplates restraint as to the obligation of contracts, not as to the application of remedy. If this restraint affects a power which the constitution did not mean to touch, it can only be when that power is used as an instrument of hostility to invade the inviolability of contract, which is placed beyond its reach. A State may use many of its acknowledged powers in such manner as to come in conflict with the provisions of the constitution. Thus the power over its domestic police, the power to regulate commerce purely internal, may be so exercised as to interfere with regulations of commerce with foreign nations, or between the States. In such cases, the power which is supreme must control that which is not supreme, when they come in conflict. But this principle does not involve any self-contradiction, or deny the existence of the several powers in the respective governments. So, if a State shall not merely modify, or withhold a particular remedy, but shall apply it in such manner as to extinguish the obligation without performance, it would be an abuse of power which could scarcely be misunderstood, but which would not prove that remedy could not be regulated without regulating obligation.

The counsel for the plaintiff in error put a case of more difficulty, and urge it as a conclusive argument against the existence of a distinct line dividing obligation from remedy. It is this. The law affords remedy by giving execution against the person, or the property, or both. The same power which can withdraw the remedy against the person, can withdraw that against the property, or that against both, and thus effectually defeat the obligation. The constitution, we are told, deals not with form, but with substance; and cannot be presumed, if it designed to protect the obligation of contracts from State legislation, to have left it thus obviously exposed to destruction.

The answer is, that if the law goes farther, and annuls the obligation without affording the remedy which satisfies it, if its action on the remedy be such as palpably to impair the obligation of the contract, the very case arises which we suppose to be within the constitution. If it leaves the obligation untouched, but withholds the remedy, or, affords one which is merely nominal, it is like all other cases of misgovernment, and leaves the debtor still liable to his creditor, should he be found, or should his property be found, where the laws afford a remedy. If that high sense of duty which men selected for the government of their fellow citizens must be supposed to feel, furnishes no security against a course of legislation which must end in self-destruction; if the solemn oath taken by every member, to support the constitution of the United States, furnishes no security against intentional attempts to violate its spirit while evading its letter—the question how far the constitution interposes a shield for the protection of an injured individual, who demands from a Court of justice that remedy which every government ought to afford, will depend on the law itself which shall be brought under consideration. The anticipation of such a case would be unnecessarily disrespectful, and an opinion on it would be, at least, premature. But, however the question might be decided, should it be even determined that such a law would be a successful evasion of the constitution, it does not follow, that an act which operates directly on the contract after it is made, is not within the restriction imposed on the States by that instrument. The validity of a law acting directly on the obligation, is not proved by showing that the constitution has provided no means for compelling the States to enforce it.

We perceive, then, no reason for the opinion, that the prohibition "to pass any law impairing the obligation of contracts," is incompatible with the fair exercise of that discretion, which the State legislatures possess in common with all governments, to regulate the remedies afforded by their own Courts. We think, that obligation and remedy are distinguishable from each other. That the first is created by the act of the parties, the last is afforded by government. The words of the restriction we have been considering, countenance, we think, this idea. No State shall "pass any law impairing the obligation of contracts." These words seem to us to import, that the obligation is intrinsic, that it is created by the contract itself, not that it is dependent on the laws made to enforce it. When we advert to the course of reading generally pursued by American statesmen in early life, we must suppose, that the framers of our constitution were intimately acquainted with the writings of those wise and learned men, whose treatises on the laws of nature and nations have guided public opinion on the subjects of obligation and contract. If we turn to those treatises, we find them to concur in the declaration, that contracts possess an original intrinsic obligation, derived from the acts of free agents, and not given by government. We must suppose, that the framers of our constitution took the same view of the subject, and the language they have used confirms this opinion.

The propositions we have endeavoured to maintain, of the truth of which we are ourselves convinced, are these:

That the words of the clause in the constitution which we are considering, taken in their natural and obvious sense, admit of a prospective, as well as of a retrospective operation.

That an act of the legislature does not enter into the contract, and become one of the conditions stipulated by the parties; nor does it act externally on the agreement, unless it have the full force of law.

That contracts derive their obligation from the act of the parties, not from the grant of government, and that the right of government to regulate the manner in which they shall be formed, or to prohibit such as may be against the policy of the State, is entirely consistent with their inviolability after they have been formed.

That the obligation of a contract is not identified with the means which government may furnish to enforce it; and that a prohibition to pass any law impairing it, does not imply a prohibition to vary the remedy; nor does a power to vary the remedy, imply a power to impair the obligation derived from the act of the parties.

We cannot look back to the history of the times when the august spectacle was exhibited of the assemblage of a whole people by their representatives in Convention, in order to unite thirteen independent sovereignties under one government, so far as might be necessary for the purposes of union, without being sensible of the great importance which was at that time attached to the tenth section of the first article. The power of changing the relative situation of debtor and creditor, of interfering with contracts, a power which comes home to every man, touches the interest of all, and controls the conduct of every individual in those things which he supposes to be proper for his own exclusive management, had been used to such an excess by the State legislatures, as to break in upon the ordinary intercourse of society, and destroy all confidence between man and man. The mischief had become so great, so alarming, as not only to impair commercial intercourse, and threaten the existence of credit, but to sap the morals of the people, and destroy the sanctity of private faith. To guard against the continuance of the evil was an object of deep interest with all the truly wise, as well as the virtuous, of this great community, and was one of the important benefits expected from a reform of the government.

To impose restraints on State legislation as respected this delicate and interesting subject, was thought necessary by all those patriots who could take an enlightened and comprehensive view of our situation; and the principle obtained an early admission into the various schemes of government which were submitted to the Convention. In framing an instrument, which was intended to be perpetual, the presumption is strong, that every important principle introduced into it is intended to be perpetual also; that a principle expressed in terms to operate in all future time, is intended so to operate. But if the construction for which the plaintiff's counsel contend be the true one, the constitution will have imposed a restriction in language indicating perpetuity, which every State in the Union may elude at pleasure. The obligation of contracts in force, at any given time, is but of short duration; and, if the inhibition be of retrospective laws only, a very short lapse of time will remove every subject on which the act is forbidden to operate, and make this provision of the constitution so far useless. Instead of introducing a great principle, prohibiting all laws of this obnoxious character, the constitution will only suspend their operation for a moment, or except from it pre-existing cases. The object would scarcely seem to be of sufficient importance to have found a place in that instrument.

This construction would change the character of the provision, and convert an inhibition to pass laws impairing the obligation of contracts, into an inhibition to pass retrospective laws. Had this been the intention of the Convention, is it not reasonable to believe that it would have been so expressed? Had the intention been to confine the restriction to laws which were retrospective in their operation, language could have been found, and would have been used, to convey this idea. The very word would have occurred to the framers of the instrument, and we should have probably found it in the clause. Instead of the general prohibition to pass any "law impairing the obligation of contracts," the prohibition would have been to the passage of any retrospective law. Or, if the intention had been not to embrace all retrospective laws, but those only which related to contracts, still the word would have been introduced, and the State legislatures would have been forbidden "to pass any *retrospective* law impairing the obligation of contracts," or "to pass any law impairing the obligation of contracts previously made." Words which directly and plainly express the cardinal intent, always present themselves to those who are preparing an important instrument, and will always be used by them. Undoubtedly there is an imperfection in human language, which often exposes the same sentence to different constructions. But it is rare, indeed, for a person of clear and distinct perceptions, intending to convey one principal idea, so to express himself as to leave any doubt respecting that idea. It may be uncertain whether his words comprehend other things not immediately in his mind; but it can seldom be uncertain whether he intends the particular thing to which his mind is specially directed. If the mind of the Convention, in framing this prohibition, had been directed, not generally to the operation of laws upon the obligation of contracts, but particularly to their retrospective operation, it is scarcely conceivable that some word would not have been used indicating this idea. In instruments prepared on great consideration, general terms, comprehending a whole subject, are seldom employed to designate a particular, we might say, a minute portion of that subject. The general language of the clause is such as might be suggested by a general intent to prohibit State legislation on the subject to which that language is applied—the obligation of contracts; not such as would be suggested by a particular intent to prohibit retrospective legislation.

It is also worthy of consideration, that those laws which had effected all that mischief the constitution intended to prevent, were prospective as well as retrospective, in their operation. They embrace future contracts, as well as those previously formed. There is the less reason for imputing to the Convention an intention, not manifested by their language, to confine a restriction intended to guard against the recurrence of those mischiefs, to retrospective legislation. For these reasons, we are of opinion, that, on this point, the District Court of Louisiana has decided rightly.

February 19, 1827

SEEING WASHINGTON AT A DISTANCE

To Timothy Pickering

My dear Sir   Washington March 15th. 1827
   I was much obliged by your favour of the 14th. of Feby. through our friend Mr. Mercer. I am always gratified at being recollected by my old friends, for I find myself incapable of making new ones.

   I have seen in the papers the discussions between my brother Johnson and yourself respecting Count Pulaski and the battle of Germantown. It is not a little gratifying to us who are treading close upon your heels to observe how firmly you step, & how perfectly you retain your recollection. You are a little before me and I find myself almost alone in the world. With the exception of Judge Peters yourself & Mr. Wolcot I can scarcely find any person who was conspicuous on the great theatre of our country when I first began to mix in public affairs. Things are very much changed as well as men.

   Is it probable that you will ever travel as far south as Washington? Few things would give me so much pleasure as to see you, but that is a pleasure which I scarcely dare promise myself. It is probable that the line which circumscribes your movements to the south will never intersect that which bounds me on the north.

   You give a great many interesting anecdotes of General Washington which serve to develope his character. Your opportunities of personal observation enable you to take a near view of the man. I have seen him only at a distance. I have looked at him through those actions which were the result of mature deliberation, and consultation with those to whom he gave his confidence. The conclusion to which this view of him has conducted me is extremely favourable to his judgement, his wisdom and his virtue. If he did not possess that rapidity of decision which distinguishes many men of genius, there seems to have been a solidity in his mind which fitted him in a peculiar manner for occupying the high place he filled in the United States in the critical times in which he filled it. No feature in his character was more conspicuous than his firmness.

Though prizing popular favour as highly as it ought to be prized, he never yielded principle to obtain it, or sacrificed his judgement on its altar. This firmness of character added to his acknowledged virtue enabled him to stem a torrent which would have overwhelmed almost any other man, and did I believe save his country.

Such is my impression of Washington, an impression certainly not formed on a near view of him, but on a very attentive consideration of his character his conduct, and his papers. You could take a closer view of him, especially as a military man than was in my power, and have consequently better means of judging correctly than I possess.

With the best wishes for your health and happiness, and with sincere and respectful esteem, I am dear Sir your Obedt.

EDUCATION AND PAUPERISM

To Charles F. Mercer

My dear Sir   Richmond April 7th. 1827

I had the pleasure of receiving while in Washington your "discourse on popular education" delivered at Princeton in September 1826; but was then too much pressed with official duties to afford time for its perusal, and therefore deferred my acknowledgements for the favor. Since my return to this place I have read it with the interest to which the subject is entitled; and surely none is entitled to greater. It is more indispensable in governments entirely popular than in any other, that the mass of the people should receive that degree of instruction which will enable them to perform with some intelligence the duties which devolve on them; and you have certainly placed the subject on its proper ground.

I was peculiarly struck with the melancholy future you draw of English pauperism, a picture which I fear is as just as it is sombre. Is this gloomy state of things to be ascribed entirely to an overflowing population, or does it proceed from the policy of the laws? The accumulation of landed property in the hands of a few individuals, and its continuance in those hands by the law of entails and of descent may contribute to this effect, but cannot produce it entirely. The extremes of wealth and poverty in personal estate have perhaps more influence on the mass of the people, than the extremes in real estate. The doctrines of entails and primogeniture do not reach this part of the subject. When population becomes very dense, agriculture alone will not afford employment for all the inhabitants of the country. The surplus hands must find employment in some other manner. As the supply exceeds the demand the price of labour will cheapen until it affords a bare subsistence to the labourer. The super added demands of a family can scarcely be satisfied, and a slight indisposition, one which suspends labour and compensation for a few days produces famine and pauperism. How is this to be prevented? What is the state of the poor on the continent of Europe?—especially in Holland and Flanders? I believe with you that education—that degree of education which is adapted to the wants of the labouring class, and which prevails generally in the United States—especially in those of the north—is the surest preservation of the morals, and of the comforts of human life. In the present state of our population, and for a long time to come it may be relied on with some confidence. But as our country fills up how shall we escape the evils which have followed a dense population?

The systems of education which have been adopted in the different states form a subject for useful reflection and will I hope attract the attention of our legislature. I have always thought and I still think, whatever importance may be attached to our university and colleges, and I admit their importance, the primary schools are objects of still deeper interest.

Accept my thanks for this flattering mark of your attention, and believe me to be with sincere & respectful esteem, Your Obedt.

SLAVERY AND COLONIZATION

To Marquis de Lafayette

My dear General   Richmond May 2d. 1827

I had the pleasure a day or two past of receiving your letter of the 25th. of February accompanied by the valuable notes you had the goodness to send me, and the speech of the Duke de Broglie in the House of Peers on the subject of the slave trade. I have read the notes with great attention and thank you for them, as well as for your permission to avail myself of them in the event of publishing a revised edition of The Life of Washington. I perceive I was mistaken in supposing that the Court of France, while ostensibly discountenancing your engaging in the service of the United States, privately connived at that measure. The notes contain several other interesting details not previously understood.

The applause of an unknown American citizen cannot flatter a Peer of France; but to you who allow me to beleive that you do not view my opinions with absolute indifference, I will say that I think the speech of the Duke de Broglie has great merit. I have read it with equal admiration of the justness of its sentiments and the solidity of its arguments. The subject deeply interests humanity. Should France engage seriously and earnestly in the great work of abolishing this flagitious traffic in human flesh, it must be accomplished; and one of the foulest stains on the character of Christendom will exist only in history. In the United States the trade itself is sufficiently execrated; but the disposition to expel slavery from our bosom, or even to diminish the evil if practicable, does not I think gain strength in the south. I am not sufficiently acquainted with the climate and situation of our more southern states to form any decided opinion on the practicability of carrying on the agriculture of the country with the labour of white men; but I say without hesitation that in Maryland, Virginia, Kentucky, and Missouri, and even in Tennessee, and North Carolina unless it be immediately on the sea board, white labour might be substituted for black with advantage. The positive prosperity and happiness of these states, as well as their relative power and weight in the union, would, I confidently believe, be promoted by this change. But it is impossible to impress this opinion on those who might contribute to the establishment of this beneficial policy. An excessive jealousy of the free states, and an extreme apprehension of the domestic evils which might grow out of any measure having even a remote tendency to effect the object, stifles any attempt towards it.

I do not know enough of the interior of Mexico to form any opinion on the possibility of giving our coloured population that direction; but I am persuaded that it cannot be safely located on any lands within the United States. The only secure asylum within our reach—beneficial for them and safe for us—is Africa. The colony of Liberia is rapidly advancing to a state of solidity and permanent prosperity which will make it so great an object to our people of colour to migrate thither as to justify the hope that the colonization society may soon be relieved from the expence of transporting those who wish to remove to that country. They receive rich lands which they can cultivate in safety; and the prospect of a profitable commerce is very flattering. Under these encouraging circumstances, the hope that voluntary emigration will releive us from our free coloured people may, I trust, be indulged without the charge of being over sanguine.

Measures are now taking by some of our extreme southern states which must have a material influence on the value of our slaves, and may produce effects not to be foreseen. They are prohibiting the introduction of slaves among them for sale under heavy penalties. The sales in the south have upheld the price in the middle states; and the withdrawal of this market will reduce the price so low as to bring it in the farming country to a level with the expence of raising them under the humane course which at present generally prevails. Should this policy become universal, we cannot predict its effects with certainty.

I persuade myself you will excuse my indulging in conjecture on this subject, because I know it is very near your heart.

I hear with regret your opinion that the English government does not take a sincere interest in the cause of gallant and suffering Greece. The information, or rather the speculations of the papers, had cherished the belief that a combined interference of the Christian powers of Europe to terminate the present desolating war, and guarantee the partial independence of Greece on the payment of a tribute which might compensate Turkey for her loss of territory was to be expected. I fear however that this hope, so consoling to humanity, will be disappointed.

Our papers have informed you that the debates of the last session of Congress have been scarcely less tempestuous than those of 1805-6. We dare not indulge the hope that those of the ensuing session will be more temperate. It is infinitely to be deplored that the contests concerning the election of the President, and the factions they generate; should mingle themselves with the legislation of the country. I fear however it is a disease for which no remedy is attainable.

While I hear with real sympathy the family loss you have sustained, I trust I may congratulate you on the health as well as happiness you enjoy at la Grange. That charming seat has been described to me as having every claim to the preference you bestow upon it. The United States and her citizens still look with their accustomed and grateful affection to every thing which concerns you.

Allow me to charge you with my sincere compliments to Messieurs Lafayette and le Vasseur, and to assure you that I remain with great and respectful esteem and attachment, Your Obedt

AN EXTENDED AUTOBIOGRAPHICAL SKETCH

To Joseph Story

My Dear Sir

The events of my life are too unimportant, and have too little interest for any person not of my immediate family, to render them worth communicating or preserving. I felt therefore some difficulty in commencing their detail, since the meer act of detailing, exhibits the appearance of attaching consequence to them;—a difficulty which was not overcome till the receipt of your favour of the 14th. inst. If I conquer it now, it is because the request is made by a partial and highly valued friend.

I was born on the 24th. of Septr. 1755 in the county of Fauquier, at that time one of the frontier counties of Virginia. My Father possessed scarcely any fortune, and had received a very limited education; but was a man to whom nature had been bountiful, and who had assiduously improved her gifts. He superintended my education, and gave me an early taste for history and for poetry. At the age of twelve I had transcribed Pope's essay on man, with some of his moral essays.

There being at that time no grammar school in the part of the country in which my Father resided I was sent, at fourteen, about one hundred miles from home, to be placed undr. the tuition of Mr. Campbell a clergyman of great respectability. I remained with him one year, after which I was brought home and placed under the care of a Scotch gentleman who was just introduced into the parish as Pastor, and who resided in my Fathers family. He remained in the family one year, at the expiration of which time I had commencd. reading Horace and Livy. I continued my studies with no other aid than my Dictionary. My Father superintended the English part of my education, and to his care I am indebted for anything valuable which I may have acquired in my youth. He was my only intelligent companion; and was both a watchfull parent and an affectionate instructive friend. The young men within my reach were entirely uncultivated; and the time I passed with them was devoted to hardy athletic exercises.

About the time I entered my eighteenth year, the controversy between Great Britain and her colonies had assumed so serious an aspect as almost to monopolize the attention of the old and the young. I engaged in it with all the zeal and enthusiasm which belonged to my age; and devoted more time to learning the first rudiments of military exercise in an Independent company of the gentlemen of the county, to training a militia company in the neighbourhood, and to the political essays of the day, than to the classics or to Blackstone.

In the summer of 1775 I was appointed a first lieutenant in a company of minute men designed for actual service, who were assembled in Battalion on the first of September. In a few days we were ordered to march into the lower country for the purpose of defending it against a small regular and predatory force commanded by Lord Dunmore. I was engaged in the action at the Great Bridge; and was in Norfolk when it was set on fire by a detachment from the British ships lying in the river, and afterwards when the remaining houses were burnt by orders from the Committee of safety.

In July 1776 I was appointed first Lieutenant in the 11th. Virginia regiment on continental establishment; and, in the course of the succeeding winter marched to the north, where, in May 1777, I was promoted to the rank of Captain. I was in the skirmish at iron hill where the Light Infantry was engaged; and in the battles of Brandy Wine, German town, and Monmouth.

As that part of the Virginia line which had not marched to Charleston was dissolving by the expiration of the terms for which the men had enlisted, the officers were directed to return home in the winter of 1779–80, in order to take charge of such men as the legislature should raise for them. I availed myself of this inactive interval for attending a course of law lectures given by Mr. Wythe, and of lectures of Natural philosophy given by Mr. Madison then President of William and Mary College. The vacation commenced in july, when I left the University, and obtained a license to practice law. In October I returned to the army, and continued in service until the termination of Arnolds invasion after which, in February 1781, before the invasion of Phillips, there being a redundancy of Officers, I resigned my commission. I had formed a strong attachment to the young lady whom I afterwards married; and, as we had more officers than soldiers, thought I might without violating the duty I owed my country, pay some attention to my future prospects in life.

It was my design to go immediately to the bar; but the invasion of Virginia soon took place, and the courts were closed till the capitulation of Lord Cornwallis. After that event the courts were opened and I commenced practice.

In the spring of 1782 I was elected a member of the legislature; and, in the autumn of the same year was chosen a member of the Executive Council. In January 1783 I was married to Miss Ambler the second daughter of our then Treasurer, and in april 1784 resigned my seat at the Council board in order to return to the bar. In the same month I was again elected a member of the legislature for the county of Fauquier of which I was only a nominal resident having resided actually in Richmond as a member of the Council. Immediately after the election I established myself in Richmond for the purpose of practising law in the superior courts of Virginia.

My extensive acquaintance in the army was of great service to me. My numerous military friends, who were dispersed over the state, took great interest in my favour, and I was more successful than I had reason to expect. In April 1787, I was elected into the legislature for the county in which Richmond stands; and though devoted to my profession, entered with a good deal of spirit into the politics of the state. The topics of the day were paper money, the collection of taxes, the preservation of public faith, and the administration of justice. Parties were nearly equally divided on all these interesting subjects; and the contest concerning them was continually renewed. The state of the Confederacy was also a subject of deep solicitude to our statesmen. Mr. James Madison had been for two or three years a leading member of the House of Delegates, and was the parent of the resolution for appointing members to a general Convention to be held at Philadelphia for the purpose of revising the confederation. The question whether a continuance of the Union or a separation of the states was most to be desired was sometimes discussed; and either side of the question was supported without reproach. Mr. Madison was the enlightened advocate of Union and of an efficient federal government; but was not a member of the legislature when the plan of the constitution was proposed to the states by the general Convention. It was at first favorably received; but Mr. P. Henry, Mr. G Mason, and several other gentlemen of great influence were much opposed to it, and permitted no opportunity to escape of inveighing against it and of communicating their prejudices to others. In addition to state jealousy and state pride, which operated powerfully in all the large states, there were some unacknowledged motives of no inconsiderable influence in Virginia. In the course of the session, the unceasing efforts of the enemies of the constitution made a deep impression; and before its close, a great majority showed a decided hostility to it. I took an active part in the debates on this question and was uniform in support of the proposed constitution.

When I recollect the wild and enthusiastic democracy with which my political opinions of that day were tinctured, I am disposed to ascribe my devotion to the union, and to a government competent to its preservation, at least as much to casual circumstances as to judgement. I had grown up at a time when a love of union and resistance to the claims of Great Britain were the inseparable inmates of the same bosom; when patriotism and a strong fellow feeling with our suffering fellow citizens of Boston were identical; when the maxim "united we stand, divided we fall" was the maxim of every orthodox American; and I had imbibed these sentiments so thoughroughly that they constituted a part of my being. I carried them with me into the army where I found myself associated with brave men from different states who were risking life and every thing valuable in a common cause beleived by all to be most precious; and where I was confirmed in the habit of considering America as my country, and Congress as my government. I partook largely of the sufferings and feelings of the army, and brought with me into civil life an ardent devotion to its interests. My immediate entrance into the state legislature opened to my view the causes which had been chiefly instrumental in augmenting those sufferings, and the general tendency of state politics convinced me that no safe and permanent remedy could be found but in a more efficient and better organized general government. The questions too which were perpetually recurring in the state legislatures, and which brought annually into doubt principles which I thought most sacred, which proved that everything was afloat, and that we had no safe anchorage ground, gave a high value in my estimation to that article in the constitution which imposes restrictions on the states. I was consequently a determined advocate for its adoption, and became a candidate for the convention to which it was to be submitted.

The county in which I resided was decidedly antifederal; but I was at that time popular, and parties had not yet become so bitter as to extinguish the private affections.

A great majority of the people of Virginia was antifederal; but in several of the counties most opposed to the adoption of the constitution, individuals of high character and great influence came forward as candidates and were elected from personal motives. After an ardent and eloquent discussion to which justice never has been and never can be done, during which the constitution was adopted by nine states, the question was carried in the affirmative by a majority of eight voices.

I felt that those great principles of public policy which I considered as essential to the general happiness were secured by this measure & I willingly relinquished public life to devote myself to my profession. Indeed the county was so thoroughly antifederal, & parties had become so exasperated, that my election would have been doubtful. This however was not my motive for withdrawing from the legislature. My practice had become very considerable, and I could not spare from its claims on me so much time as would be necessary to maintain such a standing in the legislature as I was desirous of preserving. I was pressed to become a candidate for Congress, and, though the district was unequivocally antifederal I could have been elected because that party was almost equally divided between two candidates who were equally obstinate and much embittered against each other. The struggle between the ambition of being engaged in the organization of the government, and the conviction of the injury which would he sustained by my private affairs was at length terminated in the victory of prudence, after which the federalists set up and elected Colonel Griffin, who obtained rather more than one third of the votes in the district which constituted a plurality.

Colonel Griffin named me to General Washington as the attorney for the district, an office which I had wished, but I declined accepting it because at that time the circuit courts of the United States were held at two distinct places far apart, and distant from the seat of government where the superiour courts of the state sat. Consequently I could not attend them regularly without some detriment to my state practice. Before this inconvenience was removed the office was conferred on another gentleman.

In December 1788 the legislature passed an act allowing a representative to the city of Richmond, and I was almost unanimously invited to become a candidate. The city was federal. I yielded to the general wish partly because a man changes his inclination after retiring from public life, partly because I found the hostility to the government so strong in the legislature as to require from its friends all the support they could give it, and partly because the capitol was then completed, and the

courts and the legislature sat in the same building, so that I
could without much inconvenience [   ] the bar to take part
in any debate in which I felt a particular interest.

I continued in the assembly for the years 1789 & 1790 &
1791, during which time almost every important measure of
the government was discussed, and the whole funding system
was censured; that part of it especially which assumes the state
debts was pronounced unconstitutional. After the session of
1791 I again withdrew from the assembly, determined to bid a
final adieu to political life.

The arrival and conduct of Mr. Genet excited great sensation
throughout the southern states. We were all strongly attached
to France—scarcely any man more strongly than myself. I sincerely beleived human liberty to depend in a great measure on
the success of the French revolution. My partiality to France
however did not so entirely pervert my understanding as to
render me insensible to the danger of permitting a foreign
minister to mingle himself in the management of our affairs,
and to intrude himself between our government and people.
In a public meeting of the citizens of Richmond, some of the
earliest if not the very first resolutions were passed expressing
strong disapprobation of the irregular conduct of Mr. Genet,
our decided sense of the danger of foreign influence, and our
warm approbation of the proclamation of neutrality. These
resolutions, and the address to the President which accompanied them, were drawn and supported by me.

The resentments of the great political party which led Virginia had been directed towards me for some time, but this
measure brought it into active operation. I was attacked with
great virulence in the papers and was so far honoured in Virginia as to be associated with Alexander Hamilton, at least so
far as to be termed his instrument. With equal vivacity, I defended myself and the measures of the government. My constant effort was to show that the conduct of our government
respecting its foreign relations were such as a just self respect
and a regard for our rights as a sovereign nation rendered indispensable, and that our independence was brought into real
danger by the overgrown & inordinate influence of France.
The public & frequent altercations in which I was unavoidably
engaged gradually weakened my decision never again to go

into the legislature, & I was beginning to think of changing my determination on that subject, when the election in the spring of 1795 came on.

From the time of my withdrawing from the legislature two opposing candidates had divided the city, the one was my intimate friend whose sentiments were very much those which I had entertained, and the other was an infuriated politician who thought every resistance of the will of France subserviency to Britain, and an adhesion to the coalition of despots against liberty. Each election between these gentlemen, who were both popular, had been decided by a small majority; & that which was approaching was entirely doubtful. I attended at the polls to give my vote early & return to the court which was then in session at the other end of the town. As soon as the election commenced a gentleman came forward and demanded that a poll should be taken for me. I was a good deal surprized at this entirely unexpected proposition & declared my decided dissent. I said that if my fellow citizens wished it I would become a candidate at the next succeeding election, but that I could not consent to serve this year because my wishes & my honour were engaged for one of the candidates. I then voted for my friend & left the polls for the court which was open and waiting for me. The gentleman said that he had a right to demand a poll for whom he pleased, & persisted in his demand that one should be opened for me—I might if elected refuse to obey the voice of my constituents if I chose to do so. He then gave his vote for me.

As this was entirely unexpected—not even known to my brother who though of the same political opinions with myself, was the active & leading partisan of the candidate against whom I had voted, the election was almost suspended for ten or twelve minutes, and a consultation took place among the principal freeholders. They then came in and in the evening information was brought me that I was elected. I regretted this for the sake of my friend, in other respects I was well satisfied at being again in the assembly.

Throughout that part of the year which followed the advice of the senate to ratify Mr. Jays treaty, the whole country was agitated with that question. The commotion began at Boston and seemed to rush through the Union with a rapidity and violence which set human reason and common sense at defiance. The first effort was to deter the President from ratifying the instrument—the next to induce Congress to refuse the necessary appropriations. On this occasion too a meeting of the citizens of Richmond was convened and I carried a series of resolutions approving the conduct of the President.

As this subject was one in which every man who mingled with public affairs was compelled to take part, I determined to make myself master of it, and for this purpose perused carefully all the resolutions which were passed throughout the United States condemning the treaty and compared them with the instrument itself. Accustomed as I was to political misrepresentation, I could not view without some surprize the numerous gross misrepresentations which were made on this occasion; and the virulent asperity, with which the common terms of decency in which nations express their compacts with each other, was assailed. The constitutionality of the treaty was attacked with peculiar vehemence, and, strange as it may appear, there was scarcely a man in Virginia who did not beleive that a commercial treaty was an infringement of the power given to Congress to regulate commerce. Several other articles of the treaty were pronounced unconstitutional; but, on the particular ground of commerce, the objectors beleived themselves to be invulnerable.

As it was foreseen that an attempt would be made in the legislature to prevent the necessary appropriations, one or two of my cautious friends advised me not to engage in the debate. They said that the part which it was anticipated I would take, would destroy me totally. It was so very unpopular that I should scarcely be permitted to deliver my sentiments, and would perhaps be treated rudely. I answered that the subject would not be introduced by me; but, if it should be brought before the house by others, I should undoubtedly take the part which became an independent member. The subject was introduced; and the constitutional objections were brought forward most triumphantly. There was perhaps never a political question on which any division of opinion took place which was susceptible of more complete demonstration; and I was fully prepared not only on the words of the constitution and the universal practice of nations, but to show on the commercial proposition especially, which was selected by our antagonists as their favorite ground, that Mr. Jefferson, and the whole delegation from Virginia in Congress, as well as all our leading men in the convention on both sides of the question, had manifested unequivocally the opinion that a commercial treaty was constitutional. I had reason to know that a politician even in times of violent party spirit maintains his respectability by showing his strength; and is most safe when he encounters prejudice most fearlessly. There was scarcely an intelligent man in the house who did not yield his opinion on the constitutional question. The resolution however was carried on the inexpediency of the treaty.

I do not know whether the account given of this debate, which was addressed to some members of Congress in letters from Richmond, and was published, was written by strangers in the gallery or by some of my partial friends. Be this as it may my arguments were spoken of in such extravagant terms as to prepare the federalists of Congress to receive me with marked attention and favour, the ensuing winter when I attended in Philadelphia to argue the cause respecting British debts before the Supreme court of the United States. I then became acquainted with Mr. Cabot, Mr. Ames, & Mr. Dexter & Mr. Sedgewic, of Massachusetts, with Mr. Wadsworth of Connecticut, and with Mr. King of New York. I was delighted with these gentlemen. The particular subject which introduced me to their notice was at that time so interesting, and a Virginian who supported with any sort of reputation the measures of the government was such a *rara avis*, that I was received by them all with a degree of kindness which I had not anticipated. I was particularly intimate with Ames, & could scarcely gain credit with him when I assured him that the appropriations would be seriously opposed in Congress.

It was about or perhaps a little after this time that I was invited by General Washington to take the office of Attorney General of the United States. I was too deeply engaged in the practice in Virginia to accept this office, though I should certainly have preferred it to any other.

I continued in the assembly though I took no part in the current business. It was I think in the session of 1796–97 that I was engaged in a debate which called forth all the strength and violence of party. Some Federalist moved a resolution expressing the high confidence of the house in the virtue, patriotism, and Wisdom of the President of the United States. A motion was made to strike out the word "wisdom." In the debate the whole course of the administration was reviewed, and the whole talent of each party was brought into action. Will it be believed that the word was retained by a very small majority. A very small majority in the legislature of Virginia acknowledged the Wisdom of General Washington.

When the cabinet decided on recalling Mr. Monroe from France, the President invited me to succeed him. But I thought my determination to remain at the bar unalterable, and declined the office. My situation at the bar appeared to me to be more independent and not less honorable than any other, and my preference for it was decided.

In June 1797 I was placed by Mr. Adams, then President of the United States, in the commission for accomodating our differences with France, and received a letter requesting my attendance in Philadelphia in order to receive the communications of the government respecting the mission previous to my embarcation. It was the first time in my life that I had ever hesitated concerning the acceptance of office. My resolution concerning my profession had sustained no change. Indeed my circumstances required urgently that I should adhere to this resolution because I had engaged with some others in the purchase of a large estate the arrangements concerning which were not yet made. On the other hand I felt a very deep interest in the state of our controversy with France. I was most anxious and believed the government to be most anxious for the adjustment of our differences with that republic. I felt some confidence in the good dispositions which I should carry with me into the negotiation, and in the temperate firmness with which I should aid in the investigations which would be made. The subject was familiar to me, and had occupied a large portion of my thoughts. I will confess that the *eclat* which would attend a successful termination of the differences between the two countries had no small influence over a mind in which ambition, though subjected to controul, was not absolutely extinguished. But the consideration which decided me was this. The mission was temporary, and could not be of long duration. I should return after a short absence, to my profession, with no diminution of character, & I trusted, with no diminution of practice. My clients would know immediately that I should soon return & I could make arrangements with the gentlemen of the bar which would prevent my business from suffering in the meantime. I accepted the appointment and repaired to Philadelphia where I embarked for Amsterdam. I found General Pinckney at the Hague, and we obtained passports from the Minister of France at that place to secure our passage in safety to Paris. While at the Hague intelligence was received of that revolution which was effected in the French government by the seizure of two of the Directory and of a majority of the legislature by a military force acting under the orders of three of the Directory combined with a minority of the councils. This revolution blasted every hope of an accomodation between the United States and France.

On reaching Paris General Pinckney and myself communicated our arrival to Mr. Talleyrand & expressed a wish to suspend all negotiation till our colleague should be united to us. In a week or ten days Mr. Gerry joined us, and we immediately addressed ourselves to the minister. The failure of our attempts at negotiation is generally known. A journal which I kept exhibits a curious account of transactions at Paris. As soon as I became perfectly convinced that our efforts at conciliation must prove abortive I proposed that we should address a memorial to Mr. Talleyrand in which we should review fully the reciprocal complaints of the two countries against each other, and bring the whole controversy, at least our view of it before the French government in like manner as if we had been actually accredited. My motive for this was that if the memorial should fail to make its due impression on the government of France, it would show the sincerity with which we had laboured to effect the objects of our mission, and could not fail to bring the controversy fairly before the American People and convince them of the earnestness with which the American government sought a reconciliation with France. General Pinckney concurred with me in sentiment and we acted most cordially together. I found in him a sensible man, and one of high and even romantic honour. Mr. Gerry took a different view of the whole subject. He was unwilling to do anything, and it was with infinite difficulty we prevailed on him to join us in the letter to the minister of exterior relations. It was with the same difficulty we prevailed on him to sign the reply to this answer of the Minister. We were impatient to hasten that reply from a fear that we should be ordered to leave France before it could be sent. We knew very well that this order would come and there was a trial of skill between the minister and ourselves, (Genl. Pinckney & myself) he endeavouring to force us to demand our passports, we endeavouring to impose on him the necessity of sending them. At length the passports came and I hastened to Bordeaux to embark for the United States. On my arrival in New York I found the whole country in a state of agitation on the subject of our mission. Our dispatches had been published and their effect on public opinion had fully equalled my anticipations.

I returned to Richmond with a full determination to devote myself entirely to my professional duties, and was not a little delighted to find that my prospects at the bar had sustained no material injury from my absence. My friends welcomed my return with the most flattering reception, and pressed me to become a candidate for Congress. My refusal was peremptory, and I did not believe it possible that my determination could be shaken. I was however mistaken.

General Washington gave a pressing invitation to his nephew, the present Judge, & myself, to pass a few days at Mount Vernon. He urged us both very earnestly to come into Congress & Mr. Washington assented to his wishes. I resisted, on the ground of my situation, & the necessity of attending to my pecuniary affairs. I can never forget the manner in which he treated this objection.

He said there were crises in national affairs which made it the duty of a citizen to forego his private for the public interest. We were then in one of them. He detailed his opinions freely on the nature of our controversy with France and expressed his conviction that the best interests of our country depended on the character of the ensuing Congress. He concluded a very earnest conversation, one of the most interesting I was ever engaged in, by asking my attention to his situation. He had retired from the Executive department with the firmest determination never again to appear in a public capacity. He had communicated this determination to the public, and his motives for adhering to it were too strong not to be well understood. Yet I saw him pledged to appear once more at the head of the American army. What must be his convictions of duty imposed by the present state of American affairs?

I yielded to his representations & became a candidate. I soon afterwards received a letter from the secretary of state offering me the seat on the bench of the supreme court which had become vacant by the death of Judge Iredell; but my preference for the bar still continued & I declined it. Our brother Washington was intercepted in his way to Congress by this appointment.

My election was contested with unusual warmth, but I succeeded, and took my seat in the House of Representatives in Decr. 1799. There was a good deal of talent in that Congress both for and against the administration, and I contracted friendships with several gentlemen whom I shall never cease to value. The greater number of them are no more.

In May 1800, as I was about to leave Philadelphia (though Congress was still in session) for the purpose of attending the courts in Richmond, I stepped into the war office in order to make some enquiries respecting patents for some of my military friends, and was a good deal struck with a strange sort of mysterious coldness which I soon observed in the countenance of Mr. McHenry, the secretary of war, with whom I had long been on terms of friendly intimacy. I however prosecuted my enquiries until they brought me into conversation with Mr. Fitzsimmons the chief clerk, who congratulated me on being placed at the head of that department, and expressed the pleasure it gave all those who were engaged in it. I did not understand him, and was really surprized at hearing that I had been nominated to the senate as secretary of war. I did not believe myself to be well qualified for this department, and was not yet willing to abandon my hopes of reinstating myself at the bar. I therefore addressed a letter to Mr. Adams making my acknowledgements for his notice of me, and requesting that he would withdraw my name from the senate, as I was not willing openly to decline a place in an administration which I was disposed cordially to support. After writing this letter I proceeded immediately to Virginia.

Mr. Adams did not withdraw my name, & I believe the

nomination was approved. I had not been long in Virginia when the rupture between Mr. Adams and Mr. Pickering took place, and I was nominated to the senate as secretary of state. I never felt more doubt than on the question of accepting or declining this office. My decided preference was still for the bar. But on becoming a candidate for Congress I was given up as a lawyer, and considered generally as entirely a political man. I lost my business all together, and perceived very clearly that I could not recover any portion of it without retiring from Congress. Even then I could not hope to regain the ground I had lost. This experiment however I was willing to make, and would have made had my political enemies been quiet. But the press teemed with so much falsehood, with such continued and irritating abuse of me that I could not bring myself to yield to it. I could not conquer a stubbornness of temper which determines a man to make head against and struggle with injustice. I felt that I must continue a candidate for Congress, and consequently could not replace myself at the bar. On the other hand the office was precisely that which I wished, and for which I had vanity enough to think myself fitted. I should remain in it while the party remained in power; should a revolution take place it would at all events relieve me from the competition for Congress without yielding to my adversaries, and enable me to return once more to the bar in the character of a lawyer having no possible view to politics. I determined to accept the office.

I was very well received by the President, and was on very cordial terms with all the cabinet except Mr. Wolcot. He at first suspected that I was hostile to the two exsecretaries, & to himself, because they were all three supposed to be unfriendly to the President to whom I was truely attached. My conduct soon convinced him however that I had no feeling of that sort, after which I had the satisfaction of finding myself on the same cordial footing with him as with the rest of the cabinet.

On the resignation of Chief Justice Ellsworth I recommended Judge Patteson as his successor. The President objected to him, and assigned as his ground of objection that the feelings of Judge Cushing would be wounded by passing him and selecting a junior member of the bench. I never heard him assign any other objection to Judge Patteson, though it was afterwards suspected by many that he was believed to be connected with the party which opposed the second attempt at negotiation with France. The President himself mentioned Mr. Jay, and he was nominated to the Senate. When I waited on the President with Mr. Jays letter, declining the appointment he said thoughtfully "Who shall I nominate now?" I replied that I could not tell, as I supposed that his objection to Judge Patteson remained. He said in a decided tone "I shall not nominate him." After a moments hesitation he said "I believe I must nominate you." I had never before heard myself named for the office and had not even thought of it. I was pleased as well as surprized, and bowed in silence. Next day I was nominated, and, although the nomination was suspended by the friends of Judge Patteson, it was I believe when taken up unanimously approved. I was unfeignedly gratified at the appointment, and have had much reason to be so. I soon received a very friendly letter from Judge Patteson congratulating me on the occasion and expressing [   ] hopes that I might long retain the office. I felt truely grateful for the real cordiality towards me which uniformly marked his conduct.

I have my dear Sir been much more minute and tedious in detail than the occasion required, but you will know how to prune, condense, exclude, and vary. I give you the materials of which you will make some thing or nothing as you please— taking this only with you, that you will be sure to gratify me by pursuing precisely the tract you had marked out for yourself, & admitting nothing which may overload the narrative according to the original plan. Do not insert any thing from the suspicion that I may look for it because I have introduced it into my narrative.

It would seem as if new and perplexing questions on jurisdiction will never be exhausted. That which you mention is one of the strongest possible illustrations, so far as respects the original act, of the necessity in some instances of controuling the letter by the plain spirit of the law. It is impossible that a suit brought by the U.S. can be within the intention of the exception. There is however great difficulty in taking the case out of the letter. The argument you state is very strong and I am much inclined to yield to it. As no private citizen can sue in a district court on a promissory note I am much inclined to restrain the exception to those district courts which have circuit court jurisdiction. But the difficulty is I think removed by the act of the 3d. of March 1815 and by the decision of the last term. I speak of that decision however from memory as I have not yet received 12th. Wheaton.

Farewell. With the highest respect & esteem, I am your

July 1827

A "FLATTERING BIOGRAPHY"

To Joseph Story

My dear Sir   Richmond Decr. 30th. 1827

I have received your flattering letter and the still more flattering Biography which accompanied it. You will not I am persuaded consider me as affecting diffidence when I express a consciousness that your friendship has given an importance to the incidents of my life to which they have no just pretensions. This consciousness is mingled with a fear that many may ascribe to me such an excess of vanity as fully to counterbalance any good quality I may be allowed to possess. These fears however do not chill the warm and grateful sentiments with which I receive every mark of your good opinion. The belief that the writer of this sketch views me through a medium which magnifies whatever may deserve commendation, and diminishes those failings which others may deem serious faults, is dearer to my heart than any impression which eulogy, were it even deserved, might make on others. Mutual esteem and friendship confer reciprocally on those who feel the sentiment, one of the most exalted pleasures of which the human mind is susceptible.

When the Review appears I shall not name the author, because there is a part of it concerning which I wish to have some conversation with you. It is that which bestows negative praise by declaring the absence of certain qualities which are undoubtedly not very desirable. I fear that this may be suspected to affirm the presence of these same qualities in another work which has produced a good deal of excitement. You will readily conceive the effect of such a suspicion. If therefore any of my particular friends should enquire, as possibly they may, what artist has drawn the portrait so flattering to myself, I shall not name him for the present.

I congratulate you on the prospect of a more agreeable winter than you have heretofore passed at Washington. I trust accomodations may be found for Mrs. Story at Mrs. Rapines, and that she may be tempted by gracing our table to shed the humanizing influence of the sex over a circle which has sometimes felt the want of it. She must however be forewarned that she is not to monopolize you, but must surrender you to us to bear that large portion of our burthens which belongs to you.

I have received your letter of the 22d. of December, and am greatly obliged by the examination you have given the subject concerning which I enquired. I had hoped that the point was settled in the commercial towns. My mind had a strong leaning in the direction which yours seems to have taken, and you confirm the opinion I was previously disposed to adopt.

I participate in the serious feelings which you suggest as growing out of the present contest for the Presidency. I begin to doubt whether it will be long practicable peaceably to elect a chief Magistrate possessing the powers which the constitution confers on the President of the United States, or such powers as are necessary for the government of this great country with a due regard to its essential interests. I begin to fear that our constitution is not doomed to be so long lived as its real friends have hoped. What may follow sets conjecture at defiance. I shall not live to witness and bewail the consequences of those furious passions which seem to belong to man. Yours truely & affectionately

INTERNAL IMPROVEMENTS AND THE CONSTITUTION

To Timothy Pickering

Dear Sir   Washington March 18th. 1828

I had yesterday afternoon the pleasure of receiving your letter of the 10th. I have always supposed there must be an error in pointing the section you recite. I have always supposed that there ought to be a comma instead of a semicolon after the word excises. I have never beleived that the words "to pay the debts and provide for the common defence and general welfare of The United States" were to be considered as a substantive grant of power, but as a declaration of objects for which taxes &c might be levied. I am much gratified by the information you give that in your copy of the journals of the Old Congress for 1787 that the clause in question was pointed as we both think it ought to have been. The information is new to me and I am much obliged by your giving it.

I have no doubt of the correctness of your opinion that a general power to make internal improvements would not have been granted by the American people. But there is a great difference between a general power and a power to make them for military purposes or for the transportation of the mail. For these objects the power may be exercised to great advantage and, there is much reason for thinking, consistently with the constitution; farther than this, I know not why the government of The United States should wish it, nor do I beleive it is desired.

I concur entirely with you on the proposition to replenish the treasuries of the States from the treasury of The United States. If our revenue should exceed the wants of the government the ready mode for extricating ourselves from the difficulty is to diminish the taxes. I can scarcely reconcile the arguments in favor of taxing for the use of the States with the argument that you cannot tax for the general welfare. And yet they sometimes proceed from the same quarter.

We closed a laborious session yesterday, and I am on the wing for Virginia.

It gives me great pleasure to hear from you and greater still to know that you still retain your powers of body and mind. Except yourself I know no man who was active in our revolution that is older than I am. With respectful and affectionate esteem,

I am dear Sir your Obedt

HUMANITY TOWARD INDIANS

To Joseph Story

My dear Sir   Richmond Oct. 29th., 1828

I have just finished the perusal of your centennial discourse on the first settlement of Salem, and while fresh under its influence, take up my pen to thank you for the pleasure it has given me. You have drawn a vivid portrait, and I believe a faithful likeness of those extraordinary men who first peopled New England; and my feelings as well as my judgement have accompanied you in your rapid sketch of the character and conduct of their descendants. I wish the admonitory part may have its full effect on others as well as on those to whom it was particularly addressed. Some of our southern friends might benefit from the lesson it inculcates.

But I have been still more touched with your notice of the red man than of the white. The conduct of our Fore Fathers in expelling the original occupants of the soil grew out of so many mixed motives that any censure which philantropy may bestow upon it ought to be qualified. The Indians were a fierce and dangerous enemy, whose love of war made them sometimes the aggressors, whose numbers and habits then made them formidable, and whose cruel system of warfare seemed to justify every endeavour to remove them to a distance from civilized settlements. It was not until after the adoption of our present government that respect for our own safety permitted us to give full indulgence to those principles of humanity and justice which ought always to govern our conduct towards the aborigines when this course can be pursued without exposing ourselves to the most afflicting calamities. That time however is unquestionably arrived; and every oppression now exercised on a helpless people depending on our magnanimity and justice for the preservation of their existence, impresses a deep stain on the American character. I often think with indignation on our disreputable conduct (as I think it) in the affair of the Creeks of Georgia; and I look with some alarm on the course now pursuing in the North west. Your observations on this subject are eloquent, and are in perfect accordance with my feelings.

But I turn with most pleasure to that fine passage respecting the lady Arabella Johnson. I almost envy the occasion her sufferings and premature death have furnished for bestowing that well merited eulogy on a sex which so far surpasses ours in all the amiable and attractive virtues of the heart—in all those qualities which make up the sum of human happiness, and transform the domestic fireside into an elysium. I read the passage to my wife, who expresses such animated approbation of it as almost to excite fears for that exclusive admiration which husbands claim as their peculiar privilege. Present my compliments to Mrs. Story and say for me that a lady receives the highest compliment her husband can pay her when he expresses an exalted opinion of the sex, because the world will believe that it is formed on the model he sees at home.

I have read with much interest the character you have drawn of our deceased friend and brother the lamented Judge Trimble. Most richly did he merit all you have said of him. His place I fear cannot be completely supplied. I was desirous of having the character republished in our papers; but was restrained by the flattering introduction of my name. My modesty was alarmed by the apprehension that the request for its publication might be ascribed as much to vanity as to my deep feeling for departed worth.

Most cordially do I congratulate you on the appointment of our friend Hopkinson. With affectionate esteem I am dear Sir your

ELECTING THE VIRGINIA CONVENTION

To John Randolph

My dear Sir   Richmond Decr 24th. 1828

I have deferred making my acknowledgements for the message and other public documents for which I am indebted to you, in the hope of being enabled to accompany my thanks for this flattering attention—not with any information of what is passing in our legislature, for the papers communicate every thing, but with some speculations on the future which might possibly amuse. I despair however of making even this return for your kindness. On the all engrossing subject of the convention, there, is so much diversity as well as contrariety of opinion that even those who mingle freely with the members, and converse intimately with them, can only conjecture what will be the result of legislative deliberation respecting it. A man who has not these advantages, who has heard the sentiments only of the few, can scarcely hazard even a conjecture.

It is supposed, and with some reason, that the principle on which the convention may be constituted will have no inconsiderable influence on the character of that body, and consequently on the character of the constitution it may devise. You have seen the plan recommended by the committee. It assumes the principle on which the state has been divided into congressional districts as the basis of representation in convention. The delegates from the great slave holding counties consider this proposition as an advance on their part which ought to be met by the tramontaine gentlemen. The members from the West think very differently. In their opinion the free white population is the only legitimate basis of representation, and they consider themselves as having advanced to the extreme limit which can be marked by the spirit of conciliation when they offer to elect the members of the convention from Senatorial districts. On one side they adhere to the representation by county and on the other a representation according to numbers computing [   ] male adults. These however will most probably join the standard of the friends of the one district system or the other. Which of these systems will triumph cannot at present even be conjectured. One prediction may be made with some confidence. This foundation for a new arrangement of political power will not be laid without much exasperation and discontent. We cannot foresee the extent to which this discontent will be pressed. It is certainly very doubtful whether such a portion of it may not reach the people as to make it a problem not easy of solution whether this great movement may not prove abortive, or result only in angry contest and increased ill temper.

I wish you health enough to enjoy the festivities of the season and beg you to believe that I remain with great and respectful esteem, Your Obedt

To Mary W. Marshall

My dearest Polly   Washington Feby. 1st. 1829

Our sick Judges have at length arrived and we are as busy as men can well be. I do not walk as far as I formerly did, but I still keep up the practice of walking in the morning. We dined on friday last with the President, and I sat between Mrs. Adams and the lady of a member of Congress whom I found quite agreeable as well as handsome. Mrs. Adams was as cheerful as if she was to continue in the great house for the ensuing four years. The President also is in good health and spirits. I perceive no difference in consequence of the turn the late election has taken.

General Jackson is expected in the city within a fortnight, and is to put up in this house. I shall of course wait on him. It is said he feels the loss of Mrs. Jackson very seriously. It would be strange if he did not. A man who at his age loses a good wife loses a friend whose place cannot be supplied.

I dine tomorrow with the British minister and the next day again with the President. I have never before dined twice with the President during the same session of the court. That on friday was an official dinner. The invitation for tuesday is not for all the other Judges and I consider it as a personal civility. Tell Mr. Call all the secretaries are sick and Mr. Clay among them. He took cold by attending the colonization society and has been indisposed ever since.

The town it is said was never so full as at present. The expectation is that it will overflow on the 3d. of March. The whole world it is said will be here. This however will present no temptation to you to come. I wish I could leave it all and come to you. How much more delightful would it be to me to sit by your side than to witness all the pomp and parade of the inauguration.

I hear very little from Richmond but I adhere to my old rule of beleiving that every body dear to me, and especially the one dearest to me is well.

Tell Mr. Harvie I am greatly obliged by his letter.

Farewell my dearest Polly with the most ardent wish for your happiness I am your ever affectionate

To Mary W. Marshall

My dearest Polly   Washington March 5th

I have been much releived by hearing from several persons who came through or from Richmond, that there was no report in town of your being indisposed. I will resume my old confidence that you are well since I do not hear the contrary.

We had yesterday a most busy and crowded day. People have flocked to Washington from every quarter of the United States. When the oath was administered to the President the computation is that 12 or 15000 people were present—a great number of them ladies. A great ball was given at night to celebrate the Election. I of course did not attend it. The affliction of our son would have been sufficient to restrain me had I even felt a desire to go.

I am told by several that I am held up as a candidate for the convention. I have no desire to be in the convention and do not mean to be a candidate. I should not trouble you with this did I not apprehend that the idea of my wishing to be in the convention might prevent some of my friends who are themselves desirous of being in it from becoming candidates. I therefore wish you to give this information to Mr. Harvie.

I had hoped yesterday that we were about to have good weather which would enable you to take proper exercise, but today makes me fear that my hope will be disappointed.

Farewell my dearest Polly. Your happiness is always nearest the heart of your

1829

"I LOVE THE GOVERNMENT"

To Joseph Hopkinson

My dear Sir

I received some time past a small packet from Mrs. O Sullivan which she requested me to return, and I now take the liberty of doing it through you. I should not give you this trouble did I not fear that a letter addressed to her might miscarry, and she expresses a strong desire to have the papers it incloses again in her possession.

Among the many friends who rejoice at your late appointment, there is not one who takes a more sincere and lively interest in it than myself. I had at first supposed it impossible that the Senate could hesitate to give the President good advice, at least on this occasion; but I soon found I was mistaken, and the apprehension produced by the first delay was strengthened by all the intelligence which rumour gave us. We were told that a great principle, the principle of R E F O R M, must be established, that the public will required it should be universal, and we feared that not even you could escape from its all comprehensive operation. The gratification received from the dissipation of our fears was not a little increased by learning the decided majority by which the nomination was approved. Notwithstanding the strength and violence of the current, we are told that scarcely a Senator about whose good opinion you would be very solicitous, voted against you. This is pleasant, and I congratulate you upon it.

You hear from others and see in the papers more than I can tell you respecting the transactions of this lately busy place. Rumour tells us more I would hope than is true. The President it is said is not himself inclined to proscription. This I am inclined to believe, because I think a President of The United States will always be more disposed to conciliate than exasperate; and must always feel some reluctance at inflicting injury; But he is brought in by a hungry and vindictive party frequently, who do not feel his responsibility, and who demand pay for their services. His better judgement and better feelings too often yield to their importunities.

My principles lead me to wish every administration to do well, because I love the government and wish it to be well administered. I therefore hope as long as hope can find any thing to feed on. Yet I perceive much more to fear than to hope for the future. I do not mean to apply this meerly to the existing President. Farewell; That you may be happy and that Providence may continue to take care of our country is the constant prayer of your affectionate friend

March 18, 1829

PROPERTY AND SUFFRAGE

To James M. Garnett

Dear Sir   Richmond May 20th. 1829
    On my return from North Carolina I received your letter of the 10th.

My private judgement is certainly in favor of founding the right of suffrage on the basis of an interest in land. I have no objection to extending the present rule to a reversionary interest; and to leases for such a term of years as may give the lessee actual property in the soil. The state of society in a part of our country suggests this extension. Tenants in the upper part of the state are numerous; and the migratory spirit of our people creates such difficulty in ascertaining the expiration of leases for lives, as to excite some unwillingness on the part of land holders, to execute leases of that description.

I have never thrown my ideas on this subject in the shape of an argument; and they are very well expressed in your "reply to the enquiries of a free holder."

I have never, in reflecting on it, allowed all the weight which is generally ascribed by my countrymen, to the natural rights of Man. These rights exist in a state of nature, but are surrendered, as it seems to me, when he enters into a state of society, in exchange for social rights and advantages. If any original natural rights were retained (I speak not of those with which society has no concern, the exercise of which cannot affect others, such as freedom of thought, breathing the atmosphere, using our senses &c) we should expect them to be those of life and liberty. Yet both are at the disposition of society. All natural rights therefore of this description may be controuled by society, and are exercised by its permission. The wanton use of this power by the imposition of unnecessary restraints, would certainly be an abuse of it. Still the power exists, and its exercise must be regulated by the wisdom of society. On no other principle can the exclusion of females, minors, free people of colour &c from the polls be sustained.

If, as I think cannot be denied, a voice in the government of a country be the exercise of a social, not of a natural right, society must judge of the extent to which it ought to be granted, and of the individuals on whom it may be safely and beneficially conferred. It is a question of expediency, not of right.

Considering it as a question of expediency, we ought, it would seem to me, in solving it, to take into view all the great objects for which government is instituted. One of primary magnitude—security against external force devolves mainly on the government of the Union. State legislation embraces taxation for state purposes, and every thing relative to persons and property.

Personal security is undoubtedly an object of the first importance; but it is obvious to all, and has been repeatedly observed that this is an object in which all have an equal interest. However the legislature may be elected, personal liberty will be equally secure, because the legislator must be equally intent on its preservation. All persons must be equally subject to the laws; and no difference or opposition of interest can exist in this respect.

But the laws which affect our persons constitute a small portion of the code of every nation. The great mass of legislation respects property. Is it wise, is it safe, in framing the legislature, to exclude property altogether from our consideration? If power and property be separated entirely from each other, is there not reason to fear that they may be reunited by means which cannot be avowed?

To me it seems true wisdom so to constitute the legislature as to furnish the best attainable security that its opinions will lead to the preservation of the great subjects of legislation—persons and property. If it be true, as I think it is, that any representation of the people which public opinion would tolerate, or any statesman of the day could suggest, would sedulously and with equal vigilance guard our persons, we ought not entirely to overlook the safety of our property. This is I think best done by beginning at the foundation—at the right of suffrage. In the representative we may expect to see the image—the improved image, but still the image, of his constituents; and if we would form a representative body both wise and faithful, we must give its full effect, as far as human provisions can give it, to the sense of the honest yeomanry of the country —the real people—by removing the influence of those whom it would be unsafe to trust.

I know very well that among the most destitute of the human race may be found intelligence, honour, and inflexible principle; but we have no means of distinguishing them by law; and, in framing a constitution must act on general principles. It is generally true that the opposite qualities may be too often looked for among those who would be excluded from the right of suffrage by the rule which has been mentioned.

If any property qualification be required, the arguments in favour of an interest in land are so obvious and have been so often mentioned that they need not be repeated. It is so easily acquired that no person of any property who values the right of suffrage will be without it. If any discrimination be made, this is recommended additionally by the fact that we are accustomed to it.

While I express my individual judgement I must say that public opinion has, I suspect, decided the question differently. If we are to trust what we see in the papers, the disposition to abandon the principle we have hitherto maintained, and to make the right of suffrage universal, or to depend on a small property qualification, has become very extensive. Beyond the blue ridge this opinion appears to be universal. Immediately east of that mountain, it has been adopted by many. It has derived great support from the sentiments ascribed to Mr. Jefferson.

Should the friends of the present system, or of something very like it be outvoted, the question will be whether any, and if any, what other test shall be substituted in its place. The payment of taxes presents itself as the most obvious; but there is great difficulty in fixing the amount.

I am also in favour of estimating our slave population in apportioning our representation.

Most of the observations already made apply to this question as strongly as to freehold suffrage. It is among the most productive funds for taxation, it bears a great portion of the burthens of government, and has peculiar claims to consideration in the formation of that body which is to be entrusted with the power of imposing taxes. The fact that they are unequally distributed in different sections of the state gives additional strength to the claims of those who possess it to have on this account some increased weight in the legislature. It is the best, perhaps the only certain security against oppressive taxation. I would add that slaves though property, are also persons. They constitute a part of the real effective population of the country. They exclude a white population to the same extent. Although incapable of exercising the right of suffrage themselves, why may it not be exercised for them by that active part of the society which exercises the same right for others equally incapable of acting for themselves. Females, minors &c are excluded from the polls, but are included in the enumeration of persons on whom representation is apportioned.

The obvious unfitness of this sketch for publication will secure it from the public view. It is designed for your private eye. I shall of course perform that part which my duty as a citizen may require, but am not willing as a meer voluntier to emerge from that privacy and retirement to which my period of life has doomed me. I do not give this hint from any apprehension of the publication of this letter but to suggest my unwillingness that the use you mention should be made of it. Indeed this is an unnecessary precaution, as neither its matter nor its manner fit it for your purpose.

I look with anxiety for the elections in your district in the earnest hope that Virginia will have the aid of your services in the convention. With great and respectful esteem, I am dear Sir your Obedt

ACCEPTING A NOMINATION

To Joseph Story

My dear Sir   Richmond June 11th. 1829

I had the pleasure some time past of receiving your letter inclosing a copy of that which transmitted a copy of his commission to our friend Judge Hopkinson. I am the more gratified by the flattering terms of the letter when I recollect by whom the copy was taken. I am sure you told her in my name by anticipation how much I was delighted by such a letter copied by such a hand.

I am almost ashamed of my weakness and irresolution when I tell you that I am a member of our convention. I was in earnest when I told you that I would not come into that body, and really believed that I should adhere to that determination; but I have acted like a girl addressed by a gentleman she does not positively dislike, but is unwilling to marry. She is sure to yield to the advice and persuasion of her friends.

I wrote from Washington signifying my wish not to be brought forward, and desiring that the attention of the district might be directed to some other person; but the letter was mentioned to very few, and those few advised that it should not be communicated, but that I should remain free to act on my return as my judgement might direct.

The committee appointed at this place to nominate had written to me at Washington but the letter reached that place the day of my departure or the day afterwards, and of course was not received. A duplicate was transmitted to me a few days after my arrival in Richmond, which I answered immediately, acknowledging my grateful sense of the favorable opinion which had led to my nomination, but declaring my unwillingness to become a member of the convention, and declining the honour intended me. The Committee would not act upon this letter; but in the meantime it was rumoured in the town that I declined being voted for, in consequence of which I was pressed so earnestly on the subject by friends whose opinions I greatly value that my resolution began to stagger. It was said that whether I took any part in debate or not my services were counted on as of real importance. The committee addressed a second letter to me, containing assurances of their anxious desire that I would reconsider the resolution I had formed, and assent to what they were certain was the general wish of the district. As is usual, I yielded, and gave a reluctant consent to serve if I should be elected. Such is the history of the business. I assure you I regret being a member, and could I have obeyed the dictates of my own judgement, I should not have been one. I am conscious that I cannot perform a part I should wish to take in a popular assembly; but I am like Moliere's *Medicin malgré lui.*

The body will contain a great deal of eloquence as well as talent, and yet will do I fear much harm with some good. Our freehold suffrage is I believe gone past redemption. It is impossible to resist the influence, I had almost said contagion of universal example. With great esteem and affection, I am my dear Sir your Obedt

SUFFRAGE AND REPRESENTATION

To Joseph Story

My dear Sir   Richmond July 3d. 1829
　　Your favour of the 23d. of June accompanying "Mr. Brazer's discourse at the interment of Doctor Holyoke," and your very interesting address to the bar of Suffolk at their anniversary on the 4th. of Septr. 1821, reached me a few days past. It is impossible to read the first without strong impressions of the worth both of Doctor Holyoke and Mr. Brazer.

　　Your address was of course read with pleasure and attention. It takes, as is your *custom* a very comprehensive view of the subject—of the law and of the distinguished persons who have adorned it. It presents strong incentives to exertion.

　　Directly after writing my last letters I saw your appointment to the Dane professorship, and anticipated your acceptance of it. The situation imposes duties which I am sure you will discharge in a manner useful to others, and conducive to your own fame. I did not however anticipate that the labour would immediately press so heavily on you as your letter indicates. Four octavo volumes in five years is a heavy requisition on a gentleman whose time is occupied by duties which cannot be neglected. I am confident that no person is more equal to the task than yourself; but I cannot help thinking that the publication may be postponed to advantage. I presume the work will be in the form of lectures; and I suspect you will find it advisable to postpone the publication of them till they have been revised for a second course. Precipitation ought carefully to be avoided. This is a subject on which I am not without experience.

I hope your attention has been turned to the two great cases we have under advisement. I wish you would place your thoughts upon paper. I am the more anxious about this as I have myself not considered them, and fear that I shall be prevented from bestowing on them the attention they ought to receive. Mr. Thompson I presume will look thoroughly into that from New York and be prepared in it; but if the majority of the court should not concur with him, it will be necessary that preparation should be made for such an event.

We shall have a good deal of division and a good deal of heat, I fear, in our convention. The free hold principle will I beleive be lost. It will however be supported with zeal. If that zeal could be successful I should not regret it. If we find that a decided majority is against retaining it I should prefer making a compromise by which a substantial property qualification may be preserved in exchange for it. I fear the excess incident to victory after a hard fought battle contested to the last extremity may lead to universal suffrage or to something very near it. What is the property qualification for your senate? How are your senators apportioned on the state? And how does your system work?

The question whether white population alone, or white population compounded with taxation shall form the basis of representation, will excite perhaps more interest than even the free hold suffrage. I wish we were well through the difficulty. Farewell. I am my dear Sir affectionately & truely, Your

A BARKING DOG

To James Rawlings

Dear Sir   Richmond, July 25th. 1829

The distressed I might say distracted situation of my wife at length forces me very reluctantly to make a direct application to you, and to state to you her real situation. The incessant barking of your dog has scarcely left her a night of quiet since the beginning of summer. During this spell of hot weather she has been kept almost perpetually awake. Last night she could not sleep two hours. Her situation is deplorable, and if this state of things continues she cannot live.

Rather than ask what it may be disagreeable to you to do, I would without hesitation abandon my house, and have proposed it to her; but our little place in the country affords her only a confined and hot chamber in which she thinks she cannot live. She therefore insists on my communicating her situation directly to you in the hope that when it is known the cause may not be continued. It is most painful to me that any thing in the circumstances of my family should interfere in the slightest degree with the inclination of a neighbour, and I have refrained as long as possible from applying to you on this irksome subject. Very respectfully, Your Obedt

We should take refuge among our friends in the upper country, but my wife cannot travel, and cannot sleep in a house with a family.

THE DANE PROFESSORSHIP

To Joseph Story

My dear Sir   Richmond Septr. 30th. 1829

I have read with great pleasure your discourse pronounced as Dane Professor of law in Harvard University. It is in your best style of composition.

You have marked out for yourself a course of labour which is sufficiently arduous; but I beleive you love to struggle with difficulty, and you have generally the good fortune or merit to overcome it. At seventy four you will find indolence creeping over you. But we will not anticipate evil.

You have not spared the students of law more than the Professor. You have prescribed for them a most appalling course. Our southern youths would stumble at the threshhold and think such a task too formidable for even a commencement. You Yankees have more perseverance, or think more justly on the proposition that he who attempts much may accomplish something valuable, should his success not be complete.

I hope I shall live to read your lectures. They will form an exception to the plan of life I had formed for myself, to be adopted after my retirement from office—that is to read nothing but novels and poetry.

Our convention approaches. I still feel vain regrets at being a member. The chief though not the only cause of these regrets is that *non sum qualis eram*—I can no longer debate. Yet I cannot apply my mind to anything else. Farewell—with affectionate esteem I remain your

Speech in the Virginia Constitutional Convention on Apportionment

Two propositions respecting the basis of representation have divided this Convention almost equally. One party has supported the basis of white population alone, the other has supported a basis compounded of white population and taxation; or which is the same thing in its result, the basis of federal numbers. The question has been discussed until discussion has become useless. It has been argued until argument is exhausted. We have now met on the ground of compromise. It is now no longer a question whether the one or the other shall be adopted entirely but whether we shall, as a compromise, adopt a combination of the two, so as to unite the House on something which we may recommend to the people of Virginia, with a reasonable hope that it may be adopted.

Now, when on the subject of compromise, two propositions are again submitted to the Committee; one of them is, that the two principles originally proposed shall remain distinct; one of them constituting the basis of the House of Delegates, and the other of the Senate. The other proposition is, that the two principles shall be combined and made the basis of both Houses. This latter proposition presents the exact middle ground between white population exclusively, and the basis of white population combined with taxation, or what has been denominated the basis of federal numbers.

The motion of the gentleman from Augusta, (Mr. Johnson) to strike out the word "Resolved," from the proposition offered by the gentleman from Northampton, (Mr. Upshur) is intended to substitute for the combined ratio, which is the foundation of that gentleman's scheme, the proposition of the gentleman from Frederick, (Mr. Cooke) which is to introduce white population exclusively as the basis of the House of Delegates, and white population and taxation combined as the basis of the Senate. This is the question now before the Committee.

We are engaged on the subject of compromise, a compromise of principles which neither is willing to surrender. The very term implies mutual concession. Some concession must be made on both sides, but the quantum to be made by each must depend on the relative situation of the parties, and this must be considered before a right judgment can be formed on the subject. Let us enquire, then, what is the real situation of the parties on this question. On this enquiry will depend the reasonableness of any compromise that may be proposed.

The past discussion shows conclusively the sincerity with which each principle has been supported. There can be no doubt of the honest conviction of each side, that its pretensions are fair and just. The claims of both are sustained with equal sincerity, and an equally honest conviction, that their own principle is correct, and the adversary principle is unwise and incorrect. On the subject of principle nothing can be added, no advantage can be claimed by either side, for no doubt can be entertained of the sincerity of either. To attempt now to throw considerations of principle into either scale, is to add fuel to a flame which it is our purpose to extinguish. We must lose sight of the situation of parties and state of opinions, if we make this attempt.

What is that situation?

A question has been taken in the Committee on the proposition first submitted to us, and it has been carried by a majority of two. Is it possible under existing circumstances, that any confidence can be reposed in this decision? Can either the majority or minority feel any confidence that the same question will hereafter be again decided precisely in the same manner? Can we be blind to the actual working of public opinion? Do not gentlemen believe it to be more probable that at least some one of the members of this majority, may change his opinion and thus leave the House equally divided? Is it not even probable that a still greater change may take place, so as to place the present scanty majority, with the same paucity of numbers on the other side? Can any gentleman be confident how this question will be ultimately decided? None of us can be certain that its result in the House will be the same that it has been in Committee?

But let us decide one way or the other, if the majority shall be so small, if the opinions of the Convention shall be so nearly balanced, the Constitution will go forth to the people, deriving very little additional weight from the recommendation of this body. The majority and minority will have almost equal weight, and the Constitution will rest on itself. Is it possible to conceal from ourselves, that the powerful arguments of the minority conveyed to the people through the press, supported by the cooperating interest of a large district of country whose weight has been placed in the opposite scale, may produce great effect? The endeavor would be vain to conceal the fact that in a part of the Eastern country—that lying upon and South of James river near the Blue Ridge, there are interests which must and will operate with great force unless human nature shall cease to be what it has been in all time. It is impossible to say what may be the influence of those interests abroad, though they may exert none on the members of this convention. It is impossible to say how far they may affect the adoption or rejection of the Constitution. But it is by no means certain that this change in public opinion will not be felt in this body also. Admitting gentlemen to retain their theories—theories which they maintain with perfect sincerity, still there exists another theory equally republican and which they equally respect the theory, that it is the duty of a representative to speak the will of his constituents. We cannot say how far this may carry gentlemen. Neither can we say what will be the ultimate decision of this House or of the people.

Taking this view of the state of parties, it is manifest that to obtain a just compromise, concession must not only be mutual —it must be equal also. The claims of the parties are the same. Each ought to concede to the other as much as he demands from that other, and thus meet on middle ground. There can be no hope that either will yield more than it gets in return.

What is that middle ground?

One party proposes that the House of Delegates shall be formed on the basis of white population exclusively, and the Senate on the mixed basis of white population and taxation, or on the federal numbers. The other party proposes that the white population shall be combined with Federal numbers, and shall, mixed in equal proportions, form the basis of Representation in both Houses. This last proposition must be equal. All feel it to be equal. If the two principles are combined exactly, and thus combined, form the basis of both Houses, the compromise must be perfectly equal.

Is the other proposition equal? I ask the gentleman who make it if they think it so?

The party in favor of the compound basis in both Houses have declared their conviction that there is no equality in the proposition. They at least think it unequal. How can they accede to a proposition as a compromise which they firmly believe to be unequal? Do gentlemen of the opposite party think it equal? If they do, why refuse to take what they offer to us?

They consent that the Senate shall be founded on the mixed basis, and the House of Delegates on the white basis. If this be equality, why will they not take the Senate? There can be only one reason for rejecting it—they think the proposition unequal. If the Senate would protect the East, will it not protect the West also? If the proposition is equal when the Senate is tendered by them to us, is it not equal when tendered by us to them? If it is equal, it must be a matter of absolute indifference to which party the Senate is assigned. If a difficulty arises, it is because the proposition is unequal, and if it be unequal, can gentlemen believe that it will be accepted? Ought they to wish it?

After the warm language (to use the mildest phrase) which has been mingled with argument on both sides, I heard with inexpressible satisfaction propositions for compromise proposed by both parties in the language of conciliation. I hailed these auspicious appearances with as much joy as the inhabitant of the polar regions hails the re-appearance of the sun after his long absence of six tedious months. Can these appearances prove fallacious? Is it a meteor we have seen and mistaken for that splendid luminary which dispenses light and gladness throughout creation? It must be so, if we cannot meet on equal ground. If we cannot meet on the line that divides us equally, then take the hand of friendship, and make an equal compromise; it is vain to hope that any compromise can be made.

December 4, 1829

Speech in the Virginia Constitutional Convention on the Judiciary

Mr. MARSHALL now rose and addressed the committee in nearly the following terms:

The gentleman from Chesterfield, has understood the language of these resolutions correctly. No doubt was entertained in the judicial committee that the whole subject of the jurisdiction of the courts and the change of their form should be submitted entirely to the Legislature. There was no question on the subject. When I first heard the amendment of the gentleman from Norfolk, I had no objection to it except that this court of appeals had been long known to the Constitution of Virginia, and ought to be retained, unless there was some utility in the change. As to the consideration that there had been a regular and fixed construction of the Constitution of the U. States for a great length of time, that was no reason to change the title of court of appeals, because the Constitution of Virginia, had been in existence for a still longer time. But though my original objection to the change had been only that it was unnecessary, when I heard the gentleman's argument I felt more.

I shall not enter on the question, whether the construction of the Federal Constitution by the Congress of the U.S. is correct, or whether it will be adhered to or not. That question I shall not touch—it is not before the Committee. We act on the presumption, that that construction might be adopted, and we have provided against it. The argument of the gentleman goes to prove not only that there is no such thing as Judicial independence, but that there ought not to be no such thing: that it is unwise and improvident to make the tenure of the Judge's office to continue during good behaviour. That is the effect of his argument. His argument goes to prove, not only that there is no such thing, but that it is unwise that there should be. I have grown old in the opinion, that there is nothing more dear to Virginia, or ought to be dearer to her Statesmen, and that the best interests of our country are secured by it. Advert, sir, to the duties of a Judge. He has to pass between the Government and the man whom that Government is prosecuting: between the most powerful individuals in the community, and the poorest and most unpopular. It is of the last importance, that in the exercise of these duties, he should observe the utmost fairness. Need I press the necessity of this? Does not every man feel that his own personal security and the security of his property depends on that fairness? The Judicial Department comes home in its effects to every man's fireside: it passes on his property, his reputation, his life, his all. Is it not, to the last degree important, that he should be rendered perfectly and completely independent, with nothing to influence or to controul him but God and his conscience? You do not allow a man to perform the duties of a Juryman or a judge if he has one dollar of interest in the matter to be decided: and will you allow a judge to give a decision when his office may depend upon it? when his decision may offend a powerful and influential man? Your salaries do not allow any of your Judges to lay up for his old age: the longer he remains in office, the more dependant he becomes upon his office. He wishes to retain it, if he did not wish to retain it, he would not have accepted it. And will you make me believe that if the manner of his decision may affect the tenure of that office, that the man himself will not be affected by that consideration? But suppose he is not affected by it: if the mere repeal of a law, and the making some change in the organization of his Court, is to remove him, that these circumstances will not recur perpetually? I acknowledge that, in my judgment, the whole good which may grow out of this Convention, be it what it may, will never compensate for the evil of changing the tenure of the Judicial office.

The gentleman from Orange placed his argument upon this ground—that to impose such a restraint upon the legislature was to make an imputation upon the legislature which he would not make—he did not suppose it possible they would act in that manner, and he would not provide against it. For what do you make a Constitution? If your confidence is complete & no provision is necessary against misdoing, and no imputation is to be cast upon the legislature, why are we making another Constitution? Consider how far this argument extends in the 10th resolution of the Legis. Co, you say that no bill of attainder, or *ex post facto* law shall be passed. What a calumny is here upon the Legislature, of the gentleman's native state! Do you believe that the Legislature will pass a bill of attainder, or an *ex post facto* law? Do you believe that they will pass a law impairing the obligation of contracts? If not, why provide against it? Does not the principle of the gentleman from Orange apply as much to this case as to the other? You declare that the Legislature shall not take private property for the public use without just compensation. Do you believe that the Legislature will put forth their grasp upon private property, without compensation? Certainly I do not. There is as little reason to believe they will do such an act as this, as there is to believe that a Legislature will offend against a Judge who has given a decision against some favourite opinion and favourite measure of theirs, or against a popular individual who has almost led the Legislature by his talents and influence. I am persuaded there is at least as much danger that they will lay hold on such an individual, as that they will condemn a man to death for doing that which when he committed it was no crime. The gentleman says it is impossible the Legislature should ever think of doing such a thing. Why then expunge the prohibition? He replies the benefit to be obtained is this, that it is possible the Legislature may create Judges whom they afterwards discover to be useless: they discern their error, but if this clause is retained, they cannot retrace the step and abolish their own work. Is this probable? In the history of this country, Judges are known to be charged with duties they are scarcely equal to. There are no surplus Judges. The office does not descend to the family, and multiply with it. All the Judges are created by a Legislative act: and they may as well abolish a court to get rid of a Judge, as create a court to make a Judge. There can be no just fear that unnecessary Judges will be created—it is not the tendency of our situation and our Government. (The danger that they will be left dependent, is more probable:) but if it does arise, it is provided against by the 8th resolution.

I see no utility in the amendment of the gentleman from Norfolk. It will change the established appellation of the court, long settled in our own Constitution. Be this, however, as it may, nothing can be in my apprehension more mischievous than to expunge that clause with the views that gentleman entertains. His design is professedly and avowedly, to leave all the Judges: but the Judges of the Court of Appeals, (and them too, as I believe will be the fact) to the power of the Legislature. There is this difference: The removal of a Judge is an unpleasant task—it usually occasions some reluctance: but, merely to take away the foundation on which he stands, and to let him drop, is another thing: this occasions very little compunction: and as little to re-elect others and leave him unprovided for.

I feel strongly, that this Convention can do nothing that would entail a more serious evil upon Virginia, than to destroy the tenure by which her Judges hold their offices.

———

Mr. MARSHALL rejoined:

I trust the great importance of this subject, will be deemed a sufficient apology for my again troubling the Committee. Some observations have fallen from the gentleman from Norfolk, which I feel it incumbent upon to notice. The gentleman has said, that it is sufficient for the independence of the Judiciary Department, that the Judges of the Supreme Court be independent: and that there is no country on earth, where the independence of the Judges of the other Courts is secured. I will refer him to the country with which I am best acquainted—I mean Great Britain. What is the Supreme Court of Great Britain? It is the House of Lords. And are not the Judges of the Court of Common Pleas independent? Do they not hold their office during good behaviour? Yet these are Inferior Courts. I do not know so well the condition of other countries in this respect; but I believe the independence of the courts is preserved in France.

The independence of all those who try causes between man and man, and between a man and his Government, can be maintained only by the tenure of their office. Is not their independence preserved, under the present system? None can doubt it. Such an idea was never heard of in Virginia, as to remove a Judge from office. You may impose upon him any duty you please. You may say, that the Court of Appeals shall sit every day, from the 1st of January to the last of December. The Judge of a County Court may be called on to perform his duty on the bench, for a whole year: Yet he holds his office during good behaviour.

The Legislature can have no motive to impose unreasonable duties on a Judge—he may be required to do all he can do, and he can do no more. If the Judges in commission, are incompetent to the duty which is to be performed, the Legislature will create more Judges: it is within the ordinary province of Legislative action. Their independence is not impaired, by their being required to do all they can. That is their acknowledged duty.

We have heard about sinecures and judicial pensioners. Sir, the weight of such terms is well known here. To avoid creating a sinecure, you take away a man's duties, when he wishes them to remain—you take away the duty of one man, and give it to another: and this is a sinecure. What is this, in substance, but saying, that there is no such thing as judicial independence? You may take a Judge's duties away, and then discard him. What is this but saying, that there is, and can be, and ought to be, no such thing as judicial independence? The gentleman says, he is a great friend to an independent Judiciary, and his friendship extends to the Supreme Court only. The whole circuit duty is now in the Inferior Courts; would he be very willing to transfer it to the Court of Appeals? It is impossible for him to answer but in the negative. He would then have the whole criminal jurisdiction of the State, entrusted to Judges, removable from office by the Legislature at its pleasure. What would then be the condition of the court, should the Legislature prosecute a man, with an earnest wish to convict him? But more. The great mass of controversy existing in the Commonwealth, must always be decided in the Inferior Courts. We had an example in the Old General Court. What would be the consequence of giving original jurisdiction to an Appellate Court? Such a mass of causes accumulated in that court, that the great grandson of no man then living, would have seen the trial of the last cause on the docket. This will be the inevitable consequence: business will accumulate to an extent, that it will be impossible to pass through. The Inferior Courts will, therefore, try the great mass of causes, and reserve an appeal on questions of law. The gentleman would leave all these Judges unprotected by the Constitution. He declares himself a friend to Judicial Independence, and gives independence to those only, who have no criminal jurisdiction. I understand by Judicial Independence, the independence of all the members of the Judicial Department, whatever be their situation. He asks, are you to make every petty officer independent? I answer, no: but, is that the question? Are your Judges to be likened to every petty officer? Would he liken the Judges to them?

Will the gentleman recollect, that in order to secure the administration of justice, Judges of capacity, and of legal knowledge, are indispensable? And how is he to get them? How are such men to be drawn off from a lucrative practice? Will any gentleman of the profession, whose practice will secure him a comfortable independence, leave that practice, and come to take an office, which may be taken from him the next day? You may invite them, but they will not come. You may elect them, but they will not accept the appointment. You don't give salaries that will draw respectable men, unless by the certainty of permanence connected with them. But if they may be removed at pleasure, will any lawyer of distinction come upon your bench? No, Sir. I have always thought, from my earliest youth till now, that the greatest scourge an angry Heaven ever inflicted upon an ungrateful and a sinning people, was an ignorant, a corrupt, or a dependent Judiciary. Will you draw down this curse upon Virginia? Our ancestors thought so: we thought so till very lately—and I trust the vote of this day will shew that we think so still.

December 11, 1829

THE BIRTH OF A GRANDSON

To Mary W. Marshall

My dearest Polly   Jany. 31st. 1830
    Every thing goes on as usual. I take my walk in the morning, work hard all day, eat a hearty dinner, sleep sound at night and sometimes comb my head before I go to bed. While this operation is performing I always think with tenderness of my sweet barber in Richmond. It is the most delightful sentiment I have.

Edward I doubt not has informed of his fine large boy and that Rebecca is as well as could be expected. He seems to be quite as proud as I was at the birth of our first born. Thus the world goes on.

I dined on tuesday with the President in a very large mixed company. I sat by Mrs. Donalson, the Presidents niece and found her a very agreeable and Lady like woman. She is I beleive quite popular, but not so popular as Mrs. Madison was.

I saw Tom Francis about a week past but I am so occupied that I believe he thought I neglected him. I certainly saw very little of him. He has now gone to visit his brother. Judges Johnson and McClain do not live with us, in consequence of which we cannot carry on our business as fast as usual. Judge Thompson is sick. The rest of us are very well.

I have not heard one word respecting you since I parted from you; but hope dear hope paints you to my imagination as in good health and happy.

I have I fear bad news from Potowmac. I wrote to my tenant Mr. Sprigg a letter which I hoped would produce my rent but his letter brought niether money nor promise. My other tenant, at Andersons bottom, seems to expect to bring me in debt. One of my neighbours claims a valuable part of my land.

Thus it fares with those who do not look after their own affairs. It is only from you my dearest Polly that I always find things better than I had expected.

Farewell my dearest. Your happiness is the constant prayer of your ever affectionate

"GAY SPRIGHTLY AND GALLANT"

To Mary W. Marshall

My dearest Polly   Washington Feb. 14th. 1830

I have nothing to tell you but the splendid dinner parties to which we are invited. On friday we dined with the Secretary of State who gave a dinner to a Young Lady from Charleston just married to a nephew of the President. I sat between her and Mrs. Livingston of Louisiana, a very fine woman indeed with whom I was very much pleased. The bride appeared to be quite happy and to be glad that she was married. We dined after six and sat at table till after eight. When we retired to the setting room three young Ladies who professed a great desire to be acquainted with the Judges were introduced to me, and you would have been quite surprized to see how gay sprightly and gallant the wine made me. Yesterday I dined with the British minister. He always gives most excellent dinners & very superior wine, but we had no Ladies. It was some compensation for this deficiency that we sat down to table but an hour sooner than when we dined with the secretary of state. I hope very sincerely that we shall not be invited out again, as I greatly prefer remaining at home and attending to our business.

I find the influenza as prevalent here as it was in Richmond. Three of our Judges are laid up with it—not so as to prevent their going to court, but so as to prevent their going to dinner parties. Judge Duval is carried home by a relapse of his son.

I had a letter two or three days past from James. All well. Edward, he says, is the most delighted Father he ever saw. I suspect he saw one that was quite as much delighted when he looked in the glass.

I do not expect to hear from you till after the 22d. I shall be very impatient to know how you pass through the celebration of that day, and what news you collect at the farm.

Farewell my dearest wife. Your happiness is the constant prayer of your ever affectionate

PARTY SUCCESS AND FAMILY FEUDS

To Mary W. Marshall

My dearest Polly   Washington March 7th.

I am just returned from my mornings walk of three miles and all my brethren are fast locked in sleep in their rooms. I steal a few minutes from my business which I devote to you. While thus employed, my imagination transports me to Richmond and I participate in all your little solicitudes. I picture to myself every thing which passes between the time of you coming down stairs and breakfast, and wish I could breakfast with you. I was about to say that I feared the morning was too unpromising to admit of your riding out, but I recollect that you do not ride on sunday. We have had so much bad weather that I am apprehensive you have not taken as much exercise as is necessary for health. I must exhort you a little on this subject.

I dined yesterday with my old friend Mr Swan, and except that the dinner was not on the table till six every thing was delightful. Mr. Story remained at home. He thinks he is not well enough to dine out. I had some conversation with Mr. Mercer about our Nephew William. You know he is engaged in Miss Mercers school. He has I am told given over preaching. I fancy he did not succeed well in the pulpit.

Tom Francis took his seat in the stage but a few days past for Kentucky. I thought he would have preferred staying in this country, and was a little apprehensive at one time that he intended to do so. I fear he has found more of pain than pleasure in his visit. Mr. Coleman who married our niece Lucy has been to see me. He is in Congress and is a strong Jackson Man. Our Nephew Tom son of Humphry, is an equally strong Clayite and is I am told to be brought forward in opposition to Mr. Coleman at the next election. The Kentucky part of our family is I find a good deal divided in party politics and of course not very harmonious. I am sorry for it. Party success is but a poor compensation for family feuds. Farewell my dearest. I am, Your ever affectionate

1830

THE DANGERS OF PRESIDENTIAL ELECTIONS

To James Hillhouse

My dear Sir   Richmond May 26th. 1830

I have just returned from North Carolina and had this morning the pleasure of receiving your letter of the 10th. accompanying your proposition for amending the constitution of The United States as to the mode of electing the President, and your speech made on that subject in the Senate in 1808. I read your speech when first published with great pleasure and attention, but was not then a convert to either of the amendments it suggested. In truth there is something so captivating in the idea of a chief Executive Magistrate who is the choice of a whole people, that it is extremely difficult to withdraw the judgement from its influence. The advantages which ought to result from it are manifest. They strike the mind at once, and we are unwilling to beleive that they can be defeated, or that the operation of chusing can be attended with evils which more than counter balance the actual good resulting from the choice. It is humiliating too to admit that we must look, in any degree, to chance for that decision which ought to be made by the judgement. These strong and apparently rational convictions can be shaken only by long observation and painful experience. Mine are I confess very much shaken; and my views of this subject have changed a good deal since 1808, I consider it however rather as an affair of curious speculation than of probable fact. Your plan comes in conflict with so many opposing interests and deep rooted prejudices that I should despair of its success were its utility still more apparent than it is.

All those who are candidates for the Presidency either immediately or remotely, and they are more numerous than is imagined, and are the most powerful members of the community, will be opposed to it. The body of the people will also most probably be in opposition; for it will be difficult to persuade them that any mode of choice can be preferable to election mediate or immediate by themselves. The ardent politicians of the country, not yet moderated by experience, will consider it as an imputation on the great republican principle that the people are capable of governing themselves, if any other mode of appointing a chief Magistrate be substituted for that which depends on their agency. I believe therefore that we must proceed with our present system till its evils become still more obvious, perhaps indeed till the experiment shall become impracticable, before we shall be willing to change it.

My own private mind has been slowly and reluctantly advancing to the belief that the present mode of chusing the chief Magistrate threatens the most serious danger to the public happiness. The passions of men are enflamed to so fearful an extent, large masses are so embittered against each other, that I dread the consequences. The election agitates every section of The United States, and the ferment is never to subside. Scarcely is a President elected before the machinations respecting a successor commence. Every political question is affected by it. All those who are in office, all those who want office, are put in motion. The angriest, I might say the worst passions are roused and put into full activity. Vast masses united closely move in opposite directions animated with the most hostile feelings towards each other. What is to be the effect of all this? Age is perhaps unreasonably timid. Certain it is that I now dread consequences which I once thought imaginary. I feel disposed to take refuge under some less turbulent and less dangerous mode of chusing the chief Magistrate. My mind suggests none less objectionable than that you have proposed. We shall no longer be enlisted under the banners of particular men. Strife will no longer be excited when it can no longer effect its object. Neither the people at large nor the councils of the nation will be agitated by the all disturbing question who shall be President? Yet he will in truth be chosen substantially by the people. The Senators must always be among the most alert men of their states. Tho' not appointed for the particular purpose, they must always be appointed for important purposes, and must possess a large share of the public confidence. If the people of The United States were to elect as many persons as compose one senatorial class, and the President was to be chosen among them by lot in the manner you propose, he would be substantially elected by the people, and yet such a mode of election would be recommended by no advantages which your plan does not possess. In many respects it would be less eligible.

Reasoning a priori I should undoubtedly pronounce the system adopted by the convention the best that could be devised. Judging from experience I am driven to a different conclusion. I have at your request submitted my reflections to your private view and will only add that I am with great and respectful esteem Your Obedt. Servt

"MR. MADISON . . . IS HIMSELF AGAIN"

To Joseph Story

My dear Sir   Richmond October 15th. 1830

Ascribe my delay in thanking you for the sermon drawing the character of your late Chief Justice, and for the excellent addendum you have made to it, to the indolence and negligence of age, or to any cause rather than to indifference to any mark of your kind recollection. I have read both with attention and with real gratification. I had formed a high opinion of the late Chief Justice Parker from what I had heard of him, especially from yourself but that opinion was certainly raised by the more minute detail of his qualities, and by the abridged biography contained in the work for which I am thanking you. My regret for the loss of this estimable gentleman was much enhanced by the fear that Massachusetts might be able to supply his place by seducing from the federal bench a gentleman whose loss would be irreparable. I felicitate myself and my country on the disappointment of this apprehension.

While I am acknowledging favors I thank you also for a box of fish received the other day. I have not yet tasted them but have no doubt of their excellence, and shall not be long in putting it to the test.

I find our brother Mclean could not acquiesce in the decision of the court in the Missouri case. I am sorry for this, and am sorry too to observe his sentiments on the 25th. sect of the judicial act. I have read in the last volume of Mr. Peters the three dissenting opinions delivered in that case, and think it requires no prophet to predict that the 25th. section is to be repealed, or to use a more fashionable phrase, to be nullified by the Supreme court of The United States. I hope the case in which this is to be accomplished will not occur during my time, but, accomplished it will be, at no very distant period.

I am mortified at the number of causes left undecided at the last term. I am still more mortified at the circumstance that I am unable to prepare opinions in them. The cases of Soulard and of Smith I suppose must wait for additional information or for the certainty that none is to be obtained, but I had hoped to prepare something in the lottery case. I am chagrined at discovering that I have left the statement of the case behind me. It is also cause of real surprize as well as chagrin to find that the case of Cathcart and Robertson was not decided. I really thought the court had made up an opinion on it.

I have read with peculiar pleasure the letter of Mr. Madison to the Editor of the North American Review. He is himself again. He avows the opinions of his best days, and must be pardoned for his oblique insinuations that some of the opinions of our court are not approved. Contrast this delicate hint with the language Mr. Jefferson has applied to us. He is attacked with some bitterness by our Enquirer who has arrayed his report of 1799 against his letter. I never thought that report could be completely defended; but Mr. Madison has placed it upon its best ground—that the language is incautious, but is intended to be confined to a meer declaration of opinion, or is intended to refer to that ultimate right which all admit, to resist despotism, a right not exercised under a constitution, but in opposition to it.

Farewell—with the best wishes for your happiness I am yours affectionately

JEFFERSON AND THE FEDERALISTS

To Henry Lee

Dear Sir   Richmond October 25th. 1830

Your letter of the 25th. of July reached me a few days past. I am not surprized at the feeling with which you received the vote of the senate on your nomination. Although a serious perhaps successful opposition was looked for, the actual vote was not I beleive anticipated out of doors. Your mission however would I presume be now terminated, had your nomination been confirmed.

I have read, I need not say with astonishment and deep felt disgust, the correspondence of Mr. Jefferson published by his Grandson. Such a posthumous work was, I beleive, never before given to the world. The deep rooted prejudices of the American people in his favor and against those who supported the administration of General Washington would not be more fully illustrated than by the manner in which this work has been received. It has been said, I know not how truely, that the papers were selected by himself for publication.

However Mr. Jefferson may have wished to impress on the public a conviction that his charges on the federalists are the result "of his matured judgement," I never have nor do I entertain that opinion. Mr. Jefferson cannot have been himself the dupe, in his quiet retirement, of those excitements which might have imposed upon his judgement while struggling for power. A great portion of the calumny heaped upon the federalists was founded on the fact that they supported their own government against the aggressions and insults of France. This he ascribed to hostility to republicanism and a desire to introduce a monarchy on the British model. That this opinion was fallacious, that he was wrong and the federalists right on this subject of the French revolution was surely demonstrated long before his death.

I had noticed the unjust, I cannot say peculiar asperity with which he speaks of your Father. To his eminence as the supporter of the Washington administration in Virginia, this may perhaps in a considerable degree be ascribed. Those Virginians who opposed the opinions and political views of Mr. Jefferson seem to be have been considered as rebellious subjects than legitimate enemies entitled to the rights of political war. To this may probably be added the part he took in the affair of Mrs. Walker. These causes may in some measure account for the bitterness displayed with respect to him. The first cause operated against him and myself in common.

I am certainly not regardless of the repeated unwarrantable aspersions on myself. In the first moments after perusing them, I meditated taking some notice of them and repelling them. But I have become indolent, and age has blunted my feelings. The impression made at first is in some degree worn out, and I do not renew it by reperusing the work. The parts of my conduct which form the subject of his most malignant censure are in possession of the public, and every fair mind must perceive in them a refutation of the calumnies uttered against me. To unfair minds any thing I could urge would be unavailing and probably unread. Nothing is unknown or can be misunderstood by intelligent men unless it be the motives which compelled the court to give its opinion at large on the case of Marbury vs Madison.

There is one paragraph in your letter from which I dissent entirely. You say "I must in fairness declare that I believe Mr. Jeffersons theoretical opinions on government are those most in accordance with the freedom and happiness of society that have ever been given to the world."

On what, let me ask is this declaration founded? Not surely on his opinions that all political power originally resides in and must be derived from the people by their free consent, and ought to be exercised for their happiness; not from his opinions that rulers are accountable to the people for their conduct. These are common to all the people and statesmen of America. Mr. Jeffersons opinions on these subjects, though "in accordance with the freedom and happiness of society" are not more so than "have been given to the world" by every patriot of The United States. The preeminence you bestow on him then must be sustained by something else, by something peculiar to himself not possessed in common with all his country men.

What is this something?

Is his opinion, so frequently repeated and earnestly sustained, that all obligations and contracts civil and political expire of themselves at intervals of about (as well as I recollect) seventeen years, that to which you allude? Or is it the opinion, also frequently advanced, that a rebellion once in ten or twelve years, is a wholesome medicine for the body politic, tending to reinvigorate it? Or do you found this preeminence on his letter to Mr. Kerchival v 4th. p 285, in which, after a long and ingenious disquisition on the constitution of Virginia, he says "The sum of these amendments is 1. General suffrage, 2 Equal representation in the legislature. 3 An Executive chosen by the people. 4 Judges elective or amovable. 5 Justices, Jurors, and Sheriffs elective. 6 Ward divisions. And 7 Periodical amendments of the constitution." These are I believe, some of them, among the peculiar opinions of Mr. Jefferson. Do they entitle him to the superiority you assign to him?

In truth I have been a skeptic on this subject from the time I became acquainted with Mr. Jefferson as Secretary of State. I have never beleived firmly in his infallibility. I have never thought him a particularly wise sound and practical statesman; nor have I ever thought those opinions which were peculiar to himself "most in accordinance with the freedom, and happiness of society that have ever been given to the world." I have not changed this mode of thinking. I am dear Sir with great regard your Obedt

DINING WITH THE FRENCH MINISTER

To Mary W. Marshall

My dearest Polly   Washington Jany. 30th. 1831

I had the pleasure of hearing today from Colo. Lambert that you were in your usual health and that our friends in Richmond were generally well. He says you are pretty well off for snow though you have not quite so much as we have. The slays are still traversing the streets in every direction and the snow of yesterday is still on the roofs of the houses.

I beleive I told you in my last that I was to dine with the minister of France on tuesday. I did so and had a very excellent dinner but rather a dull party. Neither the minister nor his Lady could speak English and I could not speak French. You may conjecture how far we were from being sociable. Yesterday I dined with Mr. Van Buren the secretary of State. It was a grand dinner and the secretary was very polite, but I was rather dull through the evening. I make a poor return for these dinners. I go to them with reluctance and am bad company while there. I hope we have seen the last but I fear we must encounter one more. With the exception of these parties my time was never passed with more uniformity. I rise early, pore over law cases, go to court and return at the same hour and pass the evening in consultation with the Judges. Visiters sometimes drop in upon us, but their visits are short and we always return them by a card.

I saw Mr. Robinson yesterday evening and had the pleasure of hearing from him that my sister Colston and family were in good health.

Farewell my dearest Polly. Your health and happiness are my constant prayer. Your affectionate

CALLING ON CATHARINE SEDGWICK

To Mary W. Marshall

My dearest Polly   Washington Feb. 7th. 1831

I have seen—who do you think I have seen? Guess—I am sure you will not guess the person and I will therefore tell you without keeping you longer in delightful suspense. I have seen Miss Sedgewic; the author of Hope Leslie. I called on her to-day, a compliment I pay very few ladies, and she thanked me for it. She is an agreeable, unaffected, not very handsome lady, but not the reverse, of about thirty. I was surprized, though I did not tell her so, at her remaining unmarried. I am sure she would have no objection to a respectable good tempered husband, and I heartily wish her one. I was pleased with her and

shall read her new novel when I go home with the more pleasure for having seen her.

We are still bound up in snow and ice. The mail does not arrive regularly and I know nothing of what is passing in Richmond. I cling however to the hope that my friends are all well,
and that my dear wife especially continues in a state of undis-
turbed quiet and of reasonable happiness. For myself, I am too
busy to be unhappy. Except that I do not take my usual exercise, I pass my time as I always do in Washington. This winter
is just like the last so far as respects myself, and the last was just
like a dozen of its predecessors. Every body says it is excessively cold and I agree that what every body says must be true.

I suppose you have heard that we have lost our marshal.
Poor Ringold is out of office, and I greatly fear that his family
and himself will be distressed. He has just left us. Brother
Story and myself condole with him very sincerely, and he is
grateful to us for our friendly regard.

Farewell my dearest Polly. That you may be happy is the
constant prayer of your ever affectionate

Opinion in Cherokee Nation v. Georgia

THIS bill is brought by the Cherokee nation praying an injunction to restrain the State of Georgia, from the execution of certain laws of that State, which as they allege go directly to annihilate the Cherokees as a political society, and to seize for the use of Georgia the lands of the nation which have been assured to them by the United States in solemn treaties repeatedly made and still in force.

If courts were permitted to indulge their sympathies, a case better calculated to excite them can scarcely be imagined. A people once numerous, powerful, and truely independent, found by our ancestors in the quiet and uncontrolled possession of an ample domain, gradually sinking beneath our superior policy, our arts, and our arms, have yielded their lands by successive treaties, each of which contains a solemn guarantee of the residue, until they retain no more of their formerly extensive territory than is deemed necessary to their comfortable subsistence.

To preserve this remnant the present application is made. Before we can look into the merits of the case, a preliminary inquiry presents itself. Has this court jurisdiction of the cause?

The third article of the Constitution describes the extent of the judicial power. The second section closes an enumeration of the cases to which it is extended, with "controversies" "between a state or the citizens thereof, and foreign states, citizens, or subjects." A subsequent clause of the same section gives the Supreme Court original jurisdiction in all cases in which a state shall be a party. The party defendant may then unquestionably be sued in this Court. May the plaintiff sue in it? Is the Cherokee nation a foreign state in the sense in which that term is used in the constitution?

The counsel for the plaintiffs have maintained the affirmative of this proposition with great earnestness and ability. So much of the argument as was intended to prove the character of the Cherokees as a state, as a distinct political society, separated from others, capable of managing its own affairs and governing itself, has in the opinion of a majority of the judges been completely successful. They have been uniformly treated as a state from the settlement of our country. The numerous treaties made with them by the United States recognise them as a people capable of maintaining the relations of peace and war, of being responsible in their political character for any violation of their engagements, or for any aggression committed on the citizens of the United States by any individual of their Community. Laws have been enacted in the spirit of these treaties. The acts of our government plainly recognise the Cherokee nation as a state, and the Courts are bound by those acts.

A question of much more difficulty remains: Do the Cherokees constitute a foreign state in the sense of the Constitution?

Their Counsel have shown conclusively that they are not a state of the Union, and have insisted that individually they are aliens, not owing allegiance to the United States. An aggregate of aliens composing a state, must they say be a foreign state. Each individual being foreign, the whole must be foreign.

This argument is imposing, but we must examine it more closely before we yield to it. The condition of the Indians in relation to the United States is perhaps unlike that of any other two people in existence. In the general nations not owing a common allegiance, are foreign to each other. The term foreign nation is with strict propriety, applicable by either to the other. But the relation of the Indians to the United States is marked by peculiar and cardinal distinctions which exist no where else.

The Indian territory is admitted to compose a part of the United States. In all our maps, geographical treatises, histories, and laws, it is so considered. In all our intercourse with foreign nations, in our commercial regulations, in any attempt at intercourse between Indians and foreign nations, they are considered as within the jurisdictional limits of the United States, subject to many of those restraints which are imposed upon our own citizens. They acknowledge themselves in their treaties to be under the protection of the United States; they admit that the "United States" shall have the sole and exclusive right of regulating the trade with them and managing all their affairs as they think proper; and the Cherokees in particular were allowed by the treaty of Hopewell, which preceded the Constitution, "to send a deputy of their choice whenever they think fit to Congress." Treaties were made with some tribes by the state of New York under a then unsettled construction of the confederation, by which they ceded all their lands to that state, taking back a limited grant to themselves, in which they admit their dependence.

Though the Indians are acknowledged to have an unquestionable and heretofore unquestioned right to the lands they occupy until that right shall be extinguished by a voluntary cession to our Government, yet it may well be doubted whether those tribes which reside within the acknowledged boundaries of the United States can with strict accuracy be denominated foreign nations. They may more correctly perhaps be denominated domestic dependent nations. They occupy a territory to which we assert a title independent of their will, which must take effect in point of possession when their right of possession ceases. Meanwhile, they are in a state of pupilage. Their relation to the United States resembles that of a ward to his guardian. They look to our government for protection, rely upon its kindness and its power, appeal to it for relief to their wants, and address the president as their Great Father. They and their country are considered by foreign nations as well as by ourselves as being so completely under the sovereignty and dominion of the United States that any attempt to acquire their lands, or to form a political connexion with them would be considered by all as an invasion of our territory and an act of hostility.

These considerations go far to support the opinion that the framers of our constitution had not the Indian tribes in view when they opened the courts of the union to controversies between a state or the citizens thereof and foreign states.

In considering this subject, the habits and usages of the Indians, in their intercourse with their white neighbours ought not to be entirely disregarded. At the time the constitution was framed, the idea of appealing to an American Court of Justice for an assertion of right or a redress of wrong had perhaps never entered the mind of an Indian or of his tribe.

Their appeal was to the tomahawk or to the government. This was well understood by the statesmen who framed the constitution of the United States, and might furnish some reason for omitting to enumerate them among the parties who might sue in the Courts of the Union. Be this as it may, the peculiar relations between the United States and the Indians occupying our territory are such that we should feel much difficulty in considering them as designated by the term foreign state, were there no other part of the Constitution which might shed light on the meaning of these words. But we think that in construing them considerable aid is furnished by that clause in the eighth section of the third article which empowers Congress to "regulate commerce with foreign nations, and among the several states, and with the Indian tribes."

In this clause they are as clearly contradistinguished by a name appropriate to themselves, from foreign nations, as from the several states composing the union. They are designated by a distinct appellation and as this appellation can be applied to neither of the others, neither can the appellations distinguishing either of the others be in fair construction applied to them. The objects to which the power of regulating commerce might be directed, are divided into three distinct classes—foreign nations, the several states, and Indian tribes. When framing this article the convention considered them as entirely distinct. We cannot assume that the distinction was lost in framing a subsequent article unless there be something in its language to authorise the assumption.

The counsel for the plaintiffs contend that the words "Indian tribes" were introduced into the article empowering Congress to regulate commerce for the purpose of removing those doubts in which the management of Indian affairs was involved by the language of the ninth article of the confederation. Intending to give the whole power of managing those affairs to the government about to be instituted the convention conferred it explicitly, and omitted those qualifications which embarrassed the exercise of it as granted in the confederation. This may be admitted without weakening the construction which has been intimated. Had the Indian tribes been foreign nations in the view of the convention this exclusive power of regulating intercourse with them might have been and most probably would have been specifically given in language indicating that idea, not in language contradistinguishing them from foreign nations. Congress might have been empowered "to regulate commerce with foreign nations including the

Indian tribes, and among the several states." This language would have suggested itself to statesmen who considered the Indian tribes as foreign nations, and were yet desirous of mentioning them particularly.

It. has been also said, that the same words have not necessarily the same meaning attached to them when found in different parts of the same instrument: their meaning is controlled by the context. This is undoubtedly true. In common language the same word has various meanings, and the peculiar sense in which it is used in any sentence is to be determined by the context. This may not be equally true with respect to proper names. *Foreign nations* is a general term, the application of which to Indian tribes, when used in the American constitution, is at best extremely questionable. In one article in which a power is given to be exercised in regard to foreign nations generally, and to the Indian tribes particularly, they are mentioned as separate in terms clearly contradistinguishing them from each other. We perceive plainly that the constitution in this article does not comprehend Indian tribes in the general term "foreign nations"; not we presume because a tribe may not be a nation, but because it is not foreign to the United States. When, afterwards the term "foreign state" is introduced, we cannot impute to the convention the intention to desert its former meaning and to comprehend Indian tribes within it, unless the context forced that construction on us. We find nothing in the context, and nothing in the subject of the article which leads to it.

The Court has bestowed its best attention on this question, and after mature deliberation the majority is of opinion that an Indian tribe or nation within the United States is not a foreign State in the sense of the Constitution, and cannot maintain an action in the courts of the United States.

A serious additional objection exists to the jurisdiction of the court. Is the matter of the bill the proper subject for judicial enquiry and decision?

It seeks to restrain a state from the forcible exercise of legislative power over a neighbouring people asserting their independence, their right to which the state denies. On several of the matters alleged in the bill, for example on the laws making it criminal to exercise the usual powers of self government in their own country by the Cherokee nation, this court cannot interpose at least in the form in which those matters are presented. That part of the bill which respects the land occupied by the Indians, and prays the aid of the court to protect their possessions maybe more doubtful. The mere question of right might perhaps be decided by this court in a proper case with proper parties. But the court is asked to do more than decide on the title. The bill requires us to control the legislation of Georgia, and to restrain the exertion of its physical force. The propriety of such an interposition by the court may well be questioned. It savours too much of the exercise of political power to be within the proper province of the judicial department. But the opinion on the point respecting parties makes it unnecessary to decide this question.

If it be true that the Cherokee nation have rights this is not the tribunal in which those rights are to be asserted. If it be true that wrongs have been inflicted, and that still greater are to be apprehended, this is not the tribunal which can redress the past or prevent the future.

The motion for an injunction is denied.

March 18, 1831

"THE GREAT TEACHER EXPERIENCE"

To Joseph Story

My dear Sir   Richmond May 3d. 1831

By the schooner King I send you a barrel containing a few hams which are to be deposited for you with Fisher and Power of Boston. As the address is marked on the cask I hope they will reach you in safety and will be found reasonably well flavoured.

What do the wise men in the East say to the *Tabula rasa* which is made in the cabinet? Our quid nuncs were astonished at first, but soon discovered that the really voluntary resignations were proofs of unparalleled magnanimity and patriotism; and that those which were compulsory, were quite *comme il faut*. This is not only as it should be, but as it always will be.

I am apprehensive that the revolutionary spirit which displayed itself in our circle will, like most other revolutions, work inconvenience and mischief in its progress. I believe Mr. Brown does not count on boarding the Judges next winter; and if any other arrangement is made, tis entirely unknown to me. We have like most other unquiet men, discontented with the things that are, discarded accomodations which are reasonably convenient, without providing a substitute. We pull down without enquiring how we are to build up. The matter rests I understand with our younger brother, and he has probably committed it to some other person. If he had made an arrangement, we should I presume have heard some thing about it. I think this a matter of some importance, for if the Judges scatter ad libitum, the docket I fear will remain quite compact, losing very few of its causes; and the few it may lose, will probably be carried off by seriatim opinions. Old men however are timid, and I hope my fears may be unfounded.

I sent you some time past a copy of Algernon Sidney. It is rather antediluvian, but you expressed a wish to see it. The writer is among our ablest men. Most of his friends have been classed among the Jacksonians, but I think their hostility to Mr. Adams rather than their affection for General Jackson has arranged them under his banners.

The world has been so convulsed by peace that I suspect it must have war in order to be made quiet. Materials in abundance have been prepared for a general conflagration, and unless the mass of debt operates as an extinguisher I perceive nothing which can prevent the spread of the flame. I am quite in amaze at the reform in Great Britain, and can come to only one conclusion which is that I know nothing about it, and can form no opinion at all satisfactory even to myself. The great teacher experience can alone inform us what is best for themselves, and for the world.

I presume you are engaged on your circuit. I set out the last of this week. Farewell, with every wish for your happiness I am yours truely

PUBLISHING THE CHEROKEE CASE

To Richard Peters

My dear Sir   Richmond May 19th. 1831

I returned yesterday evening from Raleigh, and received this morning your letter of the 13th. asking my opinion on the propriety of your going on to execute your purpose of publishing the cherokee case entire, as a separate work.

As an individual I should be glad to see the whole case. It is one in which the public takes a deep interest, and of which a very narrow view has been taken in the opinion which is pronounced by the court. The Judge who pronounced that opinion had not time to consider the case in its various bearings and, had his time been ever so abundant, did not think it strictly proper to pass the narrow limits that circumscribed the matter on which the decision of the court turned. The dissenting opinions, it is true, go more at large into the subject, but those which were delivered in court look to one side of the question only, and the public must wish to see both sides. You have received you say the opinion of Judge Thompson; and he I doubt not, presents with ability the other side of the question. But as I have not seen his opinion I am incompetent to decide on its containing what would completely satisfy the public judgement and curiosity.

The argument was in my opinion such as does high honor to the counsel engaged in the cause. Both gentlemen did it ample justice. For reasoning and for eloquence it has been seldom equalled—never surpassed. The intelligent—those who take an interest in forensic discussions—have a right to see it. It may justly claim a place in the official volume of reports. The question seems to me rather to be whether you can withhold the argument entirely from that volume, than whether you may communicate it in another. Its publication in a distinct volume seems to me to be a matter entirely for your own consideration. I as an individual should be gratified with seeing the whole case, and I am persuaded the whole case cannot well be given with the general volume of reports.

This however is my private individual view of the subject.

There may be objections to the course you propose which I do not perceive; but you I am sure will judge rightly in the case.

I wish you a great deal of happiness and am my dear Sir with much esteem and affection Your obedt

REMEMBERING A CHILD'S DEATH

To Joseph Story

My dear Sir   Richmond June 26th. 1831

I have received your two letters of the 29th. & 31st. of May and have adopted your opinion respecting the admiralty jurisdiction, though in doing so I have reversed the decree of my brother Barbour. I felt some doubt whether the General Smith was not shaken by the case of Ramsay v Allegre, in which the court supposed that the note certainly ousted the admiralty of its jurisdiction, without deciding whether, independent of the note, jurisdiction would have existed. I think there is a good deal of force in the argument of Wirt and Meredith that the original cause of action did not merge in the note. However I have maintained the jurisdiction.

I am greatly perplexed about our board for the next winter. You know what passed while you were with us, and how much discontent was expressed at all previous arrangements. I was unwilling to say any thing for two reasons. Being at any rate a bird of passage, whose continuance with you cannot be long, I did not chuse to permit my convenience or my wishes to weigh a feather in the permanent arrangements of my brethren. But in addition, I felt serious doubts, although I did not mention them, whether I should be with you at the next term. What I am about to say is of course in perfect confidence, which I would not breathe to any other person whatever. I had unaccountably calculated on the election of P——t taking place next fall, and had determined to make my continuance in office another year dependent on that event. You know how much importance I attach to the character of the person who is to succeed me, and calculate the influence which probabilities on that subject would have on my continuance in office. This however is a matter of great delicacy on which I cannot and do not speak. My erroneous calculation of the time of election was corrected as soon as the pressure of official duty was removed from my mind, and I had nearly decided on my course, but recent events produce such real uncertainty respecting the future as to create doubts whether I ought not to await the same chances in the fall of 32 which I had intended to await in the fall of 31. This obliges me to look forward to our quarters for the next winter. This uncertainty as to my being with you which had prevented my taking any part in our previous consultations on this subject, if consultations they may be called, prevented my saying any thing on the last day. It seemed then to be conclusively determined that we did not remain with Brown, and I understood that Judge Baldwin would provide lodgings. He said something of relying on his sister to select them; to which I was perfectly agreed. He was of course to communicate any thing which might be done. Not having heard a syllable from him I conclude nothing has been done. We cannot however do any thing for ourselves till we know that he does nothing for us. In this state of uncertainty I have thought of writing to him when he comes to Philadelphia in the fall, and if he has made no arrangement, to provide for ourselves. You Judge Thompson, Judge Duval and myself may I hope contrive to mess together. Brother Duval must be with us or he will be unable to attend consultations. I have supposed you may mention this subject to our brother Thompson, and if he concurs in it write to Brother Duval to engage the old rooms for us at Browns, or to locate us at some other place in the neighborhood. This however must depend on the intelligence to be obtained from Judge Baldwin.

I hear with feelings of deepest sympathy the family affliction you have sustained, and participate sincerely in the grief which both Mrs. Story and yourself must feel. These are wounds into which time and time alone can pour its healing balm—Consolation is vain. I thank you for the verses which the melancholy occasion has produced. They are replete with the deep parental feeling it was calculated to call forth.

You ask me if Mrs. Marshall and myself have ever lost a child. We have lost four—three of them bidding fairer for health and life than any that have survived them. One, a daughter about six or seven was brought fresh to our minds by what you say of yours. She was one of the most fascinating children I ever saw. She was followed within a fortnight by a brother whose death was attended by a circumstance we can never forget. When the child was supposed to be dying I tore the distracted mother from the bed side. We soon afterwards heard a noise in the room which we considered as indicating the death of the infant. We beleived him to be dead. I went into the room and found him still breathing. I returned and as the pang of his death had been felt by his mother, and I was confident he must die I concealed his being alive and prevailed on her to take refuge with her mother who lived the next door across an open square from her. The child lived two days during which I was agonized with its condition and with the occasional hope, though the case was desperate, that I might enrapture his mother with the intelligence of his restoration to us. After the event had taken place, his mother could not bear to return to the house she had left and remained with her mother a fortnight. I then addressed to her a letter in verse in which our mutual loss was deplored, our lost children spoken of with the parental feeling which belonged to the occasion, her affection for those which survived was appealed to, and her religious confidence in the wisdom and goodness of providence excited. The letter closed with a pressing invitation to return to me and her children. This letter has been delayed for the purpose of sending you a copy. But tis lost. Your affectionate

"OUR TRANQUIL FIRE SIDE"

To Mary W. Marshall

My dearest Polly   Philadelphia Oct. 6th. 1831
    Doctor Physic has employed the time since my arrival at this place in examinations and enquiries as preparatory to making up his final opinion respecting the course to be pursued. He deliberates very much, is determined to do nothing rashly, and seems anxious to be perfectly master of my case. His inteligence, his extraordinary attention, and the deep interest he

takes in my welfare, as well as the feeling he shows, have acquired my perfect confidence, and give me the most exalted opinion of his skill and goodness. He seems to be idolized in Philadelphia, and I do not wonder at it.

I have just come out of his last examination, and I beleive he has decided on the treatment of the disease. He has not however as yet commenced with it. I have most sanguine hopes of his being able to restore me. All that man can do I am sure he will do, and I flatter myself that his efforts will be successful. I anticipate with a pleasure which I know you will share the time when I may set by your side by our tranquil fire side & enjoy the happiness of your society without inflicting on you the pain of witnessing my suffering. But it will be a long tedious time before that period can arrive. The Doctor has not spoken definitively respecting the time, but I think I cannot be with you until the meeting of the circuit court on the 22d. of Novr., if then.

I am treated with the most flattering attentions in Philadelphia. They give me pain, the more pain as the necessity of declining many of them may be ascribed to a want of sensibility. I mentioned to you the persevering earnestness with which Mr. Peters and his amiable family pressed me to take a room in his home. I have been equally pressed by Doctor Gillespie. All the gentlemen of the city, especially those of the bar have been most painfully solicitous to show their affectionate and respectful regards. These almost force me into movements which irritate my complaint. To day I am to receive a very flattering address from the young men of the city which will I ardently hope be the last.

I am not sure that the Governor may not require my subscription or a part of it for the Enginier. I forgot it or should have arranged it before my departure. May I trouble you to mention it to Mr. Harvie and to furnish him with any small sum that may be required.

I am not sure that some more lime and salt may not be necessary for steeping and retting my seed wheat. Should the overseer [   ] for any Oby can purchase it. The lime 2[   ] per barrel and the salt at the same price per sack.

Farewell my beloved wife. To hear that you are happy and in at least your usual health would be my greatest gratification. My love to our friends. Your ever affectionate

IRRESISTIBLE PEARS

To Mary W. Marshall

My dearest Polly   Philadelphia Oct. 12th. 1831
     The rains of the last two or three days have confined Doctor
Physick, whose health is delicate, to his house, and prevented
my entering on the course he has prescribed. To day we see the
sun and I hope his operations will begin. My room is now
preparing and he has just left me with directions to take a table
spoonfull of castor oil two hours after dinner. He encourages
me with the expectation of being restored to perfect health,
and my own hopes are as sanguine as usual. Every accomodation I can wish is afforded, and my Landlady is extremely attentive to me. She has engaged one of the best male nurses in
the city who now attends me altho he is not needed, and will do
every thing I can require. I still continue to receive the kindest
attentions from all who see me, and I have a prospect of being
as comfortable as is compatible with my situation.
     Cary Ambler called on me yesterday and left his card. I am
sorry that I had stepped to the office of a portrait painter who
is employed by the gentlemen of the bar to take my portrait. I
did wrong to go out, but could not resist the desire to comply
with their request. The Doctor has laid his interdict on my
going out again. I have just learned this morning that Edward
Ambler is in town. I am sorry that I cannot go to see him.
Doctor Physick I hope will be able to place him once more on
his legs.
     I have just received a long and very friendly letter from my
brother Story. He speaks of coming to this place on purpose to
see me. Mrs. Story I am told is still much depressed.
     I do not wonder that people who have time hanging on
their hands are fond of boarding houses. I find this quite agreeable. If I had my Richmond barber I should I think be quite
contented.
     I over eat myself every day in spite of the wise resolutions I
continually form. The potatoes with butter and the seckle pares
are irresistible. I must of course take some thing solid, and
after finishing my Bucks county fowl I think I will command

myself as to the farther temptations which I remain, but I have never succeeded. In spite of myself I take pare after pare till I am almost ashamed of the number I have eaten.

My affectionate love to our friends Yours ever

HEALTH CONCERNS

To Joseph Story

My dear Sir   Philadelphia Oct. 12th. 1831

I had the pleasure of receiving in the course of the mail your very friendly letter of the 6th.

I have been under the Doctors ever since my return in May from North Carolina and have been regularly growing worse. My disease, for which I have to blame myself, was mistaken. My Physician suspected it, but I was so confident against him that he never made the experiments necessary to establish the fact. At length I suffered so much pain and became so alarmed as to determine on a visit to this place. I have been here a fortnight. Doctor Physic, whom I consulted immediately proceeded very circumspectly. He made some examinations which led to the beleif that I had probably stone in the bladder and on applying the sound at different intervals has decided that I have one. The usual operation was to have been performed a day or two past, but the rainey weather has confined the Doctor whose health is extremely delicate, and I must wait till we see the return of the sun. We have now the promise of a fair day; and should our anticipations be realised I count on going through the operation tomorrow.

I place the most entire confidence in Doctor Physic. Never was man better calculated to inspire confidence in a patient than he is. His profound attention to the case, and his patient investigation of the symptoms added to his very high reputation for skill as a surgeon produce a firm conviction that nothing will be omitted which can contribute to my recovery. I look with impatience for the operation.

Our brother Baldwin is here. He seems to have resumed the dispositions which impressed us both so favorably at the first term. This is as it should be. He spoke of you in terms not indicating unfriendliness. He mentioned our next winters accomodations in such a manner as to show his decided preference for Mrs. Peytons, but he has not engaged the apartments. We must make some positive engagement before the meeting of congress or we shall separate and each be under the necessity of providing for himself. I should have urged an immediate decision had I not been restrained by some communications which have passed between Mr. Peters and Mr. Ringold. When Mr. Peters mentioned that subject to me I expressed my decided approbation to the proposal of our old friend to receive us in his house provided it was agreeable to our brothers. On reflection I suspect the situation of the house, between the palace and Georgetown—will not be to your mind, nor to the mind of the other Judges. I shall suggest this to Peters. Should this conjecture be well founded I think we shall do well to engage immediately with Mrs. Peyton.

On the most interesting part of your letter I have felt and still feel great difficulty. You understand my general sentiments on that subject as well as I do myself. I am most earnestly attached to the character of the department, and to the wishes and convenience of those with whom it has been my pride and my happiness to be associated for so many years. I cannot be insensible to the gloom which lours over us. I have a repugnance to abandoning you under such circumstances which is almost invincible. But the solemn convictions of my judgement sustained by some pride of character admonish me not to hazard the disgrace of continuing in office, a meer inefficient pageant.

In the course of the summer I resorted to different courses of medicine none of which were of any service to me but which had a sensible influence on my general health. My nerves, my digestion and my head were seriously affected. I had found myself unequal to the effective consideration of any subject, and had determined to resign at the close of the year. This determination however I kept to myself being determined to remain master of my own conduct, I at length resolved to take no more medicine, after which I was slowly restored to my former self. This occurred about the time of my leaving Richmond for this place, and notwithstanding the pain I feel, I recover strength daily. I have therefore determined to meet you at the next term and to postpone any thing definitive till then.

Present my most respectful good wishes to Mrs. Story: I indulge the hope that both of you have recovered firmness enough to receive the dispensations of providence however severe with a mindfulness of the great duties which still remain to be performed. With esteem and affection yours truely

RECOVERING FROM SURGERY

To Mary W. Marshall

My dearest Polly   Philadelphia, Nov 8th 1831

I have at length risen from my bed and am able to hold a pen. The most delightful use I can make of it is to tell you that I am getting well and have well founded hopes that I shall be entirely free from the painful disease with which I have been so long affected. I anticipate with a pleasure in which I know you share the gratification of passing with you the long evenings which are before us without any suffering on my part and I will hope without much on yours.

I cannot as yet conjecture when that time will arrive. Doctor Physick is so very anxious for my complete cure that I fear he will be disposed to detain me longer than I shall think necessary. I have not yet ventured to say any thing to him on the subject, but I form an ill augury from the fact that he restrains the exertions I am disposed to make and seems unwilling for me to sit up as long as I wish. I felt so strong while in bed as to think that I should be able at once to leave my room and walk about, but when I got upon my legs I was quickly undeceived. I tottered so as to be scarcely able to walk a step without assistance. I soon however found myself to strengthen and can walk across my room without aid. I have received a letter from Mr. Fisher for which I am greatly obliged to him. Nothing delights me so much as to hear from my friends and especially from you. How much was I gratified at the line from your own hand in Mary's letter: Those only who receive a line from much loved and long absent friends can tell how much. Tell Mary I was infinitely obliged by her letter, but very sorry to hear that William was in delicate health. I fear his digestion is feeble.

I fear I shall not be able to see Doctor Physic today. His constitution is very frail and his health feeble. Yesterday he was confined. When he is sufficiently recovered I shall sound him respecting my return to Richmond. His conversation as yet, though nothing direct has been said rather indicates the impression that I must remain some time longer. Perhaps a fortnight or three weeks. I shall however be able to speak more certainly by the time I write to you again.

I am much obliged by your offer to lend me money. I hope I shall not need it but can not as yet speak positively as my stay has been longer and my expenses greater than I had anticipated on leaving home. Should I use any part of it, you may be assured it will be replaced on my return. But this is a subject on which I know you feel no solicitude. I eat heartily and sleep sound. My wounds are almost healed. I find the use of my limbs by inabling [   ] the better to use them. Under the circumstances I think I must strengthen rapidly.

God bless you my dearest Polly love to all our friends. Ever yours most affectionately

"THE PRIVATIONS OF AGE"

To Joseph Story

My dear Sir   Philadelphia Novr. 10th. 1831

I learn with much regret from our friend Mr. Peters that you have been seriously indisposed. I fear your various duties confine you too closely. You must my dear Sir be careful of your health. Without your vigorous and powerful cooperation I should be in despair, and think the "ship must be given up."

I have had a most tedious confinement. At length however I leave my bed and walk across my room. This I do with a tottering feeble step. It is however hourly improving and I hope next week to take the boat for Richmond in time to open my court on the 22d. Doctor Physick has added to consummate skill the most kind and feeling attention. I shall never forget him.

There has been some difficulty about our next winter's arrangement. You perceive I speak confidently of meeting you. At length it seems fixed that we are to quarter with Ringold. Mr. Peters has written you all about it. I was a little apprehensive that you would be unwilling to locate yourself so far out of the center of the city, but your other friends seem to think you will be greatly pleased. I am told that our accomodations as to rooms will be convenient, and as to every thing else you know they will be excellent. Mr. Johnson I am told will quarter by himself—and our brother McLain will of course preserve his former position. The remaining five will I hope be united.

The circuit court is in session in Philadelphia. Our brother Baldwin has called on me frequently. He is in good health and spirits, and I, always sanguine, hope that the next term will exhibit dispositions more resembling those displayed in the first than the last.

I am at present and have been all the summer, very unfit for serious business. I was not one moment free from pain from the time I parted with you till the operation was performed which extracted about 1000 calculi. You may judge how much I suffered. The pain increased daily and disqualified me for serious thought. Thank Heaven I have reason to hope that I am relieved. I am however under the very disagreeable necessity of taking medicine continually to prevent new formations. I must submit too to a severe and most unsociable regimen. Such are the privations of age. You have before you I trust many very many years unclouded by such dreary prospects.

Farewell. You have the best wishes of him who is with affectionate esteem Your

COLONIZING FREED SLAVES

To Ralph R. Gurley

Dear Sir   Richmond Decr. 14th. 1823

I recieved your letter of the 7th. in the course of the mail, but it was not accompanied by the documents you mention.

I undoubtedly feel a deep interest in the success of the society, but if I had not long since formed a resolution against appearing in print on any occasion, I should now be unable to comply with your request. In addition to various occupations which press on me very seriously, the present state of my family is such as to prevent my attempting to prepare any thing for publication.

The great object of the society I presume is to obtain pecuniary aids. Application will undoubtedly be made, I hope successfully, to the several state legislatures by the societies formed within them respectively. It is extremely desirable that they should pass permanent laws on the subject and the excitement produced by the late insurrection makes this a favourable moment for the friends of the colony to press for such acts. It would be also desirable if such a direction could be given to state legislation as might have some tendency to incline the people of colour to migrate. This however is a subject of much delicacy. Whatever may be the success of our endeavours to obtain acts for permanent aids I have no doubt that our applications for immediate contributions will receive attention. It is possible though not probable that more people of colour may be disposed to migrate than can be provided for with the funds the society may be enabled to command. Under this impression I suggested some years past to one or two of the board of managers to allow a small additional bounty in lands to those who would pay their own passage in whole or in part. The suggestion however was not approved.

It is undoubtedly of great importance to retain the countenance and protection of the general government. Some of our cruisers stationed on the coast of Africa would at the same time interrupt the slave trade—a horrid traffic abhorred by all good men, and would protect the vessels and commerce of the colony from pirates who infest those seas. The power of the government to afford this aid is not I beleive contested. I regret that its power to grant pecuniary aid is not equally free from question. On this subject I have always thought and still think that the proposition made by Mr. King in the senate is the most unexceptionable, and the most effective that can be devised.

The fund would probably operate as rapidly as would be desirable when we take into view the other resources which might come in aid of it, and its application would be perhaps less exposed to those constitutional objections which are made in the south than the application of money drawn from the treasury and raised by taxes. The lands are the property of The United States and have heretofore been disposed of by the government under the idea of absolute ownership. The cessions of the several states convey them to the general government for the common benefit without prescribing any limits to the judgement of Congress, or any rule by which that judgement shall be exercised. The cession of Virginia indeed seems to look to an apportionment of the fund among the states "according to their usual respective proportions in the general charge and expenditure." But this cession was made at a time when the lands were beleived to be the only available fund for paying the debts of the United States and supporting their government. This condition has probably been supposed to be controuled by the existing constitution which gives Congress power to dispose of, and make all needful rules and regulations respecting the territories or this property belonging to The United States. It is certain that the donations made for roads and colleges are not in proportion to the part born by each state of the general expenditure. The removal of our coloured population is I think a common object, by no means confined to the slave states although they are more immediately interested in it. The whole union would be strengthened by it and relieved from a danger whose extent can scarcely be estimated. It lessens very much in my estimation the objection in a political view to this application of this ample fund that our lands are becoming an object for which the states are to scramble and which threaten to sow the seeds of discord among us, instead of being what they might be—a source of national wealth.

I am dear Sir with great and respectful esteem Your Obedt

1831

NATIONAL AND STATE CONTROVERSIES

To Edward C. Marshall

My dear Son   Washington Feby. 15th. 1832

Your letter of the 10th. gave me great pleasure because it assured me of the health of your family and of the health of the other families in which I take so deep an interest. My own has improved. I strengthen considerably and am able without fatigue to walk to court a distance of two miles and to return to dinner. At first this exercise was attended with some difficulty, but I feel no inconvenience from it now.

The sympathetic feeling to which you allude has sustained no diminution. I fear it never will. But I perceive no symptoms, and I trust I never shall of returning disease.

The question on Mr. Van Burens nomination was not exempt from difficulty. Those who opposed him I beleive thought conscienciously that his appointment ought not to be confirmed. They feel a good deal of hostility to that gentleman from other causes than his letter to Mr. McLane. They beleive him to have been at the bottom of a system which they condemn. Whether this conviction be well or ill founded, it is their conviction, at least I beleive it is. In such a case it is extremely difficult, almost impossible for any man to separate himself from his party.

This session of Congress is indeed peculiarly interesting. The discussions on the tariff and on the bank especially will I beleive call forth an unusual display of talent. I have no hope that any accomodation can take place on the first question. The bitterness of party spirit on that subject threatens to continue unabated. There seems to be no prospect of allaying it.

The two great objects in Virginia are internal improvement and our coloured population. On the first I despair. On the

second we might do much if our unfortunate political prejudices did not restrain us from asking the aid of the federal government. As far as I can judge, that aid, if asked, would be
freely and liberally given.

The association you speak of if it could be made extensive
might be of great utility. I would suggest the addition of a resolution not to bring any slave within the county.

My love to Rebecca. I am my dear Son your affectionate
father

Opinion in Worcester v. Georgia

Samuel A Worcester
vs
The State of Georgia

This cause, in every point of view in which it can be placed, is of the deepest interest.

The defendant is a state, a member of the union which has exercised the powers of government over a people who deny its jurisdiction, and are under the protection of The United States.

The plaintiff is a citizen of the State of Vermont, condemned to hard labor for four years in the penitentiary of Georgia, under colour of an act which he alleges to be repugnant to the constitution laws and treaties of The United States.

The legislative power of a state, the controuling power of the constitution and laws of The United states, the rights, if they have any—the political existence of a once numerous and powerful people, the personal liberty of a citizen, are all involved in the subject now to be considered.

It behoves this court in every case, more especially in this, to examine into its jurisdiction with scrutinizing eyes, before it proceeds to the exercise of a power which is controverted.

The first step in the performance of this duty is the enquiry whether the record is properly before the court.

It is certified by the clerk of the court which pronounced the judgement of condemnation under which the plaintiff in error is imprisoned, and is also authenticated by the seal of the court. It is returned with and annexed to a writ of error issued in regular form, the citation being signed by one of the Associate Justices of the Supreme Court, and served on the Governor and Attorney General of the state more than thirty days before the commencement of the term to which the writ of error was returnable.

The judicial act[a] so far as it prescribes the mode of proceeding, appears to have been literally pursued.

a. Judicial act Sec. 22. 25. v. 2. p 64. 65

In February 1797, a rule[a] was made on this subject in the following words, "It is ordered by the court that the clerk of the court to which any writ of error shall be directed may make return of the same by transmitting a true copy of the record, and of all proceedings in the same under his hand and the seal of the court."

This has been done. But the signature of the Judge has not been added to that of the clerk. The law does not require it. The rule does not require it.

In the case of Martin vs Hunters lessee[b] an exception was taken to the return of the refusal of the state court to enter a prior judg. of reversal by this court because it was not made by the judge of the state court to which the writ was directed; but the exception was overruled and the return was held sufficient. In Buel vs Vanness,[c] which was also a writ of error to a state court, the record was authenticated in the same manner. No exception was taken to it. These were civil cases. But it has been truely said at the bar that, in regard to this process, the law makes no distinction between a criminal and civil case. The same return is required in both. If the sanction of the court could be necessary for the establishment of this position, it has been silently given.

MCulloch v The state of Maryland[d] was a qui tam action brought to recover a penalty, and the record was authenticated by the seal of the court and the signature of the clerk without that of a Judge. Brown & al. v The state of Maryland was an indictment for a fine and forfeiture. The record in this case too was authenticated by the seal of the court and the certificate of the clerk. The practice is both ways.

The record then, according to the judiciary act, and the rule, and the practice of the court, is regularly before us. The more important enquiry is, does it exhibit a case cognizable by this tribunal?

The indictment charges the plaintiff in error and others, being white persons, with the offence of "residing within the

a. 6 Wh Rules
b. 1st Wh 304. 361
c. 8th. Wh. 312
d. 4 Wheat 316

limits of the Cherokee nation without a license"; "and without having taken the oath to support and defend the constitution and laws of the state of Georgia."

The defendant in the state court appeared in proper person and filed the following plea. "And the said Samuel A Worcester in his own proper person comes and says that this court ought not to take farther cognizance of the action and prosecution aforesaid, because, he says, that, on the 15th day of July in the year 1831, he was, and still is, a resident in the Cherokee nation; and that the said supposed crime or crimes, and each of them, were committed, if committed at all, at the town of New Echota, in the said Cherokee nation, out of the jurisdiction of this Court, and not in the county Gwinnett, or elsewhere, within the jurisdiction of this Court: and this defendant saith, that he is a citizen of the state of Vermont, one of the United States of America, and that he entered the aforesaid Cherokee nation in the capacity of a duly authorized missionary of the American Board of Commissioners for Foreign Missions, under the authority of the President of the United States, and has not since been required by him to leave it: that he was, at the time of his arrest, engaged in preaching the gospel to the Cherokee Indians, and in translating the sacred Scriptures into their language, with the permission and approval of the said Cherokee nation, and in accordance with the humane policy of the government of the United States for the civilization and improvement of the Indians; and that his residence there, for this purpose, is the residence charged in the aforesaid indictment: and this defendant further saith, that this prosecution the state of Georgia ought not to have or maintain, because, he saith, that several treaties have, from time to time, been entered into between the United States and the Cherokee nation of Indians, to wit, at Hopewell, on the 28th day of November 1785; at Holston, on the 2d day of July 1791; at Philadelphia, on the 26th day of June 1794; at Tellico, on the 2d day of October 1798; at Tellico, on the 24th day of October 1804; at Tellico, on the 25th day of October 1805; at Tellico on the 27th day of October 1805; at Washington city, on the 7th day of January 1805; at Washington City, on the 22d day of March 1816; at the Chickasaw Council House, on the 14th day of September 1816; at the Cherokee Agency, on the 8th day of July 1817; and at

Washington City, on the 27th day of February 1819: all which treaties have been duly ratified by the Senate of the United States of America; and, by which treaties, the United States of America acknowledge the said Cherokee nation to be a sovereign nation, authorised to govern themselves, and all persons who have settled within their territory, free from any right of legislative interference by the several states composing the United States of America, in reference to acts done within their own territory; and, by which treaties, the whole of the territory now occupied by the Cherokee nation, on the east of the Mississippi, has been solemnly guarantied to them; all of which treaties are existing treaties at this day, and in full force. By these treaties, and particularly by the treaties of Hopewell and Holston, the aforesaid territory is acknowledged to lie without the jurisdiction of the several states composing the union of the United States; and, it is thereby specially stipulated, that the citizens of the United States shall not enter the aforesaid territory, even on a visit, without a passport from the governor of a state, or from some one duly authorised thereto, by the President of the United States: all of which will more fully and at large appear, by reference to the aforesaid treaties. And this defendant saith, that the several acts charged in the bill of indictment were done, or omitted to be done, if at all, within the said territory so recognized as belonging to the said nation, and so, as aforesaid, held by them, under the guarantee of the United States: that, for those acts, the defendant is not amenable to the laws of Georgia, nor to the jurisdiction of the Courts of the said state; and that the laws of the state of Georgia, which profess to add the said territory to the several adjacent counties of the said state, and to extend the laws of Georgia over the said territory, and persons inhabiting the same; and, in particular, the act on which this indictment against this defendant is grounded, to wit, 'An act entitled an act to prevent the exercise of assumed and arbitrary power, by all persons, under pretext of authority from the Cherokee Indians, and their laws, and to prevent white persons from residing within that part of the chartered limits of Georgia occupied by the Cherokee Indians, and to provide a guard for the protection of the gold mines, and to enforce the laws of the state within the aforesaid territory,' are repugnant to the aforesaid treaties; which, according to the Constitution of the United States, compose a part of the supreme law of the land; and that these laws of Georgia are, therefore, unconstitutional, void, and of no effect; that the said laws of Georgia are also unconstitutional and void, because they impair the obligation of the various contracts formed by and between the aforesaid Cherokee nation and the said United States of America, as above recited: also, that the said laws of Georgia are unconstitutional and void, because they interfere with, and attempt to regulate and control the intercourse with the said Cherokee nation, which, by the said constitution, belongs exclusively to the Congress of the United States; and because the said laws are repugnant to the statute of the United States, passed on the —— day of March 1802, entitled 'An act to regulate trade and intercourse with the Indian tribes, and to preserve peace on the frontiers:' and that, therefore, this court has no jurisdiction to cause this defendant to make further or other answer to the said bill of indictment, or further to try and punish this defendant for the said supposed offence or offences alleged in the bill of indictment, or any of them: and, therefore, this defendant prays judgment whether he shall be held bound to answer further to said indictment."

This plea was overruled by the court, and the prisoner, being arraigned, pleaded not guilty. The jury found a verdict against him and the court sentenced him to hard labour in the penitentiary for the term of four years.

By overruling this plea, the court decided that the matter it contained was not a bar to the action. The plea therefore must be examined for the purpose of determining whether it makes a case which brings the party within the provisions of the 25th. section of the "act to establish the judicial courts of The United States."

The plea avers that the residence charged in the indictment was under the authority of the President of The United States and with the permission and approval of the Cherokee nation. That the treaties subsisting between The United states and the Cherokees acknowledge their right as a sovereign nation to govern themselves and all persons who have settled within their territory, free from any right of legislative interference by the several states composing The United States of America.

That the act under which the prosecution was instituted is repugnant to the said treaties, and is therefore unconstitutional and void. That the said act is also unconstitutional because it interferes with and attempts to regulate and controul the intercourse with the Cherokee nation which belongs exclusively to Congress; and because also it is repugnant to the statute of The United states entitled "an act to regulate trade and intercourse with the Indian tribes and to preserve peace on the frontiers."

Let the averments of this plea be compared with the 25th. Sec. of the judicial act.

That section enumerates the cases in which the final judgement or decree of a state court may be revised in the Supreme court of The United States. These are "where is drawn in question the validity of a treaty or statute of, or an authority exercised under, The United states and the decision is against their validity; or where is drawn in question the validity of a statute of, or an authority exercised under any state on the ground of their being repugnant to the constitution, treaties or laws of The United States, and the decision is in favor of such their validity; or where is drawn in question the construction of any clause of the constitution, or of a treaty, or statute of, or commission held under The United States, and the decision is against the title right privilege or exemption specially set up or claimed by either party under such clause of the said constitution, treaty, statute, or commission."

The indictment and plea in this case draw in question, we think, the validity of the treaties made by The United States with the Cherokee Indians: if not so, their construction is certainly drawn in question, and the decision has been, if not against their validity, "against the right, privelege or exemption specially set up and claimed under them." They also draw into question the validity of a statute of the state of Georgia "on the ground of its being repugnant to the constitution treaties and laws of The United States, and the decision is in favor of its validity."

It is then we think too clear for controversy that the act of Congress by which this court is constituted, has given it the power, and of course imposed on it the duty, of exercising jurisdiction in this case. This duty, however unpleasant, cannot be avoided. Those who fill the judicial department have no discretion in selecting the subjects to be brought before them. We must examine the defence set up in this plea. We must enquire and decide whether the act of the legislature of Georgia under which the plaintiff in error has been prosecuted and condemned, be consistent with or repugnant to the constitution laws and treaties of The United States.

It has been said at the bar that the acts of the legislature of Georgia seize on the whole Cherokee country, parcel it out among the neighboring counties of the state, extend her code over the whole country, abolish its institutions and its laws, and annihilate its political existence.

If this be the general effect of the system let us enquire into the effect of the particular statute and section on which the indictment is founded.

It enacts that all white persons residing within the limits of the Cherokee nation on the first day of March next, or at anytime thereafter, without a license or permit from his Excellency the Governor, or from such agent as his Excellency the Governor shall authorize to grant such permit or license, and who shall not have taken the oath herein after required, shall be guilty of a high misdemeanor, and, upon conviction thereof, shall be punished by confinement to the penitentiary at hard labor for a term not less than four years.

The 11th. section authorizes the Governor, "should he deem it necessary for the protection of the mines or the enforcement of the laws in force within the Cherokee nation, to raise and organize a guard" &c.

The 13th. section enacts "that the said guard or any member of them shall be and they are hereby authorized and empowered to arrest any person legally charged with or detected in a violation of the laws of this state, and to convey as soon as practicable, the person so arrested before a justice of the peace, Judge of the superior, or Justice of inferior court of this state to be dealt with according to law."

The extraterritorial power of every legislature being limited in its action, to its own citizens or subjects, the very passage of this act is an assertion of jurisdiction over the cherokee nation, and of the rights and powers consequent on jurisdiction.

The first step then in the enquiry which the Constitution

and laws impose on this court, is an examination of the rightfulness of this claim.

America, separated from Europe by a wide ocean, was inhabited by a distinct people, divided into separate nations, independent of each other and of the rest of the world, having institutions of their own, and governing themselves by their own laws. It is difficult to comprehend the proposition that the inhabitants of either quarter of the globe could have rightful original claims of dominion over the inhabitants of the other, or over the lands they occupied; or that the discovery of either by the other should give the discoverer rights in the country discovered, which annulled the preexisting rights of its ancient possessors.

After lying concealed for a series of ages, the enterprize of Europe, guided by nautical science, conducted some of her adventurous sons into this western world. They found it in possession of a people who had made small progress in agriculture or manufactures, and whose general employment was war, hunting and fishing. Did these adventurers by sailing along the coast and occasionally landing on it, acquire for the several governments to whom they belonged or by whom they were commissioned, a rightful property in the soil from the Atlantic to the pacific, or rightful dominion over the numerous people who occupied it? Or has nature or the great creator of all things conferred these rights over hunters and fishermen on agriculturists and manufacturers?

But power, war, conquest give rights which, after possession, are conceded by the world, and which can never be controverted by those on whom they descend. We proceed then to the actual state of things, having glanced at their origin because holding it in our recollection might shed some light on existing pretensions.

The great maritime powers of Europe discovered and visited different parts of this continent at nearly the same time. The object was too immense for any one of them to grasp the whole, and the claimants were too powerful to submit to the exclusive or unreasonable pretensions of any single potentate. To avoid bloody conflicts which might terminate disasterously to all, it was necessary for the nations of Europe to establish some principle which all would acknowledge and which should decide their respective rights as between themselves. This principle—suggested by the actual state of things—was "that[a] discovery gave title to the government by whose subjects or by whose authority it was made, against all other European governments, which title might be consummated by possession."

This principle, acknowledged by all Europeans because it was the interest of all to acknowledge it, gave to the nation making the discovery, as its inevitable consequence, the sole right of acquiring the soil, and of making settlements on it. It was an exclusive principle which shut out the right of competition among those who had agreed to it, not one which could annul the previous rights of those who had not agreed to it. It regulated the right given by discovery among the Europeans discoverers; but could not affect the rights of those already in possession either as aboriginal occupants or as occupants by virtue of a discovery made before the memory of man. It gave the exclusive right to purchase, but did not found that right on a denial of the right of the possessor to sell.

The relation between the Europeans and the natives was determined in each case by the particular government which asserted and could maintain this preemptive privilege in the particular place. The United States succeeded to all the claims of Great Britain both territorial and political, but no attempt so far as is known, has been made to enlarge them. So far as they existed meerly in theory, or were in their nature only exclusive of the claims of other European nations, they still retain their original character and remain dormant. So far as they have been practically exerted, they exist in fact, are understood by both parties, are asserted by the one, and admitted by the other.

Soon after Great Britain determined on planting colonies in America, the King granted charters to companies of his subjects who associated for the purposes of carrying the views of the crown into effect, and of enriching themselves. The first of these charters was made before possession was taken of any part of the country. They purport generally to convey the soil from the Atlantic to the south sea. This soil was occupied by numerous

a. 8 Wh. 573

and warlike nations equally willing and able to defend their possessions. The extravagant and absurd idea that the feeble settlements made on the sea coast or the companies under whom they were made, acquired legitimate power by them to govern the people or occupy the lands from sea to sea did not enter the mind of any man. They were well understood to convey the title which according to the common law of European sovereigns respecting America, they might rightfully convey and no more. This was the exclusive right of purchasing such lands as the natives were willing to sell. The crown could not be understood to grant what the crown did not affect to claim. Nor was it so understood.

The power of making war is conferred by these charters on the colonies, but defensive war alone seems to have been contemplated. In the first charter to the first and second colonies they are empowered "for their several *defences* to encounter expulse repel and resist all persons who shall without license attempt to inhabit" within the said precincts and limits of the said several colonies "or that shall enterprize or attempt at any time hereafter the least detriment or annoyance of the said several colonies or plantations."

The charter to Connecticut concludes a general power to make defensive war with these terms "and, upon *just causes* to invade and destroy the natives or other enemies of the said colony."

The same power in the same words is conferred on the government of Rhode Island.

This power to repel invasion and upon just cause to invade and destroy the natives, authorizes offensive as well as defensive war, but only "on just cause." The very terms imply the existence of a country to be invaded, and of an enemy who has given just cause of war.

The charter to William Penn contains the following recital. "And because in so remote a country near so many barbarous nations the incursions as well of the savages themselves as of other enemies, pirates and robbers may probably be feared, therefore we have given" &c. The instrument then confers the power of war.

These barbarous nations whose incursions were feared and to repel whose incursions the power to make war was given; were surely not considered as the subjects of Penn, as occupying his lands during his pleasure.

The same clause is introduced into the charter to Lord Baltimore.

The charter to Georgia professes to be granted for the charitable purpose of enabling poor subjects to gain a comfortable subsistence by cultivating lands in the American provinces "at present waste and desolate." It recites "And whereas our provinces in North America have been frequently ravaged by Indian enemies, more especially that of South Carolina, which, in the late war by the neighboring savages, was laid waste by fire and sword, and great numbers of the English inhabitants miserably massacred; and our loving subjects who now inhabit there by reason of the smallness of their numbers will, in case of any new war be exposed to the like calamities in as much as their whole southern frontier continueth unsettled and lieth open to the said Savages."

These motives for planting the new colony are incompatible with the lofty ideas of granting the soil and all its inhabitants from sea to sea. They demonstrate the truth that these grants asserted a title against Europeans only, and were considered as blank paper so far as the rights of the natives were concerned. The power of war is given only for defence, not for conquest.

The charters contain passages showing one of their objects to be the civilization of the Indians and their conversion to christianity, objects to be accomplished by conciliating conduct and good example, not by extermination.

The actual state of things, and the practice of European nations on so much of the American continent as lies between the Mississipi and the Atlantic, explain their claims and the charters they granted. Their pretensions unavoidably interfered with each other. Though the discovery of one was admitted by all to exclude the claim of any other, the extent of that discovery was the subject of unceasing contest. Bloody conflicts arose between them which gave importance and security to the neighboring nations. Fierce and warlike in their character, they might be formidable enemies, or effective friends. Instead of rousing their resentments by asserting claims to their lands or to dominion over their persons, their alliance was sought by flattering professions, and purchased by rich presents.

The English, the French, and the Spaniards, were equally competitors for their friendship and their aid. Not well acquainted with the exact meaning of words, nor supposing it to be material whether they were called the subjects or the children of their Father in Europe, lavish in professions of duty and affection in return for the rich presents they received; so long as their actual independence was untouched, and their right to self government acknowledged they were willing to profess dependence on the power which furnished supplies of which they were in absolute need and restrained dangerous intruders from entering their country: and this was probably the sense in which the term was understood by them.

Certain it is that our history furnishes no example, from the first settlement of our country, of any attempt on the part of the crown to interfere with the internal affairs of the Indians farther than to keep out the agents of foreign powers who, as traders, or otherwise, might seduce them into foreign alliances. The King purchased their lands when they were willing to sell, at a price they were willing to take, but never coerced a surrender of them. He also purchased their alliance and dependence by subsidies, but never intruded into the interior of their affairs, or interfered with their self government so far as respected themselves only.

The general views of Great Britain with regard to the Indians were detailed by Mr. Stuart superintendent of Indian affairs in a speech delivered at Mobile in presence of several persons of distinction soon after the peace of 1763. Towards the conclusion he says "Lastly I inform you that it is the King's order to all his Governors and subjects to treat Indians with justice and humanity, and to forbear all encroachments on the territories allotted to them. Accordingly all individuals are prohibited from purchasing any of your lands; but as you know that your white brethren cannot feed you when you visit them unless you give them grounds to plant it is expected that you will sell lands to the King for that purpose. But whenever you shall be pleased to surrender any of your territories to his Majesty, it must be done for the future at a public meeting of your nation, when the governors of the provinces, or the superintendent shall be present, and obtain the consent of all your people. The boundaries of your hunting grounds will be accurately fixed, and no settlement permitted to be made upon them. As you maybe assured that all treaties with you will be faithfully kept, so it is expected that you also will be careful strictly to observe them."

The proclamation issued by the King of Great Britain in 1763 soon after the ratification of the articles of peace forbids the governors of any of the colonies to grant warrants of survey or pass patents upon any lands whatever which not having been ceded to or purchased by us (the King) as aforesaid, are reserved to the said Indians or any of them.

The proclamation proceeds "And we do farther declare it to be our royal will and pleasure for the present as aforesaid, to reserve under our sovereignty protection and dominion for the use of the said Indians all the lands and territories lying to the westward of the sources of the rivers which fall into the sea from the west and northwest as aforesaid; and we do hereby strictly forbid on pain of our displeasure all our loving subjects from making any purchases or settlements whatever or taking possession of any of the lands above reserved without our special leave and license for that purpose first obtained.

And we do farther strictly enjoin and require all persons whatever who have either willfully or inadvertantly seated themselves upon any lands within the countries above described, or upon any other lands which, not having been ceded to or purchased by us, are still reserved to the said Indians as aforesaid forthwith to remove themselves from such settlements."

A proclamation issued by Governor Gage in 1772 contains the following passage "Whereas many persons, contrary to the positive orders of the King upon this subject, have undertaken to make settlements beyond the boundaries fixed by the treaties made with the Indian nations, which boundaries ought to serve as a barrier between the whites and the said nations"; particularly on the ouabache, the proclamation orders such persons to quit those countries without delay.

Such was the policy of Great Britain towards the Indian nations inhabiting the territory from which she excluded all other Europeans, such her claims, and such her practical exposition of the charters she had granted. She considered them as nations capable of maintaining the relations of peace and war, of governing themselves under her protection; and she made treaties with them the obligation of which she acknowledged.

This was the settled state of things when the war of our revolution commenced. The influence of our enemy was established, her resources enabled her to keep up that influence, and the colonists had much cause for the apprehension that the Indian nations would, as the allies of Great Britain, add their arms to hers. This, as was to be expected became an object of great solicitude to Congress. Far from advancing a claim to their lands, or asserting any right of dominion over them, Congress resolved "that the securing and preserving the friendship of the Indian nations appears to be a subject of the utmost moment to these colonies."

The early journals of Congress exhibit the most anxious desire to conciliate the Indian nations. Three Indian departments were established and commissioners appointed in each, "to treat with the Indians in their respective departments in the name and on behalf of the United Colonies, in order to preserve peace and friendship with the said Indians and to prevent their taking any part in the present commotions."

The most strenuous exertions were made to procure those supplies on which Indian friendship was supposed to depend and every thing which might excite hostility was avoided.

The first treaty was made with the Delawares in September 1778.

The language of equality in which it is drawn evinces the temper with which the negotiation was undertaken, and the opinion which then prevailed in The United States.

1st.   "That all offences or acts of hostilities by one or either of the contracting parties against the other be mutually forgiven, and buried in the depth of oblivion, never more to be had in remembrance.

2d.   That a perpetual peace and friendship shall, from henceforth take place and subsist between the contracting parties aforesaid through all succeeding generations: and if either of the parties are engaged in a just and necessary war with any other nation or nations, that then each shall assist the other, in due proportion to their abilities, till their enemies are brought to reasonable terms of accomodation" &c.

3d. The third article stipulates among other things a free passage for the American troops through the Delaware nation, and engages that they shall be furnished with provisions and other necessaries at their value.

4th. "For the better security of the peace and friendship now entered into by the contracting parties against all infractions of the same by the citizens of either party to the prejudice of the other, neither party shall proceed to the infliction of punishments on the citizens of the other, otherwise than by securing the offender or offenders by imprisonment, or any other competent means till a fair and impartial trial can be had by judges or juries of both parties, as near as can be to the laws, customs, and usages of the contracting parties, and natural justice" &c.

5 The 5th. article regulates the trade between the contracting parties in a manner entirely equal.

6th. The 6th article is entitled to peculiar attention, as it contains a disclaimer of designs which were at that time ascribed to The United states by their enemies, and from the imputation of which Congress was then peculiarly anxious to free the government. It is in these words. "Whereas the enemies of The United States has endeavoured by every artifice in their power to possess the Indians in general with an opinion that it is the design of the states aforesaid to extirpate the Indians and take possession of their country; to obviate such false suggestion the United states do engage to guaranty to the aforesaid nation of Delawares and their heirs, all their territorial rights, in the fullest and most ample manner, as it hath been bounded by former treaties as long as the said Delaware nation shall abide by, and hold fast the chain of friendship now entered into."

The parties farther agree that other tribes friendly to the interest of The United States may be invited to form a state whereof the Delaware nation shall be the head, and have a representation in Congress.

This treaty in its language and in its provisions, is formed, as near as may be, on the model of treaties between the crowned heads of Europe.

The 6th. article shows how Congress then treated the injurious calumny of cherishing designs unfriendly to the political and civil rights of the Indians.

During the war of the revolution the Cherokees took part

with the British. After its termination, The United States though desirous of peace, did not feel its necessity so strongly as while that war continued. Their political situation being changed, they might very well think it advisable to assume a higher tone and to impress on the Cherokees the same respect for Congress which was before felt for the King of Great Britain. This may account for the language of the treaty of Hopewell. There is the more reason for supposing that the Cherokee chiefs were not very critical judges of the language from the fact that every one makes his mark. No chief was capable of signing his name. It is probable the treaty was interpreted to them.

The treaty is introduced with the declaration that "The commissioners plenipotentiary of The United States give peace to all the Cherokees and receive them into the favor and protection of The United States of America on the following conditions."

When The United States gave peace did they not also receive it? Were not both parties desirous of it? If we consult the history of the day, does it not inform us that The United States were at least as anxious to obtain it as the cherokees? We may ask farther, did the Cherokees come to the seat of the American government to solicit peace, or did the American commissioners go to them to obtain it. The treaty was made at Hopewell, not at New York. The word "give" them has no real importance attached to it.

The first and second articles stipulate for the mutual restoration of prisoners, and are of course equal.

The 3d. article acknowledges the Cherokees to be under the protection of The United States of America and of no other power. What is the real meaning of this article?

This stipulation is found in Indian treaties generally. It was introduced into their treaties with Great Britain, and may probably be found in those with other European powers. Its origin may be traced to the nature of their connexion with those powers, and its true meaning is discerned in their relative situation.

The general law of European sovereigns respecting their claims in America, limited the intercourse of Indians in a great degree, to the particular potentate whose ultimate right of domain was acknowledged by the others. This was the general state of things in time of peace. It was sometimes changed in war. The consequence was that their supplies were derived chiefly from that nation, and their trade confined to it. Goods indispensable to their comfort in the shape of presents, were received from the same hand. What was of still more importance, the strong hand of government was interposed to restrain the disorderly and licencious from intrusions into their country, from encroachments on their lands and from those acts of violence which were often attended by reciprocal murder. The Indians perceived in this protection only what was beneficial to themselves—an engagement to punish aggressions on them. It involved practically no claim to their lands, no dominion over their persons. It merely bound the nation to the British crown as a dependent ally, claiming the protection of a powerful friend and neighbor and receiving the advantages of that protection without involving a surrender of their national character.

This is the true meaning of the stipulation, and is undoubtedly the sense in which it was made. Neither the British government nor the Cherokees ever understood it otherwise.

The same stipulation entered into with The United States is undoubtedly to be construed in the same manner. They receive the Cherokee nation into their favor and protection. The Cherokees acknowledge themselves to be under the protection of The United States and of no other power. Protection does not imply the destruction of the protected. The manner in which this stipulation was understood by the American government is explained by the language and acts of our first President.

The 4th. article draws the boundary between the Indians and the citizens of The United States. But in describing this boundary the term "allotted" and the term "Hunting ground" are used. Is it reasonable to suppose that the Indians who could not write, and most probably could not read, who certainly were not critical judges of our language, should distinguish the word "allotted" from the words "marked out." The actual subject of contract was the dividing line between the two nations, and their attention may very well be supposed to have been confined to that subject. When in fact they were ceding lands to The United States and describing the extent of their cession, it may very well be supposed that they might not understand the term employed as indicating that instead of granting they were receiving lands. If the term would admit of no other signification, which is not conceded, its being misunderstood is so apparent, results so necessarily from the whole transaction, that it must we think be taken in the sense in which it was most obviously used.

So with respect to the words "hunting grounds." Hunting was at that time the principal occupation of the Indians, and their land was more used for that purpose than for any other. It could not however be supposed that any intention existed of restricting their full use of the lands they reserved. To The United States it could be a matter of no concern whether their whole territory was devoted to hunting ground, or whether an occasional village, and an occasional cornfield, interupted, and gave some variety to the scene.

These terms had been used in their treaties with Great Britain and had never been misunderstood. They had never been supposed to imply a right in the British government to take their lands, or to interfere with their internal government.

The 5th. article withdraws the protection of The United States from any citizen who has settled or shall settle on the lands allotted to the Indians for their hunting grounds, and stipulates that if he shall not remove within six months the Indians may punish him.

The 6th. & 7th. articles stipulate for the punishment of the citizens of either country who may commit offences on or against the citizens of the other. The only inference to be drawn from them is that The United States considered the Cherokees as a nation.

The 9th. article is in these words. "For the benefit and comfort of the Indians, and for the prevention of injuries or oppressions on the part of the citizens or Indians, The United States in Congress assembled shall have the sole and exclusive right of regulating the trade with the Indians, and *managing all their affairs*, as they think proper."

To construe the expression "managing all their affairs" into a surrender of self government would be, we think a perversion of their necessary meaning, and a departure from the construction which has been uniformly put on them. The great subject of the article is the Indian trade. The influence it gave made it desirable that Congress should possess it. The commissioners brought forward the claim with the profession that their motive was, "the benefit and comfort of the Indians, and the prevention of injuries or oppressions." This may be true as respects the regulation of their trade, and as respects the regulation of all affairs connected with their trade, but cannot be true as respects the management of *all their affairs*. The most important of these is the cession of their lands, and security against intruders on them. Is it credible that they could have considered themselves as surrendering to The United States the right to dictate their future cessions and the terms on which they should be made? Or to compel their submission to the violence of disorderly and licencious intruders? It is equally inconceivable that they could have supposed themselves, by a phrase thus slipped into an article on another and most interesting subject, to have divested themselves of the right of self government on subjects not connected with trade. Such a measure could not be "for their benefit and comfort" or for "the prevention of injuries and oppression." Such a construction would be inconsistent with the spirit of this and all subsequent treaties. Especially of those articles which recognize the right of the Cherokees to declare hostilities, and to make war. It would convert a treaty of peace covertly into an act annihilating the political existence of one of the parties. Had such a result been intended it would have been openly avowed.

This treaty contains a few terms capable of being used in a sense which could not have been intended at the time, and which is inconsistent with the practical construction which has always been put on them; but its essential articles treat the Cherokees as a nation capable of maintaining the relations of peace and war; and ascertain the boundary between them and The United States.

The treaty of Hopewell seems not to have established a solid peace. To accomodate the differences still existing between the State of Georgia and the Cherokee nation, the treaty of Holstein was negotiated in July 1791. The existing constitution of The United States had been then adopted, and the government, having more intrinsic capacity to enforce its just claims, was perhaps less mindful of high sounding expressions denoting superiority. We hear no more of giving peace to the Cherokees. The mutual desire of establishing permanent peace and friendship, and of removing all causes of war is honestly avowed, and, in pursuance of this desire, the first article declares that there shall be perpetual peace and friendship between all the citizens of The United States of America and all the individuals composing The Cherokee Nation.

The 2d. article repeats the important acknowledgement that the Cherokee nation is under the protection of The United States of America, and of no other sovereign whosoever.

The meaning of this has been already explained. The Indian nations were from their situation necessarily dependent on some foreign potentate for the supply of their essential wants, and for their protection from lawless and injurious intrusions into their country. That power was naturally termed their protector. They had been arranged under the protection of Great Britain. But the extinguishment of the British power in their neighborhood, and the establishment of that of The United States in its place, led naturally to the declaration on the part of the Cherokees that they were under the protection of The United States and of no other power. They assumed the relation with The United States which had before subsisted with Great Britain. This relation was that of a nation claiming and receiving the protection of one more powerful, not that of individuals abandoning their national character and submitting as subjects to the laws of a master.

The 3d article contains a perfectly equal stipulation for the surrender of prisoners.

The 4th. article declares that "the boundary between The United States and the Cherokee nation shall be as follows. "Beginning &c." We hear no more of "allotments" or of "hunting grounds." A boundary is described between nation and nation by mutual consent. The national character of each, the ability of each to establish this boundary is acknowledged by the other. To preclude forever all disputes, it is agreed that it shall be plainly marked by commissioners to be appointed by each party, and in order to extinguish forever all claims of the Cherokees to the ceded lands, an additional consideration is to

be paid by The United States. For this additional consideration the Cherokees release all right to the ceded land forever.

By the 5th. article the Cherokees allow The United States a
road through their country, and the navigation of the Tenessee
river. The acceptance of these cessions is an acknowledgment
of the right of the Cherokees to make or withhold them.

By the 6th. article it is agreed on the part of the Cherokees
that The United States shall have the sole and exclusive right
of regulating their trade. No claim is made to "the management of all their affairs." This stipulation has already been explained. The observation may be repeated that the stipulation
is itself an admission of their right to make or refuse it.

By the 7th. article The United States solemnly guaranty to
the Cherokee nation all their lands not hereby ceded.

The 8th. article relinquishes to the Cherokees any citizen of
The United States who may settle on their lands. And the 9th.
forbids any citizen of The United States to hunt on their lands
or to enter their country without a passport.

The remaining articles are equal, and contain stipulations
which could be made only with a nation admitted to be capable of governing itself.

This treaty thus explicitly recognizing the national character
of the Cherokees and their right of self government, thus
guarantying their lands, assuming the duty of protection, and
of course pledging the faith of The United States for that protection, has been frequently renewed and is now in full force.
To the general pledge of protection have been added several
specific pledges deemed valuable by the Indians. Some of these
restrain the citizens of The United States from encroachments
on the Cherokee country, and provide for the punishment of
intruders.

From the commencement of our government Congress has
passed acts to regulate trade and intercourse with the Indians
which treat them as nations, respect their rights, and manifest a
firm purpose to afford that protection which treaties stipulate.
All these acts, and especially that of 1802 which is still in force,
manifestly consider the several Indian nations as distinct political communities, having territorial boundaries within which
their authority is exclusive and having a right to all the land

within those boundaries which is not only acknowledged but guarantied by The United States.

In 1819 Congress passed an act for promoting those humane designs of civilizing the neighboring Indians which had been long cherished by the Executive. It enacts "that for the purpose of providing against the farther decline and final extinction of the Indian tribes adjoining to the frontier settlements of The United States, and for introducing among them the habits and arts of civilization, the President of The United States shall be and he is hereby authorized, in every case where he shall judge improvement in the habits and condition of such Indians practicable, and that the means of instruction can he introduced *with their own consent*, to employ capable persons of good moral character to instruct them in the mode of agriculture suited to their situation; and for teaching their children in reading writing and arithmetic, and for performing such other duties as may be enjoined according to such instructions and rules as the President may give and prescribe for the regulation of their conduct, in the discharge of their duties."

This act avowedly contemplates the preservation of the Indian nations as an object sought by The United States, and proposes to effect this object by civilizing and converting them from hunters into agriculturists. Though the Cherokees had already made considerable progress in this improvement, it cannot be doubted that the general words of the act comprehend them. Their advance in the "habits and arts of civilization," rather encouraged perseverance in the laudable exertions still farther to meliorate their condition. This act furnishes strong additional evidence of a settled purpose to fix the Indians in their country by giving them security at home.

The treaties and laws of The United States contemplate the Indian territory as completely separated from that of the states, and provide that all intercourse with them shall be carried on exclusively by the government of the Union.

Is this the rightful exercise of power, or is it usurpation?

While these states were colonies this power, in its utmost extent, was admitted to reside in the crown. When our revolutionary struggle commenced Congress was composed of an assemblage of deputies acting under specific powers granted by the legislatures or conventions of the several Colonies. It was a great popular movement not perfectly organized, nor were the respective powers of those who were entrusted with the management of affairs accurately defined. The necessities of our situation produced a general conviction that those measures which concerned all, must be transacted by a body in which the representatives of all were assembled, and which could command the confidence of all. Congress therefore was considered as invested with all the powers of war and peace, and Congress dissolved our connexion with the mother country and declared these United colonies to be independent states. Without any written definition of powers, they employed diplomatic agents to represent The United States at the several courts of Europe, offered to negotiate treaties with them, and did actually negotiate treaties, with France. From the same necessity, and on the same principles Congress assumed the management of Indian affairs first in the name of these United Colonies and afterwards in the name of The United States. Early attempts were made at negotiation, and to regulate trade with them. These not proving successful, war was carried on under the direction and with the forces of The United States, and the efforts to make peace by treaty were earnest and incessant. The confederation found Congress in the exercise of the same powers of peace and war in our relations with the Indian nations as with those of Europe.

Such was the state of things when the confederation was adopted. That instrument surrendered the powers of peace and war to Congress and prohibited them to the states respectively, unless a state be actually invaded, "or shall have received certain advice of a resolution being formed by some nation of Indians to invade such state, and the danger is so imminent as not to admit of delay till The United States in Congress assembled can be consulted." This instrument also gave The United States in Congress assembled the sole and exclusive right of "regulating the trade and managing all affairs with the Indians not members of any of the states; provided that the legislative power of any state within its own limits be not infringed or violated."

The ambiguous phrazes which follow the grant of power to The United States were so construed by the States of North Carolina and Georgia as to annul the power itself. The discontents and confusion resulting from these conflicting claims produced representations to Congress which were referred to a committee who made their report in 1787. The report does not assent to the construction of the two states, but recommends an accomodation by liberal cessions of territory, or by an admission on their part, of the powers claimed by Congress. The correct exposition of this article is rendered unnecessary by the adoption of our existing constitution. That instrument confers on Congress the powers of war and peace, of making treaties, and of regulating commerce with foreign nations and among the several states, and *with the Indian tribes.* These powers comprehend all that is required for the regulation of our intercourse with the Indians. They are not limited by any restrictions on their free actions. The shackles imposed on this power in the confederation are discarded. The Indian nations had always been considered as distinct independent political communities, retaining their original natural rights as the undisputed possessors of the soil from time immemorial, with the single exception of that imposed by irresistable power, which excluded them from intercourse with any other European potentate than the first discoverer of the coast of the particular region claimed; and this was a restriction which those European potentates imposed on themselves as well as on the Indians. The very term "nation" so generally applied to them means "a people distinct from others." The constitution, by declaring treaties already made was well as those to be made, to be the supreme law of the land, has adopted and sanctioned the previous treaties with the Indian nations; and consequently, admits their rank among those powers who are capable of making treaties. The words "treaty" and "nation" are words of our own language, selected in our diplomatic and legislative proceedings by ourselves, having each a definite and well understood meaning. We have applied them to Indians as we have applied them to the other nations of the earth. They are applied to all in the same sense.

Georgia herself has furnished conclusive evidence that her former opinions on this subject concurred with those entertained by her sister states, and by the government of The United States. Various acts of her legislature have been cited in the argument, including the contract of cession made in the year 1802, all tending to prove her acquiescence in the universal conviction that the Indian nations possessed a full right to the lands they occupied until that right should be extinguished by The United States with their consent, that their territory was separated from that of any state within whose chartered limits they might reside by a boundary line established by treaties, that within their boundary they possessed rights with which no state could interfere, and that the whole power of regulating the intercourse with them was vested in The United States. A review of these acts on the part of Georgia would occupy too much time and is the less necessary because they have been accurately detailed in the argument at the bar. Her new series of laws, manifesting her abandonment of these opinions appears to have commenced in December 1828.

In opposition to this original right possessed by the undisputed occupants of every country, to this recognition of that right which is evidenced by our history in every change through which we have passed, is placed the charters granted by the monarch of a distant and distinct region, parcelling out a territory in possession of others whom he could not remove and did not attempt to remove, and the cession made of his claims by the treaty of peace.

The actual state of things at the time, and all history since, explain these charters; and the King of Great Britain, at the treaty of peace could cede only what belonged to his crown. These newly asserted titles can derive no aid from the articles so often repeated in Indian treaties extending to them first the protection of Great Britain and afterwards that of The United States. These articles are associated with others recognizing their title to self government. The very fact of repeated treaties with them recognizes it, and the settled doctrine of the law of nations is that a weaker power does not surrender its independence—its right to self government, by associating with a stronger and taking its protection. A weak state, in order to provide for its safety, may place itself under the protection of one more powerful without stripping itself of the right of government, and ceasing to be a state. Examples of this kind are not wanting in Europe. "Tributary and feudatory states, says Vattel, do not thereby cease to be sovereign and independent states, so long as self government, and sovereign and independent authority is left in the administration of the state." At the present day more than one state may be considered as holding its right of self government under the guaranty and protection of one or more allies.

The Cherokee nation then is a distinct community, occupying its own territory, with boundries accurately described, in which the laws of Georgia can have no force, and which the citizens of Georgia have no right to enter, but with the assent of the Cherokees themselves, or in conformity with treaties, and with the acts of Congress. The whole intercourse between The United States and this nation is by our constitution and laws vested in the government of The United States.

The act of the state of Georgia under which the plaintiff in error was prosecuted is consequently void, and the judgement a nullity. Can this court revise and reverse it?

If the objection to the system of legislation lately adopted by the legislature of Georgia in relation to the Cherokee nation was confined to its extraterritorial operation, the objection, though complete, so far as respected meer right, would give this court no power over the subject. But it goes much farther. If the review which has been taken be correct, and we think it is, the acts of Georgia are repugnant to the constitution, laws and treaties of The United States.

They interfere forcibly with the relations established between The United States and the Cherokee nation, the regulation of which according to the settled principles of our constitution, are committed exclusively to the government of the union.

They are in direct hostility with treaties, repeated in a succession of years, which mark out the boundary that separates the Cherokee country from Georgia, guarantee to them all the land within their boundary, solemnly pledge the faith of The United states to restrain their citizens from trespassing on it, and recognize the preexisting power of the nation to govern itself.

They are in equal hostility with the acts of Congress for regulating this intercourse and giving effect to the treaties.

The forcible seizure and abduction of the plaintiff in error who was residing in the nation with its permission, and by authority of the President of The United States, is also a violation of the acts which authorize the Chief magistrate to exercise this authority.

Will these powerful considerations avail the plaintiff in error? We think they will. He was seized and forcibly carried away, while under the guardianship of treaties guarantying the country in which he resided, and taking it under the protection of The United States. He was seized while performing, under the sanction of the chief Magistrate of the Union, those duties which the humane policy adopted by Congress had recommended. He was apprehended tried and condemned under colour of a law which has been shown to be repugnant to the constitution laws and treaties of The United States. Had a judgement liable to the same objections been rendered for property none would question the jurisdiction of this court. It cannot be less clear when the judgement affects personal liberty, and inflicts disgraceful punishment, if punishment could disgrace when inflicted on innocence. The plaintiff in error is not less interested in the operation of this unconstitutional law than if it affected his property. He is not less entitled to the protection of the constitution laws and treaties of his country.

It is the opinion of this court that the judgement of the superior court for the county of Gwinnett in the state of Georgia condemning Samuel A Worcester to hard labor in the penitentiary of the state of Georgia for four years was pronounced by that court under colour of a law which is void as being repugnant to the constitution treaties and laws of The United States and ought therefore to be reversed and annulled.

March 3, 1832

The Life of George Washington
Second Edition, Volume I

PREFACE

The author persuades himself that no apology will be required for offering to his fellow-citizens a revised edition of the LIFE OF GENERAL WASHINGTON.

The period during which he lived, and acted a conspicuous part in American affairs, was the most interesting of American history. The war of our revolution, the very instructive interval between its termination and the adoption of our present constitution, the organization of the new government, and the principles which were developed in its first operation, form great epochs, claiming the attention not only of every statesman, but of every American unwilling to remain ignorant of the history of his country, and the character of his countrymen.

The transactions of this period constitute the subject of the following pages. In compiling them, the Author has relied chiefly on the manuscript papers of General Washington. These have supplied the requisite information respecting all facts immediately connected with himself. But as many occurrences are unavoidably introduced in which he acted no direct part, it has been drawn occasionally from other sources.

The history of General Washington, from the time of his appointment to the command of the American armies, is the history of his country. Yet the peculiar character of biography seemed to require that his private opinions, and his various plans, whether carried into execution or neglected, should be given more in detail than might be deemed proper in a general history. Copious extracts have, therefore, been made from his correspondence. Many political events, too, especially during the war, while his particular duties were of a military character, seem less appropriate to his biography, than to a professed history of the United States. These are alluded to incidentally.

The great questions which were debated in Congress during the first operations of the government, have not yet lost their

interest. Deep impressions were then made respecting the subjects themselves, and the persons by whom the various important propositions then discussed were supported or opposed,
which are not yet entirely effaced. Justice to the patriot statesmen, who then devoted their time and talents to the public
service, requires that the reasons on which they acted should
be known. The arguments, therefore, for and against those
measures which had most influence over the opinion of the nation, are substantially stated. They are necessarily collected
from the papers of the day.

Other transactions of immense importance at the time, conveying lessons as instructive as experience can give, in which
almost every individual took some part, passed under the view
of the nation, and are detailed, in some degree, from the observation of the author himself. In stating these, which belong
equally to history and biography, his endeavour has been to
represent sentiments and actions, leaving it to the reader to
draw his own conclusions from them.

The work was originally composed under circumstances
which might afford some apology for its being finished with
less care than its importance demanded. The immense mass of
papers which it was necessary to read, many of them interesting
when written, but no longer so, occupied great part of that
time which the impatience of the public could allow for the appearance of the book itself. It was therefore hurried to the
press without that previous careful examination, which would
have resulted in the correction of some faults that have been
since perceived. In the hope of presenting the work to the
public in a form more worthy of its acceptance, and more satisfactory to himself, the author has given it a careful revision.
The language has been, in some instances, altered—he trusts
improved; and the narrative, especially that part of it which details the distresses of the army during the war, relieved from
tedious repetitions of the same suffering. The work is reduced
in its volume, without discarding any essential information.

CHAPTER VIII.

General Washington commences his march to the Delaware.—Takes measures for checking Burgoyne.—Expedition against Staten Island.—British army lands at Elk River.—General Washington advances to Brandywine.—Retreat of Maxwell.—Defeat at Brandywine.—Slight skirmish near the White Horse, and retreat to French Creek.—General Wayne surprised.—General Howe takes possession of Philadelphia.—Removal of Congress to Lancaster.

On receiving intelligence that the British fleet had sailed from New York, the American army commenced its march to the Delaware. About the time of its departure, a letter from Sir Willam Howe, directed to General Burgoyne at Quebec, was delivered to General Putnam by the person who had received it, as was said, for the purpose of carrying it to Quebec, and was transmitted by Putnam to the Commander-in-chief. In this letter, General Howe said that "he was exhibiting the appearance of moving to the southward, while his real intent was against Boston, from whence he would co-operate with the army of Canada." This stratagem entirely failed. General Washington, at once, perceived that the letter was written with a design that it should fall into his hands, and mislead him with respect to the views of the writer.

1777. July.

While the utmost vigilance and judgment were required to conduct the operations of the army under the immediate command of General Washington, the transactions in the north were too vitally interesting not to engage a large share of his attention. He not only hastened the march of those generals who were designed to act in that department, and pressed the governors of the eastern states to reinforce the retreating army with all their militia, but made large detachments of choice troops from his own;—thus weakening himself in order to strengthen other generals whose strength would be more useful. The fame of being himself the leader of the victorious army did not, with false glare, dazzle his judgment, or conceal the superior public advantage to be derived from defeating the plans of Burgoyne.

On the 30th of July, all doubts respecting the destination of the British fleet were supposed to be removed by its appearance off the capes of Delaware; and orders were immediately given for assembling the detached parts of the army in the neighbourhood of Philadelphia. Scarcely were these orders given, when the aspect of affairs was changed, and they were countermanded. An express from Cape May brought the information that the fleet had sailed out of the bay of Delaware, and was proceeding eastward. From this time, no intelligence respecting it was received until about the 7th of August, when it appeared a few leagues south of the capes of Delaware, after which it disappeared, and was not again seen until late in that month. The fact was, that on entering the capes of Delaware, the difficulties attending an attempt to carry his fleet up that bay and river, determined General Howe to relinquish his original design, and to transport his army to the Chesapeake. Contrary winds prevented his gaining the mouth of that bay until the 16th of August.

The several divisions of the army were immediately ordered*
to unite in the neighbourhood of Philadelphia, and the militia

---

*These orders were received by General Sullivan, who had been encamped about Hanover, in Jersey, on his return from an expedition to Staten Island. The British force on that island amounted to between two and three thousand men, of whom nearly one thousand were provincials, who were distributed along the coast, opposite the Jersey shore. The Europeans occupied a fortified camp near the watering place; and General Sullivan thought it practicable to surprise the provincials, and bring them off before they could be supported by the Europeans. Only six boats had been procured for the conveyance of his troops; yet they crossed over into the island before day undiscovered, and completely surprised two of the provincial parties, commended by Colonels Lawrence and Barton, both of whom, with several officers and men were taken. The alarm being given, Sullivan attempted to withdraw from the island. The number of boats not being sufficient for the embarkation of all his troops at the same time, some confusion obtained among them. General Campbell advanced in force on the rear guard while waiting for the return of the boats, which was captured after making a gallant resistance.

This enterprise was well planned, and in its commencement, happily executed; but ought not to have been undertaken without a number of boats sufficient to secure the retreat.

The loss of the British in prisoners amounted to eleven officers, and one hundred and thirty privates. That of the Americans, is stated by Sullivan, at one major, one captain, one lieutenant, and ten privates killed, and fifteen wounded, and nine officers, and one hundred and twenty-seven privates prisoners. General Campbell, in his account of the action says, that he made two hundred and fifty-nine prisoners, among whom were one lieutenant colonel, three majors, two captains, and fifteen inferior officers.

of Pennsylvania, Maryland, Delaware, and the northern counties of Virginia, were directed to take the field.

The British fleet, after entering the Chesapeake, sailed up it with favourable winds, and entered Elk river, up which the admiral proceeded as high as it was safely navigable; and on the 25th of August the troops were landed at the ferry.

The British army, at its disembarkation, has been generally computed at eighteen thousand men. They were in good health and spirits, admirably supplied with all the implements of war, and led by an experienced general, of unquestionable military talents.

The day before Sir William Howe landed, the American army marched through Philadelphia, and proceeded to the Brandywine. The divisions of Greene and Stephen were advanced nearer to the Head of Elk, and encamped behind White Clay creek.

Congress had directed General Smallwood and Colonel Gist to take command of the militia of Maryland, who had been ordered by General Washington to assemble near the head of the bay. The militia of the lower counties of Delaware, commanded by General Rodney, were directed also to assemble in the British rear, and to co-operate with those of Maryland. Colonel Richardson's continental regiment, which had been stationed on the Eastern shore, was ordered to join this corps.

The militia of Pennsylvania, commanded by Major General Armstrong, were united with the main body of the army. Great exertions were used to bring them promptly into the field, and they came forward generally with some degree of alacrity. Although the numbers required by congress did not assemble, more appeared than could be armed.

The real strength of the American army can not be accurately stated. It was estimated by Sir William Howe at fifteen thousand, including militia; and this estimate did not far exceed their real total, as exhibited by the returns. But it is a fact, attributable in some degree to the badness of their clothing, and scarcity of tents, and in some degree to the neglect of the commissary department, to provide those articles of food which contribute to the preservation of health, that the effective force was always far below the total number. The effectives, including militia, did not exceed eleven thousand.

Morgan's regiment of riflemen having been detached to the northern army, a corps of light infantry was formed for the occasion, the command of which was given to General Maxwell. This corps was advanced to Iron Hill, about three miles in front of White Clay creek. The cavalry, consisting of four regiments, amounting to about nine hundred men, including persons of every description, were employed principally on the lines.

One division of the British army, commanded by Sir William Howe in person, had taken post at Elkton, with its van advanced to Gray's Hill. General Knyphausen, with a second division, had crossed the ferry and encamped at Cecil Court House. He was directed to march up on the eastern side of the river, and to join Sir William Howe seven or eight miles south of Christiana. The intention to make this movement being disclosed by the preparatory arrangements, General Washington advised Maxwell to post a choice body of men in the night on an advantageous part of the road, in order to annoy him on his march. In the morning of the third of September, the two divisions under Lord Cornwallis and General Knyphausen, moved forward and formed a junction at Pencader, or Atkins' tavern, where they encamped. In their way, the column led by Lord Cornwallis fell in with and attacked Maxwell, who retreated over White Clay creek, with the loss of about forty killed and wounded.

The whole American army, except the light infantry, took a position behind Red Clay creek, on the road leading from the camp of Sir William Howe to Philadelphia. On this ground, the general thought it probable that the fate of Philadelphia, and of the campaign, might be decided; and he resorted to all the means in his power to encourage his troops, and stimulate them to the greatest exertions.

On the 8th of September, the British army was again put in motion. The main body advanced by Newark, upon the right of the Americans, and encamped within four miles of that place, extending its left still farther up the country. Meanwhile, a strong column made a show of attacking in front, and, after manœuvring some time, halted at Milton, within two miles of the centre.

General Washington was soon convinced that the column in front was designed only to amuse, while the left should effect the principal and real object. Believing that object to be to turn his right, and cut off his communication with Philadelphia, he changed his ground, and, crossing the Brandywine early in the night, took post behind that river, at Chadd's Ford. General Maxwell was advanced in front, and placed, advantageously, on the hills south of the river, on the road leading over the ford. The militia under General Armstrong, were posted at a ford two miles below Chadd's; and the right extended some miles above, with a view to other passes deemed less practicable. In this position, General Washington attended the movements of the adverse army.

In the evening, Howe marched forward in two columns, which united, early the next morning, at Kennet's Square; after which he advanced parties on the roads leading to Lancaster, to Chadd's Ford, and to Wilmington.

Sept. 10.

The armies were now within seven miles of each other, with only the Brandywine between them, which opposed no obstacle to a general engagement. This was sought by Howe, and not avoided by Washington. It was impossible to protect Philadelphia without a victory, and this object was deemed throughout America, and especially by congress, of such magnitude as to require that an action should be hazarded for its attainment.

In the morning of the 11th, soon after day, information was received that the whole British army was in motion, advancing on the direct road leading over Chadd's Ford. The Americans were immediately under arms, and placed in order of battle, for the purpose of contesting the passage of the river. Skirmishing soon commenced between the advanced parties; and, by ten, Maxwell's corps, with little loss on either side, was driven over the Brandywine below the ford. Knyphausen, who commanded this column, paraded on the heights, reconnoitred the American army, and appeared to be making dispositions to force the passage of the river. A skirt of woods, with the river, divided him from Maxwell's corps, small parties of whom occasionally crossed over, and kept up a scattering fire, by which not much execution was done. At length one of these parties, led by Captains Waggoner and Porterfield, engaged the British flank guard very closely, killed a captain with ten or fifteen privates, drove them out of the wood, and were on the point of taking a field piece. The sharpness of the skirmish soon drew a large body of the British to that quarter, and the Americans were again driven over the Brandywine.*

About eleven in the morning, information reached General Washington that a large column with many field pieces, had taken a road leading from Kennet's Square, directly up the country, and had entered the great valley road, down which they were marching to the upper fords of the Brandywine. This information was given by Colonel Ross of Pennsylvania, who was in their rear, and estimated their numbers at five thousand men.

On receiving this information, Washington is said to have determined to detach Sullivan and Lord Stirling to engage the left division of the British army, and with the residue of his troops, to cross Chadd's Ford in person, and attack Knyphausen. Before this plan could be executed, counter intelligence was received inducing an opinion that the movement of the British on their left was a feint, and that the column under Lord Cornwallis, after making demonstrations of crossing the Brandywine above its forks, had marched down the southern side of that river to reunite itself with Knyphausen.

Not long after the first communication was made by Colonel Ross, information was received from Colonel Bland of the cavalry, which produced some doubt respecting the strength of this column. He saw only two brigades; but the dust appeared to rise in their rear for a considerable distance. A major of the militia came in, who alleged that he left the forks of the Brandywine so late in the day that it was supposed Lord Cornwallis must have passed them by that time, had he continued his march in that direction, and who asserted that no enemy had appeared in that quarter. Some light horsemen who had been sent to reconnoitre the road, returned with the same information.

The uncertainty produced by this contradictory intelligence was at length removed; and about two in the afternoon, it was ascertained that the column led by Lord Cornwallis, after making a circuit of about seventeen miles, had crossed the river above its forks, and was advancing in great force.

A change of disposition was immediately made. The divisions

---

*The author was an eye-witness of this skirmish.

commanded by Sullivan, Stirling, and Stephen, took new ground, advanced further up the Brandywine, and fronted the British column marching down that river. The division commanded by Wayne remained at Chadd's Ford, to keep Knyphausen in check; in which service Maxwell was to co-operate. Greene's division, accompanied by General Washington in person, formed a reserve, and took a central position between the right and left wings.

The divisions detached against Lord Cornwallis formed hastily on an advantageous piece of ground, above Birmingham Meeting House, with their left near the Brandywine, and having both flanks covered by a thick wood. The artillery was judiciously posted, and the disposition of the whole was well made. Unfortunately, Sullivan's division, in taking its ground, made too large a circuit, and was scarcely formed when the attack commenced.

On perceiving the Americans, the British army was formed in order of battle; and, about half past four, the action began. It was kept up warmly for some time. The American right first gave way, and by its flight exposed the flank of the remaining divisions to a galling fire. The line continued to break from the right, and, in a short time, was completely routed. The right wing made some attempts to rally, but, being briskly charged, again broke, and the flight became general.

On the commencement of the action on the right, General Washington pressed forward with Greene, to the support of that wing; but, before his arrival, its rout was complete, and he could only check the pursuit. For this purpose, the 10th Virginia regiment commanded by Colonel Stevens, and a regiment of Pennsylvania commanded by Colonel Stewart, neither of which had been in action, were posted advantageously on the road taken by the defeated army. The impression made by the fire of these regiments, and the approach of night, induced Sir William Howe, after dispersing them, to give over the pursuit.

When the American right was found to be fully engaged with Lord Cornwallis, Knyphausen made real dispositions for crossing the river. Chadd's Ford was defended by an intrenchment and battery, with three field pieces, and a howitzer. After some resistance, the work was forced; and, the defeat of the right being known, the left wing also withdrew from its ground. The whole army retreated that night to Chester, and the next day to Philadelphia.

The loss sustained by the Americans in this action, has been estimated at three hundred killed, and six hundred wounded. Between three and four hundred, principally the wounded, were made prisoners.

As must ever be the case in new raised armies, unused to danger, and from which undeserving officers have not been expelled, their conduct was not uniform. Some regiments, especially those which had served the preceding campaign, maintained their ground with the firmness and intrepidity of veterans, while others gave way as soon as they were pressed. The authors of a very correct history of the war,* speaking of this action, say, "a part of their troops, among whom were particularly numbered some Virginia† regiments, and the whole corps of artillery, behaved exceedingly well in some of the actions of this day, exhibiting a degree of order, firmness, and resolution, and preserving such a countenance in extremely sharp service, as would not have discredited veterans. Some other bodies of their troops behaved very badly."‡

The official letter of Sir William Howe stated his loss at rather less than one hundred killed, and four hundred wounded. As the Americans sustained very little injury in the retreat, this inequality of loss can be ascribed only to the inferiority of their arms. Many of their muskets were scarcely fit for service; and, being of unequal caliber, their cartridges could not be so well fitted, and, consequently, their fire could not do as much

---

*Annual Register.

†The third Virginia regiment commanded by Colonel Marshall, which had performed extremely severe duty in the campaign of 1776, was placed in a wood on the right, and in front of Woodford's brigade, and Stephen's division. Though attacked by much superior numbers, it maintained its position without losing an inch of ground, until both its flanks were turned, its ammunition nearly expended, and more than half the officers, and one third of the soldiers were killed and wounded. Colonel Marshall, whose horse had received two balls, then retired in good order to resume his position on the right of his division; but it had already retreated.

‡Deboore's brigade broke first; and, on an inquiry into his conduct being directed, he resigned. A misunderstanding existed between him and Sullivan, on whose right he was stationed.

execution as that of the enemy. This radical defect was felt in all the operations of the army.

From the ardour with which the Commander-in-chief had inspired his troops before this action, it is probable that the conflict would have been more severe, had the intelligence respecting the movement on the left of the British army been less contradictory. Raw troops, changing their ground in the moment of action, and attacked in the agitation of moving, are easily thrown into confusion. This was the critical situation of a part of Sullivan's division, and was the cause of the right's breaking before Greene could be brought up to support it; after which, it was impossible to retrieve the fortune of the day.

But had the best disposition of the troops been made at the time, which subsequent intelligence would suggest, the action could not have terminated in favour of the Americans. Their inferiority in numbers, in discipline, and in arms, was too great to leave them a probable prospect of victory. A battle however was not to be avoided. The opinion of the public, and of congress, demanded it. The loss of Philadelphia, without an attempt to preserve it, would have excited discontents which, in the United States, might be productive of serious mischief; and action, though attended with defeat, provided the loss be not too great, must improve an army in which, not only the military talents, but even the courage, of officers, some of them of high rank, remained to be ascertained.

Among the wounded was the Marquis de la Fayette, and Brigadier General Woodford.

The battle of Brandywine was not considered as decisive by congress, the General, or the army. The opinion was carefully cherished that the British had gained only the ground; and that their loss was still more considerable than had been sustained by the Americans. Congress appeared determined to risk another battle for the metropolis of America. Far from discovering any intention to change their place of session, they passed vigorous resolutions for reinforcing the army, and directed General Washington to give the necessary orders for completing the defences of the Delaware.

From Chester, the army marched through Darby, over the Schuylkill bridge, to its former ground, near the falls of that river. General Greene's division, which, having been less in action, was more entire than any other, covered the rear; and the corps of Maxwell remained at Chester until the next day, as a rallying point for the small parties, and straggling soldiers, who might yet be in the neighbourhood.

Having allowed his army one day for repose and refreshment, General Washington recrossed the Schuylkill, and proceeded on the Lancaster road, with the intention of risking another engagement.

Sir William Howe passed the night of the 11th on the field of battle. On the succeeding day, he detached Major General Grant with two brigades to Concord meeting-house; and on the 13th, Lord Cornwallis joined General Grant, and marched towards Chester. Another detachment took possession of Wilmington; to which place the sick and wounded were conveyed.

To prevent a sudden movement to Philadelphia by the lower road, the bridge over the Schuylkill was loosened from its moorings, and General Armstrong was directed, with the Pennsylvania militia to guard the passes over that river.

On the 15th, the American army, intending to gain the left of the British, reached the Warren tavern, on the Lancaster road, twenty-three miles from Philadelphia. Intelligence was received, early next morning, that Howe was approaching in two columns. It being too late to reach the ground he had intended to occupy, Washington resolved to meet and engage him in front.

Both armies prepared, with great alacrity, for battle. The advanced parties had met, and were beginning to skirmish, when they were separated by a heavy rain, which, Sept. 16. becoming more and more violent, rendered the retreat of the Americans a measure of absolute necessity. The inferiority of their arms never brought them into such imminent peril as on this occasion. Their gun-locks not being well secured, their muskets soon became unfit for use. Their cartridge-boxes had been so inartificially constructed, as not to protect their ammunition from the tempest. Their cartridges were soon damaged; and this mischief was the more serious, because very many of the soldiers were without bayonets.

The army being thus rendered unfit for action, the design of giving battle was reluctantly abandoned, and a retreat commenced. It was continued all the day, and great part of the night, through a cold and most distressing rain, and very deep roads. A few hours before day, the troops halted at the Yellow Springs, where their arms and ammunition were examined, and the alarming fact was disclosed, that scarcely a musket in a regiment could be discharged, and scarcely one car- Sept. 17. tridge in a box was fit for use. This state of things suggested the precaution of moving to a still greater distance, in order to refit their arms, obtain a fresh supply of ammunition, and revive the spirits of the army. The General therefore retired to Warwick furnace, on the south branch of French Creek, where ammunition and a few muskets might be obtained in time to dispute the passage of the Schuylkill, and make yet another effort to save Philadelphia.

The extreme severity of the weather had entirely stopped the British army. During two days, General Howe made no other movement than to unite his columns.

From French Creek, General Wayne was detached with his division, into the rear of the British, with orders to join General Smallwood and, carefully concealing himself and his movements, to seize every occasion which this march might offer, of engaging them to advantage. Meanwhile, General Washington crossed the Schuylkill at Parker's ferry, and encamped on both sides of Perkyomy Creek.

General Wayne lay in the woods near the entrance of the road from Darby into that leading to Lancaster, about three miles in the rear of the left wing of the British troops encamped at Trydruffin, where he believed himself to be perfectly secure. But the country was so extensively disaffected that Sir William Howe received accurate accounts of his position and of his force. Major General Gray was detached to surprise him, and effectually accomplished his purpose. About eleven, in the night of the 20th, his piquets, driven in with charged bayonets, gave the first intimation of Gray's approach. Wayne instantly formed his division; and while his right sustained a fierce assault, directed a retreat by the left, under cover of a few regiments who, for a short time, withstood the violence of the shock. In his letter to the Commander-in-chief, he says that they gave the assailants some well-directed fires which must have done considerable execution; and that, after retreating from the ground on which the engagement commenced, they formed again, at a small distance from the scene of action; but that both parties drew off without renewing the conflict. He states his loss at about one hundred and fifty* killed and wounded. The British accounts admit, on their part, a loss of only seven.

When the attack commenced, General Smallwood, who was on his march to join Wayne, a circumstance entirely unexpected by General Gray, was within less than a mile of him; and, had he commanded regulars, might have given a very different turn to the night. But his militia thought only of their own safety; and, having fallen in with a party returning from the pursuit of Wayne, fled in confusion with the loss of only one man.

Some severe animadversions on this unfortunate affair having been made in the army, General Wayne demanded a court martial, which, after investigating his conduct, was unanimously of opinion, "that he had done every thing to be expected from an active, brave, and vigilant officer;" and acquitted him with honour.

Having secured his rear, by compelling Wayne to take a greater distance, Sir William Howe marched along the valley road to the Schuylkill, and encamped on the ^{Sept. 21.} bank of that river, from the Fatland ford up to French Creek, along the front of the American army. To secure his right from being turned, General Washington again changed his position, and encamped with his left near, but above the British right.

General Howe now relinquished his plan of bringing Washington to another battle; and, thinking it adviseable, perhaps, to transfer the seat of war to the neighbourhood of his ships, determined to cross the Schuylkill, and take pos- ^{Sept. 22.} session of Philadelphia. In the afternoon, he ordered one detachment to cross at Fatland ford which was on his right, and another to cross at Gordon's ford, on his left, and to take possession of the heights commanding them. These orders were executed without much difficulty, and the American troops placed to defend these fords were easily dispersed.

This service being effected, the whole army marched by its

---

*The British accounts represent the American loss to have been much more considerable. It probably amounted to at least three hundred men.

right, about midnight, and crossing at Fatland without opposition, proceeded a considerable distance towards Philadelphia, and encamped, with its left near Sweed's ford, and its right on the Manatawny road, having Stony run in its front.

It was now apparent that only immediate victory could save Philadelphia from the grasp of the British general, whose situation gave him the option of either taking possession of that place, or endeavouring to bring on another engagement. If, therefore, a battle must certainly be risked to save the capital, it would be necessary to attack the enemy.

Public opinion, which a military chief finds too much difficulty in resisting, and the opinion of Congress required a battle; but, on a temperate consideration of circumstances, Washington came to the wise decision of avoiding one for the present.

His reasons for this decision were conclusive. Wayne and Smallwood had not yet joined the army. The continental troops ordered from Peekskill, who had been detained for a time by an incursion from New York, were approaching; and a reinforcement of Jersey militia, under General Dickenson, was also expected.

To these powerful motives against risking an engagement, other considerations of great weight were added, founded on the condition of his soldiers. An army, manœuvring in an open country, in the face of a very superior enemy, is unavoidably exposed to excessive fatigue, and extreme hardship. The effect of these hardships was much increased by the privations under which the American troops suffered. While in almost continual motion, wading deep rivers, and encountering every vicissitude of the seasons, they were without tents, nearly without shoes, or winter clothes, and often without food.

A council of war concurred in the opinion the Commander-in-chief had formed, not to march against the enemy, but to allow his harassed troops a few days for repose, and to remain on his present ground until the expected reinforcements should arrive.

Immediately after the battle of Brandywine, the distressed situation of the army had been represented to congress, who had recommended it to the executive of Pennsylvania to seize the cloths and other military stores in the ware houses of Philadelphia, and, after granting certificates expressing their value, to convey them to a place of safety. The executive, being unwilling to encounter the odium of this strong measure, advised that the extraordinary powers of the Commander-in-chief should be used on the occasion. Lieutenant Colonel Hamilton, one of the general's aids, a young gentleman already in high estimation for his talents and zeal, was employed on this delicate business. "Your own prudence," said the General, in a letter to him while in Philadelphia, "will point out the least exceptionable means to be pursued; but remember, delicacy and a strict adherence to the ordinary mode of application must give place to our necessities. We must, if possible, accommodate the soldiers with such articles as they stand in need of, or we shall have just reason to apprehend the most injurious and alarming consequences from the approaching season."

All the efforts however of this very active officer could not obtain a supply, in any degree, adequate to the pressing and increasing wants of the army.

Colonel Hamilton was also directed to cause the military stores which had been previously collected to a large amount in Philadelphia, and the vessels which were lying at the wharves, to be removed up the Delaware. This duty was executed with so much vigilance, that very little public property fell, with the city, into the hands of the British general, who entered it on the 26th of September. The members of congress separated on the eighteenth, in the evening, and reassembled at Lancaster on the twenty-seventh of the same month.

From the 25th of August, when the British army landed at the Head of Elk, until the 26th of September when it entered Philadelphia, the campaign had been active, and the duties of the American general uncommonly arduous. The best English writers bestow high encomiums on Sir William Howe for his military skill, and masterly movements during this period. At Brandywine especially, Washington is supposed to have been "outgeneraled, more outgeneraled than in any action during the war." If all the operations of this trying period be examined, and the means in possession of both be considered, the American chief will appear, in no respect, inferior to his adversary, or unworthy of the high place assigned to him in the opinions of his countrymen. With an army decidedly inferior, not only in numbers, but in every military requisite except courage, in an open country, he employed his enemy near thirty days in advancing about sixty miles. In this time he fought one general action; and, though defeated, was able to reassemble the same undisciplined, unclothed, and almost unfed army; and, the fifth day afterwards, again to offer battle. When the armies were separated by a storm which involved him in the most distressing circumstances, he extricated himself from them, and still maintained a respectable and imposing countenance.

The only advantage he is supposed to have given was at the battle of Brandywine; and that was produced by the contrariety and uncertainty of the intelligence received. A general must be governed by his intelligence, and must regulate his measures by his information. It is his duty to obtain correct information; and among the most valuable traits of a military character, is the skill to select those means which will obtain it. Yet the best selected means are not always successful; and, in a new army, where military talent has not been well tried by the standard of experience, the general is peculiarly exposed to the chance of employing not the best instruments. In a country, too, which is covered with wood, precise information of the numbers composing different columns is to be gained with difficulty.

It has been said "that the Americans do not appear to have made all the use that might be expected of the advantages which the country afforded for harassing and impeding the British army."

In estimating this objection, it ought to be recollected that General Smallwood was directed, with the militia of Maryland and Delaware, supported by a regiment of continental troops, to hang on and harass the rear of the enemy: that General Maxwell, with a select corps consisting of a thousand men, was ordered to seize every occasion to annoy him on his march: that General Wayne with his division, was afterwards detached to unite with Smallwood, and command the whole force collected in the rear, which would have been very respectable.

If the militia did not assemble in the numbers expected, or effect the service allotted to them, their failure is not attributable to General Washington. His calls on them had been early and energetic; and the state of his army did not admit of his making larger detachments from it to supply the place they had been designed to fill.

Loud complaints had been made against General Maxwell by the officers of his corps; and a court was ordered to inquire into his conduct, by whom he was acquitted. Whether that officer omitted to seize the proper occasions to annoy the enemy, or the cautious and compact movements of Sir William Howe afforded none, can not be easily ascertained. General Washington felt the loss of Morgan, and wrote pressingly to Gates, after his success against Burgoyne, to restore him that officer, with his regiment, as soon as possible.

CHAPTER IX.

Measures to cut off the communication between the British army and fleet—Battle of Germantown.—Measures to intercept supplies to Philadelphia.—Attack on fort Mifflin.—On Red Bank.—The Augusta blows up.—General Washington takes post at White Marsh. —Fort Mifflin evacuated.—Fort Mercer evacuated.—Skirmish at Gloucester Point.—The British open the communication with their fleet.—Washington urged to attack Philadelphia.—General Howe marches out to Chesnut Hill.—Returns to Philadelphia.—General Washington goes into winter quarters.

Philadelphia being lost, General Washington sought to make its occupation inconvenient and insecure, by rendering it inaccessible to the British fleet. With this de- [1777.] sign, works had been erected on a low marshy island in the Delaware, near the junction of the Schuylkill, which, from the nature of its soil, was called Mud island. On the opposite shore of Jersey, at a place called Red Bank, a fort had also been constructed which was defended with heavy artillery. In the deep channel between, or under cover of these batteries, several ranges of frames had been sunk, to which, from their resemblance to that machine, the name of chevaux-de-frise had been given. These frames were so strong and heavy as to be destructive of any ship which might strike against them, and were sunk in such a depth of water as rendered it equally difficult to weigh them or cut them through; no attempt to raise them, or to open the channel in any manner could be successful until the command of the shores on both sides should be obtained.

Other ranges of these machines had been sunk about three miles lower down the river; and some considerable works were in progress at Billingsport on the Jersey side, which were in such forwardness as to be provided with artillery. These works and machines were farther supported by several galleys mounting heavy cannon, together with two floating batteries, a number of armed vessels, and some fire ships.

The present relative situation of the armies gave a decisive importance to these works. Cutting off the communication of General Howe with his fleet, they prevented his receiving supplies by water, while the American vessels in the river above fort Mifflin, the name given to the fort on Mud island, rendered it difficult to forage in Jersey, General Washington hoped to render his supplies on the side of Pennsylvania so precarious, as to compel him to evacuate Philadelphia.

The advantages of this situation were considerably diminished by the capture of the Delaware frigate.

The day after Lord Cornwallis entered Philadelphia, three batteries were commenced for the purpose of acting against any American ships which might appear before the town. While yet incomplete, they were attacked by two frigates, assisted by several gallies and gondolas. The Delaware, being left by the tide while engaged with the battery, grounded and was captured; soon after which, the smaller frigate, and the other vessels, retired under the guns of the fort. This circumstance was the more interesting, as it gave the British General the command of the ferry, and, consequently, free access to Jersey, and enabled him to intercept the communication between the forts below, and Trenton, from which place the garrisons were to have drawn their military stores.

All the expected reinforcements, except the state regiment and militia from Virginia, being arrived, and the detached parties being called in, the effective strength of the army amounted to eight thousand continental troops, and three thousand militia. With this force, General Washington determined to approach the enemy, and seize the first favourable moment to attack him. In pursuance of this determination, the army took a position on the Skippack road, about twenty miles Sept. 30. from Philadelphia, and sixteen from Germantown,—a long village stretching on both sides the great road leading northward from Philadelphia, which forms one continued street nearly two miles in length. The British line of encampment crossed this village at right angles near the centre, and Lord Cornwallis, with four regiments of grenadiers, occupied Philadelphia. The immediate object of General Howe being the removal of the obstructions in the river, Colonel Stirling, with two regiments, had been detached to take possession of the fort at Billingsport, which he accomplished without opposition. This service being effected, and the works facing the water destroyed, Colonel Stirling was directed to escort a convoy of provisions from Chester to Philadelphia. Some apprehensions being entertained for the safety of this convoy, another regiment was detached from Germantown, with directions to join Colonel Stirling.* Oct. 3.

This division of the British force appeared to Washington to furnish a fair opportunity to engage Sir William Howe with advantage. Determining to avail himself of it, he formed a plan for surprising the camp at Germantown, and attacking both wings, in front and rear, at the same instant.

The divisions of Sullivan and Wayne, flanked by Conway's brigade, were to march down the main road, and, entering the town by the way of Chesnut Hill, to attack the left wing; while General Armstrong, with the Pennsylvania militia, was to move down the Manatawny road† by Vanduring's mill, and turning the left flank to attack in the rear. The Commander-in-chief accompanied this column.

The divisions of Greene and Stephens, flanked by M'Dougal's brigade, were to take a circuit by the Lime Kiln road, and, entering the town at the market house, to attack the right wing.

The militia of Maryland and Jersey, under Generals Smallwood and Forman, were to march down the old York road, and turning the right to fall upon its rear.

The division of Lord Stirling, and the brigades of Nash and Maxwell, were to form a corps de reserve.

Parties of cavalry were silently to scour the roads to prevent observation, and to keep up the communication between the heads of the several columns.

---

*Annual Register.—Stedman.
†Better known as the Ridge road.

The necessary arrangements being made, the army moved
from its ground at seven in the afternoon. Before sun-
Oct. 4. rise the next morning, the advance of the column led
by Sullivan, encountered and drove in a picket placed at
Mount Airy, the house of Mr. Allen.* The main body followed
close in the rear, and engaging the light infantry and the 40th
regiment, posted at the head of the village, soon forced them
to give way, leaving their baggage behind them. Though closely
pursued, Lieutenant Colonel Musgrave threw himself with five
companies of the 40th regiment into a large stone house belonging to Mr. Chew, which stood directly in the way of
Wayne's division, and poured on the Americans an incessant
and galling fire of musketry from its doors and windows. After
making some unsuccessful, and bloody attempts to carry this
house by storm, and then battering it for a few minutes with
field artillery, which was found too light to make any impression on its walls, a regiment was left to observe the party within
it, while the troops who had been checked by Colonel Musgrave again moved forward, passing to the left of the house.

In rather more than half an hour after Sullivan had been engaged, the left wing, having formed the line, came also into action; and, attacking the light infantry posted in front of the
British right wing, soon drove it from its ground. While rapidly pursuing the flying enemy, Woodford's brigade,† which
was on the right of this wing, was arrested by a heavy fire from
Chew's house, directed against its right flank. The inefficiency
of musketry against troops thus sheltered being instantly perceived, the brigade was drawn off to the left by its commanding officer, and the field-pieces attached to it were ordered up
to play on the house, but were too light to be of service. Some
time was consumed in this operation, and the advance of the
brigade was, of course, retarded. This part of the line was consequently broken, and the two brigades composing the division of Stephens were not only separated from each other, but
from the other division which was led by General Greene in
person. That division, consisting of the brigades of Muhlen-

*Since Robinson's.
†The author was in this brigade, and describes this part of the action from
his own observation.

berg and Scott, pressing forward with eagerness, encountered and broke a part of the British right wing, entered the village, and made a considerable number of prisoners.

Thus far the prospect was flattering. The attack had been made with great spirit; several brigades had entered the town; and such an impression had been made on the British army as to justify the expectation that its wings might be separated from each other, and a complete victory be obtained. Had the American troops possessed the advantages given by experience; had every division of the army performed with precision the part allotted to it, there is yet reason to believe that the hopes inspired by this favourable commencement would not have been disappointed. But the face of the country, and the darkness of the morning produced by a fog of uncommon density, co-operating with the want of discipline in the army, and the derangements of the corps from the incidents at Chew's house, blasted these flattering appearances, and defeated the enterprise.

The grounds over which the British were pursued abounded with small and strong enclosures, which frequently broke the line of the advancing army. The two divisions of the right wing had been separated at Chew's house; and immediately after their passing it, the right of the left wing was stopped at the same place, so as to cause a division of that wing also. The darkness of the morning rendered it difficult to distinguish objects even at an inconsiderable distance; and it was impossible for the Commander-in-chief to learn the situation of the whole, or to correct the confusion which was commencing. The divisions and brigades separated at Chew's house could not be reunited; and, even among those parts which remained entire, a considerable degree of disorder was soon introduced by the impediments to their advance. Some regiments pursuing with more vivacity than others, they were separated from each other, their weight lessened, and their effect impaired. The darkness which obstructed the reunion of the broken parts of the American army, also prevented their discerning the real situation of the enemy, so as to improve the first impression; and, in some instances, some corps being in advance of others, produced uncertainty whether the troops, seen indistinctly, were friends or foes.

The attacks on the flanks and rear, which formed a part of the original plan, do not appear ever to have been made. The Pennsylvania militia came in view of the chasseurs who flanked the left of the British line, but did not engage them closely. The Maryland and Jersey militia just showed themselves on the right flank, about the time Greene was commencing a retreat.

These embarrassments gave the British time to recover from the consternation into which they had been thrown. General Knyphausen, who commanded their left, detached two brigades to meet the right of Sullivan which had penetrated far into the village, before his left, which had been obtained at Chew's house, could rejoin him; and the action became warm in this quarter. The British right also recovered from its surprise, and advanced on that part of Greene's division which had entered the town. After a sharp engagement these two brigades began to retreat, and those which were most in advance were surrounded and compelled to surrender. About the same time the right wing also began to retreat. It is understood that they had expended their ammunition.

Every effort to stop this retrograde movement proved ineffectual. The division of Wayne fell back on that of Stephens, and was for an instant mistaken for the enemy. General confusion prevailed, and the confidence felt in the beginning of the action was lost. With infinite chagrin General Washington was compelled to relinquish his hopes of victory, and turn his attention to the security of his army. The enemy not being sufficiently recovered to endanger his rear, the retreat was made without loss, under cover of the division of Stephens, which had scarcely been in the engagement.

In this battle, about two hundred Americans were killed, near three times that number wounded, and about four hundred were made prisoners. Among the killed was General Nash of North Carolina; and among the prisoners, was Colonel Matthews of Virginia, whose regiment had penetrated into the centre of the town.

The loss of the British, as stated in the official return of General Howe, did not much exceed five hundred in killed and wounded, of whom less than one hundred were killed; among the latter were Brigadier General Agnew and Colonel Bird.

The American army retreated the same day, about twenty

miles, to Perkiomen Creek, where a small reinforcement, consisting of fifteen hundred militia and a state regiment, was received from Virginia; after which it again advanced towards Philadelphia, and encamped once more on Skippack creek.

The plan of the battle of Germantown must be admitted to have been judiciously formed; and, in its commencement, to have been happily conducted. But a strict adherence to it by those who were entrusted with the execution of its several parts, was indispensable to its success.

Major General Stephen, who commanded the right division of the left was cashiered for misconduct on the retreat, and for intoxication.

Congress expressed, in decided terms, their approbation both of the plan of this enterprise, and of the courage with which it was executed; for which their thanks were given to the general and the army.*

*On hearing that General Howe had landed at the head of the Chesapeake, Sir Henry Clinton, for the purpose of averting those aids which Washington might draw from the north of the Delaware, entered Jersey at the head of three thousand men. On the approach of General M'Dougal with a body of continental troops from Peekskill, and on hearing that the militia were assembling under General Dickinson, he returned to New York and Staten Island with the cattle he had collected, having lost in the expedition only eight men killed and twice as many wounded.

M'Dougal continued his march towards the Delaware; and the utmost exertions were made both by Governor Livingston and General Dickinson to collect the militia for the purpose of aiding the army in Pennsylvania. The success of their exertions did not equal their wishes. The militia being of opinion that there was danger of a second invasion from New York, and that their services were more necessary at home than in Pennsylvania, assembled slowly and reluctantly. Five or six hundred crossed the Delaware at Philadelphia, about the time Sir William Howe crossed the Schuylkill, and were employed in the removal of stores. On the approach of the British army, they were directed to avoid it by moving up the Frankford road; but the commanding officer, having separated himself from his corps, was taken by a party of British horse employed in scouring the country; on which the regiment dispersed, and returned by different roads to Jersey. With much labour General Dickinson assembled two other corps amounting to about nine hundred men, with whom he was about to cross the Delaware when intelligence was received of the arrival at New York of a reinforcement from Europe. He was detained in Jersey for the defence of the state, and the militia designed to serve in Pennsylvania were placed under General Forman. About six hundred of them reached the army a few days before the battle of Germantown, immediately after which they were permitted to return.

The attention of both armies was now principally directed to the forts below Philadelphia.

The loss of the Delaware frigate, and of Billingsport, greatly discouraged the seamen by whom the gallies and floating batteries were manned. Believing the fate of America to be decided, an opinion strengthened by the intelligence received from their connexions in Philadelphia, they manifested the most alarming defection, and several officers as well as sailors deserted to the enemy. This desponding temper was checked by the battle of Germantown, and by throwing a garrison of continental troops into the fort at Red Bank, called fort Mercer, the defence of which had been entrusted to militia. This fort commanded the channel between the Jersey shore and Mud Island; and the American vessels were secure under its guns. The militia of Jersey were relied on to reinforce its garrison, and also to form a corps of observation which might harass the rear of any detachment investing the place.

To increase the inconvenience of General Howe's situation by intercepting his supplies, six hundred militia, commanded by General Potter, crossed the Schuylkill, with orders to scour the country between that river and Chester; and the militia on the Delaware, above Philadelphia, were directed to watch the roads in that vicinity.

The more effectually to stop those who were seduced by the hope of gold and silver to supply the enemy at this critical time, congress passed a resolution subjecting to martial law and to death, all who should furnish them with provisions, or certain other enumerated articles, who should be taken within thirty miles of any city, town or place, in Jersey, Pennsylvania, or Delaware, occupied by British troops.

These arrangements being made to cut off supplies from the country, General Washington reoccupied the ground from which he had marched to fight the battle of Germantown.

Meanwhile, General Howe was actively preparing to attack fort Mifflin from the Pennsylvania shore. He erected some batteries at the mouth of the Schuylkill, in order to command Webb's ferry, which were attacked by Commodore Hazlewood, and silenced; but, the following night, a detachment crossed over Webb's ferry into Province Island, and constructed a slight work opposite fort Mifflin, within two musket shots of the blockhouse, from which they were enabled to throw shot and shells into the barracks. When day-light discovered this work, three gallies and a floating battery were ordered to attack it, and the garrison surrendered. While the boats were bringing off the prisoners, a large column of British troops were seen marching into the fortress, upon which the attack on it was renewed, but without success; and two attempts made by Lieutenant Colonel Smith to storm it, failed. In a few nights, works were completed on the high ground of Province Island which enfiladed the principal battery of fort Mifflin, and rendered it necessary to throw up some cover on the platform to protect the men who worked the guns.

The aids expected from the Jersey militia were not received. "Assure yourself," said Lieutenant Colonel Smith, in a letter pressing earnestly for a reinforcement of continental troops, "that no dependence is to be put on the militia; whatever men your excellency determines on sending, no time is to be lost." The garrison of fort Mifflin was now reduced to one hundred and fifty-six effectives, and that of Red Bank did not much exceed two hundred.

In consequence of these representations, Colonel Angel, of Rhode Island, with his regiment, was ordered to Red Bank, and Lieutenant Colonel John Greene, of Virginia, with about two hundred men, to fort Mifflin.

Immediately after the battle of Brandywine, Admiral Howe sailed for the Delaware, where he expected to arrive in time to meet and co-operate with the army in and about Philadelphia. But the winds were so unfavourable, and the navigation of the bay of Delaware so difficult, his van did not get into the river until the 4th of October. The ships of war and transports which followed, came up from the sixth to the eighth, and anchored from New Castle to Reedy Island.

The frigates, in advance of the fleet, had not yet succeeded in their endeavours to effect a passage through the lower double row of chevaux-de-frise. Though no longer protected by the fort at Billingsport, they were defeated by the water force above, and the work was found more difficult than had been expected. It was not until the middle of October that the impediments were so far removed as to afford a narrow and intricate passage through them. In the mean time, the fire from the

Pennsylvania shore had not produced all the effect expected from it; and it was perceived that greater exertions would be necessary for the reduction of the works than could safely be made in the present relative situation of the armies. Under this impression, General Howe, soon after the return of the American army to its former camp on the Skippack, withdrew his troops from Germantown into Philadelphia, as preparatory to a combined attack by land and water on forts Mercer and Mifflin.

After effecting a passage through the works sunk in the river at Billingsport, other difficulties still remained to be encountered by the ships of war. Several rows of chevaux-de-frise had been sunk about half a mile below Mud Island, which were protected by the guns of the forts, as well as by the moveable water force. To silence these works, therefore, was a necessary preliminary to the removal of these obstructions in the channel.

On the 21st of October, a detachment of Hessians, amounting to twelve hundred men, commanded by Colonel Count Donop, crossed the Delaware at Philadelphia, with orders to storm the fort at Red Bank. The fortifications consisted of extensive outer works, within which was an intrenchment eight or nine feet high, boarded and fraized. Late in the evening of the twenty-second, Count Donop appeared before the fort, and attacked it with great intrepidity. It was defended with equal resolution. The outer works being too extensive to be manned by the troops in the fort, were used only to gall the assailants while advancing. On their near approach, the garrison retired within the inner intrenchment, whence they poured upon the Hessians a heavy and destructive fire. Colonel Donop received a mortal wound; and Lieutenant Colonel Mengerode, the second in command, fell about the same time. Lieutenant Colonel Minsing, the oldest remaining officer, drew off his troops, and returned next day to Philadelphia. The loss of the assailants was estimated by the Americans at four hundred men. The garrison was reinforced from fort Mifflin, and aided by the galleys which flanked the Hessians in their advance and retreat. The American loss, in killed and wounded, amounted to only thirty-two men.

The ships having been ordered to co-operate with Count Donop, the Augusta, with four smaller vessels, passed the lower line of chevaux-de-frise, opposite to Billingsport, and lay above it, waiting until the assault should be made on the fort. The flood tide setting in about the time the attack commenced, they moved with it up the river. The obstructions sunk in the Delaware had in some degree changed its channel, in consequence of which the Augusta and the Merlin grounded, a considerable distance below the second line of chevaux-de-frise and a strong wind from the north so checked the rising of the tide, that these vessels could not be floated by the flood. Their situation, however, was not discerned that evening, as the frigates which were able to approach the fort, and the batteries from the Pennsylvania shore, kept up an incessant fire on the garrison, till night put an end to the cannonade. Early next morning it was recommenced, in the hope that, under its cover, the Augusta and the Merlin might be got off. The Americans, on discovering their situation, sent four fire ships against them, but without effect. Meanwhile, a warm cannonade took place on both sides, in the course of which the Augusta took fire, and it was found impracticable to extinguish the flames. Most of the men were taken out, the frigates withdrawn, and the Merlin set on fire; after which the Augusta blew up, and a few of the crew were lost in her.

This repulse inspired congress with flattering hopes for the permanent defence of the posts on the Delaware. That body expressed its high sense of the merits of Colonel Greene of Rhode Island, who had commanded in fort Mercer; of Lieutenant Colonel Smith of Maryland, who had commanded in fort Mifflin; and of Commodore Hazlewood, who commanded the galleys; and presented a sword to each of these officers, as a mark of estimation in which their services were held.

The situation of these forts was far from justifying this confidence of their being defensible. That on Mud Island had been unskilfully constructed, and required at least eight hundred men fully to man the lines. The island is about half a mile long. Fort Mifflin was placed at the lower end, having its principal fortifications in front for the purpose of repelling ships coming up the river. The defences in the rear consisted only of a ditch and palisade, protected by two block houses, the upper story of one of which had been destroyed in the late cannonade. Above the fort were two batteries opposing those constructed by the British on Province and Carpenter's Islands, which were separated from Mud Island only by a narrow passage between four and five hundred yards wide.

The vessels of war, engaged in the defence of the Delaware, were partly in the service of the continent, and partly in that of the state of Pennsylvania, under a Commodore who received his commission from the state. A misunderstanding took place between him and Lieutenant Colonel Smith, and also between him and the officers of the continental navy; and it required all the authority of the Commander-in-chief to prevent these differences from essentially injuring the service.

The garrison of fort Mifflin consisted of only three hundred continental troops, who were worn down with fatigue, and constant watching, under the constant apprehension of being attacked from Province Island, from Philadelphia, and from the ships below.

Having failed in every attempt to draw the militia of Jersey to the Delaware, General Washington determined to strengthen the garrison by farther drafts from his army. Three hundred Pennsylvania militia were detached, to be divided between the two forts; and, a few days afterwards, General Varnum was ordered, with his brigade, to take a position about Woodbury, near Red Bank, and to relieve and reinforce the garrisons of both forts as far as his strength would permit. The hope was entertained that the appearance of so respectable a continental force might encourage the militia to assemble in greater numbers.

Aware of the advantage to result from a victory over the British army while separated from the fleet, General Washington had been uniformly determined to risk much to gain one. He had, therefore, after the battle of Germantown, continued to watch assiduously for an opportunity to attack his enemy once more to advantage. The circumspect caution of General Howe afforded none. After the repulse at Red Bank, his measures were slow but certain; and were calculated to insure the possession of the forts without exposing his troops to the hazard of an assault.

In this state of things, intelligence was received of the successful termination of the northern campaign, in consequence of which great part of the troops who had been employed against Burgoyne, might be drawn to the aid of the army in Pennsylvania. But it was feared that, before these reinforcements could arrive, Sir William Howe would gain possession of the forts, and remove the obstructions to the navigation of the Delaware. This apprehension furnished a strong motive for vigorous attempts to relieve fort Mifflin. But the relative force of the armies, the difficulty of acting offensively against Philadelphia, and, above all, the reflection that a defeat might disable him from meeting his enemy in the field even after the arrival of the troops expected from the north, determined General Washington not to hazard a second attack under existing circumstances.

To expedite the reinforcements for which he waited, Colonel Hamilton was despatched to General Gates with directions to represent to him the condition of the armies in Pennsylvania; and to urge him, if he contemplated no other service of more importance, immediately to send the regiments of Massachusetts and New Hampshire to aid the army of the middle department. These orders were not peremptory, because it was possible that some other object (as the capture of New York) still more interesting than the expulsion of General Howe from Philadelphia, might be contemplated by Gates; and Washington meant not to interfere with the accomplishment of such object.

On reaching General Putnam, Colonel Hamilton found that a considerable part of the northern army had joined that officer, but that Gates had detained four brigades at Albany for an expedition intended to be made in the winter against Ticonderoga.

Having made such arrangements with Putnam as he supposed would secure the immediate march of a large body of continental troops from that station, Colonel Hamilton proceeded to Albany for the purpose of remonstrating to General Gates against retaining so large and valuable a part of the army unemployed at a time when the most imminent danger threatened the vitals of the country. Gates was by no means disposed to part with his troops. He could not believe that an expedition then preparing at New York, was designed to reinforce General Howe; and insisted that, should the troops then embarked at that place, instead of proceeding to the Delaware, make a sudden movement up the Hudson, it would be in their power, should Albany be left defenceless, to destroy the valuable arsenal which had been there erected, and the military stores captured with Burgoyne, which had been chiefly deposited in that town.

Having, after repeated remonstrances, obtained an order directing three brigades to the Delaware, Hamilton hastened back to Putnam, and found the troops which had been ordered to join General Washington, still at Peekskill. The detachment from New York had suggested to Putnam the possibility of taking that place; and he does not appear to have made very great exertions to divest himself of a force he deemed necessary for an object the accomplishment of which would give so much splendour to his military character. In addition to this circumstance, an opinion had gained ground among the soldiers that their share of service for the campaign had been performed, and that it was time for them to go into winter quarters. Great discontents too prevailed concerning their pay, which the government had permitted to be more than six months in arrear; and in Poor's brigade, a mutiny broke out, in the course of which a soldier who was run through the body by his captain, before he expired, shot the captain dead who gave the wound. Colonel Hamilton came in time to borrow money from the governor of New York, to put the troops in motion; and they proceeded by brigades to the Delaware. But these several delays retarded their arrival until the contest for the forts on that river was terminated.

The preparations of Sir William Howe being completed, a large battery on Province Island of twenty-four and thirty-two pounders, and two howitzers of eight inches each, opened, early in the morning of the 10th of November, upon fort Mifflin, at the distance of five hundred yards, and kept up an incessant fire for several successive days. The blockhouses were reduced to a heap of ruins; the palisades were beaten down; and most of the guns dismounted and otherwise disabled. The barracks were battered in every part, so that the troops could not remain in them. They were under the necessity of working and watching the whole night to repair the damages of the day, and to guard against a storm, of which they were in perpetual apprehension. If in the day, a few moments were allowed for repose, it was taken on the wet earth, which, in consequence of heavy rains, had become a soft mud. The garrison was relieved by General Varnum every forty-eight hours; but his brigade was so weak that half the men were constantly on duty.

Colonel Smith was decidedly of opinion, and General Varnum concurred with him, that the garrison could not repel an assault, and ought to be withdrawn; but General Washington still cherished the hope that the place might be maintained until he should be reinforced from the northern army. Believing that an assault would not be attempted until the works were battered down, he recommended that the whole night should be employed in making repairs. His orders were that the place should be defended to the last extremity; and never were orders more faithfully executed.

Several of the garrison were killed, and among them Captain Treat, a gallant officer, who commanded the artillery. Colonel Smith received a contusion on his hip and arm which compelled him to give up the command, and retire to Red Bank. Major Fleury, a French officer of distinguished Nov. 11. merit, who served as engineer, reported to the Commander-in-chief that, although the block houses were beaten down, all the guns in them, except two, disabled, and several breaches made in the walls, the place was still defensible; but the garrison was so unequal to the numbers required by the extent of the lines, and was so dispirited by watching, fatigue, and constant exposure to the cold rains which were almost incessant, that he dreaded the event of an attempt to carry the place by storm. Fresh troops were ordered to their relief from Varnum's brigade, and the command was taken, first by Colonel Russell, and afterwards by Major Thayer. The artillery, commanded by Captain Lee, continued to be well served. The besiegers were several times thrown into confusion, and a floating battery which opened on the morning of the 14th, was silenced in the course of the day.

The defence being unexpectedly obstinate, the assailants brought up their ships as far as the obstructions in the river permitted, and added their fire to that of the bat- Nov. 15. teries, which was the more fatal as the cover for the troops had been greatly impaired. The brave garrison, however, still maintained their ground with unshaken firmness. In the midst of this stubborn conflict, the Vigilant and a sloop of war were brought up the inner channel, between Mud and Province Islands, which had, unobserved by the besieged, been deepened by the current in consequence of the obstructions in the main channel; and, taking a station within one hundred yards of the works, not only kept up a destructive cannonade, but threw hand grenades into them; while the musketeers from the round top of the Vigilant killed every man that appeared on the platform.

Major Thayer applied to the Commodore to remove these vessels, and he ordered six galleys on the service; but, after reconnoitring their situation, the galleys returned without attempting any thing. Their report was that these ships were so covered by the batteries on Province Island as to be unassailable.

It was now apparent to all that the fort could be no longer defended. The works were in ruins. The position of the Vigilant rendered any farther continuance on the island a prodigal and useless waste of human life; and on the 16th, about eleven at night, the garrison was withdrawn.*

A second attempt was made to drive the vessels from their stations with a determination, should it succeed, to repossess the island; but the galleys effected nothing; and a detachment from Province Island soon occupied the ground which had been abandoned.

The day after receiving intelligence of the evacuation of fort Mifflin, General Washington deputed Generals De Kalb, and Knox, to confer with General Varnum and the officers at fort Mercer on the practicability of continuing to defend the obstructions in the channel, to report thereon, and to state the force which would be necessary for that purpose. Their report was in favour of continuing the defence. A council of the navy officers had already been called by the Commodore in pursuance of a request of the Commander-in-chief made before the evacuation had taken place, who were unanimously of opinion that it would be impracticable for the fleet, after the

---

*In stating the defence of Mud Island, the author has availed himself of the journal of Major Fleury.

loss of the island, to maintain its station, or to assist in preventing the chevaux-de-frise from being weighed by the ships of the enemy.

General Howe had now completed a line of defence from the Schuylkill to the Delaware; and a reinforcement from New York had arrived at Chester. These two circumstances enabled him to form an army in the Jerseys sufficient for the reduction of fort Mercer, without weakening himself so much in Philadelphia as to put his lines in hazard. Still deeming it of the utmost importance to open the navigation of the Delaware completely, he detached Lord Cornwallis about one in the morning of the 17th, with a strong body of troops to Chester. From that place, his lordship crossed over to Billingsport, where he was joined by the reinforcement from New York.

General Washington received immediate intelligence of the march of this detachment, which he communicated to General Varnum with orders that fort Mercer should be defended to the last extremity. With a view to military operations in that quarter, he ordered one division of the army to cross the river at Burlington, and despatched expresses to the northern troops who were marching on by brigades, directing them to move down the Delaware on its northern side until they should receive farther orders.

Major General Greene, an officer who had been distinguished early in the war by the Commander-in-chief for the solidity of his judgment and his military talents, was selected for this expedition. A hope was entertained that he would be able, not only to protect fort Mercer, but to obtain some decisive advantage over Lord Cornwallis; as the situation of the fort, which his lordship could not invest without placing himself between Timber and Manto Creeks, would expose the assailants to great peril from a respectable force in their rear. But, before Greene could cross the Delaware, Lord Cornwallis approached with an army rendered more powerful than had been expected by the junction of the reinforcement from New York; and fort Mercer was evacuated.

A few of the smaller galleys escaped up the river, and the others were burnt by their crews.

Washington still hoped to recover much of what had been lost. A victory would restore the Jersey shore, and this object was deemed so important, that General Greene's instructions indicated the expectation that he would be in a condition to fight Lord Cornwallis.

That judicious officer feared the reproach of avoiding an action less than the just censure of sacrificing the real interests of his country by engaging the enemy on disadvantageous terms. The numbers of the British exceeded his, even counting his militia as regulars; and he determined to wait for Glover's brigade, which was marching from the north. Before its arrival, Lord Cornwallis took post on Gloucester Point, a point of land making deep into the Delaware, which was entirely under cover of the guns of the ships, from which place he was embarking his baggage and the provisions he had collected for Philadelphia.*

Believing that Lord Cornwallis would immediately follow the magazines he had collected, and that the purpose of Sir William Howe was, with his united forces, to attack the American army while divided, General Washington ordered Greene to recross the Delaware, and join the army.

Thus after one continued struggle of more than six weeks, in which the continental troops displayed great military virtues, the army in Philadelphia secured itself in the possession of that city, by opening a free communication with the fleet.[†]

---

*While Lord Cornwallis lay on Gloucester Point, about one hundred and fifty men of Morgan's rifle corps under Lieutenant Colonel Butler, and an equal number of militia, the whole under the Marquis de la Fayette, who still served as a volunteer, attacked a picket consisting of about three hundred men, and drove them with the loss of twenty or thirty killed, and a greater number wounded, quite into their camp; after which the Americans retired without being pursued.

†While these transactions were passing on the Delaware, General Dickinson projected another expedition against the post on Staten Island. He collected about two thousand men, and requested General Putnam to make a diversion on the side of Kingsbridge, in order to prevent a reinforcement from New York.

Knowing that success depended on secrecy, he had concealed his object even from his field-officers, until eight of the night in which it was to be executed. Yet by three next morning, information of his design was given to General Skinner, who, being on his guard, saved himself and his brigade, by taking refuge, on the first alarm, in some works too strong to be carried by assault. A few prisoners were made and a few men killed, after which General Dickinson brought off his party with the loss of only three killed and ten slightly wounded.

While Lord Cornwallis was in Jersey, and General Greene on the Delaware above him, the reinforcements from the north being received, an attack on Philadelphia was strongly pressed by several officers high in rank; and was in some measure urged by that torrent of public opinion, which, if not resisted by a very firm mind, overwhelms the judgment, and by controlling measures not well comprehended, may frequently produce, especially in military transactions, the most disastrous effects.

It was stated to the Commander-in-chief, that his army was now in greater force than he could expect it to be at any future time; that being joined by the troops who had conquered Burgoyne, his own reputation, the reputation of his army, the opinion of congress, and of the nation, required some decisive blow on his part. That the rapid depreciation of the paper currency, by which the resources for carrying on the war were dried up, rendered indispensable some grand effort to bring it to a speedy termination.

The plan proposed was, that General Greene should embark two thousand men at Dunks' ferry, and descending the Delaware in the night, land in the town just before day, attack the enemy in the rear, and take possession of the bridge over the Schuylkill. That a strong corps should march down on the west side of that river, occupy the heights enfilading the works of the enemy, and open a brisk cannonade upon them, while a detachment from it should march down to the bridge, and attack in front at the same instant, that the party descending the river should commence its assault on the rear.

Not only the Commander-in-chief, but some of his best officers, those who could not be impelled by the clamours of the ill-informed to ruin the public interests, were opposed to this mad enterprise.

The two armies they said were now nearly equal in point of numbers, and the detachment under Lord Cornwallis could not be supposed to have so weakened Sir William Howe as to compensate for the advantages of his position. His right was covered by the Delaware, his left by the Schuylkill, his rear by the junction of those two rivers, as well as by the city of Philadelphia, and his front by a line of redoubts extending from river to river, and connected by an abbattis, and by circular works. It would be indispensably necessary to carry all these redoubts; since to leave a part of them to play on the rear of the columns, while engaged in front with the enemy in Philadelphia, would be extremely hazardous.

Supposing the redoubts carried, and the British army driven into the town, yet all military men were agreed on the great peril of storming a town. The streets would be defended by an artillery greatly superior to that of the Americans, which would attack in front, while the brick houses would be lined with musketeers, whose fire must thin the ranks of the assailants.

A part of the plan, on the successful execution of which the whole depended, was, that the British rear should be surprised by the corps descending the Delaware. This would require the concurrence of too many favourable circumstances to be calculated on with any confidence. As the position of General Greene was known, it could not be supposed that Sir William Howe would be inattentive to him. It was probable that not even his embarkation would be made unnoticed; but it was presuming a degree of negligence which ought not to be assumed, to suppose that he could descend the river to Philadelphia undiscovered. So soon as his movement should be observed, the whole plan would be comprehended, since it would never be conjectured that General Greene was to attack singly.

If the attack in front should fail, which was not even improbable, the total loss of the two thousand men in the rear must follow; and General Howe would maintain his superiority through the winter.

The situation of America did not require these desperate measures. The British general would be compelled to risk a battle on equal terms, or to manifest a conscious inferiority to the American army. The depreciation of paper money was the inevitable consequence of immense emissions without corresponding taxes. It was by removing the cause, not by sacrificing the army, that this evil was to be corrected.

Washington possessed too much discernment to be dazzled by the false brilliant presented by those who urged the necessity of storming Philadelphia, in order to throw lustre round his own fame, and that of his army; and too much firmness of temper, too much virtue and real patriotism, to be diverted from a purpose believed to be right, by the clamours of faction or the discontents of ignorance. Disregarding the importunities of mistaken friends, the malignant insinuations of enemies, and the expectations of the ill-informed; he persevered in his resolution to make no attempt on Philadelphia. He saved his army, and was able to keep the field in the face of his enemy; while the clamour of the moment wasted in air, and is forgotten.

The opinion that Sir William Howe meditated an attack on the American camp, was not ill founded. Scarcely had Lord Cornwallis returned to Philadelphia, and Greene to the American army, when unquestionable intelligence was received that the British general was preparing to march out in full strength, with the avowed object of forcing Washington from his position, and driving him beyond the mountains.

On the 4th of December, Captain M'Lane, a vigilant officer on the lines, discovered that an attempt to surprise the American camp at White Marsh was about to be made, and communicated the information to the Commander-in-chief. In the evening of the same day, General Howe marched out of Philadelphia with his whole force; and, about eleven at night, M'Lane, who had been detached with one hundred chosen men, attacked the British van at the Three Mile Run, on the Germantown road, and compelled their front division to change its line of march. He hovered on the front and flank of the advancing army, galling them severely until three next morning, when the British encamped on Chestnut Hill, in front of the American right, and distant from it about three miles. A slight skirmish had also taken place between the Pennsylvania militia under General Irvine, and the advanced light parties of the enemy, in which the general Dec. 6. was founded, and the militia, without much other loss, were dispersed.

The range of hills on which the British were posted, approached nearer to those occupied by the Americans, as they stretched northward.

Having passed the day in reconnoitring the right, Sir William Howe changed his ground in the course of the night, and moving along the hills to his right, took an advantageous position, about a mile in front of the American left. Dec. 7. The next day he inclined still farther to his right, and, in doing so, approached still nearer to the left wing of the American army. Supposing a general engagement to be approaching, Washington detached Gist with some Maryland militia, and Morgan with his rifle corps, to attack the flanking and advanced parties of the enemy. A sharp action ensued, in which Major Morris, of Jersey, a brave officer in Morgan's regiment, was mortally wounded, and twenty-seven of his men were killed and wounded. A small loss was also sustained in the militia. The parties first attacked were driven in; but the enemy reinforcing in numbers, and Washington, unwilling to move from the heights, and engage on the ground which was the scene of the skirmish, declining to reinforce Gist and Morgan, they, in turn, were compelled to retreat.

Sir William Howe continued to manœuvre towards the flank, and in front of the left wing of the American army. Expecting to be attacked in that quarter in full force, Washington made such changes in the disposition of his troops as the occasion required; and the day was consumed in these movements. In the course of it, the American chief rode through every brigade of his army, delivering, in person, his orders, respecting the manner of receiving the enemy, exhorting his troops to rely principally on the bayonet, and encouraging them by the steady firmness of his countenance, as well as by his words, to a vigorous performance of their duty.* The dispositions of the evening indicated an intention to attack him the ensuing morning; but in the afternoon of the eighth, the British suddenly filed off from their right, which extended beyond the American left and retreated to Philadelphia. The parties detached to harass their rear could not overtake it.

The loss of the British in this expedition, as stated in the official letter of General Howe, rather exceeded one hundred in killed, wounded, and missing; and was sustained principally in the skirmish of the 7th, in which Major Morris fell.

On no former occasion had the two armies met, uncovered by works, with superior numbers on the side of the Americans. The effective force of the British was then stated at twelve thousand men. It has been since declared by an author† who

---

*The author states this on his own observation.
†Stedman.

then belonged to it, but who, though a candid writer, appears to have imbibed prejudices against Sir William Howe, to have amounted to fourteen thousand. The American army consisted of precisely twelve thousand one hundred and sixty-one continental troops, and three thousand two hundred and forty-one militia. This equality in point of numbers, rendered it a prudent precaution to maintain a superiority of position. As the two armies occupied heights fronting each other, neither could attack without giving to its adversary some advantage in the ground; and this was an advantage which neither seemed willing to relinquish.

The return of Sir William Howe to Philadelphia without bringing on an action, after marching out with the avowed intention of fighting, is the best testimony of the respect which he felt for the talents of his adversary, and the courage of the troops he was to encounter.

The cold was now becoming so intense that it was impossible for an army neither well clothed, nor sufficiently supplied with blankets, longer to keep the field in tents. It had become necessary to place the troops in winter quarters; but in the existing state of things the choice of winter quarters was a subject for serious reflection. It was impossible to place them in villages without uncovering the country, or exposing them to the hazard of being beaten in detachment.

To avoid these calamities, it was determined to take a strong position in the neighbourhood of Philadelphia, equally distant from the Delaware above and below that city; and there to construct huts, in the form of a regular encampment, which might cover the army during the winter. A strong piece of ground at Valley Forge, on the west side of the Schuylkill, between twenty and thirty miles from Philadelphia, was selected for that purpose; and some time before day on the morning of the 11th of December, the army marched to take possession of it. By an accidental concurrence of circumstances, Lord Cornwallis had been detached the same morning at the head of a strong corps, on a foraging party on the west side of the Schuylkill. He had fallen in with a brigade of Pennsylvania militia commanded by General Potter, which he soon dispersed; and, pursuing the fugitives, had gained the heights opposite Matron's ford, over which the Americans had thrown a bridge for the purpose of crossing the river, and had posted troops to command the defile called the Gulph, just as the front division of the American army reached the bank of the river. This movement had been made without any knowledge of the intention of General Washington to change his position, or any design of contesting the passage of the Schuylkill; but the troops had been posted in the manner already mentioned for the sole purpose of covering the foraging party.

Washington apprehended, from his first intelligence, that General Howe had taken the field in full force. He therefore recalled the troops already on the west side, and moved rather higher up the river, for the purpose of understanding the real situation, force, and designs of the enemy. The next day Lord Cornwallis returned to Philadelphia; and, in the course of the night, the American army crossed the river.

Dec. 12.

Here the Commander-in-chief communicated to his army, in general orders, the manner in which he intended to dispose of them during the winter. He expressed, in strong terms, his approbation of their conduct, presented them with an encouraging state of the future prospects of their country, exhorted them to bear with continuing fortitude the hardships inseparable from the position they were about to take, and endeavoured to convince their judgments that those hardships were not imposed on them by unfeeling caprice, but were necessary for the good of their country.

The winter had set in with great severity, and the sufferings of the army were extreme. In a few days, however, these sufferings were considerably diminished by the erection of logged huts, filled up with mortar, which, after being dried, formed comfortable habitations, and gave content to men long unused to the conveniences of life. The order of a regular encampment was observed; and the only appearance of winter quarters, was the substitution of huts for tents.

1832

POLITICAL NEWS AND A LAW LIBRARY

To Joseph Story

My dear Sir   Richmond August 2d. 1832
I am greatly in your debt, more especially for the first volume of the American library of useful knowledge, and have so
long neglected to acknowledge my obligations that I am not
sure I should not, according to the practice of insolvents, have
put it off altogether, had I not been placed in a situation to ask
further assistance from you.

Congress has passed an act to increase and improve its law
library, a copy of which has just been transmitted to me by the
librarian. It appropriates 5000$ for the present year, to be ex-
pended in the purchase of law books by the librarian, in pursuance of such catalogue as shall be furnished him by the Chief
Justice of The United States. I wish it had been "as shall be
furnished him by Mr. Justice Story." However, we must correct this erratum as well as we can.

As I know your appetite for labor, I feel the less compunction in offering you a very large share of this. Indeed if you can
take the whole I can readily spare it. Will you then transmit me
a list of such law books as you would wish (or rather as ought
in your judgement) to be added to the law library. You probably recollect enough of them without seeing a catalogue, to
supply a list of those which are wanting. Say if you think there
ought to be duplicates of particular books.

The librarian informs me that he has already ordered a continuation of those British reports which are in progress, of
which he has the beginning volumes; and of the American
reporters.

I ascribe the honor now done me to our friend Peters, and
therefore think I may ask him also for aid in my difficulty. I
shall probably write to him.

We are up to the chin in politics. Virginia was always insane
enough to be opposed to the bank of The United States, and
therefore Hurra's for the veto. But we are a little doubtful how
it may work in Pennsylvania. It is not difficult to account for
the part New York may take. She has sagacity enough to see

her interest in putting down the present bank. Her mercantile position gives her a controul, a commanding controul over the currency and the exchanges of the country, if there be no Bank of The United States. Going for herself, she may approve this policy. But Virginia ought not to drudge for her benefit.

We show our wisdom most strikingly in approving the veto on the harbor bill also. That bill contained an appropriation intended to make Richmond a sea port, which she is not at present for large vessels fit to cross the Atlantic. The appropriation was whittled down in the House of Representatives to almost nothing, in consequence of the total misunderstanding of the case by Mercer. Yet we wished the appropriation because we were confident that congress, when correctly informed would add the necessary sum. This too is vetoed; and for this too our sagacious politicians are thankful. We seem to think it the summit of human wisdom, or rather of American patriotism, to preserve our poverty.

Our great political and party guide, The Enquirer, has not been able to make Mr. Barbour pull in the traces. He has broke loose and is fairly in the field. I do not precisely know how this will work. He is supported by the most violent of the state right party, who are also strong for the existing President. There might be some difficulty in managing this tangled business were not the Jackson majority so overwhelming as to leave his friends nothing to fear from a division. Some of the friends of Barbour are secretly for Calhoun; but though attached to nullification in principle, they dare not favor the name. Besides, the basement story is so firm that those who are supported on it dare not totter.

Things to the south wear a very serious aspect. If we can trust appearances, the leaders are determined to risk all the consequences of dismemberment. I cannot entirely dismiss the hope that they may be deserted by their followers—at least to such an extent as to produce a pause at the Rubicon. They undoubtedly beleive that Virginia will support them. I think they are mistaken both with respect to Virginia and North Carolina. I do not think either state will embrace this mad and wicked measure. New Hampshire and Maine seem to belong to the tropics. It is time for New Hampshire to part with Webster and Mason. She has no longer any use for such men.

I am just preparing for my usual excursion to the mountains. Would that I could meet you there. It would secure you from the cholera. Our whole sea board will I fear be overrun with it. In New York it has I perceive been carried to the western frontier. It is too visiting our lakes. You are surrounded by it. That providence may protect us, especially Boston and Richmond, is the earnest prayer of your truely affectionate

"OUR CONSTITUTION CANNOT LAST"

To Joseph Story

My dear Sir   Richmond September 22d. 1832
    I am greatly indebted to you for your favor of the 14th. Without your assistance I should have found it impossible, or at least very difficult, to comply with the duty assigned me by congress. I have given you a great deal of trouble which I regret—the less because you love law and love labor. Forty years hence your passion for the one and the other may be somewhat diminished.

    I have curtailed your list of books very much for two reasons. One that by far the greater number of those you have mentioned are already in the library, and I am unwilling to exhaust the fund by procuring duplicates,—the other that we may supply what is required by a better selection of duplicates when we meet this winter, if we should meet, and shall have the advantage of knowing precisely how much money remains to be employed. I have said nothing about the American reports because I understand from the librarian that he has already directed all of them to be purchased. In my letter inclosing the list I have said that I so understand his communication, and have requested, if I have misunderstood him, that he will correct the error by purchasing all the American reports not in the library. This is a fund of information on which the supreme court must be always at liberty to draw ad libitum.

    I am very much gratified at hearing that you are so near completing your course on constitutional law, and enriching the political and legal literature of your country with it. The task was arduous but not above your strength, and you have engaged in it with hearty good will. I anticipate much pleasure as well as information from perusing the work, and can assure you in anticipation that I shall not be among the growlers you may expect to hear. I shall not be among those who bring on you the charge of "*apostasy*" and *ultraism*. I shall like to see how in your quotations from the sage you mention you imitate the bee in extracting honey from poison. I have no doubt, however dexterous the operation, that you will be well stung in requital for your skill and industry.

If the prospects of our country inspire you with gloom how do you think a man must be affected who partakes of all your opinions, and whose geographical position enables him to see a great deal that is concealed from you. I yield slowly and reluctantly to the conviction that our constitution cannot last. I had supposed that North of the Potowmack a firm and solid government, competent to the security of national liberty might be preserved. Even that now seems doubtful. The case of the south seems to me to be desperate. Our opinions are incompatible with a united government even among ourselves. The union has been prolonged thus far by miracles. I fear they cannot continue. Yours affectionately

JACKSON'S NULLIFICATION PROCLAMATION

To Joseph Story

My dear Sir   Richmond Decr. 25th. 1832

I had yesterday the pleasure of receiving your letter of the 19th. inclosing a proof sheet of the title page &c of your great work. I anticipate the pleasure its perusal will give me.

Truely sensible as I am that the commendation bestowed on the Chief justice both in the dedication and the preface greatly transcends his merit, and confident as I am that the judgement of the public will confirm this opinion, I am yet deeply penetrated by the evidence it affords of the continuance of that partial esteem and friendship which I have cherished for so many years, and still cherish, as one of the choicest treasures of my life. The only return I can make is locked up in my own bosom, or communicated in occasional conversation with my friends.

I congratulate you on the accomplishment of your purpose, and on finishing the Herculian task you had undertaken. I know no person but yourself who could have sustained properly this vast additional labor. I cannot doubt either the ability or correctness with which it is executed, and am certain, in advance, that I shall read every sentence with entire approbation. It is a subject on which we concur exactly. Our opinions on it are I beleive identical. Not so with Virginia, or the south generally.

Our legislature is now in session, and the dominant party received the message of the President to Congress with enthusiastic applause. Quite different was the effect of his proclamation. That paper astonished, confounded, and for a moment silenced them. In a short time however the power of speech was recovered; and was employed in bestowing on its author the only epithet which could possibly weigh in the scales against the name of "Andrew Jackson," and countervail its popularity. Imitating the Quaker who said the dog he wished to destroy was mad, they said Andrew Jackson had become a Federalist,—even an ultra federalist. To have said he was ready to break down and trample on every other department of the government would not have injured him but to say that he was a Federalist—a convert to the opinions of Washington was a mortal blow under which he is yet staggering.

The party seems to be divided. Those who are still true to their President, pass by his denunciation of all their former theories; and, though they will not approve the sound opinions avowed in his proclamation, are ready to denounce nullification, and to support him in maintaining the union. This is going a great way for them,—much farther than their former declarations would justify the expectation of, and much farther than meer love of union would carry them.

You have undoubtedly seen the message of our Governor, and the resolutions reported by the committee to whom it was referred—A message and resolutions which you will think skillfully framed had the object been a civil war. They undoubtedly hold out to South Carolina the expectation of support from

Virginia: and that hope must be the foundation on which they have constructed their plan for a southern confederacy, or league. A want of confidence in the present support of the people will prevent any direct avowal in favor of this scheme by those whose theories and whose secret wishes may lead to it; but the people may be so entangled by the insane dogmas which have become axioms in the political creed of Virginia, and involved so inextricably in the labyrinth into which those dogmas conduct them, as to do what their sober judgement disapproves.

On thursday these resolutions are to be taken up, and the debate will, I doubt not, be ardent, and tempestuous enough. I pretend not to anticipate the result. Should it countenance the obvious design of South Carolina to form a southern confederacy, it may conduce to a southern league—never to a southern government. Our theories are incompatible with a government for more than a single state. We can form no union which shall be closer than an alliance between sovereigns. In this event there is some reason to apprehend internal convulsion. The northern and western section of our state, should a union be maintained north of the Potowmac, will not readily connect itself with the south. At least such is the present beleif of their most intelligent men. Any effort on their part to separate from Southern Virginia, and unite with a northern confederacy, may probably be punished as treason. "We have fallen on evil times."

I thank you for Mr. Websters speech. Entertaining the opinion he has expressed, respecting the general course of the administration, his patriotism is entitled to the more credit for the determination he expressed at Faneuil Hall, to support it in the great effort it promises to make for the preservation of the union. No member of the then opposition avowed a similar determination during the western insurrection, which would have been equally fatal had it not been quelled by the well timed vigor of General Washington. We are now gathering the bitter fruits of the tree even before that time planted by Mr. Jefferson, and so industriously and perseveringly cultivated by Virginia.

You have doubtless heard from Mr. Peters the affliction with which our brother Baldwin has been visited. It cannot I trust be of long continuance.

We shall meet once more at Washington. Till then adieu. Your faithful and affectionate friend

Eulogy for Mary Marshall

December 25th. 1832

This day of joy and festivity to the whole Christian world is, to my sad heart, the anniversary of the keenest affliction which humanity can sustain. While all around is gladness, my mind dwells on the silent tomb, and cherishes the remembrance of the beloved object it contains.

On the 25th. of December 1831, it was the will of Heaven to take to itself the companion who had sweetened the choicest part of my life, had rendered toil a pleasure, had partaken of all my feelings, and was enthroned in the inmost recess of my heart. Never can I cease to feel the loss and to deplore it. Grief for her is too sacred ever to be profaned on this day which shall be during my existence, devoted to her memory.

On the 3d. of January 1783 I was united by the holiest bands to the woman I adored. From the hour of our union to that of our seperation, I never ceased to thank heaven for this its best gift. Not a moment passed in which I did not consider her as a blessing from which the chief happiness of my life was derived. This never dying sentiment, originating in love, was cherished by a long and close observation of as amiable and estimable qualities as ever adorned the female bosom.

To a person which, in youth, was very attractive; to manners uncommonly pleasing, she added a fine understanding, and the sweetest temper which can accompany a just and modest sense of was due to herself.

I saw her first the week she attained the age of fourteen, and was greatly pleased with her. Girls then came into company much earlier than at present. As my attentions though without any avowed purpose, nor so open or direct as to alarm, soon became ardent and assiduous, her heart recieved an impression which could never be effaced.

Having felt no prior attachment, she became, at sixteen, a most devoted wife. All my faults, and they were too many, could never weaken this sentiment. It formed a part of her existence.

Her judgement was so sound and so safe, that I have often relied upon it in situations of some perplexity. I do not recollect ever to have regretted the adoption of her opinion. I have sometimes regretted its rejection. From native timidity, she was opposed to every thing adventurous; yet few females possessed more real firmness. That timidity so influenced her manners, that I could rarely prevail on her to display in company the talents I knew her to possess. They were reserved for her husband and her select friends. Though serious as well as gentle in her deportment, she possessed a good deal of chaste delicate and playful wit; and if she permitted herself to indulge this talent, told her little story with grace, and could mimic very successfully the peculiarities of the person who was its subject. She had a fine taste for belle lettre reading, which was judiciously applied in the selection of pieces she admired.

This quality by improving her talents for conversation, contributed, not inconsiderably, to make her a most desirable and agreeable companion. It beguiled many of those winter evenings during which her protracted ill health, and her feeble nervous system, confined us entirely to each other. I can never cease to look back on them with deep interest and regret. Time has not diminished; and will not diminish this interest or this regret.

In all the relations of life she was a model which those to whom it was given, cannot imitate too closely. As the wife, the mother, the mistress of a family, and the friend, her life furnished an example to those who could observe it intimately which will not be forgotten. She felt deeply the distress of others, and indulged the feeling liberally on objects she believed to be meritorious.

She was educated with a profound reverence for religion, which she preserved to her last moment. This sentiment, among her earliest and deepest impressions, gave a colour to her whole life. Hers was the religion taught by the Saviour of man.

Cheerful, mild, benevolent, serious, humane, intent on self improvement, and on the improvement of those who looked to her for precept or example. She was a firm believer in the faith inculcated by the church in which she was bred; but her soft and gentle temper was incapable of adopting the gloomy and austere dogmas which some of its professors have sought to engraft on it.

I have lost her! And with her I have lost the solace of my life! Yet she remains still the companion of my retired hours;—still occupies my inmost bosom.

When alone and unemployed, my mind unceasingly recurs to her. More than a thousand times since the 25th of December 1831, have I repeated to myself the beautiful lines written by General Burgoyne under a similar affliction, substituting Mary for Anna.

> Encompassed in an Angels frame
> An angels virtues lay;
> Too soon did Heaven assert its claim,
> And take its own away.
>
> My Mary's worth my Mary's charms
> Can never more return,
> What now shall fill these widowed arms?
> Ah me! my Mary's Urn;
> Ah me! Ah me! my Mary's Urn!!!

Opinion in Barron v. Baltimore

THE judgment brought up by this writ of error having been rendered by the court of a state, this tribunal can exercise no jurisdiction over it, unless it be shown to come within the provisions of the twenty-fifth section of the judicial act.

The plaintiff in error contends that it comes within that clause in the fifth amendment to the constitution, which inhibits the taking of private property for public use, without just compensation. He insists that this amendment, being in favour of the liberty of the citizen, ought to be so construed as to restrain the legislative power of a state, as well as that of the United States. If this proposition be untrue, the court can take no jurisdiction of the cause.

The question thus presented is, we think, of great importance, but not of much difficulty.

The constitution was ordained and established by the people of the United States for themselves, for their own government, and not for the government of the individual states. Each state established a constitution for itself, and, in that constitution, provided such limitations and restrictions on the powers of its particular government as its judgment dictated. The people of the United States framed such a government for the United States as they supposed best adapted to their situation and best calculated to promote their interests. The powers they conferred on this government were to be exercised by itself; and the limitations on power, if expressed in general terms, are naturally, and, we think, necessarily applicable to the government created by the instrument. They are limitations of power granted in the instrument itself; not of distinct governments, framed by different persons and for different purposes.

If these propositions be correct, the fifth amendment must be understood as restraining the power of the general government, not as applicable to the states. In their several constitutions they have imposed such restrictions on their respective governments as their own wisdom suggested; such as they deemed most proper for themselves. It is a subject on which they judge exclusively, and with which others interfere no farther than they are supposed to have a common interest.

The counsel for the plaintiff in error insists that the constitution was intended to secure the people of the several states against the undue exercise of power by their respective state governments; as well as against that which might be attempted by their general government. In support of this argument he relies on the inhibitions contained in the tenth section of the first article.

We think that section affords a strong if not a conclusive argument in support of the opinion already indicated by the court.

The preceding section contains restrictions which are obviously intended for the exclusive purpose of restraining the exercise of power by the departments of the general government. Some of them use language applicable only to congress: others are expressed in general terms. The third clause, for example, declares that "no bill of attainder or ex post facto law shall be passed." No language can be more general; yet the demonstration is complete that it applies solely to the government of the United States. In addition to the general arguments furnished by the instrument itself, some of which have been already suggested, the succeeding section, the avowed purpose of which is to restrain state legislation, contains in terms the very prohibition. It declares that "no state shall pass any bill of attainder or ex post facto law." This provision, then, of the ninth section, however comprehensive its language, contains no restriction on state legislation.

The ninth section having enumerated, in the nature of a bill of rights, the limitations intended to be imposed on the powers of the general government, the tenth proceeds to enumerate those which were to operate on the state legislatures. These restrictions are brought together in the same section, and are by express words applied to the states. "No state shall enter into any treaty," &c. Perceiving that in a constitution framed by the people of the United States for the government of all, no limitation of the action of government on the people would apply to the state government, unless expressed in terms; the restrictions contained in the tenth section are in direct words so applied to the states.

It is worthy of remark, too, that these inhibitions generally restrain state legislation on subjects entrusted to the general government, or in which the people of all the states feel an interest.

A state is forbidden to enter into any treaty, alliance or confederation. If these compacts are with foreign nations, they interfere with the treaty making power which is conferred entirely on the general government; if with each other, for political purposes, they can scarcely fail to interfere with the general purpose and intent of the constitution. To grant letters of marque and reprisal, would lead directly to war; the power of declaring which is expressly given to congress. To coin money is also the exercise of a power conferred on congress. It would be tedious to recapitulate the several limitations on the powers of the states which are contained in this section. They will be found, generally, to restrain state legislation on subjects entrusted to the government of the union, in which the citizens of all the states are interested. In these alone were the whole people concerned. The question of their application to states is not left to construction. It is averred in positive words.

If the original constitution, in the ninth and tenth sections of the first article, draws this plain and marked line of discrimination between the limitations it imposes on the powers of the general government, and on those of the state; if in every inhibition intended to act on state power, words are employed which directly express that intent; some strong reason must be assigned for departing from this safe and judicious course in framing the amendments, before that departure can be assumed.

We search in vain for that reason.

Had the people of the several states, or any of them, required changes in their constitutions; had they required additional safeguards to liberty from the apprehended encroachments of their particular governments: the remedy was in their own hands, and would have been applied by themselves. A convention would have been assembled by the discontented state, and the required improvements would have been made by itself. The unwieldy and cumbrous machinery of procuring a recommendation from two-thirds of congress, and the assent of three-fourths of their sister states, could never have occurred to any human being as a mode of doing that which might be effected by the state itself. Had the framers of these amendments intended them to be limitations on the powers of the state governments, they would have imitated the framers of the original constitution, and have expressed that intention. Had congress engaged in the extraordinary occupation of improving the constitutions of the several states by affording the people additional protection from the exercise of power by their own governments in matters which concerned themselves alone, they would have declared this purpose in plain and intelligible language.

But it is universally understood, it is a part of the history of the day, that the great revolution which established the constitution of the United States, was not effected without immense opposition. Serious fears were extensively entertained that those powers which the patriot statesmen, who then watched over the interests of our country, deemed essential to union, and to the attainment of those invaluable objects for which union was sought, might be exercised in a manner dangerous to liberty. In almost every convention by which the constitution was adopted, amendments to guard against the abuse of power were recommended. These amendments demanded security against the apprehended encroachments of the general government—not against those of the local governments.

In compliance with a sentiment thus generally expressed, to quiet fears thus extensively entertained, amendments were proposed by the required majority in congress, and adopted by the states. These amendments contain no expression indicating an intention to apply them to the state governments. This court cannot so apply them.

We are of opinion that the provision in the fifth amendment to the constitution, declaring that private property shall not be taken for public use without just compensation, is intended solely as a limitation on the exercise of power by the government of the United States, and is not applicable to the legislation of the states. We are therefore of opinion that there is no repugnancy between the several acts of the general assembly of Maryland, given in evidence by the defendants at the trial of this cause, in the court of that state, and the constitution of the United States. This court, therefore, has no jurisdiction of the cause; and it is dismissed.

February 16, 1833

"THE HERESIES OF YOUR COMMENTARIES"

To Joseph Story

My dear Sir   Richmond April 24th. 1833

I had the pleasure some days past of receiving your favor of the 11th., but deferred my answer till I could also acknowledge your very valuable present which it announced. The Lucy & Abigail is now arrived, and has delivered the package containing your commentaries and Allisons sermons for both of which I thank the donors.

As favors generally beget a disposition to make farther demands on the kindness which confers them, I have ventured to impose on you the trouble of distributing some books among your friends and neighbors to whom I wish to be civil, and have sent a few copies of the Life of Washington for that purpose. One you will perceive is for Mr. Webster, and one for Mr. Adams.

In looking over some old papers the other day to determine how many of them were worthy of being committed to the flames, I found a totally forgotten letter (you need not communicate this) from the Historical society of Massachusetts (or Boston) announcing that I had been elected an honorary member. To show my gratitude for this distinction, I ask them to accept my book—a poor return indeed, but the only one I can make.

You know what a compliment has been paid me by your Athenæum. I have been truly flattered by it, and hope the society will receive my book,—not surely as anything like an equivalent—but as a testimonial of my grateful sense of the favorable sentiment that society has manifested for me. The widows mite you know proved the heart more than the rich gifts of the wealthy.

I wish you to present the copy intended for Mrs. Ledyard in your very best manner. Tell her how infinitely I feel the obligation she has conferred on me. I was extremely anxious to obtain Allisons sermons for the reasons I mentioned to you, and you may assure Mrs. Ledyard that their value is enhanced greatly by the hand which gives them.

In the receipt which I took for the freight Captain New-comb promised to deliver the box to his owners—I think he calls them George Thresher & Co. or George Thorcher & Co. —Long Wharf. Though you New England men all or most of you beat copper plate in your writing, this Captain rather poses me. If I mistake his letters you however probably know his owners.

I am truly delighted that your commentaries are published. I shall read them eagerly myself, and wish most ardently that they may be read by others to whom they would be still more useful. The copy intended for the schools will do much good where the teachers introduce it. I greatly fear that, south of the Po-tomack, where it is most wanted, it will be least used. It is a Mahomedan rule, I understand, "never to dispute with the ignorant," and we of the true faith in the South abjure the con-tamination of infidel political works. It would give our ortho-dox Nullifyer a fever to read the heresies of your commentaries. A whole school might be infected by the atmosphere of a single copy should it be placed on one of the shelves of a book case.

By the way, since I have breathed the air of James River I think favorably of Clays bill. I hope, if it can be maintained, that our manufactures will still be protected by it. Have you ever seen any thing to equal the exhibition in Charleston and in the far south generally? Those people pursue a southern league steadily or they are insane. They have caught at Clays bill, if their conduct is at all intelligible, not as a real accomo-dation, a real adjustment, a real releif from actual or supposed oppression, but as an apology for avoiding the crisis and defer-ring the decisive moment till the other states of the South will unite with them. With affectionate esteem I am your

THE HISTORY OF THE UNION

To Humphrey Marshall

My dear Sir   Richmond May 7th. 1833
I am much indebted to you for your pamphlet on our fed-eral relations, which I have read with much satisfaction. No

subject, as it seems to me, is more misunderstood, or more perverted. You have brought into view numerous important historical facts which, in my judgement, remove the foundation on which the nullifyers and seceders have erected that superstructure which overshadows our union. You have I think shown satisfactorily that we never have been perfectly distinct independent societies, sovereign in the sense in which the nullifyers use the term. When Colonies we certainly were not. We were parts of the British empire, and, although not directly connected with each other so far as respected government, we were connected in many respects, and were united to the same stock. The steps we took to effect a separation were, as you have fully shown, not only revolutionary in their nature, but they were taken conjointly. Then as now, we acted in many respects as one people. The representatives of each colony acted for all. Their resolutions proceeded from a common source, and operated on the whole mass. The army was a continental army, commanded by a continental General, and supported from the continental treasury. The declaration of independence was made by a common government, and was made for all the states.

Every thing has been mixed. Treaties made by Congress have been considered as binding all the states. Some powers have been exercised by Congress, some by the states separately. The lines were not distinctly drawn. The inability of Congress to carry its legitimate powers into execution, has gradually annulled those powers practically, but they always existed in theory. Independence was declared "in the name and by the authority of the good people of these colonies." In fact we have always been united in some respects, separate in others. We have acted as one people for some purposes, as distinct societies for others. I think you have shown this clearly and in doing so have demonstrated the fallacy of the principle on which either nullification or the right of peaceable constitutional secession is asserted.

The time is arrived when these truths must be more generally spoken or our union is at an end. The idea of complete sovereignty in the states converts our government into a league, and if carried into practice, dissolves the union. I am dear Sir yours affectionately

CHRISTIANITY AND CIVIL GOVERNMENT

To Jasper Adams

Reverend Sir   Richmond May 9h. 1833.

I am much indebted to you for the copy of your valuable sermon on the relation of Christianity to civil government preached before the convention of the Protestant Episcopal Church in Charleston, on the 13h. of Feby. last. I have read it with great attention & advantage.

The documents annexed to the sermon certainly go far in sustaining the proposition which it is your purpose to establish. One great object of the Colonial charters was avowedly the propagation of the Christian faith. Means have been employed to accomplish this object, & those means have been used by government.

No person, I believe, questions the importance of religion to the happiness of man even during his existence in this world. It has at all times employed his most serious meditation, & had a decided influence on his conduct. The American population is entirely Christian, & with us, Christianity & Religion are identified. It would be strange, indeed, if with such a people, our institutions did not presuppose Christianity, & did not often refer to it, & exhibit relations with it. Legislation on the subject is admitted to require great delicacy, because fredom of conscience & respect for our religion both claim our most serious regard. You have allowed their full influence to both. With very great respect, I am Sir, your Obedt.

MASONRY

To Edward Everett

My dear Sir   Richmond July 22d. 1833

I have just received your favor of the 16th. inclosing a printed copy of your letter respecting masonry to Mr. Atwill, accompanied by printed copies of letters from General Washington and Mr. Madison on the same subject.

Soon after entering the army I was made a mason. In addition to the motives which usually actuate young men, I was induced to become a candidate for admission into the society by the assurance that the brotherly love which pervaded it, and the duties imposed on its members, might be of great service to me in the vicissitudes of fortune to which a soldier was exposed. After the army was disbanded, I found the order in high estimation; and every gentleman I saw in this part of Virginia was a member. I followed the croud for a time without attaching any importance to its object, or giving myself the trouble to enquire why others did. It soon lost its attraction; and, though there are several lodges in the city of Richmond, I have not been in one of them for more than forty years, except once on an invitation to accompany General Lafayette: nor have I been a member of one of them for more than thirty. It was impossible not to perceive the useless pageantry of the whole exhibition. My friend Mr. Story has communicated my opinions to you truly. I thought it however a harmless play thing which would live its hour and pass away, until the murder or abstraction of Morgan was brought before the public. That atrocious crime, and, I had almost said the still more, atrocious suppression of the testimony concerning it, demonstrated the abuse of which the oaths prescribed by the order were susceptible, and convinced me that the institution ought to be abandoned as one capable of producing much evil, and incapable of producing any good which might not be effected by safe and open means.

I give you my sentiments without reserve, but in confidence. I have attained an age when repose becomes a primary wish. I am unwilling to embark on any tempestuous sea, or to engage as a volunteer in any controversy which may tend to rouse the angry passions. I am unwilling to appear in the papers on any question—especially if it may produce excitement.

The antimasonic controversy has not crossed the Potowmack. With you it has become a party question which a public man cannot escape, and on which a decent and manly opinion must be firmly and frankly expressed. But I am not a public man; and, if I were, many and extravagant as are the tests by which we try the fitness of agents for the service of our country, this has not, as yet, become one of them. Several of my personal friends are masons, some few of them more zealous than myself. You will therefore pardon the unwillingness I express that any allusion to this letter should be made in the papers.

Receive the assurances of the great and respectful esteem with which I remain Your Obedt

STORY'S COMMENTARIES

To Joseph Story

My dear Sir   Richmond July 31st. 1833

The day after my last letter was written, I received a copy of your discourse pronounced at the funeral obsequies of Professor Ashmun which I read as I do everything proceeding from your pen,—with deep interest. I had not the pleasure of knowing the deceased, but you have made me acquainted with him, and taught me to respect his memory.

I have finished reading your great work; and wish it could be read by every statesman, and every would be statesman in the United States. It is a comprehensive and an accurate commentary on our constitution, formed in the spirit of the original text. In the South, we are so far gone in political Metaphysics that I fear no demonstration can restore us to common sense. The word "State Rights," as expounded by the resolutions of 98 and the report of 99, construed by our legislature, has a charm against which all reasoning is vain. Those resolutions and that report constitute the creed of every politician who hopes to rise in Virginia, and to question them, or even to adopt the construction given by their author is deemed political sacrilege. The solemn and interesting admonitions of your concluding remarks will not I fear avail as they ought to avail against this popular frenzy.

I have received also a copy of your abridgement which I have glanced over but have not read regularly.

I am grateful for the very flattering terms in which you speak of your friend in many parts of this valuable work as well as in the dedication. In despite of my vanity I cannot suppress the fear that you will be supposed by others as well as myself to have consulted a partial friendship farther than your deliberate judgement will approve. Others may not contemplate this partiality with as much gratification as its object.

I have received the 3d. No. of the National Portrait Gallery and know not in what terms to express my obligations to you for the more than justice you have done the character of your brother Judge. In this instance too, all must perceive the partiality of a friend. Be assured that he on whom that partiality is bestowed will carry with him to the grave a deep sense of it. I am particularly gratified by the terms in which you speak of my Father. If any cotemporary who knew him in the prime of manhood survived, he would confirm all you say of him.

I have received the paper containing your opinion in the very important case of Allen vs McKean. It is impossible a subject could have been brought before you on which you are more completely *au fait*. It would seem as if the state legislatures, (many of them at least) have an invincible hostility to the sacredness of charters. From the paper I should conjecture that this case will proceed no farther.

I am doomed I beleive to submit to applications made to me singly which I could particularly wish to avoid. You have probably observed that the Attorney for the District of Columbia has issued a rule against John H. Pleasants to show cause why an attachment should not issue against him for a contempt of the court in not obeying a subpœna to give testimony in the affair of Randolph. So far as the papers inform us, the object is not to obtain any testimony from the witness applicable to the prosecution, but information which may guide the prosecuting [   ] in his search for testimony. This I think rather novel. I have [   ] that an attachment will issue, in which event I am certain that an application will be made to me for a writ of Habeas corpus. [   ] of course turned my attention in some degree to the subject, and my present impression rather is that the application ought not to prevail. It appears to me that the court for the District of Columbia possesses the power to issue subpœnas to be served out of the District. If so the court is the Judge without appeal of the punishment for contempt in case of disobedience and neither the supreme court or a Judge of the Supreme court can interpose. Is it doubtful whether the officer of the District can serve the process in a state?

I have formed no positive opinion. If you think differently I shall be greatly obliged by any suggestion from you. Your affectionate friend

NAPOLEON BONAPARTE

To Henry Lee

Dear Sir   Richmond September 21st. 1833

On my return a few days past from an annual visit to our mountains, I found your favor of the 21st. of July, and immediately addressed the letter to Judge Hopkinson you requested. My expectations of its success are not sanguine. The subject is one of peculiar delicacy; and it is probable that the Judge will feel some difficulty in asking Mr. Bonaparte to place his papers in the hands of a gentleman not known to himself. It is also probable that he has already selected the Biographer of his brother, if the work is in contemplation. Lucien you know is a writer. However, the letter is sent, and must take its chance.

I inclose you a letter of introduction to General Lafayette. Is it possible that you can be unknown to him?

I can readily suppose that, had young Napoleon lived, circumstances might have elevated him to the throne. All speculations of this kind must however be buried with him, and the family of the hero at whose name Europe trembled, is now mixed with the common mass of mankind. "*Sic transit gloria mundi.*" But his personal glory has not and will not pass away. It will live in history, and will long be cherished in France. I cannot however withhold the opinion that you ascribe more to the enthusiasm manifested on replacing his statue on the top of the column of Austerlitz in *the place Vendome* than sober reality will justify. No people on earth possess more national or military pride than the French. None display that ruling passion with more vivacity. Those now live who witnessed and enjoyed the height of grandeur and of power to which France was elevated while her

Eagles soared under the auspices of the victor of Marengo, and of so many other bloody fields;—who saw all the potentates of the continent bending beneath her power;—heard her distinguished by the preeminent appellation of "The Great Nation"; —and anticipated, not without reason, her ascendency over all the nations of the earth. The same generation connects the fall of French power with the fall of Bonaparte. They see France reduced by that event to a level with her neighbors. Is it wonderful that extravagant demonstrations of joy and enthusiasm should accompany the raising of his statue?—That the veterans who fought under him, who shared his fame and contributed to his victories, should boast of their wounds, show their wooden legs, and consider their own fame as being still embodied with his? The exhibition of strong feeling on such an occasion is natural, but does not, I am disposed to think, prove conclusively that Bonaparte has taken stronger hold of the public feeling than any of the heroes who preceded him.

The sentiment excited by the name of Washington has on more than one occasion, shown itself with great strength. After the capture of Burgoyne, a powerful party was raised against him. Had you witnessed the emotion it excited, even in the army of Gates, you would have been convinced that he had taken very strong hold of the public feeling. All the great scenes of his eventful life demonstrate the same fact. It was not until the French revolution maddened the world, and gave efficacy to the machinations of one of our most skilful politicians, that the devotion of his fellow citizens was in any degree impaired. Even then, the affection of the great body of the people remained unshaken. Only the party leaders deserted him.

Alexander was poisoned. This was the act of an individual, or at any rate of a few. Bonaparte might have been the victim of the infernal machine. If his Generals partitioned his dominions, this only shows the supremacy of self over their respect for the memory of their departed chief. Bonaparte might have been the victim of the infernal machine, and none can conjecture what would in that event have been the destiny of France.

Hanibal was not less the idol of his army than Napoleon. But Carthage perished with him, Rome triumphed; and we cannot suppose that Hanibal was beloved by the Romans.

Caesar too was not less the idol of Rome than Bonaparte

was of Paris. He perished like Henry IV of France by the hands of an assassin. But this did not prove that he was not enthroned in the hearts of the people. His influence, imparted to Mark Anthony and Augustus, subdued the republic. Yet Cæsar added only Gaul to the Roman empire. Bonaparte carried the Eagles of France in triumph through the continent of Europe. I beleive that he possessed immense influence over the hearts of Frenchmen; but not more than military fame, and immense genius have bestowed on others.

Our canvass for the successor of President Jackson has commenced. A strong foundation has been laid for the election of Mr. VanBuren, but he will encounter much opposition. Many counties of Virginia have shown a disposition to bring forward our friend Mr. Leigh. Should he be taken up by the legislature, which is not improbable, he bids fair to be supported by the south. I however know very little of what is passing in the political world. I am my dear Sir with respectful esteem Your Obedt

PLANS FOR A NEW HOUSE

To James K. Marshall

My dear Son   Richmond October 14th. 1833

I received my great coat by Colo. Ambler for which I am much obliged both to you and him. I have also received your letters by Colo. Ambler and Mary Harvie.

The plan of the house is indeed a very commodious one. It is probably larger than is necessary, but I am not a judge of the saving which may be made by any reduction of its dimensions. I daresay 18 feet square would be sufficient for the sitting room and 14 feet wide would be enough for the chamber. This alteration would reduce the house two feet each way and would leave it large enough for my purposes. I however can occupy it only for a few years. It will I hope be of some service to you long after I shall be deposited by the side of your mother. It is my wish therefore that in making any reduction you should be governed entirely by your views for the future. I shall be entirely pleased with the present plan or with the reduction I have suggested. The cellar I think had better be coextensive with the house, but one fire place will undoubtedly be enough. That should be in the outer cellar which will be under the setting room. It is not improbable that the outer cellar may be a lodging for a servant, the inner for spirits &c

I perceive so much difficulty in moving that I almost repent having decided on it. However I shall stick to my resolution.

I am anxious to know what is the probability with respect to Jetts lease, and whether if it has actually expired, he will surrender the possession or compel me to eject him. Should he give it up I should be disposed to rent it on the shares from year to year though I should not be disposed to change the tenant during my life. If Jett gives up quietly and wishes to remain on the place I should be disposed to give him the preference unless strong objections should exist against him.

We have had a fine rain lately, and are very busy seeding.

Give my thanks to Claudia for the stockings she sent me by Mary Harvie. I am now wearing them, and they are very pleasant.

I have expected to hear from Edward informing me when I may look for Mrs. Nelson, Rebecca & himself.

With my love to Claudia and the children I am your affectionate Father

THE DIVIDING LINE BETWEEN PARTIES

To Thomas S. Grimké

My dear Sir   Richmond october 6th. 1834

On my return to this place a few days past from an annual summer visit to our mountain country, I had the pleasure of receiving your letter of the 14th. of July together with the papers containing Judge Harper's opinion on the constitutional question which has so much agitated South Carolina. I had previously received the opinions of Judges Johnson and Oneale and am much indebted to you for these truly interesting documents, which I have read with great attention.

Judges Johnson and Oneale appear to have decided the question on the constitution of the state; Judge Harper takes into view the constitution of the United States. His opinion unquestionably displays talent and acute reasoning powers, but is obviously founded on the assumption that our constitution is essentially a L E A G U E and not A   G O V E R N M E N T.

This is the true and substantial dividing line between parties in the United States. One of more vital importance cannot be drawn. As the one opinion or the other prevails, will the union, as I firmly beleive, be preserved or dissolved. If a meer league has never been of long duration, if it has never been of sufficient efficacy to preserve a lasting peace between its members, we must be irrationally sanguine to indulge a hope that ours will furnish an exception to any and every thing which has heretofore occurred in the history of man. If such be the true spirit of the instrument such must be its construction, but we cannot I think fail to ask ourselves for what purpose was it made? Was it worth the effort of all the wisdom virtue and patriotism of the country meerly to exchange one league for another? Did the convention did the people beleive that they were framing a league and not a government?

The first volume of The Life of Washington as in the first edition, termed in that edition an "Introduction," contains the same matter with the History of the colonies. I was induced to think that many who would be desirous of seeing the Biography of Washington might not consider this extrinsic matter as a necessary appendage to it, and therefore determined to separate them.

I am not informed whether my attempts to forward to you the 2d. edition of this work have succeeded. Should they have failed, and you will have the goodness to suggest any person with whom it may be deposited so as to reach you I will avail myself of the information. With great and respectful esteem I am your Obedt

VIRGINIA POLITICS

To Joseph Story

My dear Sir   Richmond Decr. 3d. 1834

I am so accustomed to rely on you for aid when I need it that you must not be surprised at the present application. I trust however that it will not give you much trouble.

You will perceive in the 2V. of the Life of Washington 2d. Ed. p 307–8. an account of the defeat of Harden. It is stated that the battle was fought on the St. Joseph. I have received a letter from a gentleman in Chilicothe which gives probability to the opinion that it was really fought on Paint creek, a stream which empties into the Scioto not far from Chilicothe. Will you have the goodness at your leisure to make some enquiries of Mr. Sparks and learn whether the letter to general Washington giving an account of this battle states it to have been fought on the St. Joseph or on Paint creek. You need not hurry yourself on this subject. The information will be in full time when I meet you in Washington where I purpose to be as usual in January.

I perceive you have been much employed in dispatching a batch of Pirates. I trust I may congratulate you on having finished it to your own satisfaction. My circuit duties are not arduous and will terminate this week.

You will perceive that our House of Delegates has reelected their Jackson Speaker. This however is not absolutely a test of the strength of parties. The decisive battle will be fought on the election of a Senator. Both parties appear to be sanguine. The administration has undoubtedly a majority in the senate—the opposition in the House of Delegates. We are insane on the subject of the Bank. Its friends who are not numerous, dare not, a few excepted, to avow themselves. You will perceive by the message of our Governor that he is a compete nullifier in the Georgia sense of the term.

I conjecture from Symptoms in the papers, that Mr. Van-Buren gains strength in Virginia. This opinion is founded on the fact that the papers in his interest did not for a long time allude to him as their candidate. They emptied their cup of

Malignant calumny on every other person who was named as a candidate, hoping by the destruction of others to sustain him. They now begin to bring him forward. This shows that in their opinion he is stronger than he was.

I anticipate with much pleasure our meeting at Washington. It is among the most painful of the emotions excited by the prospect of my leaving public life, an event which though not intended to be immediate, cannot be very distant, that I shall part forever from friends most dear to me. I am my dear Sir with true and affectionate esteem Your

A GRANDSON'S EDUCATION

To John Marshall, Jr.

My dear Grandson   Richmond Novr. 7th. 1834

I had yesterday the pleasure of receiving your letter of the 29th. of November, and am quite pleased with the course of study you are pursuing. Proficiency in Greek and Latin is indispensable to an accomplished scholar; and may be of great real advantage in our progress through human life. Cicero deserves to be studied still more for his talents than for the improvement in language to be derived from reading him. He was unquestionably, with the single exception of Demosthenes, the greatest orator among the ancients. He was too a profound Philosopher. His "de officiis" is among the most valuable treatises I have seen in the latin language.

History is among the most essential departments of knowledge; and, to an American, the histories of England and of the United States are most instructive. Every man ought to be intimately acquainted with the history of his own country. Those of England and of the United States are so closely connected that the former seems to be introductory to the latter. They form one whole. Hume, as far as he goes, to the revolution of 1688, is generally thought the best Historian of England. Others have continued his narative to a late period, and it will be necessary to read them also.

There is no exercise of the mind from which more valuable

improvement is to be drawn than from composition. In every situation of life the result of early practice will be valuable. Both in speaking and writing, the early habit of arranging our thoughts with regularity so as to point them to the object to be proved, will be of great advantage. In both, clearness and precision are most essential qualities. The man who by seeking embellishment hazards confusion, is greatly mistaken in what constitutes good writing. The meaning ought never to be mistaken. Indeed the reader should never be obliged to search for it. The writer should always express himself so clearly as to make it impossible to misunderstand him. He should be comprehended without an effort.

The first step towards writing and speaking clearly is to think clearly. Let the subject be perfectly understood, and a man will soon find words to convey his meaning to others. Blair, whose lectures are greatly and justly admired, advises a practice well worthy of being observed. It is to take a page of some approved writer and read it over repeatedly until the matter, not the words, be fully impressed on the mind. Then write, in your own language, the same matter. A comparison of the one with the other will enable you to remark and correct your own defects. This course may be pursued after having made some progress in composition. In the commencement, the student ought carefully to reperuse what he has written. Correct, in the first instance, every error of orthography and grammar. A mistake in either is unpardonable; afterwards, revise and improve the language.

I am pleased with both your pieces of composition. The subjects are well chosen and of the deepest interest. Happiness is pursued by all; though too many mistake the road by which this greatest good is to be successfully followed. Its abode is not always in the palace or the cottage. Its residence is the human heart, and its inseparable companion is a quiet conscience. Of this, Religion is the surest and safest foundation. The individual who turns his thoughts frequently to an omnipotent omniscient, and all perfect being, who feels his dependence on, and his infinite obligations to that being, will avoid that course of life which must harrow up the conscience. My love to your mother & the family Your affectionate Grand Father

December 7, 1834

REMEMBERING A CONVERSATION
WITH WASHINGTON

To James K. Paulding

Sir   Richmond April 4th. 1835
    Your favour of the 22d. of March was received in the course
of the mail, but I have been confined to my room, and am only
now resuming my pen.

    The single difficulty I feel in complying with your request
arises from my repugnance to any thing which may be construed into an evidence of that paltry vanity which, if I know
myself, forms no part of my character. To detail any conversation which might seem to insinuate that General Washington
considered my engaging in the political transactions of the
United States an object of sufficient consequence to induce
him to take an interest in effecting it, may look like boasting
that I held more favorable place in the opinion of that great
man than the fact would justify. I do not however think that
this, perhaps, fastidious feeling would justify a refusal to answer
an enquiry made in terms entitled to my sincere acknowledgements.

    All who were then old enough to notice the public affairs of
the United States, recollect the arduous struggle of 1798 and
1799. General Washington, it is well known, took a deep interest in it. He beleived that the real independence, the practical
self government of our country, depended greatly on its issue
—on our resisting the incroachments of France.

    I had devoted myself to my profession, and, though actively
and zealously engaged in support of the measures of his administration in the legislature of Virginia, had uniformly declined any situation which might withdraw me from the bar. In
1798 I was very strongly pressed by the federalists to become a
candidate for Congress, and the gentleman of that party who
had offered himself to the district, proposed to resign his pretensions in my favor. I had however positively refused to accede
to the proposition, and beleived that I could not be induced to
change my determination. In this state of things, in August or
September 1798 as well as I recollect, I received an invitation

from General Washington to accompany his nephew, the late Judge Washington on a visit to Mount Vernon. I accepted this invitation, and remained at Mount Vernon four or five days. During this time the walk and conversation in the Piazza mentioned by Mr. Lewis took place.

General Washington urged the importance of the crisis, expressed his decided conviction that every man who could contribute to the success of sound opinions was required by the most sacred duty to offer his service to the public, and pressed me to come into the Congress of the ensuing year.

After the very natural declarations of distrust in my ability to do any good, I told him that I had made large pecuniary engagements which required close attention to my profession, and which would distress me should the emoluments derived from it be abandoned. I also mentioned the assurance I had given to the gentleman then a candidate, which I could not honorably violate.

He thought that gentleman would still willingly withdraw in my favor, and that my becoming a member of Congress for the present, would not sacrifice my practice as a lawyer. At any rate the sacrifice might be temporary.

After continuing the conversation for sometime, he directed my attention to his own conduct. He had withdrawn from office with a declaration of his determination, never again, under any circumstances, to enter public life. No man could be more sincere in making that declaration, nor could any man feel stronger motives for adhering to it. No man could make a stronger sacrifice than he did in breaking a resolution thus publicly made, and which he had beleived to be unalterable. Yet I saw him, in opposition to his public declaration, in opposition to his private feelings, consenting, under a sense of duty, to surrender the sweets of retirement, and again to enter the most arduous and perilous station which an individual could fill.

My resolution yielded to this representation. After remarking that the obligation which had controuled his course was essentially different from that which bound me—that no other man could fill the place to which his country had called him, whereas my services could weigh but little in the political balance, I consented to become a candidate, and have continued, ever since my election, in public life.

This letter is intended to be private, and you will readily perceive the unfitness of making it public. It is written because it has been requested in polite and obliging terms, and because I am willing, should your own views induce you to mention the fact derived from Mr. Lewis, to give you the assurance of its truth. With very great respect I am Sir Your Obedt. servt.

"MY OLD WORN OUT FRAME"

To Richard Peters

My dear Sir   Richmond April 30th. 1835
    I had yesterday the pleasure of receiving your favor of the 26th. and am truly grateful for the kindness both of Doctor Chapman and yourself. You cannot estimate too highly my confidence in the medical gentlemen of Philadelphia. All that human skill can do, I should expect from them, but my old worn out frame cannot I beleive be repaired. Could I find the mill which would grind old men, and restore youth, I might indulge the hope of recovering my former vigor and taste for the enjoyments of life. But as that is impossible, I must be content with patching myself up and dragging on as well as I can. I must beg both yourself and Doctor Chapman to receive my thanks for your very friendly dispositions by letter, since they cannot be tendered in person.

    I condole with you on the state of the health of Mrs. Peters. I had heard that her situation was dangerous. Too well do I know the affliction to which you are subjected.

    I am glad to heard that the reports of the last session of the supreme court are in such forwardness.

    Present me most affectionately to those valuable friends of Philadelphia who honor and flatter me by their enquiries and beleive me to be dear Sir with much esteem Your Obedt.

To Thomas P. Devereux

My dear Sir   Richmond May 30th. 35

I was highly gratified by your letter of the 15th. but have been so much indisposed since its receipt that I have not till now taken up my pen to answer it. I derive infinite satisfaction from learning that my absence has produced no sort of inconvenience to the public business. It would have given me much regret had it been otherwise. It was however absolutely impossible for me to have been conveyed in any manner to Raleigh.

You need not doubt that I have bid an eternal adieu to the stage.

I understand Mr. Gastons memorandum perfectly. Tell him I acknowledge that Newburn potatoe stands supported by unassailable testimony.

I shall leave Richmond for Fauquier late in June or early in July. It will give me more pleasure than I can express to see Judge Gaston at my retreat. If it should accord with his convenience to visit me I could wish to receive some intimation of the time because my state of health will induce me to pass a large portion of the summer at the sulphur spring near Warrenton; and, should he not take that fashionable watering place in his route he might not find me at home. This woud be to a me a serious misfortune. I am dear Sir with great regard & esteem Your Obedt

Epitaph

John Marshall
son of Thomas and Mary Marshall
was born the 24th of September 1755
Intermarried with Mary Willis Ambler
the 3d of January 1783
Departed this life
the ——— day of —— 18

July 4, 1835

CHRONOLOGY

NOTE ON THE TEXTS

NOTES

INDEX

Chronology

1755　Born September 24 in a cabin near Germantown, Prince William County (after 1759, part of Fauquier County), Virginia, the first of 15 children of Thomas Marshall and Mary Randolph Keith Marshall. (Father, born 1730, was the son of a farmer. Mother, born 1737, was the daughter of an Anglican minister. They married in 1754, shortly after father moved from Westmoreland County.) Father becomes a prominent planter, surveyor, and magistrate in Fauquier County and serves in the House of Burgesses.

1756　Sister Elizabeth born.

1757　Sister Mary born.

1761　Brother Thomas born.

1764　Brother James born.

1765　Family moves to The Hollow, wood house on leased land in northwestern Fauquier County.

1766　Sister Judith born.

1767　Twin brothers William and Charles born.

1768　Sister Lucy born.

1769　Attends school in Westmoreland County run by Archibald Campbell, an Anglican clergyman.

1770　Returns home. Tutored in Latin by James Thomson, a Scottish-educated Anglican clergyman. Brother Alexander born.

1772　Begins reading William Blackstone's *Commentaries on the Laws of England*.

1773　Father purchases 1,700 acres of land and moves family to Oak Hill, a seven-room wood-frame house about ten miles east of The Hollow. Brother Louis born.

1775　Revolutionary War begins on April 19. Sister Susan born. Marshall is commissioned in early September as first lieutenant of a company of Fauquier County riflemen in the Culpeper Minuteman Battalion. Marches with the battalion to Williamsburg in early October and remains encamped there until late November, then marches to Great Bridge, Virginia, in early December. Participates in the American victory at Great Bridge on December 9.

1776   Witnesses the burning of Norfolk by Lord Dunmore's forces on January 1. Remains in the area until his discharge from the Minuteman Battalion in late March. Commissioned as a first lieutenant in the Continental Army on July 31, and spends the remainder of the year recruiting enlistees in Fauquier County. Assigned to the 11th Virginia Regiment, commanded by Colonel Daniel Morgan.

1777   Marches with his company to Philadelphia in January for smallpox inoculation. Sister Charlotte born. 11th Virginia Regiment joins Washington's army in New Jersey in April. Marshall serves as regimental adjutant, April–May. Marches with his regiment through New Jersey to the Hudson Highlands and back in June and July, covering 300 miles in 18 days. Assigned for duty with light infantry unit commanded by General William Maxwell in late August. British land troops in northern Maryland on August 25, beginning campaign to capture Philadelphia. Marshall fights in skirmish at Cooch's Bridge, Pennsylvania, September 3, and at Chadd's Ford during the American defeat at the battle of Brandywine, September 11. (Marshall's father commands the 3rd Virginia Regiment at Brandywine.) British occupy Philadelphia on September 26. Marshall returns to his regiment after light infantry duty and is wounded in the hand at the battle of Germantown, October 4. Appointed as a deputy judge advocate in November. Army goes into winter quarters at Valley Forge in December.

1778   Remains encamped with the army at Valley Forge until mid-June. Drills his company in new tactics instituted by General von Steuben. Present at the battle of Monmouth Court House, June 28, but does not see action. Promoted to captain in the now-renamed 7th Virginia Regiment. Serves at various postings in New Jersey until he is furloughed on November 30. Goes home to Fauquier County.

1779   Returns to army in New Jersey in May. Serves in reserve force during General Anthony Wayne's capture of the British fort at Stony Point in the Hudson Highlands, July 16, and in detachment that covers Major Henry Lee's withdrawal after the American raid on Paulus Hook, New Jersey, August 19. Sister Jane born. Marshall is assigned to various posts in New York and New Jersey during the fall. Walks home to Virginia in December on indefinite furlough as a supernumerary officer.

1780   Joins father, now commander of the state artillery regiment, at Yorktown in late February. Attends lectures on law by George Wythe and on natural philosophy by the Reverend James Madison (a cousin of the future president) given at the College of William and Mary in Williamsburg, May–July. Begins courting Mary ("Polly") Ambler, born 1766, daughter of Virginia treasurer Jaquelin Ambler. Obtains law license in Richmond and is admitted to practice in Fauquier County Court on August 28. Travels to Philadelphia in early October, seeking to resume active service. Returns to Richmond in December with Steuben and assists him in recruiting men for service in the Southern Department under General Nathanael Greene.

1781   Sees action in skirmish at Hood's Landing following Benedict Arnold's raid on Richmond in early January. Unable as a supernumerary officer to obtain a new assignment in the Continental Army, Marshall resigns his commission on February 12. Sister Nancy born. (All of Marshall's siblings lived into adulthood, and five are known to have survived him.) Marshall continues his courtship of Polly Ambler and commences law practice when the county courts reopen following the British surrender at Yorktown on October 19.

1782   Elected on April 22 to represent Fauquier County in the House of Delegates of the Virginia Assembly. Attends legislative sessions in Richmond, May 25–July 2 and November 9–29. Elected by the legislature to serve on the eight-man executive council that assists the governor in administering the state. Takes oath on November 30 and sits on the council through December.

1783   Marries Polly Ambler on January 3 in Hanover County. Serves on council, January–July and from late September through the end of the year.

1784   Resigns from council on April 1 to return to his law practice. Wins election in April to represent Fauquier County in the House of Delegates. Attends legislative sessions, May–June and October–December. Son Thomas born, July 24. Makes Richmond his permanent residence in order to practice in the state superior courts.

1785   Receives title to Oak Hill when his parents and younger
        siblings move to Kentucky. Admitted to practice in the
        Virginia Court of Appeals on April 29. Elected in July to
        a seat in the Common Hall, Richmond's governing body,
        and serves as recorder and justice of the city hustings
        court until his resignation in March 1788.

1786   Argues *Hite v. Fairfax* in the Court of Appeals on May 5,
        appearing for the heirs of Lord Fairfax in major case in-
        volving contested land titles in the Northern Neck of
        Virginia. Court rules in favor of Hite interests while rec-
        ognizing the legal validity of Fairfax titles. Daughter Re-
        becca born June 15 and dies five days later. Polly has
        mental breakdown after suffering miscarriage in Septem-
        ber. Marshall is narrowly defeated by James Innes in elec-
        tion for state attorney general in November.

1787   Elected in April to the House of Delegates representing
        Henrico County. Philadelphia convention sends the Con-
        stitution to Congress on September 17 and proposes that
        it be submitted to ratifying conventions in each state.
        Marshall takes seat in assembly on October 15. After the
        House of Delegates debates whether Virginia ratifying
        convention should have the power to propose amend-
        ments, Marshall introduces a successful compromise reso-
        lution calling for a "free and ample discussion" of the
        Constitution. Supports legislation to settle debts owed to
        British creditors under the 1783 treaty of peace and to re-
        organize the court system. Son Jaquelin Ambler Marshall
        born December 3.

1788   Elected on March 3 as a delegate from Henrico County
        to the state ratifying convention. Attends the convention
        in Richmond, June 2–27. Delivers three speeches sup-
        porting the Constitution, including an extended defense
        of the judiciary article. Convention votes 89–79 in favor
        of ratification on June 25. Marshall serves on committee
        that prepares form of ratification and text of 40 proposed
        amendments. Declines to run for Congress as a Federalist,
        choosing instead to continue his prosperous law practice.

1789   Wins election in April to the House of Delegates as rep-
        resentative for the city of Richmond. Admitted to practice
        in newly established state district courts at Fredericks-
        burg, Petersburg, and Richmond. Declines appointment
        as United States Attorney for Virginia. Attends House of
        Delegates session, October–December, and serves on
        committee of eight judges and lawyers preparing a new

edition of the laws of the commonwealth. Admitted to practice in the U.S. Circuit and District Courts in Richmond. Purchases lot near the state capitol and begins constructing Federal-style house that will become his permanent home. Daughter Mary Anne Marshall born November 24.

1790   Reelected to the House of Delegates. Attends General Assembly session, October–December. Opposes Patrick Henry's resolution denouncing federal assumption of state debts as "repugnant to the Constitution." Law practice continues to expand as Marshall becomes the principal attorney for Virginia debtors sued by British creditors in the U.S. Circuit Court.

1791   Does not stand for reelection to the General Assembly, intending to "bid a final adieu to political life." Attends to his busy practice in the state and federal courts. Commissioned colonel of the Richmond regiment of the state militia in May. Argues *Jones v. Walker*, major case involving British debts, in the U.S. Circuit Court in November, joining Patrick Henry and other attorneys appearing for the defense (term ends without a decision).

1792   Son John James Marshall, born February 13, dies June 10. Daughter Mary Anne Marshall dies August 1.

1793   Marshall and his brother James contract to purchase 215,000 acres of the Fairfax estate in the Northern Neck of Virginia for £20,000. Attends hearing held in Cumberland County Court on April 29 to examine accusation that Richard Randolph had killed his sister-in-law Nancy's newborn child; the examination ends with the dismissal of all charges. (It is unclear whether Marshall joined Patrick Henry in defending Richard Randolph, or observed the proceedings for other reasons.) Joins Patrick Henry in arguing *Ware v. Hylton,* new test case concerning British debts, before the U.S. Circuit Court in May. The case is appealed to the U.S. Supreme Court after the Circuit Court rules in favor of the creditors on most of the disputed questions. Marshall drafts public address and resolutions in August supporting President Washington's proclamation of neutrality in the war between France and Britain. Publishes "Aristides" and "Gracchus" newspaper essays, September–November, defending neutrality policy in response to Republican attacks on the administration. Joins other members of the Richmond bar in seeking clemency for Angela Barnett, a free black woman sentenced to death for killing a white man in self-defense (Barnett is pardoned by Governor Henry Lee). Elected Grand Master of the Grand Lodge of Virginia Masons in October (serves until 1796). Appointed brigadier general of Virginia militia in December.

1794   Elected to Richmond city government in July (serves until 1796). Leads militia expedition to Smithfield, Virginia, in late July to seize vessel being outfitted as French privateer in violation of the federal Neutrality Act. Serves as acting attorney general of Virginia, October 1794–March 1795, while James Innes is absent from the state.

1795   Travels to Philadelphia to argue *Ware v. Hylton* and is admitted to practice in the U.S. Supreme Court on February 2; the case is postponed until the following term. In the spring the Richmond freeholders unexpectedly elect Marshall, not originally a candidate, to the House of Delegates. Declines offer of appointment as U.S. Attorney General in August. Daughter Mary born September 13. Attends General Assembly session, November–December. Successfully defends the constitutionality of the commercial clauses in the recently ratified Jay Treaty with Great Britain. Published accounts of Marshall's role in the debate gain attention of northern Federalists.

1796   Makes only appearance before the U.S. Supreme Court when he argues *Ware v. Hylton* in February. The court rejects his argument, ruling that wartime Virginia law on the discharge of British debts contravenes the 1783 peace treaty with Britain. Marshall is warmly received in Philadelphia by several influential northern Federalists serving in Congress. Reelected to House of Delegates. Speaks at public meeting in Richmond on April 25 in favor of resolution urging the House of Representatives to appropriate money for implementation of the Jay Treaty. Declines offer of appointment as minister to France as successor to James Monroe. Attends General Assembly session, November–December. Devises legislative compromise under which Virginia yields claims to Fairfax manor lands while Marshall and the other purchasers of the Fairfax manors concede the right of state to the unappropriated lands of the Northern Neck.

1797   Obtains deed to South Branch, one of the Fairfax manors, on payment of purchase money in February. Reelected to the House of Delegates in April. American relations with France worsen as the French navy increases its seizures of American ships trading with Britain. President John Adams appoints Marshall, Charles Cotesworth Pinckney, and Elbridge Gerry as special envoys in June and instructs them to negotiate treaty with France. Marshall accepts appointment and meets with Adams in Philadelphia before sailing for Europe on July 18. Arrives in Amsterdam on August 29 and reaches Paris on September 27. The three envoys have a short informal meeting with Talleyrand, the French foreign minister, on October 8, and are then approached by three of Talleyrand's agents, who solicit $240,000 bribe as precondition for further negotiations. The agents also demand that the Americans agree to loan France $12 million and repudiate critical remarks about French policy made by Adams. Marshall keeps journal of these transactions and serves as principal drafter of two lengthy dispatches sent to Secretary of State Timothy Pickering on October 22 and November 8.

1798   Son John Marshall Jr. born January 13. Marshall drafts lengthy memorandum to Talleyrand defending American neutrality policy and asserting U.S. claims against France. Talleyrand's reply convinces Marshall of futility of prolonging mission. Publication of the envoys' dispatches causes sensation in United States. Marshall leaves France on April 23 and arrives in New York June 17. At banquet held in Philadelphia for Marshall, Congressman Robert Goodloe Harper proposes toast—"Millions for Defense but not a cent for Tribute"—that becomes Federalist rallying cry. On his way to Virginia Marshall is greeted with public demonstrations praising his defense of American honor in the "XYZ Affair" (in the published texts of envoys' dispatches, the French agents were referred to as X, Y, and Z). Arrives June 28 in Winchester, Virginia, and reunites with Polly, then recovering from breakdown following the birth of John Jr. Returns to Richmond on August 9 and resumes law practice. United States begins limited undeclared naval war with France. Visits Mount Vernon in early September and is persuaded by George Washington to run for Congress. Writes "To a Freeholder," public letter defending the administration's policy toward France and declaring his opposition to the Alien and Sedition Acts. Declines appointment to U.S. Supreme Court to replace James Wilson. In December Virginia Assembly adopts resolutions denouncing Alien and Sedition laws as "palpable infractions" of the Constitution.

1799 Supporters of Marshall and his Republican opponent John Clopton, a two-term incumbent, wage heated campaign through newspaper essays and pamphlets. Marshall secures important endorsement from Patrick Henry and wins election on April 24 by slightly more than 100 votes. Travels to Kentucky, July–August, to visit his aging parents. Returns to Richmond in time to attend fall sessions of state and federal courts. Arrives in Philadelphia with Polly in early December to attend first session of the Sixth Congress. Emerges as leader of the moderate Federalists who support Adams. Establishes friendly relations with Theodore Sedgwick, leader of the High Federalists who bitterly oppose the President's renewed attempts to negotiate an agreement with France, and with Republican leader Albert Gallatin. Drafts reply to the President's address to Congress that preserves party harmony and pleases Adams. Announces death of George Washington in speech on December 18 and eulogizes him in the House the following day.

1800 Son James Keith Marshall born in Philadelphia February 13. Republicans move to censure Adams for approving the extradition of Thomas Nash, a British seaman charged with mutiny and murder; Nash, who claimed to be Jonathan Robbins, an American impressed into the British navy, was subsequently tried and hanged by the British. Marshall delivers lengthy speech on March 7 articulating distinction between political and judicial questions and defending Nash's extradition as a legitimate exercise of executive power. House rejects censure motion and adopts resolution approving the President's conduct. Marshall joins with Republicans in unsuccessful attempt to repeal Sedition Act, and also opposes Federalist-sponsored bill establishing joint committee of the House and Senate to settle disputed presidential elections. Adams forces resignation of Secretary of War James McHenry on May 6 and names Marshall as his successor. Marshall declines position, but accepts appointment as secretary of state after Adams dismisses Pickering on May 12. Arrives in June at the new seat of government in Washington, D.C., and involves himself in ongoing negotiations with France and Great Britain. Supports proposal to settle outstanding debts owed to British creditors with a lump-sum payment. Writes lengthy dispatch to Rufus King, the U.S.

minister to Great Britain, explaining American policy of
"exact neutrality" between belligerent powers. Becomes
confidential adviser to Adams and drafts his November 22
address to Congress. Administration receives treaty,
signed in France on September 30, ending the undeclared
naval war and suspending the 1778 treaty of alliance
between France and the United States. Presidential election results in electoral tie between Republican candidates
Thomas Jefferson and Aaron Burr. Chief Justice Oliver
Ellsworth resigns on December 15. Adams nominates
John Jay, who had previously served as Chief Justice from
1789 to 1795, as his successor.

1801   Jay declines appointment. Adams nominates Marshall as
Chief Justice on January 20, and he is confirmed by the
Senate on January 27. Treaty with France is ratified in
amended form on February 3. Marshall takes oath as
fourth Chief Justice of the United States on February 4
while continuing to serve as Secretary of State. (The associate justices of the Supreme Court are William Cushing,
appointed 1789; William Paterson, appointed 1793; Samuel
Chase, appointed 1796; Bushrod Washington, a nephew
of George Washington, appointed 1798; and Alfred
Moore, appointed 1799.) Court holds brief session before
adjourning on February 10. Congress passes judiciary act
relieving Supreme Court justices from circuit duty and
creating 16 circuit court judgeships, as well as act creating
42 justices of the peace for the District of Columbia. Federalist-controlled House of Representatives elects Jefferson
president on February 17 after 36 ballots; Burr becomes
vice-president. Adams nominates, and the Senate confirms, new federal judges and justices of the peace; the
"midnight appointments" anger Jefferson and the Republicans. Marshall, acting as secretary of state, fails to deliver the signed and sealed commissions for the District of
Columbia justices of the peace before he leaves office.
Administers presidential oath to Jefferson on March 4
(will administer oath of office at every subsequent inauguration through 1833). Returns home to Richmond and
begins writing *The Life of George Washington,* having
agreed to undertake project at behest of Bushrod Washington. Jefferson witholds 17 of the 42 undelivered commissions for justices of the peace on the grounds that the
number of appointments was excessive. Marshall attends
Supreme Court sessions in Washington, August 4–11 and
December 8–31. Institutes practice of delivering decisions

through a single "opinion of the court," often unanimous, instead of having each justice issue an individual opinion. He also arranges for the justices to board together while in Washington, and begins practice of having them wear black robes while on the bench. William Marbury asks the Court for an order requiring Secretary of State James Madison to show cause why writ of mandamus should not be issued commanding him to deliver Marbury's commission as justice of peace. (The Supreme Court is authorized to issue writs of mandamus as part of its original jurisdiction under section 13 of the Judiciary Act of 1789.) Marshall grants order to show cause on December 18, postponing until June 1802 arguments as to whether mandamus should be issued.

1802   In March the Republican-controlled Congress repeals the Judiciary Act of 1801 and eliminates separate circuit court judgeships. New judiciary act, passed in April, reinstates circuit-riding by Supreme Court justices and abolishes summer term of the Supreme Court, postponing its next meeting until February 1803. Marshall doubts constitutionality of Supreme Court justices holding circuit courts without distinct commissions. Solicits views of fellow justices as to whether they should attend fall circuits; consensus is reached that the question was settled by the practice of the justices riding circuit before 1801. Father Thomas Marshall dies in Kentucky on June 22. In September Bushrod Washington contracts with Philadelphia publisher Caleb P. Wayne to publish *The Life of George Washington*. College of New Jersey (Princeton) awards Marshall honorary L.L.D. on September 29. Marshall attends his first session of the U.S. Circuit Court for Virginia in Richmond, November 22–December 10, sitting with U.S. District Court judge Cyrus Griffin. (Circuit Court for Virginia meets each year on or about May 22 and November 22, and usually sits for two to three weeks each term.) Dismisses challenge to the constitutionality of the repeal of the 1801 Judiciary Act made by the appellant in *Stuart v. Laird*. Travels to Raleigh in December to attend U.S. Circuit Court for North Carolina, where he sits with U.S. District Court judge Henry Potter. (Circuit Court for North Carolina meets on or about June 15 and December 29, and sits for less than a week each term.)

1803   Attends Supreme Court session in Washington, February 8–March 2. Son Charles William Marshall born in Richmond February 11. Supreme Court delivers decision in

Marbury v. Madison on February 24, holding an act of Congress unconstitutional for the first time. Speaking for unanimous court, Marshall rules that Marbury is entitled to both his commission and writ of mandamus commanding its delivery, but that the Supreme Court cannot issue the writ because section 13 of the 1789 Judiciary Act unconstitutionally expanded its original jurisdiction. Marshall's criticism of the administration for not delivering commissions angers some Republicans, who denounce judicial interference with executive matters. With Marshall not participating, the Court upholds his Circuit Court decision in *Stuart v. Laird*. Marshall works on *The Life of George Washington* between Circuit Court terms. Infant son Charles dies in October.

1804   Justice Alfred Moore resigns in January. Marshall attends Supreme Court in Washington, February 6–March 6. Federalist district judge John Pickering is impeached by House of Representatives and convicted by the Senate for abusive court room behavior. Articles of impeachment against Justice Samuel Chase are introduced in the House in March, accusing him of prejudicial and partisan conduct while serving as circuit court judge. William Johnson is appointed to succeed Moore. Volume I of *The Life of George Washington* published on June 11, volume II on September 3, and volume III on November 26; eventually 7,000 copies of the work are sold by subscription. House of Representatives approves impeachment articles against Chase in December.

1805   Son Edward Carrington Marshall born January 13. Marshall attends Supreme Court term, February 5–March 6. Testifies before the Senate on February 16 regarding Chase's conduct of the trial of James Callender in 1800 for violating the Sedition Act. In *United States v. Fisher* Marshall briefly expounds on the doctrine of implied powers in upholding the constitutionality of a 1797 act concerning receivers of public money. Senate acquits Chase of all charges on March 1. Spends summer in the Virginia mountains between spring and fall circuit court sessions (will continue to do so when possible for remainder of his career). Volume IV of *The Life* published August 12.

1806   Attends Supreme Court session in Washington, February 3–March 4. Prevented by illness from attending June session of the Circuit Court in Raleigh. Spends summer with family in the Allegheny mountains at White Sulphur Springs and Sweet Springs. Harvard College awards Marshall honorary L.L.D. on August 21. Justice William Paterson dies September 9. Marshall and other Fairfax land purchasers obtain deed to Leeds Manor in October after making their final payment. On November 27 President Jefferson proclaims existence of a conspiracy to foment war with Spain and detach western states from Union.

1807   Jefferson sends message to Congress on January 22 accusing former Vice-President Aaron Burr of treason in connection with the western conspiracy. Marshall attends Supreme Court session in Washington, February 2–28. Brockholst Livingston joins Court as successor to Paterson. Supreme Court hears habeas corpus motions by Burr's associates Erick Bollman and Samuel Swartwout. Marshall grants motions and discharges them for lack of probable cause for commitment on charges of treason; his opinion is the first Supreme Court commentary on the law of treason under the Constitution. Congress passes law increasing number of Supreme Court justices to seven, and Thomas Todd is confirmed as new associate justice. Burr is arrested in Mississippi Territory and transported to Richmond for hearing on treason and misdemeanor charges. (Case is heard in Richmond because a crucial assemblage of the conspirators took place on island in the Ohio River within the boundaries of Virginia.) As examining magistrate, Marshall hears arguments on charges against Burr, March 30–31. Marshall delivers opinion on April 1, rejecting Burr's commitment for treason but holding him to bail on misdemeanor charge for staging a military expedition against Spanish territory. Volume V of *The Life* published in April and arouses controversy for its treatment of the political disputes between Federalists and Republicans during the Washington administration. Circuit Court for Virginia meets, May 22–June 30. Marshall rules on June 13 in favor of Burr's motion for subpoena duces tecum requesting documents in the President's possession (Jefferson complies with the subpoena without conceding that as President he is bound to obey it). Grand jury indicts Burr on June 24 for treason and for instigating war with Spain. Marshall presides at treason trial that begins on August 3. Delivers opinion on August 31 narrowly defining the crime of treason and excluding most of the evidence against Burr. Jury finds Burr not guilty of treason on September 1. Marshall presides over trial on misdemeanor charge, September 9–15, ending in Burr's acquittal. After hearing motion to send Burr for trial in another federal court for acts committed in a different jurisdiction, Marshall refuses to commit Burr for treason, but orders him to stand trial for misdemeanor in Ohio (case is never prosecuted). Republican press denounces Marshall for twisting the law to free Burr, and a Baltimore mob hangs the Chief Justice in effigy. Stress of the Burr trial exacerbates Polly's mental condition, and she becomes increasingly reclusive and sensitive to noise. Marshall begins attending Circuit Court in Raleigh under new schedule, with terms beginning on or about May 12 and November 12.

1808   Attends Supreme Court in Washington, February 1–March 16.

1809   Supreme Court meets in Washington, February 6–March 15. In *United States v. Peters* the Court orders Pennsylvania to enforce federal district court ruling upholding Revolutionary War decree of a prize court established by the Continental Congress. Marshall's opinion in *Bank of the United States v. Deveaux* holds that the capacity of a corporation to sue in federal court under diversity of citizenship depends on the citizenship of its shareholders. President James Madison declares his intention to enforce the Supreme Court's order in *United States v. Peters,* effectively ending resistance to the ruling by the Pennsylvania state government. Marshall is elected to the Massachusetts Historical Society, August 29. Mother Mary Marshall dies in Kentucky on September 19. Son Thomas marries Margaret Lewis October 19 and receives Oak Hill as a wedding gift from Marshall.

1810   Travels to Washington for Supreme Court term, February 5–March 17. In *Fletcher v. Peck* Marshall strikes down Georgia law rescinding controversial Yazoo land purchases as violation of the obligation of contracts clause of Constitution. Virginia Court of Appeals rules in April against Marshall and other Fairfax land purchasers in *Hunter v. Fairfax's Devisee*. Marshall arranges for an appeal to the Supreme Court. Justice William Cushing dies September 13, and Cyrus Griffin, U.S. District Court judge for Virginia, dies December 14.

1811   Supreme Court meets February 4, but with only Marshall, Livingston, and Bushrod Washington present, it adjourns for lack of quorum. John Tyler (father of future president John Tyler) succeeds Griffin and joins Marshall on the U.S. Circuit Court for Virginia. Justice Samuel Chase dies June 19. Senate confirms appointments of Joseph Story and Gabriel Duvall to Supreme Court in place of William Cushing and Samuel Chase.

1812   Marshall breaks collarbone in stagecoach accident on way to Washington. Takes seat on February 13 and sits for remainder of session to March 14. Congress declares war on Great Britain on June 18. Marshall serves as chairman of Virginia state commission surveying water and land routes to the west. Leads expedition that departs from Lynchburg, September 2, and reaches Great Falls of Kanawha River on October 9. Returns in time to attend fall terms of Circuit Courts in Raleigh and Richmond. Prepares report of expedition that becomes important document in Virginia's internal improvements program.

1813   John Tyler dies January 6. Marshall attends Supreme Court in Washington, February 1–March 17. Does not sit in *Fairfax's Devisee v. Hunter's Lessee*; Story delivers opinion upholding Fairfax title. Marshall is joined on the Circuit Court for Virginia by Tyler's successor, St. George Tucker. Serves on Richmond Committee of Vigilance, formed in late June after a British naval incursion up the James River, and prepares report arguing that attempts to fortify the city are impractical. Daughter Mary marries her cousin and neighbor Jaquelin Harvie on September 18. Marshall does not attend fall Circuit Court in Raleigh. Elected member of American Antiquarian Society.

1814   Attends Supreme Court session in Washington, February 7–March 12. Holds in *Brown v. United States* that confiscation of enemy property requires Congressional authorization. Marshall dissents in prize case *The Venus*, advocating a less rigid application of principle that the national character of a merchant is determined by his domicile. British raid Washington, August 24–25, burning the Capitol and other government buildings. Marshall does not attend fall session of Circuit Court in Raleigh.

1815   Awarded honorary L.L.D. from University of Pennsylvania, January 7. Attends Supreme Court session in Washington, February 6–March 11; because of the destruction of its chamber in the Capitol, the Court meets in the home of its clerk, Elias B. Caldwell. Senate ratifies Treaty of Ghent on February 16, ending war with Britain. Marshall delivers opinion in *The Nereide*, holding that neutral goods are protected from condemnation by prize courts even if they are taken from armed belligerent ships resisting capture. In April Marshall learns that his son John has been dismissed from Harvard for "immoral & dissolute conduct." Directs son James, who has also had disciplinary problems at Harvard, to leave Cambridge and enter Philadelphia counting house of Willing & Francis as apprentice. Marshall and Bushrod Washington plan edition of George Washington's correspondence. Misses fall term of Circuit Court in Raleigh because of wife's illness. In December the Virginia Court of Appeals refuses to comply with the Supreme Court's decision in *Fairfax's Devisee v. Hunter's Lessee*. Marshall drafts petition for writ of error and sends record of case, now styled *Martin v. Hunter's Lessee*, in time for hearing at next Supreme Court term.

1816   Attends Supreme Court in Washington, February 5–March 22. Does not participate in *Martin v. Hunter's Lessee*, in which Story delivers opinion affirming Supreme Court's appellate jurisdiction over state courts in cases arising under the Constitution, federal law, and treaties. Marshall plans revised edition of *The Life of Washington*.

1817   Attends Supreme Court in Washington, February 3–March 15. Court returns to Capitol, meeting in temporary chambers in the basement room.

1818   In Washington for Supreme Court session, February 2–March 14. Prepares autobiographical sketch for *Delaplaine's Repository*.

1819   Son Jaquelin marries Eliza Clarkson on January 1. Attends Supreme Court in Washington, February 1–March 12. Court resumes meeting in its now-restored chamber beneath the Senate. Marshall delivers opinions in *Dartmouth College v. Woodward*, affirming that the Constitution protects corporate charters from state legislative impairment; in *Sturges v. Crowninshield*, striking down New York bankruptcy law as unconstitutional under the contract clause; and in *McCulloch v. Maryland*, upholding doctrine of implied powers and voiding Maryland state tax on the Second Bank of the United States. Attacks on bank decision in Richmond newspapers prompt Marshall to respond anonymously. With Bushrod Washington's assistance, publishes two "Friend to the Union" essays in Philadelphia *Union*. Misses spring session of North Carolina

Circuit Court because of family illness. Spencer Roane, the leading judge of the Virginia Court of Appeals, publishes "Hampden" essays in Richmond *Enquirer* denouncing *McCulloch* for destroying the rights of states. In June and July, Marshall replies to "Hampden" with ten "Friend of the Constitution" essays in Alexandria *Gazette*.

1820   Presides at Supreme Court in Washington, February 7–March 17. Attends son John's wedding to Elizabeth Alexander in Baltimore on February 8. Continues revising *The Life of George Washington* for second edition and preparing edition of Washington's correspondence. Injured in fall from horse in late October, but is still able to attend fall Circuit Court sessions at Raleigh and Richmond.

1821   Travels to Washington for Supreme Court session, February 7–March 16. Marshall delivers opinion in *Cohens v. Virginia* broadly affirming federal judicial power over state court decisions in cases involving federal questions. Story delivers opinion in *Green v. Biddle* striking down Kentucky's occupying claimant land laws. The two opinions provoke outrage from states' rights proponents, and the Richmond newspapers publish numerous denunciations of *Cohens,* including "Algernon Sidney" essays by Spencer Roane. Son James marries Claudia Burwell on December 22.

1822   Attends Supreme Court session in Washington, February 4–March 22.

1823   In Washington for Supreme Court term, February 3–March 14. Delivers opinion in *Johnson v. McIntosh* expounding legal nature of Indian land title. Justice Brockholst Livingston dies March 18. Marshall's youngest son, Edward Carrington, enters Harvard College. Holds special session of U.S. Circuit Court in Norfolk, Virginia, for trial of accused pirate (defendant is convicted and sentenced to death, but is pardoned by President James Monroe). Asks Speaker of the House Henry Clay to help block proposed legislation restricting appellate jurisdiction of the Supreme Court (legislation is not passed). Elected president of the Richmond branch of the American Colonization Society, founded in 1816 to settle free blacks in Africa. (Marshall has owned a small number of household slaves since the 1780s.) Smith Thompson appointed to Supreme Court in place of Livingston.

1824   Attends Supreme Court session in Washington, February 2–

March 24. Dislocates shoulder in fall on the ice, February 19. Returns to court on March 2 to deliver opinion in *Gibbons v. Ogden,* giving expansive reading to commerce clause while striking down New York law granting steamboat monopoly. Reaffirms broad view of federal court jurisdiction and principle of national supremacy in *Osborn v. Bank of the United States,* upholding the Bank's exemption from state taxation. Revised version of the first volume of *The Life of George Washington* is published in July as *A History of the Colonies.* Marshall gives speech on October 27 in honor of Lafayette's visit to Richmond.

1825   Attends Supreme Court term in Washington, February 7–March 21. Delivers opinion in *The Antelope,* case involving slave ship captured in international waters by an American revenue cutter. The Court's ruling results in 39 of the surviving slaves being sold to an owner in Georgia, while the remaining 130 slaves are freed and sent to Liberia. Elias B. Caldwell, clerk of the Supreme Court since 1800, dies in June. St. George Tucker resigns his judgeship and is replaced on the Virginia Circuit Court by George Hay, who had prosecuted Burr in 1807. Marshall gives speech on August 23 during Lafayette's visit to Fauquier County.

1826   Presides at Supreme Court in Washington, February 6–March 21. Justice Thomas Todd dies February 7; Robert Trimble is appointed to the Court as his successor. Marshall and Bushrod Washington abandon their plan to publish George Washington's correspondence in favor of more extensive edition proposed to them by Jared Sparks, editor of the *North American Review.*

1827   Attends Supreme Court session, January 8–March 16 (term now begins on the second Monday in January). William T. Carroll is appointed as new Supreme Court clerk. Marshall delivers his only dissent in a constitutional case when the Court upholds prospective state bankruptcy laws in *Ogden v. Saunders.* Delivers opinion in *Brown v. Maryland,* broadly construing the constitutional prohibition of state import duties to void state law imposing licensing tax on importers. Presides at special session of U.S. Circuit Court for Virginia, July 16–18, that tries three Spanish subjects accused of piracy; the defendants are convicted and hanged. Writes long autobiographical letter to Justice Story, recounting his life and career to 1801.

1828   Attends Supreme Court session in Washington, January 14–

March 17. Drafts memorial and resolutions adopted by internal improvements held at Charlottesville in July. Justice Robert Trimble dies on August 25.

1829   Presides at Supreme Court session, January 13–March 20. Son Edward marries Rebecca Peyton on February 12. Marshall delivers opinion in *Foster and Elam v. Neilson* affirming judicial deference to Congressional understanding of national rights acquired under treaties. In *Weston v. City Council of Charleston*, a 4-2 decision, Marshall voids local tax on federal debt certificates as an unconstitutional interference with the borrowing power of Congress. Delivers opinion for unanimous Court in *Willson v. Black Bird Creek Marsh Company*, upholding Delaware law authorizing the damming of a tidal creek as valid exercise of state police power consistent with the federal power to regulate interstate commerce. John McLean is appointed to Supreme Court in March in place of Trimble. In May Marshall is elected as a delegate to Virginia state constitutional convention. Attends convention in Richmond, beginning October 5. Supports compromise measures on suffrage and legislative apportionment, and consistently defends principle of an independent judiciary. Does not attend fall session of Circuit Court in Raleigh. Justice Bushrod Washington dies November 26.

1830   Delays trip to Washington to complete business of Virginia convention. Elected to American Philosophical Society. Attends Supreme Court, January 18–March 22. Henry Baldwin takes seat vacated by death of Bushrod Washington. Marshall speaks for 4-3 majority in *Craig v. Missouri* in striking down state loan office certificates as bills of credit prohibited by Constitution. Delivers opinion for unanimous Court in *Providence Bank v. Billings*, upholding state tax on corporations not explicitly exempted from taxation by their charters. Publication of Jefferson's correspondence provokes Marshall's "astonishment and deep felt disgust" over his accusations against the Federalist party. George Hay dies on September 21 and is replaced on the Virginia Circuit Court by Philip Barbour.

1831   Presides at Supreme Court in Washington, January 10–March 18. Marshall speaks for divided Court in *Cherokee Nation v. Georgia,* ruling that as a "domestic dependent" nation, the Cherokee lack standing to sue as a foreign state. During summer Marshall suffers from increasing pain caused by bladder stones. Attends Anti-Masonic party convention in Baltimore as spectator while traveling to Philadelphia for medical treatment. Undergoes lithotomy performed by surgeon Philip Syng Physick on October 13. Departs Philadelphia by steamboat on November 19 and returns to Richmond in time to hold Circuit Court. Wife, Polly, dies on December 25.

1832   Attends Supreme Court session in Washington, January 10–March 17. Delivers opinion in *Worcester v. Georgia* overturning several Georgia laws for violating federal treaties with the Cherokee and ordering the release of missionaries imprisoned for violating one of the voided statutes. Philadelphia firm of Carey & Lea publishes revised edition of *The Life of George Washington* in two volumes. Marshall heads Richmond commission to raise stock subscriptions for James River and Kanawha Canal Company, and publishes address urging fellow citizens to invest in the company. Provides in his will for the emancipation of his longtime personal servant Robin Spurlock; the remainder of his slaves are to be distributed among his heirs.

1833   Governor of Georgia pardons missionaries on January 14, averting possible confrontation between the Supreme Court and the Jackson administration over enforcement of *Worcester v. Georgia*. Marshall attends Supreme Court session, January 14–March 15. Delivers opinion in *Barron v. Baltimore* holding that the Bill of Rights restrains only Congress and does not limit action by state governments. Completes abridged edition of *The Life of George Washington* for use in schools (published posthumously in 1838). Son John dies on November 25.

1834   Attends Supreme Court term in Washington, January 13–March 19. Justice William Johnson dies on August 4.

1835   Attends Supreme Court, January 12–March 17. James M. Wayne joins Court in place of Johnson. Justice Gabriel Duvall resigns January 14. Marshall is severely injured in stagecoach accident while returning to Richmond. Makes preparations to move to Fauquier County. Suffers pain and loss of appetite as health gradually declines in spring. Unable to attend spring term of Circuit Court in Raleigh but holds court in Richmond. Accompanied by his son Edward, Marshall arrives in Philadelphia on June 11 for medical treatment. Spared news of his son Thomas, who dies on June 29 after being fatally injured by falling chimney in Baltimore while on his way to Philadelphia. Marshall dies in Philadelphia on July 6 of complications from enlarged and abscessed liver. Buried beside his wife, Polly, in Shockoe Hill Cemetery in Richmond on July 9.

Note on the Texts

This volume prints the texts of 196 letters, speeches, essays, resolutions, reports, legal arguments, and judicial opinions written or delivered by John Marshall between 1779 and 1835, as well as the preface to the first edition of his biography *The Life of George Washington* (1804–7); the preface to *A History of the Colonies* (1824); the preface to, and two chapters from, the second edition of *The Life of George Washington* (1832); and the text of a memorandum written in 1826 by the editor Jared Sparks recording a conversation with Marshall. With the exception of the two chapters from the second edition of *The Life of George Washington*, the texts printed here—including the prefaces to the first and second editions of *The Life of George Washington*, the preface to *A History of the Colonies*, and the memorandum written by Sparks—are taken from *The Papers of John Marshall* (12 volumes; Chapel Hill: The University of North Carolina Press, 1974–2006), volume 1 edited by Herbert A. Johnson, volume 2 edited by Charles T. Cullen and Herbert A. Johnson, volume 3 edited by William C. Stinchcombe and Charles T. Cullen, volume 4 edited by Charles T. Cullen, volumes 5–12 edited by Charles F. Hobson. The texts of chapters VIII and IX of volume I of *The Life of George Washington*, which contain descriptions of the battles of Brandywine and Germantown based in part on Marshall's personal experiences, are taken from the second edition (2 volumes; Philadelphia: Carey & Lea, 1832), pp. 152–86.

Although the majority of these documents existed only in manuscript at the time of Marshall's death, many of them were printed during his lifetime. Marshall published newspaper essays both under his own name and under a variety of pseudonyms; speeches he made in the Virginia ratifying convention and the Virginia state constitutional convention were recorded in shorthand and then published in book form or in newspapers; and some of the diplomatic dispatches he wrote while serving as an envoy in France and later as secretary of state were printed in official collections of American state papers. The opinions Marshall delivered as Chief Justice were published in *Reports of Cases*, a series of volumes edited by the Supreme Court reporters William Cranch (1801–15), Henry Wheaton (1816–27), and Richard Peters (1828–42). His opinions in cases that aroused public interest were sometimes printed in their entirety in newspapers, as were many of the rulings Marshall made as a circuit court judge while presiding over the Aaron Burr case.

In 1800 Marshall agreed to write a biography of George Washington at the request of Washington's nephew and literary executor, Supreme Court Justice Bushrod Washington, and he began work on the project the following year. The first edition of *The Life of George Washington* was published by Caleb P. Wayne of Philadelphia in five volumes between 1804 and 1807, with volume I devoted to the history of the colonies before the Revolution, volumes II–IV to the Revolutionary War, and volume V to Washington's life after the Revolution. Marshall subsequently revised and corrected the work, and published a revised version of the first volume as *A History of the Colonies* in 1824; his revision of the remaining four volumes appeared in the form of a two-volume second edition of *The Life of George Washington* in 1832.

William E. Dodd of Randolph-Macon College and Waldo G. Leland, an archivist with the Carnegie Institution, began work in 1906 on an edition of Marshall's writings and correspondence. Although their project did not result in publication, some of the material they collected was later used by Albert J. Beveridge in writing his biography *The Life of John Marshall* (4 volumes, 1916–19). The bicentennial of Marshall's birth in 1955 renewed interest in the possibility of collecting and publishing his papers, and in 1960 the College of William and Mary and the Institute (now the Omohundro Institute) of Early American History and Culture began their joint sponsorship of *The Papers of John Marshall*. Although Marshall did not carefully attend to the organization and preservation of his papers—unlike many of his contemporaries, he did not keep drafts or letter-book copies of his outgoing correspondence—the editors of *The Papers of John Marshall* were able to locate and obtain copies of thousands of personal and legal documents written by Marshall. Documents presented in *The Papers of John Marshall* are transcribed and printed without alteration in their paragraphing, and with minimal alterations in their spelling, capitalization, and punctuation, mostly in the substitution of periods for dashes used to end sentences, and, in volumes 1–4, in the substitution of "etc." for "&c" and "&ca."

This volume prints texts as they appeared in *The Papers of John Marshall* and in the 1832 edition of *The Life of George Washington*, but with a few alterations in editorial procedure. The bracketed conjectural readings of the editors of *The Papers of John Marshall*, in cases where original manuscripts or printed texts were damaged or difficult to read, are accepted without brackets in this volume when those readings seem to be the only possible ones; but when they do not, or when the editors made no conjecture, the missing word or words are indicated by a bracketed two-em space, i.e., [   ]. In cases where *The Papers of John Marshall* supplied in brackets punctuation, letters, or words that were omitted from the source text by an obvious slip of the pen or printer's error, this volume removes the brackets and accepts the editorial emendation. Bracketed editorial insertions used in *The Papers of John Marshall* to supply place names and dates at the beginning of documents have been deleted in this volume. In some cases where Marshall made changes in a document, the canceled text, if decipherable, was presented in *The Papers of John Marshall* within single angle brackets; this volume omits the canceled material.

In presenting the text printed in *American Historical Review* (January 1907) of Marshall's letter to James Wilkinson of January 5, 1787, *The Papers of John Marshall* reproduced a typographical error in their source; the error is corrected in this volume at 17.21, so that "these" becomes "those." An error of transcription in *The Papers of John Marshall* is corrected at 140.17, so that "affected" becomes "effected." In addition, three of Marshall's errors in letters are treated as slips of the pen and corrected in this volume, even though they were not corrected in *The Papers of John Marshall*: at 190.24, "act," becomes "act)"; at 340.28–29, "canditates" becomes "candidates"; at 568.1, "malicnity" becomes "malignity." In the texts of the Virginia river commission report, "A Friend of the Constitution No. III," and the opinion of the court in *Johnson v. McIntosh* presented in *The Papers of John Marshall*, three errors in the printed source texts are corrected in footnotes; in this volume, these corrections have been accepted and incorporated into the text printed here: at 364.24, "28th November" becomes "28th September," at 477.36, "parts" becomes "pacts," and at 581.26, "1703" becomes "1713."

This volume presents the texts of the editions chosen as sources here but does not attempt to reproduce features of their typographic design. Some headings have been changed, and John Marshall's name at the end of letters has been omitted. The texts are printed without alteration except for the changes previously discussed and for the correction of typographical errors. Spelling, punctuation, and capitalization are often expressive features, and they are not altered, even when inconsistent or irregular. The following is a list of typographical errors corrected, cited by page and line number: 53.36, executed,; 53.37, interests."; 103.28, persued; 110.34, preceeded; 119.29, Horttingguer; 124.25, M Talleyrand; 125.29, rereturned; 130.22 Declerations; 130.23, motive; 130.35, stepted; 161.29, says but; 161.32, land."; 164.35, it is; 178.14, case,; 183.12, No. 4; 187.4, abondon; 188.2, there; 304.25, military a; 370.6, to; 438.23, not; 446.38, without,; 660.29, by made; 671.37, that; 686.3, work; 703.5, but; 722.4, every; 732.30, regulations in; 735.35, decision.; 747.23, your; 749.30, addtional; 757.24, virdict; 765.4, alsowill; 839.13, you; 851.30, my.

Notes

In the notes below, the reference numbers denote page and line of this volume (the line count includes headings). No note is made for material included in the eleventh edition of *Merriam-Webster's Collegiate Dictionary*. Footnotes in the text are Marshall's own. For further biographical background, references to other studies, and more detailed notes, see Albert J. Beveridge, *The Life of John Marshall* (4 vols., Boston and New York: Houghton Mifflin Company, 1916–19); Jean Edward Smith, *John Marshall: Definer of a Nation* (New York: Henry Holt and Company, 1996); *The Papers of John Marshall*, edited by Charles F. Hobson et al. (12 vols., Chapel Hill: The University of North Carolina Press, 1974–2006).

SOLDIER, STATE LEGISLATOR, LAWYER, AND FEDERALIST, 1779–1797

3.2   *Thomas Posey*]   Posey (1750–1818), a Continental Army officer from Virginia, commanded a light infantry battalion during the American capture of Stony Point on July 16, 1779, and was the sixth or seventh man to enter the British fort. He later served as lieutenant governor of Kentucky, 1805–7, as a U.S. senator from Louisiana, 1812–13, and as territorial governor of Indiana, 1813–16.

3.4   Genl. Wayne's]   General Anthony Wayne (1745–1796), who had commanded the attack on Stony Point.

4.8   *milk & sopaun*]   Probably an abbreviated form of "sop in the pan," a piece of bread soaked in the drippings from roasting meat.

4.11   *William Pierce*]   Pierce (1740–1789), an officer in the Continental Army, attended the College of William and Mary with Marshall in 1780. After the war, Pierce established himself in business in Savannah, Georgia, and served as a delegate to Congress in 1786–87 and as a delegate to the Federal Convention in 1787.

5.2   The financier]   Probably a reference to Robert Morris (1734–1806), who served as superintendent of finance under the Articles of Confederation, 1781–84, and was commonly referred to as "the financier."

5.16   evacuation of Charles Town]   The British army evacuated Charleston, South Carolina, on December 14, 1782.

5.21   rice birds & polloos]   Bobolinks and parakeets.

5.30   saint James's]   The royal court in London.

5.33   Mrs. Marshall]   The marriage of John Marshall and Mary ("Polly") Willis Ambler (1766–1831) had taken place on January 3, 1783.

5.36   this letter. [   ]]   The remainder of the postscript is obscured by binding.

6.2   *Charles Simms*]   Simms (1755–1819) was a Continental Army officer who later practiced law in Alexandria and served in the Virginia legislature.

6.4   Major Powel]   Leven Powell (1737–1810), a Continental Army officer who later served in the Virginia legislature and as a Federalist congressman, 1799–1801.

6.7   receive commutables]   A Virginia act of 1782 declared tobacco and other commodities to be "commutable" articles, receivable in payment of taxes.

7.10   Unkle Keith]   James Keith (1734–1824), oldest brother of Marshall's mother.

7.13   *James Monroe*]   Monroe (1758–1831), the future president, had recently sat with Marshall on the Virginia executive council and was now serving as a delegate to Congress.

7.15–17   Genl. Clark & Mr. Banks . . . Majr. Crittenden]   George Rogers Clark (1752–1818), who had captured the British outposts at Kaskaskia and Vincennes during the Revolutionary War, had resigned his military command and was about take up his new post as surveyor of western lands reserved for Virginia military veterans; John Banks and Henry Banks were Richmond merchants; John Crittenden (1756–1806), a Continental Army officer, later moved to Kentucky.

7.22–24   Colo. R. H. Lee . . . Colo. Harry Lee]   Richard Henry Lee (1732–1794) served in Congress in 1774–79, 1784–85, and 1787. He opposed ratification of the Constitution at the 1788 Virginia convention and served as a U.S. senator, 1789–92. Henry ("Light Horse Harry") Lee (1756–1818) commanded a force of cavalry and infantry known as "Lee's Legion" during the Revolutionary War. He served as a delegate to Congress, 1786–88, and supported ratification at the Virginia convention. Henry Lee later served as governor of Virginia, 1791–94, and as a Federalist in Congress, 1799–1801.

7.32   Taylor, Colo. Nicholas]   John Taylor of Caroline (1753–1824), a member of the House of Delegates who later served in the U.S. Senate, 1792–94, 1803, and 1822–24. In 1820 he published *Construction Construed, and Constitutions Vindicated*, criticizing the Marshall Court for its nationalist rulings. George Nicholas (1754–1799) served in the House of Delegates, 1778–79, 1781–84, and 1786–88. A supporter of ratification at the 1788 Virginia convention, Nicholas later moved to Kentucky, where he helped draft the first state constitution.

8.1   Mr. Jones]   Joseph Jones (1727–1805), Monroe's uncle, was a member of the House of Delegates who later served as a judge of the General Court, 1789–1805.

8.4–5   Mr. Henry . . . The Speaker]   Patrick Henry (1736–1799) served as governor of Virginia, 1776–79 and 1784–86, and in the House of Delegates, 1780–84 and 1787–90. John Tyler Sr. (1747–1813), father of President John Tyler, was speaker of the Virginia House of Delegates, 1781–85. Tyler later served as governor of Virginia, 1808–11, and as federal district judge for Virginia, 1811–13.

8.12   Statute Staple men]   Presumably, foreign merchants who, under a statute staple (a law regulating towns engaged in the trade of commodities), would be restricted to conducting trade in certain port towns.

8.16   with respect to the 'cession]   Virginia offered in 1781 to cede to Congress its territory northwest of the Ohio River; the terms of the cession were agreed to in 1784.

8.18   My Father]   Thomas Marshall (1730–1802).

8.25–26   career of the greatest Man . . . closed]   General Washington resigned his commission on December 23, 1783.

9.29   Colo. Mercer]   John Francis Mercer (1759–1821) was a Virginia delegate to Congress, 1782–85.

9.35   exertions of the Treasurer]   Jaquelin Ambler (1742–1798) was treasurer of Virginia and Marshall's father-in-law.

10.9   warmly by Ege]   Probably Samuel Ege (1742–1801), an inspector of flour in Richmond.

10.19–20   Little Stewart . . . Kitty Hair]   John Stewart, a Richmond merchant, and Catherine Hare.

10.27   Carrington . . . his forces]   Edward Carrington (1749–1810), soon to be elected to the House of Delegates, subsequently married an older sister of Polly Marshall.

10.36–38   Lomax . . . Short]   Thomas Lomax, Meriwether Smith, William Nelson Jr., Beverley Randolph, and William Short were Marshall's current or recent colleagues on the Virginia executive council.

11.11–13   Wilson Nicholas . . . Bullitt]   Wilson Cary Nicholas (1761–1820), brother of George Nicholas, was a U.S. senator, 1799–1804, and governor of Virginia, 1814–17; William Grayson (1736–1790) was a U.S. senator, 1789–90; Alexander S. Bullitt served two terms in the House of Delegates before moving to Kentucky.

11.14–16   Wallace . . . Lee]   William Brent, Jr., defeated Gustavus B. Wallace for the Stafford seat; Mann Page, Jr., served frequently in the House of Delegates during the 1770s and 1780s; Richard Bland Lee (1761–1827), after three terms in the House of Delegates, went on to serve in the U.S. House of Representatives, 1789–1795.

11.17–18   Wilkinson . . . Mayo] Nathaniel Wilkinson defeated John Mayo, Jr., in the Henrico County election.

11.32   Mr. Henderson] Alexander Henderson represented Fairfax County in the House of Delegates.

13.5–6   safe return . . . our world] Monroe had returned from a tour of the Northwest.

13.8   resolutions . . . British debts] In June 1784 the Virginia legislature resolved to inhibit the recovery of debts owed to British creditors until the British made reparations for slaves they had removed from the state during the war.

13.10–11   the British . . . forts on the lakes] Under the terms of the peace treaty signed in 1783, the British were required to evacuate their garrisons from frontier outposts in the Northwest, while American debtors were required to pay their British creditors.

13.18–19   your Unkle] Joseph Jones.

13.23   privilege given to Rumsey] The legislature granted James Rumsey (1743–1792) a ten-year monopoly to develop his design for a mechanical riverboat. Rumsey subsequently designed a steam-powered boat that had a successful trial on the Potomac River in 1787.

13.31–36   General Assessment . . . less real importance & power] Consideration of Henry's bill for a "general assessment," levying a tax for the support of Christian ministers of all denominations, was postponed until the next session, when it was defeated. At the time Marshall wrote this letter, Henry had just left the legislature to begin serving a new term as governor.

14.5–6   Mr. Roane] Spencer Roane (1762–1822), who later served as a judge of the General Court, 1789–94, and of the Virginia Court of Appeals, 1794–1822.

14.19–20   Mr. Humphry Marshall a Cousin & Brother] Humphrey Marshall (c. 1756–1841) moved to Kentucky after the war and married Marshall's sister Mary (Anna Maria). He served in the Kentucky House of Representatives, 1793–94, and as a Federalist in the U.S. Senate, 1795–1801, and later became a newspaper publisher and historian of Kentucky.

15.2   *George Muter*] Muter (d. 1811) served in the Virginia state artillery regiment during the Revolution and was also commissioner of the state war office. He became a judge of the Kentucky district in 1785 and was chief justice of the Kentucky Court of Appeals, 1792–1806.

15.14–15   Mr. Innes]   Harry Innes (1752–1826) was chief justice for the Kentucky district, 1782–84, and attorney general for the district, 1784–89. He later served as a federal district judge in Kentucky, 1789–1816.

15.18   Cyrus Griffin]   Griffin (1748–1810) declined the appointment and Muter was named to the position instead. Griffin later served as U.S. District Judge for Virginia from 1789 until his death.

16.2   *James Wilkinson*]   Wilkinson (1757–1825), a leader in the Kentucky statehood movement, was attempting to persuade the Spanish authorities at New Orleans to open the Mississippi River to American trade. In 1805 Wilkinson became governor of the Louisiana Territory and involved himself in Aaron Burr's western schemes before accusing Burr of treason in a message to President Jefferson.

16.5   the passport]   Wilkinson was apparently seeking a passport for travel down the Mississippi to New Orleans.

16.6   the Governor]   Edmund Randolph (1753–1813) was governor of Virginia, 1786–88. He later served as U.S. Attorney General, 1790–94, and as secretary of state, 1794–95.

16.13   the Governor]   Presumably Rodriguez Esteban Miró (1744–1795), the Spanish governor of New Orleans, 1785–91.

16.18   two expeditions against the Indians]   In response to a series of Indian raids across the Ohio, the Virginia government sent two militia expeditions into the Northwest Territory from Kentucky in September 1786. One, led by George Rogers Clark, was unable to advance beyond Vincennes because of internal dissension, but succeeded in persuading the Wabash Indians to agree to a truce; the other, led by Benjamin Logan, burned seven Shawnee towns along the Miami River before returning to Kentucky.

16.28–29   Massachusetts . . . equal factions]   Protests by farmers in western Massachusetts against farm foreclosures and tax collections led in September 1786 to the outbreak of "Shays' Rebellion," named after one of its leaders, the Revolutionary War veteran Daniel Shays (1747?–1825). The uprising was suppressed by Massachusetts militia in February 1787.

17.5–6   Bowdoin and Hancock]   James Bowdoin (1726–1790), governor of Massachusetts, 1785–87, and John Hancock (1736–1793), his predecessor, 1780–85, and successor, 1787–93, as governor.

18.3–4   navigation of the Mississippi . . . the treaty]   In 1784 Spain closed the lower Mississippi to American navigation until the United States and Spain reached an agreement on the boundaries of Louisiana and the Floridas. John Jay, the secretary for foreign affairs under the Confederation, began negotiations with Spanish envoy Diego de Gardoqui in 1785 and was instructed by Congress to secure American navigation of the river. In August 1786 Jay recommended that the United States forgo its navigation claim for

25 or 30 years in return for securing a commercial treaty with Spain. After weeks of heated debate, Congress voted 7–5 to amend Jay's previous instructions, with all of the Southern states opposed; because the votes of nine states were required to ratify a treaty under the Articles of Confederation, the Jay-Gardoqui agreement was never signed.

18.18   *Arthur Lee*] Lee (1740–1792), brother of Richard Henry Lee and a cousin of Henry Lee (see note 7.22–24), was a political pamphleteer before the Revolution and an American diplomat in Europe, 1776–80. He served in Congress, 1782–84, and on the Board of Treasury, 1785–89.

18.21   Mr. Imlay] Probably Gilbert Imlay (1754–1828), a Kentucky land speculator.

18.31   conduct of General Clarke] Clark had seized the property of Spanish traders at Vincennes in order to supply his troops during his expedition against the Wabash Indians in 1786.

19. 8–9   fortiter . . . suaviter in re] Marshall reversed the Latin motto *fortiter in re, suaviter in modo* ("resolutely in deed, gently in manner").

20.1–3   *Speech . . . Adopting the Constitution*] The Virginia ratifying convention met in Richmond, June 2–27, 1788. The texts of Marshall's speeches are taken from David Robertson, *Debates and Other Proceedings of the Convention of Virginia* (3 vols., 1788–89; second edition, 1805), based on Robertson's shorthand notes.

20.4   Mr. Chairman] George Wythe (1726–1806), chairman of the committee of the whole, and an eminent judge of the Virginia High Court of Chancery.

20.36–37   man . . . struck out of existence] The bandit leader Josiah Phillips was condemned to death for treason by a bill of attainder passed in 1778 by the Virginia Assembly during Henry's first term as governor. (Under Article I, Section 9 of the Constitution, states are prohibited from passing bills of attainder.) Phillips was subsequently captured, tried for robbery, and hanged.

21.3–4   the person was not a Socrates?] In discussing the case of Phillips during the convention debate on June 7, Henry had said: "That man was not executed by a tyrannical stroke of power. Nor was he a Socrates."

21.8   *secundum artem*] According to the art, i.e., in accordance with the law.

23.9–13   Holland, . . . disturbances in that country?] Stadtholder William V of Orange (1748–1806), who was blamed by the Patriots' Movement in the Netherlands for Dutch defeats in the 1780–84 Anglo-Dutch war, left The Hague in 1785 for the less hostile province of Gelderland as the Patriots assumed power in Holland and Utrecht. In 1787 a Prussian army restored William V to power in The Hague, and thousands of Patriots fled to France.

23.27–28   the Gentleman who was last up] James Monroe.

25.11   appoint a Dictator] During the British invasion of 1781 the Virginia Assembly briefly considered appointing a dictator with full military and civil powers.

26.17–18   the Gentleman who opened the debate] Edmund Randolph was the first speaker on June 10.

29.17–18   New-Hampshire and Rhode-Island have rejected it,] The New Hampshire ratifying convention met on February 13, 1788, but then voted, 56–51, to adjourn until June 18 after the supporters of ratification discovered that many delegates had been instructed by their towns to vote against the Constitution. The reassembled convention voted, 57–47, on June 21 to approve the Constitution, ensuring ratification by the requisite nine states. Rhode Island rejected the Constitution in a popular referendum held on March 24, 1788; a convention held in 1790 voted for ratification.

29.35–36   The Gentleman tells us,] Patrick Henry, in his speech on June 9.

34.23   the ten miles square] The federal district provided for in Article I, Section 8.

38.7   (Mr. *Mason*)] One of the drafters of the 1776 Virginia state constitution, George Mason (1725–1792) attended the Federal Convention, but refused to sign the proposed Constitution because he believed it gave the federal government too much power and because it lacked a bill of rights.

44.17–18   the quitrents in the Northern Neck] Thomas, sixth Lord Fairfax (1693–1781), held Virginia's Northern Neck (the land between the Potomac and Rappahannock rivers) in proprietary until his death. In 1782 the Virginia Assembly ordered quitrents due at the time of Fairfax's death to be sequestered until the title to the proprietary was settled, and in 1785 the legislature discharged all Northern Neck landholders from paying further quitrents.

48.23   *Archibald Stuart*] Stuart (1757–1832), a lawyer and state legislator, was a judge of the General Court, 1800–31.

49.1   news . . . about Zach.] Evidently a reference to Zachariah Johnson (1742–1800), a member of the House of Delegates from Augusta County in the Shenandoah Valley.

49.20   *Albert Gallatin*] Gallatin (1761–1849), a Swiss immigrant, was then settled in western Pennsylvania but had spent time in Virginia in recent years (in later life he recalled that Marshall had proposed in 1786 to take him on as a law clerk). In May 1789 Gallatin married Sophia Allegre of Richmond, but she died only a few months later. He later served as a Republican congressman from Pennsylvania, 1795–1801, as secretary of the treasury, 1801–14, and on the commission that negotiated the peace treaty with Britain in 1814.

51.10–11 *Resolutions . . . Proclamation*] The resolutions were printed in the Richmond *Virginia Gazette, and General Advertiser* on August 21, 1793.

51.15 late Proclamation] On learning of France's declaration of war against Great Britain, President Washington consulted with his cabinet on April 19 and issued a proclamation of neutrality on April 22, 1793.

52.7 Marshall reported an address] In 1827 Marshall wrote that he had drafted the "resolutions and the address . . . which accompanied them."

52.20 the intervention of foreign ministers,] Edmond-Charles Genet, the first diplomatic minister sent to the United States by the French Republic, arrived in April 1793 to an enthusiastic public welcome. He soon angered the administration by arming and commissioning privateers in American ports in defiance of the neutrality proclamation and by threatening to make a direct appeal to the American public against the neutrality policy. The administration asked for Genet's recall in August 1793.

53.1–2 *Address . . . Proclamation*] The address to President Washington was printed in the Richmond *Virginia Gazette, and General Advertiser* on September 11, 1793.

54.28 *Aristides*] Aristides (c. 530–c. 468 BCE) was an Athenian soldier and statesman known as "The Just."

54.29 MR. DAVIS] Augustine Davis (1752–1825) was editor of the Richmond *Virginia Gazette, and General Advertiser*, a Federalist newspaper.

55.8 AGRICOLA] The pseudonym used by James Monroe in a series of newspaper essays published in Richmond on September 4, October 9, and November 13, 1793.

56.9 publication of Mr. Jay and Mr. King] Chief Justice of the Supreme Court John Jay (1745–1829) and New York senator Rufus King (1755–1827) published a letter in the New York *Diary* on August 12, 1793, confirming reports that Genet "had said he would appeal to the people from certain decisions of the President."

56.13 Burlington] Burlington, New Jersey.

61.23–24 followed by a writer] In addition to the two "Aristides" essays printed in this volume, Marshall published two "Gracchus" essays in response to "Agricola" that appeared on October 16 and November 13, 1793.

71.9–10 Counsellor Duval] William DuVal (1748–1832) was a Richmond lawyer who practiced in the state superior courts and in the federal courts.

71.22   ne exeat]   A legal writ restraining a person from leaving the jurisdiction of a court. Stuart lived in the Shenandoah Valley town of Staunton.

71.36   We fear . . . a war.]   British seizures of American merchant ships
trading with the French West Indies had caused a crisis in Anglo-American
relations. In response, President Washington appointed Chief Justice Jay as
special envoy to Britain on April 16, 1794.

72.7   Mr. Campbell]   Alexander Campbell (c. 1762–1796) and Marshall
represented the Virginia debtors in the British debts case of *Ware v. Hylton*.
Arguments in the appeal in the U.S. Supreme Court began on February 6,
1796.

72.8–9   My own cause . . . be taken up]   In June 1795 Marshall had
obtained a judgment in the U.S. Circuit Court for Virginia establishing the
validity of the Fairfax title to the Northern Neck. As he anticipated, the
Supreme Court postponed consideration of the appeal in the case, *Hunter v.
Fairfax*, until the next term. Marshall was an interested party because he had
contracted, along with his brother James and other investors, to purchase the
Fairfax estate.

72.15–17   Mrs. Marshall . . . Mrs. Bignal]   Mrs. Marshall and her husband were popular English actors and singers who for several years had been
touring in America. Anne West Bignall (d. 1805) was an actress with the Virginia Company of Richmond.

72.19   my brother & his wife]   James M. Marshall (1764–1848) and his
wife, Hester Morris Marshall (1774–1817), daughter of Robert Morris, had
sailed for England late in 1795.

72.21   sweet little Poll]   Mary Marshall (1795–1841), Marshall's only
daughter to survive infancy. She later married Jaquelin Harvie (1788–1856).

72.22–23   Tom . . . Jaquelines great improvement]   Thomas Marshall
(1784–1835) and Jaquelin Ambler Marshall (1787–1852), Marshall's oldest sons.

72.25–26   *Argument* . . . Ware v. Hylton]   Marshall's only argument
before the Supreme Court was a test case to determine the legal validity of a
special plea put in by Virginia debtors to claims of British creditors seeking
recovery of their prewar debts. Beginning in 1790, Marshall had represented
numerous Virginia debtors in suits brought by British creditors in the U.S.
Circuit Court. As a prominent member of the defense team, Marshall had
succeeded in upholding his client's plea in the lower federal court in 1793. On
March 7, 1796, the Supreme Court rejected his plea, ruling 4–0 that the 1783
treaty of peace required the payment of debts at full sterling value.

72.28–29   the act . . . is a bar]   A Virginia act of 1777 sequestered debts
owed to British creditors, allowing Virginians to pay their debts into the state
loan office with depreciated currency and obtain a receipt discharging them

for the amount paid. It was adopted as a wartime measure designed to bolster the state's depleted finances.

73.31   att. B. 3, S.292, 295]   Emmerich de Vattel (1714–1767), *The Law of Nations* (1758).

78.14–15   case cited . . . *Jenkins*]   This is a reference to an anonymous case decided by the English Court of Exchequer in 1567, reported in David Jenkins, *Eight Centuries of Reports; or, Eight Hundred Cases solemnly adjudged . . .* (3d ed., 1777).

78.16   *Old Law of Evidence*]   William Nelson, *The Law of Evidence* (3rd ed., 1744).

78.22–23   temper of the house of representatives]   In June 1795 the Senate had ratified the controversial treaty with Great Britain signed by Chief Justice Jay in November 1794. Opponents of the treaty in the House of Representatives then sought to block the appropriations needed for its implementation. After an intense debate, the House voted 51–48 on April 30, 1796, to appropriate the necessary funds.

78.30–33   A meeting was calld . . . in favor of a resolution]   Earlier that day Marshall had spoken in favor of the treaty at a large public meeting in Richmond.

79.13   Mr. Hillhouse]   James Hillhouse (1754–1832), a Federalist, served as a congressman from Connecticut, 1791–96, and as a senator, 1796–1810.

79.20   Mr. H.]   Patrick Henry.

79.25   *James Iredell*]   Iredell (1751–1799), a native of England who settled in North Carolina before the Revolution, was appointed to the Supreme Court in 1790 and served until his death.

80.1   Mr. Nimmo]   James Nimmo was elected as the presidential elector for the district composed of Northampton and Accomac counties (on the eastern shore of Virginia) and Princess Anne County (on the mainland, south of Norfolk).

80.3–4   Clinton . . . Pinkney]   George Clinton (1739–1812), former governor of New York; Thomas Pinckney (1750–1828), former governor of South Carolina.

80.6–7   Mr. Adams . . . cannot be elected]   John Adams was elected with 71 electoral votes, including one from Virginia and one from North Carolina; Thomas Jefferson received 68 electoral votes and was elected vice-president.

80.9–10   denied *wisdom* to the administration]   At the fall 1796 session of the Virginia legislature, Marshall and his Federalist colleagues proposed an address commending President Washington's conduct as "strongly marked by wisdom in the Cabinet, by valor in the field, and by the purest patriotism in both." The address as finally adopted omitted the reference to "wisdom." For Marshall's recollection of this incident in 1827, see pp. 685.38–686.8 in this volume.

80.17   Mr. Dallas]   Alexander J. Dallas (1759–1817), a Pennsylvania lawyer and court reporter.

80.26   thus far on my way to Philadelphia]   Marshall had accepted President Adams's appointment as special envoy to France, serving with Charles Cotesworth Pinckney (1746–1825) of South Carolina and Elbridge Gerry (1744–1814) of Massachusetts.

81.9   sending away Dick]   Dick, one of Marshall's slaves, carried this letter to Polly Marshall in Richmond.

81.21–22   Genl. Young . . . Mr. Hopkins]   Henry Young, a Continental Army veteran, had co-signed Marshall's marriage bond in 1783; John Hopkins was U.S. commissioner of loans for Virginia.

82.1   dearest life]   Marshall wrote "dearest life," but probably meant "dearest wife."

82.8   a heavy gloom hangs]   Robert Morris had been financially ruined as a result of land speculation and would be sent to a debtors' prison in February 1798, remaining there until August 1801.

83.27   situation shoud be as expected]   John Marshall Jr. (1798–1833) was born the following January, while Marshall was still in Paris.

83.30   Colo. Gamble]   Robert Gamble (1754–1810), a Revolutionary War veteran, was a prosperous Richmond merchant.

84.18   your mother]   Rebecca Burwell Ambler (1746–1806).

84.26   Mr. Marshall]   Possibly Humphrey Marshall, John Marshall's cousin and brother-in-law, then a U.S. senator from Kentucky.

84.30–31   Mrs. Merry]   Anne Brunton Merry (1769–1808), an English actress who was making her American debut.

84.32   Mrs. West]   Anne West Bignall; see note 72.15–17.

85.4   Englishman named Baring]   Either Alexander Baring (1774–1848), or his brother Henry Baring (1776–1848), of the English banking family of that name. Alexander Baring married Anne Bingham, the older daughter of William Bingham, in 1798, and Henry Baring married her sister, Maria, in 1802.

86.8   Mr. Brown]   John Brown (1750–1810) had resigned as clerk of the General Court to serve as Marshall's secretary for his French mission.

86.18   Mr. Bingham]   William Bingham (1752–1804), a wealthy Philadelphia merchant and land speculator who served as a senator from Pennsylvania, 1795–1801. Bingham and his wife, Anne Willing Bingham (1764–1801), were at the center of fashionable Philadelphia society.

87.24–25   Mr. Gamble] John G. Gamble, son of Marshall's Richmond friend Robert Gamble.

DIPLOMAT, CONGRESSMAN, AND SECRETARY OF STATE, 1797–1801

92.12–13   saw Genl. Pinckney] In July 1796 President Washington had appointed Pinckney to replace James Monroe as the American minister to France. When Pinckney arrived in Paris in December 1796, the Directory refused to receive him, and he was ordered to leave the country in January 1797.

93.10–11   a daughter . . . Mrs. Pinckney] Eliza Lucas Pinckney (1783–1851), Pinckney's daughter by his first wife, Sarah, and namesake of his mother, who had helped introduce indigo cultivation to South Carolina; Mary Stead Pinckney (1751–1812), Pinckney's second wife.

93.19   Madame deGazon] French actress and operatic mezzo-soprano Louise-Rosalie Lefebvre Dugazon (1755–1821).

93.22–23   The Directory . . . put in arrest] Three members of the Directory, the five-man council that held executive power in France from 1795 to 1799, used the army to execute a coup d'état on 18 Fructidor (September 4, 1797).

94.22   situation of Holland] In 1795 the French invaded the Netherlands and forced the Dutch to sign a treaty allying the Netherlands with France in its war against Britain. Under its terms, the Netherlands ceded Dutch Flanders, agreed to pay an indemnity of 100 million guilders, and accepted a French occupation army of 25,000 men.

95.14–15   for & against the stadtholder] In January 1795 William V fled to England during the French invasion of the Netherlands and the revolutionary uprising that accompanied it. William subsequently established a government in exile, while the new Batavian Republic abolished the position of stadtholder.

97.26   arrêté] Decree, order.

97.29   Moreau] General Jean Victor Moreau (1763–1813) was recalled to Paris and relieved of his command after admitting knowledge of General Jean-Charles Pichegru's contacts with royalist émigrés. Moreau was restored to duty in 1798, but was convicted of plotting against Napoleon in 1804 and banished to the United States. He returned to Europe in 1813 as an adviser to Tsar Alexander I and was mortally wounded at Dresden.

97.36   Genl. Hoche] General Louis Lazare Hoche (1768–1797), the commander of the French army of the Rhine, died at his headquarters at Wetzlar from a respiratory illness on September 18, 1797.

97.37   Carnot]   General Lazare Nicholas Marquerite Carnot (1753–1823), one of the two Directors removed by the coup d'état, escaped into exile. He returned to France after Napoleon Bonaparte overthrew the Directory in 1799.

98.16   the election of the new third,]   Elections were held in March–April 1797 for one-third of the seats in the two legislative chambers established under the 1795 constitution.

98.28   Barthelemy]   François Barthélemy (1747–1830), the other Director removed by the coup, was deported to French Guiana, but escaped and returned to France after the overthrow of the Directory.

99.8–9   the limits prohibited by the constitution,]   Under the 1795 constitution, troops of the regular army were not permitted within 25 miles of Paris except by express permission of the legislature.

99.11   council of five hundred]   The lower chamber of the legislature.

99.16–17   Tronçon . . . Thibideau]   Guillaume Alexandre Tronson du Coudray (1750–1798) was a member of the upper legislative chamber, the council of ancients, which was composed of 250 deputies over the age of 40. Du Coudray was arrested during the coup of 18 Fructidor and deported to French Guiana, where he died from fever. Antoine-Claire Thibaudeau (1765–1854) narrowly escaped deportation after the coup.

99.28   Pichegru]   Jean-Charles Pichegru (1761–1804) served as a general, 1793–96, and was elected to the council of five hundred in 1797. He was deported to French Guiana after 18 Fructidor, but escaped and joined the royalists in England. Pichegru secretly returned to France in 1804 as part of a plot to overthrow Napoleon, but was arrested and either committed suicide, or was murdered, in prison.

100.1   Prince of Condé]   Louis Joseph de Bourbon, prince of Condé (1736–1818), a cousin of Louis XVI and a leader of the royalist émigrés.

101.16–17   Merlin . . . Neufchatel]   Phillipe Antoine Merlin de Douai (1754–1838) and Nicholas-François de Neufchâteau (1750–1828) replaced Carnot and Barthélemy as Directors.

102.20   Massena]   General André Masséna (1758–1817).

102.22   *Timothy Pickering*]   Pickering (1745–1829) served as secretary of state, December 1795–May 1800. This dispatch, drafted by Marshall, was received by Pickering on the evening of March 4, 1798.

102.27   Minister of Foreign Affairs]   Charles Maurice de Talleyrand-Périgord (1754–1838) had been appointed foreign minister of France in July 1797.

102.30   Major Rutledge]   Henry M. Rutledge was Pinckney's secretary and the son of his brother-in-law, the South Carolina political leader Edward Rutledge.

103.41   Major Mountflorence] James C. Mountflorence (c. 1745–1820) also served as a secretary to Pinckney.

104.1   mr. Osmond] Antoine-Eustache, baron d'Osmond (1754–1823).

104.4–5   President's Speech . . . Session of Congress] President Adams addressed a special session of Congress on May 16, 1797.

104.15   In the morning] Beginning with this paragraph and continuing to the end of the paragraph preceding the complimentary close (page 114.8 in this volume), the original dispatch sent to Pickering was almost entirely written in code.

104.15   M. Hubbard] Nicholas Hubbard. In the copy of this dispatch submitted to Congress by Pickering on April 3, 1798, Hubbard was identified as "W."

104.17–18   Mr. Horttinguer] Jean Conrad Hottinguer (1764–1841), identified by Pickering as "X" in the copy submitted to Congress; the secretary of state also omitted all the descriptive information about his background. (Throughout Marshall's letters and dispatches, Hottinguer is referred to as "Horttinguer.")

104.32   M. Talleyrand in America;] Talleyrand lived in the United States from 1794 to 1796.

105.31   M. Bellamy] In the copy submitted to Congress, Pierre Bellamy was identified as "Y" and the name of his banking house was omitted.

106.10–11   treaty with England] The 1794 Jay Treaty.

107.14–15   General Marshalls] Marshall had been a brigadier general of the Virginia militia since 1793.

108.8   President Barras] Paul François Nicholas, vicomte de Barras (1755–1829), president of the Directory.

110.3   Lord Malmesbury] James Harris, first Earl of Malmesbury (1746–1820), had recently engaged in futile peace negotiations with the Directory at Lille.

110.8–9   rôle d'equipage] A list of a ship's crew and passengers. French warships and privateers often used the absence of this document as a pretext for seizing American vessels.

114.8   be made public] The coded portion of the dispatch ends here.

114.14–15   Definitive Articles of Peace . . . Emperor] The treaty of Campo Formio was signed on October 18, 1797. Under its terms, Austria ceded the Rhineland and territory in northern Italy to France.

114.19–20   Tribunal of Cassation]   Tribunal of appeal.

114.36   Exhibit A]   This enclosure, dated October 20, 1797, is entitled
"Paragraphs of the President's Speech, referd to in letter no. 1 under title Ex-
hibit A." The paragraphs are from President Adams's special address to the
Senate and House, May 16, 1797.

114.38–115.1   the late minister]   James Monroe, who served as U.S. minister to France, 1794–96.

116.5   Capt. Izzard]   Henry Izard (1771–1826), the son of Ralph Izard
(1742–1804), who served as a senator from South Carolina, 1789–95.

117.35   fusillerd]   Shot.

119.6   Buonaparte]   Napoleon Bonaparte had negotiated the treaty of
Campo Formio.

119.14   Venice . . . fate of Poland.]   Bonaparte had occupied Venice in
May 1797. Under the treaty of Campo Formio, the Venetian Republic was
suppressed and the city was given to Austria. Russia, Prussia, and Austria carried out their third and final partition of Poland in 1795.

119.27   Account of Negotiation Proceedings]   The remainder of this dispatch, including the two attached exhibits, was originally written almost entirely in code. It was drafted by Marshall, who took much of the text directly
from the private journal he kept during his mission to France.

123.37   M. Hautval]   Lucien Hauteval, identified as "Z" in the copy of
the dispatch given to Congress.

128.33   Pitt]   William Pitt (1759–1806) was prime minister of Britain, 1783–
1801 and 1804–6.

129.14   Rastadt]   Rastatt, a town in western Germany south of Karlsruhe.

129.17   naval victory over the Dutch]   The battle of Camperdown, fought
in the North Sea on October 11, 1797.

131.21   recalls her own minister,]   Pierre Auguste Adet (1763–1834) informed Pickering in November 1796 that he had been recalled.

133.27   Colonel Burr and Mr Madison]   Aaron Burr and James Madison.

134.14   M. D'Aranjo]   Antonio de Araujo de Azevedo (1754–1817).

137.21   Mr. Wickham]   John Wickham (1763–1839), a Richmond lawyer.

138.4–5   a very amiable lady]   Reine-Philiberte, Marquise de Villette
(1757–1822), was Voltaire's adopted daughter and had tended to him in his final days. She was a widow with two young children at the time of Marshall's
Paris mission.

139.16–17   batavian & cisalpine republics]   The Batavian Republic was established in the Netherlands following the French invasion of 1795; the Cisalpine Republic was created in northern Italy by Napoleon Bonaparte in July 1797.

139.39–140.1 person high in the confidence] Probably Pierre Bellamy, who had gone to London.

141.5 Augereau] General Pierre François Charles Augereau (1757–1816), who had helped the Directory carry out the coup of 18 Fructidor.

141.37 Berne has submitted] The French army occupied Berne on March 5, 1798.

142.1 *To Citizens of Richmond*] Marshall delivered these remarks at a banquet held in his honor.

142.4 return to my native country] Marshall arrived in New York on June 17 and reached Richmond on August 8, 1798.

144.33 addressed to Mr. Gerry] Gerry had remained in Paris after the departure of Marshall and Pinckney in April 1798. He sailed from France on August 8 and landed in Boston on October 1, 1798.

145.29 alien & sedition laws] Congress had enacted the Alien and Sedition Acts in June and July 1798. The Alien Acts extended the period required for naturalization from five to 14 years and gave the president power to expel or, in time of declared war, to imprison dangerous aliens, while the Sedition Act made publication of "false, scandalous, and malicious writing" attacking the federal government, the president, or the Congress a crime punishable by two years in prison and a $2,000 fine.

146.23 you were entirely restord] Polly Marshall was still in Winchester, where she had been under a physician's care. Her health had deteriorated following the birth of John Marshall Jr. in January 1798.

146.24–25 your mama . . . conversation discomposes her] Jaquelin Ambler, Rebecca Ambler's husband and Polly Marshall's father, had died in January 1798.

146.28–29 substitute for her lovely sister] Mary Anne Marshall (1789–1792). Marshall recounted the circumstances of her death, and that of an infant son, in a letter written to Joseph Story on June 26, 1831; see pp. 740.38–741.26 in this volume.

147.4 look at the picture] Presumably the miniature, done in Paris by an unidentified painter, that is the earliest known likeness of Marshall.

147.21 *To a Freeholder*] Marshall had recently decided to become a candidate for Congress. "A Freeholder" addressed five questions to Marshall in a letter dated September 19 that was published along with Marshall's reply in the Fredericksburg *Virginia Herald* on October 2, 1798. "To a Freeholder" was the only public statement Marshall made during the campaign.

148.17   memorial addressed by the late envoys] The memorial from the envoys to Talleyrand, drafted by Marshall and dated January 17, 1798, was sent to Congress by President Adams on May 4 and subsequently published.

150.24   charge of judge Addison] Alexander Addison, *Liberty of Speech and of the Press. A Charge to the Grand Juries of the County Courts of the Fifth Circuit of the State of Pennsylvania* (1798), a defense of the Sedition Act. A staunch Federalist, Addison (1759–1807) served as a state judge in western Pennsylvania from 1791 to 1803, when he was impeached and removed from the bench by the state legislature.

150.30   Mr. Washington] Bushrod Washington (1762–1829), George Washington's nephew, had just been nominated and confirmed as associate justice of the Supreme Court in place of the late James Wilson.

150.31   regret the passage of one of the acts] The Sedition Act.

151.9   paper produc'd by Colo. Taylor of Caroline] The Virginia Resolutions, adopted on December 24, 1798, were drafted by James Madison and introduced into the House of Delegates by John Taylor.

151.14   Mr. George K. Taylor] Taylor (1769–1815), a Federalist lawyer and legislator who later married Marshall's sister Jane.

151.19   Colo. Nicholas of Albemarle] Wilson Cary Nicholas.

153.4   encourage Davies] Augustine Davis (see note 54.29) had lost his position as public printer in 1797.

153.11   Doctor Conrod] Daniel Conrad of Winchester was the defendant in the ejectment suit that Marshall mentioned earlier in this letter.

153.28   situation of Genl. Morgan] Daniel Morgan (c. 1735–1802), the celebrated Revolutionary War general, had recently left Congress in poor health and was living in Winchester.

153.31   my sister Jane] Jane Marshall (1779–1866) and George K. Taylor were married in December 1799.

155.1–2   *Speech . . . Thomas Nash*] Nash, an Irish seaman, was imprisoned in Charleston, South Carolina, in February 1799 at the request of the British consul and accused of having participated in the bloody mutiny on board the Royal Navy frigate *Hermione* in September 1797. When the British requested Nash's extradition for murder under the Jay Treaty, Secretary of State Pickering wrote to U.S. District Judge Thomas Bee and told him President Adams had given "his advice and request" that Nash be extradited. At a hearing held in Charleston, Nash claimed to be Jonathan Robbins, a native-born American impressed into the Royal Navy, but Bee rejected his claim and had Nash turned over to British authorities. Nash was taken to Jamaica, court-martialed, and hanged on August 19, 1799. The Nash affair became a political cause célèbre, and on February 20, 1800, New York Republican congressman Edward Livingston (1764–1836) introduced resolutions calling for Adams to be censured for his conduct of the case. The text printed here is taken from a pamphlet, *Speech of the Hon. John Marshall . . . Relative to Thomas Nash, Alias Jonathan Robbins* (1800).

155.12   (Mr. Bayard)] James A. Bayard (1767–1815) was a Federalist congressman from Delaware, 1797–1803, and a senator, 1805–13.

155.35   casus foederis] Case of the alliance, i.e., a situation that causes a treaty provision to come into effect.

156.23   Rutherforth] Thomas Rutherforth (1712–1771), *Institutes of Natural Law, Being the Substance of a Course of Lectures on Grotius de Jure Belli et Pacis* (1754–56).

156.37   (Mr. Gallatin)] Albert Gallatin; see note 49.20.

158.3   the then secretary of state] Thomas Jefferson.

160.4   Mr. Nicholas] John Nicholas (c. 1757–1819), brother of George Nicholas and Wilson Cary Nicholas, was a Republican congressman from Virginia, 1793–1801.

160.29–30   I. Hawk. P.C. . . . Woodison] William Hawkins (1673–1746), *A Treatise of the Pleas of the Crown* (7th ed., 1797); Edward Coke (1552–1634), *The Third Part of the Institutes of the Laws of England* (6th ed., 1680); Richard Wooddeson (1745–1822), *A Systematical View of the Laws of England* (1792–93).

161.29–30   Statutes 27. H. 8th. C 4. . . . C. 15.] Chapter 4 of the statutes enacted in the 27th year of the reign of Henry VIII (his reign began in 1509); chapter 15 of the statutes enacted in the 28th year of the reign of Henry VIII.

163.10   trials at Trenton] Three members of the crew of the *Hermione* were jailed in New Brunswick, New Jersey, in March 1798. When Secretary of State Pickering asked Attorney General Charles Lee if the men should be extradited, Lee advised that they should be tried in an American court for murder and piracy under the 1790 Crimes Act. A federal grand jury indicted all three men for piracy, and returned an additional indictment against one of them, William Brigstock, for murder. The three men were tried and acquitted on the piracy charges in the U.S. Circuit Court for New Jersey on April 9, 1798, and the murder charge against Brigstock was dropped two months later.

165.3–4   the gallant Truxton] Under the command of Thomas Truxton (1755–1822), the U.S. frigate *Constellation* fought and severely damaged the French frigate *La Vengeance* near Puerto Rico on February 1, 1800.

165.29   gentleman from New-York] Edward Livingston.

169.40   The consular convention with France] The convention was signed in 1788 and ratified by the Senate in 1789.

171.18   Mr. Morris] Gouverneur Morris (1752–1816) was U.S. minister to France, 1792–94.

175.13–14   7th article of the amendments to the constitution] The present Fifth Amendment. (Twelve amendments were originally proposed to the states by Congress in 1789. Ratification of the third through the twelfth proposed amendments was completed in 1791, and they became the first ten amendments to the Constitution.)

183.11   *Rufus King*] King served as U.S. minister to Great Britain, 1796–1803, and as a senator from New York, 1789–96 and 1813–25. Marshall assumed his duties as secretary of state in early June 1800.

183.14   Lord Grenville] William Wyndham Grenville, first Baron Grenville (1759–1834), was foreign secretary of Great Britain, 1791–1801, and prime minister, 1806–7.

183.24   secession of two commissioners] Article 6 of the Jay Treaty established an arbitration commission for hearing claims made by British creditors for losses resulting from legal impediments to the recovery of their debts. Composed of three British and two American members (each nation appointed two commissioners, and the fifth was chosen by lot), the commission met in Philadelphia beginning in 1797. In July 1799 the board was dissolved by the withdrawal of the American commissioners.

185.17–18   4th Article of the treaty of Peace] The article read: "It is agreed that creditors on either side shall meet with no lawful impediment to the recovery of the full value in sterling money of all bona fide debts heretofore contracted."

189.6–7   *four million of Dollars . . . One Million*] The words printed in italics were written in code in the original letter.

190.18   *a sacrafice we make*] The italicized words in the text of this letter were originally written in code.

191.8–9   *the Election of N Y*] In May 1800 the Republicans gained control of the New York legislature, which would choose the state's presidential electors in November.

192.5   7th. article of the treaty] Article 7 of the Jay Treaty provided for a joint commission to hear American claims resulting from British captures of American ships. This commission met in London but its work, like that of the board established under Article 6, had recently been suspended.

193.1–2   recommencement of negotiations with France] After the failure of the diplomatic mission on which Marshall served, President Adams appointed William Vans Murray as a special envoy to France in February 1799, and later named William Davie and Chief Justice Oliver Ellsworth as additional negotiators.

194.31   Force therefore was resorted to] The United States began fighting a limited and undeclared naval war with France in 1798.

195.26–27   Victory of Massena] General André Masséna defeated the Austrians and Russians at Zurich, September 25–26, 1799.

197.11–12   ticklenberg, oznaburgs] Ticklenburg, a coarse, mixed linen fabric; osnaburg, a coarse type of plain fabric.

200.9   treaty with Spain] The treaty, signed by Thomas Pinckney in October 1795 and ratified by the Senate in March 1796, opened the lower Mississippi to American navigation.

206.29   *Richard Peters*] Peters (1744–1828) was U.S. District Judge for Pennsylvania, 1792–1818, and for the eastern district of Pennsylvania, 1818–28.

206.31–34   the book . . . the direct tax] In July 1798 Congress enacted a direct tax on houses, land, and slaves in order to finance military preparations for war with France. Resistance to the house tax in eastern Pennsylvania culminated in Fries' Rebellion in March 1799, during which armed protesters forced a federal marshal to release a group of tax resisters from custody. Peters had presided at the subsequent trials in U.S. Circuit Court in which John Fries and two other men were convicted of treason and sentenced to death (they were pardoned by President Adams in May 1800). The book Peters sent to Marshall may have been an account of the case published by Thomas Carpenter, *The Two Trials of John Fries on an Indictment for Treason* (1800).

207.4–5   Legislature of Pennsylvania . . . concurrent vote] The Pennsylvania legislature was divided over a procedure for choosing presidential electors, with the Republican-controlled House favoring a joint vote by both chambers and the Federalist-controlled Senate a concurrent vote in each chamber. A method was eventually adopted that resulted in the selection of eight Republican and seven Federalist electors.

207.13   *St. George Tucker*] Tucker (1752–1827) served as a judge of the Virginia General Court, 1788–1803, on the Virginia Court of Appeals, 1803–11, and as a U.S. District Judge for Virginia, 1813–25.

207.22–23   Fennos attack on Mr. Adams . . . Genl. Hamilton] John Ward Fenno (1778–1802), a Federalist newspaper editor, wrote *Desultory Reflections on the New Political Aspects of Public Affairs in the United States of America, since the Commencement of the Year 1799* (1800). Alexander Hamilton had published his pamphlet *Letter from Alexander Hamilton, concerning the Public Conduct and Character of John Adams, Esq. President of the United States* on October 24, 1800.

207.25–26   the Prospect before us] Tucker wrote Marshall on behalf of the imprisoned Republican journalist James T. Callender, whose pamphlet *The Prospect before Us* had led to his conviction under the Sedition Act in the U.S. Circuit Court for Virginia in June 1800.

208.31–32 pamphlet written by you] *Examination of the Question, "How Far the Common Law of England is the Law of the Federal Government of the United States?"* (1800).

209.19–21 report of a committee . . . author of this report] James Madison wrote the report defending the resolutions opposing the Alien and Sedition Acts adopted by the Virginia legislature in December 1798. The report was published as *Report of the Committee to Whom was Committed the Proceedings of Sundry of the Other States, in Answer to the Resolutions of the General Assembly* (1800).

209.36–37 Judge Ellesworth] Oliver Ellsworth (1745–1807), Chief Justice of the Supreme Court, 1796–1800, presided at the trial of Isaac Williams in the U.S. Circuit Court for Connecticut in September 1799. Williams was convicted and sentenced to eight months in prison and ordered to pay a $2,000 fine. He was pardoned by President Adams in 1800.

211.21–23 Mr. Manton of Rhode Island . . . Genl. Hamiltons pamphlet] Simeon Martin, a Federalist elector who cast his votes for Adams and John Jay. Martin presumably withheld his vote from Charles Cotesworth Pinckney, the Federalist candidate for vice-president, because Hamilton had urged Federalists to elect Pinckney as president.

211.25 treaty with France] The treaty, known as the Convention of 1800, was signed on September 30, 1800, and ratified by the Senate in amended form in February 1801.

211.30–31 nominate the senior Judge] William Cushing (1732–1810), associate justice of the Supreme Court, 1789–1810.

212.12 proposition receivd from Mr. Craig] Robert Craig wrote to Marshall on December 22 proposing to buy his property in Buckingham County, Virginia.

212.18 Copland] Charles Copland (c. 1756–1836) was a Richmond lawyer.

213.27 letter to Mazzei] Jefferson wrote a letter on April 24, 1796, to Philip Mazzei (1730–1816), a Florentine merchant and horticulturist who had once been his neighbor in Albemarle County, that included a passage of political commentary. Mazzei gave a copy of the political portion of the letter to a friend, who arranged for the publication of a French translation in the *Gazette Nationale ou le Moniteur Universal* in January 1797. An English translation from the Paris newspaper appeared in the American press in May 1797, setting off a fierce partisan controversy. In the newspaper text, the letter spoke of how "an Anglo-Monarchio-Aristocratic party has arisen.—Their avowed object is to impose on us the *substance*, as they have already given us the *form*, of the British government. . . . I should give you a fever, if I should name the apostates who have embraced these heresies; men who were Solomons in council, and Sampsons in combat, but whose hair has been cut off by the whore England."

CHIEF JUSTICE OF THE SUPREME COURT, 1801–1819

217.2   *William Paterson*]   Paterson (1745–1806) was associate justice of the Supreme Court, 1793–1806.

217.14   question on the judicial bill]   The Judiciary Act of 1801, passed by the Senate on February 7 and signed by President Adams on February 13, relieved Supreme Court justices from circuit duty, established six judicial circuits, and created 16 new circuit court judgeships. After the bill was signed, Adams and the Federalist Senate began to rapidly fill the new judgeships with "midnight" appointments.

218.9–17   Mr. Madison . . . Mr. Lincoln]   James Madison served as secretary of state, 1801–09; Henry Dearborn (1751–1829) as secretary of war, 1801–09; Albert Gallatin as secretary of the treasury, 1801–14; Abraham Baldwin (1754–1807) was a senator from Georgia, 1799–1807; Samuel Smith (1752–1839), a Maryland congressman and later a senator, declined to serve as secretary of the navy, and in July 1801 the appointment went to his brother, Robert Smith (1757–1842); Levi Lincoln (1749–1820) served as attorney general, 1801–1805.

219.10   Judge Bay]   Elihu Hall Bay (1754–1838) was a South Carolina state judge from 1791 until his death.

220.7   Mr. Cranch's commission]   William Cranch (1769–1855), John Adams's nephew, had been confirmed and commissioned as a judge of the new circuit court for the District of Columbia on March 3 and served until his death. Cranch also reported the cases heard by the Supreme Court, 1801–15.

220.22   Mr. Wagner]   Jacob Wagner was chief clerk of the Department of State, 1798–1807.

220.33–34   Mr. Johnston . . . Mr. Swan]   Thomas Johnson (1732–1819), who served as associate justice of the Supreme Court, 1791–93, had been nominated by Adams as chief judge of the circuit court for the District of Columbia, along with Cranch and James M. Marshall as assistant judges and Thomas Swann (1765–1840) as U.S. attorney. Johnson declined the appointment too late for the outgoing administration to name a replacement. (James M. Marshall resigned his judgeship in November 1803.)

221.2   Mr. Colston]   Rawleigh Colston (1747–1823) was the husband of Marshall's sister, Elizabeth (1756–1842).

221.17–18   interests of Princeton College . . . the misfortune]   A fire had destroyed the interior of Nassau Hall, the college's main building, on March 6, 1802. Paterson was a trustee of the college, and Marshall's son, Thomas, was a student at Princeton at the time.

221.21   bill lately reported to the Senate]   In March 1802 Congress repealed the Judiciary Act of 1801, which had established separate circuit courts (see note 217.14). A new Judiciary Act, passed by the Senate on April 8 and signed into law on April 29, reinstated circuit riding by Supreme Court justices.

221.29   the loss of the next June term]   Under the Judiciary Act of 1801 the Supreme Court was to meet in June and December, but the Judiciary Act of 1802 provided for only one session of the court, convening on the first Monday in February. As a result the Supreme Court, which had last met in December 1801, would not sit again until February 1803.

222.30–31   original law . . . courts of the United States]   The Judiciary Act of 1789.

224.6   Judge Bensons]   Egbert Benson (1746–1833), a New York state judge, had been appointed to a federal circuit court judgeship under the Judiciary Act of 1801.

224.9   the papers]   George Washington's papers, which were in the custody of Bushrod Washington.

225.13   Judge Chase]   Samuel Chase (1741–1811), associate justice of the Supreme Court, 1796–1811.

225.20   Judge Moore]   Alfred Moore (1755–1810), associate justice of the Supreme Court, 1799–1804.

226.6   General Lincoln]   Benjamin Lincoln (1733–1810) commanded the failed attempt to recapture Savannah on October 9, 1779.

226.10   Colonel Laurens]   John Laurens (1754–1782), a former aide to Washington who fought at Savannah.

226.17   D Estaings]   Charles Hector d'Estaing (1729–1794) commanded the French expeditionary force at Savannah, where he was wounded.

226.23   Pulaski]   Casimir Pulaski (1745–1779), a Polish volunteer serving with the Continental Army, was fatally wounded leading a cavalry charge at Savannah.

226.32   Long island & Sullivans island]   Islands at the entrance to Charleston harbor.

226.32   Clinton]   Sir Henry Clinton (1730–1795) commanded the British army that captured Charleston on May 12, 1780.

227.8–11   certain eminent personage . . . national frigate]   In March 1801 President Jefferson had offered safe passage on an American warship to

Thomas Paine, who wished to return to the United States from France but feared capture by the Royal Navy. When Jefferson's offer became public, it was widely denounced by the Federalist press, which described Paine as a "drunken atheist" and "loathsome reptile." Paine eventually returned to the United States on October 30, 1802, sailing on a civilian vessel after the treaty of Amiens ended the war between Britain and France.

227.18   example of Pennsylvania] Pennsylvania law permitted some congressional districts to elect two representatives.

227.27   Rawleigh] Marshall was then attending his first session of the U.S. Circuit Court in Raleigh, North Carolina.

229.1   *Opinion in* Marbury v. Madison] The text printed here appeared in the *Washington Federalist,* March 14 and 16, 1803, the first newspaper report to print the opinion in full.

229.8   No cause has been shewn,] Madison refused to respond to the Supreme Court's order to show cause and did not present a case at oral argument.

237.12   commentaries . . . Blackstone] William Blackstone (1723–1780), *Commentaries on the Laws of England* (4 vols., 1765–69).

242.4   Lord Mansfield] William Murray, first Earl of Mansfield (1705–1793), chief justice of the Court of King's Bench, 1756–88.

244.25–26   which act, . . . was deemed unconstitutional] Chief Justice John Jay and justices William Cushing, James Iredell, James Wilson, and John Blair wrote to President Washington in 1792, expressing their opinion that the pension act assigned duties to circuit judges that were not properly judicial. (Jay and Cushing agreed to voluntarily act as pension commissioners performing nonjudicial duties.) In 1793 Congress passed a new act that relieved the circuit courts from hearing pension claims.

253.2   *Caleb P. Wayne*] Wayne (1776–1849) was the Philadelphia publisher of Marshall's *The Life of George Washington* (5 vols., 1804–7).

254.1–2   Johnsons mode of spelling] Samuel Johnson (1709–1784), *A Dictionary of the English Language* (1755).

254.21   Mr. Morgan] John Morgan, a Philadelphia bookseller, was the agent for the British publishers of *The Life of George Washington.*

256.37   general Lee] Henry Lee; see note 7.22–24.

258.28–29   Doddesly's Annual Register, . . . Stedman] *The Annual Register, or, A View of the History, Politics, and Literature, for the Year . . . ,* first published by London bookseller and author Robert Dodsley (1703–1764) in 1758, and later continued by his brother James (1724–1797); William Belsham (1752–1827), whose historical works included *Memoirs of the Reign of George III. to the Session of Parliament Ending A.D. 1793* (4 vols., 1795);

William Gordon (1728–1807), *The History of the Rise, Progress, and Establishment, of the Independence of the United States of America* (4 vols., 1788); David Ramsay (1749–1815), *The History of the American Revolution* (2 vols., 1789); Charles Stedman (1753–1812), *The History of the Origin, Progress, and Termination of the American War* (2 vols., 1794).

260.5   mr. Belknap, mr. Hutchinson and mr. Minot] Jeremy Belknap (1744–1798), *The History of New-Hampshire* (3 vols., 1784–92); Thomas Hutchinson (1711–1780), *History of Massachusetts from the First Settlement Thereof in 1628, until the Year 1750* (2 vols., 1791); George Richards Minot (1758–1802), *Continuation of the History of the Province of Massachusetts Bay, from the Year 1748* (2 vols., 1798–1803).

260.7–8   Mr. Trumbull] Benjamin Trumbull (1735–1820), *A Complete History of Connecticut, Civil and Ecclesiastical, from the Emigration of Its First Planters from England in MDCXXX, to MDCCXIII* (2 vols., 1797).

260.10   mr. Smith] William Smith (1728–1793), *The History of the Province of New-York, from the First Discovery to the Year M.DCC.XXXII* (2d ed., 1792).

260.11   mr. Stith, and mr. Beverly] William Stith (1707–1755), *The History of the First Discovery and Settlement of Virginia: Being an Essay towards a General History of this Colony* (1747); Robert Beverley (c. 1673–1722), *The History and Present State of Virginia* (1705).

260.15   mr. Chalmer] George Chalmers (1742–1825), *Political Annals of the Present United Colonies, from Their Settlement to the Peace of 1763* (1780).

260.25   mr. Robertson] William Robertson (1721–1793), *The History of America, Books IX. and X. Containing the History of Virginia, to the Year 1688; and the History of New England, to the Year 1652* (1796).

262.9–10   my brother & to Mr. Wickham] William Marshall (1767–1815) was clerk of the U.S. Circuit Court in Richmond; John Wickham was a leading Richmond attorney.

262.10–11   Colo. Taylors testimony] The House of Representatives appointed a committee on January 7, 1804, to investigate the judicial conduct of Justice Samuel Chase. During the sedition trial of James T. Callender in the U.S. Circuit Court for Virginia in 1800, Chase had excluded the testimony of John Taylor, a material witness for Callender. The House impeached Chase in December 1804, but he was acquitted by the Senate on March 1, 1805.

262.18–19   Colo. Gamble . . . John Bassett] Robert Gamble (d. 1810) was a Richmond merchant. When called to serve on the jury, John Bassett declared that he had already formed the opinion that Callender's pamphlet *The Prospect before Us* was seditious. Chase nonetheless allowed him to serve as a juror after Bassett stated that he did not have an opinion regarding the charges alleged in the indictment.

262.25   liable to an attaint] A legal process by which a special grand jury could reverse the verdict of a petit jury and punish the jurors for their wrongful decision.

263.1–2   the other charges except the 1st. & 4th.] The first charge brought against Chase accused him of improper conduct as a circuit court judge in the treason trial of John Fries in 1800 (see note 206.31–34), while the fourth charge contained several general accusations regarding his conduct of the Callender sedition trial. In addition, Chase was accused of trying to secure an indictment for sedition against a Delaware newspaper editor in 1800, and of having delivered an "intemperate and inflammatory political harangue" to a Baltimore grand jury in 1803.

263.3–4   little finger . . . than the loins] Cf. 2 Chronicles 10:10: "My little finger shall be thicker than my father's loins." In the first blank space Marshall appears to have written "democracy," but then deleted it.

263.9   Mr. Nelson] Thomas Nelson (1764–1803) was the U.S. attorney who prosecuted Callender.

263.29–30   critique in the political & commercial register] A review of Volume I of *The Life of George Washington* appeared in the Philadelphia *Political and Commercial Register* on July 9, 1804, written by its editor, William Jackson.

268.2–3   United States v. Burr . . . *Subpoena*] A grand jury was convened in the U.S. Circuit Court for Virginia on May 22, 1807, to consider treason and misdemeanor charges against Aaron Burr. Marshall delivered this opinion in response to Burr's motion for a subpoena duces tecum ordering President Jefferson to turn over certain documents. The text is from the Richmond *Enquirer,* June 17, 1807.

268.7–8   letter from Gen. Wilkinson] Burr sought the letter his former associate General James Wilkinson had sent to Jefferson from Natchitoches, Louisiana, on October 21, 1807, warning the President that Burr was mounting an expedition down the Mississippi.

269.34   8th amendment to the constitution] The present Sixth Amendment; see note 175.13–14.

270.11–12   words of the law] The 1790 Crimes Act.

271.38–39   attorney for the United States] George Hay (1765–1830).

274.15   mind of the judges] The judges of the U.S. Circuit Court for Virginia were Marshall and U.S. District Court Judge Cyrus Griffin.

276.9   whose loss as a friend and as a judge] Justice William Paterson, who shortly before his death in 1806 had presided over the trials of William S. Smith and Samuel G. Ogden in the U.S. Circuit Court for New York. Smith and Ogden were indicted under the 1794 Neutrality Act for aiding a military expedition against the Spanish colony of Venezuela. They claimed to have been acting with the tacit approval of the Jefferson administration, and subpoenaed Secretary of State Madison, Secretary of the Navy Robert Smith, and several other government officials. When Madison and Smith declined to testify in person, Justice Paterson ruled their testimony to be immaterial and refused to compel their appearance. Smith and Ogden were subsequently acquitted.

277.1   COLDEN proceeded] Cadwallader Colden (1769–1834), attorney for Smith and Ogden. Marshall quoted from Thomas Lloyd's *The Trials of William S. Smith, and Samuel G. Ogden, for Misdemeanours . . . in July, 1806* (1807).

277.26   Mr. Sandford] Nathan Sanford (1777–1838), U.S. attorney for the district of New York.

283.7–8   argument of Judge Tucker . . . his 4th. Blackstone] St. George Tucker's *Blackstone's Commentaries: With Notes of Reference, to the Constitution and Laws, of the Federal Government of the United States; and of the Commonwealth of Virginia* (5 vols., 1803). Tucker's note "Concerning Treason" is in an appendix to the fourth volume.

283.10–11   opinion of the supreme court . . . Bollman & Swartwout] Marshall delivered the opinion in *Ex parte Bollman* and *Ex parte Swartwout* on February 21, 1807, discharging two of Burr's associates for lack of probable cause.

283.37   2d. McNally] Leonard MacNally (1752–1820), *The Rules of Evidence on Pleas of the Crown . . .* (2 vols., 1804).

284.10   Foster] Michael Foster (1689–1763), *A Report of Some Proceedings on the Commission for the Trial of the Rebels in the Year 1746 . . . and of Other Crown Cases . . .* (3d ed., 1792).

286.1–3   Opinion . . . on the Law of Treason] George Hay opened the case for the government on August 17, 1807, by examining the first in a number of proposed witnesses. Burr's lawyers moved on August 20 to exclude testimony that did not directly prove that Burr committed treason by levying war on Blennerhassett's Island in the Ohio River on December 10, 1806. This motion provoked an extensive argument on the law of treason that continued through August 29. The text of Marshall's opinion on this motion, delivered on August 31, is from the Richmond *Enquirer*, September 5 and 9, 1807.

288.18   Hale] Matthew Hale (1609–1676), *Historia Placitorum Coronæ. The History of the Pleas of the Crown . . .* (2 vols., 1736).

289.23–25   precedent found in Tremaine . . . Duke of Monmouth]
John Tremaine (d. 1694), *Pleas of the Crown in Matters Criminal and Civil
. . .* (1793–94). The Duke of Monmouth (1649–1685), an illegitimate son of
Charles II, led an unsuccessful rebellion against James II in 1685.

292.10   one of them]   Justice Samuel Chase.

292.16–17   three who were absent]   Justices William Cushing and Brockholst Livingston did not participate in *Ex parte Bollman* and *Ex parte Swartwout*. Congress added a seventh seat to the Supreme Court shortly after the
cases were decided, and Thomas Todd was confirmed as the new associate
justice in March 1807.

294.25   Vaughan's case]   Captain Thomas Vaughan, the commander of a
French privateer, was tried and executed in England for treason in 1696.

296.27–28   *bellum levatum but not percussum.*]   Levying war, but not
waging it.

297.34   cases of Damaree and Purchase]   Daniel Damaree and George
Purchase were convicted of high treason in 1710 for leading mobs that attacked Dissenting meeting houses during a London riot. Both men were later
pardoned.

297.40   *Furor arma ministrat.*]   Rage provides arms.

299.11   the Chief Justice]   Sir John Holt (1642–1710), lord chief justice of
the King's Bench, 1689–1710.

300.26–28   John Fries . . . Judge Iredell]   James Iredell and Richard
Peters presided over the first trial of John Fries in 1799. Fries was convicted,
but the verdict was overturned because of prejudicial statements made by one
of the jurors. His second trial in 1800 was presided over by Samuel Chase and
Peters.

300.37–38   Judge Patterson, . . . two different cases,]   Paterson conducted the trials of John Mitchell and Phillip Vigol in the U.S. Circuit Court
for Pennsylvania in 1795. Both men were convicted of treason and sentenced
to death for their involvement in the "Whiskey Rebellion" of 1794, but were
pardoned by President Washington.

301.6   Judge Peters . . . opinion]   In Peters' charge to the jury in the
first trial of John Fries in 1799.

301.8–9   Judge Chase . . . an opinion]   In Chase's charge to the jury in
the second trial of John Fries in 1800.

309.28–31   To the judge . . . required to give an opinion]   Burr was
brought to Richmond under guard in March 1807 and appeared before Marshall for a preliminary examination on charges of treason and misdemeanor.
On April 1 Marshall found probable cause to commit Burr only on the misdemeanor charge.

313.30   East]   Edward Hyde East (1764–1847), *A Treatise of the Pleas of the Crown* (2 vols., 1803).

314.8–9   cited from Stamford]   William Stanford, Stamford, or Staundford (1509–1558), *Les Plees del Coron . . .* (1607).

317.12   case of the lord Dacre]   Thomas Fiennes, Lord Dacre (1516–1541) was hanged after leading a poaching expedition in a neighbor's park that resulted in the death of a gamekeeper.

319.40   in '15 and '45]   The Jacobite rebellions of 1715 and 1745.

320.29   2 Dal. 348]   Alexander J. Dallas (1759–1817), *Reports of Cases Ruled and Adjudged in the Several Courts of the United States, and of Pennsylvania . . .* (4 vols., 1790–1807).

322.6   name of Jeffries]   George Jeffreys (1648–1689), lord chief justice of England, 1683–85, conducted the notorious "Bloody Assizes" following Monmouth's Rebellion in 1685 that resulted in about 200 executions.

322.40   a special verdict]   A verdict in which the jury decides only the factual issues in a case, leaving the judge to determine the legal effect of the verdict.

325.36   Keeling]   John Kelying (d. 1671), *A Report of Divers Cases in Pleas of the Crown . . .* (1789).

326.5–6   *quodam modo*]   In a certain way, in a certain measure.

333.26   Leach]   Thomas Leach (1746–1818) was editor of the sixth (1787) and seventh (1795) editions of Hawkins, *Treatise of the Pleas of the Crown.*

338.31   the Jury to do theirs.]   On the following day, September 1, the U.S. attorney told the court that he had no further evidence to present. The jury then acquitted Burr of the charge of treason after a brief deliberation.

339.6   your admiralty decisions]   *Admiralty Decisions in the District Court of the United States, for the Pennsylvania District* (1807).

339.19–20   commitment of Colo. Burr for a misdemeanor]   On October 20, 1807, Marshall ordered Burr to stand trial in Ohio for having organized a military expedition at the junction of the Ohio and Cumberland rivers. The case was never prosecuted.

339.25–26   attentions paid me in Baltimore]   Effigies of Marshall, Burr, Harman Blennerhassett, and Burr's attorney Luther Martin had been paraded through the streets of Baltimore in early November before being hanged and burned.

340.2   *Charles Cotesworth Pinckney*]   Pinckney was the Federalist candidate for president in 1808.

340.12–13   rival democratic candidates for the Presidency]   James Madison, James Monroe, and Vice-President George Clinton.

341.8   Mr. Snyders election]   Simon Snyder (1759–1819), a Jeffersonian Democrat, was elected governor of Pennsylvania on October 11, 1808.

341.19   our rulers have unfortunately adopted.]   In December 1807 President Jefferson secured the passage of a bill banning all American overseas trade. The Embargo Act was repealed in March 1809.

342.1   *Opinion in* Fletcher v. Peck]   This case arose from the state of Georgia's sale of some 35 million acres of land, comprising much of present-day Alabama and Mississippi, under the authority of a 1795 act of the state legislature. In response to charges of wholesale bribery, a newly elected legislature in 1796 repealed the earlier act and declared all sales made under it null and void. Robert Fletcher of New Hampshire and John Peck of Massachusetts were nominal parties in an arranged case that was first brought in the U.S. Circuit Court at Boston in 1803. (Because Fletcher and Peck resided in different states, their case could be heard in federal court under the diversity of citizenship clause in Article III, Section 2 of the Constitution.) In 1807 the case was appealed to the Supreme Court, which heard arguments in 1809 and again in 1810. The text of Marshall's opinion of March 16, 1810, is taken from the Washington *National Intelligencer,* March 28, 1810.

352.1–2   This feature is no . . . the constitution;]   The Eleventh Amendment, proposed in 1794 and ratified the following year, removed from federal jurisdiction any suit "commenced or prosecuted" against a state by a citizen of another state, or by a foreigner.

352.26   the South sea.]   The Pacific Ocean.

355.2   *Robert Smith*]   Smith (1757–1842) was secretary of the navy, 1801–09, and secretary of state from March 1809 until March 1811, when President Madison dismissed him.

355.5   The paper you mention]   Smith had recently published an essay, signed "A Spectator," in a Baltimore newspaper criticizing Madison's conduct of relations with France.

355.8–9   the edict . . . 28th. of April 1811]   The decree of St. Cloud, allegedly signed by Napoleon on April 11, 1811, declared that the decrees of Berlin and Milan had been rescinded on November 1, 1810. Although both Madison and Joel Barlow, the U.S. minister to France, believed the decree had been backdated, the administration publicly accepted its date as genuine.

355.33–34   declaration of the Prince Regent . . . Berlin & Milan]   Napoleon signed a decree in Berlin in 1806 imposing a complete blockade against Great Britain and Ireland. The British government responded by issuing orders-in-council prohibiting neutral commerce with ports closed to

British shipping and requiring vessels trading with open European ports to make prior stops in British ports. Napoleon then signed a decree in Milan in 1807, making neutral ships complying with the orders-in-council subject to seizure. On April 21, 1812, the British privy council announced that it would revoke its orders restricting American shipping if the Berlin and Milan decrees were repealed.

356.10   Proclamation of the 2d. of Novr. 1810] Congress passed legislation in May 1810 reopening commerce with Britain and France while authorizing the President to prohibit trade with one nation if the other removed its restrictions on American shipping. When Madison received a letter from the Duc de Cadore, the French foreign minister, falsely stating that the Berlin and Milan decrees would be revoked as of November 1, 1810, the President responded on November 2 by issuing a proclamation closing off commerce with Great Britain.

358.1–2   Report of the Virginia River Commission] Marshall drafted this report and submitted it to Governor James Barbour (1775–1842) on December 26, 1812. The text is taken from the Richmond Enquirer, January 7 and 9, 1813.

380.14–15   Your own judgement . . . heard the argument] Washington had heard arguments in the U.S. Circuit Court at Philadelphia in Golden v. Prince, a case challenging a Pennsylvania insolvency statute. In his opinion, Washington held the law to be an unconstitutional impairment of the obligation of contract and to be incompatible with the power of Congress to enact uniform bankruptcy legislation.

380.18   an Unknown Correspondent] Possible recipients of this letter are John Thornton Kirkland (1770–1840), president of Harvard College, 1810–28, and Joseph G. Cogswell (1786–1871), then a tutor in Latin at Harvard.

380.22   my culpable son] John Marshall Jr., a member of the Harvard class of 1817, had recently been dismissed from the college for engaging "in a course of immoral & dissolute conduct, which had been long continued & under circumstances that left little hope of his reform."

382.6   your agricultural character] Peters was the author of Agricultural Enquiries on Plaister of Paris (1797) and numerous papers on agricultural methods. He published A Discourse on Agriculture in 1816.

382.9   Doctor Adams] John Adams (1772–1825), a Richmond physician.

383.34   Brown] Arthur Browne (1756?–1805), A Compendious View of the Civil Law, and of the Law of the Admiralty (2d ed., 1802).

385.4   Louis Marshall] Marshall (1773–1866) ran a classical school for boys at his home in Woodford County, Kentucky.

385.6   son of our Sister Taylor] Thomas M. Taylor, son of Jane Marshall Taylor and the late George K. Taylor.

386.4   *Dudley Chase*]   Chase (1771–1846) was a senator from Vermont, 1813–17 and 1825–31, and chief justice of the Vermont supreme court, 1817–21. At the time Marshall wrote this letter, Chase was the chairman of the Senate judiciary committee.

387.28–29   British minister . . . French minister]   Charles Bagot (1781–1843) was British minister to the United States, 1815–20. Jean-Guillaume Hyde de Neuville (1776–1857), French minister to the United States, 1816–21, and his wife, Anne-Marguerite Hyde de Neuville, were a popular couple in Washington society.

388.3   Mr. Wirt]   William Wirt (1772–1834) was attorney general of the United States, 1817–29. Wirt had helped prosecute Aaron Burr in 1807, and appeared as a private attorney before the Supreme Court in numerous cases.

388.8   chiccahominy]   Marshall's farm on the Chickahominy River, a few miles northeast of Richmond.

388.15   *Joseph Delaplaine*]   Delaplaine (1777–1824), a Philadelphia publisher, was then compiling *Delaplaine's Repository of the Lives and Portraits of Distinguished Americans*, which combined engraved portraits with short biographies. The series ceased publication because of financial problems before Marshall's entry was published.

388.18–19   Mr. Wood . . . Mr. Lawrence]   Joseph Wood (c. 1778–1830) and Charles B. Lawrence (1790–1864). Wood executed a portrait of Marshall in 1816 that has not been found, though an engraving taken from the painting was published in a magazine in 1817.

390.30   Peales Museum]   Charles Willson Peale (1741–1827), the American portraitist, opened a museum and portrait gallery in Philadelphia in 1786.

391.1–2   *Opinion in* Dartmouth College v. Woodward]   The Dartmouth College case came by appeal from the New Hampshire Superior Court and was argued in March 1818. (William H. Woodward, the defendant, was the secretary-treasurer of Dartmouth.) The text is taken from Timothy Farrar, *Report of the Case of the Trustees of Dartmouth College against William H. Woodward* (1819).

397.38   Black. Comm.]   Blackstone's *Commentaries on the Laws of England*.

412.1   *Opinion in* McCulloch v. Maryland]   *McCulloch v. Maryland* was an arranged case brought to challenge a Maryland act laying a stamp tax on all banks "not chartered" by the state legislature. When James McCulloch, cashier of the Baltimore branch of the Second Bank of the United States, circulated bank notes that had not been issued on special stamped paper as prescribed by state law, the state sued him in the local court and obtained judgment. This judgment was subsequently affirmed by the Maryland Court of Appeals in 1818 and then appealed by McCulloch to the Supreme Court.

After an argument extending over nine days, Marshall delivered his opinion on March 6, 1819. The text is taken from the Washington *Daily National Intelligencer,* March 13, 1819.

413.13–17 The original act . . . the present law.] The original Bank of the United States was chartered in 1791. Congress allowed its charter to expire in 1811, then chartered the Second Bank of the United States in 1816. James Madison, who had opposed the bank on constitutional grounds in 1791, signed the 1816 charter into law as president.

434.4–5 the Federalist . . . authors of that work] Of the 85 "Federalist" essays originally published between October 1787 and May 1788, Alexander Hamilton wrote 51, James Madison 29, and John Jay five.

434.18–32 "that an indefinite . . . the state governments."] The passage quoted is from *The Federalist No. 31,* written by Alexander Hamilton.

437.29 *A Friend to the Union*] Marshall wrote his "A Friend to the Union" essays in response to the attacks on the Supreme Court's opinion in *McCulloch v. Maryland* that appeared in the Richmond *Enquirer* in March and April 1819. (In a letter to Justice Joseph Story of March 24, Marshall observed that the *McCulloch* opinion "has roused the sleepy spirit of Virginia—if it ever sleeps.") The Chief Justice arranged for Bushrod Washington to have the "Friend to the Union" essays published in the Philadelphia *Union.* They appeared on April 24 and 28, and were reprinted in the Alexandria *Gazette and Daily Advertiser* on May 15, 17, and 18, 1819.

438.4 Amphyction] Two "Amphyction" essays had appeared in the Richmond *Enquirer* on March 30 and April 2, 1819. Marshall believed their author to be William Brockenbrough (1778–1838), a judge of the Virginia General Court. Amphyction was the legendary founder of the Amphyctonic League, which sought to settle disputes among the ancient Greek states.

438.24 Cerberus] In Greek mythology, a three-headed dog that guarded the gates of Hades.

438.38 The Editor] Thomas Ritchie (1778–1854) edited the Richmond *Enquirer,* 1804–45.

440.9 Nereid] *The Nereide,* a prize case decided on March 11, 1815, in which Marshall delivered the opinion of the court, William Johnson delivered a concurring opinion, and Joseph Story dissented.

440.13–14 Olivera v. the Union Ensurance Co.] Marshall delivered the opinion of the court in *Olivera v. Union Insurance Company* on February 19, 1818.

441.9–10 four of whom have no political sin] Justices William Johnson (1770–1834) and Brockholst Livingston (1757–1823) were appointed by Jefferson; Joseph Story (1779–1845) and Gabriel Duvall (1752–1844) were appointed by Madison. Thomas Todd (1765–1826), appointed by Jefferson, did not attend the February 1819 term of the Supreme Court.

445.34–35   Certain resolutions . . . Virginia in 1798] The resolutions against the Alien and Sedition Acts drafted by James Madison.

446.2 Madison's report]   See note 209.19–21.

453.32–34   and the lessor sows . . . yet the lessor shall] The quotation is derived from a passage in Edward Coke, *The First Part of the Institutes of the Laws of England; or, A Commentary upon Littleton* . . . (16th ed., 1809). The original text reads: "and the lessee sows the land, and the lessor, after it is sown and before the corn is ripe, put him out, yet the lessee shall . . ."

463.2   *Joseph Story*] Story (1779–1845) was an associate justice of the Supreme Court, 1811–45.

463.8   the correction you propose] Story's letter of April 16 has not been found, so it is unclear which passage in the opinion he was referring to.

463.31–32   decision of Martin & Hunter] Story's opinion for the court in *Martin v. Hunter's Lessee* (1816) affirmed the power of the Supreme Court to review judgments of state courts in cases involving a federal question. Marshall did not participate in the decision.

464.3   severe affliction] Story's six-year-old daughter, Caroline, had died on April 1.

464.14–18   Mr. Bronson . . . in the first] Enos Bronson (1774–1823) was editor of the Philadelphia *Union*. The errors Marshall describes were corrected by the editors of *The Papers of John Marshall*, the source of the texts presented in this volume.

467.4   *in pais*] Outside of court.

467.16–17   signature of Hampden] Judge Spencer Roane of the Virginia Court of Appeals published four "Hampden" essays in the Richmond *Enquirer* between June 11 and June 22, 1819. His pseudonym alluded to John Hampden (1594–1643), a leader of the parliamentary opposition to Charles I.

467.32   society for colonization . . . Mr. Caldwell] Bushrod Washington was the first president of the American Colonization Society, founded in 1816 to promote the colonization of free blacks in Africa. Elias B. Caldwell (1776–1825), the clerk of the Supreme Court, was secretary of the Society.

469.13   Pickering] Timothy Pickering instituted several prosecutions under the Sedition Act while serving as secretary of state in the Adams administration.

469.24   ship money] A tax levied by Charles I without the consent of parliament.

470.13   Montesquieu] Charles de Secondat, Baron de Montesquieu
(1689–1755), *The Spirit of the Laws* (1748).

472.26   Lloyd, or Sheffy] James Lloyd (1745–1820) was a Federalist senator from Maryland, 1797–1800, who had advocated passing a more severe version of the Sedition Act in 1798. Daniel Sheffey (1770–1830) was a Federalist
congressman from Virginia, 1809–17.

476.34   Grotius] Hugo Grotius (1583–1645), *The Law of War and Peace*
(1625).

479.1–2   "by the grant of a house . . . may pass"] The quoted passage
is from Matthew Bacon, *A New Abridgment of the Law* (1st Am. ed., 1811),
citing Coke, *Commentary on Littleton*.

486.12–13   opinions . . . by the cabinet ministers] In an appendix to
the fifth volume of *The Life of George Washington,* Marshall paraphrased at
length the opinions of Secretary of State Jefferson, Attorney General Edmund Randolph, and Secretary of the Treasury Hamilton on the constitutionality of the bank bill.

492.27–28   late treaty with England] The Anglo-American Convention
of 1818.

492.29–30   our unratified treaty with Spain] The Adams-Onís Treaty,
signed in Washington on February 22, 1819, was not ratified by Spain until
1820.

502.38   Federalist, No. 39] The essay was written by James Madison.

507.39   15th No. . . . . the author] Alexander Hamilton.

508.34–35   those gentlemen] The attorneys for Maryland were Joseph
Hopkinson (1770–1842), a Federalist congressman from Pennsylvania who
had helped defend Samuel Chase at his impeachment trial; Walter Jones
(1776–1861), a leading member of the Supreme Court bar who also served as
the U.S. attorney for Washington, 1804–21; and Luther Martin (1748–1826),
who served as attorney general of Maryland, 1818–22.

512.21–35   the 80th No. . . . . the 82d No.] Both essays were written by
Hamilton.

513.10   Hunter *v.* Fairfax] In *Hunter v. Martin, Devisee of Fairfax* (1815),
the Virginia Court of Appeals declared unconstitutional section 25 of the Judiciary Act of 1789, which conferred on the Supreme Court appellate jurisdiction over the highest state courts in cases involving federal questions. The
Supreme Court reversed this decision in *Martin v. Hunter's Lessee* (1816).

513.11   Pennsylvania *v.* Cobbett] *Respublica v. Cobbett* was decided by the
Pennsylvania Supreme Court in 1798.

514.15–16   chief justice McKean]   Thomas McKean (1734–1817), chief justice of Pennsylvania, 1777–99, and its governor, 1799–1808.

520.4   the Federalist, (No. 45)]   The quoted passage is from *The Federalist No. 44*, written by Madison.

521.19   affairs of the society]   Possibly a reference to the Mutual Assurance Society of Virginia.

521.26   the case of the pirates]   In July 1819 Marshall tried a piracy case involving the crew of the privateer *Irresistible* in the U.S. Circuit Court for Virginia. After the jury returned a special verdict, Marshall and U.S. District Judge St. George Tucker disagreed as to whether the offenses committed by the defendants could be punished under a piracy statute recently passed by Congress. Their division brought the case to the Supreme Court, which ruled in 1820 that the defendants had committed piracy under the terms of the act of March 1819. Marshall subsequently sentenced the convicted men to be hanged, but they either received pardons or were indefinitely reprieved.

522.7   Hortensius]   The "Hortensius" essays written by George Hay appeared in the Richmond *Enquirer* on July 23, July 27, and August 3, 1819. While also critical of the Supreme Court's reasoning in *McCulloch*, Hortensius sought to distance himself from the extreme states' rights views of Amphyction and Hampden.

CHIEF JUSTICE OF THE SUPREME COURT, 1820–1835

525.32   Elizabeth]   Elizabeth Alexander Marshall (1802–47), wife of John Marshall Jr.

526.21   the case from Virginia]   *Cohens v. Virginia*.

527.7   March 26th.]   Marshall misdated the letter, which was postmarked in Washington on February 27.

527.11   noisy rejoicings of the 22d]   The celebration of Washington's birthday. Because of her nervous condition, Polly Marshall could not tolerate loud noises. She customarily left Richmond for the Chickahominy farm during holiday celebrations, including Christmas and the Fourth of July.

528.1   *Opinion in* Cohens v. Virginia]   In September 1820 the Norfolk borough court fined the brothers Philip and Mendez Cohen $100 for selling District of Columbia lottery tickets in violation of Virginia law. The Cohens appealed their conviction to the Supreme Court, claiming a right to sell the tickets by virtue of the federal law authorizing lotteries in the District of Columbia. The case raised important constitutional issues regarding the appellate jurisdiction of the Supreme Court in cases involving federal questions. Marshall's opinion for the court was delivered in response to a motion to dismiss the case for lack of jurisdiction. The text is taken from the Washington *Daily National Intelligencer*, March 15, 1821.

528.25   by writ of error.] At Marshall's direction, Supreme Court reporter Henry Wheaton (1785–1848) subjoined a note here in his report of this
case: "The plaintiff in error prayed an appeal from the judgment of the Court
of Hustings, but it was refused, on the ground that there was no higher State
tribunal which could take cognizance of the case."

528.34–36   The counsel who opened . . . counsel who followed] Philip
P. Barbour (1783–1841) was a congressman from Virginia, 1815–25 and 1827–30,
a U.S. district judge, 1830–36, and an associate justice of the Supreme Court,
1836–41. Alexander Smyth (1765–1830) was a congressman from Virginia,
1817–25 and 1827–30.

529.15   either intentionally or inadvertently] As directed by Marshall,
Wheaton dropped this phrase from his report of the case.

531.1   25th section of the judicial act] Section 25 of the Judiciary Act of
1789 provided for appeals to the Supreme Court from state courts in cases involving federal questions. The act specified that cases concerning the Constitution, treaties, or federal laws must first be decided by a state's highest court
before being appealed to the Supreme Court, and restricted appeals to cases
where the state courts ruled against the validity of a treaty or federal law;
where they ruled in favor of a state law that had been challenged as being
contrary to the Constitution, treaties, or federal law; or where they denied a
right or privilege claimed under the Constitution, treaties, or federal law.

549.24–27   the Mirror . . . right of prosecuting &c.] Blackstone refers
to the ancient English legal treatise known as *Mirror of Justices*; to Bracton
(Henry of Bratton, c. 1210–68), *De Legibus et Consuetudinibus Angliae (On
the Laws and Customs of England)*; and to another ancient English legal treatise, *Fleta seu Commentarius Juris Anglicani*. The quotation from Justinian
reads: "The right of prosecuting to judgment, which is due to everyone."

554.28   says a very celebrated statesman] Marshall quotes from *The Federalist No. 80*, written by Alexander Hamilton.

556.32–33   the Federalist says,] In *The Federalist No. 82*, written by
Hamilton.

564.15   the motion be overruled.] Marshall delivered a second opinion
for the court in *Cohens v. Virginia* on March 5, 1821, ruling that the federal
act authorizing the lottery did not give the Cohens the right to sell District
of Columbia lottery tickets in Virginia.

564.20   course of this term] The May term of the U.S. Circuit Court for
Virginia.

565.7   Algernon Sydney] Spencer Roane published five "Algernon Sidney" essays attacking the opinion in *Cohens v. Virginia* in the Richmond
Enquirer in May and June 1821. Algernon Sidney (1622–1683), an English

republican executed for allegedly plotting to assassinate Charles II, was the author of *Discourses concerning Government* (1698).

565.22–23   that amendment . . . Mr. Webster] Daniel Webster (1782–1852) was then a leading advocate in the Supreme Court who had appeared in the Dartmouth College case and in *McCulloch v. Maryland.* In the Massachusetts constitutional convention of 1820–21, Webster and Story opposed an amendment that would have changed the basis of representation in the Massachusetts senate from taxable property to population. Story wrote Marshall on June 27 that the proposal had been rejected by the voters.

565.26   *Edward C. Marshall*] Edward Carrington Marshall (1805–1882), the Chief Justice's youngest son, was attending school in Fauquier County. He entered Harvard College in 1823 and graduated in 1826.

567.12   gratiful] Marshall probably meant to write "gratifying."

567.15   Mr. Jeffersons letter] Story had seen a copy of a letter written by Jefferson in September 1820 to William Charles Jarvis, a Massachusetts lawyer, who used it to promote his book *The Republican* (1820). In the letter, Jefferson wrote that "to consider the judges as the ultimate arbiters of all constitutional questions . . . would place us under the despotism of an oligarchy."

567.35   case of the mandamus] *Marbury v. Madison.*

567.36   the batture] Edward Livingston (see note 155.1–2) moved to New Orleans in 1803 and acquired a portion of its "batture," a valuable alluvial deposit along the Mississippi River. In 1808 President Jefferson asserted public ownership of the batture and had the U.S. marshal evict Livingston from his property. After Jefferson left office, Livingston sued him for trespass in the U.S. Circuit Court for Virginia. Marshall and U.S. District Judge John Tyler heard *Livingston v. Jefferson* in December 1811 and ruled that the court had no jurisdiction to decide the case. In his opinion, Marshall expressed regret that jurisdictional issues left Livingston without a legal remedy.

568.28   Mr. Hall] John E. Hall (1783–1829), a Philadelphia lawyer and legal publisher, had been asked by Jefferson to publish Spencer Roane's "Algernon Sidney" essays together with Marshall's opinion in *Cohens v. Virginia.* Hall's *Journal of Jurisprudence* ceased publication before any material about *Cohens* could appear.

569.20–21   answer of Mr. Wheaton] Henry Wheaton wrote seven "A Federalist of 1789" essays that appeared in the New York *American,* July–August 1821.

570.14   statute of jeofails] A statute allowing mistakes or oversights in legal pleadings to be amended.

571.10   Mr. Hansford] Theodosius Hansford (1768–1824), clerk of the Virginia Senate from 1802 until his death.

571.12   Charles Marshall]   Charles C. Marshall (1799–1849), son of the
Chief Justice's late brother Charles Marshall (1767–1805).

571.16   act of compromise]   In 1796 the Virginia legislature passed an act
under which the state yielded its claims to the Fairfax manor lands and the
purchasers of the Fairfax estate, including John and James M. Marshall, conceded the state's right to the ungranted Northern Neck lands.

571.18   your son]   Thomas Marshall (1796–1826) was preparing to argue a
case involving the Fairfax title before Judge Robert White (1759–1831) in the
state superior court at Winchester.

572.15   case of Hunter & Fairfax]   In April 1810 the Virginia Court of Appeals upheld a challenge to the Fairfax title in *Hunter v. Fairfax's Devisee*.
The decision was reversed in 1813 by the Supreme Court in *Fairfax's Devisee v. Hunter's Lessee*. Justice Story based much of his opinion on a provision in the Jay Treaty of 1794. (Marshall did not participate in the case.)

572.17–19   Smith v The State . . . Hodgson 4 Wheaton]   The cases were
decided by the Supreme Court in 1810, 1818, and 1819.

572.20   Judge Johnson assenting.]   William Johnson had dissented from
Story's decision in *Fairfax's Devisee v. Hunter's Lessee*.

572.25   dicta of Judge Roane]   Spencer Roane was one of the judges who
decided *Hunter v. Fairfax's Devisee* in the Virginia Court of Appeals in 1810.

572.27   Happy creek]   James M. Marshall's estate, near Front Royal, Virginia.

572.30   Mr. Colstons]   Rawleigh Colston (1747–1823), Marshall's brother-
in-law and business partner, resided near Martinsburg (now in West
Virginia).

572.31   Bath]   Berkeley Springs (now in West Virginia).

573.17   James]   Marshall's son, James Keith Marshall (1800–1862).

573.33–34   Richard Martyr]   Martyr, an apprentice in the office of the
Washington *National Intelligencer*, was the son of Frances Martyr, a house-
keeper and companion to Polly Marshall.

573.37–574.1   young couple, . . . secretary of the navy]   Charles de Bres-
son (1798–1847), secretary to the French legation, and Catharine Livingston
Thompson, daughter of Secretary of the Navy Smith Thompson (1768–1843).

575.1   *Opinion in* Johnson v. McIntosh]   This case began as a land title
dispute between Joshua Johnson and Thomas J. Graham, whose claim derived from land company purchases made in Illinois in 1773 and 1775, and
William McIntosh, who held a patent issued by the United States in 1818 that
fell within the boundaries of the land company purchases. *Johnson v. McIntosh*
came to the Supreme Court on appeal from the U.S. District Court for Illi-

nois. The text of the opinion is taken from the eighth volume of Henry Wheaton's *Reports of Cases Argued and Adjudged in the Supreme Court of the United States* (1823).

581.15   a Bourbon on the throne of Spain] Philip V (1683–1746) became king of Spain in 1700.

581.31   treaty of Aix la Chapelle,] The treaty was signed in 1748, ending the War of the Austrian Succession (1740–48).

585.12   late acquisitions from Spain] Under the Adams-Onís Treaty of 1819, Spain ceded Florida and its claims to the Pacific Northwest to the United States.

590.8–9   case of *Campbell . . . Cowper*] In *Campbell v. Hall* (1774) Lord Mansfield held void an export duty imposed on Grenada without parliamentary consent. The case was reported by Henry Cowper (1758–1840) in *Reports of Cases Adjudged in the Court of King's Bench, 1774–1778* (1783).

592.38–39   opinion of the Attorney General . . . Yorke] The opinion was issued in 1757 by Attorney General Charles Pratt (1714–1794) and Solicitor General Charles Yorke (1722–1770).

593.10–11   pamphlet . . . "*Plain Facts,*"] *Plain Facts: Being an Examination into the Rights of the Indian Nations of America, to Their Respective Countries* (1781) by Samuel Wharton (1732–1800), a prominent speculator in western land.

593.13–14   Chalmers, in whose collection] George Chalmers, *Opinions of Eminent Lawyers on Various Points of English Jurisprudence concerning the Colonies, Fisheries, and Commerce of Great Britain* (1814).

597.8   Mr. Small] Abraham Small of Philadelphia was the publisher of the second edition of Bushrod Washington's *Reports of Cases Argued and Determined in the Court of Appeals of Virginia* (1823) and the prospective publisher of the second edition of *The Life of George Washington*. In 1824 Small published the first volume of Marshall's biography of Washington as a separate work, *A History of the Colonies Planted by the English on the Continent of North America, from their settlement, to the commencement of that war which terminated in their Independence.*

598.5–6   your friendly attention to my son] Edward Carrington Marshall had just entered Harvard College as a member of the class of 1826.

598.14   case concerning the securities] Marshall had recently decided the case of *Bank of the United States v. Dandridge* in the U.S. Circuit Court for Virginia. In 1827 Story delivered the Supreme Court's opinion reversing his decision.

598.23–24   plea of non est factum] Literally, "not his deed"; a general plea denying the debt on a bond.

599.38–39   successor of our much lamented friend]   Justice Brockholst Livingston died in March 1823. President Monroe offered to nominate Secretary of the Navy Smith Thompson in Livingston's place, but Thompson postponed giving an answer until he could determine whether he was a viable candidate for the presidency in 1824. Story probably heard a rumor that Monroe was considering appointing Martin Van Buren (1782–1862), then a senator from New York, to Livingston's seat. Thompson eventually accepted the judicial appointment and was confirmed in December 1823.

600.4   To Joseph Story]   The dateline of this letter was evidently cut off. At the top of the manuscript someone wrote the date "[Sept. 26. 1823]."

600.18   brother Johnson . . . has hung himself]   In August 1823 Justice William Johnson ruled in circuit court that South Carolina's Negro Seamen Act, which required free black sailors to be jailed while their ships were in port, violated the commerce clause of the Constitution.

601.8–12   case was brought . . . of the act]   In The Brig Wilson v. United States, a case heard in the U.S. Circuit Court for Virginia in 1820, Marshall ruled that the ship had not violated the Virginia statute prohibiting the admission or importation of free blacks into the state.

601.28   squadron under Commodore Porter]   The West India Squadron was formed in 1822 to suppress piracy in the Caribbean; it was commanded at the time by David Porter (1780–1843).

602.26   I have read the correspondence]   Correspondence between the Hon. John Adams, late President of the United States, and the late Wm. Cunningham, Esq., Beginning in 1803, and Ending in 1812 (1823), published by Cunningham's son without Adams' permission. In his letters, the former president bitterly attacked Jefferson, Hamilton, and Timothy Pickering.

602.36   non est qualis erat]   He is not what he was.

603.4   Henry Clay]   Clay (1777–1852) was then serving as Speaker of the House of Representatives.

603.14–15   Mr. Johnson's proposition]   Senator Richard M. Johnson of Kentucky had recently introduced a resolution proposing that the number of Supreme Court justices be increased from seven to ten, and that the concurrence of at least seven justices be required to invalidate state laws or acts of Congress. Johnson's proposal reflected the intense opposition in Kentucky to the Supreme Court's decisions in 1821 and 1823 in Green v. Biddle that invalidated state laws allowing actual settlers ejected by nonresident titleholders to secure compensation for their crops and improvements.

604.39–40   memorable distinction as to tenure of office]   During the congressional debate over the repeal of the Judiciary Act of 1801, which had created 16 new circuit court judges, opponents of the measure argued that it unconstitutionally removed judges from office, while its supporters contended that Congress had the constitutional power to abolish, as well as create, inferior federal courts.

605.27   my fall] Marshall stumbled over a cellar door while returning to his lodgings on the evening of February 19, dislocating his shoulder and suffering a concussion that left him unconscious for 15 minutes. He was able to return to the Supreme Court on March 2 with his arm in a sling.

606.29   Major Dick] Alexander Dick had served as an officer in the Continental Army during the Revolution.

606.30   the cottage, the lock of hair] The Cottage was the residence of John Ambler (1762–1836), in Hanover County, where Marshall and Polly Ambler were married in January 1783. According to family tradition, Marshall's first attempt to court Polly was unsuccessful, but her cousin John Ambler intervened by giving Marshall a lock of her hair. Believing that Polly herself had sent the lock, Marshall renewed his suit. (The lock is now on display at the Marshall House in Richmond.)

607.1   *Opinion in* Gibbons v. Ogden] The case between Thomas Gibbons and Aaron Ogden involving New York's steamboat monopoly began in 1818. When the New York Court of Errors in 1820 issued a decree in Ogden's favor, Gibbons appealed to the Supreme Court. After several delays, the appeal was argued over a period of five days in February 1824. Marshall wrote most of his opinion before his accident on February 19 and completed it during his recovery. He delivered the decision on March 2, his first day back in court. The text is taken from the Washington *Daily National Intelligencer,* March 5, 1824.

608.7   Council of Revision] The council consisted of the governor, chancellor, and Supreme Court judges, and had the power to veto legislation. It was established by the New York constitution of 1777 and abolished in 1821.

632.1–31   Thomas Gibbons . . . dismissed accordingly] The text of the decree issued by the Supreme Court in *Gibbons v. Ogden* is taken from the original autograph document in the National Archives.

633.11   Rockets] Rocketts Landing.

635.14   *Thomas W. White*] White (1788–1843), a Richmond printer, provided a copy of this letter to the Richmond *Enquirer,* where it appeared on December 2, 1824.

635.16   Mr. Garnetts lectures] James Mercer Garnett (1770–1843), *Seven Lectures on Female Education, Inscribed to Mrs. Garnett's Pupils, at Elm-Wood, Essex County, Virginia* (1824). The book was published by Thomas White, who sent Marshall a copy of the second edition.

637.8–9   Aunt Keith . . . much affected] Elizabeth Contee Keith (1745–1827) had lost her husband, James Keith, in October 1824.

637.10   William Marshall]   William Louis Marshall (1803–1869).

638.1–2   my old and good aunt]   Elizabeth Keith.

638.14   Lucy Fisher]   Lucy Marshall Fisher (1807–1774), daughter of
George Fisher (d. 1857) and Ann Ambler Fisher (1772–1832), Polly's younger
sister.

639.6   Governour of Georgia]   George M. Troup (1780–1856) had obtained the cession of the remaining Creek lands in Georgia in February 1825.
President John Quincy Adams initially approved the cession, but then repudiated it as fraudulently obtained.

639.8–9   rejection of the last treaty.]   A treaty signed in Washington,
D.C., on January 31, 1826, repudiated the earlier cession and allowed the
Creeks to retain some of their Georgia lands. Although it was ratified by the
Senate on April 22, Governor Troup and the Georgia legislature refused to
abide by the treaty, and the administration of John Quincy Adams failed to
enforce it.

639.10   Mr. Giles]   William Branch Giles (1762–1830), was a congressman
from Virginia, 1790–98 and 1801–03, and a senator, 1804–15. He later served
as governor of Virginia, 1827–30.

640.1   *Memorandum by Jared Sparks*]   Sparks (1789–1866) was then editor
of the *North American Review*. He later edited *The Writings of George Washington* (12 vols., 1834–37). This account of his conversation with Marshall is
taken from Herbert B. Adams, *The Life and Writings of Jared Sparks, Comprising Selections from His Journals and Correspondence* (2 vols., 1893).

640.24   Mr. Burk]   John Daly Burk (d. 1808), *The History of Virginia,
From its First Settlement to the Present Day* (4 vols., 1804–16).

640.31   Henning]   William Waller Hening (c. 1767–1828) compiled *The
Statutes at Large; Being a Collection of all the Laws of Virginia, from the First
Session of the Legislature, in the Year 1619* (13 vols., 1809–23).

641.26   Stannard . . . Johnson]   Robert Stanard (1781–1846) and Chapman Johnson (1779–1849).

641.27   Leigh]   Benjamin Watkins Leigh (1781–1849) later served as a senator from Virginia, 1834–36.

642.8–9   bill for multiplying . . . a majority]   The House and Senate
each passed bills increasing the number of Supreme Court justices to ten, but
were unable to reconcile their differing versions before Congress adjourned
in late May.

642.14–15 brother Tremble . . . Mr. Rowan]   Robert Trimble (1777–
1828) had been nominated to replace Thomas Todd on the Supreme Court.
Senator John Rowan of Kentucky opposed the nomination, which was eventually approved by the Senate, 27–5.

642.16–17   brother Washington . . . the Sabbath]   Bushrod Washington had refused to allow an excursion party of senators and congressmen to land at Mount Vernon on a Sunday.

642.31   *Samuel Fay*]   Fay (1778–1856) was a Massachusetts judge and close friend of Justice Story.

642.34–35   your daughter]   Harriet Howard Fay (1810–1885), the eldest daughter of Samuel Fay and Harriet Howard Fay.

645.28   *To Joseph Story*]   The text of this letter is taken from William Wetmore Story, *Life and Letters of Joseph Story* (2 vols., 1851).

645.30   your Discourse]   *A Discourse Pronounced before the Phi Beta Kappa Society, at the Anniversary Celebration, on the Thirty First Day of August 1826* (1826).

647.1   *Opinion in* Ogden v. Saunders]   The Supreme Court had held in *Sturges v. Crowninshield* (1819) that retrospective bankruptcy laws violated the contracts clause of the Constitution. *Ogden v. Saunders*, a case raising the constitutionality of prospective bankruptcy laws, was appealed from the U.S. District Court for Louisiana to the Supreme Court in 1820. The case was argued in 1824 and reargued in January 1827. On February 19 the Court upheld, 4–3, the constitutionality of prospective bankruptcy laws. Justices Washington, Johnson, Thompson, and Trimble delivered their individual opinions seriatim, while Marshall dissented for the first, and only, time in a case involving an important constitutional question. The text is taken from Henry Wheaton, *Reports of Cases Argued and Adjudged in the Supreme Court of the United States*, volume 12 (1827).

648.16–20   *M'Neil* v. *M'Millan*, . . . *Pennsylvania* v. *Smith*]   The cases were decided by the Supreme Court in 1819 and 1821.

656.30   case cited from 9 *Wheat. Rep.*]   *Renner v. Bank of Columbia*, decided by the Supreme Court in 1824.

657.3   *Bank of Columbia* v. *Oakley*,]   The case was decided by the Supreme Court in 1819.

657.14   *Strange*]   John Strange (1696–1754), *Reports of Adjudged Cases in the Courts of Chancery, King's Bench, Common Pleas and Exchequer* (2 vols., 1755).

661.30   defined by a writer,]   William Blackstone, in volume I of *Commentaries on the Laws of England*.

671.5   Mr. Mercer]   Charles Fenton Mercer (1778–1858) was a congressman from Virginia, 1817–39.

671.8–10   my brother Johnson . . . battle of Germantown]   Pickering had published a letter in the October 1826 *North American Review* that criticized the account of Germantown included in William Johnson's *Sketches of the Life and Correspondence of Nathanael Greene* (1822) and defended Count Pulaski against Johnson's accusations. Johnson and Pickering continued the controversy in an exchange of letters printed in the Washington *National Intelligencer*.

671.14 Mr. Wolcot] Oliver Wolcott Jr. (1760–1833), governor of Connecticut, 1817–27, had served as comptroller of the treasury, 1791–95, and as secretary of the treasury, 1795–1800.

671.24–25 interesting anecdotes of General Washington] In his letter to Marshall of February 14, Pickering recounted his personal observations of Washington during the Philadelphia campaign of 1777, and described him as "strikingly deficient" in the qualities of "*quick discernment*, and *instant decision*" needed by a military commander.

672.19 "discourse on popular education"] Charles Fenton Mercer, *A Discourse on Popular Education; Delivered in the Church at Princeton, the Evening before the Annual Commencement of the College of New Jersey, September 26, 1826* (1826).

674.6–7 speech of the Duke de Broglie] Achille Charles Léonce Victor, duc de Broglie (1785–1870), *Discours Prononcé par M. le Duc de Broglie à la Chambre des Pairs le 28 mars 1822, sur la Traite des Nègres* (1822).

676.14 the family loss] Louis de Lasteyne, Lafayette's son-in-law, had died in December 1826.

676.22 Messieurs Lafayette and le Vasseur] George Washington Lafayette (1779–1849), Lafayette's son, and Auguste Levasseur, who served as Lafayette's secretary during his 1824–25 tour of the United States.

676.35 request . . . highly valued friend] Story had agreed to review *A History of the Colonies* for the *North American Review* and intended to include a biographical sketch of Marshall.

677.8 Pope's essay on man, . . . moral essays.] Alexander Pope (1688–1744), *An Essay on Man* (1733–34) and *Moral Essays* (1731–35).

678.18–19 Mr. Madison then President . . . College] James Madison (1749–1812), a cousin of President James Madison, was president of the College of William and Mary, 1777–1812.

681.21–22 Colonel Griffin] Samuel Griffin (1746–1810) was a member of Congress, 1789–95.

683.5–6 my intimate friend] John Harvie. Marshall's daughter Mary later married his son, Jaquelin Harvie.

685.21–22 Mr. Cabot . . . Mr. Wadsworth] George Cabot (1751–1823), Fisher Ames (1758–1808), Samuel Dexter (1761–1816), Theodore Sedgwick (1746–1813), and Jeremiah Wadsworth (1743–1804) were all serving in the House of Representatives at the time.

689.8 death of Judge Iredell] Marshall was offered an appointment following the death of James Wilson in 1798; James Iredell died in 1799.

689.24 Mr. McHenry] James McHenry (1753–1816) was secretary of war, 1796–1800.

692.12–13 flattering Biography] Story's unsigned biographical sketch of Marshall appeared in the January 1828 number of the *North American Review*.

692.34–35 in another work] William Johnson's controversial *Sketches of the Life and Correspondence of Nathanael Greene* (1822).

693.7 Mrs. Rapines] Charlotte Rapine (d. 1835), widow of Daniel Rapine (d. 1826), late postmaster of the House of Representatives.

695.4 your centennial discourse] *A Discourse Pronounced at the Request of the Essex Historical Society, on the 18th of September 1828 in Commemoration of the First Settlement of Salem, in the State of Massachusetts* (1828).

696.2 lady Arabella Johnson] Arbella Johnson, the daughter of the Earl of Lincoln, accompanied her husband, Isaac Johnson, on the voyage across the Atlantic. She died in August 1630, two months after arriving in Massachusetts. *Arbella*, the flagship of the Puritan fleet, was named in her honor.

696.16–17 lamented Judge Trimble] Story's sketch of Justice Robert Trimble, who had died in August 1828, was published in the Boston *Columbian Centinel* on September 17.

696.24–25 appointment . . . Hopkinson] Joseph Hopkinson (1770–1842) had been appointed U.S. District Judge for Eastern Pennsylvania in place of Richard Peters, who died in August 1828.

696.28 *John Randolph*] Randolph (1773–1833) served in the House of Representatives, 1799–1813, 1815–17, 1819–25, and 1827–29, and in the Senate, 1825–27.

697.28 systems will triumph] The legislature eventually called for four convention delegates to be chosen by the freeholders in each of the 24 senate districts.

698.16 loss of Mrs. Jackson] Rachel Donelson Jackson had died of heart failure in Nashville on December 22, 1828.

698.24 Mr. Call] Daniel Call (1765–1840), a Richmond lawyer and court reporter, had been married to Lucy Ambler (1776–1797), a sister of Polly Marshall.

699.1 Mr. Harvie] Jaquelin B. Harvie (1788–1856), Marshall's son-in-law.

699.16–17 affliction of our son] Margaret Lewis Marshall, wife of Thomas Marshall, had died in childbirth on February 2, along with her newborn son.

700.4–5   Mrs. O Sullivan]   Barbara O'Sullivan (1783–1851), also known as Barbara O'Sullivan Addicks, was a writer and educational reformer then living in Philadelphia.

701.26–27   "reply . . . freeholder."]   *A Reply to the Inquiries of a Free-holder . . . on the Subject of the Convention* (1829). Garnett was elected as a convention delegate.

706.21–22   "Mr. Brazer's discourse . . . Holyoke,"]   John Brazer, *A Discourse Delivered in the North Church, in Salem, on Saturday, 4th of April 1829 . . . at the Interment of Edward Augustus Holyoke* (1829).

706.23   address to the bar of Suffolk]   *An Address Delivered before the Members of the Suffolk Bar . . . on the 4th of September, 1821* (1829).

706.31–32   appointment to the Dane professorship]   Harvard had appointed Story as the first Dane Professor of Law on June 11.

708.30   your discourse]   *A Discourse Pronounced upon the Inauguration of the Author, as Dane Professor of Law in Harvard University, on the Twenty-fifth Day of August, 1829* (1829).

709.19   *non sum qualis eram*]   I am not what I used to be.

709.22–23   *Speech . . . on Apportionment*]   The Virginia Convention opened on October 5, 1829, as Marshall and James Madison escorted James Monroe to the presiding officer's chair. Marshall subsequently addressed the question of legislative apportionment, which proved to be the most intractable issue before the convention. The text of Marshall's speech is taken from the *Richmond Enquirer,* December 8, 1829.

709.28–29   basis of federal numbers]   The entire white population, plus three-fifths of the slave population.

710.11   (Mr. Johnson)]   Chapman Johnson (1779–1849), a lawyer who served in the state senate, 1810–26

710.13   (Mr. Upshur)]   Abel P. Upshur (1790–1844), a judge on the Virginia General Court who later served as secretary of the navy and secretary of state in the Tyler administration.

710.16   (Mr. Cooke)]   John R. Cooke (1788–1854) was a Winchester lawyer and leader of the reform party at the convention.

711.4   the Committee]   The committee of the whole.

713.18–19   *Speech . . . on the Judiciary*]   As chairman of the judiciary committee, Marshall sought to ensure the principle of judicial independence by including in the revised constitution an explicit provision that any legislative modification or abolition of courts would not deprive a judge of his office during good behavior. The text of this speech is taken from the *Richmond Enquirer,* December 12, 1829.

713.22   gentleman from Chesterfield] Benjamin Watkins Leigh (1781–1849), an attorney who served as the reporter for the Virginia Court of Appeals, 1829–41.

713.27–28   gentleman from Norfolk] Littleton W. Tazewell (1774–1860) served as a U.S. senator, 1824–32, and as governor of Virginia, 1834–36. Tazewell had proposed changing the name of the Court of Appeals to "Supreme Court," with a view to protecting the tenure of judges on the highest court while giving the legislature control over inferior court judges.

714.4–5   construction of the Federal Constitution] Tazewell and other delegates had cited the 1802 repeal of the Judiciary Act of 1801 as a precedent for legislative abolition of judicial offices.

715.10   gentleman from Orange] Philip P. Barbour; see note 528.34–36.

716.31   Mr. MARSHALL rejoined] Marshall resumed speaking after Tazewell's remarks.

719.14   fine large boy] John Marshall, the first child of Edward C. Marshall and Rebecca P. Marshall, was born on January 17.

719.19   Mrs. Donalson] Emily Donelson, a niece of President Jackson's late wife, served as the hostess at the Executive Mansion.

719.22   Tom Francis] Thomas Francis Marshall (1801–1864), Marshall's nephew and son of Louis Marshall.

719.25   McClain] John McLean (1785–1861) was appointed and confirmed to the Supreme Court in March 1829, replacing Robert Trimble.

719.31–32   tenant Mr. Sprigg] Joseph Sprigg (1793–1864) was a tenant and rent collector on Marshall's land in Hampshire County (now in West Virginia), across the Potomac River from Cumberland, Maryland.

720.10–11   Secretary of State] Martin Van Buren.

720.13   Mrs. Livingston of Louisiana] Louise Davezac Livingston (1782–1860), second wife of Edward Livingston, then serving in the U.S. Senate.

721.24–25   Nephew William . . . Miss Mercers school] William Louis Marshall of Baltimore, son of Louis Marshall and brother of Thomas Francis Marshall. Margaret Mercer (1791–1846), a cousin of Charles F. Mercer, ran a school near Baltimore.

721.31   Mr. Coleman] Nicholas D. Coleman (1800–74), then a member of the House of Representatives from Kentucky, was married to Lucy Ambler Marshall, daughter of Marshall's brother Thomas Marshall. He lost his seat at the next election to Thomas A. Marshall (1794–1871), son of Humphrey Marshall.

722.7   *To James Hillhouse*] Hillhouse (1754–1832), a senator from Connecticut, 1796–1810, had sent Marshall a copy of his *Propositions for Amending the Constitution of the United States, Providing for the Election of President and Vice-president, and Guarding against the Undue Exercise of Executive Influence, Patronage, and Power* (1830). Much of this pamphlet reprinted a speech Hillhouse had given in the Senate in April 1808 proposing that the president should be chosen by lot from the senior class of senators and serve for a term of one year (the presidential term was extended to two years in his 1830 pamphlet).

724.15   *To Joseph Story*]   Story had sent Marshall a copy of John Gorham Palfrey's *A Sermon Preached in the Church in Brattle Square, Boston, August 1, 1830: The Lord's Day after the Decease of the Honourable Isaac Parker, Chief Justice of Massachusetts* (1830), as well as a newspaper article containing Story's biographical sketch of Parker.

725.1–2   brother Mclean . . . Missouri case.]   Marshall had written the opinion for the court in *Craig v. Missouri*, decided in March 1830, striking down a state law authorizing loan certificates as an unconstitutional issue of bills of credit. Justices McLean, Johnson, and Thompson dissented, and both McLean and Thompson expressed a willingness to narrow the scope of section 25 of the Judiciary Act of 1789.

725.4   last volume of Mr. Peters]   Richard Peters Jr. (1779–1848), the son of the late federal judge, succeeded Henry Wheaton as Supreme Court reporter in 1828.

725.21   letter of Mr. Madison]   James Madison's letter to Edward Everett of August 28, 1830, published in the October 1830 *North American Review*, refuted the doctrine of nullification and criticized nullification advocates who appealed to Madison's Virginia report of 1800.

726.2   *To Henry Lee*]   Lee (1787–1837), son of "Light-Horse Harry" Lee, had served in the House of Delegates, 1810–13, and as an army officer during the War of 1812. He wrote pamphlets and newspaper essays in support of Andrew Jackson during the 1828 campaign, and in 1829 received a recess appointment as consul general to Algiers. The Senate unanimously refused to confirm him in March 1830.

726.12–13   correspondence of Mr. Jefferson . . . Grandson]   Thomas Jefferson Randolph, *Memoirs, Correspondence, and Miscellanies from the Papers of Thomas Jefferson* (4 vols., 1829).

727.5–6   affair of Mrs. Walker]   As a young unmarried man, Jefferson had attempted to seduce Elizabeth Walker, the wife of his friend and neighbor, John Walker. The affair was made public by the journalist James T. Callender in 1802, forcing John Walker to seek "satisfaction" from the President. Henry Lee acted as Walker's agent in negotiations that resulted in Jefferson writing statements admitting his improper behavior.

728.8–9   letter to Kerchival]   Jefferson wrote the letter on July 12, 1816.

728.30   Colo. Lambert] William Lambert (1790–1853), a Richmond
lawyer.

729.1–2   minister of France] Jean Baptiste Gaspard Roux de Rochelle
(1762–1849) was French minister to the United States, 1830–33.

729.17   Mr. Robinson] Conway Robinson (1805–1884), then a clerk of
the Virginia General Court, subsequently married a granddaughter of Elizabeth Marshall Colston (1756–1842), Marshall's sister.

729.28   Miss Sedgewic] Catharine Maria Sedgwick (1789–1867), daughter
of the Federalist leader Theodore Sedgwick, was a novelist and author of
Hope Leslie (1827) and *Clarence* (1830).

730.14   Poor Ringold] Tench Ringgold had been marshal for the District of Columbia since 1818. When his commission expired in January 1831,
President Jackson named another man to the office.

731.1   *Opinion in* Cherokee Nation v. Georgia] In the fall of 1830 the
Cherokee brought a suit against Georgia in the Supreme Court, claiming sta-
tus as a foreign nation under the Court's original jurisdiction. The case was
argued and decided in March 1831. Marshall wrote the opinion for the court,
Justice Henry Baldwin and Justice Johnson delivered concurring opinions,
and Justice Thompson wrote a dissenting opinion that was joined by Justice
Story. The text of Marshall's opinion is taken from a copy in the Library of
Congress and, in part, from the printed account prepared by Richard Peters.

736.30–31   *Tabula rasa . . .* cabinet] With the exception of the postmaster general, President Jackson's entire cabinet resigned in April 1831.

736.32–33   really voluntary resignations] Secretary of State Van Buren
and Secretary of War John Eaton resigned voluntarily; the remaining cabinet
members were asked to resign by President Jackson.

737.3–4   Mr. Brown] Jesse Brown was the proprietor of the Indian
Queen Hotel, where the justices had resided during the preceding decade.

737.10   our younger brother] Henry Baldwin (1780–1844) joined the
Supreme Court in January 1830 as the successor to Bushrod Washington.

737.18   Algernon Sidney] *The Letters of Algernon Sydney, in Defence of
Civil Liberty and Against the Encroachments of Military Despotism . . .*
(1830), written by Benjamin Watkins Leigh.

738.6–7   publishing the cherokee case entire] Peters would soon publish
The Case of the Cherokee Nation Against the State of Georgia (1831), which included the pleadings, the arguments of John Sergeant (1779–1852) and
William Wirt (1772–1834), the opinions of Marshall, Johnson, and Baldwin
as delivered in court, Thompson's subsequent written opinion, and four
appendices.

739.10–11 my brother Barbour] Philip P. Barbour was appointed U.S. District Judge for Virginia in 1830 and sat with Marshall on the U.S. Circuit Court for Virginia.

739.16 Meredith] William M. Meredith (1799–1873), a Philadelphia lawyer, was later secretary of the treasury in the administration of Zachary Taylor.

740.31 the family affliction] Louisa Story, Justice Story's youngest daughter, had died in May at age ten.

741.3 She was followed . . . a brother] The deaths of Mary Anne Marshall and John James Marshall occurred in the summer of 1792.

741.30 Doctor Physic] Marshall had arrived in Philadelphia in late September to seek treatment for excruciating pain, which Dr. Philip Syng Physick (1768–1837) diagnosed as caused by bladder stones. Physick performed a lithotomy on October 13, removing about 1,000 minute stones.

742.29–30 my subscription . . . the Enginier] In June 1831 Marshall drafted resolutions calling for the hiring of an experienced engineer to assist the governor of Virginia in planning internal improvements.

743.18 Cary Ambler] Richard Cary Ambler (1810–77) and his half-brother Edward Ambler (1783–1846) were sons of John Ambler, Polly Marshall's cousin.

743.19 portrait painter] Henry Inman (1801–1846) had been commissioned by the Philadelphia bar to paint Marshall's portrait.

745.4 Mrs. Peytons] Ann Eliza Peyton kept a boardinghouse on Capitol Hill. In 1832 and 1833 the justices boarded at the home of Tench Ringgold, about two miles west of the Capitol.

749.2 *Ralph R. Gurley*] Gurley (1797–1872) was secretary of the American Colonization Society. Marshall, who was president of the Colonization Society of Virginia, erroneously dated the letter in 1823.

749.10–11 present state of my family] Polly Marshall was critically ill. She died on December 25, 1831.

749.18 the late insurrection] The insurrection in Southampton County, Virginia, led by Nat Turner in August 1831.

750.5 proposition made by Mr. King] Senator Rufus King of New York proposed in 1825 to use public land sales to establish a fund in support of emancipation and colonization.

751.18 Mr. Van Burens nomination] President Jackson had made a recess appointment of Van Buren as minister to Great Britain in June 1831. His nomination was defeated by the deciding vote of Vice-President John Calhoun after a bitter debate in the Senate in January 1832.

751.22 letter to Mr. McLane] While serving as secretary of state, Van Buren sent instructions in July 1829 to Louis McLane (1786–1857), his predecessor as minister to Great Britain. Van Buren's opponents accused him of ordering McLane to dishonorably repudiate the policy of the John Quincy Adams administration in negotiations with the British over reopening the West Indian trade.

753.1 *Opinion in* Worcester v. Georgia] Georgia authorities convicted Samuel A. Worcester (1798–1859) and ten other missionaries in September 1831 of violating a law excluding white persons from living in the Cherokee territory without obtaining a license from, and taking an oath of allegiance to, the state. Most of the missionaries accepted pardons, but Worcester and Elizur Butler chose to remain in prison and challenge the statute in court. John Sergeant and William Wirt, the lawyers who had represented the Cherokees in 1831, argued Worcester's case in the Supreme Court in February 1832. On March 3, 1832, Marshall delivered the opinion of the court, while Justice McLean delivered a concurring opinion and Justice Baldwin dissented. The text of the opinion is taken from Marshall's autograph manuscript in the National Archives.

754.23 qui tam action] An action in which a private person sues for a penalty that will be shared with the government.

761.3–6 "that a discovery . . . by possession."] Marshall quotes from his opinion for the court in *Johnson v. McIntosh* (1823).

765.34 the ouabache] The Wabash.

779.27 reversed and annulled.] The Gwinnett County superior court refused to recognize the mandate sent by the Supreme Court in *Worcester v. Georgia*. Official notice of its noncompliance did not reach the Supreme Court before its adjournment in March 1832, and Worcester and Butler ended the case by accepting pardons shortly before the Court reconvened for its January 1833 session.

783.20 provincials] Loyalists.

785.2 corps of light infantry] Marshall was selected as an officer of this corps.

789.29 Colonel Marshall] Thomas Marshall, Marshall's father.

795.4–5 Lieutenant Colonel Hamilton] Alexander Hamilton.

807.25–26 Colonel Greene of Rhode Island,] Christopher Greene (1737–1781) was distantly related to General Nathanael Greene. He was killed by a Loyalist raiding party in Westchester County, New York, in May 1781.

821.5 American library of useful knowledge] *American Library of Useful Knowledge* (1831), which contained a piece by Story, "Developments of Science and Mechanic Art."

821.35   Hurra's for the veto.]   President Jackson had vetoed a bill rechartering the Second Bank of the United States on July 10, 1832.

822.6–7   veto of the harbor bill]   Jackson pocket vetoed a harbor improvements bill in July 1832.

822.19   Mr. Barbour]   Philip P. Barbour was being discussed as a possible Democratic candidate for vice-president.

822.37–38   this mad and wicked measure]   An ordinance of nullification, declaring the federal tariff null and void within the state.

822.40   Mason]   Jeremiah Mason (1768–1848), a prominent New Hampshire attorney who had served in the U.S. Senate, 1813–17.

824.7   the sage you mention]   Thomas Jefferson.

824.27–28   your great work]   *Commentaries on the Constitution of the United States* (3 vols., 1833).

825.15–16   his proclamation]   President Jackson's proclamation of December 10 asserted the supremacy of federal authority and denounced as illegal the nullification ordinance adopted by South Carolina on November 24.

825.36   message of our Governor,]   John Floyd (1783–1837), governor of Virginia, 1830–34, had submitted the South Carolina nullification ordinance to the legislature on December 13.

826.39–827.1   the affliction . . . brother Baldwin]   Justice Baldwin had suffered a nervous collapse that caused him to miss the entire 1833 term of the Supreme Court.

829.13–14   beautiful lines . . . General Burgoyne]   John Burgoyne (1722–1792) wrote the lines as part of his libretto for the comic opera *Lord of the Manor* (1780).

830.1   *Opinion in* Barron v. Baltimore]   The plaintiff in this case contended that improvements undertaken by the city of Baltimore had diminished the value of his wharf property, thereby violating the "takings clause" of the Fifth Amendment. The case came to the Supreme Court from the Maryland Court of Appeals and was argued in February 1833. Marshall delivered the opinion of a unanimous court on February 16. The text of the opinion is taken from the seventh volume of Richard Peters, *Reports of Cases Argued and Adjudged in the Supreme Court of the United States* (1845).

834.8   Allison's sermons]   Archibald Alison (1757–1839), *Sermons, Chiefly on Particular Occasions* (2 vols., 1815–16).

834.32   Mrs. Ledyard]   Susan Livingston Ledyard (1789–1864), daughter of the late Justice Brockholst Livingston.

835.21   Clays bill]   The compromise tariff measure, introduced by Henry Clay, that became law on March 2, 1833.

835.34–35   pamphlet on our federal relations] Humphrey Marshall, *Federal Relations and State Rights, As They Are and Should Be in the Constitution* (1833).

837.2   *Jasper Adams*] Adams (1783–1841), then president of the College of Charleston, had just published *The Relation of Christianity to Civil Government in the United States* (1833).

837.28   *Edward Everett*] Everett (1794–1865) was serving as a congressman from Massachusetts.

837.31   Mr. Atwill,] Hermann Atwill published the *Yeoman's Gazette, Mechanic's Journal & Middlesex Advertiser* in Concord, Massachusetts.

838.21–22   murder or abstraction of Morgan] The disappearance and presumed murder of William Morgan in upstate New York in 1826 was widely attributed to a Masonic conspiracy designed to prevent Morgan from exposing the secrets of the order.

839.11   your discourse] *A Discourse Pronounced at the Funeral Obsequies of John Hooker Ashmun, Esq., Royall Professor of Law in Harvard University . . .* (1833).

840.5   3d. No. of the National Portrait Gallery] "John Marshall, LL.D., Chief Justice of the United States," an unsigned biographical sketch written by Story, appeared in James B. Longacre and James Herring, *National Portrait Gallery of Distinguished Americans,* a series that began appearing monthly in the spring of 1833.

840.27   affair of Randolph] Robert B. Randolph (1790–1869), a disgruntled former naval officer, assaulted President Jackson on May 6, 1833, by tweaking his nose.

841.14   Mr. Bonaparte] Joseph Bonaparte (1768–1844), Napoleon's brother, lived in the United States, 1815–1832.

841.21   young Napoleon] François Charles Joseph Bonaparte (1811–1832), son of Napoleon I.

842.32   the infernal machine] An attempt to assassinate Napoleon was made in Paris on December 24, 1800, by means of a bomb placed in a cart.

843.20   *James K. Marshall*] James Keith Marshall, Marshall's fourth son, lived at Leeds, an estate in Fauquier County.

844.18   Claudia] Claudia Burwell Marshall (1804–1884), wife of James Keith Marshall.

844.22   Mrs. Nelson] Mary C. Nelson (1791–1853) lived with her daughter, Rebecca, and her son-in-law, Edward C. Marshall.

844.26   *Thomas S. Grimké*] Grimké (1786–1834) was a South Carolina lawyer and social reformer who supported the union during the nullification controversy.

844.31–34   Judge Harper's opinion . . . Oneale] In June 1834 the South Carolina Court of Appeals struck down a recently passed law requiring new militia officers to swear "faithful and true allegiance" to the state. Judges David Johnson and John B. O'Neall formed the majority, while Judge William Harper dissented.

846.8   defeat of Harden] Colonel John Hardin (1753–1792) of the Kentucky militia was ambushed by Miami Indians near present-day Churubusco, Indiana, on October 19, 1790.

846.32   our Governor] Littleton W. Tazewell.

847.12   *John Marshall, Jr.*] Marshall (1821–1872) was the son of the Chief Justice's late son, John Marshall.

848.15   Blair,] Hugh Blair (1718–1800), Scottish clergyman and author of *Lectures on Rhetoric and Belles Lettres* (2 vols., 1784).

849.3   *James K. Paulding*] Paulding (1778–1860), a prolific New York writer of novels, stories, essays, and poems, was about to publish *A Life of Washington* (2 vols., 1835).

850.5   Mr. Lewis] Lawrence Lewis (1767–1839), Washington's nephew and the husband of Eleanor Parke Custis, granddaughter of Martha Washington.

851.13–14   Doctor Chapman] Nathaniel Chapman (1780–1853), an eminent Philadelphia physician, attended Marshall in his final illness and conducted a post mortem examination.

852.2   *Thomas P. Devereux*] Devereux (1793–1869) was serving as U.S. Attorney for North Carolina.

852.13   Mr. Gastons memorandum] William Gaston (1778–1844), a prominent North Carolina lawyer and politician, was then serving as a judge of the North Carolina Supreme Court.

Index

THE LIBRARY OF AMERICA SERIES

The Library of America fosters appreciation and pride in America's literary heritage by publishing, and keeping permanently in print, authoritative editions of America's best and most significant writing. An independent nonprofit organization, it was founded in 1979 with seed money from the National Endowment for the Humanities and the Ford Foundation.

To subscribe to the series or to order individual copies,
please visit www.loa.org or call (800) 964.5778.

This book is set in 10 point Linotron Galliard,
a face designed for photocomposition by Matthew Carter
and based on the sixteenth-century face Granjon. The paper
is acid-free lightweight opaque and meets the requirements
for permanence of the American National Standards Institute.
The binding material is Brillianta, a woven rayon cloth made
by Van Heek-Scholco Textielfabrieken, Holland. Compo-
sition by Dedicated Business Services. Printing by
Malloy Incorporated. Binding by Dekker Book-
binding. Designed by Bruce Campbell.